STEPHEN MCA

MUSIC BUSINESS HANDBOOK *and career guide*

DAVID BASKERVILLE, Ph.D.

UNIVERSITY OF COLORADO AT DENVER

THIRD EDITION

MUSIC BUSINESS HANDBOOK

and career guide

FOREWORD By STAN CORNYN, Senior Vice-President

WCI (Warner Communications Inc.) Record Group

THE SHERWOOD COMPANY   *Los Angeles / Denver*

Library of Congress Catalog Card Number 81-51753

ISBN 0-933056-02-8

THE SHERWOOD COMPANY
P.O. Box 21645, Denver, CO 80221

Editorial Consultant — Roberta Baskerville
Special Photography — Leigh Wiener
Graphic Art — Roger Miller
Book design by the author

Permission from the following sources to reprint photographs and graphic art is gratefully acknowledged: Ampex Corp. (pp 158, 494, 502), A & M Records (pp 264, 334, 342,), BMI (pp 22, 45, 114, 126, 139), Arp Corp. (pp 158, 278, 290), RCA (pp 174, 229), Warner Bros. Records (pp 320, 332, 333), ASCAP (pp 116, 139), KBIG (pp 204, 355, 360, 365), CBS-TV/KNXT (pp 374, 377), Manufacturers Hanover Trust (p. 24), Eastern Sound Ltd. (p. 308), Broadcast Electronics (p. 372), Magnasync/Moviola (p. 412), CBS (p. 2), Akai (p. 390), Sound Stream Inc. (p. 263), Selmer Co. (p. 190), Metrina Corp. (p. 244).

Printed in the United States of America

*To my family, and to those in the business
who care about the music, too.*

— EDITORIAL ADVISORY BOARD —

CONTENTS

ACKNOWLEDGMENTS
FOREWORD

6 - MUSIC COPYRIGHT 79

PART THREE-BUSINESS AFFAIRS

PART FOUR - THE RECORD INDUSTRY

PART SEVEN - APPENDIX

ACKNOWLEDGMENTS

Most of the information in this book comes from personal experience of the author and research covering a professional career now pushing 40 years. But along the way, I have acquired invaluable information from dozens of professional associates, teachers and students. If this book is useful, it is they who are entitled to a share of the credit.

First, I want to acknowledge those who pioneered in the music business education field, Dr. William Lee and Dr. Alfred Reed of the University of Miami. They established the first university degree program in music merchandising, which now includes graduate study.

We should all be grateful to Sidney Shemel, M. William Krasilovsky and the late Paul Ackerman for writing the basic books years ago on the music business. I acknowledge my debt to these writers.

The section of the book on the record industry was enhanced by extensive interviews with executives of CBS Records. At Capitol Records, I learned how a major label negotiates artists' royalty contracts — from the man who signs them, Robert Young, Vice-President of Business Affairs.

My section on record marketing benefits in a major way from a study of Warner Bros. Records merchandising division, where I acquired extensive information on how that giant firm sells its records. My generous host at Warner Bros. was Adam Somers, Vice-President of Creative Services and Operations.

My chapter on music publishing includes information supplied by John Devarion of Chappell Music Company, Sam Trust, President of ATV Music Corporation, Ralph Peer II, First Vice-President of the Peer-Southern Organization, and Jay Morgenstern of ABC Dunhill.

Information here on music copyright and music business law has been given authority through my extensive contacts with a number of the leading attorneys practicing law in these fields. This includes such distinguished lawyers as Daniel Webb Lang, Esq., of the Los Angeles law firm of Wyman, Bautzer, Rothman, Kuchel & Silbert; Peter Thall, Esq., partner in the New York law firm of Levine and Thall; Jay L. Cooper, Esq., and Phalen G. Hurewitz, Esq., partners in the Beverly Hills law firm of Cooper, Epstein, and Hurewitz; Harold Streibich, Esq., an authority on foreign copyright and member of the faculty of Memphis State University; and David A. Braun, Esq., now President of Polygram Records.

The chapter on studios and engineers is based, in part, on invaluable information I acquired from Brian Ingoldsby and Bones Howe, both of whom helped me design and equip my Hollywood recording studio.

Throughout the book I draw on what I learned about studio musicians and recording from dozens of distinguished artists who worked with me or for me in the Los Angeles studios. The chapter on film scoring reflects insights shared by Mario Castelnuovo-Tedesco, the late Hugo Friedhofer, Dave Grusin, Tom Scott, Nelson Riddle, Patrick Williams and Bill Stinson.

At ASCAP, background information was given me by board member and distinguished songwriter Gerald Marks. ASCAP's legal department checked the accuracy of my information on music licensing. The lawyers and other officers at BMI were equally helpful on matters relating to music performance rights.

I gained an understanding on how top concert promoters operate from Feyline Presents, Inc., one of the country's leading firms in this field.

My section on arts administration is informed by extensive interviews with Roger Stevens, head of the John F. Kennedy Center for the Performing Arts, Washington, D.C., and John Mazzola, President of New York's Lincoln Center. Additional background was gained from Professor John Cauble of UCLA's arts administration faculty, also from Oleg Lubonov, Manager of the National Symphony Orchestra, Washington, D.C. In describing how a manager for a symphony orchestra should function, I have borrowed heavily from the views of Ralph Black, Executive Director of the American Symphony Orchestra League.

I want to say how much I learned from Henry Pleasants' brilliant book, *Serious Music — And All That Jazz,* which offers an indictment of those musicians and professors who still refuse to recognize that the mainstream of today's music is Afro-American. Thank you, Henry, for your helpful suggestions about my manuscript.

Much of the content of this book has been shaped by the feedback I have received from testing the material with students, a number of whom have had more on the ball than their mentor.

One of the reasons this book has been widely accepted as a college text is that instructors who teach in this field have generously shared their views with me for this latest edition. Their names appear on my Editorial Advisory Board.

Special thanks, too, to Stan Cornyn, Senior Vice-President of WCI Record Group, for agreeing to write the Foreword to this book. Mr. Cornyn, one of the industry's most penetrating thinkers, has offered courageous statements on the commercialism rampant in music and broadcasting, reminding us all that there can be more to this enterprise than a fast buck.

This list of acknowledgments cannot conclude without mention of the invaluable help given me by my wife, Roberta, without whom this project could not have been completed. She has given this writer so many ideas over the years he has come to believe they were his own.

FOREWORD

STAN CORNYN, Senior Vice-President
WCI (Warner Communications Inc.) Record Group

It's never easy. The road to success in the music business is as rife with ruts and detours as that of any other field. No pat personality profile, no set philosophy guarantees entry to the big time. The men and women who've carved out positions of respect and influence in the industry are an amalgam of many different styles, psyches, temperaments. Some have come a long way; others took shortcuts. Some are incredulous that they are where they are; for others, the goal was inevitable.

One certainty unites them all: that nothing in this business is certain. The achievers have all exhibited, in one form or another, an ability to adapt, to alter long-standing opinions, to substitute professional intuition for conventional logic. They take chances.

There are two kinds of people in the world, talkers and doers, men and women of action, of inaction. I don't want to downgrade a very critical element of this business — one very near and dear to me — that of articulating your point, but for some people that's as far as it goes. Anyone can think of a great idea and pin your ear to the wall detailing it, and most people at some time do. But only doers can take a plan out of the grey matter and put it into action. The individuals who attain some level of leadership in the record community are as good as their word — and deed.

Record companies do not, however, turn people loose in their corridors just because they have a few plans to carry out. Those who have ideas had better also have quite a few facts at their disposal. And it takes years to develop a full understanding of all the elements needed to make a hit record, from recording it, to packaging it, to publicizing it, to airing it, to selling it.

Recently, a young up-and-comer suggested an idea he thought was sure-fire — putting flyers into record jackets listing an artist's collected works. He had no idea of the time, money and manpower involved in getting flyers into jackets. His scheme would have raised the cost of an album six cents per unit which would have meant a reasonably large loss of net profit.

We're concerned, then, with the nuts and bolts side of our operation as well as with the more nebulous concept of "art" in our industry, an equally ongoing dilemma in the realms of literature and film. Selling music is not exactly selling blenders. I won't deny an album's objective presence. We at Warner Bros. follow that chunk of vinyl's every move until it shows up, hopefully, on our computer runs in the "sold" column. That's what we're here for.

But not completely. We're dealing with artists, personalities — not objects — and that makes this business quite unlike any other. We're selling taste and emotion, not Landau tops or rear-window defoggers. This casts much of what we do in a very subjective light, raising age-old questions about the relationship between art and commerce. If it's not commercial, how do we sell it? Don't certain "uncommercial" works of music deserve to exist on artistic merit alone? If so, which ones? And how do you persuade the public, even your own staff, of the value and viability of unfamiliar, challenging musical concepts?

In contrast to other businesses, some of whom have been in operation for hundreds of years, the record industry as recently as 30 years ago was by and large a back-room affair. Street-corner groups were sent into dingy one- and two-track studios with a $400 budget to turn out hits that made millions for the label, but not a cent for them. Serious recordings were never expected to be profitable.

Today the record business is coming of age and we have the first generation of college texts on the subject to prove it. Those entering the business have the challenge of giving it new form and focus. An exciting, rewarding, clearly upbeat experience awaits you. That you can *almost* be sure of.

MUSIC BUSINESS HANDBOOK *and career guide*

Part One

MUSIC IN THE MARKETPLACE

1

OVERVIEW

I never cared much for poverty.
IGOR STRAVINSKY

**Did someone say "the music *business*"? What happened to the *art* of
music?** The shortest possible answer to that question is, "About $20
billion!" — the amount of money swirling around the art and business
of music today. But the question of what has happened to musical art
in recent times calls for a serious answer, and that is what this book is
all about. We will examine not only the radical changes in music and
its audiences, but set forth in detail just who produces the music, who
"consumes" it, and how the artists and merchants share that $20 billion.

Art and commerce make very strange bedfellows. This linkage, omnipresent in the late twentieth century, is inherently contradictory, for
musicians and merchants are, in many respects, natural enemies. They
hold generally conflicting views on what music should be and do. But
when communications technology developed into "mass media" in the
1940s, the artists and the money changers learned how to find accommodation. Since World War II, musicians and merchants have been
engaged in a red hot romance, living in sin. Their union has begat
countless offspring, without benefit of clergy. In recent years, art and
commerce have been shoved into a kind of shotgun marriage. But this
improbable union will last, not because the parties share an eternal
passion, but because they can no longer live without each other, at least
not in the manner to which they have become accustomed.

Musicians and merchants work together because they share a basic
concern: where can one find a regular supply of bread? Despite
abundant evidence to the contrary, many musicians are almost normal.
Like other people, they favor three meals a day and at least minimal
shelter from the elements. Given these mundane concerns for survival,

many musicians do all they can to postpone direct confrontation with the real world, tending to the view that if their music is good enough, the world will beat a path to their studio door. This happens sometimes. But for most musicians trying to function as full-time professionals, they find it desirable, even imperative, to cooperate with a number of helpers to assist them in their careers and their search for steady income. Today, *these musicians' "helpers" outnumber the composers and performers,* and they are indispensable in today's world of music-making. The successful musician can hardly function without the ongoing professional assistance of a whole array of associates — agents, managers, promoters, producers, sound engineers, broadcasters, merchants, attorneys, business advisors and accountants. These practitioners often see themselves as more important than the musicians they serve. They are often correct in that conceit. In our consumer-oriented economy, the packaging of a "product" is often more important than its contents.

Not even a Hollywood press agent could invent enough adjectives to describe the vitality of the music business in the late twentieth century. In recent decades, it has grown so rapidly, it could be said that no one has yet found time to figure out how to run the store. Music is produced and consumed today at a rate that could not have been imagined before the development of mass communication technology. The "music business" (the term will be used here to include the art, the profession and the business of music) now grosses a figure exceeding $20 billion worldwide. But of all the recognized professions, of all the major components in the world economy, the music business is the most inadequately researched. We have had two or three useful books written by copyright attorneys, but they do not even attempt to cover such fundamental aspects of the field as music in broadcasting and music merchandising. To this day, no thorough study of music *as a profession* has been published. The present book is the first comprehensive account of the music business and today's music profession.

Perceptions of the profession and business of music are usually at wide variance from reality. This is partly due to the fact that the field is so diverse and changes so rapidly. But it *can* be understood. It is argued that the music business, particularly the record industry, is fundamentally irrational. The music business does appear to have more than its share of lunatics. But most of what really goes on in the business and the profession does submit to rational analysis.

As with any large and diverse enterprise, a beginning of understanding can occur with an examination of its components. That is our method here. But before we do this, let's consider the overall magnitude of the music business today. These facts can provide a perspective:

- *Americans spend more money buying records and tapes than they do going to the movies or attending sporting events.*

- *One out of five Americans plays a musical instrument. These musicians spend $2 billion a year on instruments, accessories and sheet music.*

- *The annual sales of records combined with its prime delivery medium, radio, exceed the GNP of over 80 countries in the United Nations.*

- *We own more radios and record players than bathtubs.*

This pervasive interest in music and entertainment begins with a young audience: by the time a youngster has escaped from high school, he has spent more time watching television and listening to records than he has *in school!* The rational mind has difficulty handling this kind of information. But the facts can be demonstrated. Our task is to discover what they mean.

MORE THAN POP

A glance at the world of music-making today might suggest that the new mass audience is found only in the field of popular music. This is not true. The American Symphony Orchestra League reports that, in the last 10 years, the number of concerts by professional symphony orchestras has doubled. This particular audience now exceeds 23 million paying customers each season. Opera continues to attract its loyal audience, now being served by 45 professional and semiprofessional companies in this country (up from 27 companies 12 years ago). As for dance (ballet, modern), this ancient art attracted about one million paying customers in 1965. Ten years later, that audience had grown 15 times over. As for the sale of records of "classical" music, NARM (National Association of Recording Merchandisers) reports that sales figures for this repertoire is about equal to those for jazz (each comprising about five percent of the total market for records).

The tremendous growth in music production and consumption is not unique to the USA. The rate of growth is even faster in some foreign countries, e.g., Japan.

One of the mysteries of the music scene is that many of those involved in it, composers, performers, business people, educators, do not understand how huge it has become, nor does the majority of the participants understand how it really works. Many artists and music merchants lack even basic information. Worse yet, much of what they believe they "know" is either out-of-date or incorrect. The most disturbing aspect of this lack of understanding is that it is apparent in our schools and colleges. The result of this pervasive ignorance about the business and the profession has been tragic. Only about 10 percent of the 327,000 members of the AFM work steadily in music. Top graduates of our conservatories fail to get their careers even started. The turnover among personnel already working in the business end of music is alarming. Many of these operatives resign or get fired because they do not know enough about their own jobs to hold them. Employers keep searching for people who know how to function effectively in the field.

Does this all mean that musicians are dumbbells? Not at all. What it does mean is that the profession and the business have changed so radically, few people, including the educators, have been able to keep up with it. As Arthur Schlesinger Jr. and Alvin Toffler have expressed it, we are all bewildered by the rate of change, the velocity of history.

So what does the artist or the businessman do about this predicament? How can he get the information he needs to function effectively in this field? Four sources are suggested. First, he can read "the trades," the music business magazines and papers. I have rarely seen a music business office that did not have these publications in evidence; their presence is as predictable as a Gideon Bible in a hotel room. Who reads the trades? Everybody, from "gofors" to presidents. Since the business changes so rapidly, the trades are an indispensable source for current information. Another source is the various professional meetings. These regional and national affairs are sponsored by artists' unions, industry associations, merchants and trade magazines. *Billboard* has been the most active sponsor of industry-wide professional meetings. Certain information can be found in a handful of books on such subjects as copyright, radio programming, etc.

The serious investigator should be able to attend a university and get thoroughly prepared for a career in the music business. Bad news. Almost to the present day only a few colleges and universities offer complete curriculums in this field. Following the leadership in 1967 of the University of Miami, other accredited institutions have been unbelievably slow in setting up comprehensive studies in the music business field. But this picture is improving.

FINDING A PAYING AUDIENCE

History books provide only spotty information on how the musician fared in earlier times as a professional. Music historians, most of them tenured behind the protective walls of universities, have rarely shown concern for the bread-and-butter needs of the working musicians. This traditional lack of concern for the professional status and financial condition of musicians dates from earliest times. In the beginning, music-making was undertaken by individuals and groups simply for their own pleasure. The performer was also his own composer. If there was an audience, it was only a social gathering; it did not occur to the early musicians that they might develop an audience that would pay to hear them sing their songs.

The first professional musicians in western civilization were the mimes of the Greek and Roman theatre. They were singing-dancing actors. Roman law held them to be disreputable types, calling them *infami* (outlaws). In the Middle Ages the minstrels of Germany and the jongleurs of France were the first professionals. Accounts of their activities read like a review from *Variety*. These musicians were actually vaudevillians, and their acts might include, not only singing and dancing, but juggling, card tricks, even knife throwing and trained animals. Show business had begun — in the Middle Ages.

A handful of musicians involved in secular music managed to earn at least part of their livelihood during the Middle Ages and Renaissance periods. But in the religious sector, almost no musicians enjoyed real professional status. The choirboys and men of the western church sang for free. The male voice parts were usually sung by resident monks or other church worthies who performed in the cathedral choirs as just another part of their Christian service. The first professional composers in the religious field seem to have first appeared in Paris around 1100 A.D. at the Notre Dame cathedral. But musicologists cannot provide a satisfactory account of how the profession of composing music took shape in the following centuries. To this day, church musicians in most communities are either unpaid or paid below professional rates. It would appear that they are still expected to offer their professional services for the glory of God. That may be an admirable calling, but doesn't pay the rent.

Conditions for the working musician were somewhat better in Germany in the fifteenth and sixteenth centuries. The tradition of guilds included the music "trade." Musicians' guilds were organized and influenced, not only working conditions, but creative and artistic standards. These early guilds were active in organizing composition and singing contests and formulated elaborate rules for them (an accurate account of these proceedings may be found in Richard Wagner's opera, *Die Meistersinger Vön Nürnberg*).

In the following period in Europe, increasing numbers of artists were employed by nobility as house musicians. Composers and performers were put on the royal payroll to make music in the salons, ballrooms and chapels of these fancy pads. But nobility looked upon these artists as servants, and they were expected to enter the buildings of these royal estates from rear doors. Rehearsals of the resident orchestras and opera companies would be delayed until the hired hands had cleaned the rooms, polished the boots and shoveled out the stables. During Haydn's 30-year tenure at Esterháza, one wonders if he also did windows. Despite some advances in status, modern-day musicians sometimes complain they are still working too close to the barnyard.

In our own time, the champion for elevating the status of the music profession has been the American Federation of Musicians of the United States and Canada. The 609 locals of the AFM receive requests regularly from sponsors of civic events, political rallies and community benefits. These requests are usually sung in the same key: ". . . please, would you just send over some musicians for our event? They'll really enjoy it and, of course, we'll have some nice refreshments for them." Most musicians have been willing to play benefits, but they have also been exploited by those who would have them "share their art" just for the inherent pleasure of it. AFM locals have developed an effective response for unreasonable requests of this kind: they offer to supply union musicians without fee, provided the other trades and professions — stagehands, waiters, teamsters bartenders — also work without pay. It is a fair offer; there are no takers.

Gradually, musicians acquired recognition as professionals with the development of a new phenomenon, the paying audience. This first occurred in the musical theatre and opera, particularly in Italy and England. When the public began to pay its way into a room to hear music, *the music business had begun.* By the 1800s, the public had accepted the idea that you had to buy a ticket to hear a professional. Increasing numbers of paid concerts developed, not only in European cities such as Vienna, London and Paris, but in New York, Philadelphia and Boston.

We lack reliable accounts of who organized and promoted the earliest paid employment for professional musicians. Perhaps the earliest notable artist's manager or agent was Mozart's father, Leopold Mozart. Young Mozart's talent was discovered by his father before the youngster had barely graduated from diapers. Starting when Wolfgang was six years old, father Leopold started presenting his son to all of Europe, peddling the kid's talent like the valuable merchandise it was. But Mozart's father did not teach his son much about career management. Mozart junior earned considerable sums in his short lifetime but seems to have died a pauper. Mismanagement of money and careers is not unique to the twentieth century.

A more recent ancestor of today's music entrepreneur was the circus genius, P. T. Barnum. In 1850, when Jenny Lind, "The Swedish Nightingale," came to America, Barnum presented her around the country as if she were a star acrobat. Barnum's bookings earned the artist $130,000 in her American tour which, in today's dollars, would amount to about half a million.

Since the days of Barnum (and Barnum was right), the development of a growing audience for music took place in a circus atmosphere. The public likes a good show, and the music business grew, even in the classical field, in a razzle-dazzle, show biz atmosphere. At the same time Barnum was touring opera star Jenny Lind, other entrepreneurs were developing enthusiastic audiences for that unique American contribution to theatre — the minstrel show. This is not the place to treat the racist overtones of that phenomenon; our interest in minstrelsy here must be limited to how it fostered the development of the popular music business. While most of the performers were white, increasing numbers of blacks began to take part (as early as the Middle Ages, musicians from Africa were in Europe entertaining whites). But it was not until the mid-nineteenth century, with the development of the minstrel show, that blacks began to find a place in the white musical world as full professionals. This development turned out to be of historical significance, for it would be impossible to even conceive of music in the twentieth century without the pervasive influence of black musicians. I would agree with the brilliant American historian—critic Henry Pleasants in naming the music of the twentieth century the Afro-American epoch. No full understanding of the music of our time, popular or classical, is possible, in my view, for anyone who has not read Pleasants' landmark book, *Serious Music - And All That Jazz.*

The increasing popularity of minstrelsy in the 1850-1900 period enlarged public awareness and appreciation of popular music and the entertainment business. Near the end of the Reconstruction period, the size and affluence of the middle class grew. By the 1890s, the piano was a standard adornment in the parlors of upper middle class white families. On thousands of piano racks across the land, one would probably find, in addition to some Stephen Foster songs and a hymnal, a copy of *After the Ball*. The year was 1892, and this song was the first million-seller (in a 12-month period). It eventually sold 10 million copies of sheet music.

By this time, a number of large publishing houses had developed, e.g., E. B. Marks, Witmark Bros., T. B. Harms, Leo B. Feist, Mills, Shapiro and

Bernstein. Some of these firms remain active and prosperous today. These popular music publishers took pride in being able to spot potential hits. When they couldn't find them, the publishers wrote the songs themselves or put composers on weekly salaries to work in-house.

These late nineteenth century publishers developed, through trial and error, the merchandising methods that prevailed until radio came in strong in the 1920s. Songs were introduced in a number of ways. In the final days of minstrelsy (which died of its own excesses c. 1900), song pluggers would attempt to persuade the performers to use material coming off the presses. When vaudeville and burlesque began to displace the minstrel shows, pluggers contacted the headliners and even the lesser acts to try to get them to use the songs their firms were pushing at the time. A publisher who would come up with a piece of material that some vaudeville headliner like Al Jolson or Eddie Cantor would sing was almost assured of a hit, for these were the superstars of their day (1920s, 1930s).

In the 1920s, the music industry felt the huge impact of new media of mass communication. The sale of records was excellent; the first million-seller came along. Industry leaders misjudged radio broadcasting; they held a view exactly opposite the conventional wisdom of today. When radio started in the 1920s, the publishers fought it, believing that "giving music away" through this medium would hurt sheet music sales. Overexposure, they argued, via radio broadcasting was killing songs in six weeks; potential customers could not get down to the store to make a purchase before the song's popularity had waned. It should be pointed out that publishers' incomes from broadcast performances at that time were zero.

Another significant development in the entertainment field occurred in 1927 when "the talkies" began. Movie producers discovered, with the very first sound film (a musical titled *The Jazz Singer* starring Al Jolson), that audiences would buy a lot of theatre tickets to hear songs sung on "the silver screen." The major studios began scrambling for synchronization rights to enable them to turn out musical films in rapid succession.

During The Great Depression of the 1930s, million-selling records disappeared, and sales of sheet music dropped way down also. Attendance at vaudeville theatres dropped too, with the growing popularity of the movie musical. Concurrent with these depressions in the music market, radio broadcasting grew rapidly. Music publishers now shifted their attention from plugging vaudeville performers to the new stars of radio. The network broadcasts at that time emanated mostly from New York, Chicago and Los Angeles. Publishers closed their regional offices across the land and focused their plugging efforts on these new broadcasting centers. It worked. The publishers required about 24 hours to discover that they should now point their promotional efforts toward the big bands and their singers who had weekly, sometimes nightly, radio broadcasts (which, at that time, were referred to as "remotes"). Songplugging had grown from a local to a national enterprise with the development of network radio.

Publishers were not the only ones to benefit from the coming of network broadcasting. Big bands became name bands because of network radio. Then the name bands became the record stars. Management noticed that the best-selling big band records featured the band's singer. So alert talent handlers pulled the singers off the bandstand (Frank Sinatra, Doris Day, Ella Fitzgerald, etc.) and started them working alone — for much more money. This was the beginning of the present era of the dominance of the popular singer; they became the new stars and superstars, with the help of recordings and films.

During World War II, the whole world seemed to discover the appeal of America's popular music. Much of this world-wide popularity was fostered by the Armed Forces Radio network. With over 90 stations broadcasting American-made records around the world, millions of listeners, not just the G.I.'s for whom the broadcasts were intended, heard the great entertainment available from this kind of music. By the late 1940s, the American style had become a *world* style. And so it is today.

When the G.I.'s returned home, they bought large quantities of records. Music instrument factories, shut down earlier to produce weapons, were now spewing out guitars, organs, pianos, wind and percussion instruments in quantity. The music industry was now reaching a mass market.

Record companies were moving millions of singles in the 1940s. When Columbia came out with the long-playing record, the music business again experienced a development of overwhelming significance. Now, instead of two songs per record, songwriters and publishers could place 12 songs on each release. Income could thus be increased by 600 percent. On the new LP, record buyers could hear an entire Broadway show; opera buffs could now carry home an entire opera in a box; complete symphonies could easily fit on one LP. The dollar volume of classical records grew to 10 percent of the market.

Concurrent with the growing popularity of LPs was the increasing availability of low-cost tape recorders. Add to this the boom in hi-fi. For relatively low cost, consumers could now hear recorded or broadcast music with a quality of sound that was better, audiophiles believed, than their local concert hall.

The music business was getting so good, it attracted not only new venture capital, but a new breed of merchants, some of whom knew what they were doing. New distribution and merchandising methods were developed. The most significant marketing development at the time was the discovery that people would buy records wherever they shopped. Enter *the rack jobber.* This new kind of music merchant set up record racks in supermarkets, variety stores, department stores — anywhere shoppers passed by. So it was, by the 1960s, music came to be vended like cornflakes.

Large corporations began to notice that people in the music publishing and record business were making more money than the filmmakers. They decided to buy in. By the 1970s, even the conservative Beverly Hills bankers got the message: music enterprise was now an acceptable risk. They began making loans to music publishers, record producers and artists' managers, types of people they used to classify with street vendors. The main attraction to these new investors was record production. In what other kind of business enterprise could an individual or a bank invest, say, $10,000 in a master tape, then receive from it royalties one hundred times that amount, if the record hit? To the inexperienced investor, the music business began to look like a money tree.

Investors of all types tried to buy into the music industry, whether or not they knew anything about its hazards. The buying and selling of music companies by the 1970s resulted in the majority of firms becoming controlled by a handful of giant corporations. This trend continues.

INFLUENCE OF MASS MEDIA

The unique phenomenon in music in the twentieth century is the discovery of new audiences. The world has always been full of music lovers, but it was not until the development of mass communication technology that so many "new" audiences were uncovered. Through mass media, *everybody* could be reached, most of them at the speed of light. Until the 1920s, most professional music-making was addressed to a small, elite audience that was accustomed to buying tickets to attend the opera, the symphony, perhaps a Broadway musical. When radio, records and television came along, that elite audience not only continued, it grew. But now it was joined and immeasurably augmented by whole new audiences for folk music, country and western songs, blues and jazz. Mass media forever changed the size and composition of "the music audience," and merchants were quick to respond to the new millions of paying customers.

Diverse as these audiences are, the largest segment of consumers is still found "in the middle." For now, we shall refer to this group as the popular audience. Music addressed to this audience experienced its greatest change in the 1950s when performers such as Elvis Presley began to merge the styles of country, gospel, rhythm and blues. Then the Beatles came along and the new style rocked and rolled around the world like a sonic boom. An entire generation of music lovers was electrified. Mother and father were outraged at first by this aural corruption. But the Beatles soon won over just about everybody. This can be attributed to their natural talent, brilliant record production, and personalities that viewed the whole phenomenon with a disarming sense of humor. Perhaps rock and roll wasn't so outrageous after all, if you didn't take it too seriously.

The Beatles had a great sense of theatre, as did Elvis. Without knowing it, they established what I call rock theatre, where the performer engages the eye as much as the ear. Purists abhor this mix of music and show business, but it has been a favorite of audiences since the Middle Ages.

Just about everybody has offered to explain the overwhelming popularity of rock and the rock culture of the 1960s. Probably the most sensible explanation is that rock and roll music emerged simultaneously with "The Movement" and the feelings young people had about the military draft, Vietnam war, racism and anyone over 30. Part of The Movement was expressed in what Daniel Yankelovich calls "the new naturalism," a desire to return to nature, even primitivism. The rock audience turned to record stars as if they were messiahs, imitating and emulating their appearance, language, and social attitudes. When this happened, the performers and the audience became *as one*, indistinguishable. With this merger, the music business became big business.

2

THE MUSIC BUSINESS SYSTEM

The harder I work, the luckier I get.
NFL COACH

As I pointed out, it has been alleged that the music business is now too big and too complicated to submit to systematic investigation. More than a handful of observers has characterized the industry as one big zoo. After 22 years in the middle of the Los Angeles scene, I can attest that this characterization of the business is often close to the mark. On the business side, a sizable percentage of individuals in the field appear to have come directly into their executive offices from careers in the used car business. As for the artists, many seem to do all they can to avoid reality. The music business does appear to have more than its share of unstable personalities — nuts and geniuses work side by side in the peculiar enterprise of selling dreams. But if the business were dominated by irrational types, it could not really function today, because the apparatus is now so large and complicated.

The industry can be conceived as being comprised of two basic elements: *the musician and the audience.* Drawing them together is the business of music. Despite evidence of a prevailing anarchy, the music industry operates much like other large commercial enterprises, for example, the automobile business. The main difference between the two is, of course, the product. The car people change models only once a year; the music industry changes its product every day. The car salesmen have time to figure out how to move their merchandise. Musicians and their agents don't seem to have time to visit the rest room. And if they do, they take along a trade paper to study the latest charts. In examining the business aspects of music, it is this rapid change of "product" that makes it unique.

GETTING THROUGH THE MAZE

Because of the unique problems of marketing music, practitioners have developed, through trial and error, a modus operandi. In short, they figured out a system. More accurately, the music industry today is a group of subsystems. Each of these subsystems can be analyzed and understood. This study will proceed accordingly and examine how each subsystem relates to the other systems comprising the whole. Before pursuing this plan in detail, let's begin with a simple overview. Here is a sequence of events that might occur to a new song today as it finds its way to market:

1- *The composer writes the song.*

2- *The publisher publishes the song.*

3- *The publisher persuades a producer to record the song.*

4- *The record producer matches the song to a suitable recording artist, produces a master tape.*

5- *The record company releases the record.*

6- *The record promoter persuades the radio program director to broadcast the record.*

7- *The merchant sells the record, perhaps the sheet music, for the song.*

8- *The recording artist's personal manager recommends a concert tour, contacts a talent agency.*

9- *The talent agency books the tour.*

10- *The attorneys have negotiated the contracts.*

11- *The concert promoters promote the concerts, sell the tickets.*

12- *The road manager moves the people and the equipment.*

13- *The concert producer (or production manager) dresses the stage, lights it, reinforces the sound.*

14- *The artist performs.*

15- *ASCAP and BMI collect performance royalties on the music.*

16- *The accountant counts the money.*

17- *The managers, agents and promoters pay their bills.*

18- *The government collects the taxes.*

And, we could frequently add, the psychiatrist seeks to heal those who have taken part.

If we were to add to this scenario all the related activities and support personnel that become involved, we would have a cast of thousands. Most of the actors in this drama know little about what the others are doing, the concurrent subplots and bit players. According to The Peter Principle, they have reached their level of incompetence. They are unlikely to rise to a higher station — a better job, more money, unless they study the other facets of the music business system. Those who have done this have become leaders in the field.

Universities have schools of business management which attempt to teach their students how to run complex enterprises. Business management textbooks employ a nomenclature and taxonomy that terrifies most musicians. One of the favorite terms in describing administrative methodology is "systems management." Fat textbooks treat the mystique of systems management with austere language and reverence. But when the meaning of the term is reduced to simple English, systems management means the people know what they are supposed to do, their associates understand their roles, and the participants have figured out how to work together effectively. Not exactly a new idea in administration.

Another concept of administration also has a rather arcane title: "management by objectives." Books have been written about it, too. Again at the risk of incurring wrath among my friends who are professors of management, I would suggest that "management by objectives" really means that a person can save a lot of time and money by directing his energies toward what he is *really* trying to accomplish. This sounds absurdly simple, of course. But most of us waste too much time because we have not really defined precisely what we are trying to do.

INFORMATION HANDLING

In recent times, available information has doubled about every ten years. Old methods of keeping informed are hopelessly inadequate today. This is as true for the artist as it is for the businessman. New approaches to information handling had to be found. Everyone today is snowed by a paper blizzard, and firms such as IBM have designed mechanical systems they describe as "information handling" or "word processing." In the field of accounting and market research, practitioners are dependent upon computer technology to encode and decode data. Firms in the music business are now as dependent as other industries on computer science. In record label headquarters I observe as many computers in operation as in my bank.

Even composers have invoked the aid of various "information systems," such as those of Arnold Schoenberg and Joseph Schillinger. Some composers have used computer assistance. Also, Robert Moog came along and helped musicians synthesize their information in electronic music composition. The most recent information handling technology is being applied to computer-assisted audio mixing and mixdown.

Some creative people are turned off, not on, by the increasing application of technology to music. Some individuals do not accept such systematic approaches to problem solving. When I was teaching at UCLA, I once asked our visiting lecturer, Goddard Lieberson, then president of CBS, why Columbia Records released recordings of the avant-garde school of serious composition, realizing ahead of time that the firm could not expect to recoup its investments. Without hesitation, Mr. Lieberson answered, "Sheer caprice!"

Students of record production and recording technology, *Trebas Institute of Recording Arts,* Montreal, Canada. Executive Director, David P. Leonard (right) checks on student progress on this 40-channel Harrison console. Instructor: Real LeBlanc (behind telephone).

THE NEW PROFESSIONALS

3

We have no art. We do everything as well as possible.
BALINESE MUSICIAN

As pointed out above, the music business grew so rapidly, companies could not find enough qualified people to handle their affairs. The business has never had enough of Goddard Lieberson's competence and taste to go around. The fast talkers and snake oil peddlers worked their way into executive offices; some still hide out there. On the artistic side, the shortage of genuine talent has been even more obvious. We are familiar with the results of this incompetence at all levels of the music business: thousands of pointless songs, weak records, wasted investments — and countless numbers of frustrated individuals whose careers go nowhere. But criticism of the music business in earlier years should not be too harsh, for never before had art and commerce been forced into such a strange new alliance. Certainly our schools and colleges have not been much help in preparing people for these new kinds of careers.

As the industry grew, companies had to accept people walking in off the street, then train them in-house, on the job. A system centuries old was rediscovered: masters taught apprentices. It was a slow and expensive process, but it worked reasonably well. Since the mid-1970s, it can be said that the music business has been run more and more by individuals of real ability and imagination. I call these people *the new professionals*. Their most striking attribute is their versatility: the publisher may be the songwriter; the record producer may double as the arranger or write the contracts; the recording artist may be a wizard at the mixer board; the lawyer may be an imaginative career manager.

These new professionals come into the field from all walks of life — from postal clerk to stock broker, from high school dropout to university graduate. Most of our top studio musicians not only paid their dues playing in saloons, they have graduated from such institutions as Juilliard and Indiana University. Some of our new professionals are emerging from the University of Miami, which offers two degree programs in music merchandising. A gratifying number of my own students are enjoying successful careers in the music business. The versatility of these new professionals makes it possible for them to share in the planning and execution of activities relating to the creative, artistic, managerial and business aspects of the field.

Qualified professionals can be found in various parts of the country. But the ones we hear about are located in one of the three recording centers, New York, Nashville and Los Angeles. This is because most of the music business is based on the star system — specifically the recording star system. Since it costs so much money now to launch a performer's career, produce a record, finance concert tours, investors are reluctant to put their money into any individual who lacks star potential. But predicting stardom is usually impossible, so performers and investors continue to gamble in the music game. Since only a limited number of performers can attain star status, it is fortunate that the music business system offers many opportunities for individuals needed to help make the system function. No performer today can ascend to stardom or hang there in orbit without an array of qualified supporting satellites. As this book unfolds, we shall examine how stars and their satellites make the music business work.

When a musician or businessman makes it big, how much of that success can be attributed to just plain luck? The professional manager of Chappell Music's Hollywood office told me that many of the people in the business he talks to suspect that the whole music game is "just one big crap shoot." If you get lucky, you win. This is true more often than some experts might dare to admit. Many a song, many a performer has zoomed to "overnight success." But luck can sustain an artist or a company only briefly. For any level of continuity, one must add to the luck factor genuine talent and professional competence.

ART VERSUS COMMERCE

Many who do not share in the prosperity of the music industry view it with resentment, even hostility. They suggest it be spelled "the mu$ic bu$ine$$." Some of the most bitter critics are found among the members of the American Federation of Musicians who are unemployed or underemployed. While most of these musicians are not even seeking full-time employment in music, the union comprises a large pool of frustrated professionals ("I've got a diploma from Juilliard but I clerk at Sears to pay my rent. How come this lunatic banging on that drum set makes $100,000 a year?"). Another group of unhappy professionals is found among the nation's music educators ("Most rock and roll is just pornography for the ears. How can I interest my junior high kids in anything subtle?"). Equally concerned are the graduates of our universities who majored in music education ("I can't find a job teaching school, and my university didn't offer one course in the music business. Where do I turn?"). Some of the strongest resentment of today's popular music comes from classically-trained singers ("What do you mean, 'singer'? Most of those pop recording stars don't know the first thing about tone placement or breath control."). Still further criticism of the popular music business comes from jazz musicians and jazz fans ("Jazz has lost its purity, its honesty. Everyone's gone commercial. God-damned amps and Arps!").

If the pop performers are put down, so are the pop composers. Those familiar with the great standards that came from Broadway shows and Tin Pan Alley until rock took over look upon today's popular song repertoire as a vast wasteland.

Critics of contemporary music are sometimes just as harsh when observing the blatant commercialism in the so-called classical field. What is more embarrassing than to hear an opera singer trying to swing a popular song? The spectacle is equaled only by the pop crooner who attempts to sing *The Star Spangled Banner.* Wide-scaled compromise of artistic standards in the classical field is found among our professional symphony orchestras. These groups are trying desperately to reduce their deficits by sponsoring "pops" concerts. Ludicrous bookings sometimes result ("Hear the Denver Symphony with Vincent Price in 'Halloween Night' "). The scramble for an audience includes musicians and agents from every sector of the musical world.

Criticisms of the cheap and tawdry in the music business are richly deserved. Too much of the repertoire is trash. Too many untalented composers and performers enjoy undeserved "success," at least for a while. Far too many genuinely talented people have not found their place in the profession. It is not unusual to hear musicians active in recording refer to themselves as musical whores, admitting they sometimes prostitute their talents to turn a musical trick for their employers.

I have summarized the criticisms and negative aspects of the music business. Yet, on balance, we can point out just as many good things. Today, there is much to feel positive about in the art and business of music.

One of the encouraging aspects of the music industry since the mid-1970s is that there is a diminishing tolerance, by the industry and the public, for the incompetent performer, the pointless song. The simple truth is that the untalented writers and performers and producers and agents are being found out and displaced. Some untalented individuals will continue to get by, for a while. But the public and the industry increasingly demand the real thing, genuine competence. Singers, not clowns, sell the records today. A similar cleansing of ranks is occurring among composers and lyricists. The reason the majority of new songs sound bad is because they are. The truth is that *the insatiable demands of the market exceed the creative capacity of the suppliers.* At no period in music history have composers been expected to create several hundred songs *every week.* Any turn of the radio dial proves that such an achievement is impossible. So the public rejects the weak material and selects the best of what's available. This filtering process has been used by audiences for centuries in determining what is worth hearing again.

As for the dominant musical style of our time, rock and roll, it is the most ridiculed and most loved of any genre in the history of music. Hundreds of millions of its fans, now worldwide, react to it with a devotion tantamount to religious ecstasy. But ridicule of the music and its audience reveals arrogance. We live in a time uncongenial for snobs. The best of rock is as good as, sometimes better than, other popular idioms. And quite apart from its musical content, some of the texts to the folk-rock songs from writers in the Bob Dylan league contain more meaning than many opera librettos.

Defenders of contemporary music argue that some of the songwriters since the early 1960s rank with Gershwins and Kerns of earlier decades. Some of the Beatles' best work may last as long as the great Broadway show standards; those of Michel Legrand certainly will. As for the arranger-conductors in the MOR (Middle-of-the-Road) repertoire, I would rank the stunning scores of Percy Faith and Nelson Riddle with the best orchestrations of the nineteenth century masters. What about the film composers? Until the 1960s, most of them remained reluctant to abandon reliance on the clichés of post-romanticism. Once they did, the quality of film scoring began to reach new heights. The best film composers today, e.g., Jerry Goldsmith, are producing music of a quality superior to the work of many so-called serious composers.

HELP WANTED!

Whatever aesthetic judgments are made about today's music and the music business, the field attracts more aspiring professionals than it can accommodate. Part of this attraction has been artificially induced through the show biz movies and TV shows young people have seen since early childhood. The music and entertainment fields don't look like hard work or heartbreak. It looks like so much fun! If one's professional goal is fun, better to become a golf pro.

The reason many aspirants fail to achieve their goal is not so much a shortage of opportunity as a lack of sufficient talent and an understanding of how the music business system works. But many aspiring professionals do make it, of course. Why? Luck? Timing? These factors have helped launch many successful careers in both the music and business ends of the field. I believe there are four other factors contributing to the success of those who "win" in the music business:

1- *They are strongly motivated; they really want to win.*

2- *They are talented — and they surround themselves with talented associates.*

3- *They persevere; they hang in there until they win.*

4- *They get the important information.*

If you feel you need help with the first three items, you may have to alter your genes, or see your shrink. *This book will deal only with item number four.* In that regard, I shall assert again and again in these pages that the music business offers excellent career opportunities for the really talented individual, provided that individual gets the important information — and acts upon it. That information is set forth here.

WOMEN IN MUSIC

An equal place for women in music was held back for centuries for a number of social-historical reasons, the strongest of which was the western church, which denied females the right to sing and play instruments in Christian services. This prohibition tended to limit women's opportunities also as composers and directors. But in more recent times, it is news to no one that women have figured prominently, alongside men, in all kinds of musical activity, particularly in secular music.

It is not generally understood that, in the business and administrative sector of the music industry, women have been active, even prominent, for many years. They still lack their equal share at the middle and top management levels, but a number of women can be identified who have had executive positions in music at the highest level. Theodora Zavin comes first to mind. Ms. Zavin, a graduate of Columbia Law School, joined the BMI staff in New York in 1952 as resident counsel. Rising rapidly through the ranks, in 1968 she was named senior vice president of BMI. One of Ms. Zavin's many honors was being elected to the chairmanship (chairpersonship?) of the Board of Trustees of the Educational Foundation of American Women in Radio and Television, Inc. She also served on the executive committee of the American Bar Association.

Another woman who has worked at a top level in management is Jo Walker of Nashville. She joined the staff of the Country Music Association in 1958. Shortly thereafter, Ms. Walker was named CMA's executive director, a position in which she managed to develop CMA into one of the most vital professional associations we have in all of music. Ms. Walker has also been active in the organization, American Women in Radio and Television.

One of the most influential women in music and the arts has been Nancy Hanks, the person largely responsible for developing strong financial support from Congress for the National Endowment for the Arts, particularly during the years she headed NEA.

Increasing numbers of women are rising to important executive positions in the recording industry. One such individual is Eileen Rothschild, one of the senior executives with the Robert Stigwood Organization (RSO Records). The list of women of accomplishment in music and the music business could go on and on.

These individuals have earned their prestigious positions not because they were females, but because they were qualified. Most of us men believe (with typical male vanity, of course) that we have overcome our chauvinistic hang-ups and now welcome the ladies as co-workers at all levels of professional activity. As a matter of fact, firms now appear to be actively seeking more women for middle and top management jobs, holding to the view that the female voice should be carefully listened to in an industry where the majority of consumers are girls and women.

Theodora Zavin
Senior Vice-President, BMI

Jo Walker
Executive Director, Country Music Association

Note: Throughout the book the author has used the words *he* and *his* rather than *he/she* or *his/hers,* following time-honored practice. This usage is for simplicity and is meant, of course, to include both men and women.

Part Two

SONGWRITING, PUBLISHING, COPYRIGHT

4

PROFESSIONAL SONGWRITING

There should be a single Art Exchange in the world, to which the artist would simply send his works and be given in return as much as he needs. As it is, one has to be half a merchant on top of everything else, and how badly one goes about it!

LUDWIG VAN BEETHOVEN[1]

THE MARKET

Everything begins with the songwriter. One creative individual must first produce before anyone else in the music business can make a sound. Or a dollar. New songs are the lifeblood of the industry; they must be continually pumped through the music system. The music industry continues to thrive on the great standards, but even these wonderful evergreens are not immortal. Each generation hears a different drummer; it chooses its own standards from the current repertoire, which is ever renewing itself. Besides changing preferences, the demand for new songs has increased exponentially, because mass communications media have expanded the audience tenfold. The music business gobbles up hundreds of new songs every week.

If the demand for new songs is insatiable, why do so many amateur songwriters fail to find acceptance for their material? Many reasons can be identified for a new writer's lack of success. This book will identify them, then show how the really talented writers can get started as professionals.

Publishers and performers are inundated with submissions. Eager young songwriters descend on the recording centers like locusts. Probably 10 percent of the people flowing through the Greyhound stations in Nashville and Hollywood are carrying a suitcase full of leadsheets.

1-Letter to Franz Anton Hoffmeister January 15, 1801.

Major publishers and record companies receive an average of 100 unsolicited songs *each week*. The problem is not that the industry lacks enough songs. The omnipresent concern is that *they cannot discover enough good ones*. We have abundant proof of this: a large number of weak songs get recorded. This is not so much because the producers lack taste (although they are not immune from this). Rather, it is that they publish and record the best they can find. When a weak song gains initial acceptance, everyone gets hurt. The powerful promotion machinery of a rich label can often crank up an initial enthusiasm for a new record. But note how quickly a weak song disappears from the charts. Most weak songs have a life expectancy of about one month, if they are lucky. That means that every individual and every company that has anything to do with that weak song loses money. So everyone begins the search anew for material good enough to survive long enough in public favor to generate enough income to at least break even.

Is it possible to define a "good" song? Yes, if you know what to look for. Can anyone predict professional acceptance? Quite often, if you know how. Does anyone know which songs will become lasting hits? No one on this earth. Can a creatively talented songwriter break in? Very likely — if he learns his craft and learns the business.

What makes a Franz Schubert, a Richard Rodgers or a Duke Ellington? Can we identify the elements in their songs that makes us love them? Before attempting an answer, let's first note that in today's world of music, we can recognize two different kinds of "success." The first is "artistic." The second is "commercial." It would be difficult to single out, with consistency, songs that are "artistic" successes. We would be on safe ground, though, when we identify the songs that are *well-crafted* musically and lyrically. As for commercial success, it is immediately apparent from sales figures. But how far can we go in predicting how a song will fare in the marketplace? Until the Beatles came along and turned the world on its ear, musicians and merchants had a working understanding on what a "popular song" was. They knew what a C & W song was. R & B was identifiable. Today, these tidy classifications don't serve nearly as well. From eleventh century chansons to this week's charts, the all-time favorite is the love song. But then there are an infinite number of ways to express love. The Captain and Tennille once had a big hit which concerned a hot love affair between two muskrats. So even within the love song genre, it is difficult to classify songs or to predict what might be commercially successful. Hits come from everywhere. And it is this unpredictability that encourages the amateur to try to get lucky.

Whereas we have difficulty identifying the ingredients in a song that might bring it artistic or commercial success, what we can do is critically examine the great songs of the past and see what they have in common. A really great one tends to exhibit these characteristics:

1- *The song is memorable; it sticks in the mind.*

2- *The song has immediate appeal.*

3- *The text uses some kind of special imagery. Not "Your beauty makes me love you," but perhaps "Your touching makes me tremble."*

4- *The song is well-crafted: it has a beginning, a middle and an end.*

5- *Everything lyrical and musical holds to the central theme of the song. No digressions.*

6- *A great love song has an element of mystery, an indefinable enchantment. It transports the spirit and we don't know why.*

If a song possesses at least some measure of these characteristics, it has very strong potential for making it in the marketplace. So now we are on the threshold of transforming an *artistic achievement* into a *commercial success.* This work of art, possibly "inspired in heaven," now descends from on high and plummets to the city street. It begins a second childhood. It may mature into profit-yielding merchandise if these events occur:

1- *The song gets an appealing initial performance that has been captured on tape.*

2- *The record company promotes strong airplay for the record.*

3- *The song and the record suit the taste of the current market.*

4- *The record is effectively distributed and is made readily available nationally.*

THE PROFESSION

To enjoy a share of the rewards of that market, the amateur writer must become a professional. Just what is it that makes a pro? Why do so many individuals break their necks and pocketbooks to get into professional songwriting? Well, fame and fortune aren't bad. The fact is, every year complete nobodies zoom to the top. It happens, but it is rare. I suggest that besides this yearning to climb the music money tree, these other factors motivate the millions who would become professional songwriters:

1- *Composing songs can be a reaching out for love or approval.*

2- *Escape from reality. Writing can be one way of getting away from your spouse, your boss, bills, tension.*

3- *You are a performer and feel better singing your own material than borrowing from others.*

4- *Something inside compels you to be creative. This compulsion afflicts just about everybody.*

5- *You hear a lot of poor songs and figure you can do at least as well.*

Whatever the motivation, what personality types succeed as professional songwriters? I have observed that most of the pros exhibit these personality traits and work habits:

1- *They are self-assured and confident in their music. They can handle unkindness, insult, disappointment, without caving in.*

2- *They just won't give up. They persevere until they gain acceptance.*

3- *They have strong curiosity. They may start out ignorant of both their craft and their profession. But they study, observe and ask questions.*

It is easy to distinguish between an amateur and a professional. The dictionary says an amateur does what he does for love. A professional can be defined as an individual who gets paid for what he does. How many songwriters get paid, and how much? Several years ago the AGAC made some percentage estimates. Add about 50 percent to 100 percent for inflation to these AGAC figures:

> We have in the United States about 200 songwriters — composers of the big hits of the past — who enjoy annual incomes from their profession of $100,000 on up. About 1,500 songwriters now active earn a full-time writing income of $20,000 to $40,000, and 6,500 to 7,500 writers earn something less than that, perhaps $10,000 to $19,000 a year. AGAC estimates that an additional 5,000 professional writers earn less than $5,000 a year.

AGAC has also estimated that some of the older copyrights of the great standards have a present market value of at least $1 million.

THE CRAFT

Not all songwriters have been endowed with creative gifts. We lack evidence that creativity can be taught. But we do know for sure that just about any individual possessing an IQ of something above 85 can be taught the *craft* of songwriting. This can be accomplished through formal study or through private instruction.

All colleges accredited by NASM offer at least two academic years of theory study — harmony, ear training, music reading, orchestration and counterpoint. This may be the most certain way for a musician to acquire a solid theoretical background. But college composition courses tend to focus, not on songwriting, but on composition of chamber music, orchestra music and opera. About the only ongoing courses in song-writing at the college level are offered by extension divisions, outside music departments. This failure of accredited colleges to offer courses in songwriting is a national scandal. They bemoan the limited opportuni-ties for their composition graduates and at the same time fail to train them for the one field where good composers are scarce.

Who helps the lyricists? Except for studies in English literature, almost no college offers studies in lyric writing, and certainly not in how to put text to song. The exceptions are, again, those colleges and universities that offer noncredit courses in lyric writing. Lyricists wanting to learn their craft can seldom find help from our institutions of higher learning. Baton twirling, basketweaving, yes. Lyric writing, rarely.

What about the various "how-to" books addressed to songwriters? One or two presently on the market contain useful information. But most of them are lightweight, get-rich-quick publications. Their authors seem to believe that all amateur songwriters are complete idiots, incapable of absorbing more than surface information. More helpful than these silly books are the better magazines. Publications such as *Songwriter* have useful articles written by successful composers, lyricists and publishers. What about private instruction? Excellent, if you can find good teachers and can afford it. Recommended.

Many writers have learned that the most direct route to an under-standing of the craft is through study of the repertoire. Note that I said *study,* not just scan. Probably nothing could be more useful to a songwriter, amateur or pro, than to select 100 of the leading standards, then study them phrase by phrase, line by line, chord by chord. To guide you in this kind of analysis, I urge writers to study Alec Wilder's excellent book, *American Popular Song: The Great Innovators 1900-1950.* Wilder, himself a first-rate songwriter, theorist and contemporary music histori-an, studied, not 100 songs, but several thousand. Borrow Wilder's technique. If you can examine the internal workings of 100 great melodies, 100 great lyrics, you will have at least begun a serious study of the songwriting craft. The pros I know and have worked with over the years never stop studying songs. They are not only concerned with their competition, they remain eager to go on learning. Even the millionaire songwriters have studied seriously, not in a university, but on their own and with private teachers (George Gershwin, Neil Diamond, Paul McCartney). Paul Simon, millionaire composer of dozens of fine songs, stated to a reporter from *Saturday Review* back in 1969 he felt that his creative juices had stopped flowing. In asking a musician friend what he might do to get going again, his friend bluntly told him that he really lacked full command of his craft and that he'd better undertake serious study. Simon stated that he stopped smoking pot, never went back, and undertook serious study of music theory and classical guitar.

Does formal study and systematic analysis lead to writing by formula? It can, but it should not. The composer learns the theory, studies the master composers' works, then attempts to cast his own creativity into a mold found successful by others. And the really creative writers go on from there to break new ground. They rise above craft.

Another learning opportunity occurs periodically in songwriters' workshops sponsored by publishers and professional organizations. BMI has sponsored or cosponsored such workshops. Chappell Music conducts writers' workshops from time to time.

COLLABORATION

Some of the most creative artists in the popular song field have managed to write both words and music. If you can do this as well as Irving Berlin, Cole Porter, Carole King, Neil Diamond and Paul Simon, the world waits. But if your strong point is music, find yourself a lyricist. If you are good at lyrics and lack musical talent, don't try to fake it as a composer. If you write only words or only music, don't feel that you are second class. Consider Rodgers and Hammerstein, George and Ira Gershwin, Bacharach and David — and so on.

There are no formulas for locating a collaborator. Try hanging out with other writers and performers. Get the word around town what you are looking for. Songwriters of every description will surface. Some good writing teams got started through placement of a classified ad in a trade paper. I offer one suggestion: if the collaborator you hook up with is not studying his craft as seriously as you are, drop him for someone who knows he still has a lot to learn. Learn, grow together. The business rarely accommodates a dilettante.

Whatever you do, don't *hire* a collaborator. Don't respond to ads soliciting song poems. Don't pay any so-called "publisher" to "publish" your songs or add music or add words. Legitimate publishers never charge writers a dime. They pay *you*.

When two coauthors are ready to approach publishers, they should have worked out a clear understanding, preferably in writing, covering the essential issues of their relationship. The agreement should provide answers to these questions:

1- *Is all income generated by the collaboration to be equally shared?*

2- *May one writer make changes in the material unilaterally?*

3- *Under what conditions may one writer withdraw his words or music from the collaborative work if the work remains unpublished or otherwise unsuccessful?*

4- *Under what circumstances will the collaborative relationship terminate?*

5- *May the writers concurrently write alone, or with a different collaborator?*

Before completing my observation about collaboration, I should mention a special kind of working relationship that exists between the totally illiterate composer and his arranger. Some naturally gifted songwriters never bother to learn how to read and write music. They get by in the profession with their intuitive talent for inventing appealing melodies that turn out to be commercially acceptable. They usually sing their simple tunes into a tape recorder, then hire an arranger to clean up the rhythm, fix the phrasing, add the harmony and transcribe the results onto lead sheets. Musically illiterate composers sometimes experience brief success, but the only one I know of who developed a lasting career was Irving Berlin. Unless the composer is directly wired to Divine Inspiration, he will enjoy a more successful career by getting command of his craft, thus legitimizing his claim to be a professional composer.

WORK HABITS

Few things are more terrifying for the writer than a blank piece of paper. Accomplished writers have been known to stare at a blank page for hours. Some writers get stuck for months. How does a songwriter get started? One copout is to just sit there and wait for "inspiration." But every school child knows how Thomas Edison compared the value of inspiration vs. perspiration. Few professional composers can afford the luxury of waiting for special information from God. The Heavens just might not come forth with any ideas.

Every composer develops his own work habits. Many complain that their biggest problem is just getting started. Here are some ideas that work for some writers. They might work for you, too:

1- *Think of the bills you've got to pay. You've got to write this music or fall deeper in debt.*

2- *Set your sexual fantasies to music.*

3- *You come up with just a title or idea or concept or mood or — ? Think of this beginning as a seed that grows and flowers. Hang everything on that idea. Don't digress. Don't stop for coffee. Sit there and help the tiny embryo get born.*

4- *Your collaborator gave you the first phrase. Accept it even if it appears weak. Go with it, set it. If you cannot come up with something better at the moment of beginning, you have no choice. Begin.*

Most successful songwriters write *all the time*. They write, not dozens, but hundreds of songs. Many professionals like to work out a schedule, perhaps setting aside every morning for creative work. They isolate themselves for several hours, not permitting anything or anybody to interfere with their work time. Other writers are more productive working in spurts. They might stay away from their studio for days or weeks. Then they get some ideas or have to meet a deadline. They work around the clock until their "children" are born.

The truly professional songwriter works at his profession full-time. This means that when he isn't writing he is promoting what he writes. Publishers are quick to spot a writer who understands that professional success comes only from continual hustling. I know professionals who think of their work week as about one-half writing and one-half selling. Professional songwriters not only help their publishers and record companies push their material, they are on the street and in the studios and around the watering holes where the pros gather. They spread the good word. If they don't, who will know what they have written lately? How will the writer learn what people are looking for in songs? Writing and promoting, promoting and writing. This is the professional songwriter's life.

Having described the full-time professional writer, we must recognize those professionals who divide their time between composing and performing (or between writing music and some other kind of activity relating to the business). Many writers break in as performers, particularly in the fields of rock, folk and country music. In the rock field particularly, practically every successful group includes instrumentalists and singers who also write for the act.

THE BUSINESS

Anyone who wants to be a professional songwriter must learn the business aspects of his profession. Probably the majority of writers acquire this knowledge through bitter experience. There seems to be no end to the variety of misfortunes that befall trusting songwriters and musicians: they are easy prey for songsharks, crooked publishers, disappearing agents, ignorant attorneys, bootleggers and bandits. These seamy types hang around songwriters because the man or woman who writes well is hot property. Everyone in the business is after a good song. Those who cannot find their own sources may be quite prepared to lift yours.

INCOME SOURCES

When a writer manages to get published and experiences some success, he will begin to realize income from a variety of sources. Figure 4.1 provides a convenient summary.

WRITER'S POTENTIAL INCOME SOURCES

TYPE OF MUSIC USE	WHO PAYS THE WRITER
1- Broadcast performances (radio, TV)	The writer's performing rights society
2- Other (non-dramatic) performances — clubs, hotels, stadiums, etc.	The writer's performing rights society
3- Record royalties ("mechanicals")	Record producer pays the Harry Fox Agency who pays the publisher who shares with the writer
4- Sheet music sales	The publisher
5- Film (TV films, theatrical films, TV discs, tapes)	Film producer pays the publisher who shares with the writer
6- Jukeboxes, public radio and TV, cable TV	User/producer pays the Copyright Office that disburses royalties to the copyright owner or his agency
7- Transcriptions (in-flight entertainment, background music services, syndication services)	Producer pays Harry Fox Agency (or other agency) for the publisher who shares with the writer
8- Radio, TV commercials	Advertising agency pays the publisher who shares with the writer
9- Permissions (advertising/merchandising deals)	Promoter or producer pays the publisher who shares with the writer
10- Dramatic rights ("grand rights")	Producer pays the publisher (or his agent) who shares with the writer[2]

Fig. 4.1

PUBLISHING OPTIONS

If the writer manages to compose works that appear to possess commercial potential, he may be confronted with a number of publishing options. Among the most common arrangements:

1- *The writer can simply search out an established publisher and sign that firm's contract. Here the writer would participate only in* **writer's** *income.*

2- *The writer can negotiate a contract with a regular publisher where the writer gets a piece of the* **publisher's** *share of the*

2-*Grand Rights* are usually handled separately. See Chapter 6.

income. This kind of deal is often called "splitting the publishing" — the two parties usually share equally in the **publisher's** income.

3- The writer can set up his own company. This often occurs when the writer cannot persuade anyone else to publish his music.

4- If the writer is also a recording artist, his personal manager may set up a publishing company. Here the manager may own the company, retain all of the publisher's share of the income and pay his writer-performer client only the **writer's** share. Or the writer-performer might own the firm himself and engage his personal manager to administer the publishing operation.

5- The writer may enter into a partnership or set up a corporation with others to operate a publishing company. If the writer in a corporate structure were a full-time professional writer, his corporation would probably place him on a salary as a regular employee. Whether the writer also received a salary "override" on writer's royalties would be determined by the provisions of his employment contract.

Label-affiliated Deals — The most sought-after individual in publishing is the writer-recording artist. Even if his writing talents are not strong, his copyrights will produce good income if his drawing power as a performer sells records. All publishers actively seek to sign singer-songwriters. These artists are the money trees in the business.

A large percentage of record companies actively seek, sometimes coerce, new artists to place their publishing with a publishing affiliate of the label. If the label and its publishing affiliates are well-established and strongly active, the writer-performer may be best served by signing with them.

The record company-affiliated publisher will seek one of three kinds of deal:

1- Capture 100 percent of the writer's publishing rights.

2- Negotiate a **split** (often 50-50) of the publishing with the writer.

3- Assume the **administration** of the writer's own publishing company.[3]

Under normal circumstances, this kind of publisher will consider number one above to be the most attractive proposition, the administration deal the least attractive. The parties often negotiate the number two deal — they "split" the publishing.

Independent Deals — If the writer does not sign with the publishing wing of his record label, or if the writer is not a recording artist, he must

---

3-Some newly signed singer-songwriters may not even be contacted by the label's publishing wing unless there is a belief that the material the artist records can be effectively exploited.

find an "outside solution." If he does not set up his own publishing company, he will need to carefully evaluate what alternatives remain.

How does a thoughtful writer evaluate a prospective publisher? *Very carefully.* Sharks and wolves abound where big dollars are available. Let us assume the writer is unknown. If he has struggled to gain the interest of a publisher, he may be ready to sign with just about any firm that shows interest. An unpublished writer should withstand the temptation to sign the first contract thrust before him.

To assist inexperienced composers in judging a prospective publisher, consider these options:

1- *What is the publisher's reputation for integrity? Is your information objective, trustworthy, current?*

2- *How good is the firm's leadership? Competent? Stable?*

3- *What is the firm's long-term track record? Is it coasting on its catalog of golden oldies or is it currently active with contemporary material?*

4- *Is the company making money? Says who?*

5- *Who in the company cares about you and your material? Do you know the professional manager or were you signed by a subordinate person in the firm? Is there in the firm at least one individual who likes your songs enough personally to exert real effort on your behalf? This kind of personal enthusiasm is sometimes the key to successful promotion.*

6- *What are the firm's resources? Do the professional manager and his other field promoters have valuable contacts with record producers and other important people in the business? Does the company agree to produce high quality demos of your songs? Does the company have enough working capital to carry it over lean periods?*

7- *If your songs hit, does the company understand the print business and the income available from licensing for sale a variety of different editions?*

8- *If your songs hit, does the company know how to set up licensing arrangements abroad to produce foreign income?*

An unknown writer on the verge of signing his first contract with a publisher may be afraid to pose such pointed questions for fear of blowing the deal. But he needs the answers.

Whatever publishing arrangement the writer ultimately pulls together, he should base his decision on which person or firm can most successfully exploit his music *over the long term.* Is the publisher a genuine publisher with the know-how and contacts to truly exploit those copyrights internationally? Or is he only posing as a publisher, functioning only as a collection agency for the writer's royalties? *A shockingly high percentage of so-called publishers are only collecting agents and are not qualified to offer complete and genuine publishing services.* This is one of the pervading scandals of the music business.

AGAC's "Popular Songwriters Contract" — The professional association most representative of songwriters is the *American Guild of Authors and Composers.* AGAC was originally formed in 1931 as the Songwriters Protective Association. AGAC has about 4,000 members.

The organization provides a variety of useful services to its members: 1) offers a standard writers' publishing contract; 2) collects royalties charging five percent of the first $20,000, one-half of one percent thereafter; 3) maintains a copyright renewal service; 4) administers writer-publishers' catalogs (CAP, the Catalog Administration Plan); 5) provides a collaboration service; 6) maintains the Composers and Lyricists Educational Foundation; 7) operates an Estates Administration Service; 8) provides financial evaluation of songs and catalogs (to members and nonmembers); 9) offers workshops for writers.

The AGAC "yellow" contract, originally issued in 1948, was slightly revised in 1969. It strongly favored writers over publishers and, in the ensuing years, met considerable resistance. A revised AGAC contract was prepared in 1977, a markup version of which was sent to publishers for their reactions. Early in 1978 the new AGAC contract appeared. Many publishers continue to resist, even refuse, to sign even this revised contract, arguing that its terms do not take into consideration the minimum needs of the publisher. But if a writer is in a strong negotiating position, he may be able to persuade the prospective publisher to sign it. Failing this, the writer and his lawyer can use at least some of its essential terms in negotiating their own agreement with the publisher who is anxious to sign the writer. Some provisions of the AGAC contract are not particularly weighted in favor of the writer, but are just good sense to have in any equitable publishing contract.

Here are the essential provisions of the current AGAC Popular Songwriters Contract[4]:

1- *The writer warrants that the composition is ". . . his sole, exclusive and original work . . ." and that he has the right and power to make the contract and that ". . . there exists no adverse claim to or in the composition."*

2- *The publisher pays at least some advance, deductible from the writer's royalties.*

3- *Royalties on printed editions are based on the wholesale selling price and are 10 percent on the first 200,000 copies sold in the USA and Canada, 12 percent on sales in excess of 200,000 and 15 percent when sales reach 500,000.*

4- *The publisher pays the writer 50 percent of the publisher's receipts from most sources outside the USA and Canada.*

4-Published complete in the appendix.

5- *The writer shares 50-50 with the publisher on income derived from most other sources, e.g., mechanical royalties, synchronization rights, transcriptions and block licenses. Before splitting this money in half, the publisher may discount what he pays any collecting agent, such as Harry Fox.*

6- *The publisher must obtain the writer's consent before granting use of the composition in a movie, broadcast commercial or dramatico-musical presentation.*

7- *The writer's royalties must be held in trust by the publisher and not used for any other purpose.*

8- *If the publisher fails to get a commercial record of the composition within one year, the contract terminates. But the writer may extend the first year by six months for the publisher to obtain this goal, providing the publisher pays the writer $250.*

9- *The publisher must print and offer for sale regular piano copies or provide such copies or leadsheets to the writer.*

10- *The publisher must pay the writer 50 percent of foreign advances received by the publisher.*

11- *The term (length) of the contract may be for any number of years but not more than 40 ". . . or 35 years from the date of first release of a commercial sound recording of the composition, whichever term ends earlier, unless this contract is sooner terminated in accordance with the provisions hereof."*

12- *When the contract terminates, the publisher re-vests in the writer all rights in the composition.*

13- *The publisher supplies a financial statement every six months. The writer may demand an audit of the publisher's books upon supplying appropriate notice.*

14- *All disputes between the parties are to be submitted to the American Arbitration Association, and the parties agree ". . . to be bound by and perform any award rendered in such arbitration."*

15- *The publisher may not assign (turn over to another publisher) the contract without the writer's consent.*

Contracts: Getting Out — The writer and publisher may negotiate at length to shape a contract that is equitable. The relationship may turn out to be mutually profitable, even congenial. But it is the nature of the business that writers and publishers frequently want to terminate contracts. This does not mean the songs under contract must then die for lack of promotion. Rather, the copyrights are *reassigned*. Reassignments are common, and they can be to the advantage of the writer. From the writer's point of view, a reassignment is perhaps even advantageous to the writer if the songs are included in a bona fide sale of the first publisher's catalog, or in the event of a merger, or if the assignment is to a subsidiary or affiliated company. In each of these circumstances, the writer should demand from the first publisher a written instrument which states that the assignee-publisher assumes all obligations of the original (first) publisher.

The songwriter must continually police his contract to make sure that its terms are being carried out. Default is a common occurrence. It does not necessarily mean the writer is in bed with a crook. It may not involve unfairness or dishonesty or fraud at all. More likely, a publisher defaults because he is unable to get the song recorded, or royalty statements are incorrect or incomplete, or he just can't come up with royalty payments when they are due, or he becomes so burdened working on other properties he fails to promote the material in question. If the writer believes the publisher is guilty of default, whatever the reasons, he has a number of options. First, he may unilaterally break the contract. Courts take a dim view of unilateral action of this kind, for it is the court which must determine if a breach is "material" and whether the publisher has flagrantly disregarded appeals from the writer for remedy. Second, the writer may unilaterally reassign the copyright to another publisher, then notify his performing rights organization that, henceforth, all moneys formerly payable to the first publisher are now to be paid to the new publisher. The writer and the new publisher join in this notification to ASCAP or BMI. Each of these two organizations has different policies covering response to this kind of notification. Before taking such unilateral action, the writer and his counsel would be well advised to try to learn how ASCAP or BMI would respond. This kind of notification to ASCAP or BMI concerning assignment often may be sufficient to cause the first publisher to seek settlement out of court. During periods of dispute concerning assignment, performing rights societies tend to hold accrued royalties in trust pending settlement.

DEMONSTRATION RECORDS

Demonstration records ("demos") are used in a variety of ways:

- *A songwriter records a demo in an attempt to induce a publisher to accept his songs.*

- *A publisher produces demos in an attempt to persuade an artist or record producer to record the publisher's new songs.*

- *A performer records a demo to demonstrate his talents to a prospective employer, e.g., a record company, an agent, a contractor.*

- *A composer will prepare a demo in an attempt to induce an advertising agency to use his material for broadcast commercials.*

- *An ad agency will produce a demo to show a client, or prospective client, how a broadcast commercial might sound.*

Effective demos are performed by a singer or small group. The minimum accompaniment is piano or guitar. The maximum appropriate accompaniment would include a rhythm section and one or two front-line players. Under special circumstances, elaborate demos with full instrumentation and written charts are produced. As for the style of performance, the singing should be straightforward, with a minimum amount of styling. The listener wants to judge the *song*. Of course, if the demo is not of a song but of an auditioning performer, the artist will do what he can to simulate a live performance.

Demos made for publishers or by publishers are often on open reel, at 7.5 i.p.s. Open reel tapes should be identified with grease pencil on the leader and fully identified on the reel itself as well as on the box. Each separate selection on an open reel should be leadered to facilitate location of internal selections. All selections should be logged on the box. Number the sequence; cite accurate song titles and full composers' names. Five to seven-inch reels should be used, not the smaller ones, as they are more easily misplaced.

Today, cassettes of good quality are widely accepted, and many publishers prefer them to open reels. It is not a bad idea to supply both reel-to-reel and cassette copies; an auditor might take weeks to bother to thread up a reel, but can listen to a cassette in his car or anywhere else.

As with open reel demos, cassettes should be clearly labeled — on the box as well as on the cassette itself. A complete log of songs (their sequence, titles, composers' names) should accompany the cassette. Tape one copy of the log to the outside of the case, and fold another copy inside.

Acetate discs are still used occasionally for demos, but they wear out quickly, are susceptible to damage, and can be produced only by those having access to an acetate cutting lathe.

Songwriters who sing passably well can produce their own demos — on home recording equipment, if it is of reasonably good quality. Professional demo producers are readily available in larger cities. They provide a professional singer accompanied by piano or guitar. Rates rise, of course, for more backup musicians, but producers offer special rates for more than one song. Elaborately produced demos (they are becoming more common) with written-out arrangements, full orchestra, perhaps a group of singers, recorded multitrack can cost several hundred dollars for one song. Such demos, properly mixed down and equalized, can attain the quality of a master. Some do, and are subsequently released commercially. Such releases are illegal unless properly licensed by the copyright owners of the material and the appropriate payments are made to the AFM and AFTRA artists involved.

All demos should include notice of copyright (letter P in a circle — ℗). Such notice offers some protection from unauthorized use of the tapes. Demos are frequently lost, due to inadequate I.D.'s and careless handling. In addition to the identification recommended above, mailed packages should bear a complete return address and return postage. Mail them first-class; insure the package. Send copies, of course, not masters.

Performing artists' unions have regulations concerning demo production, but circumvention in most cities is widespread. Check local practices before recording.

BREAKING IN

Breaking into the field of professional songwriting is not as mysterious as generally believed. Many unknown writers are discovered every year, but few make it on luck alone. When we check out the so-called overnight success stories, we learn that most of these individuals used certain promotion techniques. We cannot articulate a breaking-in "formula." But we can describe what works for most new writers.

SEVEN STEPS

1- *The first step is the most critical. Before spending time and money seeking a professional career, it is of overriding importance that the songwriter first find out whether or not he has what it takes. Your songs may go over just great with your family and friends. These reactions can be heart-warming — and they can be seriously misleading. What the amateur needs at this point is an objective appraisal of his creative talents.*

2- *Make certain you know your craft. A writer may not be a creative genius, but he can learn to be a craftsman.*

3- *Arm yourself with professional leadsheets, lyric sheets and demonstration records.*

4- *Focus your promotion efforts on the specific market your songs fit.*

5- *Thoroughly promote your songs in your own locale before risking a trip to The Big City.*

6- *Employ the promotion techniques outlined in these pages; learn the business.*

7- *Persist. Most of the writer's competitors will become discouraged and give up. The persistent writer can beat his competition by hanging in there.*

LOCAL PROMOTION

Three levels of promotion should be undertaken. First of all, *start where you are.* It is pointless to leave the hometown before you have proven yourself locally. The amateur needs a place to make mistakes, to experiment with different kinds of promotional efforts. The hometown provides a space more private for this breaking-in period than the Big time. Assuming the writer is familiar with what has been covered here to this point, he is ready to present his work to the marketplace.

Local contacts can start with professional performers in your area. Observe them in performance; visit their rehearsals. Hang out, get acquainted. If your songs suit their style, you may persuade them to try your material and give you their reaction. At this stage, it does not matter whether these professionals are well-known. One day they may be, and making their acquaintance may initiate a contact that will bear fruit later.

Contact your local radio stations and try to persuade program directors and music librarians to listen to your demos. They will be unable to use your songs, but their opinions of your work could be valuable to you, for they are full-time professional appraisers of records. Also, see if the local disc jockeys will listen to your music. They cannot use your records either, but the best informed disc jockeys have an ear tuned to popular tastes. Their evaluation of your songs might be useful.

Seek to collaborate with people writing and producing college shows in your area. Colleges also are among the most important bookers of visiting artists. Traveling performers often pick up useful material on the road. You may have to wait in line to get to them, but it might prove worthwhile. With some performers, it is even more effective to get your songs to people *around* the artist. Most performers rely to some extent upon the judgment of their associates in selecting new material. With some performers, the best contact for this purpose would be the performer's musical director or arranger. With other performers, it is good idea to first talk to their managers, some of whom are influential song pickers.

Some smaller cities are headquarters for publishing companies. Do not rule out the small publisher. If you evaluate them according to the guidelines listed in this chapter and if they measure up, go with them if you do not have a more attractive option at the time. Contact local advertising agencies and commercial production companies. Communities with populations of 100,000 on up will have such firms. They are in constant need of melodies and musical ideas for broadcast commercials.

If you begin to receive favorable local reaction to your writing, you just might be ready for the next step in promoting your songs.

PROMOTION BY MAIL

Direct mail selling is one of the largest industries in the economy. Even music can be sold by mail, as the success of record clubs will attest. Amateur songwriters have frequently been successful in landing their first publisher through the mail. This is a special technique and nearly all efforts of this kind fail because they are not handled effectively. But if the writer follows the procedures outlined, his chances are reasonably good.

1- Study the record charts and find out the names of publishers who are currently active in handling the type of music you write. Select a dozen or so, perhaps two dozen names.

2- Locate the addresses and telephone numbers of these publishers. Your local telephone company has directories for large cities. Or ask *Songwriter* magazine for its current directory. Yet another source is

Billboard's International Buyers Guide, published annually. Yet another source is the reference desk of your local library.

3- If you do not find from these sources the name of the particular person you want, write the firm a short letter of inquiry or place a telephone call.

4- After receiving the name of the professional manager, write him a letter requesting permission to mail in some of your songs. The letter should be short, well written, and to the point. Briefly state what reception your songs have already experienced with *professional* performers. The publisher will be uninterested in your success at that Rotary Club luncheon. Drop a name or two, if you can, of established artists who have reacted favorably to your songs. If permission is received, mail in not more than three or four songs. Don't expect any publisher to examine more than that; he will be interested only in what the writer considers his best work. Your package should contain, as a minimum, a demo recording of each song (put all three of them on the same cassette or reel) AND separate lyric sheets for each song, neatly typed or printed with your name, address and telephone number on each sheet. Inclusion of professionally prepared leadsheets is optional with some publishers, but play it safe and include them. Your package should contain a brief cover letter. Since many publishers won't bother to answer your letter, better response can probably be obtained if you mail the publisher a self-addressed, stamped postcard.

Mr. John Doe, Professional Manager
XYZ Music Publishing Company
Address

Dear Mr. Doe: Date:

Please indicate your response to my questions and then mail this card back to me (it is already addressed and stamped).

WILL YOU EXAMINE MY SONGS FOR PUBLICATION? Yes ____ No ____

SHOULD I SEND MY DEMOS ON CASSETTE ____ OR REEL-TO-REEL ____?

Your response will be sincerely appreciated.

                                        Thank you!

                                        (Signed) Mary Hopeful
                                        Address/Telephone

All mail addressed to publishers should be sent first-class. Do not send certified or registered mail; many publishers seem to feel that such mail could mean trouble, and they often refuse to accept it unless they recognize the sender's name.

Wait three weeks. If you receive no reply, continue the process with other publishers until you receive favorable reaction.

Very few publishers today will open unsolicited mail. They not only are concerned about being accused of stealing material; a greater concern is that 99 percent of unsolicited songs and demos are just awful. Publishers cannot take time to dig through the hundreds of songs received every week just in the hope that one percent might be worth serious consideration. But when a writer has been professional enough to obtain permission from the publisher to submit material, whatever is mailed in is viewed entirely differently. Publishers at least know that a well-written letter of request is authored by an individual who can read and write the English language, and the writer has demonstrated that he understands something about how a publishing company functions. An unknown writer, so appraised, is immediately elevated above the run-of-the-mill amateurs who clog the mails with unacceptable material.

CONFRONTING PUBLISHERS

While many amateur songwriters manage to create publisher interest through mail contacts, most songs get published following a direct, personal confrontation of the writer and the publisher. Since all popular music publishers have offices only in the leading recording centers, the amateur who would be professional must eventually invade the forbidding precincts of New York, Nashville or Los Angeles. Publishers in these cities vary in the manner in which they will see uninvited guests who visit their offices. My own experience in New York and Los Angeles has been that publishers are invariably courteous and receptive. This has been my experience every time, whether I was known to the publisher or not. But I doubt that my personal experience is typical. The publishers I have worked with or interviewed tell me they will see unknown songwriters, but it is unwise for the newcomer to walk directly from the Greyhound station to the publisher's office. Many publishers recommend, and I recommend, that the songwriter who is unknown first write a letter to the publisher. Here again, the postman opens the door for you. Your letter can be about the same as described above, but asking permission in this instance to present your material to the publisher in person. If you are only visiting the city, tell the publisher you would like to get an appointment soon. Don't crowd him. Give him your local telephone number. His office may find it simpler to telephone you than write you a letter. Every publisher I have asked tells me they will see people who write them a sensible letter of this kind. Does this tactic result in publishers signing new songwriters? Rarely. Why? For the reasons already stated: very few really good songs are presented to them.

Another way of getting into a publisher's office is to just walk in cold and ask the receptionist if you can see her boss. This individual has the very difficult job of being the publisher's gatekeeper. She has been instructed to protect her employers from nuisance callers. The gatekeeper must somehow figure out, while you are trying to get past her, whether her boss is going to thank her or scold her for letting you get to him. In discussing this with a number of receptionists and publishers, I find that most of them possess the patience of Job. People in these positions have developed an admirable tolerance for the unexpected, often unwelcome visitor. They accept the fact that their very jobs depend on an ongoing flow of new songs ("Perhaps this total stranger standing before me is the next George Gershwin"). If the unknown guest arrives without an appointment, it is very likely that the receptionist will ask that he leave with her his leadsheets and demos. The gatekeeper will tell the guest that the boss is tied up right now, but she will try to get him to hear the music in the next two or three weeks. At this point, there are three possibilities. The most likely one is that someone in the publisher's office will, indeed, examine your material, then reject it. The firm will mail the material to you, or you are asked to drop by and pick it up. The second possibility is that the publisher never finds time to examine your material and returns it. The third possibility is that, after hearing the first eight bars or so of the first song of the demo, the publisher hears at least craft. If he recognizes that the material is well constructed and professional, he may well listen to your whole demo and look at the leadsheets. If your material stirs up this much curiosity, you are catapulted into the top one percent of the writers who try to get the publisher thinking seriously about whether some particular material will fit his current needs.

Yet another approach to getting to a direct confrontation with a publisher is to telephone him and ask for an appointment. Here again, the receptionist must be the gatekeeper. Your chances of soliciting an appointment through a letter or a telephone call are about equal.

The foregoing promotional methods are the most effective ones a person can use, at least until that time in the writer's career when he can contact a publisher cold and say, "Your friend and mine, John Doe, suggested I get in touch with you about my songs . . ." If this John Doe is truly a mutual friend, the publisher's attitude toward seeing the unknown writer is immediately transformed, for someone whose judgment he respects has already functioned for the publisher as a preliminary gatekeeper. The publisher's door is now open, at least temporarily. If a writer can develop these kinds of inside contacts, he is on his way. But once "inside," the material had better be there, or the inside contact will prove valueless.

BMI Headquarters in NYC. These employees are shown logging data (song titles received from radio stations) directly onto a disc pack to be compiled on computer tape. This system computes how often a song is played on the air, which determines how much money a songwriter and publisher are paid.

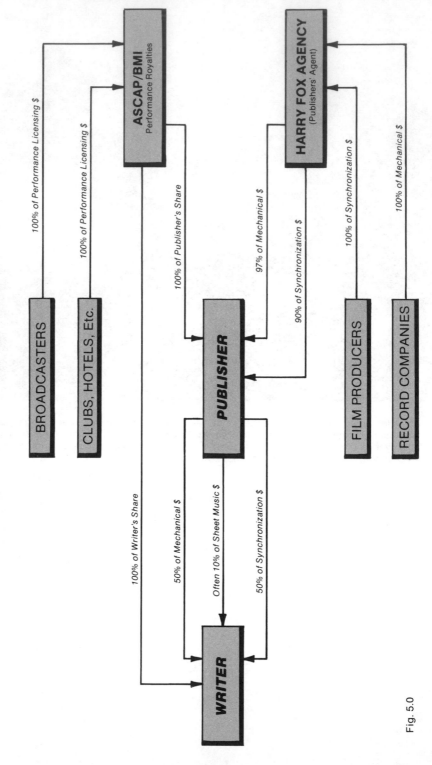

SONGWRITERS /PUBLISHERS CASH FLOW

Fig. 5.0

5

MUSIC PUBLISHING

PERSPECTIVE

When it is said that a particular copyright is *published,* that term today has quite a different meaning than in the past. Years ago, a composer know what he needed most was to locate a music "publisher" to accept his material so that copies could be printed and placed in music stores for sale to the public. This simple pattern no longer prevails. In the popular music field, *the great majority of new songs are not printed at all.* They exist, at first, only in the form of professional copies (leadsheets) that are distributed in manuscript form without cost to artists and record producers. Music publishers, then, are not printers. When they believe that a distribution of printed editions of their copyrights might prove profitable, most publishers license others to provide these services.

The heart of the music publishing business today lies, not in the print business, as it is called, but in the record industry. A publisher's principal sources of income today derive from record royalties and from money received from ASCAP, BMI, or SESAC for performances of the publisher's copyrights. Many individuals of long experience in the music business look upon publishing as the most lucrative source of income and certainly the steadiest. That is why just about everyone in the performing and recording fields is involved in some way in music publishing.

To gain a perspective on how this field has become the rich giant that it is, let's glance at how the industry developed historically:

DEVELOPMENT OF MUSIC PUBLISHING

1640 — The first book published in America — and it happens to be a music book — **The Bay Psalm Book.**

1770 — The first native-born American composer, William Billings, gets his music published.

1850-1900 — Minstrel shows are widely popular and increase public interest in popular music. Publishers begin to prosper.

1890s — The player piano becomes popular, creating a demand for player piano rolls. Large music publishing firms are established in the last two decades of the 1800s. Merchandising methods develop, and publishers begin to discover that if enough people hear a good song, it will probably be a hit. The most effective song promoters now are the performers in various theatres and vaudeville houses that develop around the turn of the century.

1900 — Popular music publishing becomes big business. In this first decade, an estimated 100 songs sell a million copies or more within a one-year period. This occurs at a time when the population of the United States is about 90 million.

The U.S. Congress passes the historic 1909 Copyright Law which provides publishers, for the first time, "mechanical rights" in recorded music. Initially, this revenue derives largely from player piano rolls.

1920s — ASCAP is established. For the first time in this country, publishers and writers begin to receive income from performances of their music. Radio broadcasting begins and is initially fought by publishers. They believe radio hurts sheet music sales. Sound movies ("talkies") begin. Film producers negotiate fees for music synchronization rights. The Harry Fox Agency is established. Sheet music sales drop with the rise of radio. Publishers now close most of their branch offices to concentrate promotion efforts on the radio network broadcasting centers which, at this time, are New York City, Chicago and Los Angeles.

1930s — The Great Depression severely hurts the music publishing business, but increasing income from movie producers helps. The "Big Bands" develop and become the most important source for plugs for new songs, particularly if the band has "a remote wire" for radio broadcasting. National Music Publishers' Association expands the Harry Fox Agency to include mechanical licensing of copyrights.

1940s — During and after World War II, people spend larger shares of their incomes on music, instruments, records, movies. The LP record appears in 1948, now producing publishers' royalties on 10 to 12 songs per record, not just two. NAB forms BMI in reaction to increasing demands from ASCAP. The big band singers (Perry Como, Frank Sinatra, Doris Day, others) go solo and become the dominant source for introducing new songs.

1950s — Rapid growth of television kills live music on the radio. Disc jockeys become the new hit-makers. Rock and roll comes to dominate popular music, exploding the record market. BMI now dominant in capturing copyrights in the rock and country fields.

1960s — Increasing dependence of publishers on radio to break new songs. The print business improves, particularly editions for the amateur and the educational field. Harry Fox Agency becomes a wholly owned subsidiary of NMPA.

1970s — Radio broadcasters shorten their play lists below "top 40," forcing companies to promote airplay in secondary and tertiary markets. The print business in the pop song folio and educational field continues to grow, but inflating costs cause many publishers to quit all print activity and assign such rights to subpublishers and licensees here and abroad. Publishers' incomes from ASCAP and BMI continue to rise. Everyone in the music business continues the search for a music to succeed rock.

1980s — In the popular music repertoire, the publishing business and the recording business increasingly become one combined enterprise.

TYPES OF PUBLISHERS

Music publishing companies today exist in all shapes and sizes — from "office-in-your-hat" operations to the multinational corporate giants. Some are full-line companies; others are specialty houses with catalogs limited perhaps to only one type of music.

PARENT COMPANIES

The music publishing business today is a maze of subpublishers, licensees, affiliated companies, administered companies, parent corporations and multinational conglomerates. When I interviewed Chappell and Company, I asked the head of its Los Angeles office how many companies were affiliated with Chappell. The professional manager first said that he didn't know; he had lost track, but asserted that "Chappell is certainly the largest music publisher in the world." As big as Chappell may be, even that huge organization is owned by yet another corporation, Polygram. Polygram, in turn, owns such giants as Polydor (Deutsch Grammophon) and Phonogram (Philips and Mercury Records). Whatever the publisher's name, it is safe to assume that it is the child of some other parent company. This trend to merge and form interlocking directorships will continue — for the same reasons firms in other fields tend to merge: tax advantages and alleged efficiency of management. This hurts smaller firms who want to maintain their independence. But independence becomes increasingly difficult in the music business, because publishing and recording share almost identical goals and because the music market is increasingly becoming one worldwide market. Firms that do not develop multinational markets risk the loss of about one-half of their income potential. Music publishers can learn a lesson from the movie producers: they have known for decades that half of their box office receipts are generated abroad.

Controlling interests in publishing companies are bought and sold quite like other business enterprises. But while control of the stock in a company changes, parent companies often leave a firm's staff intact.

FULL-LINE COMPANIES

Prior to the great expansion of the recording industry, many of the older music publishers included practically all types of music in their catalogs — classical, educational and pop. Firms with this broad a repertoire are scarce today, because the print business is so different from the business of hustling pop record releases. But a firm such as Chappell, for example, attempts to be active in all musical styles. Chappell owns or administers or subpublishes thousands of copyrights here and abroad through its subsidiaries. Each full-line firm has developed its own administrative structure, but Figure 5.1 shows a typical organization of this scope. Department names vary among companies.

RECORD COMPANY AFFILIATES

All record companies of any size own or control, or cooperate closely with, a minimum of two different publishing companies. Some of these affiliates function as if they were not dependent upon their alliance with their record company. Others are "front" organizations and are set up by record companies as a kind of depository for copyrights owned, partly owned or administered by their contract recording artists. Record companies find that they need a direct alliance with an ASCAP and BMI publishing operation in order to negotiate reciprocal contracts with their artists involving both publishing and recording rights. Critics argue that these interlocking companies involve conflicts of interest. Others argue that such cozy arrangements restrain trade and may eventually be found in conflict with antitrust laws. Newer writers and unestablished artists are sometimes coerced into placing their copyrights with a record company publisher. Those that refuse to do so sometimes find it more difficult to get recording contracts. Yet another ploy of these sweetheart contracts involves an artist-writer persuading his record company-publisher to accept more of the writer's songs for recording than he would otherwise.

The reason most of these publishing/recording deals are so common is that they are, when fairly handled, the most profitable for the participants.

ARTIST-OWNED COMPANIES

Many recording artists who write their own material have formed their own publishing companies. The reason is simple: they see no need to give up the extra income to anyone else. All recorded music must be "published." As a matter of fact, it can be said that recording a song is one way of publishing it. If an artist does record, royalties to the publisher of the copyrights accrue from the outset of record sales. As a result, artists, usually with extensive assistance from their managers, set up companies in their own names. Since most artists are largely concerned with recording and performing, their publishing activities are almost always limited to their own compositions and they do not get involved in the print business or conventional distribution.

WRITER-OWNED COMPANIES

Hundreds of very small publishing operations are owned by individual writers. Most often, these small firms have been set up by writers who have been unable to get their music accepted by other publishers. Some writer-owned firms have been set up by those who have been contract composers, but who came to believe their material was not receiving sufficient promotion — so they go it alone. Still other writers have been cheated by publishers and do not trust anyone but themselves to handle the publication of their music.

Many writer-owned firms are one-man operations. Besides the attraction of being your own boss, the writer-owner knows that no one is going to cook the books; he can get a fair count. Yet another reason for the prevalence of so many writer-owner firms is that an individual can set up shop for an absurd amount of capital — perhaps less than $100. At the end of this book I provide recommendations on how to set up your own company. Also, see Figure 5.2, which shows how very small music publishing firms can be structured.

EDUCATIONAL FIELD

Some publishers in the United States limit their catalogs to music intended for use by students, schools and colleges. This field, until the 1970s, was not large. But early in that decade, gross sales grew tremendously. School bond issues were failing and school music budgets were cut severely, some programs even being eliminated because of the unwillingness of some communities to support arts education. But educational music publishers balanced off this reduction of sales with a variety of printed materials aimed at the amateur instrumentalist and singer. The biggest sellers in these kinds of editions are for piano, organ, and guitar. Part of these sales are known as "bench packs" — educational materials given by the equipment manufacturer to the customer upon sale of a new piano or organ. The instrument manufacturer pays the copyright owners for these materials. The biggest selling editions scored for schools are for mixed chorus, pop/jazz choir, football band, stage band, and "serious" concert band compositions.

While the number of school bands and choruses may shrink, the American Music Conference believes, probably correctly, that sale reductions in those areas will be balanced by the increasing market for amateurs who will buy "how-to" books and folios. Two firms, Hal Leonard and Jam Handy, are enjoying increasing sales of materials of this kind that combine "how-to" cassettes with film strips. Audio/visual materials of this kind, when well produced, will become increasingly popular. Some school districts are using these A/V materials in place of full-time salaried live instruction.

SPECIALTY PUBLISHERS

Still other publishers maintain a policy of limiting their catalogs to just one kind of music. Some specialty publishers, for example those active only in the country field, are among the country's largest, e.g., Acuff Rose. Most specialty houses, however, are relatively small, preferring to limit their activities to a field they understand best. Typical among this kind of publisher are catalogs limited to one of the following: choral music, gospel, children's music and so-called "stage band" (big bands in schools and colleges playing pop and jazz music). One of the larger kinds of specialty publishers limits its catalog to what is called "Christian music," which might be described as white gospel. These firms, many of them located in Nashville, prosper not only through large sales of their music on records, but also do a good-sized print business.

Included on the list of specialty publishers should be those who limit their catalogs to contemporary serious ("classical") and avant-garde music. Most of these kinds of publishers are subsidized by a foundation or university; some of them "publish" only privately distributed editions. Recordings of their music are also largely subsidized.

SERIOUS MUSIC

Only a handful of publishers today limit their catalogs to serious music. Even they are now involved in the educational field. The two share much repertoire, of course. G. Schirmer is probably the best known serious music publisher. Also prominent in this repertoire: Peters, Theodore Presser and W.W. Norton. These firms sometimes borrow the plates of classics from European houses, then sell the resulting editions under their own imprimatur.

Classical music publishers do not profit much from Verdi operas and Haydn symphonies, but make up for their marginal properties with an array of special editions of the classics for school orchestras, choirs, as well as etudes for piano, organ, strings and voice.

Besides maintaining catalogs of older music, nearly all of it from Europe, these houses continue accepting losses in their publication of twentieth century serious composers. We are indebted to them for this "public service," for they know at the outset that they will rarely recover their printing costs of contemporary serious music. As stated above, some of these losses are offset by offering dramatic works and extended pieces through rental of the parts rather than through printed editions.

SUBPUBLISHERS, LICENSEES

Most publishers, including many of the largest ones, find it necessary to farm out some of their services. Firms providing these services are called subpublishers, licensees or selling agents (application of these terms is not always precise; many professionals use them interchangeably).

The service most commonly assigned to an outside firm is "the paper business," as it is often called — the production and sale of printed editions. Since few pop music publishers print and market printed editions of their copyrights, they license another company to do this for them. Among the largest publishers who include a big paper business among their activities are Charles Hansen, Warner Bros., Big 3 and Chappell. A publisher not wanting to get into the paper business will normally strike a deal with a firm such as one of the aforementioned which provides for the licensee to bear the full costs of preparing, printing and distributing the printed edition, then the licensee pays the licensor a 20 percent royalty on sales. In deals of this kind, sometimes the licensee is called a *selling agent*. A less common arrangement involves the copyright owner (publisher) bearing all preparation and printing costs, then paying the subpublisher or selling agent 20 percent. These kinds of licensing deals are most common for melodic-type popular songs that have experienced success on a hit record, and the copyright owner believes it will be profitable to make the music available in printed form. The format for such editions is usually pop song folios where the royalties are shared among the copyrights included in a particular folio. Few hard rock "songs" can be effectively rendered in print, for their success is based more on the "sound" of the recorded performance rather than the musical content.

Publisher-subpublisher arrangements are also common in print editions for the educational market. The largest licensee/selling agent in this field is Hal Leonard, Inc.

Foreign Territories — The publishing business is now worldwide, and many American publishers experience a large percentage of their income from foreign territories. Some large companies have branch offices in foreign countries that function much like the American parent firm. First, they try to exploit the American catalog by getting cover records, selling printed editions and collecting performance royalties. This may involve the branch office arranging for translations of English lyrics into the indigenous language. Second, branch offices usually involve themselves, not only in pushing the catalog of the home office, but exploiting new copyrights on their own.

An American publisher lacking branch offices abroad calls upon firms that do. Many publishers, large and small, retain the subpublishing services of such giants as Chappell and Screen Gems/EMI. While royalty splits vary from country to country, the most common sharing between the prime publisher and licensee is fifty-fifty. Percentages usually relate to how the parties share the production and promotion expenses.

A different foreign licensing arrangement involves the American publisher contracting with a foreign-based subpublisher. Deals vary, in that some countries have special requirements for incorporation, where officers (or a prescribed percentage of shareholders) might have to be nationals of that country.

American and foreign publishers may set up a partnership or joint venture. Or they may set up a simple subpublishing deal, for the life of the copyrights or for a term of years. The American company will expect the subpublisher to exploit the American copyrights through arranging cover records, providing printed editions and collecting performance royalties. Even though the performing rights society functioning in a given territory may be forwarding royalty shares to ASCAP and BMI, the American firm's subpublisher is usually expected to ascertain that performances are being fully licensed and money is paid for them.

American firms usually contract for foreign subpublishers to cover more than one country. For example, it is common for a subpublisher based in West Germany to cover all German-speaking countries in Europe. French-based subpublishers would probably service the French-speaking territories in Africa. A Scandinavian subpublisher would probably request jurisdiction over Norway, Sweden, Denmark, perhaps Iceland and Finland, too.

In respect to subpublishing in foreign territories, many American publishers employ the Harry Fox Agency, whose services abroad sometimes transcend those offered in the United States.

ADMINISTRATION

Successful music publishing companies today are structured and administered much like other commercial enterprises. The newer, smaller firms may lack a businesslike administration; their management may run company affairs by the seat of their pants. But such firms rarely survive. Today, the stakes are too high to permit a modern publishing company to operate like a mom-and-pop store. Stockholders focus on a firm's dividends. Management must produce an acceptable annual statement or be replaced by officers who are knowledgeable in contemporary business administration practices.

The major houses have a central administration comprised of a president (or vice president in charge of administration), department heads and support personnel. Firms vary in the labels they apply to departments. Here follows a description of those typical of most music publishing companies.

BUSINESS AFFAIRS

This department is managed by an individual who supervises assistants handling receipts and disbursements, accounting, data processing, payroll, insurance and purchasing. Large firms would probably try to have, as their business affairs head, a graduate of a university business school with a master's degree (MBA). An individual holding down such a job would have comparable educational credentials or extensive experience in business management. One of the most critical components of a business affairs department of a company today is computer-assisted research, particularly market research and cost accounting. Now that computers are available at costs within reach of even smaller firms, their use in the publishing business is almost universal. Managers can know, on a daily basis if need be, just where their company stands concerning royalties received and royalties paid out.

COPYRIGHT DEPARTMENT

Except for smaller firms, all publishers have at least one employee who heads a department that handles copyrights. Larger firms would have several persons in this department. A qualified department head of copyrights must know the essential parts of the U.S. Copyright Laws of 1909, the 1976 revisions, and basic international laws and agreements ("conventions") covering foreign copyrights. The firm's copyright department performs a number of essential tasks. Among the most important are:

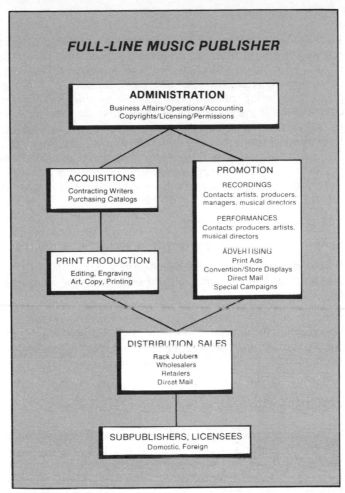

Fig. 5.1

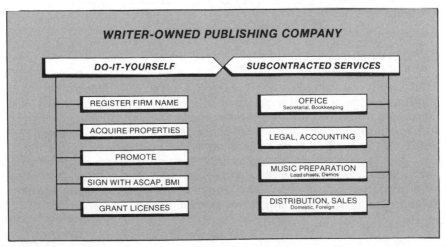

Fig. 5.2

1- *Title search: Before a publisher accepts a piece of music, his copyright department must first determine who really owns the work. The Library of Congress will assist in this research. Copyright ownership can get complicated. If the work has coauthors, what are their claims of ownership and are the claims valid? What if the work had been published before? What if the music or the words have been revised? How does a publisher determine if some of the rights have been assigned to another firm or individual or estate? After the copyright department has performed this research, questions remaining unclear are referred to a copyright attorney — who might or might not be on the staff.*

2- *Register claims of copyright.*

3- *Record transfers of copyright ownership.*

4- *Form liaison with the Harry Fox Agency, particularly in respect to mechanical licenses and the determination of synchronization fees.*

5- *Keep records of subsisting copyrights and their pending expiration dates. Recommend renewal, extension, sale or abandonment of subsisting copyrights. In matters of this importance, top management would, of course, be directly involved.*

LEGAL AFFAIRS

All music publishers must have lawyers expert in copyright law and music publishing. They also need expert tax lawyers experienced in artist management and the recording industry. Nearly all publishing transactions are based on contracts, and the ongoing services of qualified attorneys are essential in negotiating them. Small firms employ these specialists by the hour or day. Larger firms not only retain counsel part-time, as needed, but employ one or more lawyers on their staffs full-time.

OPERATIONS

After a copyright title has been cleared and the author is signed to a contract, and after the arrangers and editors have performed their tasks (assuming the work is printed), the music must go through a number of additional operations before it can be distributed and sold. Many firms group these activities, such as printing, warehousing, inventory control and shipping under an "operations" department. Some of the tasks performed here may not be glamorous or high-paying. But jobs requiring fewer skills can provide good entry levels for persons wanting to learn the music publishing business from the ground up.

DISTRIBUTION

Publishers vary in how they handle distribution and sale of printed editions. Some of the typical patterns:

- *From the publisher to subpublisher (printer) to distributor to retailer to customer.*
- *From print publisher to rack jobber to retailer to customer.*
- *From the publisher via direct mail to customer (educational field).*

Some subpublishers are licensed to handle everything for the prime publisher — arranging, editing, printing, advertising, distribution. Such printers/distributors may also work with rack jobbers who do the leg work, servicing a variety of retail outlets.

THE PROFESSIONAL MANAGER

Years ago, all publishers in the popular music field employed what were known at that time as song pluggers. Their place in the world of show business has been portrayed colorfully in the movies and other media, occasionally with accuracy. In the late 1940s, it became unfashionable to call these operatives song pluggers. Gradually, they came to be known as "professional managers." Since World War II, the professional manager has had to assume a role much broader in scope than song plugging. First, the professional manager is usually the individual who administers the office. Second, he is primarily responsible for locating new material and signing writers. Then he must somehow find an additional 40 hours a week to try to persuade record producers to record his copyrights.

Except for smaller, newer firms, most professional managers working for established publishers are individuals of long experience, lots of "street knowledge," and form that indispensable link between the composer, the artist and, particularly, the record producer. Inexperienced musicians should plan on several years of pavement pounding, listening and learning before attempting to fill the shoes of a professional manager. Still, small firms offer good training ground, and some versatile individuals managing small publishing firms rise fast.

ACQUISITIONS

Assuming the basic administrative structure is in place and functioning, the single most important enterprise of a music publisher is to locate new music and sign writers. This unending search for new talent and new materials makes the NFL draft and other talent-grabs seem like a friendly game of tag. For the music publishing business cannot manufacture its own raw material. Rather, publishers must discover talented writers among the hundreds of thousands of composers who think their music is just what the publisher wants. As a former executive editor of an ASCAP publishing firm in Los Angeles, I can attest to the fact, corroborated by others involved in selecting new material, that the ratio of material submitted to the amount acceptable is about 1,000 to one. Every publisher I have worked with or talked to about their problems of locating good new material cry the same blues: no job is more difficult than trying to locate that one-in-a-thousand song. The Los Angeles manager of Chappell told me that in his search for new songs, he estimated that *less than one percent* of the material he examined was acceptable. This aspect of music publishing is largely misunderstood by inexperienced songwriters, perhaps most of whom have come to believe, through being constantly rejected, that music publishers, as a whole, not only won't give them fair consideration, but seem to have organized a conspiracy against new writers. Quite the opposite situation prevails. Every active publisher engages in daily prayer that, somehow, the day's mail or the day's callers just might have a piece of material worth investment and presentation to the world.

Acquisition of good new material is the very lifeblood of the music publishing business. Firms that rely too heavily on their past success quickly lose their share of the market and may go out of business eventually. Chappell is an example of a giant firm that, until the 1970s, failed to continue to acquire new properties and practically ignored the rock and country fields that surged in front in the 1960s. Chappell was content to sit on its ASCAP. But Chappell got the message — late, but not too late. By running fast in the 1970s, that giant firm recovered lost ground.

In searching for new material, a publisher will first turn to writers of recent success. Such composers are as sought after as a recording star. Songwriters with songs on the current charts can pick and choose their own publishers. Publishers are quick to search out the currently successful writers, often unknown to the general public, and attempt to persuade them they should place their next new material with them. A variety of inducements are offered, and many successful writers change publishers frequently, ever seeking a better contract, stronger promotion, perhaps more congenial associates.

A second choice among publishers for good writers comes through recommendations of insiders, those in the music business whose musical judgment appears trustworthy or whose track record in the field has been impressive.

A third choice of usable new material derives from writers already under contract. Professional managers often find it necessary to prod their own staff writers, urging them to keep turning out material for the insatiable market.

Music publishers, particularly those affiliated with ASCAP, have found that one of the most important sources for catalog acquisitions has been musical theatre, particularly the Broadway stage. This incomparable repertoire, dominated by songs from the 1920 to 1960 period, is one of America's unique national treasures. Publishers holding copyrights on the great show tunes of Kern, Gershwin, Arlen, Rodgers and Bernstein, to name but a handful of masters, find that acceptance of this repertoire continues undiminished in the late twentieth century. One of the reasons publishing profits from a Broadway show are high is because of the fact that when a show hits, everyone wants to sing and play the music. A hit Broadway tune may be offered in a dozen or more arrangements, ranging from "easy piano" to school band. A second huge source of publisher revenue from Broadway show music derives from mechanical royalties from original cast albums. *A publisher's income from a Broadway show may exceed profits derived from the box office.* The latter source begins only after the initial production costs are recovered. But the publisher's profit from performances begin with opening night, and print sale profits start after recovery of initial printing costs.

By the 1970s, even somewhat earlier, publisher and record company interest in Broadway shows dropped sharply because a number of investments turned sour. Old-line ASCAP firms holding copyrights from the 1920-1960 heyday of the Broadway musical continued to earn huge profits from their catalogs. But income from current shows fell off or disappeared when public taste (or, perhaps, producers' tastes) turned away from earlier styles and began to favor rock-type shows on Broadway and in regional theatres.

The least productive source for acquisition of new material for publication is from that vast number of amateurs who believe they have what the publisher is seeking. Even though the number of unpublished writers is countless, even though most of them lack creative talent, every year amateurs catch a publisher's attention and become professional songwriters. Occasionally these breakthroughs are "overnight successes" where the unknown composer comes into fame and fortune about as simply as depicted in a bad TV show. Much more often, the "overnight success" follows years of disappointment.

CRITERIA FOR ACCEPTANCE

In the popular music field and with the repertoire usually associated with it, successful publishers have developed criteria which often serve well in distinguishing acceptable material from the chaff. Most publishers, knowingly or intuitively, seem to judge material based on these criteria:

1- *Does the demo "hit you?" If the music in the recording doesn't appeal to you in the first eight bars, that demo probably will never be heard to its end.*

2- *Has the composer been successful **lately?** Popular preferences shift so rapidly, a publisher is safer going with a currently charted writer than he would be trying to sign Leonard Bernstein.*

3- *What artists might record the song? What record producers can the publisher contact who might be persuaded to consider the song?*

4- *Does the material fill a current need in the catalog? Most publishers seek, over a period of time, some kind of balance*

*among the types of songs they accept. They have learned it is
unprofitable to try to push, say, in one season, all country songs
or all rock songs. Prudent publishers seek not only diversity, but
balance. Someone might submit a very attractive piece of
material. But if that particular publisher is currently loaded with
that kind of song, a good piece of material will probably be
rejected.*

5- *Does the material appear to show inherent quality? What's this?
Could it be that hard-nosed publishers can be motivated by
anything other than profit? Sometimes. Most of the decision-
makers in the business love music. While they can go broke if
they pander too often to their own personal tastes, many music
publishers know that the best way to build a catalog of lasting
value is to continue searching for, not just the surface appeal of a
new song, but for music that seems to have inherent quality,
music that might also appeal to listeners of the next generation.*

6- *When a publisher cannot manage to locate sufficient new
material from the sources named above, he may be reduced to
asking a simple question, "Is this piece of material I just received
about the best I can get my hands on right now?"*

CATALOG PURCHASES

Publishers who can earn income from one or more of the sources
indicated show profit. If they earn high income, they become attractive to
individuals who buy and sell whole catalogs. The sale of entire
publishing companies occurs most frequently when a small operator,
perhaps a writer-owned firm, receives an offer of purchase he can't
refuse. The little entrepreneur may not only sell his whole catalog, but
sign on with the purchaser as a contract writer, perhaps even an officer of
the firm buying him out.

Another frequent type of catalog purchase is between large, well-
established publishers, where one or the other calculates he will
experience a tax advantage in the transaction. Another buying-selling
situation develops when a large international firm buys the catalog of
another large publisher in order to obtain greater coverage of world
markets.

When whole catalogs are bought up, the seller normally assigns all his
rights of copyright and ownership, including subsisting contracts with
writers. This means that if the first publisher has contracted with a
composer to publish his music for the next several years, the new
publisher must honor that contract. AGAC contracts provide for this
kind of assignment.

Yet another buying-selling situation occurs when the seller becomes
overextended and is forced to raise quick cash. A prospective buyer can
sometimes move in with a low offer and buy up a valuable catalog for a
price below the current market. If the seller is not excessively hungry, he
may sell only a portion of his catalog.

EDITING

Nearly all music submitted for publication needs to be edited. Very few composers, even those classically trained, are familiar with the proper way to prepare manuscript for the printer. Unfortunately, in the popular field, editing standards of many publishers, including some of the major houses, are not high. Printed editions continue to be released that are mistake-ridden. Even a simple leadsheet should be prepared by an arranger qualified in this specialized field. At this stage, the arranger-editor must correct errors in notation, perhaps even rewrite portions that do not make good musical sense. Some editors are also qualified to polish lyrics, although this, too, is a specialized field that should be left to professional lyricists or "lyric doctors."

If the music is to be offered for sale in a piano-voice edition, here again a qualified arranger-editor is required, because writing is not as simple as it may appear. A musician may be well-trained in theory and orchestration, but writing quality piano-voice arrangements for publication should be assigned to specialists in this field. Major recording centers have qualified arranger-editors of this type.

When a new song becomes a big hit on records, the publisher or subpublisher will hire arrangers to prepare editions for such media as school band, chorus, solo guitar, accordion, perhaps a simplified arrangement for beginning pianists. Large publishers who are also "in the paper business" will have on staff one or more editors who will go over every notation on the arrangers' scores, editing and polishing them before plates are made.

Publishers heavily involved in the educational field have a "chief editor" who may well be a top executive in the company, possibly even the boss. The chief editor in such a firm is the gatekeeper — the individual who decides what the company will publish. If he does his gate-keeping well, the company may prosper. If he is imprudent, the firm may eventually go under. A chief editor, like others in top management, also must be well-informed on trends in the market and what his competitors are doing. If, for example, he observes that several other houses in the past year have been pushing arrangements for live synthesizer performance, he might well pass up manuscripts of this kind on his desk that have been under consideration. If, on the other hand, he observes that no other publisher is offering competition in such a specialized area, he might take a chance on such publications.

Editors are usually involved in supervising music copyists, autographers, music typists or engravers. The work of the best of these specialists must also be edited to assure standardization of style and accuracy. In all these tasks, qualified experts attempt to maintain the high quality of music editing that came to this country over a century ago from old-line European publishers. Much of today's engraving comes to us from Korea, where labor costs are low.

Editors with some publishers are assigned the additional responsibility of graphic art, packaging, and writing editorial copy such as instructions to performers.

THE PRODUCTION LINE

If a publisher determines that a newly-acquired piece of music should be offered for sale in printed form, that music goes down a production line somewhat like other products, progressing from raw material to vendable commodity. Here is a typical line of production for a piece of printed music headed for the marketplace:

1- *The publisher's acquisitions committee (or an authorized individual) determines that the piece of music should be accepted for publication and, in this instance, that it should be made available in at least one printed edition.*

2- *The publisher's copyright department determines that the title (ownership) of the music is clear (unencumbered), and a contract is negotiated with the author.*

3- *The publisher registers a claim to copyright with the Copyright Office and places copies on file with the Library of Congress, per standard procedures.*

4- *The publisher's arranger (or a free-lance arranger) scores a piano-voice version of the music. The editor makes sure it is in acceptable form, then directs a copyist, autographer, or music typist to prepare camera-ready art.*

5- *After proofreading the above, the editor orders plates made and the printer (in house or external) prints the music. First printings in the educational field are normally 1,000 copies. In the case of popular song folios, a first printing may run 25,000 copies or more.*

6- *The printer (in house or external) then ships and drop ships copies of the music in accord with instructions from the publisher. No set distribution patterns prevail, but two are fairly common. A publisher may ship directly to its jobbers and larger retail outlets. Or a publisher may assign to a subpublisher a license to promote, distribute and sell the entire edition.*

7- *Meanwhile, the publisher or licensee's promotion/advertising people have been trying to generate sales across the land, even abroad. If they have been successful, purchasers put down their money and everyone is happy.*

8- *The publisher pays the author royalties based on sales volume of the printed editions.*

EDITIONS

As pointed out, a new popular song is not published in printed form unless it achieves considerable recognition via records and tapes. But the bulk of the print music business lies, not with new pop material, but with educational materials, folk songs, how-to editions, serious music and material in the public domain. Another huge segment of the print business derives from popular standards, particularly those from Broadway shows. In the aggregate, the music print business is large today and growing, because students, schools, amateur players and professionals demand a large variety of different editions to satisfy their needs.

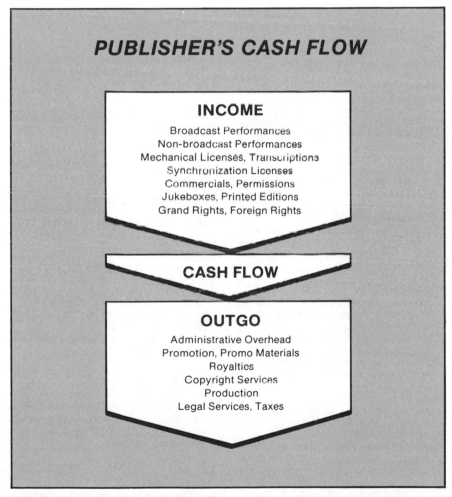

PUBLISHER'S CASH FLOW

INCOME
Broadcast Performances
Non-broadcast Performances
Mechanical Licenses, Transcriptions
Synchronization Licenses
Commercials, Permissions
Jukeboxes, Printed Editions
Grand Rights, Foreign Rights

CASH FLOW

OUTGO
Administrative Overhead
Promotion, Promo Materials
Royalties
Copyright Services
Production
Legal Services, Taxes

Fig. 5.3

EDITIONS

VOICE
Leadsheets (often called "professional copies"; these are not for sale but are given away to professionals)

Voice-piano (includes ligatures and chord symbols for guitar)

Mixed chorus (SATB, etc.), anthems, cantatas, oratorios

Men's chorus, glee club, barbershop quartet, etc.

Women's chorus (SA, SSA, etc.)

Classical songs, art songs

Pop choir or swing choir or jazz choir (with piano accompaniment, sometimes also with bass, guitar, drums)

Folk songs (usually in folio editions)

Hymns, gospel music, spirituals

PIANO
Popular songs

Easy piano arrangements of popular songs, public domain material, classical pieces

Classical (often graded from No. I-easy to No. VI-difficult)

Arrangements for piano — four hands

Beginning piano student etudes, folios

Adult beginners' editions

Classical etudes — folio editions

Jazz, jazz-rock arrangements — single arrangements or folios

Classical music editions (solo recital pieces, transcriptions of orchestra pieces, solo parts, concertos, etc.)

Improvisation study folios

ORGAN
Folios for beginners (often included are registration suggestions for electronic organs, pipe organs)

Classical works (preludes, fugues, toccatas, chorale preludes)

Solos or folios of popular songs, classical music, material in the public domain

GUITAR
Folios for beginners studying folk guitar, classical guitar, jazz-rock guitar

Song folios — folk, pop, jazz-rock

Classical pieces (issued separately or in folios)

Group study editions (some with A/V materials

ACCORDION
Folios for beginners

Song folios — folk, pop, jazz

Solo pieces

WIND, PERCUSSION INSTRUMENTS
Beginners' folios (some with A/V materials)

Standard solos (easy, medium, difficult) with piano

Popular song folios with piano

Study folios, exercises, etudes (standard, jazz-rock)

Improvisation study folios

Ensembles (duos, trios, quartets, etc.); diverse instrumentation

STRINGS
Beginners' folios

Adult beginners' folios

Etudes, various study folios for violin, viola, violin-cello, double bass

Ensembles (duos, trios, quartets, etc.)

BAND
Beginning ensemble methods (standard, jazz-rock)

Graded pieces, beginning to professional (standard, pop, jazz-rock, serious concert band music)

Marching band (often including marching maneuvers, show ideas)

Stage band, jazz-rock groups (graded from easy to very difficult)

ORCHESTRA
Beginning string orchestra study folios

Graded orchestra music (very easy to very difficult)

Concert folios (popular to classical)

String orchestra, single and folio editions (popular to classical)

Standard repertoire — overtures, symphonies, concertos, ballets, etc.

THEATRE MUSIC
School operettas, musical shows

Broadway shows (individual selections to complete productions including music, book)

Ballet scores and parts

SCORES
Operas, ballets

Symphonies, symphonic poems, overtures, etc.

Concertos

Cantatas, oratorios, etc.

Chamber music

TALENT DEVELOPMENT

The hottest publishers in the pop field are those who manage to sign, not just good composers, but composer-performers. The reason is obvious: since most recording artists who write usually record their own material, the publisher participates in the record royalties. As is well known, many composer-performers record *only* their own material, and they earn more money for themselves and their publishers than anyone in the business.

Since all publishers understand this, they compete intensely to sign composers who have recording contracts as performing artists. But the best of these writer-performers are already signed — or own their own publishing rights. So this leaves the publisher the difficult task of uncovering such versatile talent himself. Since most of this talent is raw, the publisher often finds himself in the business of talent development. In the past, this was not considered the responsibility of the publisher. Today, publishers find that talent development is one of their most productive activities.

Talent development means, not only polishing the artist's writing and performance skills, but helping him exploit all aspects of his career. So the publisher again finds himself engaged in activity practically synonymous with that of a record company: developing performances and selling records.

CONTRACTS WITH WRITERS

In the preceding chapter we discussed the AGAC contract, heavily weighted in favor of the writer. In the past at least, some publishers would not only refuse to sign it, they would require their writers to sign a contract heavily favoring the publisher. This still goes on. In an ideal world, writer and publisher would work out a contract of *equity* — one that balances the interests of both parties. In the following pages, I have attempted to achieve this ideal. It would rarely occur in the real world, because contract negotiations, by definition, are adversary relationships; each party normally goes for just about anything he can get. But the draft that follows might serve as a model for two parties coming to the table *with about equal bargaining power.* They give and take — and just might end up with something comparable to the following agreement:

ASSUMPTIONS

Any consideration of contract negotiations requires knowledge of the background of the parties and their relative bargaining strengths. In this draft contract, we shall make these assumptions:

About the Writer — *He is creative, writes both songs and instrumental pieces in the popular music genre. Prior to entering into these "negotiations" with our imaginary publisher, the writer enjoyed some publishing success through modest sales of recordings of his music. He has some music "in-the-trunk" — compositions not yet copyrighted or published, which he is prepared to assign to the publisher for the right kind of deal. He wants to advance his career, not only as a writer, but as a recording artist. The writer can be persuaded to sign over his writing talents to the publisher exclusively if the offer is good enough.*

About the Publisher — *His operation is well established and moderately successful. The firm is an ancillary operation of a parent record company with multinational distribution. The label's publishing wing has not yet fully established its operations in foreign territories. The publisher farms out all its printed music activity. The publisher has strong faith in the potential earning power of the prospective writer and seeks his exclusive services.*

DRAFT CONTRACT

This draft is for study purposes only. The author recommends that all parties entering into contract negotiations retain independent legal counsel to write the actual language of any agreement.

AGREEMENT made (date) _____ by and between

_____ , the Writer

and _____ , the Publisher

1.0 Appointment. The Publisher appoints the Writer as a composer, lyricist, arranger, orchestrator, editor, and the Writer's services as a writer shall be rendered exclusively for the Publisher and no other publisher. Services performed under this agreement shall not be deemed to be work made for hire as defined under United States copyright law.

2.0 Term. This agreement starts on (date) _____
and ends on (date) _____ .[1] The publisher is granted options to extend this agreement, by one-year increments of extension for

---

1-This kind of exclusive term contract in earlier times was often limited to one year. The author recommends two to three years to enable the publisher time to demonstrate his competence. Even enterprising publishers are often unable to develop acceptance of a composition in the first year of a contract.

additional years, but not to exceed an aggregate total of _____ years,[2] on the identical terms and conditions of the initial term. The foregoing notwithstanding, the Writer retains the option to deny these extension options unless the Publisher has obtained, directly or indirectly, _____

_____
[3]

commercially released recordings of the Controlled Compositions during the time period of _____
This shall be referred to hereafter as "The Recording Goal."[4]

2.1 If the Publisher's parent recording company terminates the Writer's contract with it as a royalty artist, this Writer's contract shall be coterminous with that recording contract.[5]

3.0 Assignment. The Writer assigns to the Publisher all rights throughout the world in the compositions listed on Schedule A attached here.[6] Throughout this contract the word "composition" shall include music, words and title.

3.1 The Writer also assigns to the Publisher all rights in the compositions created by the Writer during the term and under the conditions of this agreement. The foregoing notwithstanding, these works are offered to the Publisher on a first-refusal basis only. If the Publisher does not agree to accept them for publication and exploitation within 60 days of their being offered, the Writer reserves the right to assign them to any other publisher.

All works listed on Schedule A, together with all works described under 3.1 which the Publisher accepts, are referred to hereinafter as the Controlled Compositions.

4.0 Warranty. The Writer warrants that the Controlled Compositions are original with him, that he is the sole author and composer, and that he has not, to the best of his knowledge, borrowed, paraphrased or otherwise used any other copyrighted material for them.

4.1 The Writer indemnifies the Publisher against financial loss if a copyright infringement action or similar action is adjudicated as meritorious, or in a situation where any copyright infringement action is settled and made

---

2-In California a contract for *personal services* cannot normally be enforced for a period longer than seven years. In New York State there are precedents for contracts of this kind being enforceable for up to ten years. Five-year term contracts are probably the most common today, whatever statutory limitations might prevail.

3-The AGAC contract allows the publisher one year to obtain a commercially released recording of the particular song under contract, unless the publisher pays the writer a sum of money (currently $250) to "buy" six additional months' time to attain that goal. Failing this, all rights to the song revert to the writer.

4-A reasonable "recording goal" might be getting record deals for one-half the Controlled Compositions. See 12.0 for the consequences of the recording goal not being reached.

5-While coterminous contracts are often inadvisable, in this instance the writer would want to be released from his publishing contract in order to be free to negotiate a new publishing deal with another record company.

6-This list would probably include all of the works the writer had "in the trunk" prior to signing this contract which had not been previously published or otherwise encumbered by prior commitment. Some lawyers recommend their clients grant only *administrative rights* to a writer's available works composed prior to a term contract.

with the Writer's consent.

5.0 Royalties. In consideration of this agreement the Publisher agrees:

5.0-A To pay the Writer $ _____ in twelve equal monthly installments, and the receipt of the first installment is hereby acknowledged, as an advance against royalties, and these payments shall remain the property of the Writer and shall be deductible only from payments becoming due the Writer under this contract.

5.0-B To pay the Writer one-half of the Publisher's net receipts from the United States and Canada generated by the Controlled Compositions through the granting of licenses, rights, permits to and for all media of communication now known or later developed.

5.1 The foregoing notwithstanding, the Writer shall not receive any of the Publisher's share of any income from any performing rights society anywhere in the world. The Publisher shall not receive any of the Writer's share of any income from any performing rights society anywhere in the world.

5.2 The Publisher shall not grant any mechanical license at a rate lower than the prevailing statutory maximum to any individual or company with whom the Publisher has any affiliation or financial interest.[7]

5.3 To pay the Writer 10 percent of the wholesale price on the sale of all printed editions in the United States and Canada.[8]

5.4 Royalties are to be paid for each separate Controlled Composition and the Writer denies the Publisher the right to cross-collateralize royalties except to the extent required for recovery by the Publisher of all royalties advanced to the Writer. No cross-collateralization of any kind is permitted the Publisher in respect to any royalties or other payments made to the Writer by the Publisher's affiliated record company. If a dispute arises between the parties, the royalties applicable to the disputed Controlled Composition(s) shall not in any way limit or delay payment of royalties due the Writer from any other Controlled Composition.

5.5 Where a Controlled Composition has more than one author or composer, the share of royalties among them shall be apportioned in accord with Addendum No. _____ attached here. When the Publisher engages an author or composer to function with the Writer as a cowriter, song "doctor," or arranger, the sharing of writers' royalties shall be apportioned in accord with the relative value and extent of the creative contributions of the Writer and cowriters and these apportionments shall be negotiated by the parties in good faith.

5.6 If the Publisher engages the Writer as an arranger, orchestrator, editor or copyist, he will pay the Writer the equivalent of AFM union scale for such services, and such payments shall be over and above all other advances and royalties provided for in this contract.[9]

7-This clause prevents the publisher from offering anyone a "sweetheart" deal.

8-Instead of this, the parties might negotiate a graduated royalty rate. See the AGAC formula.

9-If the income of the writer under this contract fails to aggregate a reasonable

6.0 Foreign Rights. The parties recognize that their relationships with foreign publishers, subpublishers, affiliates and licensees are presently in flux, and the Writer and Publisher agree to determine, by mutual consent, the fair sharing of royalties and other income derived outside the United States and Canada on a territory-by-territory basis. These issues shall be negotiated in good faith, and the terms and conditions shall be set forth in addenda attached here.[10]

7.0 Promotion Expense. The Publisher shall be solely responsible for all promotion expense, including the production of audio and video demonstration tapes or discs.

7.1 If the Publisher engages the Writer to perform on any demo, he shall pay the Writer wages equivalent to applicable union scale.

7.2 If the ownership and copyright of any Controlled Composition should transfer from the Publisher and revert to the Writer, all demos on that composition become the property of the Writer.

8.0 Right to Audit. The Publisher grants to the Writer the right to engage a qualified accountant to examine the Publisher's books and related financial documents, following receipt of reasonable notice. The cost of any such audit is to be borne entirely by the Writer except that, in respect to any royalty statement rendered by the Publisher, the Writer is found to be owed a sum equal to or greater than _____ percent[11] of the sum shown on that particular royalty statement as being due the Writer, then the Publisher shall pay the entire cost of the audit, but not to exceed _____ percent[12] of the amount shown to be due the Writer.

9.0 Creative Rights. The Publisher acknowledges that the Writer's reputation and potential income relate importantly to the originality and quality of the Controlled Compositions as well as to their use. The Writer acknowledges, however, that the Publisher has the right to make unessential changes in the compositions and has the day-to-day responsibility of determining the best way to exploit the compositions. To balance these interests of the parties in this respect, it is agreed that the Publisher has the right to do any or all of the following in this context only with the consent of

---

amount, the contract may not be enforceable in some states in that the publisher has the writer completely tied up as his exclusive writing "property," thus denying him the opportunity of hustling additional writing income outside. In California, there are precedents of courts refusing to enforce exclusive services contracts of this kind where the writer's annual writing income failed to total $6000. See John T. Frankenheimer's, "The $6000 Rule"; op. cit., p 364.

10-The parent contract is left open-ended here to provide the parties an opportunity to remain flexible in response to rapidly changing foreign markets. While the parties might agree on a worldwide fifty-fifty split of income, equity might be better served by negotiating deals territory-by-territory. For a useful discussion of these issues, see John T. Frankenheimer's "Exclusive Songwriting Agreement: Analysis and Commentary," *Representing Musical Artists: Legal, Business and Practical Aspects,* p 377 f (see bibliography).

11-The AGAC contract calls for five percent here. Ten to 15 percent might be reasonable, at least from the publisher's point of view.

12-The AGAC contract calls for 50 percent here.

the Writer, whose consent shall not be unreasonably withheld:

9.0-A   Engage a lyricist to materially alter the Writer's lyrics or to write new lyrics.

9.0-B   Make substantive changes in the Writer's music.

9.0-C   Grant a synchronization license for a Controlled Composition.

9.0-D   Use the Writer's likeness, photograph, or name to exploit a product or service without the Writer's consent in respect to appropriateness and good taste and without paying the Writer a royalty commensurate with the exploitation value.

9.0-E   License a Controlled Composition for use in connection with a broadcast commercial, print advertisement or merchandising of a product or service.

9.0-F   Grant a Grand Right in connection with the production and performance of a Controlled Composition as a dramatic musical work.

10.0 Limited Power of Attorney.   The Writer appoints the Publisher as his attorney-in-fact to represent his interests, but only in respect to the Controlled Compositions. In this role the Publisher may negotiate and sign contracts, grant licenses, control trusts and otherwise act on behalf of the Writer.

The foregoing notwithstanding, the Publisher may sign contracts and other major documents only in those instances where the Writer is unavailable within a reasonable time to sign for himself.

This limited power of attorney may not be revoked at any time except when the Writer determines that the Publisher has used this limited power of attorney improperly and against the Writer's best interests.[13]

11.0 Right of Assignment.   The Publisher reserves the right to assign this contract to another fully qualified publisher capable of serving the Writer's interests in a professional manner. The Writer grants this right of assignment provided the assignee assumes all the responsibilities and obligations of the first publisher set forth in the present contract.

12.0 Reversion.   If the Recording Goal is not reached, the Writer will grant the Publisher a "run-out period" of six months beyond the initial term set forth under 2.0. If, by the end of the run-out period, the Recording Goal has still not been reached, all rights in any Controlled Composition not recorded revert totally to the Writer.

13.0 Default, Cure.   If either the Publisher or the Writer asserts that the other party is in default or breach of this contract, the aggrieved party shall provide written notice setting forth the nature of the dispute. The accused party is then allowed 30 days to cure the alleged default, during which period no default or other grievances shall be deemed incurable.

13-This limited power of attorney would be too constricting, in the view of most publishers, and they would probably accept it only from a writer whose bargaining power was stronger than their own.

14.0 Arbitration. The parties agree to submit all disputes to the American Arbitration Association and be bound by and perform any award rendered in such arbitration.

_____

Publisher

_____

Writer

County of —
State of —

SPLIT COPYRIGHTS, COPUBLISHING

The 1909 Copyright Act held that copyright was indivisible. But in actual practice, the industry has always found ways to circumvent that constraint. Today, publishing rights are very often _split,_ and when they are, we refer to them quite simply as _split copyrights._ The deals struck are said to be _copublishing_ agreements.[14] How common is this practice? In recent years, it is not unusual to find one-half or more of the songs on the pop charts "published" by two to even four or more "publishers." In reality, nearly all these split publishing deals are simply a number of persons or firms agreeing to share the publishing income, not the publishing responsibilities. They are "copublishers" in name only, as a rule. In many cases, the rightful _authors_ have probably had their arms twisted to induce them to share the publishing income — with a record label, record producer, attorney, or manager who wants to get in the act — and does — fairly or through coercion. Here is another manifestation of how irresistible music industry people find the music publishing business.

When the bundle of rights under copyright is split, administration of the property can be difficult. Where coauthors are involved and belong to the same performance licensing organization, ASCAP, BMI and SESAC will honor directions from the co-owners to divide performance royalties due the publishers involved. Performance licensing groups, however, resist these kinds of splits where more than one licensing group is involved. In respect to mechanical royalties and synchronization fees, the Harry Fox Agency is accustomed to splitting moneys in accord with instructions it receives from copyright proprietors.

Joint administration of copyright requires specific contractual arrangements for sharing of synchronization fees. While synchronization rights apply worldwide, differences of opinion prevail on how income from this source should be shared. In the past, most publishers have

---

14-Note that a _split copyright_ is not the same as _joint ownership,_ a practice long recognized in copyright registration by coauthors.

believed it equitable to attribute 50 percent of synchronization fee income to the United States, and the balance to foreign sources. Administration of copyrights outside this country should be assigned entirely to one co-owner or the other, because sharing of the responsibility leads to confusion and lack of control. This is particularly important, because in some foreign countries a unilateral commitment by one co-owner may be binding on the other.

Where a work has two authors, and two publishers split the copyright, each writer must look to his own publisher for his particular share. Unless otherwise provided in a joint administration agreement, mechanical royalties will be equally divided by the two publishers, and each publisher will then be able to pay its writer only one-half of one-half of such income, or 25 percent net.

Joint administrations of copyrights have led to coercion and abuses in the past, particularly when not all of the parties involved have been made aware of possible side agreements or under-the-table deals. The "cut-in" is an example, where the copyright proprietor does not split ownership, but cuts in someone for a piece of the pie. Under controlled circumstances, the cut-in can be fair and work even better than joint administration; a single administration is generally preferable to one that is shared. But a cut-in agreement should specify certain limitations: it should be limited to payments on mechanicals derived from a particular record by a specified artist for a finite period. If the record is taped but never commercially released, the cut-in deal should be automatically voided or the property fully recaptured.

One final note regarding alleged coauthorship. For many years, songwriters have sometimes agreed to add the name of a recording artist to a song in the expectation that such flattery (and potential income) would induce the artist to record the song. Under the 1976 Copyright Act, any falsification of the actual writers of a copyright may constitute fraudulent registration. A word to the wise.

PROMOTION, ADVERTISING

POPULAR MUSIC

The main concern of a publisher of popular songs is getting his music recorded and broadcast. Such activities are not only profitable in and of themselves, but they acquaint the public with the music, and those people then frequently go out and buy printed editions. This, in turn, generates still more income.

Publishers persuade artists and record producers to record their music generally through direct, personal contacts. Even though the publishing and recording industries are huge, much of the power and control lies in the hands of a relatively small number of "insiders" — the recording artists, record producers, established composers and important managers. Publishers place on their payrolls the kind of promotion personnel who know the insiders, the power brokers, understand their needs, keep track of market trends and changing tastes, then deliver "the right material."

Song Casting — One of the most critical functions of a publisher is to attempt to match songs with performers. A professional manager and his staff analyze each song and search out those particular recording artists they believe have a performing style that is "right" for the material. This is often called "song casting" and it is as critical a task as casting a TV show or Broadway play. This matching of artist to repertoire used to be the principal concern of staff record producers, hence their appellation, "artist and repertoire producers." Producers and publishers are, then, engaged in essentially the same enterprise — casting songs and recording them. Those persons who know how to do this well are scarce, in high demand and well paid.

Ralph Peer, II, who rose to prominence as vice-president of Peer-Southern, one of the largest popular music publishers, told me that the song casting process often works *in reverse* for prestigious publishers: *record producers* will contact *the publisher,* listing their current needs, and ask the publisher to supply material the publisher believes "right" for a particular recording project. A publisher enjoying this kind of prestige has a good share of his work done for him by producers and artists who believe the firm has good casting judgment and strong material.

Experienced publishers understand that, at the outset, only a select number of recording artists will even consider their material. This is because so many acts in popular music are "self-contained" — the individual performer or group uses only its own material. Rarely do self-contained acts accept outside songs. Accordingly, the smart publisher rarely spends much energy trying to cast his songs with an act already self-supplied.

Cover Records — The publisher who has a self-contained act under contract understands, or should understand, that once the material is initially recorded by that act, the publisher's exploitation job has only begun. Now his principal concern is getting *cover records* — inducing other recording artists to record the song. Whatever the size of a publisher's catalog, the long-range income of the firm is largely dependent upon the number of "covers" generated over the years.

Getting cover records will be very difficult unless the publisher has been discreet in the material he has placed in his catalog. This is why experienced publishers generally pass on material that appears to be just "album cuts." The unending search is for potential hit material. Most recording artists already have available, from their own hands or from insiders and friends, all the album-cut material they believe they can use. Therefore, knowledgeable song promoters generally limit the material they submit to songs they believe might make it as a single. Of course, no one can predict hit material, but successful publishers guess correctly rather often.

Another aspect of promotion is the publisher offering his services directly to record companies. The two kinds of companies, their economic interests almost identical, work out cooperative promotion campaigns for new material, frequently in connection with personal appearances of recording artists.

As for advertising in the pop field, it is almost wholly addressed to the amateur musician, students and teachers. Print advertising addressed to professionals can hardly be said to exist. With professionals, it is a word-of-mouth type of promotion, quite often one-to-one contacts.

EDUCATIONAL FIELD

Promotion of printed music intended for student and school use is accomplished in two ways. First, publishers active in the educational field spend most of their advertising budgets on direct mail campaigns. Music educators receive dozens of these promotional mailings every month, some of which include a free demo recording (pressed onto flexible plastic film). Printed samples of new releases are also included in these mailings in the form of "thematics," short extrapolations of themes from complete works. The educator, when "sold" by such mailings, proceeds to place his order either by telephone, or more likely, by mail.

A second promotional scheme involves publishers placing display ads in music education journals. Media of this type with the largest circulation include *Music Educators Journal, NAJE Educator,* the *Instrumentalist, School Music* and *Down Beat.*

A unique promotional device used in the educational field is the "reading clinic." Large retailers or an educational group will cohost day-long readings of new publications. Educators attend these readings (school ensembles are used) and subsequently place orders with their dealers to cover their needs for the school year.

CLASSICAL FIELD

Publishers of chamber music, art songs, operas and ballets have their own ways of acquainting potential buyers with their music. Unlike the pop and educational fields that focus on new music, classical music publishers are usually engaged in "reminding" customers, rather than promoting, the great music of the past. They periodically enliven their catalogs with new compositions and arrangements, but the bulk of their sales comes from reprints and new editions of the classics.

New serious works of any length are rarely printed, because anticipated sales are rarely calculated to produce enough money to cover costs of production. In lieu of direct sales, such works as new operas, ballets and symphonic works are made available through rental of the scores and parts for performance. In respect to dramatic musical works, publishers often get additional income by charging performance fees. Dramatic works by major contemporary composers produce fairly good income for both publishers and writers.

Classical music is also promoted through display ads placed in music journals. A large part of the classical and semi-classical repertoire spills over into the educational field, and most publishers sell to schools and colleges either the original scores and parts or arrangements scored specifically for school use.

Income for publishers of classical music from recordings is negligible, because most of the repertoire is in the public domain.

INCOME SOURCES

One of the reasons publishing income is large is that it is generated by so many diverse sources. The important ones are shown in Figure 5.4

As pointed out, many publishers make most of their money from performance royalties. For other publishers, their number one source is record royalties. Still others — "paper houses" — base their economic health on the sale of printed editions. If a publisher is fortunate enough to have in his catalog some of the world-renowned standards of the past, he can make thousands of dollars each time he grants some person permission simply to use the title of one of his standards — for example — for a movie or TV show title. Still more income, not huge but adding to the total, comes from compulsory licensing of jukeboxes, secondary transmissions, even school performances.

Many of the old-line publishers experience millions of dollars of income each year granting performance rights in dramatico-musical works such as musical plays, probably the biggest of all long-term money-makers.

If we were to aggregate the income of a dramatic work such as a *South Pacific*, not only from performance royalties, but from the sale of movie rights and the sale of dozens of printed editions of the score, we would be looking at a multimillion-dollar property.

PUBLISHERS POTENTIAL INCOME SOURCES

TYPE OF USE	WHO PAYS
BROADCAST PERFORMANCES	ASCAP, BMI
LIVE PERFORMANCES (clubs, hotels, theatres, etc.)	ASCAP, BMI
RECORD ROYALTIES (commercial releases for private use only)	Record Producers (usually through Harry Fox Agency)
MOTION PICTURES (for theatres or TV or home video discs, tapes)	Producers pay Harry Fox Agency or publisher directly
SHEET MUSIC SALES	Selling agents, licensees of publisher
TRANSCRIPTIONS (background music, syndications, etc.)	Producers pay publisher directly or Harry Fox Agency
PERMISSIONS (music, words, or title for commercials, merchandising)	Advertising agency or sponsor or merchandiser
PUBLIC BROADCASTING, CABLE TV, JUKEBOXES	Initially through Copyright Royalty Tribunal. Various thereafter
GRAND RIGHTS	Producers of dramatico-musical performances
FOREIGN RIGHTS	Various

Fig. 5.4

NMPA AND THE HARRY FOX AGENCY

The trade association most representative of publishers in the popular music field is NMPA — the National Music Publishers Association. While its membership is relatively small (some 200), it provides important services for more than 4000 publishers who are not NMPA members.

NMPA was originally set up to provide a clearinghouse for publishers who were being asked for rights to synchronize their music to the then-new entertainment medium, "the talkies." In the 1930s NMPA added to its services the licensing of music for electrical transcriptions for radio broadcast. In 1938 it began to license and collect fees for "mechanicals." The organization NMPA set up to provide these services became known as the Harry Fox Agency. In 1969 the Harry Fox Agency became the wholly-owned subsidiary of NMPA.

HARRY FOX AGENCY

The Harry Fox Agency, through individual authorizations and instructions from its principals, acts in the following areas:

1- *Licensing of copyrights for commercial records and tapes to be distributed to the public for private use.*
2- *Collection and distribution of royalties derived from such licensing.*
3- *Auditing the books of record manufacturers.*
4- *Licensing of musical compositions for motion picture and television synchronization.*
5- *Licensing of theatrical motion picture performing rights in the United States only.*
6- *Licensing the recording of music for other than private use, such as background music, in-flight music and syndicated radio services.*
7- *Licensing music for television and radio commercials.*

The Harry Fox Agency does not act in the area of licensing public performance (except as indicated above), grand and dramatic rights, print rights and derivative uses (music arrangements). Further information on how the agency functions is found in Chapter 7.

STUDENT TEACHES TEACHER. The author gets a lesson from former student Jim Cassell, preparing this console for a session about to begin at A & M Records, Hollywood.

6

MUSIC COPYRIGHT

SUMMARY OF THE 1976 COPYRIGHT ACT

> **Every serious student of copyright should acquire his own complete copy of the Act, together with other special publications and bulletins relating to copyright. These documents are available, without charge, from the *Information and Publications Section,* Copyright Office, Library of Congress, Washington, D.C. 20559.**

BACKGROUND

Until 1978, all USA copyrights were governed by the 1909 copyright law. During the period 1909 through 1977, copyrights came also to be governed by state statutes and common law. In 1962, Congress took action to protect copyrights about to expire, because it was anticipated that any revision of the length of term of copyright provided in the 1909 law (28 years plus a 28-year renewal option) would probably conform more closely to the more extended terms prevailing in other countries. Ten years later, in 1972, Congress provided certain copyright protection for phonorecords distributed after February 15, 1972. Also, during the 1970s many individual states passed laws limiting record piracy. This patchwork accumulation of statutes and common law was all that copyright owners had at their disposal for protection of their properties until Congress finally gave birth to the 1976 Copyright Act.

The 1909 copyright law was based largely on British law, particularly the Statute of Ann, passed by British Parliament in 1709. The Statute of Ann was the first "modern" law governing certain aspects of copyright. It provided copyright protection through a registration process to any author seeking it. It also provided two consecutive 14-year terms of copyright ownership totalling 28 years. The Statute of Ann was not so much a copyright law as a statute concerned with the regulation of trade, particularly the practices of book printers in England at that time. The statute provided a two-tiered system of protection: the statute itself covered published works, and common law offered protection for unpublished works.

The Statute of Ann's essential features were adopted by the United States Congress when it wrote the 1909 U.S. Copyright Law. The 1909 law became hopelessly inadequate to govern copyright in ensuing decades. Recording and broadcasting technologies, to cite but two media, did not even exist as we know them today. The 1909 law did not anticipate the developing technology of fast, low-cost multicopying of printed materials and sounds. Machines something like the modern jukebox did exist, but they were specifically exempted by the 1909 law. Even with the help of state statutes written since 1909, in the aggregate the laws on the books could not begin to deal with the new copyright problems. The results are well known to the owners and users of copyright during this period: confusion, frustration, cheating, bootlegging, and extensive litigation.

After World War II, the United States participated in the development of the Universal Copyright Convention and became a party to it in 1955. In that same year, Congress began efforts to revise the 1909 U.S. Copyright Law. For two years, Congress appropriated funds for copyright research; 35 monographs were published. These research efforts culminated in 1961 with the "Report of the Register of Copyrights on the General Revision of the United States Copyright Law."

From the outset of these efforts to revise the old law, Congress averred that its goal was to seek a balance of interests between copyright owners and users. This search for balance and fairness was aided yet inhibited by the special interest groups that affect most legislation. Revising the old law was a long, tough battle of opposing forces, not so much because of a concern for the creators of "intellectual property," but because multibillion-dollar industries were involved in seeking to protect their economic interests.

Through this 21-year period of argument and dispute, Congress developed a convenient copout to avoid playing the role of the bully, stating that "Congress will act when the parties in dispute reach agreement among themselves about what they want in the new law." This stance helped some, but not much. One pervasive influence usually remained unidentified: many members of Congress consistently sided with the arguments of the broadcasters, particularly in regard to that industry's strong opposition to paying performance fees for broadcasts of recorded music. It was rarely pointed out that support for this point of view apparently stemmed from the fact that many members of Congress own interests in radio and television stations.

Another strong lobby was the jukebox industry, which managed to escape with a license fee far below what copyright owners believed they were entitled to receive.

The Congressional hearings also attempted to help reduce the wholesale bootlegging of records which, by the mid-1970s, was resulting in a financial loss to legitimate record companies of an estimated $500 million per year. Legislation by Congress in 1972 and subsequent state statutes reduced some record piracy in this country.

The legislative battle ended in 1976 with a "General Revision" of the 1909 law. Most of its provisions became effective January 1, 1978. In addition to the law itself, we can gain additional insights into the intent of Congress by studying such publications as *Senate Report No. 94-474*, *House of Representative Reports No.'s 94-1476* and *94-1733*. These and other publications of the U.S. Copyright Office help clarify the 1976 Copyright Act and reveal how differing views were reconciled in the final statute.

Congress stated that a fundamental goal of the new law was to consider

> ... the relative roles of the copyright owner and user ... with respect to relative creative contribution, capital investment, cost, risk and contribution to the opening of new markets for creative expression and media for their communication ... and to afford the copyright owner a fair income under existing economic conditions.[1]

The Congress stated that its intent was that implementation of the new law would "... minimize any disruptive impact on the structure of the industries involved and on generally prevailing industry practices."[2] Whether that goal is being reached as the law is being applied is a question whose answer will be largely shaped by how special interests fare in their appeals to the Copyright Royalty Tribunal and the Congress.

ESSENTIAL PROVISIONS OF THE ACT

1- *The statute preempts nearly all other copyright laws — federal, state, and common law. This elimination of the crazy quilt of prior statutes was probably the most important gain for all concerned.*

2- *Duration of copyright was lengthened and now conforms more closely to practices prevailing throughout most of the rest of the world: life of the author plus 50 years.*

3- *Exclusive rights of copyright owners were clarified, strengthened and extended.*

1-1976 Copyright Act, Chapter 8.

2-Ibid.

4- *Protection of owners of copyright in sound recordings were clarified and extended, except that they were specifically denied a performance right.*

5- *Public broadcasters, CATV companies and jukebox operators were compelled to start paying for the use of copyrighted music, as were colleges.*

6- *"Fair Use" was defined (though not as clearly as it should have been) and extended in scope.*

7- *Policies and rates of music-use licenses are to be periodically reexamined.*

TERMS DEFINED

An understanding of copyright is dependent upon awareness of how the new law defines its terms. Definitions which follow are, for the most part, quoted directly from Section 101 of the 1976 Copyright Act. Language therein which does not relate to music has been deleted.

"AUDIOVISUAL WORKS" are works that consist of a series of related images which are intrinsically intended to be shown by the use of machines or devices such as projectors, viewers, or electronic equipment, together with accompanying sounds, if any, regardless of the nature of the material objects, such as films or tapes, in which the works are embodied.

The "BEST EDITION" of a work is the edition, published in the United States at any time before the date of deposit, that the Library of Congress determines to be the most suitable for its purposes.

"COMMON LAW" is that body of "trade customs" and decisions made by courts over the years which, through widespread acceptance, have come to be recognized as fair and equitable.

A "COMPILATION" is a work formed by the collection and assembling of preexisting materials or of data that are selected, coordinated, or arranged in such a way that the resulting work as a whole constitutes an original work of authorship. The term "compilation" includes collective works.

"COPIES" are material objects, other than phonorecords, in which a work is fixed by any method now known or later developed, and from which the work can be perceived, reproduced, or otherwise communicated, either directly or with the aid of a machine or device. The term "copies" includes the material object, other than a phonorecord, in which the work is first fixed.

"COPYRIGHT OWNER," with respect to any one of the exclusive rights comprised in a copyright, refers to the owner of that particular right.

A work is "CREATED" when it is fixed in a copy or phonorecord for the first time; where a work is prepared over a period of time, the portion of it that has been fixed at any particular time constitutes the work as of that time, and where the work has been prepared in different versions, each version constitutes a separate work.

A **"DERIVATIVE WORK"** is a work based upon one or more preexisting works, such as a translation, musical arrangement, dramatization, fictionalization, motion picture version, sound recording, art reproduction, abridgment, condensation, or any other form in which a work may be recast, transformed, or adapted. A work consisting of editorial revisions, annotations, elaborations, or other modifications which, as a whole, represent an original work of authorship, is a "derivative work."

A **"DEVICE," "MACHINE," or "PROCESS"** is one now known or later developed.

To **"DISPLAY"** a work means to show a copy of it, either directly or by means of a film, slide, television image, or any other device or process or, in the case of a motion picture or other audiovisual work, to show individual images nonsequentially.

A work is **"FIXED"** in a tangible medium of expression when its embodiment in a copy or phonorecord, by or under the authority of the author, is sufficiently permanent or stable to permit it to be perceived, reproduced, or otherwise communicated for a period of more than transitory duration. A work consisting of sounds, images, or both, that are being transmitted, is "fixed" for purposes of this title if a fixation of the work is being made simultaneously with its transmission.

To **"PERFORM"** a work means to recite, render, play, dance, or act it, either directly or by means of any device or process or, in the case of a motion picture or other audiovisual work, to show its images in any sequence or to make the sounds accompanying it audible.

"PHONORECORDS" are material objects in which sounds, other than those accompanying a motion picture or other audiovisual work, are fixed by any method now known or later developed, and from which the sounds can be perceived, reproduced, or otherwise communicated, either directly or with the aid of a machine or device. The term "phonorecord" includes the material object in which the sounds are first fixed.

A **"PSEUDONYMOUS WORK"** is a work on the copies or phonorecords of which the author is identified under a fictitious name.

"PUBLICATION" is the distribution of copies or phonorecords of a work to the public by sale or otherwise transfer of ownership, or by rental, lease, or lending. The **offering** to distribute copies or phonorecords to a group of persons for purposes of further distribution, public performance, or public display, constitutes publication. A public performance or display of a work does not of itself constitute publication.

To perform or display a work **"PUBLICLY"** means 1) to perform or display it at a place open to the public or at any place where a substantial number of persons outside of a normal circle of a family and its social acquaintances is gathered; or 2) to transmit or otherwise communicate a performance or display of the work to a place specified by clause (1) or to the public, by means of any device or process, whether the members of the public, capable of receiving the performance or display receive it in the same place or in separate places and at the same time or at different times.

"SOUND RECORDINGS" are works that result from the fixation of a series of musical, spoken, or other sounds, but not including the sounds accompanying a motion picture or other audiovisual work, regardless of the nature of the material objects, such as discs, tapes, or other phonorecords, in which they are embodied.

A *"TRANSFER OF COPYRIGHT OWNERSHIP"* is an assignment, mortgage, exclusive license, or any other conveyance, alienation, or hypothecation of a copyright or of any of the exclusive rights comprised in a copyright, whether or not it is limited in time or place of effect, but not including a nonexclusive license.

A *"TRANSMISSION PROGRAM"* is a body of material that, as an aggregate, has been produced for the sole purpose of transmission to the public in sequence and as a unit.

To *"TRANSMIT"* a performance or display is to communicate it by any device or process whereby images or sounds are received beyond the place from which they are sent.

A *"USEFUL ARTICLE"* is an article having an intrinsic utilitarian function that is not merely to portray the appearance of an article or to convey information. An article that is normally a part of a useful article is considered a "useful article."

A *"WORK MADE FOR HIRE"* is 1) a work prepared by an employee within the scope of his or her employment; or 2) a work specially ordered or commissioned for use as a contribution to a collective work, as part of a motion picture or other audiovisual work, as a translation, as a supplementary work, as a compilation, as an instructional text, as a test, as answer material for a test, **if the parties expressly agree in a written instrument signed by them** that the work shall be considered a work made for hire. For the purpose of the foregoing sentence, a *"supplementary work"* is a work prepared for publication as a secondary adjunct to a work by another author for the purpose of introducing, concluding, illustrating, explaining, revising, commenting upon, or assisting in the use of the other work, such as musical arrangements.

COVERAGE

Copyright protection subsists in *original works of authorship*. Such works must be "fixed in any tangible medium of expression, now known or later developed, from which they can be perceived, reproduced, or otherwise communicated, either directly or with the aid of a machine or device." **"Works of authorship" include:**

- *Literary works*
- *Musical works, including any accompanying words*
- *Dramatic works, including any accompanying music*
- *Pantomimes and choreographic works*
- *Pictorial, graphic, and sculptural works*
- *Motion pictures and other audiovisual works*
- *Sound recordings*

The works listed above are subject to protection under the 1976 Act *even if unpublished,* without regard to the nationality or domicile of the author. In respect to published works, protection is accorded if

1), on the date of first publication, one or more of the authors is a national or domiciliary of the United States, or is a national or domiciliary, or sovereign authority of a foreign nation that is a party to a copyright treaty to which the U.S. is also a party, or is a stateless person, wherever that person may be domiciled; or 2), the work is first published in the U.S. or in a foreign nation that, on the date of first publication, is a party to the Universal Copyright Convention.[3]

Subject matter of copyright as listed above *includes compilations and derivative works*. But it should be noted that protection here does not extend to any part of a compilation or derivative work in which such material has been used unlawfully. Also, copyright in compilations and derivative works *extends only to the material contributed by the author of such work* (as distinguished from the preexisting material employed in the work) and does not imply any exclusive right in the preexisting material. The copyright in compilations and derivative works is independent of and does not affect or enlarge the scope, duration, ownership, or subsistence of any copyright protection in the preexisting material.

It can be noted here also that copyright does not extend to publications of the U.S. Government. An individual may quote from such publications without concern for copyright infringement.

EXCLUSIVE RIGHTS

Understanding of copyright is dependent on awareness of Section 106, which specifies how the Act vests five distinct exclusive rights in the author of a work. Subject to certain limitations, the 1976 Act states that the owner of copyright has the exclusive right to do or to authorize any of the following:

THE FIVE EXCLUSIVE RIGHTS

1- *To reproduce the copyrighted work in copies or phonorecords.*

2- *To prepare derivative works based upon the copyrighted work.*

3- *To distribute copies or phonorecords of the copyrighted work to the public by sale or other transfer of ownership, or by rental, lease, or lending.*

4- *To perform the copyrighted work publicly.*

5- *To display the copyrighted work publicly.*

These five exclusive rights constitute the heart of the statute.

3-Op. cit., Section 103.

LIMITATION OF RIGHTS

If the law included only the foregoing information concerning the subject matter of copyright and the listing of exclusive rights, a non-lawyer might get along reasonably well under the 1976 Act and stay out of jail. But much of the act, particularly Sections 107 through 112, concerns the limitations of these rights.

Laws covering copyright have always been more clear for commercial users of music than they have been for private individuals and nonprofit institutions. Since the enactment of the 1909 law, the courts have held that certain kinds of uses of copyrighted material are "fair," within reason, and not an infringement or materially damaging to a copyright owner. This tradition was validated and codified, to a large extent, in the 1976 law. This law attempts to define what now constitutes *fair use*[4] and Congress, in passing the legislation, attempted to reconcile the rightful interests of the copyright owners with the legitimate, nonprofit interests of individuals, schools, libraries, churches and noncommercial broadcasters.

Notwithstanding the exclusive rights the law defines, the fair use of a copyrighted work, including such use by reproduction in copies or phonorecords, or by any other means specified by Section 106 of the law, for purposes such as criticism, comment, news reporting, teaching (including multiple copies for classroom use), scholarship, or research, "is not an infringement of copyright." In determining whether the use made of a work in any particular case is a fair use, *four criteria* have been established by prior court actions and are incorporated in the new law:

1- *The purpose or character of the use, including whether such use is of a commercial nature or is for nonprofit educational purposes.*

2- *The nature of the copyrighted work.*

3- *The amount and substantiality of the portion used in relation to the work as a whole.*

4- *The effect of the use upon the potential market for or value of the copyrighted work.*

Fair Reproduction — The law states that it is not an infringement of copyright if

1- *Libraries reproduce and distribute no more than one copy or phonorecord;*

2- *The reproduction or distribution is made without any purpose of direct or indirect commercial advantage;*

3- *The collections of the library are open and available to the public;*

4-Op. cit., Section 107.

4- *The reproduction or distribution of the work includes notice of copyright.*

The fair use section of the law further states that reproduction of one copy is alright for the purpose of replacement of a copy or phonorecord that is damaged, deteriorating, lost, or stolen, if the library has, after reasonable effort, determined that an unused replacement cannot be obtained at a fair price.

Single phonorecord copies may be made of a small part of another copyrighted work, if

1- *The phonorecord becomes the property of the user (the individual who made the request for the copy) and that the library has had no notice that the phonorecord would be used for any other than private study, scholarship, or research; and*

2- *The library displays prominently, at the place where orders are accepted, and includes on its order form, a warning of copyright in accordance with the requirements prescribed by the Register of Copyrights.*

The rights of reproduction and distribution under this section apply to the entire work, or to a substantial part of it, made from the collection of a library where the user makes his or her request or from that of another library, if the library has first determined, on the basis of a reasonable investigation, that a copy or phonorecord of the copyrighted work cannot be obtained at a fair price, if

1- *The copy or phonorecord becomes the property of the user, and the library had no notice that the copy or phonorecord would be used for any purpose other than for private study, scholarship, or research; and*

2- *The library displays prominently a warning of copyright.*

Performances — The law identifies certain kinds of performances which are considered under the concept of fair use and are not infringements of copyright:

1- *The performance or display of a work by instructors or pupils in the course of face-to-face teaching in a nonprofit educational institution.*

2- *Performance of a nondramatic literary or musical work or display of a work, by or in the course or transmission, if a) the performance or display is a regular part of the systematic instruction of a nonprofit educational institution (or government body); and b) the performance or display is directly related and of material assistance to the teaching content of the transmission; and c) the transmission is made primarily for reception in classrooms or similar places devoted to instruction.*

3- *Performances of a nondramatic literary or musical work or of a dramatico-musical work of a religious nature in the course of religious services.*

4- *Performance of a nondramatic literary or musical work (otherwise than transmission to the public) without any direct or indirect purpose of commercial advantage and without payment of any fee or other compensation for the performance to any of its performers, promoters, or organizers, if a) there is no direct or indirect admission charge; or b) the proceeds, after deducting reasonable costs of production, are used exclusively for educational, religious, or charitable purposes and not for private financial gain.*

5- *Communication of a transmission embodying the performance or display of a work by the public reception of the transmission on a home-type receiving apparatus, unless a direct charge is made to see or hear the transmission, or the transmission thus received is further transmitted to the public.*

These definitions of fair use and exempt performances have new significance for schools and other nonprofit organizations which, in the past, have enjoyed exemption from licensing and payment for performances.

Sound Recordings — The 1976 law permits certain kinds of copies of sound recordings to be made by nonprofit organizations, individuals, and broadcasters, provided the recordings are short-lived, transitory — what the law terms "ephemeral" recordings.

In respect to broadcasters, they may make one copy of an ephemeral recording provided 1) that the broadcaster is licensed to broadcast the work; 2) the copy is used only by the station that makes the copy for broadcasting within its own local service area; 3) the copy is made for security or archival purposes. Unless kept for archival preservation, the copy must be destroyed within six months of its first broadcast.

In respect to nonprofit organizations, they may make no more than 30 copies or phonorecords of a particular transmission program (broadcast) if 1) no further copies are made under this clause; 2) except for one copy for archival purposes, the copies or phonorecords are destroyed within seven years from the date the transmission program was first transmitted to the public.

Nonprofit religious organizations or government may make for distribution not more than one copy or phonorecord for any number of licensed broadcasters, or a particular transmission program embodying a performance of a nondramatic musical work of a religious nature, or of a sound recording of such musical work if 1) there is no direct or indirect charge for making and distributing any such copies or phonorecords; 2) the performance is limited to the particular transmitting organization; 3) except for one copy that may be preserved for archival purposes, the copies or phonorecords are destroyed within one year from the date the transmission program was first transmitted to the public.

COPYRIGHT OWNERSHIP[5]

INITIAL OWNERSHIP

Copyright vests initially in the author of the work. When there are joint authors, these authors own the copyright jointly. In the popular song field, it is customary for the composer (or composers) to share ownership equally with the author (or authors) of the words. However, joint authors may, through execution of a written agreement signed by them, set up disproportionate shares of ownership in a work on which they collaborated.

Copyright subsists in the "original work of authorship' and does not extend to any material objects, such as copies or phonorecords, in which the work may be embodied.

COLLECTIVE WORKS

Copyright in each separate contribution to a collective work is distinct from copyright in the collective work as a whole and vests initially in the author of the contribution. In the absence of an express transfer of the copyright (or any of the rights under it), the owner of the copyright in the collective work is presumed to have acquired only the privilege of reproducing and distributing the contribution as part of that particular collective work, any revision of that collective work, and any later collective work in the same series.

FILM MUSIC — Copyright in music scored for theatrical films and TV movies is covered by the overriding copyright in the movie itself as a composite work. Such a work carries the © type of copyright notice, in that it is classified as an audiovisual work. However, additional copyrights may preexist for music a film producer licenses for inclusion in his production. In this kind of situation, the two copyrights coexist. The film producer would be required to obtain a synchronization license for use of the preexisting copyrighted music. But the complete audiovisual work — the movie itself — would still have a blanket copyright covering its component parts.

5-Sec. 201

WORKS MADE FOR HIRE[6]

In the case of a work made for hire, the employer or the other person for whom the work was prepared is considered the author under the 1976 Act and, *unless the parties have expressly agreed otherwise in a written instrument signed by them,* owns all of the rights comprised in the copyright. Under the 1909 Act, many difficulties arose in respect to differing views on the correct legal definition of "work made for hire." This issue has been subject to considerable amounts of litigation. The Copyright Office does not even attempt to define the legal meaning of the phrase, "work made for hire," and will accept renewal registrations from both the alleged "employer" and an "author." The controversy was not solved by the 1976 law, but its language helps narrow the area of dispute and may reduce litigation of this kind.

Disputes over work made for hire often center on the first part of the definition as found in Section 101 of the 1976 Act: a work made for hire is ". . . a work prepared by an employee within the scope of his or her employment." Does the word "employee" mean an individual on the employer's regular payroll? Does "scope of employment" include work performed at home, away from the employer's place of business? What if the employee performs his services after regular working hours or on vacation? While the courts may not agree on these matters, precedents have been set for what some lawyers consider "the key question" here: *did the employer have the right to direct and supervise the manner in which the work was performed?* Courts have found that where the employer did exercise that right, the resulting work was deemed work made for hire.

Many lawyers agree that one aspect of this whole question has been clearly determined by prior court action: *a work cannot be considered made for hire if it is created as a special job assignment for which extra compensation is demanded.*

The second part of the statutory definition of "work made for hire" states that, where the work is not performed by an employee within the scope of his or her employment, it may be ". . . a work specially ordered or commissioned for use as a contribution to a collective work, as part of a motion picture or other audiovisual work, as a translation, as a compilation, as an instructional text, as a text, as answer material to a test, or as an atlas, if the parties expressly agree in a written instrument signed by them that the work shall be considered a work made for hire." This language is being interpreted by some lawyers as excluding works *not* included on the list, e.g., musical compositions, books and paintings, despite what may be a contrary intention on the part of the individuals involved.

In an article first published by the New York Law School *Law Review* of November, 1976, Dennis Angel and Samuel W. Tannenbaum assert that there are types of specially ordered and commissioned works that can be considered as works made for hire under S. 22. My own interpretation of

---

6-Sec. 201(b).

the 1976 Act is in general accord with the views expressed by Angel and Tannenbaum. Works made for hire may include

1- *Contributions to a collective work.* *The definition provided by the 1976 Act is not really limited to periodical issues, anthologies, encyclopedias and the like, and would appear to allow inclusion, for example, of a book of music.*

2- *Most audiovisual works,* *including motion pictures, TV movies, videotapes and videodiscs (excluded are unauthorized fixations of live performances or telecasts). Film strips are excluded if they fail to convey an impression of motion. In respect to movies, it was apparently the intent of Congress to include as works for hire the musical scores to motion pictures. While film composers today are practically never engaged on a regular basis by a studio or producer, their work is specially commissioned. An attorney could argue that a movie composer is "an independent contractor." Even where a film score clearly falls under a work made for hire classification, it is common practice for the film producer to retain only the "publisher's share" of the copyright and assign all the "author's share," including all author's royalties, to the film composer.*

3- *A supplementary work.* *This would be a work prepared for publication as a secondary adjunct to a work by another author for the purpose of introducing, revising, or assisting in the use of the other work, such as musical arrangements.*

4- **A compilation** — *a new work of authorship formed by the collection of preexisting materials, such as a song folio.*

Other types of works might be reasonably classified as works made for hire, but they do not qualify in that the parties have not executed a written agreement expressing such an understanding. There are still other works that can be considered works made for hire, but they are excluded here in that they are unrelated to music.

SOUND RECORDINGS

Section 114 states that the copyright owner of a sound recording has these exclusive rights:

1- *The right to reproduce the copyrighted work — to dupli-cate the sound recording in the form of phonorecords (or copies of motion pictures and other audiovisual works). Note that this right is limited to "duplicating the actual sounds fixed in the recording."*

2- *The right to prepare derivative works based on the copy-righted material — to make and distribute phonorecords which are new arrangements or versions of the copyrighted work.*

3- *The right to distribute phonorecords to the public by sale or other transfer of ownership, or by rental, lease, or lending.*

4- *The right to display the phonorecord publicly — show copies of it.*

Performance Right Exclusion — The 1976 law specifically excludes performance rights in phonorecords. This exclusion is one of the most significant and controversial sections of the law. The issue was debated at length by Congress, but the strong lobby representing broadcasters persuaded influential Congressmen to exclude payment of performing fees for phonorecords. The USA is well behind most other countries in this respect: *over 50 Western countries have laws providing for collection of such royalties or the broadcasters voluntarily pay them.*

Congress did not solve this critical issue by simply excluding performance royalty payments for recordings; it was apparently so embarrassed by its own failure, it instructed the Register of Copyrights to study the issue, hold hearings of interested parties, then report back to Congress as to whether the exclusion should be amended or eliminated. Early in 1978, the Register of Copyrights reported to Congress the results of her research, expressing the opinion that the exclusion of a performing right in phonorecords was not at all justified and that the 1976 Act should be amended accordingly. Her research pleased musicians and record companies, because it included evidence, in-dependently gathered, that there was no credibility to the old argument from broadcasters that payment of a recorded music royalty would cause financial hardship.

AFM and AFTRA have lobbied strongly in favor of a performing right in phonorecords because such a right, even if derived from a low licensing rate, would increase considerably the potential income of performers. Strong support for performance royalties from recordings comes also from RIAA.

Every session of Congress since 1977 has seen bills introduced which would provide for a performing right in records. Congressional support appears to be growing but continues to lack sufficient strength to pass such a bill. Performing artists and record companies continue their lobbying efforts.

EXCLUSION — The exclusive rights of the owner of copyright in a sound recording in respect to the preparation and reproduction of derivative works *do not extend* to the making or duplicating of another sound recording that consists entirely of an independent fixation of other sounds, even though such sounds imitate or simulate those in the copyrighted sound recording.

SOUND-ALIKE PHONORECORDS — Imitations which mimic the original record are legally permissible, but the imitative phonorecord must be an entirely independent fixation of other sounds. It cannot simply use a duplicate tape of the original.

Compulsory License — In the case of nondramatic musical works, the exclusive rights to make and distribute phonorecords of such works are subject to compulsory licensing under the conditions specified by Section 115. The main features:

1- *A person may obtain a compulsory license **only if his or her primary purpose in making phonorecords is to distribute them to the public for private use.** This sentence is very significant and clearly excludes from compulsory licensing all records that are generally classified under the term, "transcriptions." In the music field, that term is applied, not to phonorecords or tapes intended for purchase and use by the public, but to discs or tapes leased or sold for special uses, e.g., theme music for programs broadcast, wired music services such as Muzak, etc.*

2- *A person may not obtain a compulsory license for use of the work in the making of phonorecords duplicating a sound recording fixed by another, unless a) such sound recording was fixed lawfully; and b) the making of the phonorecords was authorized by the owner of copyright in the sound recording or, if the sound recording was fixed before February 15, 1972, by any person who fixed the sound recording pursuant to an express license for use of such work in a sound recording.*

A compulsory license includes the privilege of making a musical arrangement of the work to the extent necessary to conform it to the style and manner of interpretation of the performance involved, but the arrangement shall not change the basic melody or fundamental character of the work and shall not be subject to protection as a derivative work under the law except with the express consent of the copyright owner.

NOTICE OF INTENT — The 1976 law requires that the person planning to obtain a compulsory license must notify the copyright proprietor of his intention before or within 30 days after making, and before distributing, any phonorecords of the work. If the person cannot locate the owner of the work, "it shall be sufficient to file notice of intention in the Copyright Office." The notice must comply with the regulations set forth by the Register of Copyrights.

Failure to serve notice or file notice *forecloses the possibility of a compulsory license and, in the absence of a negotiated license, renders the making and distribution of phonorecords actionable as acts of infringement.*[7]

It should be noted that the copyright owner totally controls the *first* recording of the work — and he can charge any royalty or fee he wishes. He can even require the first record release be coupled with one or more of his other copyrights, as the reverse side of a single record or as components of a record album. But once the first record of the property is made and distributed, the copyright owner (normally the publisher) has no further control over the licensing rate or the manner and quality of cover records that follow the initial release. When the Congress wrote the 1976 Act, it set the statutory mechanical rate "... for each work embodied in a phonorecord at either 2.75 cents, or one-half of one cent per minute of playing time or fraction thereof, whichever amount is larger." As pointed out elsewhere in this book, the Royalty Tribunal was empowered to periodically adjust compulsory license rates. As a consequence, these figures tend to change from year to year.

ROYALTY PAYMENTS[8] — To be entitled to receive royalty payments under a compulsory license, the copyright owner must be identified in the registration or other public records of the Copyright Office. The owner is entitled to royalties for phonorecords made and distributed after being so identified, but is not entitled to recover for any phonorecords previously made and distributed.

Except as provided above, the royalty under a compulsory license shall be payable for every phonorecord made and distributed in accordance with the license. "For this purpose, a phonorecord is considered 'distributed' if the person exercising the compulsory license has voluntarily and *permanently parted with its possession.*" This language helps reduce the ambiguity prevalent until 1978 relative to liability for royalty payments. The 1976 Copyright Act makes it clear that a record manufacturer need not pay royalties on promotional copies. It also appears that the manufacturer is not liable for royalty payments on records returned to them which have not been sold, for such records did not leave the manufacturer's possession *permanently,* as the law provides.

7-See the following chapter concerning distinctions between a *compulsory* and a *negotiated* mechanical license.

8-Sec. 115(c).

DURATION OF COPYRIGHT[9]

SUBSISTING COPYRIGHTS IN THEIR FIRST TERM

Copyrights still in their first terms continue, under the 1976 law, for their original 28 years. Within one year of the expiration date, the author may renew the copyright for an additional 47 years, thus bringing the total protection period to a total of 75 years.

DEFAULT — If the author fails to file such application for renewal and extension, the copyright in that work will terminate after the original 28 years.

SUBSISTING COPYRIGHTS IN THEIR SECOND TERM

The 1976 law describes specific terms under which a copyright may be extended or recaptured if it is already in its second 28-year term. As Congress stated, the 1976 law creates here an entirely new property right. The 1909 law provided only 56 years of protection. The 1976 revision provides, in this instance, a total of 75 years of protection. Thus, a 19-year "bonus" period is created, added on. The monetary value of many old standard popular songs is high and, for this reason, authors and publishers are joined in battle to establish claims on these 19-year bonus periods. One major writer's catalog includes a standard pop song which, over the 19-year bonus period, was estimated to have a value in 1976 of over $1 million. AGAC provides its members (and, for a fee, even non-members) a catalog evaluation service to assist authors in negotiating deals with publishers covering the 19-year extension periods.

AFTER 56 YEARS

Properties whose 56-year protection would otherwise expire under the 1909 law are, under the 1976 law, automatically granted copyright protection for a total of 75 years, except that, if a writer wants to recapture a composition from a publisher, he may, within a five-year period following the original 56-year protection, set a termination date. This notice of termination must be given to the publisher not less than two years nor more than 10 years ahead of the termination date decided upon by the author. Once an author has thus reclaimed the copyright, his ownership of it is free and clear. *Failure* to exercise the option to terminate within the five-year period will permit a copyright to endure to the end of the period originally contracted between the author and the publisher.

9-Chapter 3 of the *Act*.

EXCLUSIONS — Works made for hire and sound recordings are not included in the provisions described here concerning the 19-year extension period.

PERIODIC RENEWALS — Copyrights subsisting prior to January 1, 1978 which were due to run out under the 1909 law were endangered during the protracted deliberations of Congress on the general revision of the old law. To protect copyright owners during this limbo period, Congress, from 1962, periodically extended such copyrights until the 1976 law could take effect.

LITIGATION — Termination and extension options provided in the 1976 law now create disputes among authors, coauthors, their heirs and publishers and they will be engaged in court actions that will continue for some time.

AFTER JANUARY 1, 1978

Copyright in works created on or after January 1, 1978 subsists in that work *from its creation* and, except as provided under certain conditions, endures for a term consisting of the life of the author and 50 years after the author's death.

JOINT WORKS — Where two or more authors prepared a joint work (and did not do the work for hire), they enjoy copyright for a term consisting of the life of the last surviving author and 50 years after such surviving author's death.

WORK MADE FOR HIRE — In a work made for hire, copyright holds for 75 years from the date of its first publication, or a term of 100 years from the year of its creation, whichever expires first.

RECAPTURE — The 1976 law provides that, under certain conditions, an assigned copyright can be recaptured by its author after the first 35 years (see below).

WORKS "IN THE TRUNK"

Copyright in a work created before January 1, 1978 but not theretofore in the public domain or copyrighted, subsists from January 1, 1978 and endures for the life of the author and 50 years after the author's (or coauthor's) death. In no case, however, ". . . shall the term of copyright in such a work expire before December, 2002; and, if the work is published on or before December 31, 2002, the term of copyright shall not expire before December 31, 2027."[10]

10-Sec. 303.

FORMALITIES[11]

The term formalities is used around the world in reference to the specific actions a claimant must take to validate claim to copyright. In the United States, these formalities include notice of copyright, deposit of copies and registration of claim to copyright. The 1976 law is permissive in respect to some kinds of mistakes in following through on formalities. But to be on the safe side, claimants should follow the letter of the law.

NOTICE ON PRINTED MUSIC

The term *notice* of copyright refers to the public display of information concerning the date the work was published and who registered the claim. On printed additions, the law stipulates:

1- *Notice should be placed on all publicly distributed copies. The notice imprinted should be the symbol ©(the letter C in a circle) or the word **Copyright** or the abbreviation **Copr.** and the year of first publication of the work. The types of notice most often seen:*

© **1982 John Doe**

2- *In the case of compilations or derivative works incorporating previously published material, the year date of the first publication of the compilation or derivative work is sufficient.*

3- *The notice must also include the name of the copyright owner. A recognizable abbreviation of the owner's name may be used.*

4- *The position of the notice shall be affixed to the copies so as to give reasonable notice of the claim to copyright.*

NOTICE ON SOUND RECORDINGS[12]

Whenever a sound recording protected under the 1976 law is published in the U.S. or elsewhere by authority of the copyright owner, a notice shall be placed on all publicly distributed phonorecords of the sound recording. The form of the notice consists of three elements:

1- *The symbol ℗ (the letter "P" in a circle); and*

2- *The year of the first publication of the sound recording; and*

3- *The name of the owner of the copyright in the sound recording. A recognizable abbreviation may be used. If the producer of the*

11-Chapter 4 of the *Act.*

12-Sec. 402.

> *sound recording is named on the phonorecord labels or con-*
> *tainers, and if no other name appears in conjunction with the*
> *notice, the producer's name shall be considered a part of the*
> *notice.*

Position of notice shall be placed on the surface of the phonorecord, or on the phonorecord label or container, in such a manner and location as to give reasonable notice of the claim to copyright. A typical notice for a phonorecord -

℗ **1982 Smith Records**

Audiovisual works **do not require the symbol ℗ but the symbol © because they are not considered phonorecords.**

ERRORS, OMISSIONS

As detailed in sections 401, 402 and 403, omission of notice from copies or phonorecords does not invalidate the copyright in a work if

> **1-** *The notice has been omitted from no more than a relatively small number of copies or phonorecords distributed to the public; or*
>
> **2-** *Registration for the work has been made before or is made within five years after the publication without notice, and a reasonable effort is made to add notice to all copies or phonorecords that are distributed to the public in the United States after omission has been discovered; or*
>
> **3-** *"The notice has been omitted in violation of an express require-ment in writing that, as a condition of the copyright owner's authorization of the public distribution of copies or phono-records, they bear the prescribed notice." This paragraph, a direct quote from Section 405 of the Act, is unclear to most lawyers, but it is included here for the sake of completeness. The courts will have to interpret this language.*

Any person who innocently infringes a copyright, in reliance upon an authorized copy or phonorecord from which the copyright notice has been omitted, incurs no liability for actual or statutory damages under Section 504 for any infringing acts committed before receiving actual notice that registration of the work has been made under Section 408, if such person proves that he or she was misled by the omission of the notice.

Under most circumstances, an error in the date appearing in the copyright notice does not invalidate the copyright, e.g.,

> **1-** *When the year date in the notice is earlier than the year in which the publication first occurred, any period computed from the*

*year of first publication under Section 302 is to be computed
from the year of the notice.*

2- *When the year date is more than one year later than the year in
which the publication first occurred, the work is considered to
have been published without any notice and is governed by the
provisions of Section 405.*

DEPOSIT[13]

As noted, deposit of works in the Library of Congress and registry of
works are separate formalities, and the performance of neither act is a
condition of copyright. Yet, both are important. In respect to *published
copies,* Section 407 states that the copyright owner (or his publisher)
must deposit within three months after the date of publication, two
complete copies of "the best edition" of the work. In respect to *sound
recordings,* the deposit shall include two complete phonorecords of the
best edition, together with any printed material or other visually
perceptible material published with such phonorecords.

Under certain conditions, deposits made prior to any attempt to
register the work may be used to satisfy the deposit requirements called
for when the author (or his publisher) undertakes to actually register the
work. If the author desires to have his initial deposit satisfy the deposit
requirements specified on the registration forms, he must enclose a
letter with his initial deposit specifically directing the Library of Congress
to hold those deposits for later connection with the author's registration
application. If such a letter is not enclosed, the Copyright Office will
require separate, additional deposits of a work just as called for on the
registration form. For a more detailed description of these regulations,
see *Copyright Office Circular R7A.*

Congress has authorized modifications of deposit requirements from
time to time, at the discretion of the Copyright Office. While failure to
deposit copies or phonorecords according to current regulations does
not actually endanger the copyright, the government does have the
authority to demand copies and fine the laggard up to $250 per work and
levy additional fines up to $2,500 for willful and repeated refusal to
comply.

REGISTRATION[14]

As pointed out earlier, the law states that deposits and registration are
"separate formalities." But this language can be confusing. The fact is
that deposit can be made independent of registration, but registration of
a claim to copyright *must* be accompanied by the deposit specified on

---

13-Sec. 407.

14-Sec. 408.

the application form. Also, the law states that registration "is not a condition of copyright." But that language, too, can be misleading. Registry is strongly advised because, under certain conditions, an author's work left unregistered lacks certain advantages the work would otherwise enjoy.

It is important to know that registration of copyright is a *prerequisite* (Section 411) to undertaking legal action against an alleged infringer. Lacking correct registration, the aggrieved party cannot collect statutory damages (but this condition does not extend to actual damages).

Another disadvantage in failing to properly register a musical work is that a copyright owner loses, at least temporarily, any statutory right to collect mechanical royalties under the compulsory license provision of the law.

A work may be registered at any time during the subsistence of the copyright, whether it is published or unpublished. The registration may be made by the owner or the publisher. The registrant must deliver the required deposit together with the application fee.

The material required to register a claim to copyright includes:

1- *In the case of an unpublished work, one complete copy or phonorecord;*

2- *In the case of a published work, two complete copies or phonorecords of the best edition;*

3- *In the case of a work first published outside the USA, one complete copy or phonorecord as so published;*

4- *In the case of a contribution to a collective work, one complete copy or phonorecord of the best edition of the collective work.*

The acceptance of sound recordings, not just sheet music, in registering claim to copyright was a significant advance over the 1909 law. In the popular music field, thousands of songwriters lack the ability to render their material in music notation. Now all they have to do is make a simple tape recording and submit it in lieu of sheet music. The acceptance of sound recordings also provides important advantages to persons desiring to copyright jazz improvisations, many of which do not submit to conventional music notation.

If the Register of Copyrights determines that all legal and formal requirements have been met, the Register shall send to the applicant a certificate of registration. If the claim is found invalid, the Register shall refuse registration and notify the applicant in writing the reasons for such refusal. The effective date of copyright registration is the day on which an application, deposit and fee all have been received in the Copyright Office.

If the author or the author's publisher made a mistake in an original registration of claim, or if either wants to modify it, the Register of Copyright has established procedures and set fees for the way in which these matters can be accommodated.

FEES[15]

1- *Registration of a claim* or a supplementary registration including issuance of a certificate of registration, $10.

2- *Registration of a claim to renewal* of a subsisting copyright in its first 28-year term, including issuance of a certificate of registration, $6.

3- *Recordation of a transfer* of copyright ownership (one title only), $10.

4- *Filing a notice* of intention to make phonorecords, $6.

5- *Issuance of an additional certificate* of registration, $4.

6- *Making and reporting of a search* and related services by the Copyright Office, $10 per hour.

TRANSFERS, ASSIGNMENTS[16]

The 1909 Act held the view that copyrights were indivisible. But in common practice, copyrights under the old law were transferred and assigned in a variety of ways. In recognition of common practice, the 1976 Act specifically states that the ownership of a copyright may be transferred *in whole or in part* by any means of conveyance or by operation of law and may be bequeathed by will. In explaining these rights of transfer, lawyers refer to the "bundle of rights" embraced in copyright. In this respect, they are usually referring to the rights vested initially in the author *exclusively*, e.g., the right to reproduce the original work of authorship, prepare derivative works from it, distribute copies and phonorecords, perform the work and display it. The law even provides (Section 201) for subdivision of rights. For example, the right to reproduce and publish copies might be shared by more than one publisher.

RECORDATION OF TRANSFERS[17]

It is important for individuals involved in transfers of copyright to file a *Certificate of Recordation* with the Copyright Office. When this action is taken in accord with the regulations set forth by the Register of Copyrights (Section 205), such recordation gives all persons what lawyers call "constructive notice" of the facts stated in the recorded document. Recordation is a prerequisite, under most circumstances, to

---

15-Sec. 708.

16-Sec. 201.

17-Sec. 205

initiate an infringement suit.

Occasionally, a situation arises where two transfers are in conflict. In such instances, the one executed first prevails if it has been properly recorded and otherwise conforms to the regulations of the Copyright Office.

TERMINATION OF TRANSFERS

In the case of any work other than a work made for hire, the exclusive or nonexclusive "grant of a transfer" or license of copyright or any right under a copyright, executed by the author on or after January 1, 1978, otherwise than by will, *is subject to termination* under conditions cited in Section 203. The essential conditions cited there are:

1- *Termination of the grant may be effected at any time during a period of five years beginning at the end of 35 years from the date of execution of the grant.*

2- *If the grant covers the right of publication of the work, the period begins at the end of 35 years from the date of publication of the work under the grant or at the end of 40 years from the date of execution of the grant, whichever term ends earlier.*

3- *Advance notice of intent to terminate must be in writing, signed by the number and proportion of owners of termination interests required under Section 203, or by their duly authorized agents, upon the grantee or the grantee's successor in title. The notice shall state the effective date of the termination, which shall fall within the five-year period specified in Section 203, and the notice shall be served not less than two or more than 10 years before that date. To be in effect, this notice must be recorded in the Copyright Office before the effective date of termination. An individual intending to file a notice of termination must comply with the form, content and manner of service prescribed by the Register of Copyrights.*

4- *Termination of a grant may be effected notwithstanding any agreement to the contrary, including an agreement to make a will or to make any further grant.*

5- **A derivative work prepared under the authority of a grant before its termination may continue to be utilized under the terms of the grant after its termination** *(but this privilege does not extend to the preparation after the termination of other derivative works based upon the copyrighted work covered by the termination grant). This provision is causing considerable difficulties, because parties of interest differ sharply on precisely what the term "derivative work" means.*

6- *Upon the effective date of termination, all rights under this title that were covered by the termination grant revert to the author or authors.*

7- *Unless and until termination is effected under Section 203, the grant, if it does not provide otherwise, continues in effect for the term of copyright provided by law.*

Section 203 offers further details describing the conditions under which further grants or agreements may be made following the effective date of the termination.

COPYRIGHT ROYALTY TRIBUNAL[18]

The 1976 Copyright Act provided for the establishment of an instrumentality of the Congress to serve that legislative body in matters concerning copyright. That instrumentality is the Copyright Royalty Tribunal. It is composed of five commissioners appointed by the president of the United States. They serve for seven years, but their terms are staggered. Unlike other federal regulatory bodies, the members select their own chairperson. It is also to be noted that the Tribunal serves the Congress and is not part of the executive branch of the government.

The law sets forth in detail what the Tribunal is empowered to do and how it is supposed to discharge its responsibilities. A summary:

1- *Make decisions that ". . . will afford the copyright owner a fair return for his creative work and the copyright user a fair income under existing economic conditions."*

2- *Conduct hearings of interested parties, then set royalty rates for music uses.*

3- *Periodically adjust these rates to reflect the legitimate interests of copyright owners and music users, inflation, and changing market conditions.*

4- *Determine equitable shares, then distribute royalties deposited with the Copyright Office to copyright owners or their agents.*

5- *Maximize the availability of creative works to the public.*

To learn the views of concerned parties, the Tribunal conducts extensive public hearings. It devotes much of its attention to testimony submitted by trade associations, artists' unions and guilds. Spokesmen for these organizations — usually represented by their respective presidents and high-priced attorneys — present their cases to the Tribunal, naturally enough, in order to maximize their economic interests.

18-Chapter 8 of the *Act*.

ADVOCATES BEFORE THE TRIBUNAL

INTERESTED GROUPS, PERSONS	REPRESENTATIVE ORGANIZATIONS
Composers, writers	ASCAP, BMI, AGAC
Publishers	NMPA, ASCAP, BMI, SESAC
Performing artists..................	AFM, AFTRA, AGMA
Record producers, manufacturers	RIAA
Record merchants..................	NARM, NAMM
Performing rights societies..........	ASCAP, BMI, SESAC
Radio and television broadcasters ...	NAB
Public broadcasters	PBS, others
Schools and Colleges..............	NASM, MENC
Jukebox operators	AMOA
Cable television, syndicators	Various

The major issues facing the Tribunal are summarized here, together with positions traditionally taken by proponents and opponents.

ISSUES: Proponents/Opponents

Issues	Proponents	Opponents
High mechanical royalty	AGAC, NMPA ASCAP, BMI, SESAC	RIAA, NARM
High cable TV royalty	ASCAP, BMI, SESAC, NMPA, AGAC	Cable TV Program syndicators
High performance right license	ASCAP, BMI, SESAC, NMPA	NAB, schools and colleges
High jukebox royalty	ASCAP, BMI, SESAC NMPA	Jukebox operators
Performance right in phonorecords	AFM, AFTRA, RIAA	NAB

INFRINGEMENT, REMEDY[19]

The law provides that any person who violates any of the exclusive rights of the copyright owner is an infringer. If a copyright owner believes his rights have been infringed, the statute provides him with a number of "remedies" or relief from the offending party. Even coauthors can act against an infringer: no matter how small the coauthor's ownership might be in a work, he may institute legal action.

19-Op. cit., Sec. 501.

REMEDIES

The law provides these options for action against an infringer:

1- *INJUNCTION* — *A temporary or final injunction can be sought from any court having jurisdiction to prevent or restrain infringement of copyright.*

2- *IMPOUNDMENT* — *The court may order impoundment of articles alleged to be involved with infringement. The impoundment can hold pending court determination of the merits of the claim of infringement. Impoundment could include printed copies, phonorecords, masters, plates, even manufacturing and packaging equipment.*

3- *DESTRUCTION* — *The court could order, as part of a final judgment, destruction of inventories, e.g., printed copies, phonorecords, etc.*

4- *DAMAGES* — *If the infringer is found guilty, he is liable, except as the law provides, for*
a- *Actual damages suffered by the copyright owner as a result of the Infringement.*

b- *Any additional profits gained by the infringer as a result of acts of infringement.*

c- *The copyright owner may elect to seek statutory damages instead of actual damages and profits for all infringements before final judgment is rendered, in a sum not less than $250 or more than $10,000 "as the court considers just."*

d- *"In a case where the copyright owner sustains the burden of proving, and the court finds, that infringement was committed willfully, the court in its discretion may increase the award of statutory damages to a sum of not more than $50,000." Lesser awards are made where the court finds the infringer "was not aware and had no reason to believe that his or her acts constituted infringement."*

e- *Costs and attorney's fees may be recovered by the prevailing party, at the court's discretion.*

f- *Copyright owners may choose to sue for actual damages or statutory damages and may change to the latter course at any time before final judgment of the court.*

CRIMINAL OFFENSES

A criminal offender is defined in the law as "any person who infringes a copyright willfully and for purposes of commercial advantage or private financial gain." Consequences of criminal offenses:

1- *Criminal offenders shall be fined not more than $10,000 or imprisoned for not more than one year, or both.*

2- *The above statement notwithstanding, the fines for infringement in respect to phonorecords and motion pictures are much more severe: a fine of not more than $25,000 or imprisonment for not more than one year, or both, for the first offense, and a fine of not more than $50,000 or imprisonment for not more than two years, or both, for any subsequent offenses.*

3- *In addition to the above penalties, the court may order the forfeiture and destruction of all infringing printed copies and phonorecords, including equipment used to print or manufacture the infringing articles.*

4- *Any person who, with fraudulent intent, places on any article a notice of copyright that such person knows to be false shall be fined not more than $2,500. A similar fine can be assessed for fraudulent removal of a copyright notice (see below concerning further provisions in respect to record piracy).*

5- *Any person who knowingly makes a false representation of a material fact in the application for copyright registration provided for by section 409, or in any written statement filed in connection with the application, shall be fined not more than $2,500.*

RECORD COUNTERFEITING

The 1976 law includes a supplementary provision which extends the control of counterfeited phonorecords. This is in respect to the use of counterfeit copyright notice Ⓟ (letter P in a circle) on phonorecords: "Whoever knowingly and with fraudulent intent transports, receives, or offers for sale in interstate commerce or foreign commerce any sound recording (whatever the medium) to which is fixed a counterfeit or fraudulent copyright notice . . . shall be fined not more than $10,000 or imprisoned for not more than one year, or both, for the first such offense and shall be fined not more than $25,000, or imprisoned for not more than two years, or both, for any subsequent offense." The offender may also have any counterfeit stock and manufacturing equipment confiscated and destroyed.

Note that buried in the fine print here is language that could have sweeping effect on those individuals who simply *assist* the counterfeiter — those who transport the material, receive it or offer it for sale. The courts will have to determine just how broad a net this part of the law is intended to cast. It would appear that those individuals who assist the counterfeiter in these ways may also be considered as involved in criminal action if they are engaged in the activities knowingly and with fraudulent intent. If enforcement of the law were to assume this wide a scope, record piracy in the United States might be reduced to a negligible amount.

INNOCENT INFRINGERS

A court can reduce damages to as low as $100 for "innocent infringers," even to zero when the offender employed by a nonprofit organization or noncommercial broadcasting entity can prove he believed the use was fair use.

INTERNATIONAL COPYRIGHT PROTECTION

There is no such thing as "international copyright" that will automatically protect an author's works throughout the world.

US Copyright Office

For over a century, countries of the world have been making attempts to bring their copyright laws into some kind of uniformity. Artists, publishers and governments have long recognized the mutual advantages that would redound to the benefit of all if uniform, reciprocal protection could be developed for intellectual properties. While this ideal goal may never be reached, significant progress toward worldwide agreement on copyrights has been made in the twentieth century.

Protection against unauthorized use of musical works in a particular country still depends basically on the national laws of that country. But special difficulties arise when nationals of one country seek protection of their works around the world. In the last 100 years, a number of international treaties have been developed which offer, in some instances, generally good protection internationally. The U.S. Copyright Office urges composers and publishers who wish copyright protection in a particular country to first find out the extent of protection for foreign works available in that country. If possible, this information should be acquired *before the work is published anywhere,* since protection may depend upon the particular situation prevailing at the time of first publication. While nearly all developed countries adhere to at least one international copyright agreement, the U.S. Copyright Office warns that ". . . some countries offer little or no copyright protection for foreign works under any circumstances." One major country, The People's Republic of China, did not participate in international copyright protection until 1980. While China has not joined any copyright union, in that year it negotiated a trade agreement (most favored nation status) which included reciprocal copyright protection with the United States.

The USSR joined the Universal Copyright Convention in 1973.

THE BERNE CONVENTION

The first significant international copyright agreement was reached in Berne in 1886, where the Swiss government hosted a convention of principal European countries. The agreement reached in 1886, together with subsequent "Berne conventions" comprise the International Union for the Protection of Literary and Artistic Works, better known as the Berne Union. It is administered by the World Intellectual Property Organization (WIPO).

While the United States has never joined, the Berne Convention, one century later, continues to be of vital importance internationally. This is because, over the ensuing years, the Berne countries have periodically revised and updated their agreements in response to changing international conditions and developing communications technology.

Subsequent to the initial treaty signed in 1886, the Berne Convention has held meetings to change and/or expand its initial agreements. The first of these occurred in Paris in 1896. The next meeting took place in Berlin in 1908, at which time the Berne countries completely abandoned copyright "formalities" except those required for a country's own nationals (in this context, "formalities" includes such things as copyright notice, registration, deposit and fee). The Berlin meeting also brought about an expansion of protected works to include the artistic field, including music.

The Rome revision (1928) recognized the growing importance of radio broadcasting. In addition, Rome gave recognition to the "moral rights" of authors, namely, the right of authors to object to a "distortion, mutilation or other alteration" of their work, even after a work has been assigned to another person. The moral rights of authors has been a distinguishing feature of the Berne Union and is one of the issues that has delayed Berne Union membership by the United States (some publishers, film producers and broadcasters have traditionally lobbied against constraints upon the alteration and revision of copyrighted works).

Membership in Berne is open; a nation wishing to join need only notify the Swiss government of its intent to adhere (a Union member may withdraw just as easily). Each Berne Union member is privileged, also, to adhere only to the particular portions of the conventions to which it has committed itself. Accordingly, any person testing a particular issue finds it necessary to first learn precisely which conventions (comprising the Union) have been subscribed to by a particular country.

In general, protection under the Berne Union is extended without formalities to works by nationals of any country on the sole condition that first (or simultaneous) publication takes place in a country that belongs to the Berne Union. While the United States is not a Berne country, many American nationals have sought Berne Union protection by arranging a simultaneous publication in Canada, a Berne member. This is the familiar "back door" route followed for many years by U.S. nationals. While this appears to have been generally effective in securing reciprocal copyright protection for U.S. nationals in Berne countries, the U.S. Copyright Office warns, in its publication, Circular 38 (*International Copyright Protection*), that difficult legal questions can arise as to precisely what constitutes a genuine "first" or "simultaneous" publication in a particular case. Under the Rome text of Berne, to be "simultaneous," publication must take place on the same day in the Convention and non-Convention country. But under the Brussels text, a publication is considered "simultaneous" if it occurs within 30 days of the initial one — and thus qualifies for protection. It is evident that it is imperative to know which text, Rome or Brussels, is the governing one for the intended country of simultaneous publication. In respect to Canada, Shemel and Krasilovsky point out that a claim to copyright can be officially registered in that country, and that "such registration in Canada has the virtue of being prima facie evidence of copyright."[20]

The Berne Union requires that, in respect to *publication*, works be "issued and made available in sufficient quantities to the public," but does not consider

20-*This Business Of Music*, p. 287.

performances and broadcasts as *publication.*

As pointed out above, U.S. membership in Berne has been discouraged by those nationals of this country who are against imposition of constraints on the so-called authors' "moral rights." Other persons argue against this country joining Berne because of the disparity between the Union and the USA in respect to copyright formalities. Yet another force traditionally arguing against the Berne Union focuses on the so-called "manufacturing clause" in the United States law. This clause, apparently embedded in our statutes resulting from political pressure from America's tight printing trade unions, requires U.S. nationals to print their works in this country, thus denying publishers the option of seeking lower cost printing abroad. The new copyright law, however, provides for elimination of the manufacturing clause. Beginning in 1978, foreign nationals were no longer required to have their works manufactured in this country unless they were, at the time, domiciliaries of this country. In addition, United States nationals are no longer required to comply with the old manufacturing clause if they are domiciled outside the the the USA for a continuous period of at least one year preceding the date of importation or public distribution of the work in the United States. Of greater significance was the provision in the 1976 Copyright Act that phased out the manufacturing clause after July 1, 1982.

While experts in international copyright law still see some difficulties ahead, a growing number of U.S. nationals, particularly those in music, believe this country has moved much closer to acceptance of the Berne Convention, particularly as a consequence of the enactment of the United States 1976 Copyright act. Impetus for our joining the Berne Convention increased in July, 1978 when the Register of Copyrights recommended to Congress that such action would be in the best interests of this country.

COPYRIGHT TREATIES IN THE AMERICAS

The Berne Convention was almost exclusively a union of European countries. In 1888, two years after the Berne Union was organized, South American countries met in Montevideo, Uruguay. In the following year, this meeting resulted in the Montevideo Treaty of 1889. But widespread adherence of other countries did not follow, and the Montevideo Treaty is no longer in force.

1902 saw the enactment of the Mexico City Treaty, which adopted the Berne Union concept of granting protection for authors according to the law of the territory where protection was claimed. The Mexico City Treaty differs from Berne, however, in respect to its requirement of registration and deposit of copies in the country of origin as well as in all countries where protection of the work is desired. While this treaty still governs copyrights between the United States and El Salvador (and between El Salvador and the Dominican Republic), it remains limited in importance because copyright relations between most American countries (Cuba, Mexico and Venezuela excluded) and the USA are governed by the Buenos Aires Convention of 1910. Besides the USA, members of the Buenos Aires Convention include Argentina, Brazil, Chile, Columbia, Costa Rica, the Dominican Republic, Ecuador, Guatemala, Haiti, Honduras, Nicaragua, the Republic of Panama, Paraguay, Peru, and Uruguay. The essence of this convention is expressed in the fact that compliance with the copyright law of the country of first publication qualifies the work for protection in the other member countries. The Buenos Aires Convention includes one additional stipulation to secure copyright: each work must carry a notice indicating that property rights in the work are reserved. **This requirement has been traditionally satisfied by American nationals with the inclusion of the words, "All rights reserved" as part**

of the copyright notice. The Buenos Aires Convention otherwise does not require any formalities except for those required by the country of origin.

THE UNIVERSAL COPYRIGHT CONVENTION

While the Buenos Aires Convention governs USA copyright relations with most American nations, the treaty is unlikely to attract additional members because of the establishment of the Universal Copyright Convention, which the United States joined in 1955. Initial meetings to set up UCC were sponsored by the United Nations in 1952 and took place in Geneva. The treaty came into force September 16, 1955. The UCC, as revised in Paris in 1971, took effect July 10, 1974, and was significant in that it gives the copyright owner the exclusive right to broadcast the copyrighted work.

One of the advantages of the UCC is that it reduces to a minimum the formalities for securing copyrights among participating countries. As a general rule, the UCC requires a participating country to give to foreign works the same protection it offers to the works of its own nationals. To qualify for protection under UCC, a work must have been written by a national of a participating country or must have been published for the first time in a UCC country.

The UCC requires that all copies bear the copyright symbol©, the name of the copyright proprietor and the year of first publication — in such a manner and location as to provide reasonable notice of claim to copyright. Further formalities can be waived or added by a member country for its own nationals and for works first published in its territory. Consequently, nationals of the United States are required to follow precisely the same formalities already set forth in the 1976 Copyright Act.

One of the goals of the sponsor of the UCC, the United Nations, was to attract a maximum number of adherents. To this end, the number of exclusive rights UCC grants to its members were held to a minimum level of "adequate and effective protection." The treaty's language here states that such protection includes "... basic rights insuring the author's economic interests, including the exclusive rights to authorize reproducing by any means, public performance and broadcasting." It is important to note that this protection extends to works, not only in their original form, but to any form which is recognizably derived from the original.

An important aspect of UCC is that is provides contracting states the right to grant exclusive rights of translation to foreign authors for a period of seven years. It should be pointed out that U.S. law and the Buenos Aires Convention give translation rights to authors without time limitation.

The UCC had, as one of its goals, the avoidance of competition with other prevailing international copyright agreements, particularly Berne and the Inter-American treaties. In respect to the Buenos Aires Treaty, the UCC language provides that, where there is a difference of provisions, "the most recently formulated convention" shall prevail.

BILATERAL COPYRIGHT AGREEMENTS

In addition to conventional, multinational copyright treaties, the United States has a number of bilateral understandings with other nations. Both the 1909 and 1976 U.S. copyright acts provide for the president of the United States to set up special copyright agreements by proclamation. Prior to this country's joining of UCC, such bilateral arrangements were the primary method for U.S. nationals to obtain copyright protection abroad. Actually, even where two countries are both

UCC members, prior to UCC their copyright agreements were entirely controlled by bilateral agreements.

In general, these treaties extend to foreign nationals the same protection their countries offer American citizens. But foreign nationals are required, whatever their domestic statutes may provide, to adhere to the copyright formalities stipulated in the U.S. Act of 1976.

GENEVA PHONOGRAM CONVENTION

When the Berne and UCC convention countries met in Paris in 1971 to revise their respective agreements, their governing bodies developed a new convention governing copyrights in phonograms (records and tapes). It is officially known as the "Geneva Convention of October 29, 1971, for the Protection of Producers of Phonograms against Unauthorized Duplication." The Convention defines phonograms as ", . . any exclusively aural fixation of sounds of a performance or of other sounds." The phonogram "producer" is deemed to be the person who first fixes such sounds, and the intent of the convention is to protect producers. This includes protection against importation of unauthorized phonogram copies as well as against unauthorized local manufacture. Signatories to the Convention are required to offer such protection in at least one of three areas of law: copyright, unfair competition, and penal sanctions.

To qualify for protection, the producer must print a notice on all authorized phonograms or their containers. The form of the notice is identical with one stipulated in the American Copyright Act of 1976: the symbol ℗, the copyright proprietor's name and the date of first publication. But, as with UCC, the notice is required only of member nations which call for copyright formalities as a condition of copyright. All formalities required by the Phonogram Convention are deemed fulfilled by use of the notice.

The United States ratified the Geneva Phonogram Convention in 1973, and the 1976 Copyright Act expressly includes its provisions.

COPYRIGHT SOCIETIES

A complete understanding of copyright is difficult, not only for authors and music users, but for lawyers and judges. This is largely because most individuals find it simpler to understand conventional *property rights* than rights inherent in *intellectual property*. The latter are intangible, and infringements, real or imagined, plague the music business and cause expensive trouble for its practitioners.

Enactment of the Universal Copyright Convention and the 1976 copyright law have helped to clarify copyright around the world. But interpretation and understanding of statutes, new and old, have occupied lawyers, litigants and courts for decades. One of the effective ways individuals concerned with copyright can help each other is to share information appearing in such publications as the *Bulletin of the Copyright Society*. It contains authoritative articles and opinions on copyright and is published six times a year by the Copyright Society of the USA. I recommend membership in the society to individuals and institutions, for it is a center of the American copyright community for the bar, for industry and for law schools. The society's literature states that its primary function

> ... is the gathering, dissemination and interchanging of information concerning protection and use of rights in intellectual property. The Society undertakes and engages in research in the field of copyright law in cooperation with universities, law schools, libraries, governmental agencies, lawyers and industry representatives in the United States and foreign countries. The Society also seeks to promote better understanding of copyright and the vital importance of legal and economic protection of intellectual property generally and copyright in particular among the general public, in industry and in the academic world.
>
> Leadership of the Copyright Society of the USA includes distinguished representatives of the bar, research scholars, the music industry and government. The society is a nonprofit corporation organized under the Education Law of New York State and can be contacted through its offices located at the NYU Law Center.

Individuals preferring to participate in continuing study in their own areas may find that their home state has a local copyright organization. State bar associations have this kind of information.

Part Three

BUSINESS AFFAIRS

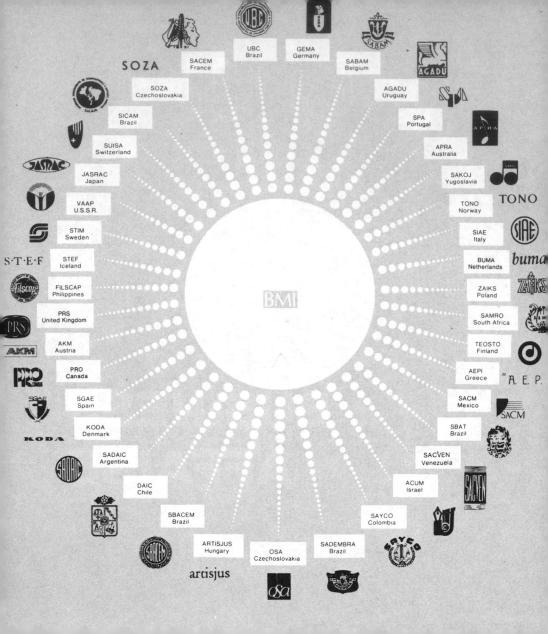

7

MUSIC LICENSING

MUSIC RIGHTS — AN OVERVIEW

Copyright law in the United States requires that a music *user* must obtain the consent of the copyright owner to make use of his property. This consent is customarily given through the granting of a license. In that there are many different kinds of music uses and applications, copyright law and industry practice have developed an array of different kinds of licenses and use permits.

The music business is far too large and diverse for each copyright owner or publisher to even attempt to handle all these licensing grants *individually*. As a consequence, it is standard industry practice for copyright owners — writers and publishers — to *engage agencies* to handle these tasks. Without these agencies, no copyright owner could possibly cover all uses of his music around the world. Even if the whole accounting process could be computerized, the individual would have no practical way to collect licensing fees and performance royalties.

To handle these far-ranging business affairs, writers and publishers not only retain collecting agencies to help them, they affiliate themselves with performing rights collecting organizations, commonly known as performing rights societies.

To assist in developing a comprehensive awareness of how music uses are licensed in the United States (and in many foreign territories), the accompanying table is instructive. In the following pages, each of these kinds of licenses is explained.

For most composers and publishers, their strongest source of income derives from licensed performances of their music. Practically all of this money comes to them from two American performing rights societies, ASCAP and BMI.

In examining how these organizations serve the industry, it is important to keep in mind that they really only do one thing: *they license music performances and distribute performance royalties to their affiliated writers and publishers.* They don't publish music[1]; they are not in the business of promoting individual copyrights; they are not responsible for their affiliates' success in the marketplace — they simply handle performing rights, nothing else.

1-BMI did publish music for a while in its early history (1940s), but no longer does so. ASCAP has never published music.

Hal David, ASCAP President

MUSIC LICENSES

TYPE OF MUSIC USE	TYPE OF LICENSE REQUIRED
Broadcast performances of nondramatic music	*Performance license* ("small right"): broadcasters obtain a blanket (annual) license from a performing rights society.
Live performances of nondramatic music	*Performance license* ("small right"): host venue or producer obtains it from a performing rights society.
Audio tapes and records for private home use only	*Mechanical license:* producers obtain it from Harry Fox Agency or directly from publishers.
Audio-visual tapes/discs for consumer home use	*Mechanical license* and *synchronization license* (or one combining both): producers negotiate with copyright owners or Harry Fox Agency.
Broadcast commercials	Publishers or Harry Fox Agency grant special use permissions.
Theatrical films, TV movies	*Synchronization license:* producers negotiate with Harry Fox Agency or directly with publishers. Performance license for USA movie theatres only: Harry Fox Agency or directly with publishers.[2]
Background music	*Transcription license* (often called a "block license" or "blanket license"): service suppliers negotiate with publishers or Harry Fox Agency.
Dramatic music	*Grand right* or *dramatic right:* producer negotiates with copyright owners or their agents. Practices vary.

2-Performing licenses for theatres outside the United States are often obtained by foreign performing rights societies directly from movie theatre operators. Cost of these kinds of licenses are scaled to a share of the box office receipts. ASCAP and BMI members sometimes share in this income through foreign performing rights societies having reciprocal arrangements with ASCAP and/or BMI.

How much money do they collect and distribute? Their income rises faster than the rate of inflation. This can be attributed to a number of factors: 1) increasing acceptance by music users that they must obey the copyright laws and pay up; 2) increasing efficiency of the collecting agencies; 3) rising licensing rates imposed by the Copyright Royalty Tribunal; 4) more efficient, more comprehensive collections from reciprocating foreign societies.[3]

The three American performing rights organizations currently collect, from all sources, foreign and domestic, something in the range of $250 million a year. ASCAP and BMI both hold back 17 percent to 19 percent of their gross earnings for overhead, then distribute the rest to their members and affiliates.[4]

ASCAP and BMI like to take out full-page tradepaper ads stating they lead the world. ASCAP's slogan "We've Always Had The Greats" might be compared to BMI's line "The World's Largest Performing Rights Organization." An impartial judge would certainly agree that ASCAP has, by far, the world's strongest catalog of great standards — great music and big money-makers. BMI has a much larger number of affiliates — both writers and publishers — and its catalog is much more extensive than ASCAP's, but its catalog is cluttered with thousands of copyrights of transitory popularity — songs that will probably never achieve the status of a standard.

So anyone searching for "the better" of the two organizations has to turn to a comparison of their relative earning power. The most objective data come from research collated by the Royalty Tribunal, which pulls together comparable statistics of all three societies in this country. The Tribunal's estimate of the relative earning power of the three: ASCAP 54 percent; BMI 43 percent; SESAC the remaining three percent.[5]

AMERICAN SOCIETY OF COMPOSERS, AUTHORS AND PUBLISHERS

The first performing rights society in the United States was ASCAP. Its founders were inspired, in part, by the renowned Italian opera composer, Giacomo Puccini (1858-1924). Puccini was making a fortune in Europe with *La Bohème, Tosca* and *Madama Butterfly.* When he visited New York in 1910, he was astonished to discover that the Americans, unlike Europeans at that time, had no effective method of collecting fees for performances of their music. His expressions of indignation over this

---

3-Among the most lucrative foreign income territories are the U.K., France, Germany, Sweden and South Africa.

4-SESAC has a different distribution ratio.

5-Percentages used by the Tribunal in the early 1980s in awarding royalty shares from cable television — a reasonably accurate indication of the three organizations' relative earnings.

injustice influenced a number of leading composers in the United States (Victor Herbert and John Philip Sousa among them) to organize a collecting agency for music performances. The organization they formed was named the *American Society of Composers, Authors and Publishers* (ASCAP).

In the early days of ASCAP's history, the organization had a difficult time of it. Music users were reluctant to start paying for music performances they had traditionally enjoyed for free. Today, after decades of "educating" music users, the concept of payment of performance fees through music licensing organizations is now broadly accepted, although frequently with great reluctance by broadcasters, clubs, hotels, restaurants, theatres — wherever music is performed publicly. The United States Supreme Court, in stating its approval in 1967 of a lower court ruling, took the position that "...a central licensing agency such as ASCAP is the only practical way that copyright proprietors may enjoy their rights under federal copyright laws and that broadcasters and others may conveniently obtain licenses for the performance of copyrighted music." In this case, the lower court had pointed out that a single copyright owner cannot deal individually with all the potential and actual users of a piece of music and stated that a single radio station may broadcast as many as 60,000 performances involving as many as 6,000 separate compositions.

ASCAP in its early history was comprised largely of composers and lyricists of music for Broadway shows and Tin Pan Alley. Most of ASCAP's initial effort in the 1920s was focused on seeking performance fees for radio network broadcasts of show music. Today, broadcast performances still generate most of the performance royalties collected, but since the 1950s the use of music on television has produced much greater performance income than radio.

MEMBERSHIP

While ASCAP's membership to the mid-1940s, at least, was comprised largely of composers of Broadway shows and movie musicals, when BMI started attracting large numbers of new composers, ASCAP found it necessary and advantageous to open its rolls to newcomers. Both organizations offer a variety of inducements to attract new writers and publishers. New members will be admitted to ASCAP if they have at least one song published and distributed or one song commercially recorded. Promising new writers as well as more established ones are offered royalty advances which are based on ASCAP's estimate of how much success the writer may experience. Well-established writers are sometimes offered substantial advances to switch from BMI to ASCAP.

ASCAP discouraged its writer members from teaming up with BMI cowriters. In the period from the late 1950s through the early 1970s, the society would not recognize such collaborations[6]. By the 1980s the practice was still discouraged by ASCAP, but tolerated. From time to time, as many as five percent to 10 percent of *Billboard's* Hot 100 charts show ASCAP and BMI writers in collaboration (and occasionally as many as three to five cowriters!).

When coauthors associated with different licensing organizations look for their share of royalties, computers must be carefully programmed to correctly calculate equitable shares, in that ASCAP and BMI do not have the same formula for royalty payments.

All of the income ASCAP collects is distributed to its members, except funds held back to cover operational expenses and reserves. From the outset, ASCAP has maintained its headquarters in New York City. The organization operates 14 field offices, the principal ones being located in Hollywood and Nashville.

Writer and publisher members pay annual dues. Twice each year, ASCAP conducts a general meeting in New York City for its members near the East coast. Similar meetings are held every six months for ASCAP members located in the Los Angeles area. ASCAP officers and board are elected by a vote of the general membership. A balance is sought between representatives of writers and publishers and between the popular field and what ASCAP calls the standard field. While all officers of ASCAP are members of the society, over 600 additional personnel are employed in ASCAP's legal, licensing, logging and membership departments.

The power of ASCAP to control the performing rights of much of the world's favorite music is great. Music users have, from time to time, looked upon this power as monopolistic and unfair. Whatever the validity of this view, the U.S. Department of Justice in 1960 entered into a court-administered control of ASCAP, with ASCAP's consent. The arrangement is legally known as a *consent decree* and was undertaken in respect to the antitrust laws of this country.[7] To this day, the court-appointed judge supervises ASCAP's affairs, particularly in respect to license weighting formulas and payments to ASCAP's members.

ASCAP conducts a public relations campaign to create goodwill among its members and the community. It offers prizes each year to composers and symphony orchestras. In addition to distribution of earned income, ASCAP has an extensive system of annual awards to its members in both the popular and standard fields. Awards of this kind range from $100 to $5,000 per year and are intended to help compensate members for performances not surveyed or accounted for through ASCAP's normal procedures.

6-BMI doesn't favor "split authorship," but has never insisted its writer affiliates eschew collaboration with ASCAP writers.

7-BMI is also under a consent decree, but it sets forth a different set of constraints.

PERFORMANCE LICENSING

The society licenses about 40,000 music users. More than one-half of ASCAP's income, about 54 percent, derives from television stations and networks; radio income yields about 32 percent. All other sources produce considerably lesser amounts. In signing TV stations, ASCAP grants a blanket license for use of its entire repertoire, usually setting its fee just under two percent of the station's adjusted gross income.

While all commercial stations are already licensed by ASCAP, BMI and SESAC, the process of signing them is ongoing, in that some 500 stations each year change ownership, and licensing negotiations with them must begin anew.

ASCAP also licenses thousands of other users of its catalog, e.g., clubs, hotels, stadiums, etc. A prospective licensee may be approached initially through the mail. ASCAP officers tell me they use persuasion rather than coercion — explaining to the music user that the law requires him to pay for the use of copyrighted music. Prospective licensees are often indignant at this request and refuse to sign. If a soft-sell approach fails, ASCAP may dispatch one of its field representatives to call upon the music user and urge him to conform to the law. Failing this, most performing rights societies either threaten, or actually undertake, legal action, sometimes via a class action suit. Licensing societies almost always win these battles, whether through persuasion or through the courts — for a simple reason: the law is on their side.

Live music performances taking place in such facilities as hotels and clubs are normally asked to sign a one-year *blanket license.* The setting of the license rate takes into account 1) the seating capacity of the venue; 2) whether it charges admission; 3) its live music weekly budget; 4) the number of hours of musical entertainment provided. It may also take into account the estimated gross income of the facility.

Where a venue, such as a stadium or arena offers musical entertainment *only occasionally,* performing rights societies attempt to collect performance fees *from the promoter or producer* renting the facility. However, where a facility offers entertainment on a regular basis, ASCAP and BMI will normally look to the management of the location to pay for the performance license.

It should be emphasized that performing artists themselves and their agents and managers normally are not expected to pay performance royalties to anyone. Rather, this responsibility and expense devolves upon either the venue management or the entertainment promoter or producer.

SAMPLING, ACCOUNTING

When a writer or publisher affiliates with ASCAP, he provides the society a complete catalog of his works. The ASCAP index department encodes this information into its computers which store information on hundreds of thousands of pieces of music. Also stored in the computers is information from a variety of sources concerning when and where each of these pieces of music is performed.

ASCAP uses two accounting systems for performances. One is a *census*, ostensibly a complete accounting of all performances taking place in a given year. The census system is used almost exclusively for TV network performances and for performances, whatever the medium or venue, of the repertoire associated with chamber music, opera, ballet and symphony. The other accounting technique is known as a *sampling system*, and it is used for practically all other kinds of performances.

Since most of ASCAP's revenue derives from *network television broadcasts*, the society tries to account totally for all network performances taking place in that medium of music licensed by the society. To accomplish this, ASCAP also requires its licensees to supply log sheets of all the music it broadcasts, and on what stations. ASCAP also counterchecks this information with program listings in *TV Guide* magazine. That research is complicated, because *TV Guide* publishes over 90 different regional editions of program listings.

ASCAP further confirms its census by audio/video taping of TV network shows. Despite all these checks and double checks, the system occasionally fails, as I can personally attest. One of my compositions was broadcast on both the NBC and CBS television networks. But when I received my quarterly report, no credit points were shown to reflect those performances. I received payment eventually, by pointing out to ASCAP its error in accounting.

In respect to accounting for music performances on *local* TV stations, ASCAP again uses program listings in *TV Guide,* cue sheets and audio tapes recorded by one of the society's field offices. This TV survey aggregates some 30,000 program hours each year.

In respect to radio, ASCAP's survey is based on a sample comprising c. 60,000 program hours per year. This is accomplished through audio tape recordings made by ASCAP's regional offices. The stations being sampled are unaware of the survey. When the sampling procedure was first set up, ASCAP engaged outside experts to design the system in an effort to acquire maximum objectivity. ASCAP and BMI both resort to sampling techniques, because *the cost of attempting a comprehensive census of all music performed would exceed all available revenue.*

While both organizations insist their sampling procedures are scientific and impartial, their accuracy and fairness are hotly debated. Some complaints of the alleged inequity of the system are apparently justified. For example, one of my students complained to a BMI executive when he was visiting my campus, stating that one of his songs registered with BMI had become a regional hit in the Seattle-Portland area but that the performances were not reflected in his BMI Check. The BMI spokesman stated that the song was apparently missed during the survey period because, at that particular time, the Pacific Northwest was excluded from sampling. My student was just unlucky that time.

To increase the accuracy of its sampling, ASCAP always includes in its survey, at least once a year, each station whose annual license fee is at least $10,000. This type of information source ASCAP calls a *self-representing* station. When ASCAP accumulates its broadcast tapes, they are audited by individuals who are expert in identifying music that may be broadcast without being identified on the air. These auditors have an enormous responsibility, but ASCAP reports that their margin of error is extremely low. This taping system is very expensive to operate, but ASCAP relies on it in the belief that it provides the best possible accounting system.

The effectiveness and equity of a sampling system is dependent on how the sampling figures are extended and interpreted. For example, if a song performance is picked up in one area which represents one-tenth of all radio stations of that class, it is *weighted* by a factor of 10, in the theory that such an extension would fairly represent actual performances if all 10 regions had been surveyed. Both ASCAP and BMI use complicated formulas in calculating what weight would be fairly given to a sampled performance.

The evaluation of the weight of a performance helps determine how many credits or "points" will be assigned to a particular writer or publisher. To offer another example of weighting, a performance on 100 TV stations will obviously earn fewer points than when heard on 200 stations. A piece of music heard during halftime at a football game will earn only about 25 percent of what it might otherwise earn when featured on camera on a TV variety show. A performance of four minutes duration will earn more credits than one lasting only one minute, and so on.

For many years, ASCAP has shown special deference to composers of serious music, regarding them and their works as valuable cultural assets. Accordingly, distribution of revenues to serious composer-members and publishers of ASCAP is heavily weighted in their favor. As stated above, ASCAP uses a census technique in accounting for performances in the symphonic, opera, concert and recital fields, and such performances earn *10 to 12 times* as many credits as a work in the popular field.

Additionally, ASCAP sets aside a large sum each year for its *Standard Awards* which are given to composers of serious music to compensate them for performances of their music that are not covered by normal survey techniques.

ASCAP has a number of additional ways it honors achlevements of authors and publishers (whether or not they are members of the society). For example, since 1968, ASCAP has given its *Deems Taylor Award* to authors and publishers of outstanding books and articles on music. Among the distinguished authors and musicians receiving this award have been Gunther Schuller, Irving Kolidin, Martin Williams, Alec Wilder, Duke Ellington and John Hammond. The present writer was added to this list in 1980 for this *Handbook*.

ROYALTY DISTRIBUTION

Performance royalties collected by ASCAP are distributed to members four times per year. At one time, members were free to choose, immediately upon joining the society, that their royalties be paid on a current performance basis or on a payment plan known as the *four-fund system.* The four-fund system takes into account, not just current performances, but "average performances" (from past quarters), "recognized works" (selections in a composer's catalog recognized by ASCAP), and length of membership. Older ASCAP members tended to prefer the four-fund system for obvious reasons — they had been members for some time, they had more recognized works, and their music had accumulated more performances over a period of time. But newer members were at a disadvantage under this system. Accordingly, in 1976, the U.S. Court decreed that all new writer members were to be on a *current* performance basis. A new writer may later elect to convert to the four-fund system, but it seems clear that most writers are better off remaining on the current performance basis. Older ASCAP members will probably prefer to remain on the four-fund basis, particularly because it provides the advantage of steadier income. ASCAP *publishers* now receive payment only on the current performance formula.

How much do ASCAP members earn? Some members do not earn sufficient performance credits to cover membership dues.[8] At the other end of the payment scale would be the famous composers of the standards from Broadway shows and films. Much of their individual wealth comes from the performance fees ASCAP has collected for them over the years. Some are millionaires.

FOREIGN COLLECTIONS

Most performing rights organizations around the world have reciprocating agreements. They collect performance royalties for foreigners while foreigners do the same for them. ASCAP and BMI have reciprocal agreements with some three dozen such organizations. In recent years, even Iron Curtain countries have begun to participate in international agreements of this kind. For example, in the 1970s ASCAP negotiated a cooperative royalty collection arrangement with *VAAP,* the agency in the USSR which most closely resembles western countries' performing rights organizations. In respect to the Peoples Republic of China, the "most favored nation" trade agreement negotiated with the United States in1980 involved reciprocal copyright protection, and this arrangement may eventually lead to shared music performance royalties.

While some publishers rely upon their subpublishers outside this country to supervise collection of performance fees, ASCAP and BMI perform a valuable service to their members who would otherwise have no agency to collect foreign performance royalties.

ASCAP and BMI have generally to deal with only one licensing agency in each country; unlike the United States, most other countries have but one licensing organization. Difficulties with collections abroad often arise with the problem of identifying songs when they are broadcast in

---

8-If this occurs, ASCAP usually drops such a writer from its rolls. ASCAP's administrators have told me the organization prefers a roster of active, earning members.

the native language or when they are performed under a different title. In any event, foreign performance royalties for American writers and publishers are increasing rapidly as surveys and accounting procedures improve. Among the most lucrative foreign sources of income at this time are Canada, Japan, West Germany, the United Kingdom, Holland, Denmark, France, Spain, Switzerland and Italy.

GRIEVANCE PROCEDURES

Following the establishment of BMI in 1939, ASCAP initiated efforts to expand its membership and repertoire to meet competition. As new members joined the society, they began to question ASCAP's distribution, alleging that it was heavily weighted in favor of the established members who enjoyed huge incomes from their music scored for Broadway, Tin Pan Alley and Hollywood. Older, more established members of ASCAP countered with the argument that public acceptance of their copyrights fully justified their high incomes. The 1960 Consent Decree included a provision calling for ASCAP to set up a Board of Review to handle members' grievances. The Board of Review is elected by the general membership, and it handles complaints, accumulates information and can demand redress of grievances, including back payments to aggrieved members when the board believes such action is justified. Most grievances center on questions of weighting of credits and distribution of royalties. The majority of ASCAP members agree that this system of handling grievances works well and is equitable.

BROADCAST MUSIC INC. (BMI)

MEMBERSHIP

BMI is structured differently from its chief competitor.[9] Unlike ASCAP, which is owned by its entire membership, BMI is owned by its stockholders, originally some 475 broadcasters in this country. While ASCAP's management is handled by a board of directors elected by its full membership, the BMI board of directors is made up of its principal stockholders, the broadcasters, who determine management policy. BMI critics allege that this structure excludes the voice of its writer members. BMI answers by pointing out that if its distribution to writers

---

9-I am frequently asked whether an individual should join ASCAP or BMI, or whether a person should consider switching from one organization to the other. While I have been treated generously by ASCAP for many years, I do not recommend ASCAP above BMI nor make recommendations either way. Each individual should examine both organizations, also SESAC, then make up his own mind.

Edward M. Cramer,
BMI President

BMI offices, Nashville

were not equitable, it could not have attracted a membership one-third larger than its principal competitor. When formation of BMI was first proposed in the late 1930s, the prospectus distributed to investors stated that stockholders could anticipate no dividends. None has ever been paid. BMI, in this sense, is a "nonprofit" organization.

Where ASCAP has *members,* BMI has no "members," only writer and publisher *affiliates.* BMI tells an applicant that he will be accepted as a writer-affiliate if he has ". . . written a musical composition, alone or in collaboration with other writers, and the work is either commercially published or recorded or otherwise likely to be performed." As for admission of new publishers, BMI literature states, in part, that affiliation with BMI ". . . will be of practical benefit only to a publisher who has the ability and financial resources to undertake broad-based exploitation of his works." BMI also requires that its publisher affiliates ". . . satisfy reasonable standards of literacy and integrity." BMI does not charge its affiliated writers any application fee or dues. BMI publisher affiliates pay an application fee.

BMI describes its attitude toward proselytizing new members as "the open door." It uses a number of publications and public relations projects to increase awareness of the advantages of BMI membership. Like ASCAP, BMI offers special awards to school composers, unknown writers and arts organizations such as symphony orchestras. Important among these goodwill projects are the Songwriters' Workshops conducted to instruct inexperienced composers in how to create, then place, their unpublished material. BMI also sponsors music business workshops in cooperation with universities. As a host for one of these sessions at the University of Colorado, I know of their value to students heading for careers in the music business.

LICENSING

BMI, like ASCAP, receives most of its income from broadcasters, particularly from television. Although the organization is owned by broadcasters, BMI states that it does not offer them preferential rates. This statement is subject to interpretation. ASCAP generally bases its blanket licenses on 1.7 percent to 1.9 percent of a station's adjusted gross income plus a "sustaining fee." While BMI rates are formulated somewhat differently, its licenses to broadcasters figure out to be about one-third lower than ASCAP's.

Like its competitors, BMI licenses a great number of other music users, from hotels to skating rinks, from symphony halls to ball parks. To avoid separate dealings with the many thousands of music users, BMI conducts basic negotiations with established trade organizations. For example, BMI periodically negotiates industry-wide rates with the American Hotel and Motel Association. In the classical field, BMI negotiates with the American Symphony Orchestra League. In respect to hotels, restaurants and clubs, BMI works out license fees based, in part, on the establishment's weekly budget for music, e.g., the size of the orchestra, if any, the number of hours the business caters to the public, its seating capacity, etc. Licenses for theatres, concert halls, stadiums, etc., are based largely on the frequency of their use and seating capacity.

BMI continues to sign new licensees. Some of my pupils have assisted BMI in auditing unlicensed facilities and "live-logged" all music heard in a club in a given evening of spot checking. These reports are turned over to BMI field representatives who then call upon the establishment owner and seek to sign him. Reluctant proprietors almost always sign a license once they learn the justification for collection of performance fees is now not only provided by statute, but widely accepted by music users. This kind of acceptance is not universal, but the efforts of ASCAP and BMI have been remarkably successful in generating this ever-growing source of income for writers and publishers.

SAMPLING, ACCOUNTING

Where ASCAP relies heavily on actual tape recordings of music broadcast, BMI uses music performance logs it receives each year from a sample number of its licensed broadcasters. During a period of 12 to 14 months, each station's programs will be logged for one week. BMI claims this provides greater accuracy than ASCAP's system of tape recordings where the disc jockey may not always identify what is being broadcast. BMI believes its broader sampling base provides more accurate information on music broadcast outside urban centers, where much of BMI's repertoire finds special favor.

Like ASCAP, BMI receives complete cue sheets or logs from producers of *network* TV shows which list all music used — theme music, cue music and songs. BMI also receives cue sheets from feature film producers. Still further information is accumulated by BMI through sampling performances taking place in such venues as hotels, clubs, theatres, etc.

Like ASCAP, BMI has made important use of TV listings in *TV Guide* magazine. It has an arrangement that links *TV Guide*'s computers with BMI computers. This large amount of TV programming information is fed directly to BMI's information processing equipment and moves this part of BMI's logging operation from one of sampling to one of nearly complete accounting, particularly of TV movies and syndicated shows. Of course, BMI receives only program titles and movie titles. It must then seek to discover exactly what BMI music was actually broadcast.

In discussing with ASCAP and BMI the need for greater application of computer technology to performance logging, everyone agrees this is the path that must be followed. Total logging of all radio broadcasts of recorded music should become possible in this generation. It is my view that attainment of this goal could be achieved through extensive use of bar coding of records and tapes. For years, record manufacturers resisted this kind of price labeling of their products. Today, it has become commonplace on record jackets. If bar codes were printed right on the disc or cartridge *labels,* it would be technically possible to make a *complete census* of all radio broadcasts of recorded music — simply by installing bar code scanners above radio station turntables. The scanner, linked to computers, could pick up sufficient data to inform ASCAP and BMI not only what music was broadcast, but the time of day and length of performance. The next step might be that performing rights societies could then weight their broadcast performances in ways that would award copyright owners certain bonus credits when their music was broadcast in prime time, or when a particular performance was extended in time.

ROYALTY DISTRIBUTION

Logging performances is only the beginning of BMI's information processing. Its computer, already encoded with data on one million songs (with up to 1,000 new titles being added every month), receives all of these bits of information, causes them to interact, generates statements, calculates appropriate totals and subtotals, distributes proper payment and writes the checks for BMI members. BMI standard contracts with writers and publishers do not cite payment rates, probably because they experience frequent revision. BMI payments are calculated by sophisticated formulas which take into account, not just current, but accumulated performances. Payments are higher for songs that originate, for example, in a Broadway show or feature film. As a song's aggregate number of performances reaches certain plateaus, the copyright owners receive bonus payments from BMI, ranging from 25 percent to 100 percent. Under certain circumstances, BMI pays bonuses of different amounts on all songs in its repertoire. Copyright owners who are presently members of a music licensing organization, or those who plan to join one, can get current distribution rates and bonuses by contacting ASCAP or BMI directly.

Established writers whose music appears on the charts have, in the past, been able to get advances on performance royalties from both ASCAP and BMI. Both organizations structure their distributions, bonuses and royalty advances not only to attract new writers, but to discourage defection of their present membership. In general, once an affiliate strikes a relationship with one licensing organization, he is better off in the long run staying with that organization, for a disruption in the flow of income from performances can be costly. Most ASCAP and BMI gains in membership occur through proselytizing of new writers and publishers, not from raiding each other's rosters.

FOREIGN COLLECTIONS

As outlined above, BMI has reciprocal arrangements with all of the important music licensing organizations abroad. BMI receives performance royalties from these foreign organizations, then pays BMI members their share, withholding five percent for servicing foreign accounts. Now that the music business is becoming more and more a worldwide industry with hits developing in many different parts of the world, it is to be anticipated that writers and publishers everywhere will welcome the further development of these reciprocating arrangements for collection of performance royalties.

As with ASCAP, BMI has set up a procedure to accommodate grievances that may arise among its members. The Consent Decree entered into between BMI and the U.S. Department of Justice sets forth a requirement that all disputes of any kind between BMI and its members or music users must be submitted ". . . to arbitration in the City of New York under the prevailing rules of the American Arbitration Association."

SESAC

SESAC (the acronym originally stood for Society of European Stage Authors and Composers) is the third performing rights organization in the United States. Unlike ASCAP and BMI, SESAC is privately owned and has been in the hands of the Heinecke family since the organization was established in 1931. It represents about 250 publishers who control some 470 catalogs, 150,000 compositions of over 1000 writers.

Unlike the distribution practices described for ASCAP and BMI, SESAC's owners retain one-half of the firm's income and distribute the other half to their affiliates. The organization is unique in the field in having a number of preset royalty amounts it pays out when a composition in its catalog attains a certain level of "chart success." In the past, the SESAC catalog has emphasized gospel music and other contemporary Christian musics. The organization is also receptive to works in the jazz idiom.

SESAC lacks the resources to sample or log performances of its repertoire on a level comparable to ASCAP and BMI. It uses weighting formulas different from its competitors for payments to affiliates. Despite its small size compared to its two stronger competitors, 98 to 99 percent of domestic broadcasters, according to SESAC, find it advantageous to have a SESAC license.

Unlike ASCAP and BMI, SESAC serves its affiliates by handling the licensing and collecting of mechanical fees and synchronization rights.

MECHANICAL LICENSES

As explained in my chapter on copyright, record manufacturers are required to obtain a *mechanical* license in order to produce and distribute records and tapes to the public. This type of license is limited to those whose intention is to make these records available only for *private* use — the kinds of records people buy and take home. Other kinds of mechanical licenses, e.g., those required for transcriptions, are discussed later in this chapter.

The copyright law sets forth procedures and fees for record producers to obtain a *compulsory* mechanical license. But in actual practice, most licensing of recordings for home use are *negotiated* mechanical licenses. Publishers and record producers bypass the compulsory licensing route and work out their own license. A negotiated mechanical license differs from a statutory compulsory license in three ways:

1- *The royalty rate may be the same as the current statutory rate or it may be lower.*

2- *Royalty accountings are usually quarterly rather than monthly as required under a statutory license.*

3- *The statutory requirement of "notice of intent" to record the copyrighted material is waived.*

Most publishers use the Harry Fox Agency to issue their mechanical licenses. Publishers instruct Fox what royalty to charge, then he negotiates the license, collects the royalties, takes out a service fee of about three percent (the rate has varied slightly over the years), then forwards the net balance to the publisher.

Royalty Rates — As set forth in my chapter on copyright, the first change in the statutory rate for a compulsory mechanical license since 1909 occurred in 1978 when Congress voted an increase to 2.75 cents, i.e., 2.75 cents "... for each work embodied in a phonorecord or one-half cent per minute of playing time or fraction thereof, whichever amount is larger." This rate is periodically adjusted by the Copyright Royalty Tribunal. Changes, if any, in the statutory rate are based on the list (retail) price of records. If suggested list prices are generally discontinued by the industry (some firms make this prediction), wholesale prices will be substituted to determine royalty rates.

Collection Services — Publishers choosing not to retain the Harry Fox Agency to collect royalties have alternatives. For example, a firm offering licensing and collecting services for mechanicals and synchronization rights is the American Mechanical Rights Association (AMRA) of New York. This organization represents a number of foreign mechanical rights societies, the largest of which is probably GEMA of West Germany. AMRA finances its operation with a five percent service charge on gross collections.

Another New York-based company is the Copyright Service Bureau Ltd. Since the 1960s it has offered services similar to AMRA and also offers copyright and accounting services for writers and publishers. Its service fees vary.

Among the firms offering a variety of copyright services are Mietus Copyright Management, also of New York. Another monitoring service for mechanical royalties is the American Guild of Authors and Composers.

American publishers requiring mechanical royalty services in Canada used to retain the Harry Fox Agency. Fox no longer operates in Canada, and services it rendered formerly are now performed by CMRRA —The Canadian Musical Reproduction Rights Agency Ltd. CMRRA charges a five percent commission on royalties it collects for its clients.

Most publishers lack strong branch offices in foreign territories and usually turn to Harry Fox's foreign service branch to handle their mechanical royalties abroad. Fox has reciprocal arrangements with most foreign collecting agencies. They normally charge Fox about 15 percent for their collecting service. Fox takes off a service fee (around three percent), then forwards the net balance to the publisher client.

COLLECTION SERVICES

TERRITORY	AGENCY
France, Belgium, Holland, Luxembourg	SDRM (Société Pour l'Administration du Droit de Reproduction Mecanique, based in France
West Germany, Austria, Bulgaria, Rumania, Israel, Turkey, the Philippines	GEMA (based in West Germany)
England, Scotland, Ireland, South Africa	MCPS (London-based Mechanical Copyright Protection Society of Great Britain)
Scandinavia	NCB (Nordisk Copyright Bureau)
Spain	SGAE
U.S.S.R.	VAAP
Switzerland	SUISA
Australia, New Zealand	ANZ Musical Copyright Agency
Japan	JASRAC

Fig. 7.2

FILM LICENSES

A producer of theatrical motion pictures must acquire two kinds of licenses in the United States. The first one is called a *synchronization license.* The term refers to the right to use music which is timed to synchronize with, or relate to, the action on the screen. Film producers ordinarily also seek a *performance license* for exhibitions in the United States.[10]

10-For this license the film producer will normally go to the publisher (or his agent). This is because a court decree has denied, to ASCAP at least, the right to require a performance license directly from movie theatres in the United States.

If the producer wants new music composed expressly for his film, he will engage a film music composer to write the original score. He often buys these creative services on a *work made for hire* basis. As pointed out in Chapter 6, in this circumstance the producer, or employer, not only owns all the rights to the original music, he is considered, under copyright law, the *author* of the work. Thus, the producer does not require a license of any kind from the composer of the music, since it is the producer's property.

If the film producer does not obtain his musical score on a work made for hire basis, he has other ways to proceed. He may engage a film composer *as an independent contractor,* pay him a fee, then negotiate publishing rights in the music. If the composer retains all publishing rights, the film producer must then obtain from him a synchronization license to use the music in a film.

Another source for film music is from music already under copyright and published. If a film producer, for example, wants to use an established pop song, he must negotiate a synchronization license with the publisher. Most American publishers handle these arrangements through the Harry Fox Agency. After the publisher instructs Fox — the Agency does not make basic decisions in this regard — on what to accept and what to charge, Fox negotiates with the film producer for the music use and the cost of the synchronization license.

Costs of synchronization licenses will be largely determined by the market value of the music, whether the music is to be performed on camera or just underscored, whether it is to be sung, and the duration of the performance in the film. When a producer does not know who owns a particular work, he knows that the Harry Fox Agency computer can not only tell him who publishes the music, but can call up on the same screen the licensing rates. If Fox doesn't have a record of the copyright, knowledgeable producers will normally engage a copyright researcher or law firm to assist.

It is very important for the film producer to obtain the broadest possible synchronization license, since a movie originally planned for theatrical exhibition in this country will probably be used later in foreign theatres, television broadcasts here and abroad, cable TV and home videodiscs and tapes. The publisher may try to grant the film producer a limited license in order to maximize his profits later when the film is used in different media.

In respect to *performance* licenses for film music, conditions in this country differ from those in Europe. It is customary for film producers to acquire from publishers a performance license for theatrical exhibition of a film in this country. But in Europe and most other countries outside the U.S.A., each country's own performance licensing society grants to theatres in that country a blanket license for the performance of music accompanying films. These licensing societies generally derive their income from film music by charging a small percentage of the net box office receipts. Nearly all performing rights societies outside this country have reciprocal agreements with ASCAP and BMI wherein the former may grant licenses for music controlled by ASCAP or BMI. American composers sometimes receive substantial performance royalties from music they have scored for films which become popular in theatres abroad.

Different performance rights problems arise in respect to films made outside the United States. For example, British and French composers' performing rights societies claim the exclusive right to collect performance royalties from all exhibitions of their films in the United States.

TV Movie Rights — A different set of licensing problems arise when a film is originally produced *for television broadcast.* The producer will certainly go for the broadest possible synchronization license, in anticipation of his production being eventually rented or sold to other media and possibly foreign territories. But in respect to a *performance* license, the producer will normally not need one for television broadcasts, in that the TV stations and networks already have a blanket performance license with ASCAP, BMI and SESAC, for all the music they broadcast.

New Use Rights — A film producer or TV movie producer frequently wants to use music already existing in a commercially released recording. One of the reasons this may appear attractive to the producer is that he knows beforehand how the music will sound and that it has been well received by the public. But obtaining permission to borrow a record for a film score can become a complicated, expensive process. Negotiations of this kind will involve not only the record company, but the performing artists, the artists' unions and music publishers. The record company contract with the artist may prohibit use of that artist's records in another medium. If so, special waivers and artist's compensation must be negotiated. Both artists' unions — AFM and AFTRA, will require *new use* payments. The music publisher will demand from the film producer a synchronization license and a performing license.

TRANSCRIPTION LICENSES

The terms "transcriptions" and "electrical transcriptions" have been used for many years in reference to special oversized discs used by radio broadcasters. These discs were licensed only for radio use and were not available to the public. Transcriptions today are now found more often on tape, and the term is applied more broadly to include syndicated programs, library services, and "wired music services" such as Muzak.

These kinds of music users require two kinds of music licenses — a mechanical license and a performance license. Copyright owners sometimes grant a combination license for just one fee. A firm seeking a transcription license may negotiate directly with the music publisher or use the services of the Harry Fox Agency. In respect to performance licenses, they negotiate terms with ASCAP, BMI or SESAC.

Muzak claims to have over 30,000 copyrights in its repertoire and finds it impractical to negotiate for each individual license. Muzak usually obtains a master (or "block") license from ASCAP and BMI with fixed annual fees based on the then current number of its franchised dealers. Firms holding Muzak franchises then make payments to ASCAP and BMI based on the number of individual customers the franchiser serves in a given year. A common term for a transcription license is three years with annual fees being in the range of $5 to $10 per song per year. Muzak-type licenses call for separate negotiations for performance rights.

The 3M Company has negotiated different kinds of transcription licenses. That firm originally only *sold,* rather than leased, its tapes. Instead of a fixed annual fee, the 3M license calls for a payment of five cents per selection for each copy of the tape that is sold. This nickel includes two cents for the mechanical license and three cents for the performance license. The latter is good for three years, after which a further payment of one cent per each additional year is required. The problem of policing collection of license fees after the end of the initial three-year contract devolves upon the performing rights organization, but 3M assists in this by providing ASCAP and BMI with the names and addresses of its customers and by notifying them when renewal payments fall due.

Except for the special contracts 3M has negotiated, other users must negotiate a separate license to "perform" transcriptions of this kind in public places such as restaurants, hotels and airports. Performance licenses of this kind are issued to the supplier of the music service and not to the ultimate user. Performance license fees are sometimes based on a percentage of the fee charged by the music supplier. Rates vary according to the size of the facilities served and whether or not they serve food and beverages. A franchised supplier is charged an annual fee for each facility he serves, such as restaurants, hotels, offices, etc.

A somewhat different kind of transcription license is obtained by program syndicators and broadcasters' library services such as described in the chapter on radio broadcasting. These packages must negotiate for transcription licenses with the Harry Fox Agency or directly with the music publishers. In respect to performance licenses, syndicators and production companies involved in these kinds of services take care of them with ASCAP and BMI, thus relieving individual broadcasters from the burden of negotiating separate performance rights for this particular music.

JUKEBOX LICENSES

Since 1978 jukebox owners have been required to obtain a public performance license for music played on their machines. This is for nondramatic music only, and is applied to equipment where admission is not charged, directly or indirectly. As explained earlier, this is a compulsory license.

The Copyright Office issues a registration certificate which the operator must attach to each of his machines in full view. While fines are assessed for noncompliance, jukebox operators in the years following enactment of the law have not complied well. One recent guess is that only about one-third of the estimated half-million boxes in the country were registered and paying the annual license. Lawsuits are pending in many instances.

The cost of the license started at $8 per box in 1978. In 1981 the Royalty Tribunal decided to raise this fee to $50, phasing it in over several years. License rates for all compulsory licenses are subject to periodic adjustment by the Royalty Tribunal.

NONCOMMERCIAL LICENSES

Since 1978, schools and colleges have been required to pay for the music they use outside the classroom. ASCAP and BMI offer colleges and universities a two-tiered payment formula. The first "tier" calls for colleges to pay a few pennies per year for each full-time student enrolled. The second tier provides for an additional charge based on ticket sales and seating capacities of campus performing facilities.

CABLE TELEVISION LICENSES

Cable television operators must operate under a compulsory licensing arrangement which became operational in 1978. Cable TV delivers what the copyright law calls *secondary transmissions* of primary program material.

The Copyright Royalty Tribunal grants the compulsory license, sets the royalty rate, collects the money and distributes it to copyright claimants. Licensing rates are currently based on a small percentage of operators' gross revenues. Royalties are shared by five major groups representing copyright owners. The largest share goes to program syndicators (75 percent); joint sports claimants are awarded around 12 percent; noncommercial broadcasters share 5.25 percent; and the three performing rights societies share 4.5 percent to 5 percent. The smallest share (3.5 percent) goes to commercial TV broadcasters.

The Tribunal may periodically adjust the royalty rate and the manner in which royalties are shared by copyright owners.

HOME VIDEODISCS, TAPES

Music owners and users are searching for ways to properly license home videodiscs and tapes. Few precedents are available to guide them. Home video entertainment is a unique medium; it may borrow (or steal) sounds from copyrighted recordings; it may borrow (or steal) portions of copyrighted films and TV shows; it may include music previously copyrighted for other media and mix it with new music, some of which may be separately copyrighted; some of it may be in public domain.

As set forth elsewhere in this book, the copyright owners and home video software producers have the difficult task of reconciling these diverse interests, then working out equitable licensing arrangements for these properties. *The software producers must acquire from copyright proprietors both mechanical licenses and synchronization licenses.* Perhaps industry leaders and their copyright attorneys can invent a new kind of *combination license* for home video.

LICENSING OF DRAMATIC MUSIC

Study of copyright law in the United States makes clear that the statute makes sharp distinctions between dramatic music and nondramatic music. Accordingly, the licensing of rights differs markedly.

The term *dramatic music* includes, for example, operas, musical plays, musical shows and revues, in whole or in part. The term may also include music that did not originate in some kind of theatrical production but was written as part of a TV or radio show where the music was integral to the plot and where it contributed to carrying the drama forward. It is customary to refer to copyrights in dramatic music as *grand rights,* and grand rights must be negotiated with copyright owners *separately* from nondramatic rights, which are sometimes termed *"small rights."*

In respect to Broadway musicals and similar productions, rights of authors, composers and lyricists are set forth in contracts based on regulations of the New York Dramatists Guild. Under these kinds of contracts, the composers and lyricists retain all publication rights of their material, and inherent in the right of publication is the right to collect both mechanical royalties and synchronization fees.

In respect to performance licensing, a show's composers receive royalties from ASCAP or BMI for performances of individual songs on radio, TV, clubs and restaurants, etc. But when a dramatic musical work is performed as a whole or a substantial portion of it is performed, e.g., a scene including music and dialogue, grand rights must be licensed. ASCAP does not involve itself in licensing grand rights of any of its repertoire. Its members usually assign that responsibility to one of the firms involved in grand rights licensing and rental of scores and parts. Among the larger firms in this field are Rodgers and Hammerstein Repertory, Tams Witmark Music Library and Music Theatre International. BMI licenses with broadcasters include dramatic music rights, but BMI reserves the right to negotiate special conditions for use of certain kinds of dramatic performances. SESAC contracts exclude dramatic music rights.

When a Broadway musical becomes a hit, its writers enjoy income from its performances long after its Broadway run. In this country there are hundreds of regional theatres offering performances of these beloved shows. Each dramatic performance of this kind requires a license and royalty payment. Going rates for one performance of an amateur or school production of a Broadway musical would range between $75 and $150. In addition, the show's book, score and parts must be rented from the licensing agency. Professional performances of Broadway shows (following a Broadway run) require a license involving a weekly minimum guarantee against 10 percent of the box office receipts. Professional productions also must rent the show's book, score and parts. The producers are generally charged higher rates than those set for amateur groups.

Performance licenses for touring companies vary. Some touring companies are under the aegis of the original Broadway producer; others are mounted independently.

Concerning licensing of a musical for an original cast recording, negotiations are normally handled by the show's producer, subject to the approval of the authors and composers. In respect to granting movie rights to a Broadway show, deals are handled by the Negotiator for the Dramatists Guild. The Dramatists Guild limits any agent involved to a 10 percent commission on the sale of any movie rights. Up to 3.5 percent of that commission may then be deducted to pay for the services of the Dramatists Guild Negotiator.

Broadway musicals are popular all over the world and, like jazz, are one of this country's most important cultural exports. Licensing of publishing rights to dramatic music is sometimes handled through foreign subpublishers. As for live performances outside the U.S.A. and Canada, dramatic music licenses are negotiated on an individual basis with the foreign producer. For productions of American-born shows in the British Isles, royalties paid to a show's authors and composers are regulated by the Dramatists Guild and vary according to who initially arranged the British production and what interval of time may have elapsed between the Broadway run and the British production.

An additional area of dramatic music licensing concerns the music composed as background to a musical show or music underscoring straight drama performed live. Depending on the stature of the composer, the producer will usually pay a flat fee in front, then possibly one-half of one percent of the box office take for the run of the production. When dramatic music is taped and used with live drama, it is customary for the producer to be charged a fee of about $25 to $50 a week by the music's publisher.

BMI computer terminals help operators compile data concerning performance royalties earned by writer and publisher affiliates.

ASCAP's regional office, Nashville

UNIONS AND GUILDS

Individuals involved in the music and entertainment fields have developed a large number of organizations to represent their interests. The number and kinds of representative organizations appear almost endless.[1] Here we have room to discuss only the larger organizations. They are structured in a variety of ways. Some, like the AFM, are real trade unions, connected with the AFL-CIO. Others are more accurately described as guilds. Still others are simply associations of independent contractors. If this were not complicated enough, we have entertainment industry "guilds" (for example, the New York Dramatists Guild) whose members may own the company with whom they are supposed to "negotiate" for their services.

The AFM, AFTRA, AGMA, SAG, and IATSE are discussed below. The AGAC is treated in Chapter 4; the CLGA is covered in Chapter 25. Smaller unions and guilds are described at the end of this chapter.

1-The following kinds of professionals are represented in some kind of association: composers, arrangers, lyricists, instrumentalists, singers, playwrights, theatrical producers, directors, stage actors, screen actors, choreographers, dancers, scenic designers, scenery builders, stagehands, electricians, personal managers, record producers, audio technicians, and educators specializing in the fields of music management, merchandising and recording technology.

AMERICAN FEDERATION OF MUSICIANS (AFM)

The full name of the AFM is *American Federation of Musicians of the United States and Canada.* It is the oldest union in the United states representing individuals professionally active in the fields of entertainment and the arts, its history dating from the nineteenth century. The AFM has around 330,000 members, some ten percent of whom are in Canada. Its "international" headquarters is in New York City, and it maintains over 600 "locals."

AFM membership includes professional instrumentalists, conductors, arrangers, orchestrators, copyists, music librarians and proofreaders. The union maintains no jurisdiction over the professional services of *composers* (although practically all composers professionally active in film, television, radio, commercials and syndication are AFM members by virtue of their services as either conductors, instrumentalists, arrangers or copyists).

If a musician *sings* professionally, he need not be an AFM member unless he also works professionally in one of the capacities listed for regular AFM membership.

Unlike a number of guilds and professional associations in the arts, the AFM is a bona fide *labor union:* its members are employees and the AFM represents the interests of its members to employers.

The AFM functions on two levels — local and national. The local offices of the union have jurisdiction over all union work for musicians which is not covered by national contracts. AFM national contracts embrace all services of musicians in the fields of recording, network broadcasting, theatrical film, television film and tape, "live-on-tape" network television, home videodiscs and tapes, syndicated programs and services, pay-TV, commercial announcements and contracts covering certain traveling productions such as circuses and ice shows. Musicians who perform outside their home local jurisdictions are also covered, to some extent, by the national AFM office in respect to a traveling tax added to local sales.

National contracts are negotiated by the union's National Contracts Division, which reports to the AFM Board of Directors. The National Contracts Division has a resident representative in New York City and Los Angeles. The division negotiates contracts, or revises contracts, with trade associations representing record manufacturers, network broadcasters, commercial announcement producers and film producers. Most of these national contracts have a two- to three-year term.

AFM contracts, whether local or national, generally include agreement on such issues as wages, hours, overtime, working conditions, orchestra size minimums, instrument "doubling," heavy-instrument cartage, "class" of venue, rehearsal fees, pay for leader and contractor, tracking scale, reuse and new use of recorded material. Contracts also stipulate that the employer will employ only AFM members, and that he agrees to pay the current surcharges for the AFM's Pension and Welfare Fund. Recording contracts also include the employer's commitment to pay into the AFM funds. Most contracts include an arbitration clause. The union requires that contracts be countersigned by a union officer, although some locals do not enforce this rule.

The local and national offices of the AFM are financed by members' initiation dues, annual dues and "tax." The term *tax* (or work dues) is used by musicians in reference to the 1.5 percent to perhaps 3.5 percent assessment made against union scale wages earned by members and paid into the AFM treasury.[2] For years, the AFM financial condition has verged near bankruptcy because many AFM locals have not required members to pay tax on local gigs. This slack policy in the past produced too little income for the union to finance its affairs. The AFM has since made it mandatory for all AFM employment to be taxed, the revenue being shared among the locals and the national office. Special kinds of employment, e.g., recording and film scoring is, from time to time, assessed a special add-on tax.

The AFM attempts to license and control talent agents through franchising them. This process is described in Chapter 9. The union also seeks to protect its members from employers who don't pay union musicians what they are due. Slow-paying or nonpaying employers are sometimes sued by the union. More often, they are simply blacklisted, in part through publication of the names of offenders in the musicians' monthly magazine, *International Musician*.

AMERICAN FEDERATION OF TELEVISION AND RADIO ARTISTS (AFTRA)[3]

Although AFTRA is only one-tenth the size of the AFM, it has jurisdiction over most *singers* — soloists, background singers and other choral ensembles. The organization was founded in the 1930s as the American Federation of Radio Artists. At that time, its membership was focused largely in New York, Chicago and Los Angeles, and was made up largely of radio announcers, singers, and sound effects technicians. Today, AFTRA has over 40 branch offices ("locals"), and its membership has expanded to include, not only thousands of artists active in television, but many others working as professional singers in the recording industry, syndicated programs, commercial spots and traveling shows. Among its membership are anonymous background singers and multimillionaire superstars.

Like the AFM, AFTRA is a real labor union: its members are employees,

---

2-Some locals require employers to forward a check directly to the union office to cover all union wages, benefits and retirement funds. Then the union deducts musicians' work dues, deposits the benefits and all other special payments into their respective accounts, and writes a net paycheck for each musician employed on the date. Under different circumstances, the AFM will permit an employer to pay musicians through an artists' payroll service company, whose services are available in large cities. AFM contractors sometimes use this kind of company to handle wages, tax accounting and benefit payments.

3-In Canada the comparable union is ACTRA, the Association of Canadian Television and Radio Artists.

and AFTRA's main business is working out labor agreements with prospective employers. As with most national labor unions, AFTRA's leadership negotiates its national contracts with industry associations representative of the major sectors of the entertainment industry — record companies, TV and radio networks, TV producers and producers of commercial spots intended for broadcast.

In the past, certain jurisdictional disputes arose between the AFM and AFTRA. In recent years, both unions have agreed that an artist who both sings and plays an instrument on records and network broadcasts is expected to hold cards in both unions and pay dues to both. AFTRA also had a jurisdictional dispute years ago with the Screen Actors Guild (SAG). Today, the two unions agree that a singer must belong to SAG if he records music *originally on film.* If the singer records *originally on videotape* (or "live-on-tape"), the artist must belong to AFTRA. This understanding holds even when one medium is later used under different circumstances — what artists' unions call *new use,* e.g., a videotape that is later transferred to film, or vice versa.

AFTRA usually tries to persuade employers to use the union's standard forms of agreement. Like most such agreements, they provide for the best interests of the employees, in respect to wages, working conditions and benefits. AFTRA contracts classify a singer on a given job as a soloist or background singer. Scales are higher for soloists. Second-highest wages are earned by soloists who "step out" of an ensemble momentarily for a featured segment. Background singers are paid somewhat more when performing with duos and trios than they are in larger choral ensembles.

Of all the artists' performing unions, AFTRA has the most complicated schedule of wages. Particularly in the commercial spot field, union stewards must be able to tell a producer what his costs will be for singers *relative to the intended market* for the spots — whether they are for local, regional or national broadcast. AFTRA wages rise according to the potential size of the market. In the commercial production industry, it is not unusual for large production companies and advertising agencies to have at least one full-time employee helping spot producers figure out the correct AFTRA scales. The only safe solution is for the producer to get current AFTRA scales directly from the union.

One of the most important components of AFTRA contracts is the provision for *new use* or *extended use.* As with most other artists' union contracts, when an AFTRA member performs on a tape intended for one particular medium, he earns additional money if that tape is later used in a different medium, e.g., when a commercial recording might be licensed for use in a movie or television show. AFTRA artists also earn additional wages in a situation where the use of a broadcast commercial extends beyond the initial term (often limited to thirteen weeks). If the spots are to be broadcast beyond that initial period, AFTRA artists are paid for "extended use" of the material. Since many spot campaigns are broadcast for long periods of time, even years after the initial use, earnings of AFTRA members from this source can become very large.

As with the AFM, AFTRA requires a union steward on the job to make sure the producer meets all his obligations to the singers under contract.

AFTRA is almost exclusively concerned with negotiating and implementing singers' activities covered by *national* contracts, particularly the recording and broadcasting industries. The singers' union has minimal influence and control over singers recording local shows or spots. Nonunion singers dominate there.

Among the major achievements of the AFTRA leadership has been the negotiation of national recording contracts that provide what are known as *contingent scale payments.* This, and other aspects of AFTRA's involvement in the recording industry, are explained in Chapter 17.

AMERICAN GUILD OF MUSICAL ARTISTS (AGMA)

The American Guild of Musical Artists was organized in the 1930s to serve the interests of singers and dancers working in the opera, ballet, concert and recital fields. AGMA's membership also includes instrumentalists who are active as *soloists* in the classical field.

AGMA employment agreements are often negotiated for a particular ensemble, such as the Met's chorus or the San Francisco Opera's corps de ballet. Such contracts cover the standard items in any labor agreement — wages, working conditions and benefits. Most AGMA contract negotiations are with nonprofit arts organizations which own the performing group, e.g., the American Ballet Theatre Foundation, which owns and sponsors the American Ballet Theatre.

ACTORS EQUITY ASSOCIATION ("EQUITY")

Professional actors and directors in the United States are represented by the Actors Equity Association — which theatre people refer to simply as "Equity." A large number of Equity members are *singing* actors (or "actors who sing") in theatrical productions.

Equity is a trade union. For actors and directors employed in the Broadway theatre, Equity negotiates with the League of New York Theatres and Producers Inc.

For many years, Equity membership was made up almost entirely of actors and directors working in New York City. Today, Equity has members all over the country. This has come about with the large growth of regional theatres, dinner theatres and acting companies in residence on college campuses.

Of all the artists' unions, Equity enjoys the best reputation, with producers at least, for being flexible about what an actor should be paid. This is because Equity leadership has understood that one of the ways the union can foster increased employment opportunities for actors is to demand full Equity scale only from producers who can afford it. Since so many productions combine casts of both professional, semiprofessional and nonprofessional actors, Equity often makes special concessions on wage scales. But if most the cast is earning union wages, or adjusted union scale wages, it is referred to in the business as "an Equity show."

One of the reasons Equity has been relatively lenient with producers concerning wage scales (and even nonpayment of actors under certain circumstances) is that the union always has more members out of work than members working. But for the Broadway productions at least, actors and singing actors cast in a show that closes on opening night get at least two weeks additional salary, because producers are required by Equity to post a bond prior to opening for that kind of emergency.

Besides the contract Equity periodically negotiates with Broadway producers, the union extends to off-Broadway producers much lower scales. For actors employed in regional theatres and companies in residence on college campuses, Equity covers their services with its so-called L.O.R.T. agreement — the acronym for League of Resident Theatres. Many of these contracts are with nonprofit entities which are supported, at least in part, by colleges, states arts councils, the National Endowment For The Arts, and private donations.

Equity cooperates with producers and theatrical companies, in presenting talent "showcases," where unknown actors and singing actors find an opportunity to gain experience and recognition.

SCREEN ACTORS GUILD (SAG)

The Screen Actors Guild is probably the most widely known artists' union, in that so many of its members are world-famous performers. SAG has jurisdiction over all actors, singers and instrumentalists who act in theatrical motion pictures and television movies. It is classified as a trade union, in that its members are employees whose services are rendered to employers through contracts negotiated by the union (guild). In Hollywood, the parent contract is negotiated with MPTPA — the Motion Picture and Television Producers Association.

Like the AFM and AFTRA, the actors' union attempts to control the behavior of actors' agents through a franchising system. Again similar to AFM and AFTRA, SAG contracts stipulate who is responsible for residual payments to actors when a production created for one medium is sold or licensed for exhibition through another medium.

To encourage producers to film their projects in the United States, SAG sometimes authorizes deferred payments of actors' wages. These agreements provide that actors' wages are not payable until the production starts to yield its first dollar of income.

INTERNATIONAL ASSOCIATION OF THEATRICAL AND STAGE EMPLOYEES (IATSE)

The IATSE is the union having jurisdiction over stagehands in the legitimate theatre and in some film productions. Many motion picture cameramen and movie projectionists also belong to the IATSE.

In the television field, IATSE is getting some competition from a rival union, NABET — the National Association of Broadcast and Electrical

Technicians. In respect to audio technicians working in recording studios and broadcasting, no one union has managed to gain complete jurisdiction. Many employers of these kinds of technicians have been able to avoid union shop status.

It should be noted that *open shop* agreements generally stipulate that individuals employed in such a situation are subject to the collective bargaining agreement in effect between the pertinent union and the employer, and that in the event of a dispute, the terms of the collective bargaining agreement would govern the employment of the nonunion employee.

OTHER UNIONS AND GUILDS

Dramatists Guild — The New York Dramatists Guild is a trade association, not a labor union. It represents composers, lyricists and "book" writers active in the musical theatre on Broadway. The guild also includes, as members, playwrights who write plays without music, or plays that use music only incidentally.

The Dramatists Guild is a division of the Authors League of America, which has two branches — the Dramatists Guild and the Authors Guild. The latter is a trade association of authors of books other than "books" for plays.

One of the principal concerns of the Dramatists Guild is the protection of the copyrights of its members. The guild requires that the ownership and control of the music, lyrics and book of a show remain in the hands of its authors and composers. The producer cannot claim publishing rights of this material. Guild members retain copyright in their material, including the licensing of performances of dramatic music (grand rights). The guild also helps its members preserve the integrity of their works, in that producers and directors are not allowed to alter music, lyrics or the book to a show without the composers' and authors' consent.

Other unions and guilds related to the music and/or entertainment fields are the Writers Guild of America, the Directors Guild of America, the Producers Guild of America, the Conference of Personal Managers, the Society of Stage Directors and Choreographers, and the United Scenic Artists.

Additional concerns relating to unions and guilds have to do with the employment of minors and the whole issue of immigration and work permits, where one country seeks to limit foreign artists from displacing its own citizens from job opportunities. Individuals needing definitive information on these kinds of problems are advised to search out current regulations and statutes through attorneys experienced in labor law.

MUSIC INDUSTRY CROSSROADS, Sunset and Vine, Hollywood. Motown Building (left) and Federal Savings Building house dozens of music industry companies.

9

AGENTS, MANAGERS AND ATTORNEYS

Most professional artists find it desirable, even imperative, to call upon others to assist them in handling their business affairs and the development of their careers. Partly because of the "glamour" of the music and entertainment fields, performers of even modest success find themselves surrounded by individuals who claim they can help the artist find the path to fame and fortune. Curiously enough, some of them can. Many performers of modest gifts have been brought from the unemployment line to at least temporary "success" through the efforts of clever management. Many others, obviously very talented, continue to flounder in the small-time for want of someone competent enough to guide their careers in the right direction.

A successful professional artist generally surrounds himself with a complete retinue of assistants, probably including a personal manager, agent, business manager, road manager, attorney and publicist. The competence of these individuals ranges from superb to zero. Some are mere hangers-on, possibly "groupie" graduates. Others may be wizards at handling money and negotiating contracts. As for their integrity, this array of music business personalities includes individuals with characters ranging from exemplary to crooked. Some are licensed and regulated; others completely lack credentials. Some have master degrees in business administration; others may have difficulty reading traffic signs. The services that support personnel render an artist overlap and intertwine. In this chapter I shall try to identify agents, managers and music business attorneys, then define their roles in the arts and entertainment industries.

AGENTS

Agents go under various names. Many people refer to them as "bookers," which most of them are. In California they are known today as "talent agents." Sometimes people in and out of the business use the term "manager" or "artists manager" interchangeably with "agent." In that these appellations are used most definitively in the state of California where a high percentage of agency work is conducted, I shall use the word "agent" here the way California statutes define "talent agent" — that person who is in the full-time business of procuring employment primarily for performers, writers, producers and directors.

The talent agent has two kinds of clients. First, he has a roster of artists. His other kind of client is the *buyer* of such talent — producers, record companies, publishers, packagers, promoters and club owners. His job is to deliver his artists to talent buyers. He serves as the middle man, the negotiator. He knows, or should know, what an artist is worth, and he must know what the buyer is willing and able to pay. If the agent prices his "merchandise" too high, the buyer won't deal. If he prices his merchandise too low, he not only earns a lower commission, he may lose clients to other agents who are more aggressive.

The agents who are most successful over the long run have earned the respect and confidence of both buyers and sellers. It is the agent's task to see to it that all his clients make a reasonable profit. And if he can attract major artists to his stable, his commissions may place him in an income bracket comparable to that of a star performer.

SMALL AGENCIES

A small-time agent often starts in a medium-sized city working alone. He quickly discovers he cannot be very effective just by himself and connects with one or two other local agents. Perhaps three of them can afford to rent a modest office and hire a secretary. Agencies of this size handle most local bookings. They try to persuade local club owners to try live music instead of a jukebox or videotaped entertainment. One of their greatest challenges is locating acts attractive enough to pull dancers and drinkers into local clubs. Most of the acts sending them demos are, at best, semiprofessional — clearly not strong enough to justify the club owner paying them even union scale. So the agent keeps searching — for buyers and qualified talents.

Until the agent can discover acts with some drawing power, he will rarely be able to build his booking business above a minimum survival level. But now and then, local acts create a local following and start to command fees high enough to earn the agent a respectable income.

Local agents with ambitions transcending the local city limits search out contacts and cooperative bookings with national, and even international, agencies. Such deals ordinarily involve commission splits.

If a local agent learns his trade and develops national contacts, he will probably try to find a job with a large international booking agency. If he is aggressive, creative and persevering, he might make it. Major booking agencies employ hundreds of people and operate with offices in the major cities of the world. Agencies such as William Morris and ICM (International Creative Management) handle hundreds of artists and gross hundreds of millions of dollars a year. Such agencies "net" commissions of 10 percent to about 20 percent of their gross.

One of the principal reasons these large international outfits do well is their power to *package* — they can pull together, for a television network or movie company, not only the star performers, but supporting players, writers, directors, composers, even choreographers. It is big business in this league, and major talents generally seek exclusive representation by one of these international firms. In addition to their ability to package, the big companies represent artists in all fields of entertainment — concerts, television, records, films, commercials and product endorsements.

Major agencies rarely sign unknown talents; they are preoccupied booking their stars. Unknown acts must struggle along with local agents, usually until they achieve some success as recording artists.

Some artists, e.g., songwriters, don't even need agents. They learn to contact publishers directly. But when a songwriter is also a performer, he usually requires a talent agent to represent him as a performer.

FULL-SERVICE AGENCIES

Large talent booking companies are sometimes described as "full-service agencies." They generally demand that their artists grant them the right of *exclusive representation in all fields*. In the process of signing an artist, a full-service agency will submit a package of ten or more contracts for the signature of the new client. Some of these agreements are *form contracts* used by that particular agency. Of the ten or more contracts submitted to prospective new clients, only four will have frequent application to a contemporary recording artist or performing group:

1- *American Federation of Musicians Exclusive Agent-Musician Agreement;*

2- *American Federation of Television and Radio Artists Standard Exclusive Agency Contract;*

3- *American Guild of Variety Artists Exclusive Agency Contract; and*

4- *The talent agency's own "general services and materials agreement." More often than not, this is broken down into two or more separate contracts which cover "materials," services, TV and movie packages and other kinds of entertainment packages.*

Most "general services and materials" agreements cover only those matters not covered by the union contracts listed here. They generally provide that the agency serve as the artist's advisor and representative in respect to the artist's activity and participation in such fields as "merchandising, testimonials and commercial tie-ups." The general services contract that has been used by the William Morris Agency, one of the world's oldest and largest, provides that the artist's approval is required prior to the agency committing the artist, that the agreement can be terminated if the agency can't find work for the artist for four consecutive months, that any disputes are to be referred to the Labor Commissioner of the state of California, that the agreement shall not negatively affect any union contracts involving the artist, and that the agency has the right to assign the contract to a third party.

A full-service agency "general materials and packages" contract covers the artist's involvement in creative properties (scripts, scenarios and packaged shows, e.g., for television and film). But it is standard practice in the industry for agreements of this kind to exclude professional activity as a composer. Accordingly, the artist's income from music publishing is also excluded.

Changing Representation — Artists frequently change agencies in the hope that new representation will further their careers. Large agencies are often criticized for neglecting the individual artist unless he is a star of some magnitude. Many lesser names feel they get lost in the shuffle of a big company attempting to find work for its huge stables. The major booking companies are aware of these negative views of their operations and attempt to offer each of their clients the personal attention of at least one particular agent on their staff who is assigned to keep the artist working and happy. The AFM agency franchise agreement *requires* that the firm name the specific individual agents who are to handle the affairs of the musician under contract.

Agents, like performers, are mobile. They frequently change companies or break off and set up their own firms. If the agent has performed well, his leaving causes consternation in the company, because the firm loses continuity of contracts and probably a lot of goodwill among talent buyers. The departure of a popular agent also is upsetting, to say the least, to the particular group of artists he was handling for the company. Often, personal relationships and confidences are built up between agent and artist. When the agent leaves, it is a common occurrence for those artists to seek relief from their contracts with the company, declaring their intention of following that agent, wherever he may go. The agency is reluctant to terminate a contract with a valuable client and might refuse to release him. A court battle may ensue. In general, in these kinds of altercations the courts have tended to find for the artist, recognizing that in the employment field, the element of personal relationships is entitled to special consideration.

REGULATION OF AGENTS

The public may have acquired its acquaintances with booking agents largely through watching show biz movies on the late show. Some of the colorful characterizations might lead one to believe that the only qualifications needed by an agent are a tolerance for cigar smoke and a pair of alligator shoes. The field is still inhabited by Damon Runyan-type characters. Many buyers and sellers of talent are convinced there is no such thing as an honest agent — that too many of them talk faster than they can deliver.

Statutory Regulation — Agents and artist managers proliferated early in this century with the rapid growth of the movie industry. In the early days, agents' abuses of performers were widespread: wages would be skimmed or never paid; collusion between agents and employers would occur. Artists would be dispatched long distances to jobs that never existed. In that agents became particularly active in the early days of the film industry, California was one of the first states to attempt to regulate them. Following first attempts in 1913 to regulate employment agencies, California enacted its Labor Code in 1937. This code made a distinction between "motion picture employment agencies" and agents active primarily in booking vaudeville acts, circus performers and actors for the legitimate stage.

In 1943 California added a new category, "artist's manager." In 1967 California repealed substantial portions of its Labor Code. "Theatrical employment agencies" and "Motion picture employment agencies" were eliminated as separate categories. But the "artist's manager" category was retained and placed under the jurisdiction of the Labor Commissioner of the Department of Industrial Relations. "Employment agency" provisions were shifted to the jurisdiction of what is now the Department of Consumer Affairs.

In 1978 California altered its artists manager statute, the principal change being one of nomenclature: "artists managers" were subsequently to be known as "talent agents."

Because of widespread abuse of artists by agents in the past, California laws today severely limit the activities of all persons involved in artist representation. Procurement of employment for artists and entertainers in California is strongly regulated by two state statutes — the *Talent Agencies Act* of 1978 and the *Employment Agency Act.*

Simply stated, all persons engaged in the procurement, or attempt of procurement, of employment of an artist must be licensed by the state to do so. Any contract can be vitiated by the state where an individual engaged in procuring employment lacks the required state license.

Union Regulation — In addition to state laws governing persons engaged in agency activity, talent agents are restricted severely on a national basis by the various performers unions and guilds. The organizations most involved here are the American Federation of Musicians (AFM), the American Federation of Television and Recording Artists (AFTRA), the American Guild of Variety Artists (AGVA), the American

Guild of Musical Artists (AGMA), and the Screen Actors Guild (SAG).

Artists' guilds and unions vary in what they require when they franchise or license a talent agent. But the following requirements are typical of most agreements:

1- *Maximum allowable commissions are stipulated. For example, AFTRA and SAG apply only a 10 percent ceiling on commissions applied to the artist's gross compensation. Artists are not permitted to pay both an agent and a manager more than an aggregate total of 10 percent.*

   The AFM allows a 20 percent commission on one night gigs, 15 percent if the job runs two days, usually 10 percent on jobs running three days or longer. Under certain circumstances the AFM will allow an additional 5 percent commission on engagements where the musician's wages equal or exceed twice the minimum union scale. Sometimes the agent is exempt from these ceilings if he has under contract only one other musical artist.

2- *AFM, AFTRA and SAG generally franchise only those agents who agree to limit their professional activity to procurement of employment for artists. This constraint is unreasonable in that the most successful and influential professionals in the entertainment industry are active concurrently in other entertainment industry enterprises such as management, production, publishing, and recording.*

3- *Lengths of contracts are limited. AFTRA allows a maximum term of three years. Under certain conditions, SAG limits its members to contracts of one year's duration.*

MANAGERS

The arts and entertainment industries engage a number of different kinds of managers. The most influential among them is the artist's personal manager. No facet of the business is so bereft of fully competent individuals. The reason is simple: they are supposed to know everything and do everything. Personal managers are expected to perform tasks ranging from negotiating million-dollar contracts to picking up the star's laundry.

In the present chapter the discussion of personal managers is limited to how they are regulated by state statutes and artists unions. In the following chapter treatment is given, in some detail, to the manner in which management contracts are negotiated and how managers advance the careers of their clients.

REGULATION OF MANAGERS

Regulation of artist's personal managers is most strict in the state of California. Since many management contracts are negotiated there, an understanding of California's regulation of managers will be most useful.

Statutory Regulation — As pointed out earlier in this chapter, in California the only person allowed to procure employment for an artist is one who is licensed as a talent agent. While personal managers are supposed to be principally concerned with advising and counseling their clients about their careers, they often become involved, directly or indirectly, in procuring jobs for their clients. Procurement of employment is supposed to be the responsibility of talent agents, but personal managers can rarely separate themselves totally from the talent agent's activities.

The California statute does not permit a personal manager to become involved *even indirectly* in procuring employment for an artist. Rulings of the California Labor Commission have held that *any* such activity of this kind by an unlicensed person is against the law.

If the personal manager wants to stay within the law and remain in the management profession, he can opt to take out a talent agent's license. But then the individual would have to function under the constraints imposed by artists unions on talent agents. If the manager decides against becoming a licensed talent agent, he has other options:

1- *The manager may voluntarily forego his commissions on all employment procured by a talent agent. But California's Labor Commission has ruled this ploy is but a camouflage for what is really going on.*

2- *The manager may go into partnership with the artist. Both parties may find this unattractive, however, in that they are exposed to liability for their partner's actions.*

3- *The manager may "employ" the artist exclusively and supply his services to third parties. This might serve the manager's interests, but will seriously disadvantage the artist by imposing restrictions on his activities that could go well beyond the terms normally encountered in a regular management agreement.*

4- *The personal manager might set up a corporation which would "deliver" the artist's services to third parties. This setup has not been fully tested by the courts. Some lawyers believe it may offer the best insulation available from the constraints of talent agent licensing requirements.*

Next to California, the state that hosts the greatest number of personal management contract negotiations is New York. That state offers a more congenial environment for these proceedings than California. New York avoids the issue of licensing personal managers, in that it defines theatrical agencies (bookers) as those who procure employment *other than incidental* to the manager-artist relationship. This would appear to exclude personal managers, in that the procurement activity most of them engage in *is* incidental.

Union Regulation — Personal managers of good reputation could obtain a franchise from an artists union, but they would then fall under regulations far more constricting than they could tolerate. The unions would impose a ceiling on their commissions, the term of their contracts with clients would be shorter, and they would probably be required by the franchise to engage in employment procurement activity full-time *and not engage in other business activities concurrently.* Few managers could function under these restrictions, in that it is the very nature of the business for them to be involved at any given time in a number of entertainment business activities, particularly publishing and recording.

The personal manager in California has one other option: he might take out a union franchise, then ignore the union's restraints. This is a temptation, in that unions rarely enforced these rules. But ignoring union rules can be risky; no one can predict when the union might start enforcing its franchising agreements. Some California lawyers have publicly stated, however, that they believe this union-ignoring ploy may still be the personal manager's most attractive option to avoid the overriding power of the state's Labor Commission.

The end result of statutory and union constraints on personal managers is that, in California at least, many established and respectable personal managers opt against both state licensing and union franchising,[2] choosing instead to be guided by their own conception of ethical professional practices.

CONFERENCE OF PERSONAL MANAGERS

The recognized professional association in the field is the Conference of Personal Managers. CPM has about 100 members in its New York City-based Conference of Personal Managers East, and about the same number in Los Angeles in its Conference of Personal Managers West. While CPM does not represent the majority of professionals in the field, it includes many of the most powerful ones.

CPM has attempted to establish ethical standards of conduct for the profession. Probably its greatest influence has been through CPM's promulgation of its "standard" contracts. An objective study of them could draw only one conclusion: they are heavily weighted in favor of the manager. A number of experienced lawyers have publicly stated that the contract CPM most often uses is not only one-sided, but seriously flawed from a legal standpoint.

2-Nelville L. Johnson and Daniel Webb Lang. "The Personal Manager in the California Entertainment Industry," p. 175. *Music Industry: Negotiations and the Law* (Toronto 1980: Board of Governors, York University).

Phalen G. Hurewitz of the Beverly Hills law firm of Cooper, Epstein, Hurewitz and Mark has written that, in the standard CPM contract, the commitment the personal manager makes to the artist is ". . . indefinite and uncertain . . .," that other sections are ". . . incongruous . . .," and that ". . . a court could conclude that the manager's duties under the contract are too indefinite and conditional to constitute consideration and that the contract is not enforceable . . ."[3] Hurewitz further asserts that the manager's commitment is so indefinite and vague, there is ". . . no mutuality of obligation and that the contract is illusory."[4]

Super-aggressive lawyers and clients risk coming up with "contracts of adhesion." Hurewitz warns negotiators: "To the extent that a management contract provides for an exorbitant commission rate in conjunction with the general power of attorney and the otherwise all-encompassing effect of additional provisions in the personal management contract, it may be argued by an artist that it is a contract of adhesion, i.e., 'a standard contract which, imposed and drafted by the party of superior bargaining strength, relegates to the subscribing party only the opportunity to adhere to the contract or reject it.' "[5] Hurewitz goes on to point out that such contracts, e.g., in the insurance field, have been modified or nullified in actions of enforcement.[6]

Lawyers and courts have viewed personal management contracts as involving laws governing *principal-agency* relationships. Where the parties have relatively equal bargaining power, the normal principal-agency type of agreement would set forth the conditions under which the principal *employs* the agent. Hurewitz believes that a personal management contract that is not in line with laws regulating principal-agency relationships may be seriously flawed.[7]

For a different approach to the personal management agreement, see the following chapter.

ASSISTANTS TO MANAGEMENT

Few artists' managers attempt to travel regularly with their clients and assign such duties to a road manager. They handle the transportation of people and equipment, arrange for meals and lodging, supervise sound reinforcement and lighting personnel, check box office receipts and collect performance income. Contrary to show business legend, road managers are usually too busy to take time to procure fringe benefits — booze, drugs and sex — for the performers and hangers-

---

3-Phalen G. Hurewitz. "Personal Management Agreement: Analysis and Commentary," p. 67, *Representing Musical Artists: Legal, Business and Practical Aspects* (USC Law Center 1975: Entertainment Law Institute).

4-Hurewitz, p. 66.

5-Op. cit., p. 85.

6-Ibid.

7-Ibid.

on. Road managers who learn the business and know how to hustle often graduate to artist management jobs. Some have become producers.

Many young people break into "show business" by signing on as "roadies," the label often used to describe persons hired to move equipment and help set it up. While some roadies possess expertise in such areas as lighting or sound, the majority of them seem to learn what is expected of them on the job.

The people hired on as road crew members usually earn minimum salaries plus their travel expenses. But traveling acts have no difficulty locating an adequate supply of individuals willing to work for low wages and high adventure.

Whether the individual is a recording artist or some other kind of professional in the field, when his income reaches a respectable level, other support personnel will be required to advance the career. This is treated in the chapter on artist management.

Herbie Hancock at the Arp 2600 synthesizer.

ATTORNEYS

Entertainment business attorneys hold positions of great power in the industry. Part of this power has come about by default. In the earlier years of the business, most executives, agents and managers lacked the education and background to run big companies and handle the affairs of millionaire clients. Even today, executives lacking strong backgrounds in business management and business law keep their lawyers close at hand to protect them against unwise decisions and flawed contracts.

As in the fields of music, theatre and broadcast journalism, law schools are turning out at least twice as many graduates as we seem to need. We already have about 470,000 lawyers in this country. In addition, we have some 130,000 students in law school (of which about 30 percent are women). Despite the fact that unemployment (or underemployment) among graduates now emerging from law schools is estimated at about 30 percent, *we have an actual shortage of lawyers fully qualified to practice in the entertainment field.* We have several dozen lawyers well-informed on copyright, but some of these practitioners get their clients into trouble when they attempt to hold their own in negotiations with a publishing company or record label.

The most experienced lawyers in copyright are found in Washington, D.C., New York City and Beverly Hills. The best-qualified lawyers in general music business practice are found in the three recording centers in the United States. In Canada, there is a handful of entertainment and sports industry lawyers practicing in Toronto and Montreal. Nationally, we probably have some 200 to 300 attorneys who limit their practice exclusively to music business matters, trademarks and patents (the prevailing legal specialization).

DEFINITIONS — A **lawyer** is defined by Black[8] as "a person learned in the law; as an attorney, counsel, or solicitor; a person licensed to practice law."

An **attorney in fact** (Black)[9] is "a private attorney authorized by another to act in his place and stead, either for some particular purpose, as to do a particular act, or for the transaction of business in general, not of a legal character. This authority is conferred by an instrument in writing, called a "letter of attorney," or more commonly a "power of attorney."

An **attorney at law** (Black) is "an advocate, counsel, or official agent employed in preparing, managing, and trying cases in the courts."[10]

RETAINING LEGAL COUNSEL

While lawyers expert in the entertainment industry are in short supply, it is possible to locate a qualified legal counselor. How can a person go about this task? These questions might be asked:

1- *What is the prospective attorney's reputation, and what is the source of your information? Is it objective? The fact that a lawyer has passed the state bar examination and offers all the appearances of respectability is insufficient reason for complete trust. The law profession has its share of crooks. The great*

8-*Black's Law Dictionary*, rev. 4th ed. (Chicago 1968: West Publishing Co.).

9-Ibid.

10-In Canada and the United Kingdom, appellations for legal practitioners differ from usage in the United States.

majority are trustworthy, but check out your prospective legal counsel with as many persons as you can.

2- *Is the prospective lawyer sufficiently experienced in the music field to look out for the musician's interests in publishing, recording, performance rights and foreign rights?*

3- *Is the prospective lawyer well-informed in copyright?*

Yet another way to check out lawyers is through the American Bar Association. But asking the local ABA for referrals will rarely be helpful outside those cities where the recording industry flourishes.

In addition to negotiating contracts, an attorney often can provide tax counseling, investment counseling, collect money, negotiate property settlements and settle disputes. In the last mentioned role, lawyers generally agree that the most skillful among them manage, whenever possible, to settle disputes without resorting to litigation.

Some clients retain attorneys primarily for their inside connections in the industry. A number of well-established music industry lawyers have told me they prefer to limit their practices to legal services and try to avoid performing the work of agents.[11]

Payment Options — One of the universal complaints against lawyers is their cost. Fees are generally so high that many individuals in need of counsel have to forego the service. But when legal services are imperative, the client has a number of payment options.

The usual arrangement is paying an hourly fee. Before running up a bill, the prospective client should simply ask the lawyer, in an exploratory meeting, what he charges. If ongoing legal services are needed, the client may place his lawyer on a monthly retainer.

An alternative to these payment procedures is the *contingent payment* plan, which is common in the entertainment industry. The client pays a relatively low hourly rate (often about one-half of the regular rate), provided the gross compensation payable to the lawyer in any calendar month is not less than a specified percentage of the client's gross earnings. Some contingent fee arrangements call for no immediate monthly retainer fee, the lawyer's compensation being deferred until the client's income attains a prescribed level. In this kind of arrangement, the lawyer might, in addition, demand a percentage of the client's gross income, often set at 5 percent to 7.5 percent. Some lawyers charge as much as 15 percent.

Are contingent fee deals ethical? Yes, under certain conditions, according to the American Bar Association's *Code of Professional Responsibility* (1970) and opinions expressed by various state bar associations and state supreme courts. But they are considered ethical, as a rule, only where a contingent fee arrangement is "to the advantage

---

11-Clients often expect their attorneys to use their contacts in the industry to promote audition tapes. Attorneys seem to find this task distasteful and believe this kind of selling job transcends the role of legal counselor.

of the client" and where the client may otherwise have no way to get legal services or was unable to pay a fixed fee.

When the client is a production company or film producer, the lawyer might "participate" — a term used in the industry to describe sharing in an investment in a project or a company. A "participating" attorney might charge no legal fee, but "take points" instead — receive a percentage of the profits, if any.

How much is a lawyer entitled to charge for his services? State bar associations publish guidelines for their members.[12] Professional ethics call for lawyers to follow them.

Legal Status — When an attorney accepts a client, one of his first tasks in many entertainment industry situations is to determine the client's legal status. In his business and legal relationships, will the client be best served by being "self-employed," a partner, proprietor, independent contractor — or would his interests be better served by forming a corporation or taking part in joint ventures? The client (the "client" may be a group of persons) will need the lawyer to explain the advantages and disadvantages of those options. And the music industry moves so rapidly, the legal status that worked well at the outset will almost certainly change with changing conditions.

Contract Negotiations — As pointed out, nearly all significant events in the entertainment industry involve the negotiation of contracts. And that is the business of lawyers. The number and kinds of contracts commonly used in the Industry is extensive. Typical agreements:

> *Composer* with a publisher, coauthor
>
> *Performer* with employer, agent, promoter, producer, contractor, performing group, lawyer, broadcaster, merchandiser, advertising agency
>
> *Producer* with a record company, performer, recording studio, production company, publisher, distributor, merchandiser, lawyer
>
> *Talent Agent* with a performer, promoter, club owner, producer, production company, record company, film company, lawyer
>
> *Artists Personal Manager* with an artist, record company, broadcaster, accountant, auditor, road manager

The Adversary Relationship — Individuals entering into contract negotiations are, by definition, adversaries. They may be the best of friends. But once they start negotiating a legal agreement, the parties should seek every legitimate advantage available. Contract negotiations need not be unfriendly encounters, but the parties are advised by their attorneys, as a rule, to go for whatever they can rightly get.

12-The California State Bar's *Rules of Professional Conduct* are typical: *A member of the State Bar shall not enter into an agreement for, charge or collect an illegal or unconscionable fee . . . when it is so exorbitant and wholly disproportionate to the service as to shock the conscience of lawyers of ordinary prudence practicing in the same community."*

Each individual entering into contract negotiations should have separate legal counsel. When one lawyer attempts to represent both parties, he may have difficulty serving them impartially. The American Bar Association's *Code of Professional Responsibility* and most state bar associations' codes of ethics assert that lawyers should not represent adversaries and should urge prospective clients to retain their own attorneys.

Independent legal counsel is particularly important in situations where collateral contracts are entered into simultaneously, e.g., an artist-manager contract and an artist-manager-publisher deal. If one of the parties to these collateral contracts happens to be a lawyer himself (very common in the industry), the potential exposures to conflicts of interest can be overwhelming. Disputes can rise out of collateral contracts. When they do, courts have sometimes found that a lawyer had taken advantage of the client's ignorance and subsequently determined that one or more of the contracts were unenforceable.

In light of this exposure of lawyers to potential conflicts of interest, they sometimes prefer to loan one of the parties money to retain independent counsel. In such a circumstance, the lawyer would carefully document such a transaction, identifying the purpose for which the loan was made.

Extralegal Services — Clients frequently ask their attorneys to recommend agents and managers. In that the good ones are in short supply, the attorney is usually hard-pressed to name qualified people. The client then often asks his lawyer to manage his career and his business. Lawyers frequently agree to do this, often protesting that the arrangement is to be only temporary. But then an interesting thing often occurs: the lawyer-manager starts making more money in that capacity than he does just practicing law. This outcome is frequent when a lawyer agrees to administer the client's publishing company. A lawyer attempting to provide a client two different kinds of professional service exposes himself to conflicts of interest. Among the sharpest critics of these practices have been lawyers themselves.

Bar associations state that lawyers shall not enter into a business transaction with a client or knowingly acquire a financial interest in an artist's enterprise potentially adverse to the client unless the transaction

> ... is fair and reasonable to the client and fully disclosed and transmitted in writing to the client in a manner and terms which should have reasonably been understood by the client ... and the client is given reasonable opportunity to seek advice of independent counsel of the client's choice on the transaction ... and the client consents in writing thereto.[13]

If a lawyer provides extralegal services and enters into business or investment deals with a client, legal ethics demand that he always conduct himself *as a lawyer.* A lawyer cannot ethically switch hats. He cannot ethically operate his law practice and a publishing company or

---

13-Op. cit. "Ethical Constraints on Contingent Fee Arrangements," p. 15.

management company as nominally distinct businesses; he cannot ethically engage in extralegal activities to feed his law practice. If the lawyer offers extralegal services, ethics of his profession demand that he always handle himself in accord with the ethical and legal constraints imposed on him *as a licensed attorney-at-law.*

Termination — The law provides that a client can discharge his lawyer at any time.[14] But some courts have held that the discharge of a lawyer does not necessarily discharge a former client's liability. For example, dismissing an attorney where a contingent fee arrangement is in place can become sticky for the client. In this kind of situation, the former client will probably have to continue paying the attorney, after disengagement, on earnings flowing from contracts negotiated before the parties went separate ways.

Whether or not a contingent fee is involved, a client who discharges his lawyer should send written notice of termination. Where the artist is retaining a new attorney, his former attorney should be asked, in the notice of termination, to forward all material in the client's file to the new lawyer. Bar associations view this kind of procedure as a matter of professional courtesy.

14-*Code of Civil Procedure,* Section 284.

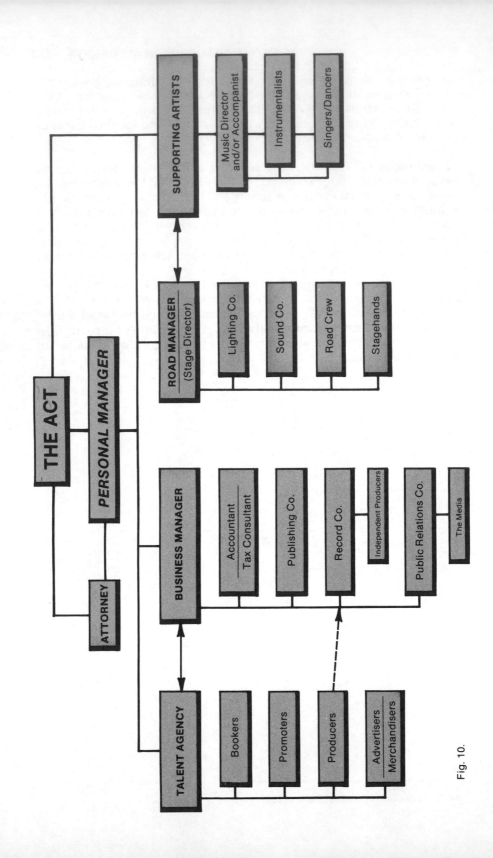

Fig. 10.

10

ARTIST MANAGEMENT

Management, too, is an art.
MOZART'S FATHER (AND MANAGER)

In the preceding chapter, personal management was discussed only from the standpoint of *regulation* by state statutes and artists' unions. In this chapter, financial relationships and the manager's functions in advancing the artist's[1] career will be examined. This part of our study closes with an examination of how the manager and his client might negotiate an equitable personal management contract.

How important is a good manager? Ask a record company. Most labels today won't even sign an artist who lacks good management. They believe it just isn't worth it to invest their time and money in an artist whose career, even his daily activities, are not thoughtfully planned. Record companies are no longer prepared to tolerate irresponsible behavior of stars, uncoordinated concert tours, inept promotional support, so often areas of concern with artists lacking competent management. Some labels will help an artist locate a good manager. Undirected talent, unfocused careers are commonplace in the music business. These performers may get lucky and land on the charts for a few weeks. But they quickly fade into oblivion, like thousands before them who lacked firm, knowledgeable management.

At what point does an artist need a manager? *About the time he discovers he can earn more than union scale;* suddenly he is in need of someone to handle his business affairs and develop his career. This can be a difficult time in an artist's life, because he soon discovers that it is

---

1-In this chapter, references to *artists* and *stars* is meant to include, not only performers, but other professionals who, from time to time, engage personal managers, e.g., writers, producers, directors, choreographers, etc.

often impossible to locate anyone qualified to do this. The reason for the acute shortage of fully qualified people is that artists' personal managers are supposed to know it all — both the artistic-creative aspects *and* business management.

DISCOVERING EACH OTHER

In searching for a competent personal manager, these qualities and competencies should be sought:

1- *He is well organized, systematic.*

2- *He is straightforward and honest, and has a reputation to prove it.*

3- *He is an effective communicator; he writes well and is an articulate, persuasive oral communicator.*

4- *He knows his limitations: if he lacks competence in certain fields, he won't try to fake his way; he'll hire outside experts when needed.*

5- *He has good industry contacts. If he doesn't, he is busy developing them.*

If a personal manager with these competencies really wants to become a successful personal manager, he will probably make it. And **professionals with this much on the ball will probably earn more money over the years than many of the artists they represent.**

Successful personal managers have one other kind of expertise: they know how to spot a *potential star*. They cannot afford to invest their time and money in anyone who lacks what the manager views as the *potential* talent to reach the top. And until a manager's clients develop strong earnings, there won't be many dollars available to produce commissionable income — the manager's livelihood.

The Personal Relationship — Experienced managers and artists all agree on one issue: the relationship is dependent on strong personal ties of friendship and trust. If that is lacking, the relationship won't last, because the parties must work intimately together on both the personal and professional levels. When a manager and artist are considering joining forces, I recommend they postpone a written agreement and simply "live together" for several months and try to find out if they can work comfortably and effectively together. During this trial period, they should search in each other for everything from horse sense to a capacity to dream. Both may be needed.

THE FINANCIAL RELATIONSHIP

Established personal managers usually insist the artist agree in writing that the manager be authorized to handle all the artist's money — what comes in and what goes out. Such a manager would relent on this important issue only if the responsibility for receipts and disbursements was handled by a business manager selected by the parties. If an artist is fearful of granting his manager complete control over the money, the artist should not sign with that person, for this kind of contract is based on complete mutual trust. If the artist has any feeling he must watch the money, the two have no prospect of a successful professional relationship.

Yet, many artists of stature insist the money be entirely handled by an independent third party — usually a business management firm. It is often a preferable arrangement where an act generates large sums of money.

ACCOUNTING

Whatever arrangements the parties agree upon for business management, the personal manager's first responsibility in this regard is setting up the financial accounting. The astute personal manager will call in the accountants even in the formative stages of contract negotiations to make sure the parties agree on how they are going to control "the count" and report the taxes. The difficulty here is that, even in the entertainment capitals of the world, there are few accounting firms fully knowledgeable in these specialized areas of entertainment and communications industries. For example, a major recording star requires a CPA who understands international tax treaties and the exchange of foreign currencies and fluctuating money markets. Lacking specialized knowledge, an act of international stature can have little confidence that his accountants are protecting him in the worldwide movement of his royalties.

While the personal manager should inform himself on who might be a qualified accountant, the selection of that individual or firm should be approved by the artist. A major act will also need auditors to periodically examine the books, not only of his own manager, but of his publisher and record company. Contracts with these parties must specify under what conditions audits will be acceptable and precisely who will be liable for the auditing expense.[2]

The artist's lawyer will recommend that audits requested by the artist must be undertaken by an individual or firm independent from his management firm.

2-When a major act audits his record company, the expense can run $20,000 to $30,000 per audit.

CONTROLLING EXPENSE

It is not generally understood that a large percentage of working artists incur expenses larger than their incomes. This may be true even of some of the artists the public thinks of as rich and famous. Since the "successful" artist will have to pay out 15 percent to 25 percent of his gross to his manager, another 10 percent or so to his booking agency, perhaps an additional 5 percent to his business manager or accountant, his best hope of realizing a profit on what little is left is to exert stringent control over all other expenses. That responsibility is supposed to devolve upon the manager. But the manager may be in the habit of spending too freely; it isn't his money. The artist's attorney should impose spending constraints on the manager when the management contract is negotiated.[3]

The artist himself is often the one throwing money around and contributing more than the manager to unacceptable expense. If the artist holds the view that those royalties are going to keep rolling in forever, a seasoned manager might persuade the artist to limit himself to a weekly allowance. Show business stories abound on how former stars went through millions only to end up financially destitute. An artist submitting to a modest weekly expense account would increase his chances of surviving the late lean years when no one even remembers his name.

Loans, Investments — The entertainment industry is still overpopulated by artists and managers who have only a dim view of the realities of the rational business world. Despite the increasing numbers of persons working in the field who demonstrate occasional periods of rationality, show business types, artists and managers alike, involve themselves in unsecured loans, huge advances and wild investment schemes. These shenanigans occur, however, among individual practitioners. *The bankers don't participate,* nor do the well-managed publishing and record companies.

But many personal managers find it necessary to loan an act money to keep it alive at least in its developing stage. The manager should demand the contract state he is, however, under no *obligation* to loan money or advance money to the artist, no matter how serious the crisis may be.

MANAGER'S COMMISSION

It is standard practice in the industry for personal managers to earn compensation for their services through commissions on the artist's *gross* income. The equity of this practice is open to question, but managers who know how the business has operated in the past will rarely accept any other arrangement. Their argument is a simple

---

3-Suppliers often try to overcharge entertainment business personalities, apparently assuming that such customers are not bright enough to critically examine their bills.

one — and persuasive: the manager may be the person principally responsible for the rise and fall of his clients' income. The manager invests his time (and often his own money) in getting a career off the ground; he is entitled to participate in the artist's prosperity, should it ever come.

The informed artist's point of view on this issue is set forth in the draft contract appearing later in this chapter.

Going Rates — In recent years, certain "going rates" have become recognized in the industry for personal managers' commissions. They range from a low of 10 percent to a high of 25 percent. Here are some of the factors influencing these rates:

1- *The stature and track record of the manager. A manager with powerful contacts in the industry is worth 25 percent to an artist. If the manager has little or no track record, he should agree to a much lower commission.*

2- *The income of the artist. If the artist has a high income, the manager will come out well even at a relatively low commission rate.*

3- *An established star signed with a strong booking agency may demand his manager reduce his commission on work obtained by that agency.*

4- *The extent of the manager's services. For example, if the manager farms out all business management, accounting services, as well as promotion services, he should not expect to earn top commission rates.*

5- *The sophistication of the parties. In most cases, the manager is experienced and knowledgeable. Most artists, at least early in their careers, are astonishingly naive. When the eager young artist hears "Just sign here, sweetheart. I'm going to make you a big star!" he may even believe it. Sometimes those TV late show movie scripts are not too far off the mark.*

An Argument For Reasonableness — A powerful manager can often get a very high commission even from an act that may be struggling to pay his rent. But if that artist later develops high income, he may well remember the early days and seek to renegotiate those commissions and reduce them to a reasonable level. More likely, the successful artist will be ready to dump his former manager and sign with a less expensive one. The manager who was greedy in the earlier relationship may well have lost an opportunity to come into really good earnings, had he been patient. Managers are well-advised to keep their demands reasonable, because most artists are quick to discontinue association with support personnel, particularly personal managers, who fail to treat them fairly.

Commission Base — Personal manager's commissions are usually based on the artist's gross income from all activity relating to the entertainment industry. In this context, "income" includes, not only wages, but whatever is of value that comes to the artist from the entertainment industry, directly or indirectly, including such sources as royalties, an interest in, or ownership of, a production company, TV package, film, publishing or recording company, stock in a corporation, the right to buy stocks, interest in a partnership, bonuses, even gifts.

*The commission **base** is more important than the commission **level**.* If the artist has a competent, aggressive attorney, and if the personal manager lacks the clout of the artist, the commission base can sometimes be limited to what I call the *adjusted gross income.* An artist negotiating from strength should be able to convince the manager that he is entitled only to a commission based on the artist's *actual* income, not on all the money simply passing through his hands to support other persons and other activities. The pros and cons of this fundamental issue are set forth in the draft contract later in this chapter.

The Money Flow — The artist and his manager may work together successfully for many years. But one day, the relationship will end. As difficult as it may be, they should anticipate the problems of disengagement. Like marriage, an artist-manager partnership is easier to enter into than to leave. When the artist and manager get divorced, they will suffer, not only the wrenching experience of ending a close personal relationship, they will have to negotiate some kind of "property settlement." While a divorcing couple can eventually agree on "who gets the house, who gets the car," etc., the artist and manager have a much more complicated set of financial problems.

The essential difficulty here is that an established act has money flowing in from contracts the manager negotiated, and when the couple disengage (for whatever reason) *that money continues to flow.* Should the departing manager continue to receive commissions therefrom? Some lawyers make the argument that, unless negotiated otherwise, such commissions continue into perpetuity.

The richest source of these funds usually comes from publishing and recording contracts probably worked out by the departing manager during his period of service. Nearly all personal management contracts state the manager is entitled to full commissions on this money, without diminution, for the full term of those contracts. Part of the problem this creates for the artist is encountered when he searches for *new* management. If the artist's major source of income is already tapped for years hence by the old manager, what has a manager to gain by signing on with an act so encumbered with prior commitments?

A Possible Compromise — If we assume the parties possess about equal bargaining strength, one of the simplest compromises available is an *across-the-board de-escalation of commissions* over a year or two following termination of the contract. Figure 10.1 shows how this might work: the old manager continues to enjoy 100 percent of his commissions for the first six months following disengagement from the artist.

ARTIST'S MONEY FLOW TO MANAGERS

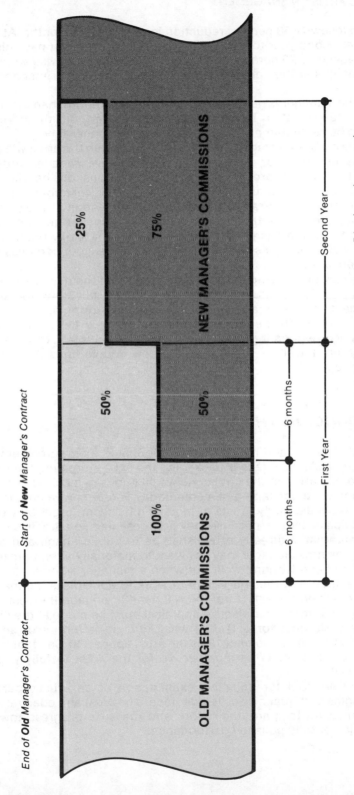

Note — The *new* manager receives 100% commission from the outset on all business *he* generates.

Fig. 10.1

Then follows a 50 percent reduction for the next six months. At the start of the second year following disengagement, the artist pays his former manager only 25 percent of what he would have otherwise earned. After six months at this rate, all commissions to the former manager would end.

If the manager is negotiating from greater strength than the artist, the same de-escalation formula might still be used, but the percentages could be set higher and stretched out over a longer time.

One clear advantage to this de-escalation plan the artist will discover when he scouts for a new manager. If the new manager understands how these games are played, one of the first questions he will put to the artist is "Are you tied up with your former manager for ongoing commissions?" The artist and his lawyer can respond simply, "No more encumbrance here than usual; my former manager gets commissions on a diminishing scale for 18 months; then I'm totally unencumbered. As my old manager's commissions de-escalate, your commissions rise. Fair enough?"

The accompanying graphic also shows that the *new* manager earns 100 percent commissions on all *new* deals he sets up for the artist.

One final advantage of a de-escalation formula: if the second manager accepts the plan suggested here, the parties should have little difficulty negotiating a similar de-escalation plan for the second manager as well — when even the *new* couple finds it necessary to disengage.

PRODUCING THE ACT

Once the artist and manager have negotiated their agreement, one of the first tasks they face is packaging the act — creating the presentation of the artist to the public. As we all know, in a consumer-oriented economy the packaging of a commodity is often more important than what is inside. Many artists of modest gifts seem to get by well in the marketplace largely because they are presented so attractively.

If an artist is already established as to public image and personal style, the new manager may not want to materially alter a presentation that has been working well. But when a manager signs on a relatively new act, both parties have a lot of work to do. Unless the manager is fully qualified himself (rare), he will need to engage the best help the artist can afford. An objective appraisal must be made at the outset on these basic questions: 1) Just what kind of performer or act do we have? 2) To what audience does the artist appeal? 3) Can that audience be expanded? 4) What must we do for the artist to fully exploit his potential?

A useful tool for objective examination of an artist's performing strengths and weaknesses is videotape. The artist and coaches can use this medium to guide their work and measure progress toward the creation of truly polished performances.

In addition to engaging voice coaches, choreographers, costumers, etc., the manager who takes the long view of his client's career will probably want to provide dramatic training, too. Nearly all musical performers who reach national prominence eventually receive opportunities to play dramatic roles.

Some managers provide important assistance to their clients when they have the ability to identify good musical material. As pointed out, few artists — including those who write much of their own material — ever seem to have a sufficient supply of high-quality songs. The manager may have to take his turn listening to demos and helping search out usable material. The act may also need "special material," songs and patter and routines created exclusively for that artist. Practically all stars booked into Las Vegas consider special material essential to a big-time presentation.

Coordinating The Elements — If the act has been fully prepared, the next move is to place it onstage, under flattering lighting, in an appropriate setting. Now the manager becomes a theatrical *producer.* If he can't handle this task, he should engage someone who can. Major acts often tour with their own stage directors who supervise lighting, staging and sound.

If the artist is cast in a touring Broadway show, he will be part of a company that travels, not only with its own sets, but its own lights, control board, audio system, even flooring.

Programming — Experienced managers representing powerful acts control the selection of opening and supporting acts, making sure that the headliner comes on at the best possible time and under the most advantageous circumstances. From the early days of vaudeville, headliners insisted on warm-up acts to preheat the audience. This sequencing of acts is called *programming* and the manager must control it when he can. If the manager's client is to be introduced by an M.C. or some other person, the manager must make sure the introducer says the right things and says them briefly. A windy M.C. can kill an act before he invites it onstage. In the pop field, touring recording artists are frequently introduced by a local disc jockey. DJs are among the worst offenders in offering overextended introductions; managers should try some tactful way of asking the announcer to be brief, then get off. More frequently, this task falls to the road manager.

ADVANCING THE CAREER

The manager's main responsibility is advancing the careers of the artists in his stable. His reputation — and his income — depend upon how effectively he does this. A first-rate manager will design and execute *a complete campaign* for each artist. In this effort, he *starts with people,* with personalities, not organizations. Top managers develop extensive lists of key personnel in the industry. Most of these potential contacts will never be used. But when a manager must move quickly — which is most of the time — an up-to-date list of power brokers will prove essential.

Since he probably operates out of one of the recording and publishing centers, he will find out who the decision-makers are in the most active companies. He will get the names of the important agents, promoters and industry lawyers. The music industry is a giant, but only a few hundred individuals have positions of real power. Many of this group of decision-makers know each other on a first-name basis. They rub shoulders together at industry conferences; they exchange information; they return each other's telephone calls; they trade favors. They even exchange jobs. When a manager is negotiating with one record company, the competing record companies for that contract have probably heard, privately, about what each side is offering. So the experienced manager discovers there are few secrets in the business at the top level. This inner circle of powerful people know who the con artists are, who will keep his word, who can deliver. ·

How does a new manager crack this inner circle? By demonstrating his credibility and his competence.

The artist's manager must also develop good contacts throughout the country where his clients will perform. He must get the names of the top disc jockeys in major cities, the important promoters and agents. If he has time, he may also develop a list of key personnel in branch offices of record labels with whom his clients are under contract.

CARE AND FEEDING OF THE MEDIA

In executing a campaign to exploit an artist, the manager must develop contacts (and friends) with the purveyors of mass communications-particularly the press and broadcast media. This would include wire service reporters, feature writers, syndicated columnists — and the "music press" — the writers and publications focusing on personalities in the music and entertainment fields. They are not difficult to contact, in that they are looking to artists, managers and publicists to feed them information.

Materials — When contact is made, the manager must feed his sources with appropriate material. This is usually done with press kits or "promo packs." They are expensive to assemble but essential to a publicity campaign. Depending on budget and circumstances, promo packets will often contain canned press releases, 8 X 10-inch photographs ("glossies" suitable for reproduction), perhaps 8 X 10-inch four-color photographs of the artist in performance; sample records and tapes, including videotapes; perhaps additional gift items and novelties. If a record company is involved, a major promotion will often include a material object (a novelty of some kind) that ties in with a new record release. The manager or the artist's publicist will help in getting these kits and trinkets to the press, disc jockeys, radio program directors, perhaps to the employees of record distributors and retail outlets.

Interviews — Managers have learned one of the most economical techniques to generate strong publicity for a touring artist is to set up telephone interviews in advance of the artist's arrival. Telephone interviews can be used in large cities when an artist lacks time to cover all the major broadcasting stations.

As the artist travels across the country, the manager or his representative will set up press conferences. Most reporters and cameraman are dispatched to these events by their assignment editors; they will appear where they are assigned to cover a story. But free-lancers and stringers can often be persuaded to cover a press conference when free food and drink are announced as available following the press conference. When the budget allows, some press conferences are planned as press *parties*. Enterprising publicists can often induce the press to show up for these happy hours even when the artist is relatively unknown (media personnel seem ever alert to offers of free nourishment and libation).

In addition to press conferences, a manager or publicist can arrange for *exclusive* interviews. If a syndicated columnist or network TV host can be lined up, one interview or guest shot of this kind can yield more good PR than a hundred open press conferences.

Artists managers rarely attempt to handle all the PR for their clients and often retain a publicity firm to assist. Services of these companies can run from $100-a-week retainers to perhaps $3500 a month, depending on the services required and the track record of the supplier. Competition among publicists is keen. In their effort to produce maximum attention, professional flacks will sometimes resort to outrageous publicity schemes. The media and the public may actually enjoy a crazy hype for a while. But it is the personal manager's responsibility to rein in PR types when they try too often to substitute promotion gimmicks for campaigns based on something approximating reality.

Billing — From the early days of the entertainment industry, it has been standard practice for managers and promoters to control what professionals call *billing*. Billing has to do with the size, emphasis and position of artists' names in print ads and screen credits. If an artist ranks as a "star," his name is set *above* the name of the production — in large, bold type.[4] If the artist is a "co-star," his name will appear *below* the name of the production, and in type smaller than that used for the star. If the artist is a "featured" player, his billing will be much less prominent and relegated to an inferior position in the layout.

As the manager's client gains prestige, he must be attentive to the possibilities of negotiating for increasingly prominent billing. An astute manager will occasionally accept a lower fee for his client if the billing is strong.[5]

CONTROLLING PERFORMANCES

One of the personal manager's most useful services is controlling his client's performance opportunities. Once a career gains momentum, it is not unusual for the artist to receive more offers to perform than he can handle. Both the artist and the manager are tempted to maximize income and accept every gig in sight. But it is the manager's responsibility to limit the frequency of performances to avoid exhausting the artist's energies and to avoid overexposure of the act. The manager will be particularly concerned with travel times between engagements.

As important as determining the frequency of performances, is the selection of the *kinds* of engagement offers. The sharp manager understands his artist's unique identity and the nature of the artist's audience. Insensitive talent agents and tasteless producers will offer the manager job opportunities from time to time that are totally unsuitable. The money might appear attractive, but miscasting an artist and placing him on a bill where the audience might have different tastes can do more harm than good for a career.

In addition to controlling the frequency and kind of job offers to accept, the manager must determine when his client is "ready." For

---

4-Similar billings are used for producers, writers and directors, etc. Some are so prestigious (or have invested so much money) that they receive star billing — their names positioned above the title of the production.

5-Contracts often specify billings in terms of relative *percentages*. For example, an artist might demand his name never be printed less than 50 percent as large as the production title — or an artist's musical director might require his name appear 25 percent as large as the artist's name. These kinds of billings can be readily observed on Las Vegas hotel billboards.

example, if the performer is primarily a singer and the job offer also requires acting, the manager, in consultation with his client, should try to determine before they sign, whether the artist can handle the role, whether the script is "right" and whether the production will be of respectable quality.

LANDING A RECORDING CONTRACT

Most young performers today find it impossible to graduate to the big time without a record contract. This has not always been true. In earlier decades, a performer might acquire a national following through such media as network radio, television, the movies, Broadway, even vaudeville in the old days. Most of our famous older stars gained fame and wealth through this kind of exposure. Today, they sell few records, but might get $100,000 a week as Las Vegas headliners.

The music business today revolves around the turntable. A new act will find it difficult to get jobs, for example, in broadcasting or film *before he has made it on records.* Personal managers of even limited experience understand this, and consider their most important responsibility is to somehow land record contracts for their clients. Many performers engage a manager *primarily for this purpose.* Occasionally, the artist's attorney will recommend that his client engage the personal manager *only if the manager can, indeed, secure a record deal.* No record contract, no personal management agreement. To most aspiring young performers, a personal manager has little to offer unless he can deliver at this level.

Even if we assume the artist in question has great talent, the manager will usually have a difficult task gaining the serious attention of an established record company. As pointed out earlier in this book, major labels commonly invest $150,000 and more to produce a debut album, and at least that much and more in promoting it. So the manager must somehow persuade a record company to invest something like a quarter of a million dollars on this unknown artist — and that amount of money is required just to get the recording career *started.*

Prospects for the manager's success in landing a record contract for a client will probably be determined by the answers to these kinds of questions:

- *How strong are the manager's contacts in the industry?*

- *How strong, how unique is the artist's talent? Is there star potential there?*

- *Is the manager's approach timely? Is the label signing anyone at this time? Is the record company undersupplied or oversupplied with artists who perform somewhat in the vein of the manager's client?*

> • *Does the record company believe in the manager? The label may love the artist but lack confidence in the manager's ability to deliver.*

The Process — Let us assume that the manager is fully qualified and is respected in the industry. Let us further assume he represents an artist who has star potential. Here is the sequence of events that might yield the securing of a record contract:

1- The manager makes a frontal attack on the label itself. If he can't gain the attention of the top decision-makers, he works on the next level down. Record companies are infested with hundreds of employees trying to make points with the boss. If a label employee, whatever his position, can participate in his company's discovering a new star, that employee believes his career will prosper. Among the lower-level contacts the manager might pursue are promotion people and field personnel for the label. The alert ones are on the lookout for new talent.

2- The manager will try to work with his client's publisher. Major publishing executives have excellent contacts with label executives and independent producers.

3- The manager fails to reach the attention of record companies and focuses on independent producers and production companies. The best of these have direct contact with record labels. The manager may determine an offer from a record production company looks more attractive than signing directly with a label; the production company may be able to present its services and the artist's services as a package to some record company. It happens often.

4- The manager arranges for third parties to catch the artist in performance — or watch a videotape demo. If some respected individual in the industry tells a friend (who tells a friend . . .) he has heard a great new talent, the word may get back to a decision-maker at some record company. Word-of-mouth may turn out to be as effective as knocking on doors.

The Result — If the manager should fail to get his client a record contract after two or three years effort, the artist may be destined to remain in the small time — unless he can find a place in some other sector of the entertainment industry. But let's assume the manager succeeds in persuading a record company to negotiate a contract. What is a "good" contract? How much dare be asked? Is the label excited and ready to get behind the new act with strong promotion and lots of money?

Let's assume the next step: the contract is signed; everyone is happy. At the moment, that is. Now the manager must badger the label to promote the records. If the effort is halfhearted, the artist's records may never gain airplay or reach the retailers. At this moment, the manager's greatest service will be *prodding the label to perform on the contract,* to deliver what was agreed. His efforts in this direction can never stop.

Let's make one more assumption in this scenario: the record label fulfills its promises of promotion and the records sell very well. Now the artist has so much money rolling in, he may say to the manager, "My friends tell me your commission is out of line. I want to renegotiate our contract. Your new rate is now 10 percent, not 25 percent. If that is unacceptable, I will sign with this other management company that will probably do more for me — and for a lower commission than I've been paying you." This kind of scenario is not uncommon. Personal managers may struggle for years establishing an act. Their biggest problem may turn out to be success: when their clients start coming into really big money, they may defect to a manager who had nothing to do with building the act to high income status.

Why do otherwise bright people go into the personal management field? Probably because the really competent managers continue to be in high demand, and they often seem able to develop sufficient loyalty among their clients to be in on the receiving end when careers prosper. These kinds of managers can become millionaires.

NEGOTIATING FOR APPEARANCES

Once a manager has developed a successful artist, other talent buyers fall into line, seeking to cash in on the performer's growing stature. Genuinely successful performing careers today often follow this sequence of events:

1- *The artist gains initial recognition as a live performer in one geographic area. He signs with a personal manager.*

2- *The manager lands his client a record contract, through his competence, contacts, good luck and timing.*

3- *The artist's records gain airplay and the label helps underwrite a concert tour. Other live performances ensue.*

4- *The successful recording artist and concert performer attracts the attention of TV network producers. They engage the artist.*

5- *The artist, now successful on records and television, may attract the interest of film producers and Broadway producers. The manager has a major star and high income. His big task now is to try to figure out how to keep all these good things happening.*

DEVELOPING PERIPHERAL INCOME

Major stars receive additional opportunities to increase their incomes from such sources as product endorsements, broadcast commercials and merchandising deals. These offers will normally be received by the artist's manager and he will need to know how to handle them to maximum advantage.

The field of product and service "merchandising" is bigger than most persons realize. For example, the NFL teams gross more from licensing the sale of football team souvenirs *than they take in at the stadium box office.* In the music segment of the entertainment industry, major recording stars may receive more income from merchandising deals of this kind than they do from record royalties.

Each music souvenir merchandiser is licensed by the artist's manager to use the artist's name and image, then pays perhaps three percent to 15 percent royalty (at retail) on each item sold. The manager may also receive invitations for his clients to appear on broadcast commercials or endorse products and services. The manager, in consultation with his client, must determine whether these kinds of offers might help or hurt the artist's career.

In summary, it becomes evident that the personal manager is the key professional in the entertainment industry, often wielding more power and influence than any one person should be expected (or entitled) to handle. All we ask of him is omniscience.

THE PERSONAL MANAGEMENT TEAM

Earlier in this chapter, it was recommended that artists and managers delay signing a contract to join forces until they had gone through some kind of "trial marriage" — to discover, if possible, whether they could work closely together in an intimate, long-term relationship. If we assume the parties have done this and remain convinced they can develop a winning team, they should both engage their own independent legal counselors and proceed to negotiate a contract.

If their attorneys are well-informed and aggressive, the artist and manager should negotiate for all they can get for themselves. Normal procedure is for one side to express his demands — from a position, quite naturally, of maximum self-interest. The second party then counters with his position — similarly biased in his favor. At this juncture, the parties are in an adversary relationship and will need to negotiate compromises.

The draft contract that follows assumes the parties start their negotiations in the sequence just described. Where issues are particularly controversial, I articulate the opening position of each party. Then follows an articulation of an *equity* position — what I believe would be a fair resolution and balance of interests if the parties had about equal bargaining strength.

The equity positions expressed here are not just my own, but a concensus of opinion prevailing among a number of distinguished entertainment industry attorneys who have shared their views with the author.

PERSONAL MANAGEMENT AGREEMENT
(Draft Only)

> *This draft agreement is for study purposes only. Its language should not necessarily be used verbatim in an actual contract. The author urges each party involved in negotiations to retain independent legal counsel to draft the actual language of a contract.*

AGREEMENT made on (date) _____ by and between

_____ , the Artist

and _____ , the Personal Manager
(hereinafter called Manager).

WITNESSETH

Whereas the Artist wishes to obtain advice and direction in the advancement of his (her) professional career, and

Whereas the Manager, by reason of his (her) knowledge and experience, is qualified to render such advice and direction,

NOW THEREFORE, in consideration of the mutual promises set forth here, the Artist and Manager do agree:

DEFINITIONS

Artist — The first party to this agreement who appoints the second party, the Personal Manager. The Artist may be one individual or more comprising the professional performing group. If more than one individual signs this Agreement as an Artist member of the performing group, then this Agreement shall be binding upon all such persons, individually and severally, and all of the representations, warranties, agreements and obligations contained herein shall be deemed to be individual, joint and several.[6]

This agreement covers all of the professional talents, activities and services of the Artist in all sectors and media of the arts and entertainment industry, as an instrumentalist, singer, actor, entertainer, composer, writer, editor, arranger, orchestrator, publisher, executive, producer, manager, audio technician, promoter and packager.

Personal Manager — is used here to describe the individual who advises and counsels and directs the Artist's career and manages the Artist's business affairs.

6-The Manager may require here that the members of the performing group are individually and severally liable for any claims against any other member of the group or the Manager.

Third Party — is any individual, company or corporation with whom the Artist and/or Manager do business related to this agreement, e.g., talent agent, producer, publisher, record company, production company, promoter, business manager, accountant, auditor, union or guild, broadcaster, merchant, advertiser.

Entertainment industry — is used here, not only in its generally understood meaning, but also includes all related aspects of literary activity, publishing, broadcasting, filming, telecommunications, promotion, merchandising, advertising, through all media of communication now known or later developed, of the arts and entertainment industry.

1.0 APPOINTMENT

Artist's Position — It is in the Artist's interest to place strong language in the agreement setting forth precisely what the personal manager is obligated to do. To offer "advice and counsel" is ambiguous. The Artist will seek a specific list of services to be rendered and require the Manager to use his "best efforts" to meet his responsibilities.

Manager's Position — The Manager will seek only a general statement regarding his appointment. He may not accept the language committing him to his "best efforts," in that his commissions under such language might not be automatic.[7] He may prefer the expression "reasonable efforts . . ."

Equity Position — The Artist appoints the Manager as his exclusive personal manager throughout the world in all fields related to the arts and entertainment industry. The Manager will offer the Artist advice and counsel and will use his best efforts to advance the Artist's career.

The Manager accepts the appointment as set forth here and agrees that, in fulfilling the appointment, he will 1) make himself available to the Artist at reasonable times and places; 2) devote his best efforts to the Artist's affairs; 3) maintain an office and staff adequate to fulfill the appointment and his responsibilities thereunder.

1.1 Exclusivity — The Artist appoints the Manager as his exclusive personal manager and will engage no other personal manager during the term of this agreement. The Manager's services to the Artist are non-exclusive; he may manage other artists concurrently and carry on other business activities, at his sole discretion.[8]

1.2 Business Management — The Manager shall be in charge of the Artist's business affairs personally or, with the consent of the Artist, engage a Third Party as business manager.

1.3 Representation — The Manager shall represent the Artist's best interests with Third Parties and supervise agreements with them.

7-Joseph Taubman. *In Tune With the Music Business* (New York 1980: Law-Arts Publishers), p. 80. Also see Hurewitz, p. 69.

8-The Artist may seek to limit the Manager's freedom here by requiring him to list his current clients and agree not to further obligate himself. This may help assure the Artist the Manager will have sufficient time to serve the Artist's best interests.

2.0 EMPLOYMENT

Artist's Position — Despite the language in most contracts of this kind, the Artist **expects** *the manager to actively procure employment for him. This is the very reason most artists sign on with a particular manager.*

Manager's Position — The Manager will insist the agreement specifically excuse him from any obligation to procure employment for the artist. If the agreement is negotiated and "performed" in the state of California, the Manager will require extra-strong language here disavowing any hint that he is **even to attempt** *to procure employment or that he will participate even indirectly in such activity.*

Equity Position — The procurement of employment, or the attempt to procure employment for the Artist is not an obligation of the Manager, and the Manager is not authorized, licensed, or expected to perform such services. But the Manager recognizes that the obtaining of employment is of the essence in advancing the Artist's career, and that the Manager shall, after consultation with the Artist, engage, direct and/or discharge such persons as talent agents, employment agents as well as other persons and firms who may be retained for the purpose of securing engagement contracts for the Artist.

3.0 ASSIGNMENT

Artist's Position — The Artist will attempt to deny the Manager the right to transfer or assign the contract to a Third Party. The Artist enters into the agreement largely because of his feeling of confidence and trust in this particular Manager. The Artist could not be assured this same confidence and trust could be found in some Third Party who was allowed to take over the contract. To protect himself, the Artist will seek a **key man** *clause (below).*

Manager's Position — The Manager will seek to avoid inclusion of a **key man** *clause, arguing that he may become disabled or otherwise unable to perform. He may develop different interests and want to be free to assign the contract. If the Manager is employed by a management* **company**, *his company will probably insist it retain the right to assign the agreement.*

Equity Position — The Manager is the *key man* in this agreement and is denied the option to assign this agreement to a Third Party without the prior written consent of the Artist. Any Third Party under consideration in this context shall agree to assume all the responsibilities assigned to the first Manager and be fully qualified, in the opinion of the Artist, to perform in a manner and at a level comparable to the first Manager.

4.0 TERM, TERMINATION

Artist's Position — Unless the Artist is in an inferior negotiating position, he will seek an initial term of one to two years. He seeks to avoid a longer first term in the belief that, should his career prosper, he will want to negotiate more favorable terms at the end of the first term — or seek to terminate his Manager and engage a new one willing to serve for a lower commission.

Manager's Position — *It is in the Manager's best interests to negotiate a maximum term allowed by state statute for personal services contracts. He seeks maximum assurance that he has the Artist tied up and can enjoy high income for years to come. He wants to recover his investment made during the lean years of the Artist's career.*

Equity Position — The term of the Agreement shall be for two years, provided the parties satisfactorily fulfill their mutual obligations. If either party has substantial cause to claim the other party has failed to perform under this Agreement, the claimant must send a written notice by registered mail, return receipt requested, citing specific reasons for the complaint, allowing the recipient of the written notice 30 days to cure and reasonably satisfy the complaint. If the aggrieved party does not receive a response that is reasonably satisfactory to the claimant, the claimant may then terminate this Agreement by sending written notice ten days in advance to the other party.[9]

4.1 Options — The Artist grants the Manager options to extend the initial term of this Agreement to a maximum aggregate total of seven years,[10] provided the Artist's gross income from the entertainment industry during the preceding year(s) aggregates these totals:

(A) First term: $ _____

(B) First Optional Extension Period of One Year (total of (A) and (B)):

   $ _____

(C) Second Optional Extension Period of One Year (total of (A) through (C)):

   $ _____

(D) Third Optional Extension Period of One Year (total of (A) through (D)):

   $ _____

(E) Fourth Optional Extension Period of One Year (total of (A) through (E)):

   $ _____

(F) Fifth Optional Extension Period of One Year (total of (A) through (F)):

   $ _____

The foregoing notwithstanding, the Artist grants these extension options only on the condition that the Manager fulfills, in the initial term and

---

9- The parties may prefer that this option to terminate not be allowed, and that all serious claims of failure to perform be referred to arbitration. But a powerful act may demand the right to terminate at any time, making the claim that he *serves at the pleasure of the artist.* But no prestigious manager would accept this, arguing that he would be too vulnerable to the artist behaving capriciously.

10-States have statutes of limitation of contracts involving "personal services."

optional extensions thereof, all his responsibilities and obligations set forth herein.[11]

5.0 POWER OF ATTORNEY

Manager's Position[12] — The Manager will attempt to get general power of attorney, including, among other powers, the complete and unrestricted right to 1) collect and disburse all the Artist's money; 2) negotiate and sign contracts on behalf of the Artist; 3) engage and discharge personnel; 4) exploit the Artist's personality, name, likeness, photographs, which would include commitment of the Artist to product endorsements and commercial announcements; 5) exert "creative control," including the selection or rejection of musical and literary materials, record producers, staging and costuming.

*Artist's Position — An experienced lawyer will seek to severely limit a grant of power of attorney. First, grant of **general** power of attorney is all-encompassing and affords exposure to conflicts of interest and abuse. The Artist will probably be most resistant to extending power of attorney to **creative control.** Unless the Manager is fully qualified to make artistic judgments, for example, the Manager could impose poor decisions in such sensitive areas as selection of music to be recorded, the manner and style of presentation and the selection of record producers.*

Whatever resolution the parties make in regard to creative control and constraints on decision-making, the Artist will probably demand that power of attorney be cancelable by the Artist at any time.

Equity Position — The Artist agrees the Manager may require limited power of attorney from time to time for his convenience. Accordingly, the Artist grants limited power of attorney to the Manager to serve as the Artist's agent and attorney-in-fact in emergency situations only and denies the Manager this power without the prior written consent of the Artist 1) to accept any performing engagement on behalf of the Artist exceeding one week in duration; 2) to sign checks drawn upon the Artist-Manager's Trust Account with a face value greater than $1000 and of an aggregate monthly amount in excess of $5000 for all such draws; 3) to sign any agreement on behalf of the Artist that is of more than incidental importance or having a term longer than one month; 4) to engage or discharge support personnel; 5) to accept on Artist's behalf any product or service endorsement; 6) to limit the Artist's creative control over such matters as the selection of musical and literary material; determination of the manner and style of performance, including staging and costuming.

The Artist may terminate this power of attorney at any time, without notice, in the event that the Manager misuses, in the sole opinion of the Artist, this power.

11-Whatever the circumstances of termination or disengagement, the lawyers will need to exchange notices of release. These releases may include *executory provisions* — requirements for performance, payments, etc. following termination of the agreement.

12-See Hurewitz. Op. cit.

6.0 ARTIST'S RESPONSIBILITIES, WARRANTIES

6.1 Encumbrance — The Artist warrants that he is under no restriction, disability or prohibition in respect to the Artist's right to execute this Agreement and perform its terms and conditions. The Artist warrants that no act or omission by the Artist will violate, to the best of his knowledge, any right or interest of any person or firm or will subject the Manager to any liability or claim to any person.

6.2 Commitment — The Artist will devote his full time and attention to the advancement of his career.

6.3 Ownership — The Artist warrants that, to the best of his knowledge, he is the sole owner of his professional name,[13] _____ and that this warranty is restricted to adjudicated breaches.

6.4 Advice — The Artist will accept in good faith the advice and counsel of the Manager, in recognition of the Manager's special knowledge and experience in the entertainment industry.

6.5 Income — The Artist shall encourage all agents and employers to make payments of all moneys due the Artist to the Manager, or to a Third Party approved by the Artist and Manager.

6.6 Employment — The Artist shall refer all offers of employment to the Manager, and the Artist shall not accept offers of employment without the consent of the Manager.

7.0 MANAGER'S COMPENSATION

Artist's Position — *The Artist will seek to sign the Manager for a 10 percent to 15 percent commission. If this is unacceptable to the Manager, the Artist may offer to increase the rate as gross income rises.*

Manager's Position — *If the Manager is new at the game and anxious to get into the field, he might accept a commission as low as 10 percent, but try for 15 percent. An unknown manager will probably only be able to attract relatively unknown artists, so the parties must agree to struggle together in the early stages of their relationship. The astute manager who accepts a low starting income will seek commission increments when he can manage to materially increase his client's income.*

Equity Position — The Artist shall pay the Manager 15 percent of the Artist's gross income for the first year of this Agreement. "Gross income" shall include, without limitation, all fees, earnings, salaries, royalties, bonuses, shares of profit, stock, partnership interests, percentages, gifts of value, received directly or indirectly, by the Artist or his heirs, executors, administrators or assigns, or by any other person, corporation or firm on the Artist's behalf, from the arts and entertainment industry.

The commission shall be 20 percent in the second year of this Agreement, provided the Artist's gross income for this second year increases _____

13-Courts have held that the legal ownership of a trade name ultimately resides, not in the person first using it, but is owned by the person or persons identified with the name when it acquires a "secondary meaning."

percent over the first year. If this Agreement is extended to a third year, the commission shall rise to 25 percent provided the Artist's gross income increases _____ percent over the prior year.

8.0 COMMISSION BASE

*Artist's Position — An unknown artist will probably have to pay an established manager on artist's **unadjusted gross** income. But an established artist with an aggressive lawyer may be able to obtain certain exclusions from that gross, such as those listed below.*

*Manager's Position — The Manager will fight for the broadest possible commission base and seek to calculate his percentage on the Artist's unadjusted gross income. But if the Artist has superior bargaining power, "gross income" will probably become an **adjusted** gross income.*

Equity Position — The foregoing definition of the Artist's "gross income" notwithstanding, the following types of income shall be deducted from the gross income for purposes of calculating the Manager's commission: 1) the first $25,000 aggregated income in any single year derived from the entertainment industry or $500 per calendar week, whichever is greater; 2) record production expense where a Third Party provides same to the Artist; 3) record producers' fees, points and percentages where a Third Party pays the Artist for same; 4) performance, production and travel expense including salaries of support personnel connected thereto where a Third Party pays the Artist for same; 5) legal fees incurred by the Artist in dealings with the Manager and Third Parties in the negotiation and performance of agreements; 6) passive income — where the Artist receives money or other things of value from sources outside the entertainment industry or the Artist's income from investments inside or outside the entertainment industry.[14]

In any circumstances where the Manager has a financial interest with a Third Party or company with whom the Artist has any kind of business relationship, the Manager shall receive no commissions on any moneys the Artist receives from such sources.[15]

When this Agreement and all extensions thereof terminate, the Artist shall pay the Manager 100 percent of his commissions for a period of one year from all income generated by contracts and agreements set up by the Manager during the term of the agreement. For the following six months, the Manager's commission is limited to 50 percent of the Artist's commissionable income. For the subsequent six months, the Manager's commission is limited to 25 percent of the Artist's commissionable income. Thereafter, all Manager's commissions on the Artist's commissionable income cease.

14-A manager with a strong track record and powerful contacts will probably not accept these commission exclusions. If he did, he would demand a higher commission rate. The author's rationale for suggesting these exclusions is simple: most of these exclusions are not the Artist's *income*, but his *overhead*. The Manager is entitled to commissions on income, but not outflow.

15-The attorneys will need to negotiate how commissions are to be paid, if any, where the Artist's services are provided by a corporation. The commission will be adjusted to reflect whether the Artist, in this circumstance, has a financial interest in the corporation, is only an employee, or both.

9.0 FINANCIAL ACCOUNTING

Within thirty (30) days following the execution of this Agreement the parties shall select, by mutual consent, a certified public accountant to provide accounting services.

9.1 Records — The parties shall exchange informal financial records of all moneys flowing through their hands that relate to this Agreement. The Manager's financial records shall account for all receipts, disbursements, commissions withheld, advances, loans and investments, if any. Copies of the parties' financial reports shall be forwarded monthly to the accountant.

9.2 Audits — The Manager shall commission independent auditors, with the consent of the Artist, to conduct periodic audits of the Artist's publisher and record company to determine if these firms are fully paying royalties due the Artist and paying in a timely manner.

9.3 Limitations — The Manager may not incur any expense on behalf of the Artist in an amount larger than $ _____ for any one expense, without the consent of the Artist. The Manager may not incur monthly expenses on behalf of the Artist that exceed $ _____ without the consent of the Artist.

9.4 Loans — The Manager is not expected or required to make loans to the Artist or advance the Artist money. The Manager shall not make loans to any other person or invest the Artist's money without the prior consent of the Artist.

If the Artist asks the Manager to loan him money, and if the Manager voluntarily agrees to do so, the Manager shall be entitled to recover when due such loaned money together with reasonable interest. If such repayments to the Manager are not made when due, the Manager may recover the amount outstanding from the Artist's current earnings from the entertainment industry.

9.5 Overhead — The Manager's office overhead is not recoupable from the Artist, nor the Manager's travel expense within a fifty (50) mile radius of his office. The Artist shall pay the Manager's travel expense outside this radius when the Manager is requested by the Artist to travel.

9.6 Liability — Neither party is liable to the other for debts and obligations they may incur that are not covered by the Agreement.

10.0 GENERAL ISSUES

The present Agreement constitutes the entire understanding between the parties, and no other agreement or commitment, oral or written, prevails between the parties, and neither party may change or modify any part of the present Agreement without the prior written consent of the other party.

If one or more parts of this Agreement is found to be illegal or unenforceable, for any reason or by any person, the same shall not affect the validity or enforceability of the remaining provisions of this Agreement.

10.1 If the Artist incorporates, he agrees to cause said corporation to sign an agreement with the Manager which provides no less favorable terms than the first agreement.

10.2 Default and Cure — If either party claims that the other is in default or breach of this agreement, the aggrieved party shall provide written notice setting forth the nature of the dispute. The accused party is then allowed thirty (30) days to cure the alleged default, during which period no default or other grievances shall be deemed incurable.

10.3 Arbitration — The parties agree to submit all disputes to the American Arbitration Association and be bound by and perform any award rendered in such arbitration.

10.4 This Agreement is made under the laws of the state of _____

IN WITNESS WHEREOF, the parties hereto have executed this Agreement as of the day and year first indicated above.

_____

Artist

_____

Personal Manager

INNOVATOR DR. ALFRED REED, University of Miami. The music merchandising program Dr. Reed established in the 1960s was the first of its kind and now offers even a masters degree. Graduates of this program occupy important positions in the music industry.

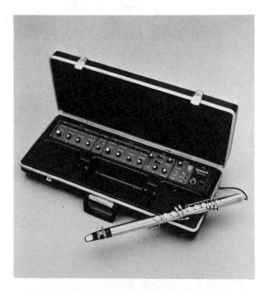

ART AND SCIENCE COMBINED. This Lyricon II from the Selmer Company combines the art of instrument design with computer science.

11

CONCERT PROMOTION

The promotion and production of live concerts employs large numbers of people and causes the flow of hundreds of millions of dollars. Those taking part hope that the money will flow in their direction. It looks so easy: you rent a facility, hire a star, and collect the money. This get-rich-quick illusion has caused more bankruptcies than exploring for oil. Promoters and producers who know the concert field do well financially; those lacking competence do not survive in it.

How big is the concert field? *Billboard* magazine estimates that the college concert and entertainment field yields a gross of $500 million a year. Add to this figure the income from non-college-sponsored concerts, and we are looking at a $1 billion enterprise. Where does all this money go? Before it can start to come in, someone must put up the money in front.

SPONSORSHIP

The promoter must invest his own money or persuade others to gamble with him. Early in this money-raising stage, the promoter must register his firm name with the county clerk, license his business and establish a business bank account. Assuming this preliminary homework has been done, an unknown concert promoter will have to provide cash deposits or surety bonds or a letter of credit to guarantee hall rentals and promotional expenses. He may also have to come up with cash deposits (usually 50 percent) required by most agents at the signing of contracts for the performers.

As explained in Chapter 13, the freshman concert promoter may establish a "limited partnership," whereby he assumes only part of the financial risk and consequently enjoys only a share in the profits, if there are any profits. Another option available is for the young promoter to set up a corporation to finance concerts (Chapter 13).

About one-half of the live concerts in the USA are sponsored or cosponsored by colleges and universities which, each year, set up student-run committees to handle the school's annual budget for campus-sponsored entertainments. Sponsoring, promoting and managing college concerts today is a big business, sometimes involving a budget of $100,00 or more for one event. College students lack sufficient experience and knowledge in the field to handle these affairs by themselves. Increasing numbers of colleges find it necessary to bring in professional promoters and managers. Artists' agents find it difficult to work with strictly amateur student committees and are always relieved when a college involves a knowledgeable professional to work with them in handling the endless details and large sums of money involved. But due credit should be given to these students, some of whom begin to learn the promotion-management-production field while in school, then go on to find their place as professionals in the concert promotion or artist agent-management fields.

Over 300 colleges have banded together in the National Entertainment Conference (NEC). Its purpose is to share information and increase cooperation among campus promoters, booking agents and others in the entertainment field. The musicians' union has recognized its special relationships with colleges by formulating the AFM-NEC standard contract.

Another organization representing college concert activities is the National Entertainment & Campus Activities Association. NECAA's magazine, *Programming* contains useful information on effective methods of producing campus entertainment. The organization also helps sponsor apprenticeships for its members with music business enterprises.

Concerts on and off campus are frequently sponsored or cosponsored by a local radio station. AFTRA frowns on its members becoming involved in concert sponsorship in the belief that such activity can be a conflict of interest. But radio stations and their employees find ways to ally themselves with live concerts, because such events are regarded by them as excellent contacts with their broadcast audience. Concert promoters welcome cosponsorship of broadcasters, because the potential audience for the live event is comprised largely of the same persons who listen to broadcast music.

For many years, the most active cosponsor of concerts in the pop and rock fields has been the record industry. Label executives know that the successful promotion of a new album may be dependent upon coordination with a concert tour. But when record sales dropped in the late 1970s, record companies cut way back on financial support of their touring artists. In recent years, touring costs have become so high, a number of experienced observers have predicted that live concerts of recording artists may become a thing of the past. They believe that a handful of superstars may still make it on the road, but that most other concert tours may phase out because of the increasing difficulty of breaking even on such ventures.

When a label does help underwrite concerts, it cooperates with the artist's management in producing and supplying promotion materials. Some labels maintain "college departments" to coordinate record company support of college-sponsored performances.

Some record companies will buy blocks of tickets for concerts, then give them away to individuals and firms who have influence, or so they believe, over the record-buying public — disc jockeys, media personnel, and employees of record distributors and record stores. In addition to spreading goodwill among influential people, giving away tickets helps fill the house, thus giving the impression to the audience that the event is a huge success. This practice has been used for a long time on Broadway, too, and is known as "papering the house."

When a record company commits even more money to a concert than is indicated above, it may fly in one of its own publicists or product managers to assist the proceedings. Yet another kind of promotional support involves the record company participating in the expense of buying broadcast spots and print ads. In these efforts, the label and concert promoter may work out a sharing of such expenses with a local record retailer who wants to take part in the promotion.

An even more elaborate involvement by a record company occurs when the label itself sets up a complete national tour. When this is undertaken for a new act, the artists may be so broke that their record company must not only finance the purchase of equipment, but advance the group or artist funds for transportation, even hotels and meals. Labels may invest $100,000 and more to finance a national tour of an act it believes may make it. Despite these descriptions of extensive tour support, artists' managers complain that their clients never get enough of this kind of backing.

BUDGETS, VENUES

Early in the cycle of events leading to a live concert, the promoter will have formulated a budget. This process separates the men from the boys, because inexperienced promoters not only estimate costs too low, they will completely overlook certain kinds of overhead. Even if they follow the production management controls suggested here and budget expenses carefully, another danger area for the new promoter is his *optimism*. Every year, hotshot new promoters jump into the field, full of confidence that they will show established promoters how it should be done. They are optimistic beyond reason because they do not yet know enough about what they might encounter.

Before a promoter can start signing acts, he must locate an appropriate facility, often referred to in the trade as a "venue." Many communities' most attractive venues are tied up by other tenants or other promoters. Securing open dates can be difficult, and available dates are useless without the coincident availability of the acts the promoter wants. In selecting a concert venue, the promoter can usually rent the facility for a flat fee, or a flat fee plus a percentage of the gross. The landlord normally furnishes the stage manager, box-office manager, maintenance crew, security personnel and ushers. The promoter's second rental option is called "four-walling": the landlord furnishes the facility and the stage manager; the promoter brings in all other personnel at his own expense — stagehands, ushers, security and box-office help.

A critical issue is the number of seats. A thousand-seat facility sold out at $10 a ticket grosses $10,000, obviously. The promoter with a budget of $7,500 (allowing $2,500 for his profit) will probably lose his shirt because few halls sell out. Even if every seat is sold, unanticipated expenses may gobble up the profit margin. Few concerts in the pop-rock fields can be put together and profit from a $10,000 gross. The promoter would be well-advised to wait until he can locate a 5,000 or 10,000 seat arena, book a headline act, and pull together enough money to finance a sizable promotional campaign. A budget of this kind may be less risky than the one described for the 1,000-seat facility.

Whatever the potential gross a particular venue might yield, the experienced promoter budgets his package to produce at least a break-even figure, not for an SRO audience, but for a *60 percent house* — meaning that the promoter estimates that 40 percent of his tickets just won't sell. Theatre managers have used this 60 percent house figure since the 1800s in planning budgets.

Let us invent a concert budget for our freshman promoter-producer:

CONCERT BUDGET

POTENTIAL INCOME

10,000 seats at $10 per seat.		
Maximum gross	$100,000	
Less 40% for unsold tickets	40,000	
Gross income		60,000

ESTIMATED EXPENSE

Hall rental (includes box office, ushers, stage crew)	5,000
Star act	29,000
Supporting act	3,250
Liability insurance	1,000
Surety bonds	250
Advertising, promotion (15% of the gross)	9,000
PA company	2,000
Lighting/staging company	1,000
Security company (rent-a-cop)	2,000
Perquisites (special food, drink, etc.) for the star	500
Cleanup	1,000

Unforeseen expense
(10% of estimated gross)   6,000
                                                              60,000

PROFIT/LOSS   0

Fig. 11.1

This young promoter is very fortunate — and probably set some kind of record for his first project: he broke even! Consider the things he handled wisely:

1- *He hired a 10,000 seat arena, thus maximizing his potential gross.*

2- *He spent a bundle on a big name act — to assure strong ticket sales.*

3- *He was well-covered against damaging lawsuits by taking out an expensive liability policy.*

4- *He budgeted 15 percent of his anticipated gross revenue for advertising and promotion, an amount often recommended as a minimum by successful promoters.*

5- *He budgeted $1,000 for cleanup, just in case his audience left more mess than the arena rental contract would normally take care of as routine maintenance.*

6- *He budgeted 10 percent of his estimated gross revenue for unforeseen expense. Astute promoters have learned this ploy from construction contractors, many of whom will protect themselves against delays, strikes, inclement weather and just bad luck by adding on 10 percent to 15 percent for "unforeseen expense."*

In addition to breaking even, a promoter this smart can probably look forward to even making a profit next time around. His first venture produced another bonus: the people he worked with — agents, managers, artists, security people all discovered this individual is a level-headed businessman who treats associates fairly. Next time around, he may well get somewhat lower fees, more complete cooperation from these people.

Our imaginary freshman promoter risked only his own money on the venture described above. It is more common for inexperienced promoters to start out to learn the business by working for others who share the financial risks. One such cooperative arrangement involves artists' agents who share the initial financial liability with a promoter. Under normal circumstances, investors can expect to profit from a business venture somewhat in proportion to the risks they accept. If the cooperative venture of the agent and the promoter shows a profit, the two parties would expect to share in the revenue in proportion to the share of the money each person risked.

Another modus operandi in the field of concert promotion occurs when a talent buyer, such as a convention group, business firm, etc., accepts the risk, puts up the money in front, then engages the promoter simply to package the show for a flat fee. In this kind of situation, the promoter functions more as a producer.

CONTRACTS

Promoters contract for artists' services through booking agencies. The promoter should try to work with agents of wide experience, because a booker can be of invaluable service. Agents, in turn, prefer to work with seasoned promoters because they are more likely to share with them a successful experience. Agents will normally limit stars' bookings to promoters with good track records. Most stars are in a position to pick and choose where they will perform and need not take a chance on unknown concert promoters. But agents handling performers of lesser magnitude are frequently looking for concert dates, and the less-than-famous promoters can work out satisfactory contracts with them. As pointed out above, smart agents set artists' fees, whenever they can, to permit the promoter to make money, too. Contracts must be mutually profitable, or the parties will shop elsewhere next time. Promoters should make preliminary inquiry of agents concerning artists' usual fees and available dates. This information can set in motion preliminary planning, such as placing a hold on a concert facility. After the promoter has worked out a preliminary budget based on this information, he again contacts the agent and starts nailing down a firm agreement. If he can negotiate an acceptable fee for his acts, the promoter can then polish his budget, double-check his estimated income and expenses, then sign the contracts.

Some promoters permit themselves the luxury of booking the acts they personally prefer — if the price is within reach. Most experienced promoters favor their personal preferences, but are more likely to follow the weekly fluctuations of the trade charts, regional sales and airplay — then do everything they can to book the acts that are the most recent successes in their concert territory. If the promoter's cosponsor aids in this research, they may develop a winning combination. Booking artists on the way down the charts has hurt many a promoter.

Once the promoter has signed his star act, he is under pressure to accept a lead-off act or other secondary acts on the bill. Agents handling both the star and a favored lead-off act will do all they can to get the promoter to buy a package deal: "You can have my star if you'll give this new act a break and let them lead off." Or the promoter may hear this appeal from the record company: "We just signed the Hitmakers group and if you buy them for your next bill, we'll fly in our promotion guy to help you really push the date, for free. The act? Cheap!" Agents are on questionable legal ground when they attempt to coerce a talent buyer to buy one act if he'll just take one in addition. In the motion picture exhibition business this is sometimes called block booking and has been judged illegal, under certain circumstances, by the courts. But the practice, usually disguised with persuasive language, continues.

Once the promoter and agent have come to terms on the acts and the prices, stars, sometimes lesser names, usually make additional demands. One concerns an agreement describing the setup and expense for the sound system, lights, staging, etc. Details covering these items are attached as an addendum to the artist's contract in the form of what is usually called a "technical rider." Stars frequently specify the companies they want engaged to supply the sound reinforcement and staging. Others leave it to the promoter to engage the best local or regional suppliers and technicians. Audio and staging is usually determined by the star act. Lesser names on the bill are accustomed to accepting whatever the star has demanded in technical services.

The promoter has signed his acts and accepted the technical demands. He is not yet through committing himself. During the peak of the rock and roll period, when big stars became accustomed to being treated like The Second Coming of Christ, they would add fine print to their contracts demanding their dressing rooms be lavishly supplied with special food and drink. The booze and mixers would have to be particular brands. The automobile chauffeured to transport the star could not just be a limousine, it had to be a particular model of Mercedes, black. Promoters also understood they should have some flunky hanging around who might help the act locate dope, possibly even young women of easy reputation. When the concert business fell off sharply in the late 1970s, experienced promoters informed stars and their managers that they would have to hustle their own fringe benefits when they were unreasonable. Smart promoters today do all they can to make their artists comfortable. But only the inexperienced promoter will waste his time and money accommodating outlandish tastes.

PROMOTION

There are only a few superstars that will draw a SRO audience just by having their forthcoming appearance announced. These giant draws require the promoter to spend practically no money on advertising. That is fortunate, for he has undoubtedly already signed away 80 to 90 percent of his gross to the visiting superstar. In a more common occurrence, the promoter signs his acts, then has to shout and scream to inform the public he has tickets, lots of tickets, for sale. Some promoters prefer to personally handle publicity and advertising responsibilities. For some, it is just this "show biz" aspect of concert promotion that first attracted them to the field, and they seem to enjoy, even thrive, on the razzle-dazzle role of the hustler, the flack. The promoter's advertising agency might have personnel to assist in the publicity campaign. More likely, the promoter will hire a publicist or

PR firm to organize a campaign that will persuade the public to buy the tickets. This process is aided by "promo kits" supplied by the managers of the artists (promotion materials are often supplied by the artist's record company).

A professionally assembled promo kit includes canned press releases, feature stories, complete biographical information ("bios"), an assortment of 8"x10" glossy photographs, and, possibly, additional promotional items such as imprinted T-shirts, souvenir items and promotional records. Kits are mailed to media personnel by the artist's management, publicist or PR company. They are timed to arrive two to three weeks before the scheduled concert. Recipients of these kits generally give items of intrinsic value to their kids, then scan the canned copy, perhaps pulling out an item that piques their interest. Reporters who are personally attracted to the artist's work will probably submit an article and the glossies to their editors for consideration. Knowledgeable promotion personnel seek at least two breaks in local newspapers: a "teaser announcement" — perhaps a one-column, one-paragraph announcement some two weeks before the concert date; then, one to three days before the event, they hope to plant a feature story and a photograph of the performer in the entertainment section of a local newspaper. Larger papers require "exclusives" to do this — a guarantee from the publicist that only that particular newspaper is being given the material for release on that particular occasion.[1] Experienced publicists never deceive newspapers with "double plants" or fake "exclusives."

Another useful kind of press is the interview: the star arrives; all newspapers and broadcast media in the concert territory are informed that at 2 p.m. in the Big Hotel The Star will hold a press conference. Reporters present may turn in interview copy; their editors may or may not print it. More effective is the "exclusive interview," where an individual reporter or newspaper columnist will be offered the exclusive right to interview The Star, provided he can offer reasonable assurance he will write the story and get it printed. Print media publicity is most effective with MOR, country acts and classical artists.

If the bill features pop recording stars, the promoter knows his most effective advertising will be on the radio — not just spot announcements but the supporting chatter of jocks who are always searching for something musical to talk about.

Rock-pop audiences are less attracted to print media. Middle America, accustomed to following the entertainment pages of their daily newspaper, may never be aware that a particular rock star has been in town, come and gone, sold out. In lieu of extensive newspaper ads, rock promoters will focus their print ads on posters, locating them wherever young people gather — schools, college campuses, bookstores, record stores, etc. Record labels sometimes help promote a concert of one of their contract artists with special record store displays, sometimes taking over whole windows to push the artist's latest release and his local concert appearance. Some promoters learn

---

1-For additional information on promotion techniques, see Chapter 10.

that ad space bought in campus newspapers pays off, and the paper will usually run editorial copy, too.

Promoters and publicists may use gimmicks when they can attract attention no other way. Publicists representing major stars tend to shy away from publicity gimmicks, having learned that the public is sometimes quick to spot hype.

How much should a promoter budget for advertising? Feyline Presents of Denver, one of the world's largest concert promotion organizations, estimates the potential box-office gross for an event, then budgets 10 percent to 15 percent of that figure for promotion. That formula works beautifully for Feyline (the firm spends much less than 15 percent when booking an act with tremendous drawing power; superstars sell themselves).

Whatever moneys are budgeted for advertising, the seasoned promoter keeps careful watch on how tickets for an event are moving. When they lag behind projected estimates, the smart promoter will quickly pump more advertising dollars into the project to bolster his campaign. But if tickets move faster than projected sales estimates, some producers will quickly pull ads, in the belief that the event will prove successful without all the originally budgeted advertising.

What kind of promotion works best? Joseph Levine, a very successful film producer, used to complain that, by his estimate, one-half of his ad budget was wasted, but that he could never figure out which half. Many experienced publicists believe the most effective promotional "gimmick," the best "press" is simply word-of-mouth. The potential audience seems ready to pass the good word along if the word — the straight information — is clearly announced at the right time.

PRODUCTION MANAGEMENT

The concert promoter is ultimately responsible, not only for booking the talent and filling the hall, but for every detail relating to the presentation of that entertainment. Anyone attempting to enter the field should first try to discover whether he has the aptitude — and the will — to assume the management of a great variety of *details.* If the promoter's talents and inclinations lean mostly to actual promotion, he should engage an associate producer to assume the responsibility for the management of the performance itself. This kind of associate producer might be called the production manager or stage director. Any individual presuming to function in this capacity must be experienced, as an amateur or professional, in theatre and staging.

While some promoters and stage managers do an adequate job with minimum controls, many of the best of them rely heavily on *lists of things to do.* After many years of touring here and abroad, I recommend promoters and production managers work up "control sheets" as written guides for what to do and when to do it. Since this book addresses amateur as well as professional people, the accompanying pages show the kind of production control sheets that can work efficiently in most situations. These forms will be particularly useful for college promoters.

The secret to effective concert promotion is to understand the importance of what I call *production back-timing*. The technique is comparable to the ones used in the construction industry, where the contractor schedules a sequence of events so that subcontractors arrive on time with the necessary deliveries and workmen.

The College Production Planning form (Fig. 11.2) identifies the myriad tasks that must be back-timed so that preparations for a performance can unfold in orderly fashion.

COLLEGE PRODUCTION PLANNING

LEAD TIME	CONTROL NUMBER	RESPONSIBILITY
6 to 12 months	1-	*Research history of concert promotions in your area. What has worked well in the past?*
3 to 6 months	2-	*Formulate budget for forthcoming school year; appeal for funding.*
	3-	*Place tentative holds on performance facilities.*
	4-	*Make preliminary contact with talent agents to learn of tentative costs, available artists and dates.*
3 months	5-	*Get school's approval of your plans, then negotiate contracts with agents. Pending formal execution of contracts, exchange confirming telegrams.*
	6-	*Confirm your hold dates on facility, then formulate a written agreement with the facility management.*
2 months	7-	*Execute contracts with agencies, including technical riders.*
	8-	*Contact artists' record companies for help with promotion. Ask for press kits, promotional materials, money for block-ticket purchases, cooperative ads, even promotion personnel.*
	9-	*Formulate promotion budget and campaign. Get print and broadcast ad costs.*
	10-	*Contract for outside suppliers, as needed, for sound reinforcement, lighting, security, caterers, etc.*
6 weeks	11-	*Place printing orders for tickets, posters, banners, etc.*
4 weeks	12-	*Contract for ticket selling outlets.*
3 weeks	13-	*Deliver printed tickets to outlets. Set strict controls for accounting.*

14- *Line up student volunteers for ushering, ticket takers, setting up/striking stage, publicity, gofors, box office, etc.*

3 weeks 15- *Line up cooperative ads with record stores, radio stations, etc. Seek store displays of posters, albums.*

16- *Clear plans with fire department: size of crowd, control of aisles, exits.*

17- *Clear security plans with police, sheriff, rent-a-cop firm, campus police. Discuss liabilities with school's legal counsel.*

18- *Distribute promotional materials to print and broadcast media. Schedule press conference, interviews. Mount banners, posters.*

2 weeks 19- *Reconfirm arrangements with outside suppliers (sound, lighting, transport, caterers, etc.)*

20- *Check ticket sales. Adjust promotion budget accordingly.*

1 week 21- *Call a production planning meeting with facility manager, stage manager, production director, student volunteers. Issue written instructions to everybody concerning their responsibilities, schedule, contingency plans.*

3 days 22- ***Reconfirm everything!***
a- With artists' road managers regarding any changes in time of arrival of personnel, equipment.
b- With outside suppliers.
c- With facility stage manager.
d- With student crew chairpersons.
e- With ticket sellers. If sales are lagging, execute preconceived last-minute promotion campaign.

Performance day 23- *Call production meeting one hour prior to scheduled arrival of equipment and roadies. Everyone charged with responsibilities relating to the production and performance attends this meeting and takes notes. Last-minute changes in plans discussed.*

24- *Set up. Confirm all personnel and equipment are arriving per plan.*

Performance day 25- *Pick up money and unsold tickets from outlets. Deposit money in bank, deliver unsold tickets to facility box office for sale there.*

26- *Welcome the performing artists and their entourage. Control issuing of backstage and auditorium passes. Save the best (free) seats for unexpected important guests.*

Post-Production	27-	*If agreed contractually, join the road manager for a count of receipts and unsold tickets shortly after the box office closes. Make agreed payment, then arrange for secure place to store cash overnight.*
	28-	*Feed your people after the show, at least your volunteers. They've earned it!*
	29-	*Confirm facility cleanup is proceeding per plan. Did the place experience more than normal wear and tear? If so, discharge your contractual responsibilities.*
	30-	*Write a summary report, following a short meeting of your key personnel: what went wrong, what went well?*
	31-	*Thank the participants by telephone or letter for their cooperation, particularly those who worked as volunteers.*
Fig. 11.2	32-	*Pay your bills promptly to assure goodwill for the school's next venture.*

As preparations for a performance unfold, persons in charge start accumulating voluminous correspondence and telephone messages. Filing folders become unmanageable. To maintain control, I recommend that promoters, stage managers and road managers pull all the data together on one sheet that relate to the performance itself. Try the one shown (Figure 11.3) or prepare your own.

College students who acquire experience promoting campus concerts are now in demand by fully professional promotion companies, provided, of course, their track records as amateurs justify the confidence of potential employers. Qualified people are needed in the field.

PRODUCTION CONTROL

PERFORMANCE FACILITY (name/address/telephone/manager) _____

_____

_____

_____

PERFORMANCE DATE/TIME _____

PRODUCER/PROMOTER/AGENT(S) _____

_____

_____

_____

FEATURED ARTIST(S) _____

   Road Manager _____

_____

STAGE (size/risers/pit/stairs/curtains/exits, etc.) _____

_____

_____

_____

_____

LIGHTING (spots/borders/foots/dimmer/voltage/supplier/operator) _____

_____

_____

SOUND (supplier/technician/description) _____

_____

_____

DRESSING ROOMS (number/size/furnishings/condition/location) _____

_____

_____

LOADING DOCK (access/parking/security) _____

_____

UNION JURISDICTIONS _____

Fig. 11.3

12

THEATRICAL PRODUCTION

PERSPECTIVE

The theatre has formed an integral part of music for centuries. Many of our master composers have experienced their greatest success in the theatre: Mozart, Wagner, Stravinsky, Gershwin. In Western civilization, "musical theatre" can be said to have started in the Jewish synagog and the Roman church; most religious ceremony would be unthinkable without music. Much religious pageantry, of itself, is choreographed music.

Musical theatre's earliest patronage, in addition to organized religion, came from the aristocracy who built and operated theatres right on their own premises. Later, men of wealth, e.g., the merchants of Venice, the Medici of Florence, became enthusiastic patrons of the arts. By the seventeenth century, public opera houses began operating, selling tickets (at about 50 cents each) to cover production costs. In the eighteenth century Handel, years before he scored his biggest hit, *Messiah,* was hustling around London, buying and managing theatres, booking talent, scoring, producing, conducting operas, even doubling as a pit musician (keyboards) in his own theatre. Competing musical shows, particularly *The Beggar's Opera,* eventually drove impressario Handel out of the musical theatre business, while other producers, whose ears were more in tune with current taste, established a musical theatre tradition in London that flourishes to this day.

By the nineteenth century, musical theatres in Europe and this country, including everything from grand opera to minstrel shows, were flourishing, selling tickets, turning a profit. Early in our own century, opera and ballet production costs began to exceed box office income, and the musical *patron,* the big giver, reappeared to keep these art forms alive. Meanwhile, imported European operetta was being transformed in this country into such forms as the musical *revue, musical comedy* and, since *Show Boat* (1927), the *musical play.* In our own time, it is musical theatre that keeps Broadway and most regional theatres from going into bankruptcy.

Today, nearly all music-making is, at least in part, musical theatre. By this I mean that most of the musical performances we experience involve events, not just for the ear, but for the eye. Even the symphony conductor choreographs his dance, consciously or unconsciously, in front of his orchestra to attract the admiration of the paying audience (ask any musician how much a conductor's gyrations actually contribute to the musical performance). The concert violinist or pianist choreographs his stage movements to impress listeners — at least all the star recitalists do; their stage presence is one of the principal reasons they become recognized as stars.

In the pop field, the working musician has learned how to appear attractive to the audience. While a performer need not become a vaudevillian, without a sense of theatre he will not graduate from the small time and may spend most of his professional life working Saturday nights at the Elks Club. All successful performers understand "musical theatre," intuitively or through training. In this sense, rock and roll has been musical theatre ever since the Beatles showed everyone how much fun it could be to *watch* music. Some popular performers are criticized for offering *only* theatre, not music.

Commercial musical theatre has even infiltrated our schools and colleges. Witness the thousands of young baton twirlers performing to adulterated rock charts played by their school marching bands. The school and college sports programs are directly bound up with commercial musical theatre — through the football stadium halftime shows and other pageantry.

The public loves to hear music with its eyes. The theatrical, even show business ingredients, so pervasive in contemporary music, is inextricably bound up with the music business and permeates music making, from saloon to university.

TYPES OF MUSICAL THEATRE

If we apply a more traditional definition to musical theatre, we still discover a great variety of expression. That piece of territory in New York known as Broadway has seen the production of contemporary music's most treasured repertoire; it has been the working place for dozens of America's most gifted composers, lyricists, playwrights, producers, directors and performers. Since 1945, Broadway would have gone into total bankruptcy had it not been for the musicals that kept it alive. Some Broadway musicals have produced more profit through LP sales and publishing income than they ever generated through ticket sales. Performance licensing of Broadway musicals has been producing excellent royalties from these shows since the 1920s. Stage musicals of genuine quality demonstrate a staying power unique in most popular music. As Lehman Engel points out in his books on the subject, the musicals that last and experience periodic revivals possess two essential ingredients: a good book and memorable songs.

Broadway musicals have always been the most expensive kind of production to mount. In 1950, a sumptuous production cost $200,000. Today, a producer has to raise $1 million to $2 million to mount a first-class Broadway musical, and the investors could not expect to break even with a 52-week run: many musical plays do not start turning a profit until they have run two, even three years.

The reason costs are now out-of-hand is that stage production is a *handcraft enterprise* in a mechanized age. No matter how carefully a show is budgeted, a producer cannot increase the "efficiency" of live singers, dancers and musicians. The live audience may total only 1000 per performance, not the 20 million available on television. Since the costs of live musical production will continue to rise with an inflating economy, this popular medium may suffer ultimate demise without subsidy. Of course, the Broadway musical has enjoyed special kinds of subsidy for years. Investors have risked their money partly in anticipation that the Broadway run is but a *preliminary phase* of the potential profitable life of a musical through original cast recordings, performance licensing, perhaps even movie rights. Broadway producers with track records like Harold Prince raise money easily. Some of them, Prince included, have a stable of investors always waiting to risk their money. Profits from a hit show compare favorably with a hit record. An investor who placed $100 with Harold Prince in 1954 to help mount *Pajama Game,* then let his money ride on Prince's *West Side Story* and *Fiddler on the Roof* saw his $100 grow to $3,000. And Prince doesn't even let his investors read the book or hear the music beforehand.

But Broadway does not have enough producers of Harold Prince's stature to generate production money sufficient to keep the Broadway musical alive indefinitely.

The death of Broadway has been predicted since the 1930s, but this lively tradition refuses to attend its own funeral. Ultimate demise of the live Broadway musical may be postponed through some kind of consortium: record companies, movie and TV producers may figure out a way of subsidizing Broadway more than they have in the past, using the live stage to perfect material and test public acceptance. It is conceivable that such a process might eventually return its investment through subsequent income generated through original cast recordings, movie and TV productions based on the original production that was born live. Forward-looking producers have been videotaping Broadway and off-Broadway shows for years, in anticipation of licensing the performances to manufacturers of videocassettes and videodiscs.

A more practical solution to keeping alive the Broadway musical began to take shape recently. Cy Coleman, Broadway writer-producer of hit shows began to experience some success with what might be called the minimusical. A minimusical can be written for two or three actors-singers, working with perhaps a trio in the pit or duo pianos. Production costs can be one-tenth those of a regular Broadway musical, and audiences may learn to accept these musical dwarfs. The Broadway hit, *I Do, I Do* had a cast of two. If the various unions claiming jurisdiction over theatrical production can accept the minimusical. their members may prefer smaller crews and lower minimums to no work at all on Broadway.

As rising costs began to reduce the number of shows mounted on Broadway, producers in the 1950s began to develop a theatrical movement that came to be known as off-Broadway. This movement away from New York's ten-block theatre district centered on drama, particularly experimental theatre. It had minimum impact on *musical* theatre. Concurrent with the off-Broadway movement, American universities began to increase their musical show production. Other regions of this country and Canada began developing indigenous theatre. At last, Broadway lost its monopoly on professional musical production. The movement is usually referred to as *regional theatre,* and it includes amateur, semiprofessional and fully professional productions. Actors, singers and dancers now use university and regional theatres to learn their craft. These establishments help fill the void left by the death of vaudeville in the 1930s where, as the show business expression has it, a performer found "a place to be bad." Schools, colleges and regional theatres now offer about the only training ground for aspiring professional singers, dancers, actors and writers. They spawn most of our new television performers, some of our writers and producers.

Regional theatres find particularly strong public acceptance for plays, dances and shows designed for children. Some children's theatres will break even at the box office. Regional theatres that focus on the classics, on experimental, noncommercial productions may receive financial support from the National Endowment for the Arts to help them stay alive and well.

For several years, Broadway has experienced further competition from *dinner theatres* that have sprung up all over the country. By 1975, Actors Equity, the union covering professional actors, reported that these dinner theatres *were producing more employment for their members than all of Broadway.* Dinner theatres find that their biggest draws are productions of hit Broadway musicals. The public does not ever seem to tire of yet another production of *Carousel* or *The Music Man.* Dinner theatres never invest in production of original musical plays.

Many of these theatres started out featuring stars or semi-stars. Since then, rising production costs have caused most dinner theatres to abandon that policy and now cast leading roles with fallen movie stars or talented college students. But the kids get paid, and in this sense, dinner theatres can be considered part of the professional theatre.

These establishments rarely have a proscenium stage. They mount their productions in-the-round, use blackouts for curtains, employ a minimum number of dancers on their small stages and put up with duo-piano accompaniment or a tiny pit band. Despite these limitations, some dinner theatres turn out very attractive shows.

Another component of musical theatre is the summer theatre, so popular across the country. Cities with particularly successful summer theatres are Chicago, Kansas City and Houston. They mount proven Broadway musicals almost exclusively. Many of these productions are first-class. They usually hire name artists for the leads, support them with the best local talent (professional and semiprofessional singers-actors-dancers), and employ a full pit orchestra of AFM musicians. Many summer theatres break even, perhaps even turn a profit, at the box office during their summer seasons, which may run from two to six weeks. Productions are mounted in old movie houses, community arts centers, parks, theatres and even tents. These productions offer short-term professional employment but some of their performing alumni go on to careers on Broadway, television, recording and film.

The Los Angeles Civic Light Opera not only mounts sumptuous productions rivaling the best of Broadway, but occasionally produces an original musical, runs it several weeks in Los Angeles and San Francisco, then sends it to Broadway. This reverses the traditional pattern, of course. With Los Angeles now the home ground for so many artists connected with the recording and broadcast industries, not to mention movies, this city may become important in mounting original musicals, then sharing them eventually with Broadway and the rest of the world.

Another important part of musical theatre is touring shows. Most Broadway hit musicals develop at least one road company that starts touring just as soon as the investors believe the public has heard about its New York success. Major hits have more than one New York-mounted road company which not only prosper on tour, but produce a lot of employment for singers, dancers and musicians. Road companies generally tour with their own musical conductor, perhaps a percussion-ist and one or two lead players, then fill in the pit orchestras with a dozen to three dozen local AFM members. The producer or musical director contacts local AFM contractors, perhaps through the local promoter, to engage the pit musicians. The AFM local sets minimums for local venues, which are generally scaled to the size of the facility. A 1000-seat theatre would probably have an AFM local minimum of a dozen to 18 musicians. Arenas and stadia in larger cities have AFM minimums of 30 to 45 musicians. These "casual" jobs provide consid-erable supplemental income for musicians across the country, many of whom are otherwise employed as music educators or as members of local symphony orchestras.

Other components of the touring show phenomenon are the various ice shows and circuses which offer supplemental employment for hun-dreds of AFM musicians every year. As with touring Broadway musi-cals, these shows travel with their own musical conductors and one to four first-chair musicians who form the nucleus of the orchestras fleshed out by local AFM musicians.

For several years, ice shows and circuses have used prerecorded tapes of vocal soloists or quartets. The conductor, working with ear phones and a sound engineer, synchronizes the canned voices with the live orchestra. A more recent phenomenon, particularly with leading ice shows, is to prerecord even some orchestral sounds, particularly strings, synthesizers and Melotron. These tapes are then synchronized to the live orchestra. The AFM exerts control over the production and use of these canned tracks. The show producers pay specially negotiated license fees for copyrighted music which has been recorded for these kinds of uses.

A significant part of musical theatre in this country is found in Las Vegas and other entertainment centers where gamblers' losses finance lavish entertainments. Las Vegas employs more live musicians and dancers, arrangers and copyists than all of Broadway. Fortunately for musicians, gambling casinos try to outdo each other in the lavishness of their stage productions and regularly employ large pit orchestras playing from manuscripts scored by AFM members.

The quality of the arrangers and players working in Las Vegas ranks with the best anywhere. A number of them were first drawn westward in search of work in Hollywood, then moved to Las Vegas and accepted steady employment there in preference to intermittent jobs in the Los Angeles area.

Another component of American musical theatre is the *industrial show.* When new products are introduced or national sales campaigns are being organized, companies like Ford and Cadillac hire a producer or a production company to create commercial entertainment packages designed to motivate and instruct their salesmen. These shows are not open to the public and are scheduled in major cities where the corporation pulls in its regional sales force. Industrial shows often have big budgets and offer seasonal employment for composers, arrangers, copyists, singers, dancers and instrumentalists. Writers and producers of industrial shows are usually found among the group that also produces broadcast commercials. Several major cities have production companies set up to turn out the kind of shows major corporations want, e.g., Detroit, Chicago, Los Angeles, New York and Philadelphia.

Classical and modern dance is a part of American musical theatre. Resident and touring companies offer at least seasonal employment for dancers and musicians who are engaged to accompany them. Most professional dancers belong to AGVA or AGMA. Many dance companies perform to recorded music, and the AFM has been unsuccessful in reducing this practice which limits live employment of union musicians.

Any list of musical theatre types should probably include the field of athletics. School and college musicians do not perform at basketball and football games on a professional basis, but their directors do — as do many of the arrangers. School and college purchases of printed music, combined with the performance licensing fees paid by arenas, stadiums, etc., constitute a level of activity involving millions of dollars. Any publisher or music licensing organization that ignores this important source is losing out on a lot of income.

Further music business interests are observed in professional football. Some NFL franchises either employ their own professional bands or invite (sometimes pay) school and college bands to entertain the sports fans at halftime and during time-out periods. All non-school musicians performing at NFL games are comprised of AFM members exclusively (local area musicians). The real money is generated by television broadcasts of the music. Since most broadcasts are either regional or national networks (sometimes international), music performance income to copyright owners from this branch of athletics is considerable. Publishers and composers struggle each week of the season to persuade NFL band leaders to broadcast their music.

PRODUCTION, PERSONNEL

Theatrical production, in many respects, is comparable to record production, in that everything begins and ends with one individual, the producer himself. All employment and all income is initially generated through the producer — his imagination and his money. In musical theatre, the producer's work begins with acquisition of a "property," which is just as bad a word as "product," the term used in the record industry. A theatrical property might only be an idea for a show, or it could be a novel or dramatic play that the producer feels might form a basis for a musical production of some kind. If the producer locates such a property, he will try to negotiate with its owner an option to produce it within a specified period of time. Then he scurries about trying to interest composers, lyricists and "book" authors (the term, "book" is used in the musical theatre to describe the scenario and dialogue of the musical drama; it excludes music and lyrics).

Producers are not the only individuals seeking musical show properties. Composers afflicted by the Broadway itch continually search various sources — novels, plays, even movies, for properties that they believe might form the basis for musical treatment. If they are successful in securing an option on a property, they then seek out a producer to assume the overall responsibility of pulling the production together and mounting the show.

If the musical is heading for Broadway, the producer must negotiate contracts with the author of the book, the composer and lyricist, in accord with standards and procedures set forth by the New York Dramatists Guild. The Dramatists Guild is powerful in controlling what gets on Broadway; its membership includes practically all important playwrights, musical show book authors, composers and lyricists active on Broadway.

The producer negotiates contracts with the show's author, composer and lyricist which specify what these writers are to receive in respect to salaries, royalties and subsidiary rights. The typical producer-writer contract provides a salary to be paid during the period the show is being created. Once the show opens, the writers normally receive equal shares (one-third each to the author, the composer and the lyricist) of six percent to eight percent of the show's gross box-office receipts during its Broadway run.

These contracts provide that when the producer is about to engage a director, conductor and dance director for the show, he must first obtain the approval of these artists from the author, composer and lyricist (by majority vote). The Dramatists Guild contract further stipulates that the producer cannot pull out a song or add one without the approval of the writers.

Concurrent with the effort to raise money for his show and sign the writers, the producer prepares at least a preliminary budget. One of the largest components of his weekly running costs will be rental of the theatre. When a producer schedules production time, he estimates what date he will open on Broadway, then tries to locate a suitable theatre. Most Broadway theatres are relatively small; the producer of a Broadway musical must locate a house that provides at least 1,000 to 1,500 seats in order to have sufficient capacity to generate adequate weekly box-office income. Broadway theatre owners know from long experience that the life expectancy of a new musical ranges from three hours to several years. They, too, must gamble with the show. A theatre owner is reluctant to sign a rental agreement with any producer in whom he lacks confidence. He will be more willing to risk tying up his theatre if the producer has a good track record, if the show's writers are well-known, if the cast includes a star. Once satisfied he should take a chance on the show, the landlord will charge the producer about 30 percent of the box-office gross receipts until that figure reaches $25,000 to $35,000 a week, then 25 percent thereafter. It is evident that a Broadway musical must do near capacity business to stay alive.

Typical weekly running costs of a full-line musical show will include most, possibly all, of the following:

1- *Royalty payments of six percent to eight percent of the box-office gross, shared equally by the author, composer and lyricist.*

2- *Salary (plus a weekly royalty) for the star.*

3- *Salaries for leading players (actors, singers, dancers).*

4- *Salaries for the stage manager and assistant stage manager.*

5- *Salaries (based on Actors Equity scale) for supporting actors, dancers, singers.*

6- *Salary (usually against a weekly royalty) for the show's director.*

7- *AFM scale for the pit musicians and any musicians that might appear on stage.*

8- *Salary for the choreographer. Big names sometimes also receive royalties.*

9- *Salaries for union stagehands, electricians (including audio technicians), carpenters, wardrobe personnel.*

10- *Office expense of the producer. Contracts typically provide for $600 to $1000 a week for this purpose plus one to two percent of the box-office gross for a management fee.*

11- *Salaries for production assistants; retainers to PR personnel; fees (or percentages) to theatre party promoters.*

Even if the show is a hit, the producer and his angels will not begin to get any of their investment returned until these weekly running costs are met. One of the reasons investors continue to put their money into this high risk field is because income from subsidiary rights sometimes will not only help crack the production nut, but exceed box-office revenue.

Production of professional shows outside of New York is now extensive. Production overhead may include most of the salaries paid to persons connected with Broadway musicals, but the rates are far below those in New York, particularly for stagehands and electricians. The "off-off-Broadway" producer is in a very different position from the producer who puts together the money to mount a Broadway show: regional theatres and dinner theatres do not really "produce" musicals, they *reproduce* them, they work only with proven material. Box-office success is almost guaranteed when a dinner theatre announces a forthcoming production of, say, an *Oklahoma!* or a *Fiddler on the Roof.*

Regional theatre producers often function in that gray area between the fully professional and the semiprofessional. Actors Equity regularly negotiates agreements with regional and community theatres which permit Equity-scale members to perform in the same cast with non-Equity members. AFM is less lenient with regional producers, except that theatre minimums (size of the orchestra required by the AFM) are generally within reason.

Regional theatres are less burdened by the absurd demands placed on them in New York by the stagehands' and electricians' unions. Regional producers often receive production money from city governments, light opera associations and regional arts councils.

Producers of material defined by statute as *dramatic music* — musical plays, operas, etc. — are required to pay performance royalties to the copyright owners. These kinds of performance licenses, known as "grand rights" (see Chapter 6), are required for both amateur and professional productions.

13

MUSIC MERCHANDISING

The world of business keeps changing its mind on how it wants to define its terms. I find little consensus in scholarly articles in business journals, and the most recent college textbooks differ in their definitions of such words as "merchandising," "marketing," "promotion" and "selling." The most recent trend is to use the term, "marketing" in a very broad sense — embracing the fields of advertising, promotion, distribution, merchandising, wholesaling and retailing of goods and services. That is alright with me, and in respect to the music business, all of these aspects are treated in this book.

Before proceeding with the present chapter on music merchandising, let me quote how that term is used at the University of Miami. Dr. Alfred Reed, cofounder and present director of that institution's baccalaureate and masters degree programs in music merchandising, defines the term broadly and stresses that music merchandising is much more than just selling goods and services. The true music merchant, he says,

> . . . must have at least a firsthand knowledge of music plus a
> fairly widespread knowledge of the place of music in our
> society . . . the merchandising of music, in any of its various
> forms, is dependent upon a grasp of changing times, fash-
> ions, tastes, and other personal and group factors which, in
> turn, create demand . . . no amount of purely business study

can make a successful merchandiser today, unless he can also make the strategic decisions that underlie the purely business side of the enterprise. And the basic foundation of successful music merchandising is to grasp and understand the place of music, all kinds of music, in our contemporary society.[1]

I agree with Dr. Reed's definition in this context. But for clarity of presentation, I present in this chapter information relevant to a narrower definition of music merchandising: *the pricing, distribution, promotion and retailing of music-related products, particularly discs, tapes, sheet music, music books and magazines, instruments and accessories.*

We should add to this such music-related merchandise as souvenir and novelty items, e.g., T-shirts, posters, bumper stickers, etc. If we add to this list music recording and reproducing equipment — audio and video — the dollar volume of the "music merchandising" business would rank it near the top among all business enterprises in this country.

The following figures provide a perspective on the scope of this sector of the music industry:

- *Retail sales of records and tapes — audio and video — aggregate about $4 billion in the U.S.A.*[2] *Aggregate sales abroad are even higher.*

- *Retail sales of instruments, equipment and accessories total over $2 billion a year in this country.*[3]

- *The number of stores in the United States specializing in the sale of instruments, equipment and accessories is over 5,000.*

- *The number of retail outlets for records and tapes is estimated to be at least 35,000 to 40,000 in the United States and Canada.*

- *Retail sales of music recording/reproducing equipment (audio and video) now aggregate about $9 billion a year in the US.*

Effective merchandising is dependent upon close cooperation among manufacturers, wholesalers, distributors and retailers. These enterprises offer employment for probably 200,000 persons. Positions are usually filled by individuals trained on the job, because our schools and colleges have lacked, until recent years, educational programs adequate to prepare individuals for this kind of employment.

1-From an interview appearing in *Music Handbook 75,* published by *Downbeat,* and the author's conversations with Dr. Reed.

2-Source: *Recording Industry Association of America* and the *National Association of Recording Merchandisers.*

3-Source: research commissioned by the *American Music Conference.*

Many individuals active at the retail level of music merchandising are musicians who need to supplement their incomes. It is interesting to observe that many musicians entering this field as an option to performing full-time discover that music merchandising becomes their number one choice for making their living.

SELLING DISCS AND TAPES

RIAA and NAMM have developed estimates indicating what kinds of retail outlets account for the greatest number of audio records and tapes sold:

Record stores	46%
Discount stores	16%
Department stores	8%
Other retail outlets	6%
Record clubs	13%
TV offers, direct mail	4%
Other	7%

RACK JOBBERS

Before we discuss the conventional record store, we will look at a different kind of supplier-merchant, the *rack jobber.* These business-men move over one-half of the records and tapes sold in the United States and Canada and are gaining in their market share abroad.

When the customer walks into a Sears store or a K-Mart, it is not possible to know just by looking around whether that record selling area is a department of the store, whether it is space leased to an outside firm, or whether it is serviced by a jobber who supplies the racks and bins. Chances are, a rack jobber is servicing that record selling operation.

Jobbers work out various kinds of contracts with the store that supplies the retail space. Among the most common:

> 1- *The jobber rents out space for his racks and bins from the retailer for a flat monthly fee. He offers complete servicing of the area and retains all the money collected from sales.*
>
> 2- *The jobber pays the host store a percentage of his sales.*
>
> 3- *The jobber and store management work out a minimum lease fee, then if sales exceed an agreed-upon figure in any given month, the jobber pays the store an override.*

Retailers like record racks on their premises because they can usually make more profit per square foot of space from this kind of merchandise than they can from other lines. Merchants also benefit from increased shopper traffic generated by the high volume of record buyers.

When rack jobbing of records was in its early stages (late 1950s, early 1960s), jobbers were content to lease small areas near checkout stands. These tiny displays had space to accommodate only a very limited variety of records. Jobbers tended to display only the current superhits — and only some of them. The balance of the limited space was given to *cutouts.* This limitation of space helped foster the hit records syndrome: only the hits were made available on the racks. Newer artists, lesser-known records never got a chance to be seen or heard.

Rack jobbers continue these small operations in some locations. But today, some installations rival in size some of the conventional record stores. When a rack jobber sets up a large number of racks and bins, he needs clerks to assist customers and restock supplies daily. Where a rack setup of this size is in operation, it is practically indistinguishable from a "leased department." When a merchant leases enough space for this kind of operation, he has a major commitment of capital, and he will probably have his own checkout counter and handle his own money rather than depend on the store's main check-out stands. Leased departments are common in department stores and discount chains. Large retailers can demand hefty lease payments from the record merchant and, at the same time, they are spared all responsibility of running the record sales department.

Large retailers and chains, observing the success on their premises of these record sales operations will, from time to time, decide to take over the same space, install their own record department management, then pocket the percentage they formerly paid out to the rack jobber. Rack jobbers try to anticipate this kind of temptation by offering the store trouble-free, profitable operations, sparing retailers the problem of trying to run a kind of retailing they do not really understand.

In recent years, large firms in the rack jobbing field have branched out into the record distribution business too. They accommodate not only their own rack installations but sell product to any other jobber or retailer who wants the merchandise.

Individuals who started out as rack jobbers or distributors are now also heavily involved in operation of retail outlets. **The lines between record distribution, jobbing and retailing are now blurred; some of the most successful merchants operate in all three areas.** This blending of record selling operations has been accelerated by the need of merchants to buy products at ever-higher discounts through volume purchasing. For this same reason, this trend in the business will continue, probably grow.

RETAIL STORES

Since the introduction of record racks and record clubs in the 1950s, the conventional retail record store has had some rough times. The small operators in the retail record business came into being in the 1960s with the rise of rock and roll and folk-rock. Many of these stores became known as "head shops" and were patronized by what we used to call hippies, young people on the prowl for new records, companionship and other sensory stimuli. Record head shops tended to disappear as the hippy generation went underground or dissolved into straight society. The only counterpart extant today for this kind of very small retail operation is the "mom-and-pop" record store.

One type of relatively small record store does well when it is well-managed. I refer to the proprietor who locates in a special neighborhood, earns the confidence of a small but loyal clientele, and stocks the particular kind of records that appeal to that community. For example, one such operation does a strong business in Boston selling polka records.

Another kind of specialized record store is found in the inner-city ghetto. The black merchant understands what his predominantly black clientele is looking for and he accommodates it. Yet another kind of specialized record store is often found in shopping communities adjoining a large university where the market for classical music is strong. When staffed by knowledgeable clerks, such stores do well.

Many small record stores, though, are disappearing. One reason is that they cannot buy enough stock to receive an adequate discount from distributors. In turn, this means they cannot discount their retail prices to compete with larger stores. Another reason the small store rarely survives today is that many customers want to browse through endless bins of merchandise. Tastes are more diverse now; a customer may favor country music, but he finds something he also wants to take home in MOR or jazz. Only a retailer with a large inventory of diverse styles can attract this kind of customer.

Retailing today is much more complicated than in the past. Even retail operations of medium size are expected to stock singles, LPs, 8-track tapes, cassettes, covering not only current releases, but past hits. To further compound the retailer's inventory problems, his stock should cover all major styles, from pop to classical. If this weren't enough, his customers will also expect him to have blank tape in open reel and cassette configurations — and a full line of accessories. Stocking, controlling and merchandising such a diverse inventory demands working capital 10 times greater than in simpler times. Record retailing today is big business.

Prices, Discounts — When a merchant manages to pull together enough working capital to set up a retailing operation, his problems have just begun. One of his greatest challenges is determining at what price he can afford to buy — and then what kind of discounts he can offer his customers. Distributors will romance him with all kinds of discount offers, seeking to induce him to buy in greater and greater volume. But if he is persuaded to buy 100 records at special discount on one release, he thereby diminishes his working capital to buy smaller amounts of a number of other hot items. The skill in balancing these conflicting interests separates the men from the boys in the retail business. When the retailer reduces his working capital through heavy purchasing, his next recourse is to persuade his banker to loan him just a little more, then a little more. His credit at the bank and with distributors can soon become overextended and he may wish he had gone into the fish business.

Many retailers I talk to complain that the record companies and distributors do not treat them well. Their complaints are voiced in the trades and at association conventions. The most prevalent complaint is labels' discounting policies; to the merchant, they are generally considered inconsistent, inadequate, sometimes unacceptable. The distributors and manufacturers counter with the argument that the retailer gets all he deserves, in that most record buyers enter a store presold anyway, through radio promotion.

Point-of-Purchase Stimuli — Record companies have great difficulty getting their releases accepted for airplay by radio stations. Even when new releases do gain airplay in some parts of the country, label promotion people find it very hard to attract record buyers *nationally,* which they must do to achieve an acceptable number of sales. Even if a new release gets good national exposure on the radio, every label that can afford it develops a variety of *visual* sales stimuli to attract customer interest. The industry often refers to these visual stimuli as "P.O.P.'s" — point-of-purchase (or "point-of-sale") merchandising aids. As every shopper knows, these P.O.P.'s assume a variety of forms, ranging from posters to mobiles to souvenir trinkets bearing evidence of some connection with the product being pushed. Some labels — Warner Bros. and CBS come to mind — spend millions of dollars a year creating, manufacturing and distributing these point-of-purchase items for use in music stores.

The retailer welcomes these label-supplied sales stimuli, because he is aware that many of his customers are not "presold" when they enter his store. The merchant tries to provide a stimulating environment for the potential customer, hoping he will feel free to browse until he locates a record to buy. Experienced merchandisers have learned that the most sales result from cooperation of the retailer, the distributor and the record company.

As record retailing becomes a business of lowering profit and increasing risk, the smaller entrepreneur becomes easy prey for sale to a retail chain. The growth of record chain operations results from the same economic pressures already cited: to make a profit, the merchants must find ever new ways to buy cheaper, and the mass merchandiser is certainly in a better position to do this than mom and pop. Chain store operators provide an additional advantage to their component units: when one store overbuys and gets stuck with inventory, it can often shift some of this product to another unit in the chain that may have run short. Chain store members help each other balance their inventories.

Bar Coding — Probably the most efficient and economical method of controlling inventory and returns is through bar coding. For several years, NARM (National Association of Recording Merchandisers) has been trying to persuade full adoption of bar coding by the industry. Many labels now imprint the codes, and merchants who have installed code-scanning equipment use these data, not only for inventory control, but for practically all other sales information: which records were sold, at what price, the "age" of the merchandise, the amount of sales charged, etc. Another value of the widescaled adoption of bar coding of records and tapes is the detection of counterfeit merchandise. Scanners can easily detect false codings.

Returns — Distributors and sales personnel regularly pressure dealers to buy more stock than they believe they can move. This pressure assumes various forms. The record company or distributors will often offer merchants liberal merchandise return privileges. In the past, practically all records and tapes in this country were sold on consignment: if you can't sell the merchandise, return it for full credit. At the start of the 1980s, most labels and distributors had tightened their returns policies. The practice now is often one that requires the merchant to return the stock within a prescribed time limit, that he is entitled to return only a prescribed percentage of records ordered, and that he will not receive credit for returns unless he pays his bills from the distributors or label within a reasonable time.

Price Cutting — The pervasive complaint of retail merchants is price cutting. Manufacturers can only recommend retail prices; they cannot control them. Competitive pricing is a basic characteristic of the capitalistic system. But some merchants not only try to underprice their competitors, they will sometimes attempt to run a rival out of business. Price wars are waged, not just among small merchants, but among the medium-sized stores, large stores and chains. Warlike tactics do not always work, because a merchant can survive but a short time selling below cost. Well-capitalized, competing merchants sometimes outwait these wild discounters and see the offending party go under. But severe discounting continues to plague record merchants. Since they are often unable to solve the problem among themselves, relief may have to come from record manufacturers and distributors in offering "favored customer" deals to merchants trying to maintain rational pricing policies.

CUTOUTS, REPACKAGING

Record manufacturers find it impossible to estimate how many records to press. If they underestimate demand, customers will ask for the record and cannot be accommodated. If they overestimate demand, they will find their warehouses stocked with dead merchandise. Once the demand drops sharply, the manufacturer will stop production. The inventory remaining is known as cutouts. Retail outlets cannot move this stock at normal prices, and the manufacturer finds it profitable to unload this merchandise at cost or below cost on buyers who specialize in cutouts. These cutout merchants buy up quantities, warehouse the records, then vend them to rack jobbers and other retailers at a very low price. Their customers, in turn, offer these cutouts at extremely low prices. Both parties usually turn a profit, and the retail customer gets a bargain.

Some record stores find that their profit margin from cutouts is better than from conventional sales. Some cutout companies buy or lease old masters, then rerelease artists, or fallen artists, who still have loyal fans ready to gobble up ancient hits at bargain prices. For example, cutout merchants and repackagers always appear able to sell "rereleases" or "new" releases of the big name band hits of the 1940s. Another perennial repertoire comes from the early rock and roll hits. Repressings of the country music continue to sell, through "new" releases, new packages or cutouts.

Perhaps the most successful merchandising of old hits repackaged is seen on television. Companies buy up or lease masters from record companies holding the rights to old hits, then repackage them under their own record labels. These repackagers favor such LP (and tape) titles as "Sinatra's Greatest Hits" or "The Best of Country Music." They produce low-cost, hardsell TV spots, buy spot time on independent TV stations and provide a local mailing address and toll-free telephone number for viewers to place their orders. Some operators in this field manage to promote repackaging deals without clearly defined licensing arrangements. But the 1976 Copyright Act made it easier to control illegal or borderline operations of this kind.

HOME VIDEO PRODUCTS

Throughout the 1970s, merchants had been told to get ready for the "new" home videocassette and videodisc business. The predicted "explosion" of this market never did occur. But in the early 1980s, hardware merchants were selling huge numbers of VCR's — videocassette recorders. This greatly increased the sale of raw videocassette tapes in record stores, and many merchants also began to sell prerecorded videocassettes.

Record store sales of *videodiscs* accelerated early in the decade, also, in part because of the increasing availability of videodisc players priced at about the same level as a regular TV set.

The market for "home video" hardware and software grew rapidly. NARM (National Association of Recording Merchandisers) urged its members to go after this market vigorously or risk losing it to the competition.

Few record stores attempt to compete with home appliance stores and TV stores for the sale of video recorders and players. But few record store merchants today have failed to greatly increase their offerings of video software. They have no real option: most market analyses predict that, in a few years, merchants may be selling more video entertainment than audio.

Record store merchants found, however, that it is not easy to add video products to their inventories and turn a profit. The market is still relatively small compared to the number of customers for audio products. Most estimates revealed that only about five percent of the music-loving public owned videodisc and tape players by 1982.

Another problem for record merchants is that the buyer of home video products is quite different from the typical buyer of recorded music. Research indicates that the "typical" home video product buyer is male, about 35 years of age, well-educated, enjoys an annual income above $35,000 — and is quite selective in his tastes.

Yet another problem for the record store merchant is the sales resistance of his customers, largely caused by indecision and confusion over incompatible playback equipment. Neither the merchant nor his customer knows whether the videocassette or videodisc will win out. Even if the disc should win the contest for the public's money, we do not know which of several videodisc systems may prevail. The merchant and customer are in a similar dilemma over whether the Betamax or VHS-type cassette will dominate. So dealers and customers in large numbers hold back — waiting for others to risk their money during the shakedown period of incompatible hardware and software.

By 1982, there were some two million VCR's in American homes. Sales of 20,000 to 30,000 prerecorded discs or tapes were considered a "hit." The International Tape/Disc Association awarded its "Golden

Videocassette" sales award when a particular release sold 17,000 units.

A typical record store will carry about 500 different titles of some 14,000 estimated to be available. The merchant would probably stock more if he could find sufficient working capital, always in short supply.

The best sellers are feature movies. But the backlog of films is a finite source. Owners of home video equipment appear ready to buy new programs when they become available.

Some movie studios are releasing videocassettes and discs of new feature films *simultaneously* with their release in movie theatres. This infuriates the movie theatre operators but delights the video merchants, in that the latter enjoy the benefit from the promotion money (often several million dollars per movie) already being spent on the film's theatre release.

Sell Or Rent? — Merchants believe that the public will look at a videodisc or cassette a few times, then tire of it much more quickly than they would after repeated playings of a regular record album. If they are correct, the mass market for video product *sales* may never be attained, because only affluent people may be willing and able to invest $30 to $50 for a few playings of a videodisc or tape. As a consequence, merchants have found that many music lovers prefer *renting* these video packages to buying them. Program suppliers try to limit rentals, of course, in that the practice reduces sales. Some suppliers require retailers to sign a sales agreement promising they will not rent this merchandise. But dealers declare they cannot profit much from video sales in that margins are thin. As a consequence, many merchants ignore the no-rent agreements and engage in the practice anyway.

Yet, the rental business has its own set of problems. One is the inconvenience and extra time required to keep track of the rentals moving in and out of the store. Many rental units come back damaged and must be discarded. Circumvention of no-rent agreements is so widespread, some manufacturers of video programs do not make a serious attempt to enforce them. Other manufacturers permit rentals, but tack on a surcharge when making the sale to the store.

In order to avoid copyright problems, some merchants take pains to make their purchases indirectly; instead of buying directly from the manufacturer, they make their purchases for rentals through a secondary supplier such as a subdistributor not connected with the manufacturer. Copyright attorneys seem to believe this buying method relieves the merchant from any entanglement with copyright law.

Some analysts believe the sell-or-rent argument will be settled in the marketplace. They anticipate that, when the volume of production increases sufficiently for suppliers to lower the sale price, the public will find that the cost difference between buying and renting will be slight enough to discourage widespread rentals.

NARM

The association most broadly representative of the interests of record sellers is NARM, the National Association of Recording Merchandisers. The organization's literature states that "Regular membership of NARM is comprised of rack jobbers, independent distributors, and retailers of phonograph records, tapes, accessories and equipment. The Associate Membership consists of the suppliers of all types of product and services to NARM's Regular and Associate Members. Virtually every record manufacturing company is an associate member of NARM. In addition, manufacturers of display fixtures, printing and packaging services and blank tape are Associate Members."

When NARM was organized in the late 1950s, it was primarily an association serving the interests of rack jobbers. Since that time, it has accepted into its membership companies and individuals engaged in all aspects of record manufacturing, distribution and retailing.

NARM issues a newsletter called *NARM Sounding Board*, which contains useful information, reports on NARM-sponsored research, and offers special articles on music business management and merchandising.

NARM assists its members by offering special seminars several times a year in various cities across the country. They are called *NARM Regionals;* they provide special training for merchants in sales promotion and store management.

Another important service is NARM's *Recording Industry Internship Program.* To encourage its members to participate in this program, NARM distributes this description to its members:

The purpose of this major program is to prepare students for entry level and middle management positions with firms just like yours. The NARM Internship Program will provide you an eager student representative from the Junior classes from the top colleges and universities across the country that offer record and music management courses.

This program affords you the opportunity to aggressively seek out and recruit quality personnel with basic music industry background and strong management potential for your future growth - with NARM supplying all the legwork. In addition, this program, should you decide to participate, will, with the help of NARM, develop the framework for an employee recruiting and training program.

The cost of this 10-week program (to our members) is $1,500 per student. This figures out over a 10-week period to an hourly rate of $3.75.

The advantages to the NARM Internship Program are many:

- It will enable NARM member companies to identify and evaluate potential employees.

- Students will have a "hands on" opportunity in an actual work situation, dealing with the reality of shipping and receiving, inventory control, pricing, returns, personnel, buying, accounting, advertising, sales, display positioning . . . and more, thus reinforcing the textbook training received in the classroom, as well as, enhancing each university's program upon student return to the school.

- It is anticipated that the success of the Internship Program will stimulate the interest of other academic institutions to include courses, as well as degree programs, in the music industry — thereby bringing more competent and well-trained people into the business.

Merchants believe that one of the most effective ideas NARM leadership has come up with in recent years is its *Give the gift of music* campaign. NARM conceived this promotion scheme in an effort to help its members sell more music merchandise *as gifts.* The promotion campaign became a success nationally. NARM supplies merchants the *Give the gift of music* logo in all shapes, sizes and colors and provides ideas on how and where to use the logo and slogan in print ads, on TV commercials, decals and for imprints on products. Research indicates that a sizable percent of music merchandise purchases are intended for gifts, and this NARM promo campaign has advanced this kind of buying.

Television

SELLING INSTRUMENTS, EQUIPMENT

Merchandising instruments and equipment is a major part of the music business. In the United States we have nearly 50 million instrumentalists — amateur and professional. These performers all need to be supplied with equipment and accessories. The American Music Conference has accumulated estimates of just who buys:

Instrument	Number of Amateur Players	Percent of Amateurs	Median Age
Piano	18.1 million	36	28
Guitar	15.1 "	30	23
Organ	6.1 "	12	31
Clarinet	2.9 "	6	19
Drums	2.7 "	6	19
Trumpet	2.2 "	5	19
Flute	2.5 "	5	19
Saxophone	1.5 "	3	22
Violin	1.7 "	4	27
Harmonica	1.5 "	3	25

Source: American Music Conference.

As to the number of school music ensembles, my research shows the following:

Concert Bands	23,000
Marching Bands	22,000
Stage Bands	16,000
Small Ensembles (Combos, etc.)	16,000
Orchestras	6,000
Choral Groups	25,000
Small Singing Ensembles	17,000

AMC research shows that about 73 percent of elementary school students and about 41 percent of high school students participate in music. When only the top four percent of academically talented high school students are evaluated, the percentage of them involved in music leaps to 88 percent.

Sales of instruments, equipment and printed music have risen almost every year since the AMC began accumulating the statistics.

INSTRUMENT	1982 Sales (est.)*
Organs	$475 million
Pianos	612 "
Electric Pianos	45 "
Synthesizers	31 "
Fretted Instruments	392 "
Woodwind Instruments	149 "
Brass Instruments	104 "
String Instruments	51 "
Percussion Instruments	92 "
Miscl. Other Instruments	178 "
Sound Reinforcement Equipment	247 "
Accessories	306 "
Printed Music	313 "

*Estimates of the author based on data supplied by the *American Music Conference.*

CHANGING MARKETS

Retail sales of instruments, equipment and printed music have been rising for decades. This huge market is comprised of three groups of customers, the smallest of which is the professional musician. The next largest group is comprised of the amateur, the music hobbyist — children and adults. The largest part of this market involves schools and colleges which host some 100,000 school ensembles. These music ensembles, in turn, have an aggregate membership of several million young musicians. Their instruments, equipment and music are bought by the schools themselves and the individual musicians' families.

The market is changing. Since the 1960s, school bond issues have been failing. Music educators have been unable to convince electorates and school boards that music is more than an educational frill — nice to have but not really important. Many Americans do not yet value highly the civilizing effect musical training can have on the human spirit and have traditionally been more inclined to sacrifice music and art budgets than, for example, sports. Marching bands continue to fare well, of course, because they are really part of athletic programs. Football bands often offer good entertainment (for the kids and their audience), but many observers view them as more involved in show business than music education.

Band uniforms and plastic sousaphones continue to sell well. But the demographics impacting on the record industry are also affecting sales of instruments, equipment and printed music. When a school budget cuts music programs, the most vulnerable area has been at the elementary level. The quickest way to chop school budgets is to fire

teachers; the elementary school music specialist is first to go. Many major cities have completely eliminated them from their budgets. Cutting music education in the early grades impacts negatively on music education in high schools. Even here, many school districts are cutting music budgets. These cuts, in turn, reduce the number and quality of students entering college level music study. The long-term result of these cutbacks is that, coming out of the educational assembly line are fewer and fewer adults who have been turned on to music through participation. We are producing a larger generation of listeners, but fewer performers than before. But the phenomenon is not fully understood. Some kids have been turned off to music through an unpleasant school music experience. While we may now turn out fewer music performers from our schools, this loss may be balanced by growth in adult interest in music performance. Signs of this development are at hand: sales of pianos and organs to adult beginners are up, as are instruction books. As adults acquire increased time for leisure, it appears likely that increasing numbers of this growing segment of our population will turn to music. They will be shopping for instruments, equipment, accessories and sheet music.

Another market impact of school music budget cuts is the increased production of self-teaching materials. The Hal Leonard company is selling increasing quantities of A/V learning kits. Students (and adults) take home a cassette tape, a correlated study book, practice their flutes with this material, and do an acceptable job of teaching themselves. The school district has saved at least part of a teacher's salary, and the kid experiences a feeling of accomplishment. Many school band directors start beginners with these A/V kits, then reinforce those experiences with ensemble practice in the school rehearsal room.

What kind of merchandise do music stores sell? The figures that follow are based on AMC studies, *U.S. Department of Commerce Census of Business* and my own research.

TYPES OF STORES

AMERICA's 5000 MUSIC STORES

Merchandise Sold	Percentage of Stores Carrying the Merchandise
Guitars, Other Fretted Instruments	80%
Pianos	70%
Organs	70%
Band Instruments	65%
Amplifiers	63%
Synthesizers	45%
Printed Music	80%
Records, Tapes	30%

MUSIC STORE LOCATIONS

Cities with populations of 250,000 and more	23%
Suburban areas near a large city	18%
Cities with populations between 50,000 and 250,000	33%
Cities with populations under 50,000	43%

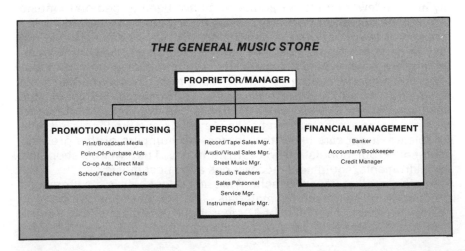

Fig. 13.1

These estimates must be read with caution. At first glance, it would appear that most stores carry just about everything. This is not true. We have very few music supermarkets. Stores tend to specialize in one area, say, pianos and organs, then they may offer printed music too, but only a few editions, not a full department. A band instrument store may report on a questionnaire that it also sells records. This will most often mean, not a record department, rather, the availability of a few learning cassettes or some "play-along" LPs for students of improvisation. Stores that report they sell synthesizers may include piano-organ stores which offer "synthesizers" as an accessory to an electric organ.

PIANOS, ORGANS — By far the largest business in terms of dollar volume is done by the stores specializing in the sale of pianos and organs. Music merchants generally group pianos and organs under "keyboards"; they are normally excluded under the appellation, "musical instruments." Piano-organ stores require large initial investments in inventory and a lot of floor space. They often advertise free lessons for their instrument buyers. Most instruments are sold to beginners and near-beginners. The market has grown rapidly with the introduction of electronic organs offering automatic production of rhythm patterns and chords or both — with the press of a button. More expensive accessories include electronic oscillators similar to performance-type synthesizers. Beginning players are attracted to these instruments in large numbers partly because the sounds produced give the manipulator a feeling of power — and most customers do not find it beyond their intelligence to press the buttons. Beginners can soon learn to sound like one-man-bands.

A piano-organ store invariably offers instrument maintenance, with a piano technician on its payroll full-time, not only to prepare instruments for sale, but to provide tuning services to customers. Old-line piano merchants were reluctant to add electronic instruments, often viewing them as just machines, not musical instruments. But their views were quickly modified as they observed the rapidly growing market. Traditional piano stores now offer not only a variety of electronic organs, but electronic pianos. This addition has brought into their stores many young rock and jazz musicians who regard the electronic piano and "rock organ" indispensable to contemporary music performance. Only the largest piano-organ stores have on staff fully qualified maintenance personnel for the various electronic instruments. Repair services on this kind of equipment are usually farmed out; qualified personnel are hard to find even free-lance.

Many piano-organ merchants offer rental agreements as an alternative to outright purchase. The most common arrangement is for the merchant to place the instrument in the buyer's home, offer him several weeks' free lessons, this package provided on a rental agreement, say, six months with option to purchase. The purchase option normally includes application of some or all of the rental fee already paid. Lending institutions sometimes cooperate with merchants in financing these plans, thus reducing the amount of capital a merchant would need to offer these options to customers.

GUITAR, DRUM STORES — Every community has at least one merchant engaged in the business of selling guitars and drums. These stores frequently become the hang-out place for young musicians active in rock, country and pop music performance. Stores selling guitars also carry amplifiers and speaker systems, even audio mixing panels, PA systems and "tone dividers." All but the smallest guitar-drum stores employ audio maintenance personnel, or they may provide such service by leasing out the department to a separate operator. Maintenance of guitar amplifying equipment can become a large part of a store's operation, because few manufacturers yet build equipment rugged enough to accept the abuse inflicted during transport.

Stores vending percussion equipment are almost invariably operated by a professional drummer who moonlights. The proprietor not only has firsthand knowledge of the kinds of paraphernalia drummers need, he can assist with maintenance. Finally, percussion merchants offer lessons on the premises to amateurs and beginning professionals. Musicians visiting the guitar-drum store find it perhaps the best place in town to hear word of auditions and potential jobs.

BAND, ORCHESTRA, INSTRUMENTS — Merchants of wind, string and brass instruments operate much like guitar-drum store proprietors. One important difference is their clientele. Most general instrument stores seek, and often obtain, the business of the local school band and orchestra directors. The educational field forms a large part of the business written by music stores, and bidding can become unfriendly among competitors. Some merchants will sell instruments and equipment to school districts at or near cost, in the hope that this activity will provide good visibility in the community to attract the non-school business. Still other instrument merchants share the school business bids through undercover "understandings" with their competitors. This is clearly illegal, but some merchants find ways to launder these activities to provide an acceptable appearance to the business community.

Instrument stores normally carry three grades of merchandise. The least expensive models are recommended to beginners and parents who are uncertain whether the youngster will stick with his newfound toy. All merchants carry school-grade instruments, too. These are ruggedly constructed, provide acceptable intonation, and are the type of instrument the merchant will normally use for rentals. As with the rent-purchase deals described above for pianos, band instrument merchants sometimes build up a very large rental business. This kind of operation can get out of hand. Quite a number of merchants have been so successful renting instruments that they become overextended financially through the need to maintain a large inventory. A balance of rentals and sales is necessary, not only to maintain an acceptable cash flow, but the confidence of bankers.

The third level of merchandise includes the first-line instruments demanded by the professional artist. This kind of equipment costs at least twice as much as the economy and student models.

One of the strongest attractions of a musical instrument store is its repair shop — if it is a good one. It not only produces a profit, but pulls potential purchasers into the store, too.

The accessory business also attracts many customers, and profit margins on this kind of merchandise are higher than for instruments. But pilferage by customers and employees is a major problem. The crime of shoplifting in this country is about out of control and costs merchants and their customers millions of dollars a year. This problem is partly controlled by the proprietor himself who almost invariably doubles as a salesperson. The busy time for music instrument stores is from 3 p.m. to 9 p.m.; after conventional stores have reached the closing hour, music stores keep busy into the evening offering music lessons.

As all store owners will attest, their toughest problem is *locating qualified help.* Apart from the question of stealing, it is not easy to locate clerks and salespersons who are not only well-informed, but have the kind of temperament suitable for dealing with the public.

Nearly all instrument salespersons divide their time between greeting customers and giving music lessons on the premises. In the larger communities, most music instrument salespersons and teachers are AFM members, and the stores become a kind of meeting place for the professional musicians in the area.

HOME ENTERTAINMENT EQUIPMENT STORES — The market for hi-fi equipment, sometimes called "componentry," received its greatest impetus with the introduction of stereo sound systems in the late 1950s. Since that period, merchants have found a growing market for all kinds of home entertainment equipment. Fortunately for the merchant, audiophiles never seem quite satisfied with last year's equipment. As ever new components appear on the market, consumers step forth to spend their money. Clearest evidence of the size of this kind of market is the fact that manufacturers now advertise, not just in specialty magazines, but *Time, Newsweek* and *Readers Digest.* The market is now so proliferated with brands and models, gadgets and accessories, that the bulk of sales are in hi-fi stores. Department stores, formerly important retailers of audio equipment now take second place to the stereo specialists found in every city.

As with record retailing, price cutting among stereo merchants is endemic, even epidemic. Big chains periodically cut their prices in apparent attempts to wipe out smaller competitors. Sometimes they succeed. The mass buying available to chain stores makes possible a retail pricing policy that the mom-and-pop stores cannot match. Most clerks in hi-fi stores are audiophiles themselves, often well-informed on the mysterious circuitry inhabiting their magic boxes. They use a jargon known only to themselves and the hi-fi fans who patronize them. It's all good for business. Also good for the stereo business are the high quality records now being produced. Modern recording-pressing technology makes possible an aural realism that challenges the live performance experience. By the mid-1970s, even the 1⅞ i.p.s. cassettes began to rival LP quality. Open reels offer the highest fi, but are fading fast from favor; consumers are even losing interest in LPs, good as they are, in favor of the new high quality cassette tapes and the convenience and quality of the newer cassette players.

Many hi-fi shops now vend what is known in the trade as semiprofessional equipment. This includes, for example, four to eight-track recording machines, comparable mixers, low cost equalizers, electronic echo devices, and high quality amps. This line of merchandise, priced about 25 percent to 50 percent higher than consumer-grade equipment, is being bought in quantities by songwriters, performers and demo recording studio operators. While the semipro equipment is not engineered to stand up under the extended periods of use in fully professional studios, its recording and reproduction specs come close to professional hardware — and most of us cannot distinguish the difference in audio quality between these two grades of equipment.

Like other music merchants, hi-fi stores do not seem able to solve equipment maintenance problems. Equipment is now so sophisticated, the fix-it-type repair person must often fake his way through the electronic maze. Stores that operate their own repair departments are regularly insulted by customers indignant about inadequate repairs. The sales business is so good, in-house repair departments often refuse outside jobs, struggling even to keep the equipment they sell in working order. Some proprietors prefer to farm out maintenance to electronic repair companies who are more likely to staff qualified personnel. This works well for the customer who is prepared to wait weeks to get his equipment repaired.

Merchants try to attend consumer electronic trade shows to inform themselves on new products and market trends. In the early 1980s, one of their strongest sellers was VCRs — videocassette recorders. Soon to follow were videodisc players. It appears certain that, as the price of this equipment comes down and as more prerecorded programs become available, the market will broaden greatly. Many market analysts believe that sales of videocassettes and disc players will one day overtake sales of both conventional TV sets and hi-fi equipment.

SELLING PRINTED MUSIC

RACKS, LEASED DEPARTMENTS

Most printed music is sold from racks or sheet music departments located in stores engaged in other kinds of retailing. The biggest seller among printed music editions is the popular song folio. Most record stores now regularly sell these printed editions along with records, tapes and accessories. Like the growth in the early 1960s of rack locations for records, folios are showing a similar expansion, including such locations as bookstores.

The second important retail outlet for printed music is found in sheet music departments located in record stores and music instrument-equipment stores. Such departments are often leased from the "host" store. The floor space may simply be subleased, or the host may charge a minimum rent against some kind of percentage of printed music sales. According to a 20-store survey of record stores offering printed music for sale, the *Music Retailer* magazine found that customers tended to fall into one of two categories: "the young adult, primarily male, who purchases Top-40 guitar and personality books and the older female who prefers organ and piano music." Many retailers find that about 40 percent of their sheet music customers are over 30 years of age, and this group of buyers demonstrates a preference for musical styles much broader than rock and roll.

The print music merchant will not only carry pop song folios but a much more varied stock, e.g., pop standards, individual sheet music, P.D. folios, how-to-play books for children and adults and vocal group pop charts. The largest sheet music operations will also carry various editions of popular classics, e.g., Mendelssohn's *Songs Without Words*, Mozart sonatas, and Hannon-Czerny-type etudes. Print music merchants buy from jobbers who carry a variety of music publishers' lines. Racks are sometimes serviced by jobbers in establishments lacking full-time clerks.

Inventory control for a print music merchant is difficult because of the great variety and quantity of merchandise. The availability of low cost computers is easing this problem for merchants who can afford the investment.

EDUCATIONAL FIELD

The sale of printed editions in the fields of educational music and serious music is markedly different from pop. The music education repertoire is now so diverse and voluminous, most educators prefer to patronize the large regional dealers who stock the major editions (and a lot of minor ones). These regional operations — some states may only have one to three serving the whole area — are often staffed by professional musicians and music educators.

Publishers attempt to presell educational materials through print ads in music education journals and through direct mail campaigns. Print music merchants in the educational field conduct a large portion of their business by mail, often priding themselves in getting phoned-in-orders in the mail within a day or two. New customers are expected to place their orders only through official school district purchase orders. Print music proprietors grieve over the traditionally slow-paying school accounts. Some have almost gone bankrupt waiting for this public money to come in from school accounting offices.

Merchants operating large educational music stores also stock various kinds of serious music — chamber music, symphonies, concert pieces, oratorios, other large choral works — either in "original" editions (often European) or in more recent editions. Since nearly all of this repertoire is in the public domain, a variety of editions is available. While a community orchestra conductor or church choir director may find standard works in these large retail operations, when he needs lesser known serious works, his dealer will usually have to contact the publisher to supply them on special order. Only the largest metropolitan centers attempt to have on their shelves a wide selection of editions of symphonies, chamber music, operas, ballet, etc.; the market is just too small, and retailers cannot afford the floor space for such slow-moving merchandise.

Larger print music retailers also stock music library supplies and various accessories, sometimes including school band supplies. Retailers sometimes promote sales by sponsoring annual reading sessions of new editions at a music camp or local college campus.

STORE OPERATION

STRUCTURE

Music stores and other kinds of business enterprises are operated according to how they have been structured financially. In our capitalistic economy, a business enterprise can be structured and capitalized in one of three ways:

sole proprietorship

partnership

corporation

Each of these forms of ownership has certain advantages of operation, and each offers certain disadvantages. An individual contemplating investment in a music store or any other kind of business venture should consider the pros and cons of these three options.

SOLE PROPRIETORSHIP — The principal advantage of sole proprietorship is that it is easy to set up and get under way. All the entrepreneur really needs is some money (his own or borrowed funds), a great amount of energy — and a lot of nerve. The sole proprietor who wants to get out fast can do that, too; he doesn't need to call a meeting of the board to make decisions. Many entrepreneurs venture forth on their own largely because they dislike working for someone else; they enjoy being their own boss. The proprietor runs his own show, sinks or swims on his own abilities. Finally, the sole proprietor enjoys the advantage of all the profits; he need not share with anyone what he makes.

That's the good news. Now for the bad news: the sole proprietor is personally responsible for all financial losses the business may ex-

TYPES OF BUSINESS OWNERSHIP

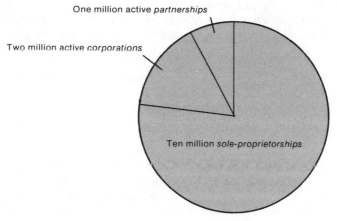

One million active *partnerships*

Two million active *corporations*

Ten million *sole-proprietorships*

Fig. 13.2   Estimates projected for 1980 based on *Statistical Abstract of the United States. 1977*

TYPES OF BUSINESS OWNERSHIP

ADVANTAGES

SOLE-PROPRIETORSHIP	PARTNERSHIP	CORPORATION
1- You are the boss 2- Easy to form, easy to dissolve 3- You retain all profits	1- Simple to organize 2- Complementary management skills 3- Expanded capitalization	1- Limited personal liability 2- Maximum capitalization 3- Lower cost per unit of doing business

DISADVANTAGES

1- Very hard work 2- Unlimited financial liability 3- Management deficiencies 4- Limited working capital 5- Potential lack of continuity of operation	1- Unlimited financial liability 2- Potential conflicts of authority 3- Potential personality conflicts	1- Expensive, complicated to form 2- Legal restrictions 3- Double taxation 4- Impersonal, insensitive

Fig. 13.3

perience. If our Horatio Alger runs out of money, his creditors can take possession of his personal property, including house and home — whatever he may own of value. The sole proprietorship has the omnipresent problem of limited capital. Even if the business is going well, the single operator may find it difficult to raise enough money to expand his business. The one-man operation will also be deficient in management capabilities; no one person can do everything well. A whirlwind salesperson-manager can pull his company under if he can't understand basic accounting principles. Finally, the sole proprietorship may have to cease operations suddenly if the owner-manager becomes physically or mentally disabled or goes through divorce or has to move away.

PARTNERSHIP — Partnerships are another form of business ownership. They are defined by the Uniform Partnership Act as "associations of two or more persons who operate a business as co-owners by voluntary legal agreement." General partnerships are established when all partners involved carry on the business as co-owners. Limited partnerships (not permitted in some states) are composed of one or more general partners and one or more limited partners. A limited partner is one whose liability to the company is limited to the amount he has invested in it. Joint ventures are a third type of partnership and are popular with investors who join together temporarily to undertake a short-term business enterprise, such as producing a show.

Partnerships offer certain advantages of ownership. First of all, they are easy to form. The partners should negotiate, at the outset, a written agreement which defines shares of ownership and spells out each partner's responsibilities to the firm. Partnerships are also likely to have, in the beginning, more working capital than sole proprietorships. It is also likely that a firm where two or more individuals are active in management will experience the advantage of having people with complementary skills. For example, one partner may be tops in sales, another may be adept at accounting.

The principal disadvantage of this form of organization is that the partners may disagree on how to run the business. Add to this the possibility that the partners may develop personality conflicts. And if the partners reach an impasse, it is difficult for them to dissolve the company; disputes may arise over disposition of inventory and how outstanding debts are going to be paid.

CORPORATIONS — Where sole proprietors and partners are people, a corporation is a thing. The impersonal aspect of a corporation was set forth in 1819 by the then Chief Justice of the United States Supreme Court John Marshall who observed that a corporation is ". . . an artificial being, invisible, intangible, and existing only in contemplation of law." Corporations are separate legal entities and they offer a number of advantages. The most obvious one is that management has more money with which to work. Corporations also have a diversity of managerial talents and the financial capability to buy in large quantities, thus reducing costs per unit of doing business. Also, a shareholder knows that his personal liability to the corporation is limited to the value of the stock he owns. Even if the company folds, shareholders' personal properties are not vulnerable to claims against the corporation.

Of the three types of business organization, the corporate structure is the most difficult to set up, the slowest and most expensive to get into operation. Each state charters corporations according to its own laws, and state and federal regulatory agencies now burden management with an unbelievable amount of bureaucratic meddling.

Another disadvantage for investors in corporations is that they experience double taxation: they pay corporate taxes plus personal income taxes on dividends received from the corporation.

SELL OR RENT? — As mentioned above, most stores offer customers the opportunity to rent an instrument with option to purchase. This option is particularly attractive to parents buying their youngster his first instrument. Dad and mom have been badgered by the kid who insists that he'll just die if he can't own a guitar. Honest merchants may inform the family that a high percentage of beginning players lose interest after their initial enthusiasm — and the family is stuck with continuing the payments on the instrument long after the kid has returned to his first true love, baseball. Mom and dad, having already experienced the changing interests of their progeny, will often be more willing to rent an instrument for a few months. Then, if the youngster loses interest, they will be out less money. If the musical interest sustains, the merchant normally applies most of the rental payments to the purchase price.

The rental-purchase option is so attractive, merchants find they can write more business than they can finance. Manufacturers know this, as do wholesalers and bankers. As a result, it is to their interest to assist the merchant in expanding his business. Few music stores can "handle their own paper." They enter into various paper-handling contracts with their suppliers of merchandise and money.

Major instrument and equipment manufacturers conduct large-scaled national promotion campaigns, often preselling the customer before he enters the store. For this reason, merchants must vie for retail *franchises,* for they are valuable. Manufacturers protect their franchised stores by limiting one to a particular geographic area. If a franchised merchant fails to perform to the satisfaction of the manufacturer, he may lose the privilege of vending that particular line to a competing retailer in his area.

STUDIO OPERATIONS — Most instrument stores assign space for the offering of private music lessons. While teaching students on the premises is less prevalent with piano-organ stores, the practice is almost universal with stores vending band and orchestra instruments. This kind of studio operation can include one to perhaps a dozen small studios. Larger operations sometimes provide space for group lessons and small ensembles. Some even set aside space for full concert band rehearsals or for accordion bands, guitar ensembles, etc.

One type of studio operation provides that the store collects lesson fees, then pays the teacher an agreed amount for each period of instruction, withholding a percentage for studio overhead. Another type of studio operation has the individual instructor collect the tuition, then pay the store $2 an hour or so for use of the studio. Members of NAMM can obtain a printed form which sets forth in writing a typical agreement between a store and a studio teacher. The agreement is part of NAMM's *Store Studio Manual.*

Merchants sometimes try only to break even on floor space they displace for studio operations, believing they will experience sufficient profit through sales and rentals to students passing through their store.

FINANCIAL MANAGEMENT

Financial management of a music store can be more critical than developing sales. Large numbers of merchants enter the field with inadequate backgrounds in money management and accounting. Frequently, a merchant will appear to be doing good business and at the same time be losing money and not even know it. His financial record keeping was inadequate — or he had the information but did not know how to interpret it. This is probably the number one reason so many businesses fail.

Music merchants need three basic record books: a *journal,* a *ledger,* and a *checkbook.* The journal (sometimes called a daybook) is a chronological daily record of business transactions. It includes the dates of transactions, a brief description, the amount of money involved and an indication of the accounts affected by the transactions (an "account" is a record of the increases and decreases in one type of asset, liability, capital, income, or expense).

The most important accounting book is the ledger. It is a book or file (or computer) in which all the merchant's accounts are maintained. Each entry made in the daily journal is later transferred (or "posted") to the proper account in the ledger. With the ready availability of computers priced low enough for even the small merchant, this description is somewhat outdated. Many stores, large and small, have "cash registers" which double as computer input terminals. The salesperson punches up the transaction — and all the merchant's record keeping is recorded instantaneously — daily journal, ledger, and inventory information.

Computers now obviate the need for old-fashioned "bookkeeping" and accounting procedures. These matters are now handled at low-cost, and at the speed of light. The merchant who lacks the capital can probably get his bank to buy the equipment, then lease it back to him.

The small merchant, new to the game, may tend to mix his personal finances with those of his business. This is unacceptable to the auditors and tax collectors. The store requires its own separate bank account and accounting procedures, including a separate checkbook. All receipts should be recorded and deposited daily. Small cash transactions are handled via a petty cash account. All stores employing two or more persons are required to maintain complete payroll records. Forms appropriate for this are available in stationery stores.

Just as critical to complete record keeping are the merchant's balance sheet and P/L statements (statements of profit and loss). The balance sheet shows the financial condition of the store at a given time, usually at the close of business on the last day of each month and the last day of the year. It lists the assets and liabilities of the business and the *owner's equity* (sometimes called "proprietorship").

A P/L statement summarizes the store's operation over a given period and shows how much profit or loss resulted. It shows how much merchandise was purchased and sold, the cost of the goods sold, the gross margin, various types of expense, any income other than that from sales, and the profit or loss for the period. Merchants do not need to be CPA's, but they do need to know how to interpret P/L statements, for they tell the proprietor not only whether he is currently making money, but these essentials:

> **Current ratio** — *Does the business have enough current assets to meet its current debts, with a margin of safety for possible losses such as inventory shrinkage or uncollectible accounts? While not a firm rule, a 2:1 ratio is often recommended.*

> **"Acid-test ratio"** — *Similar to the current ratio, but here the inventory is not included in the current assets — only cash on hand, government securities, and receivables. It helps answer the question, "If all sales revenue should disappear, could the business meet its current obligations with the readily convertible, 'quick funds' on hand?"*

P/L statements also help the merchant know how many days' sales are tied up in accounts receivable. And the proprietor and any other investors can learn from the reading of a P/L statement just what return is being realized on investment in the store. The formula:

$$\text{Return on investor's equity} = \frac{\text{Net profit}}{\text{Net worth}}$$

One of the most critical issues facing a music store is inventory turnover, the ratio of the cost of goods sold to average inventory (the cost of goods sold divided by the average inventory). A merchant must know how fast his inventory is moving. Few expenses can be more costly than wasting floor space on dormant stock. The proprietor can be guided by a survey of NAMM members who report that the average "complete" music store with sales of $100,000 to $250,000 per year showed these figures:

Department	Inventory Turnover In One Year	
	RANGE	AVERAGE
Pianos	*1.5 to 2.3*	*1.8*
Organs	*1.2 to 2.0*	*1.6*
Musical Instruments	*1.0 to 1.8*	*1.4*
Accessories	*.9 to 1.9*	*1.6*
Sheet Music	*1.1 to 2.1*	*1.3*
Records	*1.8 to 4.2*	*2.4*

Inventory turnover is a clear indicator of merchandising efficiency. The faster the turnover, the less capital is required in proportion to sales. Less money must be borrowed; new merchandise can be acquired and sold more quickly.

PROMOTION

The proprietor who has invested only his own money in his music store is not really alone financially. His investment is backed up by the far larger resources of manufacturers of the lines he sells. Manufacturers invest huge sums every year, not only in production, but in sales promotion and advertising. They know that their prosperity, their very survival, is dependent upon their franchised retailers. Musical instrument and accessory manufacturers do all they can to presell the retail customer. They try to implant their brand name in his head before the customer enters the store. Many customers are presold through national advertising campaigns shouting the merits of particular products. These national campaigns must be supplemented and localized by the retailer.

One sales promotion device is the *cooperative ad:* the manufacturer and the merchant share the cost. Another cooperative effort develops when the manufacturer supplies point-of-sale items for the merchant to display in his store — signs, banners, streamers, show cards, special display racks, window dressings, etc. Some stores regularly festoon their premises with these point-of-sale stimuli. Manufacturers normally supply these items without charge.

School and college musical directors are among the biggest buyers of instruments and equipment. Retailers find that these customers are often presold by contacts made by instrument manufacturers. Manufacturers display their wares to educators at professional meetings and conventions. These contacts sometimes develop direct factory sales that are credited to the teachers' local music store. Manufacturers often employ well-known performers as goodwill ambassadors to attend these conventions and music clinics, representing themselves, as is sometimes true, as users of the firm's instruments. Some firms supply the professional services of these clinicians to schools for benefit concerts, further developing goodwill for the firm and its products.

Local instrument merchants supplement these national promotions with their own advertising. Well-established retailers set annual ad budgets. Small stores will advertise when they can find the working capital to do so. Larger advertisers employ advertising agencies to write and place ads. But most small ads are poorly produced and ineffective, whether handled by an agency or the retailer himself. Proprietors are well-advised to study advertising, if only to learn if their money is being wisely spent.

Music store sales promotion is often most effective through direct contact with potential customers. Retailers seeking sales to schools regularly dispatch field salespersons to call on educators. In smaller communities, it is the store owner himself who legs it around the county drumming up business with schools and colleges. The objective io not only to sell to the schools but to create awareness among students that a particular store handles good merchandise and treats customers well.

Even more direct contact with potential customers occurs on the floor of the store when a family walks in to the shop. The youngster or his family may have dropped in to get something repaired — and left with a new Selmer alto. Effective salesmanship. Many large sales develop through a store's offering music accessories. Accessories offer high markup, draw a variety of customers into the store and then cause them to return, for most accessories are expendable and need replacement.

While some merchants cater largely to young musicians and school sales, most retailers also seek the business of professional musicians. They not only buy the higher-priced professional instruments and equipment, they are, when well-accommodated, probably the store's most effective sales force   for nearly all professionals, even semi-professionals, have pupils who need a recommendation on where to shop. Professionals who frequent a music store also use them for communications centers ("I need a drummer for Saturday night. Know anyone who can cut it for me?"); ("John Doe's rehearsal band is meeting Tuesday night this week. Will you help pass the word?").

In stores of all sizes, it appears that the most successful music merchants are those who are visible components of their communities. It behooves them to be on good terms, not only with their banker, but with other individuals and institutions in their area who help make the community a better place to live. The motivation may be altruistic. The result could mean more business.

14

ARTS ADMINISTRATION

THE SERIOUS MUSIC MARKET

The operation of symphony orchestras, opera and ballet companies constitutes a very large portion of the music business. The pop field gets most of the publicity, but some segments of the serious music field have experienced a more rapid growth rate in recent years than rock and roll. The production and purveyance of serious music has traditionally been separate from pop. This is because the artists and administrators generally come from different backgrounds and pursue different goals. The production and consumption of serious music today is really big business, and the artists and managers in pop and serious music are, more often than not, engaged in very similar kinds of work. "Crossing the line" is an everyday occurrence. Individuals qualified to function in the world of "art music" often end up in "commercial music." Some who start their careers in one of the pop fields may find themselves working for a symphony orchestra or perhaps in church music.

As pointed out earlier, it is difficult to set forth precise definitions for such carelessly used terms as "popular," "classical," "art music" and "serious music." The confusion prevailed long before the 1924 premiere of George Gershwin's so-called "symphonic jazz" composition, *Rhapsody in Blue*. Disputes about the correct way to classify music will continue. But to provide a framework for an understanding of the present chapter, I shall use the term "serious music," "classical music" and "art music" interchangeably and include the repertoire generally associated with the symphony orchestra, opera, ballet, recital, modern dance and church music.

It is customary to distinguish between pop and serious music by describing the former as "commercial" or profit-oriented, and the latter as nonprofit. Here again we find a lot of "crossing the line." But to keep things simple, I will generally hold to that point of view here in a discussion of arts administration.

The National Endowment for the Arts (NEA) estimated in the late 1970s that, in the preceding decade, the number of professional symphony orchestras and opera companies had nearly doubled. In the same period, the number of opera companies grew from 27 to 45, resident theatre companies from 12 to 50. In the mid-1970s the National Committee for Cultural Resources studied 343 top arts organizations (symphonies, operas, ballets, etc.). Its findings, published in *National Report on the Arts,* corroborated the many other studies conducted by the Ford Foundation, Rockefeller Foundation, federal, state and regional agencies. The study revealed that attendance at arts events was up, the number of arts performances was up, employment of artists and arts administrators was up and so were gross revenues, expenses — and deficits. Here is a tragic anomaly: *the more audience you draw to classical music, the more rapidly you increase your indebtedness.*

The audience for serious music was not reduced when rock, pop and country markets exploded in the 1960s. Rather, all these audiences grew at the same time. This apparently contradictory phenomenon is explained by a number of factors: 1) increased leisure time; 2) more discretionary income became available; 3) proliferation and accessibility of mass media; 4) broadening of audience tastes; 5) more effective distribution and marketing methods. Years ago, musical snobbery was more prevalent. Today, it is not uncommon for music lovers to include in their personal record collection anything from Beethoven to Mancini, from Louis Armstrong to Isaac Stern.

The growth in ballet and, particularly, modern dance, has been spectacular in the last 15 years. Around 1968 we had some 30 professional dance companies. Today, the number is closer to 150, and they draw audiences estimated by the NEA to exceed 15 million persons annually. This amazing growth in interest in dance can be attributed to the influence of television exposure of this art, particularly the programs on public TV.

The Public Broadcasting Service (PBS) and the Corporation For Public Broadcasting (CPB) have also helped expand the audiences for symphony and opera. There have been sponsored weekly radio broadcasts of the Metropolitan Opera for decades, as well as of symphony orchestras (San Francisco, Seattle, Los Angeles, Chicago, among others). Telecasts of the Boston Pops and Boston Symphony have drawn audiences of millions. Imaginative producers such as Emmy Award winner Allan Miller are finding ways to make symphonic music *look* interesting on film and TV.

This widely expanded exposure of serious music via radio and television has increased the sale of symphonic, opera and ballet recordings. Royalties from sales constitute a significant segment of the annual incomes of such orchestras as Cleveland, Boston, New York, Philadelphia, Chicago, Los Angeles and even the Utah Symphony.

One of the most active labels in the serious music field, Vox (with its low budget Turnabout line) explains that the familiar claim that record companies must continue to record only European orchestras to make a profit is no longer true. Vox finds that the superior skill of American orchestras often makes possible the completion of master takes in one-half the time of most European orchestras. Thus, companies can still meet the much higher union rates in the United States. After decades of resistance, the AFM has adopted a more enlightened policy for symphonic recording. The breakthrough occurred first with a contract negotiated between London Records and the Los Angeles Philharmonic Orchestra: the AFM approved a new policy of no payments required to members of the ensemble who were not needed on a particular session.

It might be noted here also that in this country we have had some of our finest university ensembles commercially recorded: not only the reknowned One O'Clock Lab Band of North Texas State University, but the M.I.T. Symphony Orchestra (on the Turnabout label).

Some serious music recordings, particularly the repertoire called "contemporary serious music," cannot profit or break even. An important group of recordings of this repertoire is found on the CRI label (Composers Recordings Inc.). CRI limits its releases exclusively to contemporary serious music. It is a commercial company but a majority of its stock is owned by the American Composers Alliance (a minority interest is owned by American Musical Associates, set up initially by a foundation). CRI's growth can be attributed to its expanding foreign sales and to its rapidly expanding number of retail record store outlets. CRI moves a sizable percentage of its merchandise through direct sales to schools and libraries.

Innovative marketing methods have greatly expanded the sale of classical music. For example, the Metropolitan Opera Company is now using a direct mailing list of 500,000 persons (accumulated from 20 record companies) known to be lovers of opera. The selling campaign, part of "The Met By Mail" project, publicizes opera music available on regular labels and on discs produced by RCA and London Records for the Met's own label.

As a rule, classical music recordings have not been big sellers. In the 1960s, Stravinsky complained that sales of records of works he had written after 1920 rarely exceeded 5,000 copies. These pieces — even of the world-famous composer — lost money. But in 1977, when RCA released a recording of Stravinsky's *Firebird* ballet suite (premiered in 1910), they were able to move 100,000 copies. Sales of serious music at this level were unheard of until the 1970s, when RCA and many other labels *learned how to promote and package releases appealing to buyers who formerly limited their purchases to pop music.* We now have the "crossover" record in the classical field reaching expanded markets worldwide. As pointed out in my coverage of the recording industry, one of the strongest markets for crossover records is with movie music — soundtrack music appeals to both classical and pop music fans here and abroad.

REPRESENTATIVE ORGANIZATIONS

The world of serious music and arts administration includes a number of important organizations that represent the special interests of professionals in the field. In respect to unions and guilds representing artists in the classical field, see Chapter 8. A number of other important organizations — not necessarily "guilds," despite some of their names, are listed below.

College and church organists are represented by the American Guild of Organists. The special interests of composers in the classical field have been served, since 1938, by the American Composers Alliance. Its American Composers Edition serves as a nonprofit music publisher for its members, making scores and parts available through loans and rentals to colleges, universities, symphonies and opera companies. ACA members are affiliates of BMI, for ACA is a publisher affiliate of BMI. As noted earlier, ACA is the principal stockholder in Composers Recordings Inc. For many years, American composers have been active in the International Society for Contemporary Music and its American component, League of Composers. Founded by Aaron Copland and other distinguished American composers, this group has fostered public acceptance of contemporary serious music by offering concerts, goodwill and publicity.

Opera is represented by the NOI (National Opera Institute) which has its national headquarters at the John F. Kennedy Center for the Performing Arts in Washington, D.C. In addition to fostering opera in this country, NOI sponsors the training of opera directors and managers through an apprenticeship program which provides stipends to individuals seeking on-the-job training under active professionals. More recently organized than NOI is Opera America, an organization whose membership includes 44 U.S. and four Canadian professional companies.

Professional music critics have formed the Music Critics' Association, which includes in its membership a large number of major critics, particularly those writing for the big eastern newspapers. The American Council for the Arts (formerly, Associated Councils for the Arts) forms a useful clearing house for information and ideas relating to state and regional arts council activities. ACA publishes useful pamphlets and books on arts administration.

Arts administrators have organized the Association of College, University and Community Arts Administrators. Educators in that field are represented by the Association of Arts Administration Educators.

The largest organization in music is the National Music Council, chartered by Congress in 1957 to serve the interests of the amateur and professional musician in all fields. It has some 60 member organizations which represent, in turn, an aggregate membership of some 1.5 million members. A partial list of its member-organizations indicates the scope of NMC: AFM, ACA, AGMA, AMC, ASCAP, ASOL, BMI, CMS, CMA, MENC, MPA, NAJE, NASM, NFMC, NMPA, RIAA, SESAC — and SPEBQSA — Society for the Preservation and Encouragement of Barbershop Quartet Singing in America!

AMERICAN SYMPHONY ORCHESTRA LEAGUE

In the field of serious music, the largest audience is for symphonic music. In the United States are found over 1,500 symphony orchestras, probably one-half of the world's total. Some two-thirds of these are banded together in the American Symphony Orchestra League. The ASOL, headquartered in Washington, D.C., is a nonprofit corporation with a strong professional staff. ASOL's annual conventions draw 1,000 enthusiastic delegates from all over the country. The organization receives most of its support from members' dues which, in turn, are scaled according to the size of the orchestra's annual budget. ASOL is research-oriented and serves as a data gathering, data distribution agency for its members who are interested in arts administration, audience building and fund raising.

One of the most useful services provided by ASOL is educational. Each year, the league staffs and sponsors regional workshops. Professional managers, symphony board members, conductors and volunteer workers attend these meetings to learn from experts how to function more effectively in their own communities. ASOL also sponsors Symphony Management Seminars where present and aspiring orchestra managers attend classes for eight days of intensive study on how to run a professional symphony orchestra. ASOL receives partial support of its educational activities from the National Endowment for the Arts.

ASOL offers what it calls Service Memberships for conductors and orchestra managers who want to exchange information concerning job openings in the symphonic field. ASOL does not run a placement service, but provides useful information to its members which often leads to employment. The league's splendid magazine, *Symphony News*, published six times a year, provides timely information to professionals and amateurs interested in the life and times of symphony orchestras.

Orchestras classified by the American Symphony Orchestra League as "major" provide their 75 to 110 contract musicians with the major source of their income. Among these 34 major orchestras are "the big five" — New York, Chicago, Philadelphia, Boston and Cleveland, each of which has about 100 AFM musicians under annual contract. Several orchestras just below "the big five" provide contracts almost as attractive. It should be noted that all of these orchestras sign contracts with some 60 percent to 90 percent of their musicians for salaries above the prevailing minimum union scale.

Orchestras classified as "metropolitan" rarely have sufficient resources to provide, for all of their musicians, salaries adequate to furnish their principal means of support. While a handful of first-chair musicians may receive annual wages in the $15,000 range, most of the musicians fill out their incomes with teaching and other kinds of employment, inside or outside music.

Orchestras that are unable to offer their musicians something in the range of $15,000 a year or more vie with each other for the best available players. While we have a surplus of qualified wind and percussion performers, the best of these are sought after by orchestras that can offer only small annual wage guarantees. In order to attract the best musicians to these orchestras with smaller budgets, communities have developed a technique of offering "security employment" as a sideline: the orchestras line up musical work or extramusical jobs in their communities, full or part-time, in order to aggregate a respectable annual income for the musicians imported. For example, a small community might line up a full-time job for a good bassoonist who would work during the week as a piano salesman. He would be available for evening rehearsals and weekend concerts with the community orchestra — which might be unable to pay him anything at all for his bassoon playing. Another community might be able to pay their imported bassoonist $5,000 a year as a musician, then line up a job for him with local industry. These moonlighting package deals may not have been the artistic goal of a Juilliard graduate, but they are more attractive than abandoning professional music altogether. Among our orchestras in smaller communities, it is these kinds of arrangements that make possible professional and semiprofessional ensembles of genuine quality.

MAJOR, REGIONAL AND METROPOLITAN SYMPHONY ORCHESTRAS IN THE UNITED STATES AND CANADA

(Classifications by the American Symphony Orchestra League)

MAJOR

Atlanta Symphony
Baltimore Symphony
Boston Symphony
Buffalo Philharmonic
Chicago Symphony
Cincinnati Symphony
Cleveland Orchestra
Dallas Symphony
Denver Symphony
Detroit Symphony
Honolulu Symphony
Houston Symphony
Indianapolis Symphony
Kansas City Philharmonic
Los Angeles Philharmonic
Milwaukee Symphony
Minnesota Orchestra
Montreal Symphony
National Symphony
New Jersey Symphony
New Orleans Phil.-Sym.
New York Philharmonic
North Carolina Symphony
Philadelphia Orchestra
Pittsburgh Symphony
Rochester Philharmonic
Saint Louis Symphony
San Antonio Symphony
San Francisco Symphony
Seattle Symphony
Syracuse Symphony
Toronto Symphony
Utah Symphony
Vancouver Symphony

REGIONAL

Birmingham Symphony
Calgary Philharmonic
Columbus Symphony
Florida Symphony
Hartford Symphony
Hudson Valley Philharmonic
Louisville Orchestra
Greater Miami Philharmonic
Nashville Symphony
Oakland Symphony
Oregon Symphony
Phoenix Symphony

REGIONAL (Continued)

Richmond Symphony
San Diego Symphony
San Jose Symphony
Toledo Symphony
Winnipeg Symphony

METROPOLITAN

Akron Symphony
Albany Symphony
Amarillo Symphony
American Symphony
Arkansas Symphony
Austin Symphony
Baton Rouge Symphony
Brooklyn Philharmonic
California Chamber
Canton Symphony
Cedar Rapids Symphony
Charlotte Symphony
Chattanooga Symphony
Chautauqua Symphony
Clarion Music Society
Colorado Springs Symphony
Corpus Christi Symphony
County Symphony of
   Westchester
Dayton Philharmonic
Des Moines Symphony
Duluth-Superior Symphony
Eastern Philharmonic
Edmonton Symphony
El Paso Symphony
Erie Philharmonic
Evansville Philharmonic
Flint Symphony
Florida Gulf Coast Symphony
Florida West Coast Symphony
Fort Lauderdale Symphony
Fort Wayne Philharmonic
Glendale Symphony
Grand Rapids Symphony
Hamilton Philharmonic
Jackson Symphony
Kalamazoo Symphony
Kitchener-Waterloo Symphony
Knoxville Symphony
Lansing Symphony
Lexington Philharmonic

METROPOLITAN (Continued)

Lincoln Symphony
London Symphony
Long Beach Symphony
Long Island Symphony
Los Angeles Chamber
Madison Symphony
Memphis Symphony
Miami Beach Symphony
Midland-Odessa Symphony
Monterey County Symphony
Music for Westchester
   Symphony
New Haven Symphony
New Mexico Symphony
Norfolk Symphony
Northeastern Pennsylvania
   Philharmonic
Omaha Symphony
Orchestra Da Camera
Greater Palm Beach Symphony
Pasadena Symphony
Portland Symphony
Puerto Rico Symphony
Quebec Symphony
Queens Symphony
Regina Symphony
Rhode Island Philharmonic
Sacramento Symphony
Saginaw Symphony
Santa Barbara Symphony
Savannah Symphony
Shreveport Symphony
South Bend Symphony
Spokane Symphony
Springfield Symphony
   (Massachusetts)
Springfield Symphony (Ohio)
Stockton Symphony
Symphony of the New World
Thunder Bay Symphony
Tri-City Symphony
Tucson Symphony
Tulsa Philharmonic
Vermont Symphony
Victoria Symphony
Wheeling Symphony
Wichita Symphony
Winston-Salem Symphony
Youngstown Symphony

FUNDING THE ARTS

It is not generally understood that even the best-managed arts organization cannot expect to break even at the box office. All symphonies, opera and ballet companies, no matter how efficiently run, are unable to earn sufficient income to cover their expenses. Simply stated, all real arts organizations are dependent upon outside funding for survival. This has been true throughout history. Among the earliest patrons of the arts were the church and the nobility. Concurrent with patronage of this kind, artists occasionally earned part of their livelihood from municipal and national governments. When public theatres and concert halls increased in number in the seventeenth and eighteenth centuries, money generated by ticket sales to the middle class helped support musicians. Concurrently, persons of individual wealth supported the arts. In modern times, arts "societies" were formed by patrons to organize financial backing for orchestras and opera companies. American arts organizations for generations have enjoyed large gifts from wealthy individuals. But when the federal tax laws changed and limited unrestricted giving to arts organizations, our orchestras and opera companies began to experience serious financial difficulties. Today, the tax laws are such that large gifts from wealthy individuals are infrequent.

Performing arts organizations can manage to earn, on the average, only about 38 percent of their costs of operation. This means that symphonies, opera and ballet companies must raise, on the average, 62 percent of their budgets from sources other than the box office. If this were not difficult enough, the gap between earned income and overhead *continues to widen,* due to inflating costs. Ticket prices *could* be raised high enough to cover all overhead, but if they were, the Business Committee for the Arts has estimated that prices would then be out of the range of most patrons: the cheapest symphony concert ticket would run about $40; opera tickets might cost $50 to $60, ballet a little less. Since such prices are out of the question at this time, arts organizations continue to search for alternative income sources.

Offering more performances each season is not the answer either — for two reasons. First, most of our performing groups are already scheduled to capacity. Second, when an arts group adds a performance, *it increases its operating indebtedness.* Here is a classic "Catch-22" situation: the greater the number of services provided, the greater the financial loss incurred.

In Europe, symphonies and opera companies enjoy large governmental subsidies. This is such a strong tradition there that music lovers do not have to worry whether their symphonies and opera companies will survive from year to year. Governmental support of the arts in the United States has been near zero throughout most of our history. In the late 1960s, government support increased measurably, and continued to rise through the 1970s. In the early 1980s, we began to feel the impact of a more fiscally conservative Congress and administration which has reduced federal funding for the arts.

NATIONAL ENDOWMENT FOR THE ARTS

The federal agency most directly concerned with helping the creative and performing arts in this country is NEA, the National Endowment for the Arts. In 1965 Congress established the National Foundation for the Arts and Humanities. Within the Foundation were established two agencies — the National Endowment for the Arts and the National Endowment for the Humanities. In 1966, Congress appropriated $5 million for these agencies to "foster the arts." Congressional support of the NEA by 1981 had reached a level of about $150 million.

The enabling legislation provided that NEA funds were to be allocated upon the advice of the National Council of the Arts, a group of twenty distinguished citizens appointed by the president to oversee the affairs of NEA and NEH. All art groups are hungry and, each year, some 13,000 of them (and individual artists) apply for federal support. Of this number, some 1,300 each year receive NEA grants. Fifteen hundred orchestras and 600 opera companies are eligible. Nearly all NEA grants are project-oriented and they are, for the most part, matching grants, meaning that $1 of federal money must be matched by $1 of local money. On the average, requests require six to nine months to process.

Individual states are eligible for block grants which they, in turn, may assign at their discretion.

Individual artists are also eligible for grants — in the range of $1,000 to $10,000. Individuals receive grants for such things as completing a composition, expenses of music preparation and residencies in schools and communities.

In the early years of NEA, jazz artists complained that they were slighted in favor of classical musicians. In recent times, the NEA has been more responsive to these complaints. Today, it is possible for a jazz student or young professional to obtain an NEA fellowship to write or perform jazz, including short-term apprenticeship programs where the individual receives a stipend and expenses to travel with a jazz musician to learn from a professional on the job. Also, established jazz professionals obtain short-term residencies in schools to bring jazz to students.

NEA grants are intended to assist local arts groups in these ways:

1- *Expand the number and kinds of their programs.*

2- *Increase public accessibility.*

3- *Provide "sustained professional opportunities" for musicians.*

4- *Present "gifted young American artists as soloists."*

5- *Foster "better management capability."*

Early on, NEA leaders were aware that the financial difficulties of arts organizations were due, in part, to inept management, and it has traditionally given support to local groups that were attempting to improve their planning, management, and control of finances. To assist arts groups in acquiring more sound management, NEA grants have gone to universities to support graduate study in arts administration. Federal money has been available to help finance "professional apprenticeship programs in arts management."

A sizable portion of federal monies are assigned through NEA's National Program Funds. NEA also provides Treasury Fund Grants. They are intended for large awards for major projects. When a local individual or group gives money for a major project, a matching grant is made by the Treasury Fund. This arrangement has the effect of doubling the amount of money available for large local projects.

A third kind of NEA grant is known as a Challenge Grant. For every $3 raised locally, Challenge Grants add $1. These kinds of grants have been effective in encouraging strong local support for the arts.

STATES ARTS COUNCILS

According to the NEA, community and regional arts councils increased in number from 150 to about 1,800 in the last ten years. Included in that total are, not only community groups, but state and regional councils on the arts. Federal law requires NEA to assign at least 15 percent of its programming funds to states and territories on an equal basis and offer an additional five percent to regional organizations.

Some state legislatures began support of the arts with great reluctance. Pressure on politicians from their constituents changed that. Many states in the union assign tax dollars to help support artists and arts organizations. New York is far in front of the other states with an annual appropriation of some $30 million to its arts councils.

New York began to appropriate far more (total) dollars for the arts than any other state years ago, after a widescaled study of cultural and economic impact of the arts on the state was undertaken. It showed the politicians that the great majority among the electorate favored generous support of cultural enterprises from tax money, and that every dollar spent in these ways redounded to the benefit of the state's economy. The results of this research appear to have convinced the New York state legislature that it is good politics to appropriate tax dollars for the arts.

Arts enthusiasts in other states have used similar evidence demonstrating the favorable economic impact of dollars paid out for symphonies, opera and ballet companies. For example, the $10 million spent each year for the Boston Symphony Orchestra produces healthy influences on the economy of the Boston area. About one-half of that huge budget will be spent around Boston through the wages paid the orchestra's artists and staff people. Other millions of that budget will be fed back into the local economy for transportation, utilities, advertising and equipment. Also, hundreds of thousands of concertgoers further feed the Boston area economy for such things as dinners out, taxicabs, even baby-sitting.

A more recent study on the favorable economic impact of giving to arts organizations was conducted by the Johns Hopkins Center for Metropolitan Planning and Research. Support for the arts was examined in 1978-79 in six cities — Columbus, Ohio; Springfield, Illinois; San Antonio, Texas; Minneapolis-St. Paul, St. Louis and Salt Lake City. The research concluded that the income for the community generated by arts organizations somtimes is nearly equal to, sometimes even greater than, the support the artists receive from donations and governmental support. Most studies show that the arts are "good business."

One of the organizations that has demonstrated its favorable impact on the economy is the Metropolitan Opera Company. After going through many seasons worrying about survival, the Met in the late 1970s got on its financial feet. This turnaround has been attributed to tighter management and to what the Met's leadership believes is "opera's increasing popularity." The Met operates at close to 98 percent seating capacity — a remarkable achievement for any performing company. It is unfortunate, however, that the Met has been forced to raise its ticket prices beyond the reach of a huge number of opera lovers.

The Met averages a radio audience of some five million listeners for its venerable Saturday afternoon broadcasts. As a result of these radio broadcasts, the membership of the Met's Opera Guild has reached over 150,000 nationwide. Guild members contribute about $2 million a year to support the company.

At present, the principal source of unearned income of arts groups comes from local private sources. Performing arts groups expend tremendous energy raising money. Their first concern is to sell tickets. The most successful efforts of this kind focus on generating subscrip tion sales. Tickets may sometimes be more easily sold for individual performances, but most major symphonies, opera and dance groups now understand their energies are best spent seeking sales of a full series of performances. Patrons who buy season tickets not only commit themselves to more money, they are much more loyal and enthusiastic people than those who attend only occasionally. The subscriber feels he is "a patron" of the arts, that the group is part his and he takes pride in its health and progress.

Where an individual ticket might cost $10 and a subscription series $100, how does a volunteer make such a sale? Danny Newman, public relations head of the Chicago Lyric Opera and consultant to the Ford Foundation on audience development, recommends "the hard sell." He favors printed materials with pizzazz and pushy sales pitches by armies of volunteers contacting potential patrons by telephone and mail. Mr. Newman has been brought in to consult with many major arts organizations and his record of results is remarkable. Following adoption of Newman's sales promotional techniques, the Denver Symphony boosted its sale of subscriptions over 90 percent in a three-year period. Newman's book on the subject is recommended (see bibliography).

Arts groups have, in recent years, adopted some of the ticket-selling techniques of professional sports. Today, it is becoming standard practice for symphonies and opera companies to attempt to sell blocks of seats to large companies. Executives are attracted to buying up a box or even a larger section of seats for the season, not only for themselves, but to give to their customers and potential customers. Corporations are also attracted more and more to creating an image in their communities of being involved in good works and cultural affairs.

As for individual gifts to arts groups, present tax laws make large gifts less attractive now than they once were. Efforts are now less on the size of gifts and more on their quantity. Armies of volunteers are active each spring and summer drumming up small donations of $1 to $100 from persons of modest means, but who are interested in helping out the local performing group. The standard method is to sell "memberships" in the sponsoring society for annual dues of, say, $20. The money usually goes, not to run the society or club, but to help support performing artists. Those giving more than the minimum dues are listed in the program as "donors" or "benefactors" or "sponsors," depending on the size of their contributions. This appeal to individual vanity produces millions each season for the arts.

There are special techniques in seeking individual gifts. One I learned from John Mazzola, president of New York's Lincoln Center For The Performing Arts. Mr. Mazzola told me he never expends energy seeking unrestricted gifts for Lincoln Center. Rather, he identifies the particular enthusiasm of a potential patron. For example, when he learns someone with money is an opera nut he'll ask for money for the Met, and not even mentioned the other performing groups connected with Lincoln Center. Mazzola finds that gifts come from particular arts lovers who will often extend themselves to support their personal favorite.

FOUNDATIONS, CORPORATIONS

At one time, foundations were a major arts funding source. They still are, but of diminishing significance. When the difficult economic period of the early 1970s hit such organizations as the Ford and Rockefeller foundations, their assets dropped to about one-half their former value, and grants were cut accordingly. But there are hundreds of foundations still making important grants to the arts. Everyone knows this, and these organizations spend much of their time receiving and processing pleas for money. Many of them are now contributors to the Foundation Center, a clearinghouse for information. The Foundation Center (888 7th Avenue, New York 10019), publishes a book, *About Foundations: How to Get the Facts You Need.* This publication includes recommended procedures for locating information on foundations in a specific area and identifying their particular interests.

In recent years, there has been a significant increase in "community foundations," those connected, not with a corporation or private wealth, but a city or some other governmental body. Since the tax reform act of 1969, community foundations hold certain advantages over private foundations. For example, community foundations pay no taxes; private foundations must pay four percent on investment income. Private foundations are also required to pay out each year a minimum amount of their earned income; community foundations face no such requirements under the tax laws. Because of decreasing resources and new tax laws, some private foundations have assigned all their assets to community foundations and have then gone out of business. Individual donors can experience a better tax advantage with gifts to community foundations than when giving to private foundations. For these reasons, community foundations are the only ones now still growing. Traditionally, they have favored health and welfare projects, but that emphasis is shifting. More and more of their support is now going to the arts.

One of the most significant growth areas in support for the arts is found among corporations. One hundred-twenty-five major U.S. corporations have formed the Business Committee for the Arts. This New York-based group assists major corporations in coordinating their support of the arts.

Corporate giving is the fastest growing kind of financial support for the arts. Business Committee for the Arts research indicates that it is the largest American corporations who are increasing their gifts most rapidly, particularly oil companies.

Fund raisers can learn useful information from Exxon Corporation, one of the major supporters of the arts and humanities. About one-half of Exxon's support dollars have been assigned to the Public Broadcasting Service.

Exxon reports that it turns down some 90 percent of the requests it receives for donations *because of the inept manner in which they are made.* Exxon has publicly stated that the firm has been astonished how ill-prepared people are when they come to ask for money; they generally lack the important information. Exxon's management often prefers to talk, not to fund raisers, but directly to artistic directors who have a clearer vision of just why the money is needed.

Corporations which support the arts prefer that the requests come to them in writing, that they be very specific about needs and that they be concise. Exxon dispels the familiar claim that corporate stockholders resist company money being given for the arts. On the contrary, Exxon's inquiry of its stockholders shows they are supportive of such policies.

When the arts groups complain about their lack of support from big corporations, the problem is often not so much stinginess but the absence of solicitation. Most of the big outfits *haven't ever been asked.* And most of them will not give away their money until someone steps forth and helps them understand why they should. In most communities, well-organized, comprehensive canvassing of large corporations generally turns out to be very profitable.

Performing arts groups that are financially alive are the ones which have developed the support of volunteer citizens who know how to ask for money. One standard procedure is to nominate wealthy executives in the community to the board, then persuade them to personally contact their wealthy friends for donations. A symphony board member might never have heard of Bartok, but he may have landed that prestigious spot on the board because people figured he knew how to contact money sources.

Another way of raising money is universally employed by art groups: they enlist large numbers of socially-conscious women to get out in the community and hustle donations, large and small. Symphony, dance and opera companies who can organize several dozen women's committees to get on the telephone and follow up mail solicitations generally find that this group of people becomes an irresistible force. The most effective campaigns of this kind are not only carefully timed and organized, but each solicitor undergoes special training — how to talk to people, what to say, how to "close the sale." The clearest manifestation of the effectiveness of support from women in the arts is found in the Women's Council of the American Symphony Orchestra League. Their enthusiasm probably does more to sustain our American orchestras than anything else. ASOL's Women's Council holds annual conventions and publishes *The Gold Book,* a reference source and how-to book for volunteer workers in the arts.

In addition to performing effective services in selling subscriptions, women's committees engage in a great variety of fund-raising projects. Typical of such undertakings are radio and TV marathon broadcasts, fashion shows, antique sales and auctions. These projects raise millions for the arts. And to hear the volunteer workers tell it, taking part is also a lot of fun. No arts enterprise anywhere could function 24 hours without the generous and enthusiastic efforts of its volunteer workers.

Funding sources for the arts include the American Federation of Musicians' Trust Fund (Chapter 17). Each year, hundreds of communities receive generous funding from this source for live music performances ranging from soloists in hospital wards to cosponsorship of the *Messiah.* The AFM not only provides money for union musicians' wages, but support money for publicity, hall rentals, etc.

Any account of subsidies for the arts should include recognition of the generous contributions *of the artists themselves* — composers, copyists, conductors, performers. In every community in the land, these individuals subsidize the arts through either working without fee or for fees below professional levels. They donate their artistry to the cause because they love music and place that above demands for financial reward. Like the volunteer workers mentioned earlier, without these generous gifts of time and talent, the production and performance of the arts would suffer greatly.

ADMINISTRATION

THE NEED

In interviewing America's leading arts administrators, I find they are in agreement on how they define their work. They say that arts administration is "the art of losing money gracefully." Until recent years, the profession was unknown. If you had the responsibility of managing an orchestra or opera company, you learned on the job and muddled through. This identical pattern prevails too often today in hundreds of arts organizations. That is one reason most of them are in serious financial trouble. The blunt fact is that the great majority of our symphonies, opera, ballet and modern dance companies are administered by well-meaning individuals who have only a dim view of what they are really supposed to be doing.

Probably the first organized movement to offer education for arts administrators occurred in 1969 when the National Endowment for the

Arts gave UCLA's Graduate School of Business $10,000 to organize two conferences, one on the west coast, one in the east to examine the problem of how to prepare people to function as arts administrators. One of the fallouts of these conferences was the establishment of a masters degree curriculum in arts management at UCLA's Graduate School of Business. Today we have a number of quality educational programs in our universities offering studies, mostly at the masters degree level, in arts administration.

Probably 300 graduates of various arts management training programs are presently employed in the field. But we still have a shortage of individuals fully qualified to manage the affairs of arts groups, many of whom have operating budgets in the millions. Ralph Black, head of the professional staff of the American Symphony Orchestra League states that we have an acute shortage of persons qualified to fill the job openings in this country for symphony orchestra management. William Dawson, Executive Director, Association of College, University and Community Arts Administrators, states that jobs await individuals possessing "professional skills" in the field. My own research corroborates Mr. Black and Mr. Dawson.

One way to gain a perspective on the need for professional arts administrators is to look at the staff of a major symphony orchestra. An organization with an annual budget in the range of $2 million to $6 million will have these professionals at work 50 weeks a year:

> General Manager or Executive Director
> Assistant Manager
> Director of Development
> Assistant Director of Development
> Two to four additional professional money raisers
> Director of Public Relations or Director of Press Relations
> Assistant Public Relations Director
> Personnel Director
> Road Manager or Stage Director
> Property Manager
> Assistant Stage Director
> Head Librarian
> Assistant Librarian
> Controller or Accountant
> Two to four assistants to the Controller (bookkeepers, etc.)
> Ticket Sales Manager
> Assistant Ticket Manager
> Office Manager
> Secretaries, stenographers, gofors

It is the responsibility of the general manager to see to it that each of these individuals understands his responsibilities and discharges them properly. If the manager's associates do function properly, that will leave him time to operate at a level for which he was really hired — thinking, planning, budgeting, promoting, following directives from the board, raising money, handling finances, and creating an environment for the symphony that makes possible ever finer artistic achievements, the reason for expenditure of all this effort in the first place.

Management, too, is an art, as Mozart's father once said. First of all, it is the art of working with people effectively. Arts organizations are unique in this respect, for they involve professionals and volunteers working side by side. The smooth cooperation of pros and amateurs is not achieved easily and some arts administrators never really get the hang of it. When an individual works for free, it isn't a good idea for the professional manager to push him around. Armies of volunteers, essential to all arts organizations, just won't work unless they believe wholeheartedly, not only in the artistic goals of the ensemble, but in its management.

In addition to possessing the ability to organize and motivate large numbers of volunteer committees, the arts administrator must be responsive to the policies of and instructions from the board of directors. ASOL's Ralph Black has declared that the number one problem of professional symphony orchestras is not money, but weak boards. Helen M. Thompson, former staff head of the American Symphony Orchestra League, directed an ASOL study some years ago which showed that truly successful symphony orchestras enjoy the support of board members who really work at it. The second finding of the ASOL research demonstrated that the really well-run orchestras "had etched out a sound basic philosophy of the value of the orchestra as a permanent institution in the life of the community."

Assuming the manager and the board see eye to eye, the administrative head has these responsibilities:

1- *Supervise the work of his staff. Hire and fire.*

2- *Organize and supervise volunteers.*

3- *Direct long-range planning.*

4- *Raise money. This is the board's responsibility, but it needs a lot of help.*

5- *Prepare budgets, including debt management, endowment funds, retirement plans, campaign funds and operations budgets.*

6- *Work with the artistic director in the conception and implementation of programs* — including casting, scheduling.

7- *Negotiate contracts for professional services. The most difficult one will be with the AFM, whose contracts normally run for two to three years. Dozens of contracts must also be negotiated with guest conductors and guest soloists. The manager who spends too much leads the organization deeper into debt. If he spends too little, artistic standard may drop.*

8- *Supervise technical matters relative to performances, the daily moving of artists and equipment; staging, lighting; booking transportation, hotels, meals for over 100 artists.*

9- *Handle press relations and public relations; keep the volunteers happy, the press happy, the politicians happy, the school children and their teachers happy, the National Endowment happy, the board happy and, above all, keep the audience happy.*

Since no individual knows how to accomplish all these things, it might be more instructive to list the specific skills and attributes required of a successful arts administrator. A summary:

1- *He doesn't just like music, he loves music.*

2 *He has great energy and enthusiasm — the kind that makes others want to work for him and with him.*

3- *He is an evangelist: developing a first-rate performing arts group is not a job to him, but some kind of religion.*

4- *He uses his energy and his time efficiently and knows how to organize the energies of others.*

5- *He knows how to run a meeting: starts on time, announces a specific agenda, keeps loquacious tongue waggers within bounds, prohibits digressions, encourages all points of view, summarizes decisions made and adjourns on time.*

6- *He keeps his attention on long-range goals, but knows what is the most important thing to do Monday morning.*

7- *He can prepare a sensible budget, present it clearly and hold within it. He may not be a CPA, but he can count and doesn't throw other people's money around.*

FINANCIAL MANAGEMENT

Management of arts organizations is difficult because most of them do not know how to handle money. They know there will never be enough so they limp along, improvising each day some kind of quick fix for impending disaster. But some arts groups manage their finances astutely. Those that do start with a well-conceived financial plan. This is a minimum requirement in avoiding serious fiscal difficulties. A financial plan for an arts organization cannot be worked out like a commercial business operation, because a symphony, opera or dance company has no way of calculating what accountants like to call "cost benefit ratios." This is a way of asking, "If we spend $1,000 here, what benefits will that money produce?" Since arts groups are nonprofit in nature, the decision about that $1,000 outlay must be calculated, not on what profit it might yield, but by what it might produce artistically — and artistic achievements cannot be listed on profit-and-loss statements. So the arts administrator must make many important financial decisions intuitively.

In many communities experts in financial management, insurance, advertising, printing, graphic arts and public relations volunteer their assistance without cost to arts organizations. These are significant contributions and help keep costs low. CPA's tell arts administrators that their money problems don't stem particularly from a need for more frugality. Indeed, many arts groups can teach commercial concerns how to get things done at minimum cost. Rather, the accountants and other financial experts observe that it is the need for boards and arts administrators to carefully *plan* income, expense, debt management and budgeting. Lack of financial planning is at the heart of many arts administration problems.

Arts administrators are indebted to the American Council for the Arts for its leadership role over the last decade in fostering better financial management in the arts. For over ten years, ACA has been assisted by the Shell Companies Foundation in making available a series of publications for the arts. Of these, one of the most useful is *Financial Management for the Arts* (see bibliography). This book, prepared with the assistance of the American Institute of Certified Public Accountants, is particularly useful for arts organizations with budgets in the $20,000 to $200,000 range and is written in language accessible to persons unaccustomed to the CPA's nomenclature. It will be instructive to glance at the chapter headings of this book: *Planning and Budgeting; Cash Management; Funds and Fund Accounting; General Accounting Scheme and Reporting; Financial Organizations.*

If an arts organization can learn good financial management, the other essential component leading to success is an infusion of love. Money and love. An unbeatable alliance.

Part Four

THE RECORD INDUSTRY

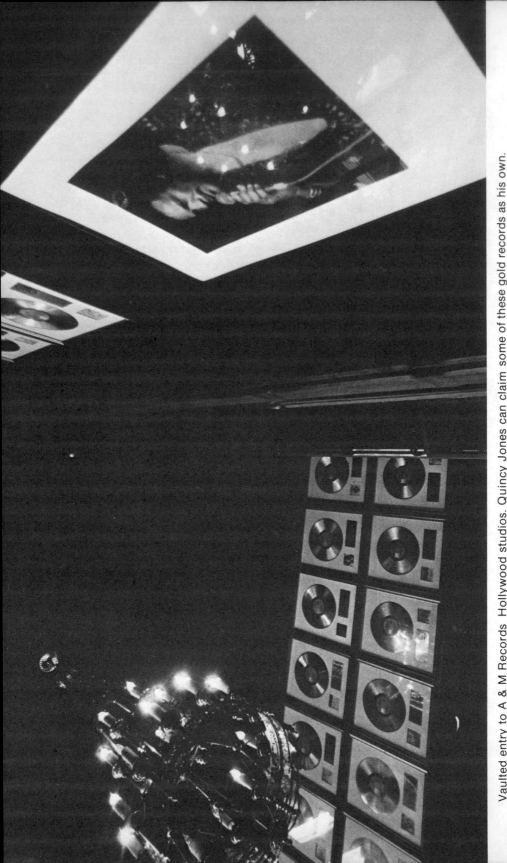

Vaulted entry to A & M Records Hollywood studios. Quincy Jones can claim some of these gold records as his own.

15

SCOPE OF THE RECORD INDUSTRY

I have learned from experience that it is easier to make a businessman out of a musician than a musician out of a businessman.

GODDARD LIEBERSON

The record industry overwhelmingly dominates the art and business of music today. Once a piece of music is composed, not much of importance can happen to it in the marketplace until it is recorded. The lives and fortunes of composers, performers, publishers, agents and merchants rise and fall with the sale of records and tapes. If records sell well, all other sectors of the business prosper. When records flop, everyone hurts.

For an understanding of how the record industry functions today, it will be helpful to consider how it grew to its present condition.

HISTORICAL BACKGROUND

1877 — *Edison invents the cylinder phonograph.*

1894 — *The first commercial disc recordings appear in the US market.*

1900s — *The Victor Talking Machine Co. is incorporated in 1901, develops 10,000 dealers. At first, opera repertoire dominates. Then dance music begins to sell well (on Victor and Columbia labels).*

1917 — *the first jazz record is released.*

1920s — *By 1921, 100 million records are produced in the USA. Large impetus from "commercial" jazz.*

1924 — *Bell Laboratories develops an electrical process for recording, in-*

creasing audible range over the earlier acoustical recordings to 100-5000 Hz. Bass instruments can now be heard.

Meteoric rise of radio popularity puts recording industry into a tailspin. 1929 — stock market crash.

1930s — The Great Depression hurts all business, particularly the record industry. Sales of discs and phonographs drop 90 percent over the 1927 peak year (total retail sales in 1933: $5.5 million).

Jukebox industry grows large, helping salvage the record business. By the late 1930s, the jukebox operators were buying 13 million discs to serve their machines.

Decca starts marketing low-cost (35¢) singles featuring artists such as Bing Crosby, The Mills Brothers, The Dorsey Brothers, Guy Lombardo; sells 19 million records in 1939.

Dealers sell record players near cost to encourage record sales.

First "albums" appear by mid-1930s, each single 78 rpm disc within the binder selling for 50¢.

Department stores introduce record and phonograph departments.

1940s — Weekly volume of new records released in the early 1940s: 10 to 20 singles (78 rpm); by the end of the decade, 40 to 100 per week, depending on the season.

AFM strike against record companies paralyzes the industry 1942-1945, damages popularity of big band recordings which, in turn, accelerates sales of records featuring pop singers.

Airplay not yet a major promotion factor except big band remote broadcasts. Jukeboxes help break new hits, particularly in the black music and country fields.

Late 1940s — one-stops come into being, mainly to accommodate jukebox operators. Rise of independent record labels, which begin to dominate the R & B field. Proliferation of distributors into smaller markets. Average dealer markup: 38 percent.

1948 — Columbia introduces the 33.3 rpm LP, retailing for $5.79.

Race records (as they were then called), C & W separate from pop records.

1950s — Television rises rapidly, grabs a large share of the radio audience. Radio loses advertising revenue. To economize, stations drop most live music and turn to recorded music. Increasing popularity of TV also sharply reduces record sales from 1949 to 1954.

R & B and C & W markets become dominated by "independent" labels.

Interest in hi-fi increases buyers of MOR records.

Rock and roll craze begins in the mid-1950s. "Cover record" concept initiated.

Record clubs begin in 1955. Columbia starts, soon followed by RCA and Capitol.

Rack jobbing begins in 1957.

Stereo is introduced in 1958.

Record retailing changes. Proliferation of labels and products burdens retailers with huge inventories. Space demands force abandonment of listening booths. Record supermarkets begin concurrently with proliferation of the small rack setups. Record retailing in chaos amidst price cutting and expanding sales.

Classical music's first million-seller (1959): Van Cliburn's performance of Tchaikovsky's Concerto For Piano and Orchestra.

1960s — Social turmoil of the decade finds its "voice" in popular music, influences large sales increases of rock, R & B, soul, country records. Rock becomes the catalyst for Woodstock-type mass concerts.

NARM formed in early 1960s by record wholesalers.

Rack jobbers cut heavily into "mom and pop" retailing and become dominant in the market; record clubs cut further into conventional retailing.

Beatles craze accelerates worldwide interest in pop-rock music; sales boom ensues.

Record supermarkets and retail chains proliferate in response to decreasing profit margins, growing inventories.

Major labels recapture some markets lost earlier to independents.

1970s — Independent record producers rise to greater importance.

Composers-singers become the superstars. Crossover records become the superhits.

Sophistication of technology increases: 16 and 24-track consoles; synthesizers, computer-assisted mixing, digital recording.

Sophistication of music increases: rock softens, classical influences on *polyphony, texture, instrumentation, form.*

1980s — *Business bounces back from 1979 downturn. Industry leaders adopt conservative management policies to control costs.*

Industry searches for its role in home video entertainment (cassettes and discs, cable TV). Music markets abroad continue to grow.

THE CHALLENGE

The production and marketing of records is one of the world's largest industries. How can a person grasp its complexities? Our approach will be to examine its major components, then set forth how the pieces fit together. One of the most direct ways of understanding a complex topic is to articulate procisely what questions need to be answered. Imagine this scenario: a room is filled with the record industry's most analytical minds — artists, producers, managers, publicists and merchants. They are asked to identify the most significant problems facing the industry. After many hours together, they reduce their findings to the following:[1]

1- How can a record company make a profit with ever-rising costs? Will inflation wipe out all but the multinational giants?

2- Musicians complain that too many records are lacking in artistic value, are burdened with redundancy, and bore all but undiscriminating audiences. Why do record companies spend most of their promotional dollars on this repertoire, neglecting much of the great music found in jazz, classical and popular music?

3- Record sales remain almost totally dependent on gaining airplay. This terribly restricting process results in a high percentage of fine records never being heard. Where can we find effective promotion alternatives to exposure on radio?

4- Merchants are burdened with an avalanche of new releases every week. How can record companies be persuaded to limit this supply and unclog the pipelines?

5- Sometimes more records seem to be returned to distributors than are being ordered for sale. How can this wasteful process be controlled?

6- Slow-paying customers plague the industry at every level. How can we limit the practice of many companies which ties up other firms' working capital?

7- Royalty artists (and personal managers) continue raising their demands. What is a reasonable limit?

8- Mechanical royalty rates are rising. How can a small label afford to stay in business with ever-rising costs?

1-This research method was used by the author, but in one-to-one interviews and small groups.

9- Records continue to rise in price. When will the buying public cry, "Halt!"

10- Label-financed tours often cost more than they earn from record sales. Is live entertainment going to become a thing of the past?

11-Record and tape counterfeiters threaten everyone. What would it take to coordinate and finance an all-out war against the crooks?

12- Home taping threatens to cost copyright owners in this country as much as the sale of counterfeit records. Who has a solution to this problem?

13- Many qualified outsiders seek careers in the industry, but find doors closed. How can they gain an opportunity to demonstrate their qualifications to share in this fascinating industry?

Any person who has workable answers to these questions will find willing followers. The record business is now well-staffed with bright, talented individuals. But the problems they face have not been solved. There is room for new ideas, new energy, new people.

MAJOR LABELS

1,200 recognized record companies operate in the United States, releasing their merchandise on more than 2,600 different labels. They range in size from tiny independent operations to multinational corporate giants. Some are full-line companies handling all kinds of repertoire. Others specialize. Ownership and control of these labels often change. It is safe to assume that, whatever a label's name, someone else owns it. It is also safe to assume that, whatever the apparent native land of the label, it will have a large number of foreign subsidiaries and licensees covering most of the globe.

As with most business enterprise existing in the capitalistic societies,

smaller firms get bought up by larger ones. Opinion varies on whether this international trend toward music cartels will eventually result in a gobbling up of all little companies. I believe the need for efficient international distribution systems will accelerate the buying up of small labels. But since a record company can get started with relatively small capitalization, and since the business offers at least the possibility of huge profits on small investments, independent entrepreneurs will continue to launch their own labels, perhaps even hoping they will later be bought by some international giant.

Major labels, together with their subsidiaries, dominate the record business here and abroad, accounting for about 75 percent of worldwide sales. No agreement exists on just how large a record company must become before it can be ranked as a "major" label. The fact is the relative rank of record companies here and abroad changes with the coming and going of monster hits. When a firm gets lucky one year with a series of platinum records, those kinds of sales can elevate a label rapidly.

The reason companies own or control large numbers of subsidiary labels is to manage distribution. All major labels own or control their own distribution networks in the United States. Outside this country, they either operate their own distribution centers or license others.

A second advantage major labels have over smaller firms is in promotion. When a big firm releases a new record, it can assign its entire field force and merchandising personnel to that particular project. This may sometimes bring to bear 200 or more individuals actively working a particular release all at the same time. While major labels rarely assign their full energies to just one release, they have the advantage of shifting their field personnel whenever they find it necessary to push particular products. The national impact of this combined force can put over even a weak record. This issue is strongly disputed, some arguing that even heavily concentrated promotion cannot persuade the public to buy a record that doesn't actually have it "in the grooves." But certainly the powerful promotional forces of the major labels have much greater success with weak material than the smaller firms. Major artists are attracted to major labels primarily because of their powerful promotion departments and well-organized distribution networks. Artists are also attracted by the prestige of being signed by a major label. They would rather be known as "a Columbia artist" than as a "Smith artist."

Yet another advantage major labels have over smaller ones is their reputations for integrity and lasting power. Firms the size of RCA and WEA aren't going to false-program their computer banks to cheat some artist out of $1,000 worth of royalties. It isn't that large firms are necessarily more wholesome in their accounting than the little fellows. It is just that it would cost them more to cook their books than it would be worth.

Finally, major labels offer stability and longevity. This can mean that they are more likely to maintain inventories and continue distribution of records perhaps years after their first release. Smaller labels may find it impossible to offer such ongoing service.

INDEPENDENT LABELS

Today there is almost no such thing as an "independent" label. But over the years it has been common practice to classify all but the major labels as independents. Despite their large size, some would continue to classify even Motown and A & M as "independents." Another large label, Arista, is often classified as an independent, even though this enterprising company claims its gross sales rank with the majors.

If labels must be classified, it would make more sense to simply describe them as small, medium and large. And even those rankings would change every year or so, for the record business is volatile.

Dependency — Most independent labels are dependent upon large record companies for

1- *Their initial financing;*

2- *Manufacture of their discs and tapes;*

3- *Distribution services.*

Large record companies frequently invest in an independent label when they have confidence in the firm's leadership. They may enter into a joint venture with a qualified independent producer and share in the capitalization needed to set up a small label. Or the large firm may wholly finance the new company, partly in anticipation of profits generated by distribution of the small label's products.

Independent labels are almost wholly dependent upon the major record companies for manufacture of their products. The majors either own or control nearly all the major pressing plants and tape duplicating facilities. The independent label often has difficulty getting prompt production when the pressing plant's parent company has the facilities tied up with its own orders. This bottleneck has seriously hurt small labels when they develop a regional hit, then can't get records produced in volume to fill the record stores with adequate stocks.

If an independent label pulls together adequate initial financing and a strong staff, it cannot go anywhere on a national basis without national distribution. Since the majors own or control most national distribution networks, the small operator is totally dependent upon the big record companies to get their products in the pipelines and into the stores.

Some major labels offer independents, not only national distribution, but promotion services. This will sharply increase costs, but an independent label may determine it is the best solution for its promotion needs. Since no independent label can afford its own national promotion staff, it has only one other alternative: engage independent record promoters.

Farming out distribution and promotion is very expensive. But when an independent record company manages to produce a few hits, the high overhead becomes manageable. Many small firms have lived through high-risk periods to develop into very profitable companies. Perhaps the most conspicuous example of a firm that started very small and grew very rich is the Chrysalis label. From the outset, that company exhibited creative leadership and determination. It turned out to be a winning combination.

SPECIALTY LABELS

The specialty labels experiencing the biggest grosses are in the classical music field, e.g., Nonesuch, Deutch Grammaphon, Westminster, Odyssey and Angel. Since all the classics have already been recorded and rerecorded by the world's greatest artists, classical labels are largely concerned with selling from existing inventories, many of which contain huge backlogs. Larger classical labels such as Columbia will, from time to time, tape "new music," the works of "serious" contemporary composers. Few such pressings return their production costs, but some of the larger companies apparently feel an obligation to the art of music to attempt to keep classical music alive in a commercial world.

Some specialty labels, particularly in the classical field of contemporary music, release their records "privately." They eschew more conventional distribution channels and seek to locate buyers of their sometimes esoteric product through the mail, addressed particularly to colleges and universities. This kind of label cannot break even and requires subsidy of some kind.

Other specialty labels limit their activities to certain ethnic markets. They find ways to reach cultural enclaves or ethnic groups in particular parts of the country and work directly with retail outlets in such communities. Another kind of specialty label is Folkways, which offers a variety of folk, blues, ethnic and jazz musics, selling mostly by mail to schools and libraries.

One of the most successful types of specialty label sells gospel music. Some people refer to this repertoire as "contemporary Christian music." Among the most effective promotional methods used by gospel record companies are the many personal appearances of their contract artists. Touring gospel singers draw large audiences and sell lots of records.

RECORD COMPANY ADMINISTRATION

Most large record companies administer their affairs in a pattern like the accompanying graphic display (Figure 15.1). Firms will vary in how they label and group departments. But whatever their structure, they must handle the kinds of tasks I describe. In simpler times, large organizations were managed in a structure that looked like a pyramid: underlings worked at the base of the triangular structure, reporting to

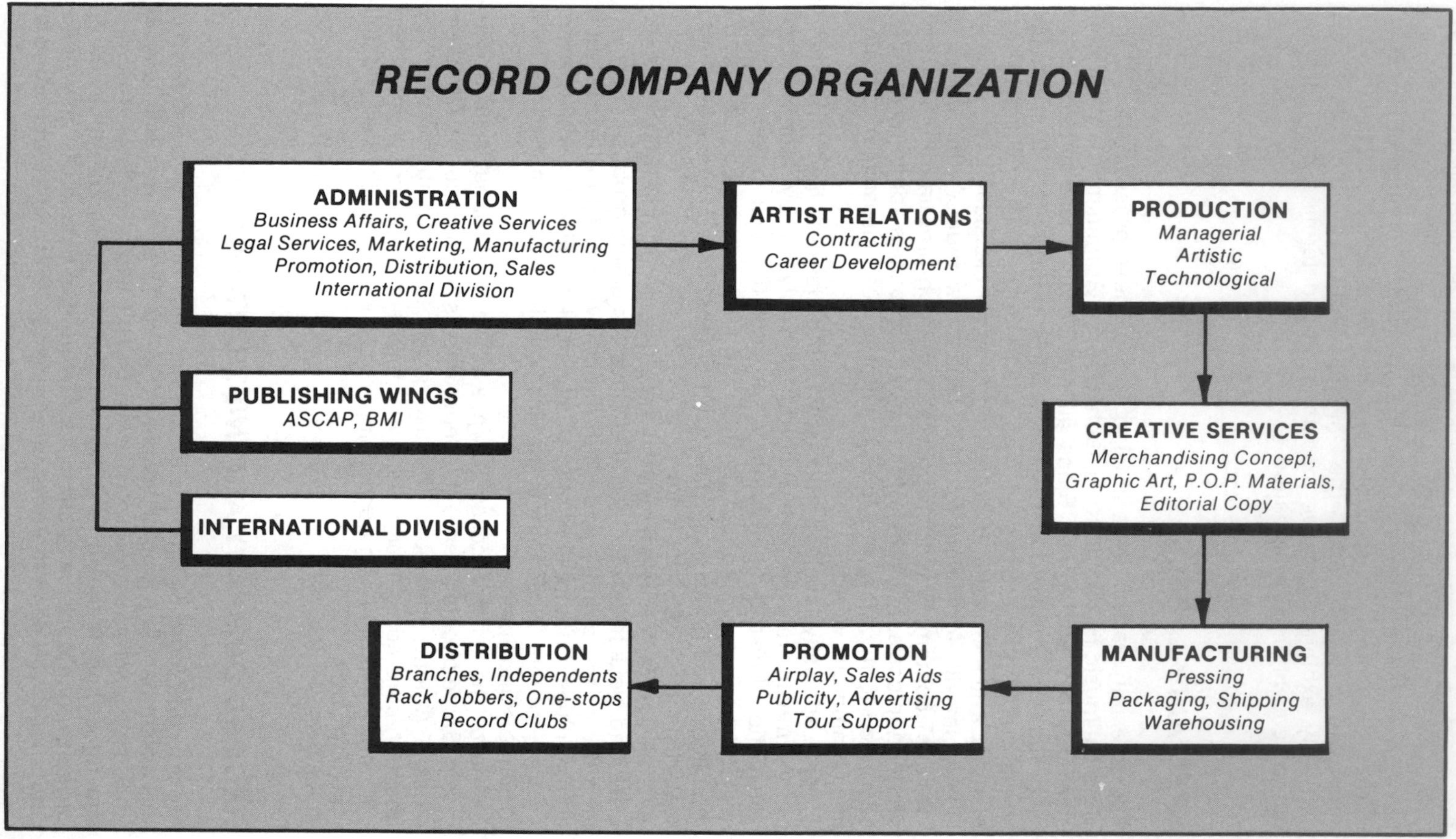

RECORD COMPANY ORGANIZATION

PRODUCTION
Managerial
Artistic
Technological

CREATIVE SERVICES
Merchandising Concept,
Graphic Art, P.O.P. Materials,
Editorial Copy

MANUFACTURING
Pressing
Packaging, Shipping
Warehousing

ARTIST RELATIONS
Contracting
Career Development

PROMOTION
Airplay, Sales Aids
Publicity, Advertising
Tour Support

ADMINISTRATION
Business Affairs, Creative Services
Legal Services, Marketing, Manufacturing
Promotion, Distribution, Sales
International Division

DISTRIBUTION
Branches, Independents
Rack Jobbers, One-stops
Record Clubs

PUBLISHING WINGS
ASCAP, BMI

INTERNATIONAL DIVISION

Fig. 15.1

their department heads who, in turn, would report to divisional managers who, in turn, would report to the boss perched at the apex. Modern business organizations rarely structure themselves in this way. As John Kenneth Galbraith puts it, *large companies run themselves by committee.* These committees can be conceived as circles; the circles interact.

Individual initiative and creativity are highly valued in the record industry, but no one I know makes any claim to omniscience. The wisest executives I have been around admit that a large portion of their success can be attributed to the fact they surround (insulate?) themselves with competent associates. As one senior vice-president told me, "Not one of us around here knows enough. The record business changes so fast, about all we can do is get together about once a week and pool our ignorance." A professor of business administration might call this "dispersed decision encounters." The process is older than the Roman senate. Decision-by-committee is favored in modern organizations because, when a decision proves wrong, at least those who took part in it have managed to spread out the blame.

Some labels have an "executive committee" which is charged with the task of formulating basic company policy and making major decisions. An executive committee for a large label might include the CEO (chief executive officer), the vice-presidents for administration, artist and repertoire, marketing, distribution, the controller (or treasurer), and the house legal counsel. The vice-presidents of the company's publishing wings and foreign operations might be included in this decision-making committee.

Artist Relations — Companies like Warner Bros. Records, with a reputation for being "artist oriented," might have a vice-president for artist relations. That department would have broad responsibilities, which might include talent search, contract negotiations, artist management and development, tour support and publicity. Other firms would disperse some of these responsibilities among other departments.

A & R Department — Most large firms appoint a vice-president to head record production. He assigns either a house producer or outside producer to record the label's contract artists. Independent producers may be selected and supervised by the vice-president for A & R. This individual would accept or reject masters brought in by independent producers.

Creative Services — Large firms which follow the Warner Bros. model have a vice-president for "creative services." This influential executive supervises a sizable staff whose main responsibility is creating marketing campaigns. Such a group of individuals first creates a marketing *concept,* conceives and executes graphic art, writes editorial copy, designs, manufactures and distributes "point-of-sale" stimuli — posters, banners, window displays, etc.

Business Affairs, Accounting — This department is usually staffed by MBA's, accountants, purchasing agents and data processors. They keep track of receipts, expenditures, payroll, royalties, purchasing, inventory and information handling.

Sales Promotion, Marketing — Record companies vary in how they group activities promoting sales of their products. Some firms group all such activities under a "marketing department." Other firms separate "marketing" from "promotion." Still other firms will group these activities under "distribution and sales." Whatever the rubric, the people attempting to promote sales are engaged in advertising, promotion, publicity, public relations — whatever is needed to persuade the public to buy the records.

Distribution — Major labels own and control their own distributing networks. Smaller labels distribute their records through independent distributors or through distributors operated by a major label.

Legal Department — Many firms have a legal department, staffed by a "general counsel" or head lawyer who supervises other lawyers who are on staff, retainer, or called in free-lance. The legal department is largely concerned with assisting in negotiating contracts with artists. These negotiations are headed by top officers in the company, some of whom are licensed attorneys themselves. Contract negotiations usually include, on the artist's side, the artist's attorney or manager or both. Many artists' managers are also attorneys. Legal departments of record companies are usually staffed by lawyers who are specialists in copyright, music and entertainment law.

Operations — If a label has a department called "operations," it would place therein such functions as scheduling and maintenance of its recording studios, record mastering and manufacture, office maintenance, warehousing and shipping.

Publishing Affiliates — All record labels own or control at least two publishing companies — one connected with ASCAP and one signed with BMI. Labels with aggressive publishing wings seek to persuade, sometimes coerce, their contract artists to grant them publishing rights to the music the artist records for the label.

International Division — All but the smallest labels maintain an active international division, usually headed by individuals knowledgeable in international copyright law, foreign licensing techniques, etc. Since foreign business now accounts for over one-half of total sales, record companies continue to expand their international offices and liaisons with licensees outside this country.

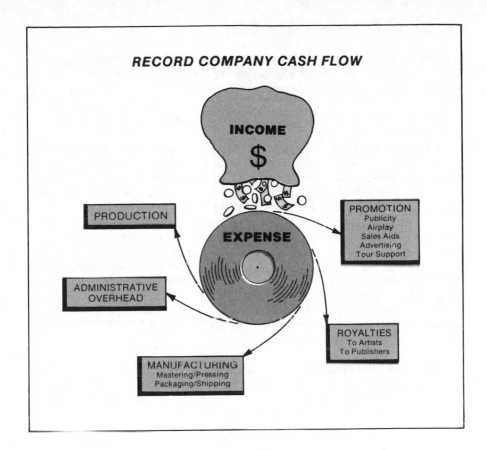

RECORD COMPANY CASH FLOW

INCOME
$

PRODUCTION

EXPENSE

PROMOTION
Publicity
Airplay
Sales Aids
Advertising
Tour Support

ADMINISTRATIVE
OVERHEAD

ROYALTIES
To Artists
To Publishers

MANUFACTURING
Mastering/Pressing
Packaging/Shipping

Fig. 15.2

PIRACY, COUNTERFEITING, BOOTLEGGING

The illegal copying and selling of phonorecords in the late 1960's became a problem so pervasive that some observers believed the counterfeiters might put legitimate companies out of business. For many years, record piracy, bootlegging and counterfeiting have been a worldwide problem of overwhelming proportions.

No accurate statistics are available on the financial drain caused by discs and tapes sold illegally. The most comprehensive, worldwide study was made in the early 1980s by *The World Intellectual Property Organization*[2] headquartered in Geneva. That group, in cooperation with the *International Federation of Producers of Phonograms and Videograms,* concluded that the worldwide sale of counterfeit, pirated and bootlegged merchandise had a value of over $1.1 billion.

The seriousness of illegal record copying varies widely from country to country. Portugal, for example, has a situation where illegal records

2-WIPO came into being in 1970 as a specialized agency of the United Nations.

and tapes appear to capture some 75 percent of the market. Italy, too, has a problem on about the same scale. In many parts of Latin America, Asia and Africa, piracy and counterfeiting of records is not a crime nor is it even regarded as a civil offense. Elsewhere, many nations do have statutes against record piracy, but enforcement is generally lax.

In the United States, significant progress has been made toward controlling the sale of counterfeit records. This can be attributed to stiffer penalties now provided in the 1976 Copyright Act, increasing vigilance of the FBI in searching out the criminals, a new alertness among record merchandisers in spotting illegal merchandise (much of it looks about the same as legitimate products), and the prosecution, fining and jailing of an increasing number of offenders. But the most recent reports of the RIAA stress that the problem in this country is far from solved. At every record industry meeting, leaders prod each other to reduce this problem which hurts everybody in the business, particularly copyright owners.

To effectively limit worldwide record counterfeiting, it is generally agreed these steps must be taken by every country genuinely interested in controlling the problem:

1- *Enlist the cooperation of record merchants who want to operate legitimately. Record company executives express the view privately that many record stores aid the crooks by buying their merchandise to save a few dollars.*

2- *Enact stronger copyright laws and impose more severe penalties.*

3- *Enforce such laws and prosecute offenders.*

Walter Yetnikoff, president of CBS Records, has stated publicly that if sufficient money and effort were spent toward solving the counterfeit problem, it could still take 10 to 20 years to eliminate the scourge.

For years, record companies have been searching for a practical device that would provide a way for honest distributors, merchants and consumers to detect counterfeit merchandise. A variety of package-marking or coding devices have been developed. Some labels have preferred to keep secret just what coding they use, to reduce the possibility of someone coming up with a code-scrambling device to defeat the system. Some records are determined as honest merchandise through electronic "wands" or scanning instruments, now widely used by retail stores. The anti-counterfeit codings cost about one cent per unit to apply.

Home Taping — A problem related to counterfeiting is the widespread practice of music lovers copying their favorite music on home tape recorders. Surveys have been made by the major labels, but they have come up with conflicting data. There is some doubt whether the avid home-taper actually buys fewer records. Some research shows that the person who is busy taping music at home may continue to buy as many records following acquisition of his recorder as he did before. Other research has estimated the loss of sales to home taping may aggregate over $700 million in the United States.

Copyright owners and some record companies have urged the Congress to establish a tax on raw tape, then share the revenue with copyright owners who suffer loss of royalties through home taping. Austria was the first country to assess such a tax for this purpose. Other countries are expected to follow Austria's lead. Pressure on Congress is increasing, and has extended to lobbying for the establishment of a sales tax on recording equipment, again with the revenue to be shared among copyright owners of the music and the sound recording. Those favoring this kind of legislation are also pushing for Congress to include videotape and video recorders in this proposed tax.

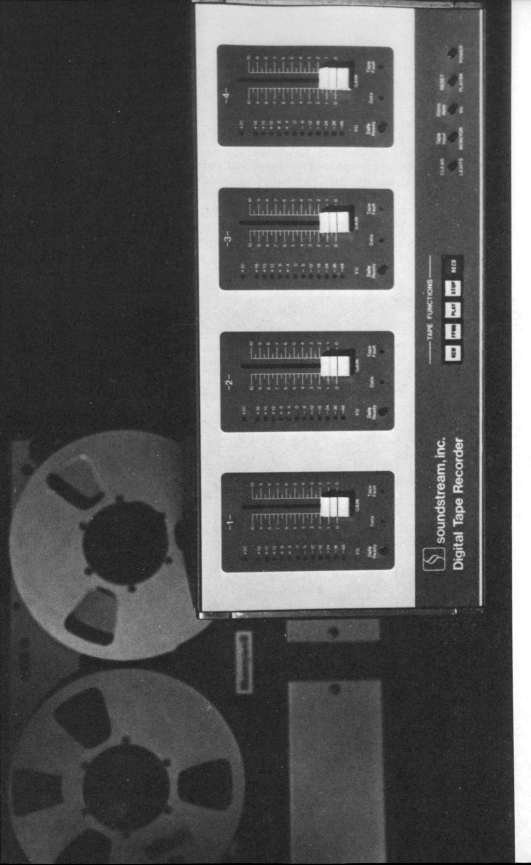

DIGITAL TAPE RECORDER developed by Sound Stream, Inc., widely used in both the classical and popular music fields.

16

RECORD MARKETS

RESEARCH METHODS

A record company must know who its customers are — who is currently buying, and who might be persuaded to buy in the future. The industry is fiercely competitive. It appears likely the companies which conduct the most thorough market research will lead the pack.

Despite the many studies that have been made by record companies, trade associations and professional journals, we do not have very accurate information. One of the reasons for this is that, until recently, research methods used in the industry have sometimes been unscientific, ill-conceived and, occasionally, just plain phony.

Of all the "research" used in the record business, the "charts" have been most suspect. As for research of record "sales," data are generally imprecise and too often fail to make clear the distinctions between the figures for merchandise actually sold as compared to the huge amounts of unsold stock returned by dealers. And when a chart or poll declares that one particular musical style outsells another, no one can really know what these figures mean because there is no concensus on just how various musical styles should be categorized. For example, it is not unusual for one record to be listed on three or more charts in the same magazine. Thus, its relative ranking becomes meaningless.

But recent research is more reliable and, consequently, more useful. Increasing numbers of qualified research analysts and scientific pollsters are becoming involved. Their computers are beginning to spew out more believable data. The record industry is beginning to understand where it is, if not just where it might be headed.

THE CHARTS

Everyone in the record business who enjoys eating regularly follows the charts published in the trade journals, *Billboard, Record World* and *Cash Box.* Profits soar or plunge, careers flourish or collapse — in direct ratio to the relative altitude certain records reach on these weekly sales reports. Music people assess the validity of the charts something like the way politicians react to political polls: when you are riding high, your faith in the data is unbounded. But when you rank low, you tend to suspect the figures are not really trustworthy and perhaps even rigged. The trade papers are aware of these suspicions and do all they can to make their charts objective, accurate and credible. But insiders believe ways can be found to hype the reports in one way or another.

Opinion varies as to the extent artificial influences may affect the validity of these reports from time to time. My own view is that when a chart fails to be objective, the problem is not so much that the chart makers have suffered a lapse of morality. Rather, invalid charts, when they appear, more often result from carelessly assembled data or incorrect interpretation of the facts.

Billboard publishes the most widely quoted charts and employs a large staff in its market research department. *Billboard*'s famous Hot 100 chart (best-selling singles) is determined through such information sources as dealers' and one-stops' weekly sales figures. The Hot 100 chart is also influenced by the extent of airplay drawn from 10 geographic areas. That person who wonders why his record doesn't crack the Hot 100 page should know *Billboard* doesn't even consider a release that is not moving at least 30,000 units a week on a reorder basis.

The trade papers gather most of their data by telephone. While this medium is faster than the mails, it permits inaccuracies inherent in verbal communication. While data are stored in computers, *Billboard* insists its data banks are used only as aids, and each record is positioned through the applied judgment of an experienced chart-making human being.

Whatever research methods a record company may use to measure the progress of a record, if a 45 rpm single picks up good airplay in major markets it has an excellent chance of landing a position on the charts, making its initial appearance probably in the bottom third of the rankings. If strong radio play for the single continues, it will probably rise on the charts. When the chart makers observe a particularly rapid rise, that record will be awarded a "bullet" or some other marking indicating suddenly increasing popularity. Records with a "bullet" tend to rise to the highest chart positions and become the biggest hits.

Albums, Album Tracks — Record album charts are a different story. This kind of chart cannot be compiled from evidence only from airplay, because no one can know which of a dozen tracks is most responsible for the popularity of an LP. Accordingly, national rankings of albums are determined largely by unit sales. The trade papers telephone representative retail outlets across the country to learn how albums are moving out of the stores. For purposes of making up "album" charts, researchers include under that category all recorded music configurations except singles. That is to say, LPs, prerecorded cassette tapes and 8-track tapes are counted as "album" units.

Until recently, record labels and radio programmers had no way to determine which tracks on an album were being most played. Some trade papers and tip sheets now offer charts which purport to identify, through research, which tracks from albums are the most popular. One example is *Billboard's 60 Top Tracks* chart, which claims to identify, in relative airplay ranking, the top 60 rock songs, *whether they are from single records or album cuts. Billboard* believes this kind of chart places individual tracks on an equal footing nationally, regardless of their actual configuration. This kind of information is particularly useful for radio program directors who broadcast a mix of singles and AOR (Album-Oriented Rock).

While this kind of chart-making has been limited to just rock records, it would be useful to have it extended to other musical styles.

A glance at any trade paper reveals that a chart is available, credible or not, to indicate the activity of singles, LP's, tapes, airplay regionally and nationally, international sales, and the comparative progress in the market of records classified by musical style. Many industry people not only compare relative rankings among *Billboard, Cash Box* and *Record World* (which often differ markedly), but compare their discrepancies with one or more "inside" publications, e.g., *Radio and Records.* Then they compare these data with "tip sheets." They vary in quality; some even accept record company advertising. *The Gavin Report* is perhaps the most respected among these "inside" publications; it seems to have a reputation for being the most objective.

Radio broadcasters and label executives compare data accumulated from these external sources with reports from their own distributors who have first-hand knowledge of how the product is faring in the market.

Reliability of sales figures might be increased if all the chart makers would feed their data into a central computer bank, then appoint an impartial staff of analysts to tell the industry what all the figures mean. While this kind of cooperation could increase comprehensiveness and objectivity, competing chart makers are not likely to take part, for the trade papers, particularly, know their existence is dependent upon their advertisers, the same people who buy the trade papers in the first place to read the charts.

Dr. Feelgood? — Today, market research methods are being used that would have been unthinkable in earlier years. One of the more unusual information sources is found at the Consumer Behavior Center in Dallas, Texas, where Dr. Thomas Turichi tests musical preferences of potential record buyers. He employs galvanic skin responses of his human test subjects as they listen to certain cuts from an album that is about to be released. Fifty-six listeners, ranging in age from 12 to 34, as a rule, are tested at one time. Each individual has electrodes attached to his fingertips, the impulses being measured for the most favorable response to records being tested in the lab. Turichi claims 93 percent accuracy with his research method. Does anyone believe him? Well, over 20 record companies have paid the good doctor $800 per album for his data. About 2,000 records have been processed in this manner in Turichi's lab.

It might be noted that Turichi, a musicologist on the faculty of Texas Women's University, employs research methods he first developed for measuring responses of listeners to classical music. But for many musicians, any thought of measuring musical response in a laboratory is horrifying. But galvanic skin response methods might prove more accurate data than less carefully controlled response measurements, for example, the so-called "passive research" methods conducted by radio stations.

For many years, music therapists have understood, sometimes with considerable precision, just what kinds of music will elicit certain responses in their patients. Why aren't record companies investigating how this kind of expertise might assist their determination of just what records are deserving of release and promotion?

RIAA

The most comprehensive market research in the record industry is carried on (or commissioned) by RIAA, the Recording Industry Association of America. The RIAA is the most representative trade association in the record manufacturing business and includes companies accounting for 85 percent to 90 percent of all records sold in this country. All major labels are members of RIAA. The organization is well-financed, deriving its funding from members' dues, which range from about $100 to several hundred thousand dollars a year, the amount being determined by a company's annual sales.

RIAA is best known to the public through its certification of records as "gold" or "platinum." When a label believes its sales justify such a certification, the RIAA conducts an independent audit (even non-RIAA members may request such an audit). If the audit shows a *single* record has actually sold one million copies, the RIA certifies the record as "gold." An *album* must sell one-half million copies to gain gold status. As record sales increased in the mid-1970s, the RIAA determined that some distinction should be made for records which sold far more than the amounts qualifying them for gold status. Thus, the "platinum" record was established, and that status is certified when a single sells two million copies and an album sells one million. Now that some records go "double" or "triple platinum," the RIAA may find it necessary to invent a still more prestigious category for monster hits. "Diamond" records?

RIAA issues annual reports of research it has conducted or farmed out to experts such as the Cambridge Research Institute. RIAA reports can be misunderstood if the reader is inexperienced. No one can misunderstand data accounting for "units sold." But when the RIAA reports "dollar amounts" of annual sales, it is difficult to know what what the word "sold" means here. This is because a high percentage of records in the United States are shipped *on consignment,* and dealers are permitted to return unsold merchandise, within a specified time limit, their only penalty being the cost of return freight.

It is in the self-interest of many individuals in the industry to report maximum sales. Some insiders allege that reports of "sales," including data labels report to RIAA, are not only hyped, but sometimes wildly inaccurate. Yet, RIAA does all it can to maintain the credibility of its summary reports.

One kind of research the RIAA has commissioned concerns estimates of how many copies of a record must sell *to break even.* Results from these studies have produced data that are depressing to anyone in the music business. While the figures change from year to year, most RIAA members report that about 70 percent to 80 percent of their releases *fail to return their investments.* Yet, some companies claim their track records are much better. Whatever the proportion of hits to flops, record companies that survive do so because their hits yield sufficient profits to cover their overhead.

One of the important services RIAA performs for the industry is the commitment of its resources to fighting record counterfeiting and piracy.

RECORD CATEGORIZATION

As pointed out repeatedly in this volume, we have no agreement on the categorization of different styles of music. This lack of concensus on classification makes it difficult, sometimes impossible, for one person in the field to know what the other person is really talking about. Difficulties with categorization are particularly apparent in understanding record charts. If a record ranks number 5 on the "Hot 100" chart, number 10 on "Easy Listening" and perhaps number 40 on the "Country" chart, what does it mean? In addition to an indication that the record is "crossing over," it also means that the trade paper could not, or would not, decide just what style of music the record really contained.

Ambiguity of categorization is hopeless now in the rock field and just about as big a problem with "country" or "soul" music. Some time ago, NARM gave up trying to distinguish certain musics, and now reports sales data under the umbrella term, "Contemporary," which now includes "rock," "pop" and "soul."

Whatever category we determine for a particular song or record, one certainty does prevail, however: *the public doesn't care very much.* For many years, the record-buying public has repeatedly demonstrated that it is attracted by the sound of the music, not its type.

The clearest evidence of the public's disinterest in categories of music is the crossover record, where the release of a record aimed at one audience attracts, by accident or design, additional audiences. Nearly all superhits today are crossover records, achieving multimillion-selling status by picking up listeners crossing traditional lines.

While conceding that precise categorization of music is impossible, perhaps even undesirable, the following classifications may help clarify terminology which, in the past, has been used too casually.

Rock — All studies show that rock continues to be the dominant musical style. As the original rock and roll developed derivative styles, someone was always ready to offer ever-new labels — "hard rock," "soft rock," "acid rock," "country rock," "folk rock," "heavy metal rock" and so on. Those with different tastes hope the ultimate development in this genre will be non-rock.

Country — Country includes what used to be called "country and western" music, country swing, bluegrass, "Nashville country," "L.A. country," pop country and popular songs with a country-type rhythm. Singing styles range from "straight Nashville" to pop.

Soul, R & B, Disco — Under "soul" we include the musical styles created and performed predominantly by black people. Most recordings of this kind tend to feature a free use of the human voice and vocal and instrumental improvisation. Contemporary music in these styles often employs a very active electric bass line.

Easy Listening, MOR — This is a broad category flanked on the left by jazz and on the right by classical music. The terms, easy listening and MOR ("middle of the road"), are sometimes used interchangeably. This middle ground includes most popular music, particularly standards and show tunes that lack a harder rock beat. This style stresses, for the most part, romantic songs and lush orchestrations. Some radio stations broadcasting this repertoire prefer to use the term "good music" or "beautiful music."

Jazz — Since much jazz is now included under such classifications as "jazz-rock," "fusion," or "soul," about the only music that can now be categorized as "pure" jazz is instrumental, not vocal, largely improvised rather than arranged, and favors acoustic instruments.

Gospel — Gospel is used as a generic term for music containing texts that make reference to the Christian faith. Some persons believe the term gospel should be applied only to the religious musical expressions of black persons. Others would include both "black" gospel and "white" gospel. Trade papers sometimes classify this repertoire under "inspirational music." Perhaps the most useful rubric for this repertoire is "contemporary Christian music," which happens to be the name of the leading professional journal covering the field (*Contemporary Christian Music*).

Classical — This is the repertoire originally intended for performance in concerts, operas, legitimate theatres, recital halls and places of worship. Musicologists favor the term "art music" for this repertoire and contrast it to what they call "commercial music." In the record and broadcast industries, semiclassical, semipopular, "symphonic jazz" and light opera are sometimes included under the classical music category.

Other — Musics not falling under any of the categories defined above can be grouped under "miscellaneous" or "other," because their share of the market is too small to figure importantly in research data. Here we can include comedy records, children's records, ethnic musics and educational materials. As for movie sound tracks, they range in style from hard rock to symphonic and defy categorization. As to original cast albums of musicals, they, too, cover a musical gamut from rock to opera.

STYLISTIC PREFERENCES

Public tastes change rapidly. The simplest way to confirm this in the music field is to compare a record chart today with one a year ago. In the rock field particularly, acts zoom to quick stardom and dominate the charts for a few months. About one year later, it appears that well over half of last year's favorites have disappeared. Except for a handful of all-time stars — the Beatles, the Rolling Stones and Bob Dylan — the mass audience finds new favorites and forgets its former idols.

This strange inconstancy in the rock audience probably derives largely from the transient nature of the material recorded — so much of it sound and fury signifying nothing, to borrow from Shakespeare. Spasms of the moment with little musical substance.

Another reason last year's stars are difficult to find on this year's charts is that many hit records appear to be artificially created. Record people become indignant when anyone suggests they can "create" a hit just through promotion. On the contrary, they argue, "It's got to be in the grooves; we can't 'create' a hit." But a strong case can be made on the other side of this argument. Large numbers of very poor records reach the top of the charts, and the only reasonable way to explain these phenomena is to conclude that the promotion people on these records are more creative than the musicians.

Public tastes in music are more constant once we leave the rock field. Some performers remain top favorites for decades — Bing Crosby, Johnny Cash, Ella Fitzgerald, the Boston Pops. Whoever may survive public favor over the years, most market studies focus, not on performers, but on musical styles. We lack clear agreement on how to categorize music, but studies by RIAA and NARM give us a general idea of public preferences (Figure 16.1).

It is useful to compare RIAA and NARM research data with a study commissioned by Warner Communications Inc. WCI claims it is ". . . the most thorough, in-depth study of the industry ever conducted,"

RECORD BUYERS' PREFERENCES
% of Dollar Volume

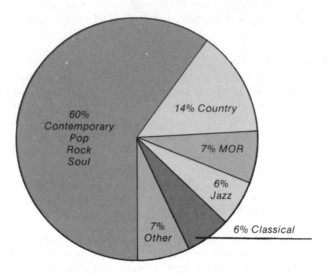

60%
Contemporary
Pop
Rock
Soul

14% Country

7% MOR

6%
Jazz

7%
Other

6% Classical

Fig. 16.1

RECORD BUYERS' PREFERENCES: ANOTHER VIEW
% of Dollar Volume

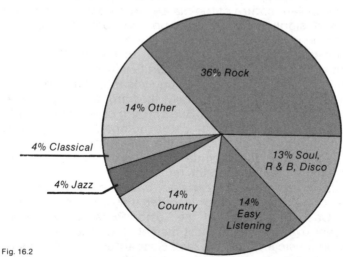

36% Rock

14% Other

4% Classical

4% Jazz

14%
Country

14%
Easy
Listening

13% Soul,
R & B, Disco

Fig. 16.2

Based on *The Prerecorded Music Market - An Industry Survey* (Kapp-Fishbein)
© Warner Communications Inc. Used by permission.

and I have no reason to question it. In comparing these statistics (Figures 16.1 and 16.2), it is essential to observe the differences in music categorization.

Since these studies were made, we have seen an increase in the size of the audience favoring country music and pop-country.

DEMOGRAPHICS

Studies of stylistic preferences provide only one part of the information available to record companies from demographic research. The *age* of record buyers is important to know, and recent studies have brought into question the old myths about kids dominating the market. Since rock and roll has had its most enthusiastic fans among teenagers since the 1950s, and because rock appears to have dominated the business ever since, industry leaders continued to assume that the kids bought the most records. They clearly did in the early periods of the development of rock and other so-called "contemporary" musics. But the WCI study, cited above, dropped like a bombshell when it was made public. Particularly shocking was the section of the study which accounted for the age groups who are now buying the most records:

WHO BUYS TAPES AND RECORDS	PERCENT OF THE MARKET
Persons 25 years and older	53%
Teenagers	23%
Persons 20-24 years of age	22%

The WCI study also showed a direct correlation between persons who listen most to radio and those who buy the most records: persons who listen to the radio at least 10 hours a week represent 54 percent of all record buyers and they account for 62 percent of the dollars spent on records.

Since the WCI-sponsored study appears to have used research methods at least as scientific as RIAA and NARM, it may alter how record companies apply their marketing energies in the coming years.

Another industry giant, CBS Records, has also engaged in extensive market research. It tends to corroborate WCI's data. CBS has found that 77 percent of all record buyers are 18 or older. It believes this same group accounts for 82 percent of all records purchased.

One of the reasons demographic studies have destroyed the old myths about kids dominating the market is that investigators in earlier years failed to take into account that record "markets" have been *aggregating*. When the record industry exploded in the 1950s and 1960s, kids were the main buyers. But these youngsters are now adults. As adults, they do buy fewer records, but still they continue to buy. When this more mature group is added to the teenagers of later years, the accumulated total of music lovers becomes very large. This accounts not only for the aging of the market, but its growth.

An increasing share of the market is being won by prerecorded audiocassettes. This growth is attributable to the greater convenience of cassettes and the enhanced sound quality available in recent years from improved tape and better playback equipment. New buyers in Asia, Africa, and Eastern Europe start out with low-cost cassette players and will probably never own a record turntable. Some industry observers believe cassettes may continue to increase their market share and perhaps wipe out other record playing modes. But other analysts believe this is unlikely, in that most music lovers possess a library of albums they will want to enjoy for years to come on the equipment they presently own.

The accompanying tables do not reveal industry concern over the impact of widescale home recording of radio broadcasts and albums. As pointed out, home recording is great for the purveyors of raw tape, but represents a major loss of sales of prerecorded tapes and discs.

WORLD MARKETS

The largest market for records and tapes is the United States, which accounts for about 35 percent to 40 percent of the world total. When we attempt to account for the size of foreign markets, available data are incomplete and unreliable. RIAA offers annual reports which account, not for total foreign sales, but for the dollar value of merchandise shipped by US companies to foreign territories. I have drawn from these RIAA figures, used data from excise tax payments, factored in US Department of Commerce information on worldwide inflation — and offer the estimates of world market shares shown in Figure 16.3.

Three of the largest record company conglomerates in the USA — RCA, CBS and WEA, along with some other labels with multinational sales operations, *gross more abroad than they do in the United States.*

Fig. 16.3

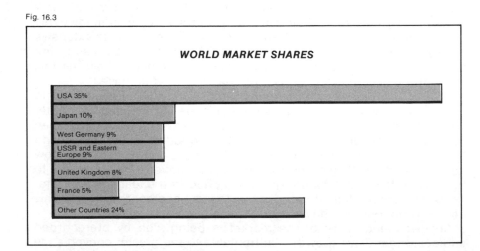

WORLD MARKET SHARES

USA 35%
Japan 10%
West Germany 9%
USSR and Eastern Europe 9%
United Kingdom 8%
France 5%
Other Countries 24%

The market shares shown in Figure 16.3 account for the *export* (or licensing) of American product abroad. But increasing numbers of foreign territories are attempting to export their own records, not only to us, but to other developing markets. Only two nations in the world, the United States and the United Kingdom, have fully developed foreign markets. A number of European countries and Japan are beginning to expand exportation of their record products internationally.

17

ARTISTS CONTRACTS

AFTRA AGREEMENTS

All recognized, nationally-distributed record labels enter into a labor contract with the American Federation of Television and Radio Artists (AFTRA) for the services of singers. This agreement, known as the *National Code of Fair Practice for Phonograph Recordings*, covers solo singers, and vocalists who are part of recognized musical groups, from duos on up. The present contract covers essential concerns of AFTRA in respect to wage scales, overdubbing, working conditions, reuse payments, royalty obligations and labels' contributions to AFTRA's Pension and Welfare Funds.

VOCAL CONTRACTORS

Where recording involves three or more AFTRA members, AFTRA requires a union contractor. That individual is usually a singing member of the group (except where the contractor's sex precludes it). The AFTRA Code defines contractors as ". . . those artists who perform any additional services, such as contracting singers, pre-rehearsing, coaching singers, arranging for sessions or rehearsals, or any other similar or supervisory duties, including assisting with and preparation of production memoranda." AFTRA makes no distinction

JOE ZAWINUL simultaneously manipulates two Arp 2600 synthesizers and a sequencer.

in this respect between a vocal contractor and a vocal director. The AFTRA contractor is required to be present at all recording sessions, whether he is or is not one of the singers, in order to supervise the adherence of the record producer to the terms of the Code.

One of the contractor's important responsibilities is to keep track of overdubbing of voices. The practice is almost universal today, and it is the task of the AFTRA contractor to log these events, then charge the producer for them. AFTRA requires that when its members become involved in any form of tracking, they are to be paid for the session "as if each overtracking were an additional side." Producers sometimes find that extensive overdubbing can run their costs higher than they would have been if additional singers had been engaged in the first place. Voices are overdubbed either "live on tape" or through electronic means, such as tape delays. These techniques are sometimes used to change the timbre, resonance or intensity of voices. Sometimes the mixing engineer can cause one to four voices to sound like many more singers are performing. In that most tracking results in a net loss of employment for union singers, AFTRA attempts to control its use through assessing extra charges for such services.

In addition to his fee as one of the group singers, the contractor receives additional compensation per hour or per side of recording, whichever is higher. An AFTRA contractor is also required when the recording of a Broadway show involves a group of three or more singers.

For all sessions involving AFTRA-member singing groups, the contractor renders the "AFTRA Members Contractor Standard Report Form," which cites the record producer's name, hours of recording, the names of AFTRA members involved and wages due them. The contractor has the producer initial this form, then turns it in to the AFTRA office.

The record company or producer must also file with AFTRA, within 21 calendar days following the last recording session, a "production memorandum" (known as "Schedule A") which sets forth the fees paid for the singers. This memorandum also sets forth information sufficient for AFTRA to calculate any fees that may be negotiated later.

Legislation is pending in Congress in respect to the payment of performance fees to recording artists whose records are broadcast. Also pending is the adoption in this country of the "International Convention for the Protection of Performers, Producers of Phonograms, and Broadcasting Organizations." This convention, which dates from 1961, has been adopted by the principal countries of Europe. The AFTRA Code has been written in anticipation of the adoption of the International Convention by this country, and provides that AFTRA members' share of any such performance fees received by American record companies will be bargained for in good faith.

SCALES, ROYALTIES

The production memorandum cited above must include an indication as to which AFTRA members on the session were *royalty artists* and which were not. A *royalty artist* receives, not only AFTRA scale, but royalties based on the number of records sold. In respect to "self-contained" acts and all other royalty artists, their maximum wage per record side is three times the minimum AFTRA scale, irrespective of the number and length of the sessions required for that side. AFTRA requires that the record company provide to *royalty artists,* at least twice a year, (and to AFTRA upon request) ". . . a full and proper accounting" of record sales in order to ascertain the royalties due the artists. These accountings are to continue so long as there are sales of the record involved.

The AFTRA Code sets forth in detail its requirements regarding minimum wages. A producer or contractor should consult an AFTRA representative for current details. Here I shall only sketch some of the more common classifications of employment and wages.

AFTRA classifies its members as 1, soloists or duos; 2, group singers; 3, soloists who "step out" of a group; 4, singers who record original cast albums (Broadway shows, etc.); and 5, choral singers recording or broadcasting classical or religious music.

Some years ago, AFTRA managed to negotiate a contract with the record producers that constituted a significant breakthrough in how extra wages were to be calculated for singers. For records made on or after December 14, 1974, AFTRA members started receiving *additional wages based on records sold.* In the past, royalty artists enjoyed no such additional rewards, no matter how successful a particular record became. When these extra payments were agreed upon, they became known as **contingent scale payments.** Here are typical payments under the current contract:

1- *When an LP record reaches a sales plateau of 157,500, non-royalty* AFTRA artists on that record receive a payment equal to 50 percent of their original wages (at scale) for those particular sessions.

2- *When a single record attains sales of 500,000, non-royalty singers receive one-third of scale.*

3- *Singers recording original cast albums receive 30 percent of scale when sales of 460,000 are reached.*

A record is considered for these payments for a period of eight years following its initial release. Payments are limited to sales in the United States which occur through normal retail channels. Sales through record clubs, premiums and mail orders are excluded. Also excluded from these calculations are records distributed for promotional purposes. In determining which record releases are subject to these payments, only the initial release of a record side in album form is included, not any subsequent inclusions of that side in albums. As for singles, only the initial release is eligible for these payments, but if a single is later included in an album it is eligible. Also, a side first released in an album is eligible when it first reappears as a single.

In respect to the AFTRA Pension and Welfare Funds, record companies are required to pay to participating AFTRA recording artists about 8 percent (the rate may vary) of their *gross* compensation for recording. The term, "gross compensation" is defined by the AFTRA Code in this respect as including even royalties paid AFTRA members by the record company. Payment into the fund is limited to the first $100,000 of gross compensation paid to the artist by the record company in any calendar year. The payment into these funds is also required in respect to the contingent scale payments described above.

ACQUIRED MASTERS

When a singer records for one of the recognized labels, AFTRA has no difficulty controlling minimum wages and working conditions. But many records are made by very small companies and by independent record producers who then attempt later to sell or lease their master tapes to a third party. This practice is widespread in the music business, and full union control is difficult, often impossible. AFTRA and the AFM do what they can, however, to protect their members from unfair practices.

The rights of performers are often abused when a producer transfers rights in a master tape to another person. The first producer may have met all the provisions of his contract with AFTRA, but royalties may still be coming in which are payable to the singers. Also, the third party acquiring rights to the master (and possibly including an inventory of merchandise unsold) is required to continue payment of singers' royalties on all sales the third party generates.

A more complicated situation arises when the original master was not recorded under the AFTRA Code. In anticipation of this kind of situation (not uncommon), the AFTRA Code requires that when a record company acquires rights to a master from an outside source, before the record is released the company must furnish to AFTRA a warranty and representation that all performances embodied in the master were recorded "in the recording territory" (USA, its territories and possessions), and that all artists have been paid the minimum rates then in effect under the AFTRA Code and that all payments due to the AFTRA Pension and Welfare Funds have been made. This warranty and representation is AFTRA's Schedule D. If the record company will not or cannot execute Schedule D, it has the option of filing AFTRA's Schedule A, described above.

If it is learned that these representations are false and the parties involved were not signatories to the AFTRA Code, the company acquiring the master must then make the minimum scale payments plus any applicable contributions due the AFTRA Pension and Welfare Funds.

When a third party acquires interest in or ownership of a master recording, his obligations for payment of royalties and contingent payments are spelled out by AFTRA. But the courts have occasionally been unpredictable in their rulings on these matters. In an attempt to dispel all ambiguities, the AFTRA Code specifies that the obligation to pay AFTRA royalties *devolves upon the transferee* and, in turn, any subsequent transferee, for sales made under such transferees or their licensees.

Artists unions do all they can to protect the interests of their members when master tapes recorded for one medium are transferred for use in another medium. Perhaps the most common occurrence of this kind involves a tape prepared for a commercial record and then transferred for use on television, where the on-camera artist lip-syncs his performance. Whatever kind of secondary use is made of a recording (called a "new-use" or "re-use"), AFTRA has set specific scale payments for its members so involved. The singers' union also permits transfers of use only when "the star or featured overscale artist," if any, grants his permission.

NONUNION RECORDING

While the singers' union comprises 36,000 members, the practice of nonunion recording is widespread. In this regard, AFTRA has the same problem as the AFM. Aspiring young performers, eager to get their professional careers off to a quick start, do not often take time to learn established professional practices. Some artists never do discover the advantages of collectivism, the concept of all union activity.

When a young performer fails to convince a recognized record label to sign him, he may take things into his own hands, produce his own masters, perhaps even press a few hundred records and attempt to place them on the market. Rarely do such entrepreneurs adhere to AFTRA or AFM regulations or scales. Many "self-produced" performers, at the start of their careers, are not even aware of the artists' unions and their traditions. Occasionally, the performer-producer-distributor-merchant experiences initial success in a limited geographic area where he may have developed a local following. Some one-man record companies manage later to sell or lease their masters to an established label with national distribution. *At that point, either the original entrepreneur or the lessee must meet the AFTRA obligations described above.* Thus, the original entrepreneur saves no money in the long run by initially circumventing AFTRA and AFM, for their members must ultimately be paid for any record to take off in the national market.

AFM AGREEMENTS

PHONOGRAPH RECORD LABOR AGREEMENT

All record companies engaged in national distribution of their products have a contract with the American Federation of Musicians for the services of instrumentalists, directors, arrangers, orchestrators and copyists. Every two to four years, the AFM Executive Board empowers its National Contracts Division, or a special negotiating committee, to work out terms of the contract with recording industry representatives. The current contract is known as the *Phonograph Record Labor Agreement*. It governs wages, benefits and working conditions for all services of musicians working in the recording industry in the United States and Canada. The Agreement provides that

> . . . only the services of members in good standing of the American Federation of Musicians of the United States and Canada shall be used for the performance of all instrumental music, and in copying, orchestrating or arranging of such music, in recording phonograph records, and, in the employment of persons eligible for membership in the Federation, only such persons as shall be members thereof in good standing shall be so employed.

In addition to wages paid for musicians' services, the contract also requires the employer to pay around $4 (amounts vary contract to contract) per session into the AFM Health and Welfare Fund (AFM H & W) and 10 percent of gross (scale) wages into the AFM-EPW, the Employers Pension and Welfare Fund.

The contract provides 200 percent of sideman's pay for the leader (musical director). Where a session calls for 12 or more musicians, an AFM contractor is required. He receives double sideman's wages. Musicians doubling on a second instrument are paid, with some exceptions, 20 percent extra for the first double, then 15 percent for each additional double. The Agreement contains many other details covering rest periods, meal breaks, restrictions on the use of electronic instruments where they displace conventional instruments, and surcharges for work performed after midnight and on holidays. Even cartage fees for heavy instruments are stipulated.

The Agreement requires that all music "prepared" for recording must be handled exclusively by arrangers, orchestrators and copyists who are members of the AFM. Since the AFM claims no jurisdiction over the work of songwriters and other kinds of composers, the Agreement does not cover their services.

Enforcement of the scales and working conditions stipulated in the Agreement can be generally managed with the well-established, recognized labels when they produce their own masters. But, as noted above, the practice is widespread in the industry for record companies to lease or buy "outside" masters. The Agreement deals with this problem in detail (Paragraph 18), but policing of these transactions is difficult, sometimes impossible. Record manufacturers are prohibited from using acquired masters unless the music was recorded under the AFM contract and the scale wages it required were paid, or the musicians have been paid equivalent wages and the required contribution to the AFM Pension and Welfare Funds has been made. The company may satisfy its obligation in respect to acquiring masters by securing a "representation of warranty" from the seller or licensor that the requirements of the AFM have been satisfied.

SPECIAL PAYMENTS FUND

When a record company signs the AFM Phonograph Record Labor Agreement, it must also simultaneously execute a Phonograph Record Manufacturers Special Payments Fund Agreement. From the beginning, the AFM recognized that the increasing impact of recording technology was devastating to the music profession — except, of course, for the AFM members who, each year, earn at least part of their livelihood from recording. Knowing that no practical way was available to prevent the rapid increase in the recording industry, the AFM managed to negotiate agreements with the record companies that return to union musicians at least a fraction of the income lost through the reduction of jobs performing music live. The Special Payments Fund Agreement also helps compensate, in a small way, for the failure of Congress to provide in the 1976 Copyright Act a performance royalty from recorded music.

Record companies make payments into the Special Payments Fund twice each year, the amounts being based on the aggregate sale of records in the company's catalog. The "royalty" due the fund is .6 percent of the suggested retail price of each record sold. Record companies are allowed discounts for packaging (up to 15 percent) and for free promotional copies distributed (up to 20 percent) and for records sold through record clubs (up to 50 percent). Companies must pay these royalties for a period of ten years dating from the initial release of a record.

All these royalties are paid by the record companies to the Administrator of the Fund. After expenses of administration are deducted, all funds are then paid to the musicians who, during the preceding five-year period, performed on any of the records covered by the Agreement. One musician in Los Angeles, particularly active as a wind player and arranger, has received checks of $50,000 or higher from the fund for five years running. About a half-dozen "supersession" AFM members receive checks in the $40,000 range. Some 400 recording musicians receive checks in the $10,000 range.

AFM members in the three major recording centers received c. 70 percent of all payments from the Special Fund: Los Angeles led with c. 36 percent; New York came in second with 20 percent; Nashville's share was 13 percent. Chicago musicians ranked fourth.

The Special Payments Fund Agreement recognizes that, during the 10 years royalties must be paid, the ownership and control of a record may change. In anticipation of these changes, the Agreement provides that "any such purchaser, assignee, lessee, licensee, transferee, or user shall become an additional first party hereto," meaning that such persons must assume the obligations to the AFM of the company first producing the masters or records. Because of the extensive changes in the record industry — companies and ownership come and go — the control and collection of these funds by the AFM is difficult and cannot always be accomplished.

TRUST FUND AGREEMENT

Record companies must also enter into a Trust Fund Agreement with the AFM. Payments are made to the fund's Trustee and are based on record sales at percentages identical to those for the Special Payments Fund. Disbursements from the Trust Fund are different, however. The Agreement provides that the Trustee is obligated to use all monies collected, except for operational expenses, to set up performances of live music performed by AFM members. In actual practice, administration of these monies is shared by each of the AFM locals who parcel out jobs to their members, irrespective of whether the members are recording musicians, and pay them prevailing local union scales. AFM locals may use some of the money for these live performances to hire halls, finance publicity and print tickets, etc. Cosponsors may be used. The intent of the fund is to foster public understanding and appreciation for live music, and most performances are for schools, hospitals, religious organizations, cultural events and patriotic celebrations. If no admission is charged, the live performances may be broadcast. Established cultural organizations, such as symphony orchestras, opera and ballet companies often call upon the Trust Fund to finance, or partially finance, live music performances.

This sponsorship of live music performances has done more to foster goodwill for the musicians' union than any other AFM activity.

NONUNION RECORDING

AFM and AFTRA have been trying to maintain strict union shops in the recording studios for decades, with uneven results. Following enactment of the Taft-Hartley law and "right-to-work" laws in various states, establishment and maintenance of a strict union shop concept has been difficult. All professional symphony orchestra recording in the United States is under the AFM, as is most MOR and pop-type recording in the major recording centers. Union control is less strong in rock, soul and country fields. Particularly with younger rock bands, quantities of master tapes are produced every year, sometimes recorded by fly-by-night producers and "managers" who promise the kids they'll get rich quick. Most of these operators disappear shortly after sundown. The AFM, from time to time activates a PR campaign to attract very young players ("Young Sounds of the AFM") with reduced fees and dues. As young musicians gain professional experience, they usually discover that working under the protection of AFM membership offers greater long-term rewards than a fast dollar picked up in nonunion sessions.

Another kind of nonunion recording, somewhat more legitimate, is the "spec" session. Producers will hire some musicians, pay them perhaps $20 per hour, then promise to make full payment later, "when the record sells," in an amount equal to AFM scale. Still other producers pay the musicians (union or nonunion) nothing in front, promising to pay full union scale later when the producer can raise the money. Both these kinds of spec recording are disapproved by the AFM. But since nonunion practices of this kind are widespread, it has been suggested the AFM find ways to recognize the honest producer who develops a reputation for eventually paying his musicians.

As noted above, the most effective point of control is found with the independent producer when he attempts to lease or sell his masters to a record company. But if that record company is not a signatory to the AFM recording agreements, or is a signatory but fails to adhere to those agreements, nonunion masters can get produced and sold. But engaging in this kind of fly-by-night activity is short-lived and rarely profitable. This follows because, should a nonunion record company experience temporary success, it will want to sign other artists, and all the established ones are AFM members recording under AFM contracts. The nonunion company will be unsuccessful in such attempts. Further, if the nonunion artist starts to experience success on a nonunion label, he will want to subsequently sign with a more stable company that can offer him much better long-range opportunities.

One of the union's most effective means of controlling nonunion recording is to penalize its own members. Some locals assess union lawbreakers fines of $1,000, $2,500, even as much as $5,000 for second and third-time offenses. In addition to heavy fines, most locals' bylaws permit the union to expel a member who fails to follow AFM rules governing recording services.

ROYALTY ARTIST CONTRACTS

Every performer who understands the music business knows that a really prosperous career is largely dependent upon obtaining a record contract. Therein lies the big money, the international reputation. Until a performer becomes recognized as a recording artist, it is almost impossible for him to attract enough notice to draw employment offers from concert promoters, major booking agencies, television and film producers. Occasionally, an artist will develop a satisfactory career in one area, for example, on Broadway, and never establish a career on records. But for most performers, bypassing the prestige and potential income gained through recording is a rarity.

While the AFM and AFTRA contracts control wages and working conditions for backup artists, the individuals and groups whose names and sounds are used to sell records negotiate contracts for their services, not through an artists union, but in *direct negotiations with a record company*. Such performers are known as *royalty artists*. The AFM defines such a performer as a musician

> . . . who records pursuant to a phonograph record contract which provides for a royalty payable to each musician at a basic rate of at least two percent of the suggested retail list price of records sold (less deductions usual and customary in the trade), or a substantially equivalent royalty, or who plays as a member of (and not as a sideman with) a recognized self-contained group . . . (which is) two or more persons who perform together in fields other than phonograph records under a group name (whether fictional or otherwise); and . . . the members of which are recording pursuant to a phonograph record contract which provides for a royalty payable with respect to the group at a basic rate of at least three percent . . . and all of the musicians of which are or become members of the American Federation of Musicians as provided in this Agreement.

The union used to require AFM approval of royalty contracts. Today it is more common for the AFM simply to require such contracts be "filed" with the union.

TYPES OF DEALS

In earlier times it was simple: a record company signed an artist, instructed one of its house A&R men to produce the records, and that was that. Today, that simple formula still prevails at times. More often, though, the record company and the artist have a number of other options in working out a contract. The reason we have different kinds of recording deals struck today is because of the presence, sometimes dominance, in the business of the *independent producer.*

Here are the most common types of deals being made today in placing an artist under contract:

1- *The label signs the artist, then has one of its producers handle the project in-house. The artist gets his royalties, the staff producer receives his salary, perhaps a royalty override.*

2- *The label already has the artist under contract, then retains an independent producer (or production company) to deliver a master tape. The record company assigns a production budget to the producer, possibly pays a production "fee" up front, and negotiates a royalty of one percent to five percent based on the retail list price of records sold by the artist.*

3- *The independent producer and an independent artist strike a deal, create a master tape, then try to induce a record company to buy it. The label accepting the master pays the parties royalties based on records sold (the artist and the producer had worked out beforehand how they would share these royalties).*

4- *A label shares its costs of producing a master tape with an independent producer or with an artist, perhaps both, in some kind of joint venture (limited partnership). Royalties here would be shared in proportion to the financial commitment of the parties.*

5- *An artist forms his own production company to deliver a master tape to a label. The producer on the project might be on the production company's payroll, or he might be engaged free-lance just for this particular project. The label pays the artist's company a royalty. The artist then pays the producer his share of those royalties.*

6- *A corporation has an employment agreement with the artist, then agrees to loan out his services to a record company. The label pays royalties directly to the corporation. The corporation, in turn, pays the artist a salary, possibly a royalty override. This arrangement could provide tax shelter for the artist, and he might also receive from the corporation certain additional benefits, even a retirement plan.*

NEGOTIATIONS

Most record companies are very selective today in determining the talent they want to sign. Unlike earlier times when a label would sign artists on a speculative basis to test public reaction, current practice is to limit signings to artists the label is reasonably certain will find strong public acceptance. Today's conservative signing policies result largely from the prohibitive costs of "breaking" new artists, which now start in the range of $250,000 for production and initial promotional expenses.

The normal procedure is for a record company executive to persuade his firm it should go after a particular artist, well-established or unknown, inquire of the performer who handles his management, then invite the two to begin discussions about a contract. Following at least one exploratory meeting, a negotiating team would meet to hammer out the fine print of the agreement.

If the artist lacks management and legal counsel, established labels will insist he be represented by advisors, one of which would be an attorney. The negotiations for the label would be handled by a senior executive and the company's legal counsel. Sometimes a company's vice-president for A&R is empowered to negotiate and finalize an artist's recording contract.

Both parties look upon the negotiations as an opportunity to maximize self-interests. The prevailing party will almost always turn out to be the one with the strongest negotiating position. In a word, clout.

THE ISSUES

Properly drawn recording contracts will cover the following issues:

Term — Until recently, the standard length of an artist's recording contract would be one year, with four one-year options for the company to extend. More common today, at least with important artists, is a period without a time limit, but the length of the contract would be tied to the timing of master tape deliveries and record release requirements. Experienced lawyers often attempt to negotiate contracts on a per-album basis, for example, a three-album contract. If the first album does not sell well, the parties are bound to each other for two follow-up releases which afford them an opportunity to amply test the effectiveness of their alliance. A per-album deal often provides for delivery of a tape every six to nine months, the contract terminating after delivery of the third album. But the parties could, of course, subsequently negotiate a new contract to extend their relationship.

In a three-album contract, should the label decline to release all three albums, the contract should provide a penalty, normally a sum of money payable to the artist. Well-drawn contracts provide guarantees of artist's delivery and the company's release of the records. Experienced lawyers try to get the label to guarantee release within 30 to 60 days following delivery of the master tape to the company.

Exclusivity — Except in the jazz field, all recording contracts require the artist to record, during the term of the contract, only for the label that has him under contract. But if the artist also records from time to time in a capacity other than as a solo artist or featured group, e.g., as a session musician or record producer, his lawyer will want the contract to permit such outside services to enable the contract artist to maximize his income.

The label's demand for the artist's exclusive services may extend to its claim on home video rights. The artist should not grant this extension without additional consideration. The label could reasonably demand, however, that it retained the right of first refusal on the artist's services in video and film. In turn, the artist should deny any *demand* of the record company that he make himself available for video recordings and filmed performances, except for video promo tapes. The artist would not only grant the latter right, he would probably insist the firm promise to produce and exploit video promo tapes of respectable quality.

Royalties, Advances — Depending on how badly the label wants to sign the artist, the royalty offer will be in the range of 10 percent of record sales based on the retail price. Major stars have been known to get 18 percent to 19 percent at retail. Sometimes a label will try to hold the initial royalty below 10 percent, then index increments in the rate as record sales rise. For example, the artist might receive 9 percent on the first 100,000 sales, perhaps 10 percent on the next 100,000, then something like 12 percent if the record went gold. Lawyers can persuade a label to start the initial royalty rate higher on a *second* album, should sales of the first album turn out to be satisfactory.

In respect to royalty advances, there is no standard policy among record companies. But it is common for a record company to estimate an artist's annual royalties, then advance one-half that amount. If a label is particularly enthusiastic about signing an unknown artist, it will probably advance the performer sufficient amounts to sustain him in respectable style until earnings enable him to survive on his own.

Record companies generally hold back royalties in a reserve account in anticipation that some records "sold" will be returned by dealers for credit. The contract should limit this reserve account and specify the maximum time period such royalties can be held back.

Attorneys with special competence in tax matters may counsel their artist clients to accept only a prescribed amount of income from royalties in a given year. Sometimes artists can gain certain tax shelters through deferred payment of royalties.

Foreign Releases — The artist and his lawyer should try to persuade the record company to specify where the record will be released in foreign territories. This is essential, in that more than half of the world's supply of new releases are sold outside the United States and Canada. In addition to getting the label to list specific foreign territories, the artist should try to get the label to effect these releases simultaneously with, or shortly after, the American release, to maximize the effectiveness of a promotion campaign.

The artist and his lawyer will want to carefully negotiate how royalties are to be paid on sales in foreign territories. Many labels pay only 75 percent of the domestic rate. When a sale takes place outside this country or Canada, the artist is entitled to an accounting within six months.

Overseas, records are rarely sold on consignment. In the UK and Europe, a sale is a sale; you get paid for what is purchased. This makes accounting simpler and obviates the need for the label or its foreign licensee holding back royalty reserves.

Knowledgeable music business lawyers also take care to have contracts stipulate when royalties are paid. A contract permitting a six or twelve-month lag might cause serious financial loss if the country's inflation rate were exceedingly high. Also, foreign royalties should be calculated and paid *at the source,* before licensees and the parent company have imposed their discounts and service fees.

If the lawyers are not informed on tax treaties, they will need to call in an accountant who is, in that the record business today is global, and tax treaties among nations impact directly on the artist's income.[1]

1-United States citizens and residents of this country are taxed on worldwide income, subject to tax treaty provisions. Nonresident aliens and foreign corporations generally are subject to tax in the jurisdiction of the *source* of income. The purpose of tax treaties between nations is to avoid imposition of double taxation on the same income.

Production Budget Minimums — Major recording artists can negotiate a commitment from a label to budget $150,000 or more per album to cover production costs. Less prominent recording artists would not be able to impose such a demand. But a promising new artist would be well-advised, if negotiating with a label of limited resources, to demand a minimum budget commitment or risk being caught in a low-quality project that could hurt a developing career.

Creative Control — Recording stars often demand, and usually receive, control over such issues as the selection of songs to be recorded, the selection of a producer, and album graphic art. Less important artists will probably have to accept the judgments of the company in such matters. The parties could compromise the question of who selects the record producer: it might be by mutual consent. As for the selection of songs, few labels would force a recording artist to record material he could not perform comfortably.

Commitment to Promote — A strong-selling recording artist will probably be able to demand the label commit sufficient money and personnel to fully exploit the records released. Most artists, including the big stars, regularly complain that the label is not providing adequate promotion. This promotion issue is the one that causes most recording contracts to break down. If the records don't sell, the label blames the artist; the artist insists the sales would have been just fine if the firm had done an adequate promotion job.

Charge-backs — Royalty contracts routinely include the stipulation that the record company does not have to pay the artist any royalties, except for advances that are negotiated, *until the firm has recovered, through a charge-back on the artist's royalties, all its out-of-pocket production costs.* Production expenses that are considered legitimate to charge back include studio rentals, the cost of blank tape, union wages to AFM and AFTRA members, music arranging and copying expense. Such costs can easily total $100,000 and more. When a royalty artist completes a project, *all he gets* (except for advances on royalties) *is union scale.* No more money comes to the artist until the record company has recouped its production costs. It is evident the records will have to sell well just for the parties to break even.

It is not unusual for an artist to complete a contract, have some good-selling records, yet leave behind a considerable debt accrued from recording expense of non-selling records under that contract. Labels rarely attempt to recover this kind of debt from an artist leaving the company roster.

Ownership of Masters — Experienced attorneys negotiate carefully for ownership of master tapes. Initially, the record company owns all rights. But when a contract is terminated, artists' attorneys often will try to negotiate transfer of ownership to their clients. If a firm believes an artist's records will continue to sell well after the term of the contract, they will be reluctant to release ownership of the masters. Master recordings of established artists have considerable residual value, particularly when a firm repackages and/or reissues old records. Master tapes are often sold or leased to secondary labels for this purpose.

Publishing Rights — Where the artist composes his own songs, many record companies will try to persuade that individual to place all his songs with a publishing company owned by or affiliated with the label. If the label's publishing wing cannot obtain full publishing rights, it will probably attempt to "split" the copyrights in some way, sharing the publishing revenue with the performer. This is sometimes called a "cut-in." The value of publishing rights can run very high, and this aspect of recording contracts is often difficult to negotiate.

Assignment — Contracts normally specify terms under which a label may assign a contract to another person. Recording companies, particularly the smaller ones, change hands, change leadership, change direction, and may want to drop an artist, perhaps even one with whom they are making money. Under such circumstances, the label may assign its contract rights. Sometimes an assigned contract can be to the advantage of an artist, particularly if the initial firm is not experiencing success with that performer, or where friction develops between an artist and company management.

Sometimes an artist signs with a label because he works particularly well with one of that company's producers. If this is the situation, the artist should try to get a *key man* clause in the contract, providing the artist has the option of walking away from the agreement, should his favorite producer no longer be with the company.

Right To Audit — The parties usually agree the artist may, upon proper written notice, demand to audit the firm's books. Royalty statements are sent to the artist semiannually. If they do not appear in order, an audit can be demanded.

Audits for major stars can cost as much as $30,000. The artist's lawyer should seek a provision in the recording contract which requires the record company to pay the entire cost of the examination if the amount found to be owing exceeds, say, five percent of the amount actually paid before the audit in the period examined.

Major music business lawyers report that audits rarely reveal the company has cheated the artist. But discovery of royalties owed is a regular occurrence. Artists' managers and music business attorneys usually recommend record companies should be audited at least once every two years.

Default, Cure — If the parties have a serious disagreement, certain remedies are available, some more satisfactory than others.

Suppose the artist is scheduled to deliver an album but decides to take a six-month vacation. The label has no firm grounds for suit, in that it will not be able to prove what it lost in record sales. But when the label believes the artist is not meeting his contractual obligations, it has these remedies available: 1) it can suspend the artist; 2) it can obtain an injunction preventing the artist from recording for another company; 3) it can sue for damages.

Since recording contracts involve "personal services," few courts will tell an artist he must perform such services against his will. If the record company enjoins the artist from recording for a competing firm during a period of dispute, the artist has three options: 1) he can give up the battle and not record at all; 2) he can attempt to renegotiate the contract; 3) he can admit defeat and continue recording for the first company.

Leading music business attorneys report that when a record company and an artist have a serious disagreement over a contract, most firms will renegotiate. Neither party can prosper in the long run when compelled to work under a contract viewed as inequitable or unfair. That would be a poor climate for making music.

Arbitration — Many contracts include a compulsory arbitration clause calling for the parties to submit disputes to the American Arbitration Association. Resolutions can be made much more promptly than through court action, but some record companies resist arbitration clauses, holding to the view that these proceedings tend to favor the individual as opposed to a corporation.

While rulings can be prompt through arbitration proceedings, their implementation may result in suits being filed anyway. Some settlements sought through arbitration can be strung out for a year or longer. Record companies may prefer, in lieu of arbitration proceedings, to ask for a *declaratory judgment* to determine if a contract has been breached.

ROYALTY DISCOUNTS

As with personal management agreements, the **royalty base** is usually more important than the **royalty rate.** For decades, record companies have been getting away with certain limitations on the royalty base that knowledgeable artists' lawyers resist. Still, some limitations on the artist's royalties can be justified, at least from the record company's point of view.

Here are commonly seen limitations on the royalty base:

1- Breakage allowance — Some labels still offer royalties based on 90 percent of sales, a practice once justified, in that about ten percent of the old 78 RPM records would become damaged in transit. Now that records are made of unbreakable vinyl, the artist should not tolerate a breakage allowance.

2- Packaging discount — Labels often charge 10 percent to cover costs of producing album cover art. Cover art does not usually cost this much; the 10 percent charge is assessed anyway.

3- Free goods — Companies usually discount royalties 12.5 percent to 15 percent for free goods — copies given away for promotional purposes. The discount runs much higher for single records, sometimes 40 percent. Some labels believe they must give away nearly one-half their singles to sell the other half.

Record companies sometimes require that royalties on free goods follow "the Harry Fox formula." Experienced lawyers recommend such demands be examined closely, arguing the Harry Fox Agency does not treat all record companies alike.

4- Tape discounts — Profits on tapes are supposed to be lower than on discs, and labels try to pay a lower royalty on them. The fact is that profits on tapes and discs are about the same.

5- Record club sales — Labels usually offer to pay 50 percent royalty on their net receipts from sales through record clubs.

6- Merchandising — Some record companies attempt to tie up merchandising deals that may come to the artist. No respectable label should make any claim on artists' royalties from this source.

7- Cross-collateralization — Record companies often demand the right to cross-collateralize royalties. If one record sells well, royalties from it are discounted to the extent necessary for the label to recoup its production costs on the artist's other records that have not sold as well. Artists with bargaining power can often deny the company this right of cross-collateralization.

The reader may come to share the views widely held by the industry's most prominent lawyers. At a UCLA Extension conference on recording contracts, music industry attorneys David A. Braun, Jay L. Cooper and Paul G. Marshall agreed that the royalty discounting policies of many record companies are indefensible, and that attorneys involved in these negotiations must be aggressive in protecting their clients' interests.

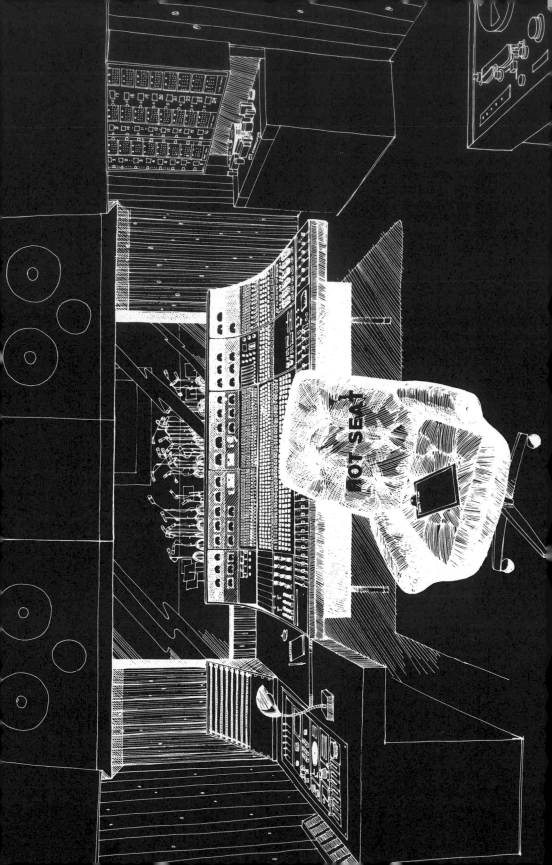

18

RECORD PRODUCTION

It is said that movie-making is "the director's art." We can say that creating sound recordings has become "the *producer's* art." We do not often hear of a successful record today that does not reveal the sure hand of a competent producer. Even if the song is great, the performance outstanding, these elements must be brought together and presented to the ear as one artistic whole.

The old label for a record producer was "A&R man." The term is usually shortened now to just *producer,* but his number one challenge remains the same: matching artist to repertoire, seeking a union of the performer and the material. Today, we have record producers who know how to achieve this unity. An imaginative producer goes beyond this: he can often contrive ways of producing a good master tape even with material that is less than great, with an artist that may not always shake the earth.

PRODUCING TALENTS

We can identify a number of different kinds of producers. Their modes of working vary from superbly organized to seat-of-the-pants. Most working producers can be identified under one of the following:

The Complete Producer — This type is rare, for he is qualified to handle all the important elements that make up record production — artistic, managerial and technological. Talents of this magnitude often operate their own production company or record company or head a creative department for a big label.

The Engineer-Producer — His competence is much narrower than "the complete producer." He is basically an engineer (audio mixer) who is engaged to run sessions for an "executive producer" or creative director who himself may lack technological skills. The engineer-producer is most adept at "getting sounds" from the console. He may lack many of the other talents and skills possessed by the more versatile producer. Grammy Award winner Bones Howe is an example of an individual who started out as an engineer — a very creative one, then learned the other aspects of the business, eventually graduating to become a complete musician-engineer-producer.

The Artist-Producer — He is probably a performing artist or writer who makes it as a producer largely through his empathy with the performers and the material. He may lack technological skills and depend wholly on his audio mixer for engineering judgments. He may have to rely on others to handle the managerial aspects of production, such as contracts, budgeting, etc.

The Promoter-Producer — He may lack musical sensitivity; he may be terrified at the options offered by the mixing console; he may not know the difference between a copyright and a birthright — but he makes it as a "producer" because he can raise money. His money (or borrowed money) forms a catalyst, drawing together diverse talents — artists, writers, mixers, etc. Master tapes get laid down here through a kind of committee action.

The Executive Producer — This appellation could be used, and often is, to identify the type of producer described just above (a money source). The distinction here may be that the real executive producer might well possess the musical sensitivity and know-how in the studio that earns the respect of the other pros involved.

The Coproducer — He is one who shares the responsibilities — either musical, technological or managerial, with other persons. Some are identified as coproducers who are performers on the sessions, and assume a leadership role during taping and mixdown.

The Non-producer — Sometimes an individual with money or some other kind of power insists on being identified on a record as the producer, but does not function in any way, in the studio or during post-production, as the real producer, except possibly to show up with the money — or take the star to lunch, perhaps to bed. In the record business, sometimes prestige can be bought.

The Independent Producer — Since about 1960, the industry has seen wide variance in employment practices concerning producers. Until the advent of rock and roll, record companies maintained a staff of full-time "house producers" who had strong control over who was recorded and precisely what material the chosen few were to record. In the 1960s, large numbers of rock stars composed their own songs and attempted to control the selection of material. They achieved this either by sheer weight of their influence or by insisting they "produce themselves," or bring in their own producers from outside. Since that time, most firms, large and small, have used a mix of in-house and independent producers.

An independent producer is sometimes a one-man company, personally supervising every facet of production. Some employ a staff of one to four or five assistants. This group of professionals is almost certainly carrying on other business activities concurrently, such as publishing and artist management.

PRODUCTION DEALS

Record producers are employed in various ways. Here are the most often seen working arrangements:

1- *A record company engages a producer as a full-time employee. He receives a weekly salary, perhaps a royalty override. The label's head of A&R (the old label lingers on) **assigns** him projects; he may have little to say about which artists or what music he records for the company.*

2- *The producer works as an "independent" — for himself or for a production company. Labels that employ him assign a budget, "deliver" the artist, and ask him to come up with a master tape. He gets a production fee, often recoupable by the label from his royalties. As with the artist, he will receive an advance on royalties.*

3- *The producer "delivers" the artist and a master tape. The two invest their time and money on the project, then set about trying to sell the master to an established label. If they succeed, the parties negotiate a **master purchase agreement** that will provide the recoupment of all or part of the production costs as well as a royalty that is shared by the producer and the artist.*

4- *The producer's services are "delivered" by the artist who has him under contract. This is sometimes called an "all-in" deal: the artist negotiates, with the help of his manager and attorney, a package which involves a royalty and an advance on royalties. The artist then shares the advance and the royalties with his producer.*

Established producers rely heavily on their attorneys in drawing up production agreements. But the producer will require legal counsel knowledgeable in this special area, since production agreements can be more complicated than artists' royalty contracts. Whatever agreement is worked out, the experienced producer will not actually start to work on the project until the document is signed.

ROYALTIES, FEES

Except on work turned out by a label's staff producers, all independent production agreements today provide a royalty for the producer. In this sector of the business, people often refer to a producer's "points," a term synonymous in this context with percentages. One point equals one percent. How many points can a producer extract from a company? It is always the same story when negotiating a contract: the party with clout prevails. A young producer just breaking in may get only *one* point. Most producers receive two to four points. A few superstars ask for and receive five and six percent on sales.

Some contracts treat the producer better than the featured artist, who must wait for his royalties until the label has recouped its production costs. The artist will normally receive a royalty two to five times higher than the producer, but the producer may have a contract that requires he receive *his* royalties from sale number one. If this kind of immediate payment is agreed upon, it is likely the record company talked the producer into fewer points.

In addition to royalties, it is standard practice for the label to pay a *production fee.* Small-time producers are fortunate to get $5,000 in front as their fee, one-half of which is normally paid before the first session begins, the other half upon delivery of the master tape. Some fees are not extra payments, but advances on the producer's royalties. Major producers can get $25,000 to $100,000 in production fees, and they are non-recoupable by the label from his royalties.

PRODUCTION BUDGETING

Whatever deal a producer works out for employment of his services, he cannot escape the responsibility of developing and controlling budgets. He will have to handle this task whether he is employed by a label or works free-lance.

It is not possible to prepare a record production budget with precision, because many of the anticipated expenses can be only roughly estimated. At budget-writing time, the producer may not even know in which city he will be recording. He may find he needs to fly in a rhythm section from Nashville. Will some of the songs on the album require an expensive complement of string players? All the budget-maker can do here is identify expense parameters.

Budget Control — Well-organized producers work up budgets on some kind of summary sheet. If the budget control sheet provides sufficient detail, it can go a long way toward helping the producer and his client handle their finances. Figure 18.1 shows one kind of budget sheet. It may be used as is, or perhaps as a model for one who prefers to set up his own.

A budget control sheet will be misleading if it fails to reflect careful research of *current* studio costs, and the latest union wage scales and surcharges. Experienced producers often call in their AFM and AFTRA contractors to help them pull together accurate figures.

Budgeting costs for taping singles is difficult enough, but when it comes to calculating the expense of recording an album, the producer enters high finance and maximum risk. Out-of-pocket expense of recording a quality master for an album today will start in the range of $100,000

Producers of rock albums often budget 10 to 20 hours of studio time *per song.* Some rock albums may clock 300 hours or more, including mixing, editing, and mastering. Producers and other record executives worried about exorbitant recording costs should compare their figures with the studio time required by *session* musicians. These superb artists sight-read the charts and are able to perform an acceptable take *on the second or third reading.* Jazz album producers may let the machines roll and catch great performances *the first time,* entirely unrehearsed — improvised.

An even more impressive comparison of recording time for rock can be made with the classical field. A professional symphony orchestra of the second or third rank can record a 15- to 25-minute work, such as Stravinsky's *Rite of Spring,* in *six to nine hours!* Of course, the orchestra would have learned the piece a few seasons back — but such an achievement is still remarkable.

Young rock and roll performers should learn how these other musicians get very complex music satisfactorily recorded in just a few hours. If they were to record as efficiently, their take-home royalties could increase by $25,000 to perhaps $50,000 per album.

High recording costs often result for one of these reasons:

1- *The group is ill-prepared; they use the recording studio for rehearsal, even for composition.*

2- *The performers can't read or can't blend or can't come up with the right style.*

3- *The producer can't decide what he really wants.*

4- *The engineer can't come up with the right sounds.*

5- *One or more of the participants is in over his head; he lacks the talent or the experience to compete professionally.*

Some of these problems will remain, no matter how well-prepared the participants may be. But as artists' royalties continue to be

RECORDING BUDGET

ARTIST/GROUP _____ DATE _____

PRODUCER _____ STUDIO _____

LABEL/CLIENT _____ PROJECT NO. _____

Contact   ENGINEER _____

	Cost Per Unit	No. of Units	Total Unit Cost	Sub-total	Extension
STUDIO					
Basic rate					
Outboard equipment					
Set up/strike					
Basic tracks					
Overdubs					
Vocals					
Mixing/editing					
Tape duplicating					
Tape					
Tax					
ENGINEERS					
1st engineer					
2nd engineer					

ARRANGING/COPYING

Music title	Arranging	Copying			
1.					
2.					
3.					
4.					
5.					
6.					
7.					
8.					
9.					
10.					
Union surcharges					

ARTISTS

	Instrumentalists	Singers	Soloists			
Rehearsals						
Basic tracks						
Sweetening						
Union surcharges						

EQUIPMENT					
Rentals					
Cartage					
Tax					

MISCELLANEOUS (Payroll tax, etc.)

UNFORESEEN EXPENSE (15% of total)

TOTAL PRODUCTION COST

Fig. 18.1

gobbled by inflating costs, it should occur to more people in the industry that huge savings can be made right in the studio.

If the project in question is being handled by a recognized production *company*, the record label will probably transfer the amount called for in the budget to that firm. But if the producer works by himself as an independent contractor, the parties may find it more efficient for the label's finance department to set up a project *draw account* — encumber the money and make it available for the producer's expenses.

Whether the production money is transferred or kept in-house, the label will assign some individual to monitor the account. That person is charged with the responsibility of keeping track of this money flow on a day-to-day basis. The producer is asked to keep this budget monitor informed whenever he incurs expense.

Some producers find controlling money flow distasteful and assign the task to their accountants. This does not work well, because the producer is the only individual on the scene daily to observe where the money goes. It is his personal responsibility.

CREATIVE CONTROL

Creative control refers to the right of the producer to make artistic judgments. The artist may have such high stature that he reserves to himself all creative control. It is more likely the producer and the featured artist will share decision-making of this kind.

Probably the most controversial "call" in matters relating to producing records is the selection of material. If the artist composes his own songs, the producer will want to hear everything the artist has in mind for the album. If the producer feels some of the songs are weak, he must figure out how to get that view across without being offensive.

The producer and the recording artist will be constantly pressured by professional associates and friends, not to mention complete strangers, to accept songs ". . . that will be just terrific for the date. Can't miss!" Producers and recording artists must ward off these assaults, or they may end up with an album of "everbody's favorites." Selecting repertoire is too serious a business to be influenced by this kind of favoritism.

With rock bands in particular, the producer, at the outset, will have the group run through all the material it presently has available. The producer has the difficult task of selecting the best material, rejecting the weakest, without offending the writers in the process. Many groups are insensitive to audience endurance. Every piece seems to include a five-minute guitar solo. The producer must persuade the musicians that material of interminable length probably won't get on the air, even with AOR stations.

The Professional Relationship — Unless the producer is new to the field and hard up for work, he will be selective in the assignments he accepts. Even if a new producer is desperate to get his career off the ground, he cannot expect to fly very far unless he and the recording artist enjoy mutual respect, and discover early on that they can work together comfortably. Record companies understand this, of course, and will not link a contract artist and producer who have any doubts, professional or personal, about their compatibility.

The experienced producer will meet with the act to learn these things before he signs for the project. Preliminary meetings are critical with a new artist or group, in that the artists probably have only a dim view of what lies ahead, are fearful of the outcome, and tend to look upon the producer as the only person in the world who can lead them to the promised land.

Producers tell me they find that at least one-half their time must be spent as resident psychologists, appraising the personality traits of the individuals, learning who they can come down on when necessary, who withdraws for hours when reproached. Producers skillful in human relationships also search for the group's resident comic. It seems that it is usually the drummer. Usually the funny man in the group can be counted on to relieve tensions all around when it is three o'clock in the morning and everyone is getting surly.

After the producer and the act have selected the material, they must lay out how each song is to be treated. Does this number need strings? Is some of the material going to be most effective when presented with complete simplicity? And so on.

When these kinds of decisions are made, the producer engages arrangers to score the charts. Producers with strong musical backgrounds will probably work with arrangers in sketching out the arrangements, to increase the likelihood that the producer's conception will be implemented.

If we assume the act and the producer have reached a working understanding on how the material is to be treated, rehearsals normally follow, to make sure the music is prepared before going into the studio. Organized groups rehearse for free, of course. But if the charts call for added instruments such as horns and strings, established session musicians will expect to be paid, often at straight recording scale, just for rehearsals. Let us hope our producer figured this expense into his budget.

If the charts call for outside singers, the producer needs to know which AFTRA contractors can deliver what is required. If session singers are used, it is likely the contractor will either score the voice parts himself, or work alongside the instrumental music arranger to assure coordination.

SELECTING THE STUDIO

We are oversupplied with good recording studios, many of which are going broke and are actively searching for producers with money to spend. The producer of long experience will have accumulated *rate cards* of good studios located in cities where he anticipates he may one day record. This kind of rate card is similar to those used by broadcasters to explain the various kinds of time costs for services. But rate cards quickly become out-of-date; the producer could be in trouble with his budget if he calculated studio expense on last year's data.

The producer has a more important decision to make than the cost of studio rentals: he needs to contract for facilities where his artist *wants* to record. "Wanting" for most artists has more to do with subjective feeling about the recording environment than any appraisal of the equipment or acoustics. No seasoned producer will ever insist an artist record in a room where he does not feel comfortable, or where he has had unpleasant dealings with studio personnel.

In addition to the need for congenial atmosphere, the producer will make his studio selection on where he knows he can get a good sound and where the maintenance of the hardware is reliable. He might tolerate untidy rest rooms, but he insists on clean recording heads. If he knows a particular studio has a staff engineer who can meet his needs, he may favor that facility over one with more sophisticated equipment. If the producer brings in his own free-lance engineer, he can expect an experienced mixer to adapt quickly to a new console.

A producer who is particular about equalization and timbre will usually go into a studio a day or two early with his engineer to check out the console, the monitoring system and the acoustics. Some conscientious producers even come in with graphic equalizers to check playback systems. One who goes to this effort (not uncommon among top pros) will bring in a tape and/or disc with which he is intimately familiar. If the playback does not sound exactly as he knows it should, he will work with his engineer and a house engineer to adjust equalization of speakers and amplifiers. He must know precisely what he is hearing when the monitors speak to him.

Seasoned producers are usually prepared for at least one disaster every 24 hours. One of their biggest problems is down time in the studio. When the machines are not working properly, the loss is not so much in dollars as in momentum; the recording artists may be unable to regain what they had going prior to the equipment failure. Studio managers know how serious down time can be and are quick to compensate for time lost when billing the customer.

The Recording Process — The producer just getting started in the field will learn early on that his success is largely dependent on how well he works with studio personnel. As one successful producer put it to me, "Those people can help you or they can kill you."

As for the recording process itself, no book, no teacher can tell you how to pull great music out of a performing artist. This can be done only by gifted producers, most of whom rely heavily on intuition, instinct.

As the recording process goes forward, the producer will be challenged from all sides. While his first concern will be the music, he is supposed to know enough about recording technology to work effectively with his engineer. The self-confident producer will encourage his engineer to contribute creatively to the recording process. When the producer cannot come up with a solution to a problem, perhaps his engineer can bail him out. I have observed that the most successful producers take all the creative input they can find, whatever the source.

POST-PRODUCTION

Even when the producer has survived production of the master tape, his job is far from over. If we assume he has been retained by a record company, the firm now imposes upon him specific *delivery requirements:*

1- *The master tape must be mixed down to two-channel stereo, and formatted for sides one and two of an album. The label will probably also expect the producer to pull out several bands for possible release as singles. If so, the singles must be edited to appropriate lengths.*

2- *Letters of consent must be obtained from all individuals involved in the project, allowing the label to use their names and photographs in promoting the records. Release letters must also state that the artists are unencumbered by conflicting recording agreements with any other firm.*

3- *The producer must deliver letters of consent from all photographers and graphic artists for use of their works.*

4- *The producer must furnish evidence that all copyrights are clear and the owners have granted mechanical licenses for each cut on the album.*

5- *Lyric sheets must be submitted. Labels want to see in writing whether the song texts are acceptable for radio broadcast.*

6- *A technical credits summary sheet is required — setting forth such details as the names of the engineers, where the master was recorded, who the arrangers and musical director were, the names of the union contractors, who mastered the tapes, and identities of artists' personal managers and booking agents.*

7- *A sign-off statement is required from the producer providing evidence he has paid his bills, and knows of no liens or encumbrances that might prevent the label from releasing the record.*

8- *The producer must collect W-4 forms for every individual involved on the project to whom wages were paid.*

If the producer has handled his affairs in a businesslike manner, he will probably be able to fulfill these delivery requirements without difficulty.

The smart producer won't mail in his master tape; he will want to make an appointment with the person who hired him, then walk in with his tape and present it personally. He will want to deliver, at the same time, at least two or three cassette transfer copies to enable the A&R people and other executives with the firm to hear his work at their convenience.

Assuming the label accepts the master, the producer will then be paid the other half of his production fee or advance on royalties. He has now met all his responsibilities under the production agreement, but the seasoned producer will want to take part in controlling *mastering* of the tape. It is customary for the record company to pay for mastering and all subsequent steps leading to manufacture of the records. But some companies will try to charge mastering to the artist's and producer's royalties. This is improper and should not be allowed.

Some conscientious producers continue their post-production services up to and including the checking on test pressings, to make sure all the effort invested in the project will be reflected in the ultimate sound of the music.

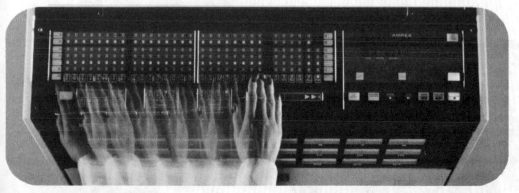

TM AMPEX CORPORATION

19

RECORD MERCHANDISING

THE MARKETING PLAN

Record companies will go to extreme lengths to get the best possible sounds on tape. But to this point, *all they really have is debt*. The only way they can begin to recover their production expense is to get the word out — try to get people interested enough to buy the record. This should be easy; millions of music lovers do this every week. For many people, recorded music is their first choice for entertainment. If the audience has the desire and the buying habit, why do record companies go through such wholesale agony in trying to get people to buy?

Agony it is, because everyone knows that the stakes are high. If you win, you win very big. If you lose, you can drop a half million dollars on one campaign. Worse yet, contract artists will defect if your marketing people cannot move a lot of records.

To understand how records are promoted, it is important to remember the point made earlier: this is a mass market business. You must develop sales, not only nationally, but all over the world. Because of production and promotion costs going out of sight, a company has to move several hundred thousand records quickly *just to break even*.

◀ Adam Somers, Warner Bros. Records Vice-President for Creative Services and Operations, discusses schedule with production assistant.

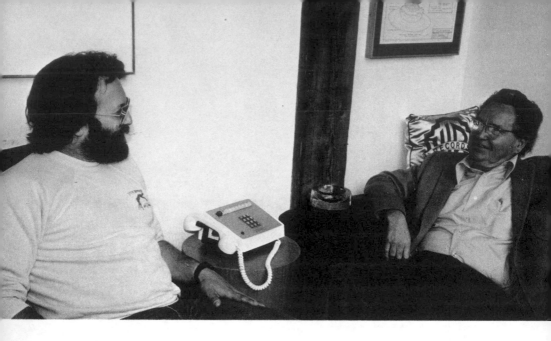

Warner Bros. Records merchandising head Adam Somers (above, left) discusses with the author how his firm sells records.
(Below) Somers examines graphic art planned for a new Warner Bros. album.

No one knows where the break-even line falls today. All top management can tell its promotion people is, "This time out, ladies and gentlemen, we have to sell more records than we ever thought possible before." Through most of the 1970s, many firms did just that. The gold record became so common, the "platinum record" was conceived. Then superhits began to go double, even "triple platinum." But these are the superhits of the superstars. I asked several major labels what percentage of their releases paid their way. They gave very divergent estimates, ranging from Columbia ("Our creative people don't know; ask the computer guys.") to Elektra/Asylum, a firm whose ads in the trades claim that practically everything they touch turns to gold. Many labels think they are holding their own if something like 20 percent of their releases break even, with perhaps five percent earning enough money to finance their whole operation.

Personnel — With some labels, promotion efforts are supervised by a top officer of the company, probably someone holding a title such as "Vice-President, Marketing." No agreement exists on distinctions among such terms as "promotion," "marketing," "merchandising," "publicity" and "sales promotion." In practice, some of these labels are used interchangeably. This accounts for the variance among record companies concerning department names and job titles. Whatever the label a company attaches to a particular department, whatever job titles they use, everyone active in this general area has the same objective — to get people to buy records. Large labels might include in their marketing department, the following personnel:

- **Merchandisers** — *They conceive, then execute, sales campaigns and provide sales aids to distributors and retailers.*

- **Promoters** — *Located in the home office and in regional offices. Main task: get records on the radio.*

- **Publicists** — *They work mostly out of Los Angeles and New York City, trying to plant stories and "news" releases with print and broadcast media.*

- **Advertisers** — *They conceive, produce and place ads in print and broadcast media.*

The Concept — The only hope a record company has of attracting attention with a new record is to conceive a *unique marketing plan.* This is difficult for a firm such as Warner Bros., which releases over 20 albums a month. That figures out to about one album per working day. Such a demand for fresh marketing ideas challenges the most creative staffs.

Whether the record company calls its marketing division "creative services" or "merchandising department," it attempts to put together a marketing campaign that ties in with the nature of the music and the style of performance. Conscientious merchandising people usually start their thinking by listening to the music they are going to try to sell. At this early stage, the company's marketing people try to come up with a "hook." Those invited to help conceive the marketing plan might include the producer, head of merchandising, the art director, and the heads of promotion and publicity for the label. This group might decide the whole campaign should be hung on one simple slogan.

Once this group invents the marketing concept, the head of merchandising directs his art department to render sketches; a photographer or painter is engaged, the copy is written and the "mechanical" (assembled graphic elements) is rendered.

Meanwhile, other merchandising people are trying to implement the marketing plan in the form of P.O.P.'s — industry shorthand for "point-of-purchase" stimuli. P.O.P.'s might include posters, banners, cutouts, standups, special display racks, window displays, flags and streamers, perhaps souvenir items the record merchant can give away to shoppers. Each of these P.O.P.'s carries out the basic merchandising idea.

P.O.P.'s are very costly to produce, but record companies seem to believe the investment in these sales stimuli pays off.

While the packaging art and P.O.P.'s are being produced, the firm's advertising department is inventing print ads, perhaps broadcast spots, too. This advertising, properly conceived, will further bear out the marketing approach being used for album art and P.O.P.'s.

RECORD PROMOTION

Record promotion means getting new releases broadcast on the radio. Promoters descend on the stations like locusts, each of them pleading for a share of the broadcast time. Just about everything is wrong with this system; it results in a ludicrous waste of time and money. But those who have tried to change it have not made much progress. Getting airpay for a new record in the "Top 40" field was very difficult when such a thing as Top 40 radio existed. Even though many in the industry still use that label out of habit, Top 40 programming no longer exists. From about 1975, rock stations have reduced their play lists by 15 to 50 percent. The national average play list of "contemporary" or "rock" stations today is now below 30 records. This means that a station can add only *two to five records every week*. Compare those figures with the number released. If we average the estimates of NARM, RIAA and surveys made by the trades, it would appear that about 1,000 records are being dumped on the market every seven days. It is clear there is no relationship between the number of records released and the time available to broadcast them. Any other kind of business enterprise would go broke overnight if it attempted to survive in this absurd marketing environment.

A promoter does not have to twist arms to persuade even major market stations to go with a new release of a superstar. Such product is largely presold, and program directors will add a new release from an artist of international stature even before receiving word that other stations are also going with the record. But new releases of a performer below superstar status require promoters to really hustle, because competition for airpay is fierce.

The most difficult task of all for promoters is to break new artists. Why should a radio station risk precious air time on unknown performers when they can accommodate but a tiny share of the established names?

Large record companies employ a staff of full-time people to handle promotion in-house. When a special campaign is set up, outside promoters may be brought in to assist.

Reporting Stations — Knowledgeable promoters focus nearly all their attention on *reporting stations.* A reporting station is one that the trade papers and tip sheet publishers telephone each week to learn which records have been programmed. *This is the information that causes a particular record to land on the charts* — or fall off and disappear. In the United States and Canada, we have 200 to 300 reporting stations (their number fluctuates). Their program directors are asked by the chart makers, not only what records (singles, album cuts) are on their play lists, but their "rotation" — how often particular records are scheduled in a 24-hour period. Reporting stations are also asked which records are "add-ons" for the week and which ones are being dropped.

If a new release can gain airplay on influential reporting stations, *it may land a position on the charts.* If that first appearance should occur, say, in the mid-range of a national chart, the promotion people may have a potential hit on their hands. At this point, most record companies accelerate their efforts and instruct their promoters all over the country to intensify their campaigns, call on program directors, show them the charts and tip sheets, and try to persuade the station to add the record. The promoter is in a position to prove what he has been saying —that the new release is starting to break nationally. The P.D. may now be persuaded. Many stations, too timid weeks ago to take a chance, decide to jump on the bandwagon, not wanting to miss out on a potential hit. The promotion campaign could start to snowball. When strong national airplay develops, a hit is born. *It happens all the time.*

Sometimes there is a catch to this. Occasionally we have "turntable hits": a record manages to get good airplay, but people just don't walk into the stores and buy it. No one has come up with a satisfactory explanation for the turntable hit phenomenon.

To gain the confidence of radio program directors, promoters must establish a reputation for credibility. What the P.D. needs most is useful *information,* not fast talk. The station needs to know whether a new release fits its programming and whether the record is gaining airplay elsewhere. If a promoter cannot provide these assurances to the station, he has one other hope: the music might appeal to the personal tastes of the P.D. or musical director. Occasionally, these decision-makers will program a new release just because they like it, but few stations permit personal tastes to influence these important decisions.

Direct Mail — With over 8000 radio stations in this country, it is obvious that only a small percentage of them can be reached through personal contacts. This effort has to be supplemented by direct mail promotion. Staff and independent personnel mail free promotional records to broadcasters. Many stations want three copies of a new release: a clean copy for the library, one for the station programmer, and one in the bins for the DJs to hear.

Mailing out this many free records is extremely expensive, and experienced promoters use a very select mailing list, one that includes mostly "reporting stations" or stations where the promoter has personal contacts.

Mail campaigns need to be followed up by telephone calls. ("Hello, Frank. Did my stuff come in? How'd you like it? What did you find time to listen to? What have you added? No? How about next week? So-and-so is breaking big in Toledo; you won't want to miss out on it. How can I help you . . ." and so on.) The success of this kind of telephone call follow up depends, not only on the suitability of the records mailed, but the rapport between the caller and the station programmer.

Campaign Management — Most labels assign one particular individual to manage a promotional campaign. He receives a budget from the company's promotion director, and is expected to develop regional, then national airplay. He may also have the responsibility of assigning particular promotion personnel to certain geographic areas and to coordinate the efforts of staff promoters working out of the label's branch offices. The director of national promotion will put out the word on timing of the campaign and how much attention and emphasis it is to receive.

This "campaign manager" is sometimes called a "tracker," because his responsibilities include keeping track of what radio stations are adding or dropping the new release. If the tracker observes good airplay developing in a particular geographic area, he may double his efforts there in an effort to develop a regional hit. If a regional breakout occurs, it can sometimes be built into a national one.

The tracker or project director also has the task of following the progress of a new release on the trade charts. The entry, rise and fall of a record on the charts provides guidance on how to spend (or withdraw) the money available for a particular campaign. For example, if an album is pulled for exploitation as a single, that promotion campaign may generate only a weak chart position. The tracker reports that the single does not seem to be really going anywhere following its initial chart appearance, and recommends to the marketing people they drop the campaign and go for a different album cut. They do, and it might not even land on a national chart. Does the label now give up on this campaign, too? If it has invested $150,000 in producing the album, and perhaps a like amount in promoting each single drawn from it, the label has the option to write off its $500,000 investment or risk pulling a third selection from the album. Many labels go to a second and third album cut today before they write off their investment on the whole undertaking.

Some labels may pull as many as three and four singles from an album, not so much because the first tracks do not sell, but rather to prolong the chart life of the album itself.

PUBLICITY

Many record companies have "publicity" departments separate from their promotion operation; others combine these two activities under a "marketing" division. Some record companies handle their publicity activities in-house; others have a small resident staff and engage publicists and PR firms to help out. A small label may depend totally on an outside firm for PR.

Even the most imaginative publicist cannot catch public attention unless he can persuade the public that *something is happening* — a new record is released, the artist is on tour, or a TV appearance is scheduled — whatever. When the publicist has no story, he will invent one. His activities center around the task of getting the artist and his records talked about. Many merchants believe the most effective sales force is word-of-mouth. If the record buyer hears the talk and catches the music on the radio, he might enter a store and make a purchase.

As discussed elsewhere in this book, the publicist's responsibilities include the production and distribution of press kits or "promo packs." The record company and the artist's management will share this task. Their efforts will probably be most effective when they follow the marketing plan adopted earlier to coordinate such activities.

ADVERTISING

Advertising can be an important component of record promotion. A variety of media have been found effective — print, broadcast, point-of-sale, direct mail, "hitchhikers," and "specialty" campaigns. All advertising seems to help sales, but the difficulty is measuring whether the resulting sales justify the expense. Now that records are a mass consumer product, large labels find it profitable, from time to time, to place ads in mass print media — magazines and newspapers. To justify the high expense, several records are pushed in one ad, thus pulling down the "cost-per-thousand" expense per record. Print ads in newspapers are sometimes paid for by a local record store or chain. But all or part of such ads may be paid for by the record company. Sometimes record stores request that a label finance a print media campaign in their area. Or, the label itself initiates print ads, particularly when it is trying to coordinate advertising with the promotion of local concert appearances of a contract artist.

Opinions differ concerning the dollar return from records advertised on radio and television. Among the most common and apparently effective types of broadcast ads are for reissues of repackaged records ("Mail $8.95 to station XYZ and get your double album of 25 country hits!") Purveyors of this merchandise have bought the masters at probably 10¢ on the dollar, saving 90 percent of their budget for broadcast ads.

Another type of broadcast ad occurs in a special promotion by a big label on a major artist, where the overall promotion campaign may be budgeted at, say, $500,000. Campaigns of this size spend a healthy portion of their ad dollars with radio and television. More than a few record labels have admitted that some of their gold records have lost money, simply because the firm spent more on promotion than the hit produced in revenue. Promotional costs must be proportional to sales.

INTERNATIONAL PROMOTION

Multinational record companies may spend as much money and effort promoting releases abroad as they do in this country. This is justified, in that foreign sales aggregate over one-half of world sales.

Increasing numbers of artists are becoming international stars. They have had the good fortune of being with a record company that has a worldwide promotion setup, or one that licenses its foreign releases to others. A multinational entertainment conglomerate must determine, each time out, whether to have foreign releases occur simultaneously with the American release, or whether to test the record here before promoting it abroad.

Sometimes the record company does not have the option of delaying foreign releases: the star's contract may require, not only the simultaneous release of his records abroad, but specific countries where the label must make his records available.

The big record companies maintain a number of regional offices in foreign territories which have the responsibility of releasing and promoting the firm's records. Among the strongest European markets for breaking new American records are The Netherlands, the UK, the Federal Republic of West Germany and France. American firms with international operations know the special promotional techniques that are most effective in these countries.

Foreign promotions cannot be handled like those in this country. In all these territories, far fewer radio stations are available for record exposure. The stations that do exist may be state-controlled and allow no advertising; time buys may be unavailable. The press in some countries — Holland would be an example — look upon promotion campaigns that involve trinkets and other giveaways to media people as bribery. Dutch journalists will not participate, for example, in press junkets. These, too, are viewed as some kind of bribery to persuade writers to say nice things about a commercial release. On the other hand, a country like Japan is often ahead of the American promoters in hyping new records by showering gifts and favors on media personnel.

Some record promotions are so heavily financed, the American promoters fly in the foreign media people to cover press parties and other special events tied in with the campaign. These junkets for the foreign press are to the west coast ("Fly to Hollywood and meet the star!") for Japanese media, and to New York for European writers and broadcasters.

When a promotion campaign is financed at this level, it could be said that the record company is "manufacturing" a star — "inventing" success. If often works — for a while. But a "manufactured" career will not sustain for long unless the public hears some measure of talent behind the hype.

RECORD DISTRIBUTION

If the promotion people have created interest in a new record, the manufacturer must find a way to get the product to potential customers — wherever they may be, at the right time and in sufficient quantities. This is a very difficult thing to do well, for the record market is totally unpredictable and widely dispersed. After fifty years of trial and error, even major labels are still trying to figure out a better distribution system. As for small labels, it has been the lack of effective distribution that has caused so many to fall in the marketplace.

Until about mid-century, only a handful of companies were in the record business. Each had its own procedure for delivering its products to customers. With the rapid proliferation of labels in the 1950s, newcomers to the market often lacked an understanding of the essential need for a *national network* of distributors to get their products to retail outlets. Smaller labels would seek larger ones to distribute their records. Other new labels contracted the services of the growing number of independent distributors which were setting up operations in most markets. Many of the distribution problems that have troubled the industry since the 1920s remain today.

As pointed out elsewhere in this volume, record retailing is plagued by price wars among merchants, and this impacts directly upon the distributors. Merchants fighting to remain afloat amidst irrational retail pricing competition appeal to their distributors for better discounts to help them survive the competition. Distributors can respond to these appeals most often when they can sell at high volume. But when a merchant overextends himself in his buying, he regularly finds himself stuck with unsold merchandise and must again appeal to the distributor for lenient "return privileges."

Distributors try to strike a balance between overselling their customers or offering an undersupply. With the former, both parties suffer the inconvenience and expense of "returns"; only the shipping industry profits with returns. But when a distributor's customers buy too conservatively and a record hits suddenly, both parties miss out on sales when the merchandise is not available to the buying public. Smart distributors try to guide retailers in their buying so as to minimize returns, because when merchandise flows in the wrong direction, everyone gets hurt.

MAJOR LABEL DISTRIBUTION

Large record companies handle distribution through their own branch offices located in major cities across the country. They distribute their number one label and affiliated labels. Some large firms also contract to distribute products of independent record companies.

Major label branch offices normally have two divisions. One handles regional promotion, the other concerns itself with distribution and sales. Promotion people working out of these branch offices invest most of their time pushing the company's main label. Of secondary concern is promotion of the company's affiliated labels. If the company has agreed to also promote "associated" and independent labels, the promotion people also try to perform a respectable job for them as well.

Branch offices of large record companies employ salespeople, too. Some companies call them "merchandisers" or "route men." Their task is to call upon retailers, try to sell them, perhaps deliver the actual records, help set up promotional displays and do what they can to help the retailer attract customers. Record route people work on salary or commission, or a salary plus an override. These are not the most glamorous jobs in the music business, but a number of ambitious routemen have graduated to management positions and gone on up the corporate ladder to earn their key to the executive washroom.

Distributors or the home office set up sales contests from time to time to motivate their field forces. Winners sometimes enjoy not only a pair of theatre tickets, but occasional trips to Hawaii. Large labels also set up national sales meetings for their distributors, usually paying their expenses for a weekend in Las Vegas or the Bahamas. Most of these meetings are about an equal mix of work and play. A record company's contract stars are asked to perform live for these select audiences of distributors, promotion people and salesmen. These meetings cost a fortune, but the labels find that offering their people this kind of motivation produces sufficient action back home to justify the cost.

INDEPENDENT DISTRIBUTION

WEA, CBS, RCA and other multinational firms handle a sizable share of record distribution, but they don't do it all. A respectable share of the business is in the hands of independent distributors. They provide services for hundreds of independent labels. In cities where a major label lacks a branch office, an independent distributor accommodates its needs as well.

Independent distributors usually provide promotion services, too. Some independents are just order-takers. Others have a staff of enterprising salespeople and merchandisers who call on record stores, deliver merchandise, set up displays, etc., much like the major label branch offices do.

Large independent distributors are confronted with pleas from new firms to take on yet another line. If they consider adding new labels, management must determine whether it has the capacity to handle the increased inventory, and they need to calculate how much additional working capital they can risk on unproven companies. If they stocked every record that appears promising, they would go broke in 30 days. But it they fail to stock new product that suddenly bursts wide open at the retail level, their local accounts will sometimes bypass their favorite local distributor and buy directly from the record manufacturer. These kinds of management decisions have been poorly handled by many distributors. They are now out of business.

Since 1972, the interests of these independent companies have been represented by NAIRD, the National Association of Independent Record Distributors. It represents about 200 firms. The association was originally organized to set up a distribution network and to form a unified voice in the industry for small labels and independent distributors. Its national conventions provide small firms a convenient place for exchange of information and for the forming of distribution arrangements for companies not affiliated with the major labels and their distribution networks.

Distribution Chains — As the less well-run independent distributors go under, their places are taken by yet other investors who believe they can make it. In recent years, smaller distributors have been bought by distribution chains. As with other store chains, conventional wisdom has it that bigger is better; distributors linked together can buy more records

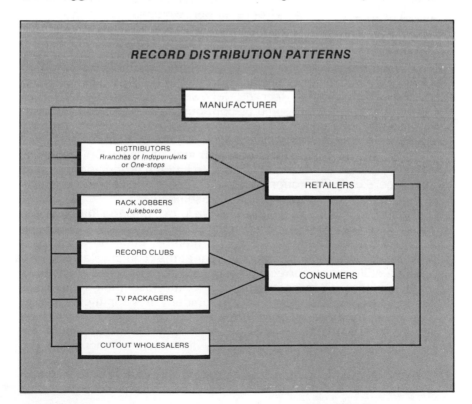

Fig. 19.

at a greater discount, then pass along these savings to their retailers — or put the money in their own pockets.

The proliferation of independent distribution chains will continue because they can operate at lower cost. They also can offer stronger competition to the distribution networks owned and operated by the major labels.

Independent distribution has accounted in recent years for some of the all-time best sellers, including hits by Stevie Wonder and Peter Frampton.

One-Stops — One-stops are a special kind of distributor. They came into being in the 1940s mainly to accommodate the needs of jukebox operators. A one-stop is a distributor who handles all labels, including the majors. He is set up to service not only jukebox operators, but small rack jobbers and mom-and-pop retailers. Most of his customers place small orders, often dropping by to pick up the merchandise themselves. Because of the low volume of sales per customer, one-stops cannot offer as good discounts as a full-line distributor. But their customers pay higher prices because they appreciate the convenience of a one-stop operation.

Rack Jobbers — Rack jobbers are the individuals and companies who contract with retailers — department stores, discount stores, etc., for the rental of space to set up display racks of records which are intended to attract retail sales from shoppers who pass by. Rack jobbing and record retailing are discussed in Chapter 13.

Record Clubs — In 1955 Columbia got the idea that records could be sold directly through the mail. It was right; the Columbia Record Club has been running well ever since. Shortly after CBS got started in the field, RCA, then Capitol Records, followed in establishing its own record clubs (Capitol has since discontinued this kind of promotion). When record clubs began, retailers threatened court action, arguing that a big company pushing sales of only its own label through the mail constituted unfair competition and restraint of trade. Columbia responded by expanding its club offerings to include products from other labels. Record clubs now offer for sale any record that proves sufficiently popular to earn a listing in their advertisements.

Club memberships are developed, as we know, through full-page ads in national magazines offering a starter supply of records below cost, together with a commitment from the "member" that he will subsequently purchase several records per year at the regular retail price.

Retailers still believe, correctly, that record clubs cut heavily into their walk-in business. Clubs are reluctant to disclose their grosses. A Chicago-based consulting firm, Sruge Company, has conducted market research which indicates record clubs gross around half a billion dollars a year. With the cost of transportation continuing to rise, it appears likely that, in years to come, selling records by direct mail will increase.

Another distribution route for records is through "TV packagers." They are discussed in Chapter 13.

Warner Bros. Records Creative Services department staff artists designing album covers, sales aids.

20

STUDIOS AND ENGINEERS

One of the most important sectors of the record industry is the operation of recording studios, only a small portion of which are owned by record manufacturers. Except to industry insiders, the operation of recording studios is largely a hidden industry, most of the best of them remaining unknown to the public. But with over 5,000 albums being laid down each year just in the United States, and with album production budgets ranging from $50,000 to $150,000-plus, it would be reasonable to estimate that the recording studio business grosses something like $300 million a year.

Some 175 professional studios are functioning in California. New York City has about 90 studios, Nashville 40 to 50 (they come and go). Thousands of individuals find full-time employment in this unique industry that requires the cooperative services of business entrepreneurs, technicians, scientists, designers, acousticians, managers and musicians. Here, art and technology must find accommodation.

While most sound recording studios limit their services to audio recording, in the major music centers it is now expected they will also offer film and television producers complete audio services for synchronizing sound with pictures. With the rapid expansion of various modes of video entertainment, increasing numbers of sound facilities in New York, Los Angeles and Nashville find it necessary (and profitable) to offer a complete range of recording services. Some studios are full production centers where audio is but one component of the operation. There are facilities which provide recording and processing for digital computer animation and "visual synthesis." Musicians, audio mixers and video producers work side by side in these studios.

SEMIPROFESSIONAL RECORDING

Recording occurs in every conceivable kind of environment, from the semiprofessional setup in a residential garage, to the 24-track monster studios which can now be found in dozens of cities in this country and abroad. As equipment has become more sophisticated, professional studios were forced to raise their rates to amortize their investments. Hourly rental rates climbed out of reach for many potential users. In recent years, this has caused, not only an increase in home recording with amateur equipment, but a proliferation of what we can call semiprofessional recording. When a producer runs up a recording studio bill of $5,000 in a week or so, it does not take him long to consider whether he might be smarter to arrest that outflow and divert it to setting up his own recording operation.

To accommodate the individuals who are attempting to do this, and to serve the investor who requires something better than consumer-quality equipment, manufacturers now have on the market an array of hardware that is called *semiprofessional equipment*. Most of this hardware is superior to the best home-type machines, yet cannot perform or withstand the constant use of fully professional equipment. The machinery we are discussing here fills that middle gap and is priced well below fully professional hardware.

Most of this kind of recording is four-track, and it serves well those individuals who have no need for 16- and 24-track studios with their $175-per-hour fees.

Semipro setups are frequently used by songwriters, publishers, performers and independent producers. Many of these individuals manage to amortize their investments after a year or so of recording their own material.

Semiprofessional recording, however, has its own problems. The AFM doesn't like it, because the union has no way of policing these operations. The neighbors (residential and office) don't appreciate it, because few semiprofessional recording studios have adequate sound isolation. Sometimes the investors regret having entered the field, because they are often unwilling or unable to continue buying the ever-new equipment the leading professional plants try to provide. But semiprofessional recording will increase, not only because of the rising rental costs of conventional studios, but because it serves the needs of many individuals so effectively.

DEMO STUDIOS

One notch above the converted garage facilities are those studios, found in hundreds of communities, that specialize in demo recordings. Nearly all of them offer four to eight-track equipment and a studio large enough to handle small ensembles. Since demo studios can offer hourly rates far lower than full commercial studios, they service the bulk of demo recording needs of writers and publishers.

Well-managed demo studios can profit. But financial difficulties occur when the small operator tries to keep abreast of the latest expensive equipment. When a demo studio operator leaps that gap between, say, a modest four-track facility to 16-track with all its attendant gadgetry, he can overextend himself, and soon find his fancy hardware in the hands of his bank, awaiting auction.

Some demo studios stay alive and prosper by becoming a headquarters for small production companies, small labels, beginning publishers, even artists managers and agents trying to get established. Whether or not these persons share ownership or management, the people involved often find it mutually advantageous to work together, sharing their expertise and contacts.

Another kind of recording operation might be called "in-house" studios, which have become increasingly popular with publishers, even advertising agencies. They are private operations, rarely open to the public, and are intended to serve the host company and its business associates. They range in size from 8- to 16-track and provide in-house production for everything from simple demos to master tapes.

An example of this kind of in-house studio is found in the Toronto office of Chappell Ltd., a music publisher component of Unichappell. Chappell of Canada wanted to be able to produce, in-house, elaborate demos, and the firm invested in two full 16-track studios to do this. Many other publishers now have similar facilities, finding them of great convenience to record their copyrights.

Cedarwood Publishing Company of Nashville has an in-house studio that not only produces elaborate demos and master tapes, but is involved in its own production of sound tracks for broadcast commercials. As the various facets of the music business continue to fuse, it is inevitable that in-house studios will proliferate.

INDEPENDENT STUDIOS

The step above the demo studio is the full-line independent studio, which has at least 24-track consoles and recorders, together with other outboard equipment sufficient to compete with plants operated by the major record labels.

To attract knowledgeable producers, the independent studio must have a lot going for it. First, it must be heavily capitalized in order to acquire adequate space, buy the latest equipment, and have enough cash flow to carry it over lean times when bookings are light. To compete today, an entrepreneur trying to set up a full-line independent recording studio should be able to get his hands on at least $500,000, with more under his mattress readily available. It also makes it increasingly difficult for even well-established studios to turn a profit.

A full-line independent studio will normally have one or two large rooms capable of handling a big studio orchestra, several rooms for smaller groups, mixdown and editing rooms, an acoustical reverberation chamber, equipment rack rooms, maintenance shop, traffic control office, and lockers for equipment storage. In New York City and Los Angeles, the largest independent recording studios also have movie projection equipment for synchronization of music to film.

A studio with all the latest hardware is in trouble if it lacks good acoustics in two critical areas — the control rooms and the studios themselves. The science of acoustics has now advanced to the stage where qualified engineers can predict how sounds will behave in a given space. Unfortunately, investors continue to throw money away on bad designs. And where the designs were right, the construction may be faulty. When the elaborate RCA studios opened in Hollywood, they were replicas of RCA's outstanding facilities in Rome. But when RCA's Hollywood Studio A first opened, I saw a blanket casually hung on the wall behind the mixing console. The acoustician had not bothered to design that surface properly to diffuse the sounds bouncing around behind the mixing console.

Modern control rooms are difficult to design, because proper balancing of stereo is largely dependent on where the mixer sits in the room — and the producer, perhaps only three feet away from the mixer, hears a different balance. Further compounding these problems, engineers and producers forget sometimes that the programs they monitor over a $700 JBL speaker system have only slight resemblance to what the music lover hears on his $35 transistor radio.

Studios often sink or swim on whether the performing musicians feel comfortable in them. One essential acoustical requirement for orchestral playing and ensemble singing is that the sounds be diffused so each performer hears a fair amount of what sounds are occurring around him. The precise opposite circumstance occurs in tracking: very short reverberation times are desired when performers are using earphones. They want to hear only themselves and the program coming over the phones.

Whatever the studio may offer in equipment and acoustics, many artists and producers tend to patronize those facilities where they like the atmosphere. Is the environment comfortable? Is the staff congenial? Is pressure felt? One of the reasons smaller cities have prosperous studios is because many artists feel more relaxed recording anywhere outside of New York City and Los Angeles. Anyone recording in the easy-going environment of Nashville or, say, James Guercio's Caribou Ranch in Colorado, favors the atmosphere of these more comfortable venues over the pressure cookers of New York City and Los Angeles.

A studio can be well-equipped and offer a comfortable atmosphere, but its profitability may depend merely on superstition. Many producers and recording artists refuse to book time in a studio that has not produced hit records. They suspect that hits are really just "sounds," and what they must do is go to that studio which produces those sounds. When I was running my own studio (since sold to Warner Bros.) in Los Angeles, I learned this lesson the hard way: until my studio produced its first hit, many major and minor stars remained reluctant to book time. Following the first hit out of those facilities, business doubled.

Some independent studio operators, such as Wally Heider of Los Angeles, become so successful they are bought out by large corporations. The Heider operation, today known as Filmways/Heider, is undoubtedly the largest recording operation of its kind: in the Los Angeles area it has 10 recording studios, two disc mastering facilities, three 24-track mobile units, and it also operates five studios in San Francisco.

LABEL-OWNED STUDIOS

Most of the large record companies own and operate their own studios in Los Angeles and Nashville. Several continue to operate studios in New York. In the beginning of the industry, there were no independent studios, and record companies built their own. The practice continues today with the older, larger companies.

The large labels want their own facilities because the best independent studios are often booked up, sometimes for months in advance. Few record companies can accept such delays, so they set up their own recording operation. Their traffic office reserves time first for the label's own producers and artists. If any studio time remains open, it is usually made available for rent by outsiders. Physical facilities and equipment are generally equal to, sometimes superior to, what can be found in major independent studios.

STUDIO OPERATION

Label-owned studios and the larger independent studios maintain a full-time staff of perhaps 20 to 50 or more persons. The manager of a recording studio is primarily "credit manager" whose workday is often filled either trying to collect delinquent accounts or determining who should be extended credit in the first place. Studios in Los Angeles, dating from the late 1960s, have had a communication network set up informally among themselves to share information on credit ratings of prospective clients. This seems to work better than more conventional credit rating sources.

Studios have traffic managers who book studio time. These individuals are sometimes put under heavy pressure by producers who assert that, if they can't get into the studios in ten days, the world will end.

Traffic managers must sometimes schedule week-long sessions months in advance, booking time for acts, for example, that will be coming off the road and who are determined to lay down an album at a specific time of the year. Besides these long-range booking problems, the studio traffic department must be adept at estimating when a session may run overtime.

Studio profit depends on how closely contiguous hours can be booked. When sessions fail to start and end on schedule, serious financial losses can hit both the studio and the producer. Major accounts planning to record an album often "block book" studio time. The producer estimates how many days or weeks he may need to lay down 10 or more songs, then persuades the studio to reserve a particular room exclusively for that project. In block booking, the artists can leave all their equipment in place overnight and not waste time the following day trying to rediscover the setup that worked well yesterday. Also, studios that block off a room for several days or weeks will offer the producer a much lower price for the project than if he were charged by the hour.

In addition to the traffic manager and credit manager a full-line studio will have a chief engineer, a staff of house engineers, mixers, editors, mastering engineers/technicians, perhaps a video/film projectionist/technician, maintenance personnel, people handling setups and the movement of equipment. An office crew completes the staff of a full-line studio.

Few recording studios have sales departments or promotion people. Management finds that business comes or goes based largely on the word-of-mouth reputation of a studio. Ads do not help much.

CHANGING TECHNOLOGY

When stereo recording was introduced in 1958, it was welcomed in the recording field as perhaps the ultimate achievement in audio technology. But studios were concerned about the inconvenience and expense of converting to stereo. Convert they did, only to learn that oncoming technological change was to be unending. Following in rapid sequence were a quantity of scientific and technological advances that affected sound recording, particularly in such areas as noise reduction, tape delays, sound synthesis, improved tape, better recording heads, improved speakers, more acoustical control, digital search-and-find systems, and computer-assisted mixing and mixdown.

The application of laser beam technology is increasing. We already have on the market several applications of laser beams in optical scanners being used for videodiscs. Research continues in the effort to discover practical application of lasers in recording itself. Progress toward this goal may be aided through further study of how to apply PCM (pulse code modulation) and VHD (video high density), not only for video playback, but for audio and video recording. Engineers report these areas of research may lead to the practical application of recording technologies well in advance of present analog methods. Some engineers believe that, at some future time, it may be possible to use lasers to record 24 hours on one side of a 12-inch disc, combining both audio and video.

As predicted, analog recording is now giving way to digital recording technology. One firm leading in digital recording has been Sound Stream Inc. of Salt Lake City, which employs some of my former students. Record buyers appear ready to pay the extra cost of digitally-recorded discs (and other audiophile recordings) to get a quality of sound believed well above that available on conventional recordings.

The technique is directly dependent upon interface with digital computers, and engineers aspiring to work in the digital recording field will have to have strong educational backgrounds in computer science.

The increasing availability of low-cost microprocessors and minicomputers has accelerated the advance of ever-more sophisticated audio mixing consoles. It is fashionable to refer to such boards as "automated." Some mixing boards come "completely automated," it is claimed, providing producers and engineers with an impressive array of presets, search-and-find systems, and instant, accurate recall of prior mixes. Less automated mixing consoles offer fewer options, but still provide engineers and their clients recording services well in advance of what was available only a few years ago.

Digital recording was largely limited to classical music at the start, but its use in the pop field has increased greatly. Application of the technique would accelerate more rapidly if it weren't for its high cost, the incompatibility of equipment with present hardware, and the shortage of fully-qualified engineers. In an effort to circumvent some of these problems, an increasing number of digital equipment manufacturers are offering their products *for rent,* usually with an option to purchase. Producers can also find available increasing numbers of digital recording service companies which have no studios of their own, but can be retained to do "remotes" — record on location.

Smaller studios will be unable to find the capital to invest in digital recorders and the other advanced hardware becoming increasingly available. This will cause a shift of business from the "good" studio to the "state-of-the-art" facility. Even the well-capitalized facilities will be hard-pressed to stay abreast of oncoming technological developments.

THE ART AND SCIENCE OF MIXING

Before getting carried away with the importance of fancy recording hardware, it might be well to remember that one of the significant achievements in the art and science of recording, the Beatles' *Sergeant Pepper's Lonely Hearts Club Band* (1967) was done on a four-track board with a four-track machine. Another reminder that excellent recording is not always dependent on the latest technology is the return, after one-half a century, of direct-to-disc recording. This an-

A & M Records Studio A, Hollywood. Engineer preparing presets for this Trident Automated Console.

cient technique, where the performance and recording must be accomplished live and in one continuous take, is now being used in both the symphonic and popular fields. Buyers appear willing to pay several extra dollars for direct-to-disc recordings with their startlingly pure quality of sound.

Whatever technology may be employed in the recording process, much more important to the final musical result is the man sitting at the mixing console. Almost no studio has a surplus of fully-qualified mixers, or "engineers," as they are usually called. Until recent years, these audio "engineers" were usually just handymen technologists, most of whom lacked formal training. They learned mixing hit-and-miss, on the job. Some of these individuals have learned more about mixing, through long experience, than most electrical engineers could aspire to know. They combine the talents of a competent technician with an intuitive ear for music. Still others in audio "engineering" come, not from the radio and TV repair shop fraternity, but from the musical world. Some of the musician-mixers do a better job at the console than anyone else, for they may bring to the task a university-trained background in orchestration, arranging and performance. These musicians then hang around enough recording scenes to learn how to mix and master.

Studios have difficulty finding mixers and engineers who are thoroughly qualified and sufficiently versatile because, until recent years, there has been no place for them to adequately prepare. The difficulty is obvious: no other group of professionals is expected to be fully educated in two different disciplines — electrical engineering and music. Since this has rarely been possible, studios regularly hire individuals who *approximate* these special qualifications. This compromise results in frustration among professionals — and a lot of wasted money and time in waiting for mixers and "engineers" to figure out how to perform adequately.

The mixers most in demand are those with the magic ears. They may not understand how to trace a short in an amp or adjust the azimuth on a recording head, but they surely know how to lay down sounds. They ride those sliders with a sure touch, pulling from the console much more interesting sounds than the microphones deliver to it. In short, the top mixers are sensitive musicians, working their electronic wizardry like sound sorcerers — which they are. Besides being able to ride a console with sensitivity and even creativity, these artists have one additional attribute without which they would race screaming from the control room after the first hour: they possess a temperament that can handle high tension. Consider: this one individual has, at his fingertips, $500,000 worth of equipment; the act on the other side of the glass gets $20,000 a night to perform, and the record company plans to spend $200,000 promoting the record the engineer is mixing. He has total control over the final result. The buck stops at the console. A normal human being would soon go out of his mind under this pressure. The top mixers feel the pressure, but they can handle it.

While the industry is surfeited with thousands of mixers, the musician-engineer who has "the ears" and a cool temperament is the individual most likely to find regular employment and high income. These musicians-artists-engineers are not in oversupply; they should be guarded by the Secret Service as national treasures.

Versatile talents will surface. One of my former students, Jim Cassell, started in the maintenance department of A & M's studios in Hollywood. He advanced to assistant engineer, then full engineer, passing over strong competition. How? His own talent, ability to work with people under pressure, and an educational background that includes a degree in electrical engineering *and* music management.

Those less adept at mixing well will find work if they are thoroughly qualified to *maintain* audio equipment. Now that the equipment is becoming increasingly sophisticated, particularly the interface with computer technology, jobs coming down the line in audio engineering will be filled, more and more, not by talented fix-it men, but by graduate electrical engineers. People with this kind of background will be needed, not only to keep the hardware operating, but to design new equipment and installations. Electrical engineers engaged in studio design will be working with acousticians specializing in electro-acoustics. Recording studios will be staffed in the future, not just by graduates of Juilliard, but MIT.

21

WIRED MUSIC SERVICES

A substantial portion of music produced today is not really meant for listening. Rather, it is intended to remain in the background of consciousness, providing an "extramusical" service. Background music drones on, as we all know, just about everywhere people can be found — restaurants, supermarkets, airports, even toilets. Some of these sounds are almost as interesting as the hum of the air conditioner (but usually provide less comfort).

Another kind of background music also goes largely unnoticed, but can be of real musical value: the music underscoring TV and film drama. This kind of music is discussed in Chapter 25. Here I will discuss Muzak-type background music, which is sometimes referred to as "wired music service."

APPLICATIONS

BMI defines background music as "unobtrusive accompaniment to work, shopping, conversation, dining and relaxation." Management has been convinced by wired music suppliers that appropriate music pouring over the house PA system puts shoppers in a buying mood, perhaps even a euphoric state which tends to reduce buyer resistance. *Market research shows this to be true.* Company managers believe that music piped into offices increases workers' productivity. We also know that the incessant drone of low-level music masks the distracting sounds of office machines and uninteresting conversations. Studies of manufacturing plants show that workers exposed to background music are more productive and happier than when the Muzak is turned off. Muzak salespersons used to claim their tapes were programmed so that just the right music was heard at certain times of the day. For example, just before lunch, when productivity tends to lag, Muzak programs tend more toward energetic music to give the workers a lift.

Some canned music suppliers provide their customers the option of selecting their own programming. We know from the research of music therapists that the controlled "application" of music can modify human behavior. Now that the practice of music therapy is a recognized profession, if not a science, wired music service suppliers would be well-advised to retain on their staffs licensed music therapists to lift their "scientific programming" above its present guesswork level.

SERVICE COMPANIES

The wired music business in the USA is dominated by three large firms — Muzak, Seeburg and the 3M Company. Many cities have smaller companies competing with "The Big Three," but they find it difficult to match the low rates and extensive repertoires of the larger firms.

Muzak, founded in 1934, is the acknowledged leader in the field. It is now owned by TelePrompTer Corporation but functions as an independent division. Muzak claims to reach an audience of over 100 million persons per day. It claims a library of over 33,000 selections, adding c. 600 each year. Muzak relies largely upon FM multiplex broadcast signals to deliver its service from its franchisers' transmitters to the FM receivers supplied to the franchisers' customers. In some locations where FM broadcasting is impractical, Muzak's franchisers will deliver the programs to their customers via leased telephone lines.

Music libraries of this type tend to package their tapes in eight-hour segments, thus affording users programs that cover the average working day. Tapes are shipped like theatrical films: one customer is instructed to ship to the next-scheduled user.

Muzak contracts its services to about 300 franchised dealers, often on contracts running 10 years with options to renew. Local franchise operators are, in effect, distributors who put salespersons in the field to line up users of the service — restaurants, hotels, offices, factories — wherever people gather. Hotel chains spend several thousand dollars each month for canned music services.

Passenger airlines are constant users of these transcription services, and they are serviced by such suppliers as Music in the Air (a division of Billboard Publications Inc.), John Doremus Inc., and Transcom (a division of Sunstrand Data Control Inc.). Contracts negotiated in 1978 shifted music performance licensing to the music suppliers. Theretofore, performing rights organizations negotiated performance licenses directly with the airlines. Aggregate performance fees paid by the airlines are in the range of $300,000 a year. ASCAP's contract provides escalation of rates in accord with the Consumer Price Index.

Muzak, Seeburg and 3M Company find themselves in competition with a large number of smaller firms offering similar services via leased telephone lines or exclusive FM broadcast channels. The Big Three lose some business to these smaller firms because of the latter's lower rates. The rates of some of these music supply companies should be low, because some of their programs sound like they were recorded on used typewriter ribbons. Where the recording quality is acceptable, the musical arrangements and performances are often third-rate. It is obvious that thousands of hours of these tapes have been laid down in makeshift studios by pickup bands populated by incompetent performers.

Even well-performed, well-recorded background music is hated by most musicians, for they view it as the primary reason for the virtual disappearance of live music jobs formerly offered in hotels, restaurants and clubs. To many professional musicians, it is particularly galling to observe that even the recording jobs in background music often go to nonunion musicians or to Europeans.

PRODUCTION

Suppliers differ in how they obtain their master tapes. Muzak claims that all of its recording is under an agreement with the AFM and that it uses only AFM—licensed recording studios. Other background music suppliers obtain their masters from two other sources, both lower in cost than AFM scale. One is simply nonunion recording done in this country. For many years, some of the best AFM musicians have recorded these kinds of tracks for around $20 per hour. Sometimes AFM members and non-AFM members will work side by side in these kinds of sessions. Musicians who accept these low wages sometimes find that on pay day their employers seem to have just left for Las Vegas, and the master tapes, recorded in Cleveland, are now in the hands of a firm in Toledo which claims they were imported from East Germany.

More experienced musicians learn that recording sessions at AFM scale may be much less frequent than they would wish, but that most AFM locals and the international AFM representatives do all they can to collect money due their members from the producers.

A second source of miles of tracks is Europe. For decades, European musicians have been willing to work for shamefully low rates, turning out hundreds of hours of tapes for use on the Continent and, particularly, for export to the USA. European producers turn out not only background music tapes, but tracks for library services used by film producers and broadcasters. The AFM and other AFL-CIO affiliates have sought cooperation of various artists unions in Europe to limit, if not eliminate, these kinds of abuses — fine artists practically giving away their talents for others to exploit. But this kind of international control appears unattainable soon.

Whether background music is recorded under union or nonunion conditions, companies often engage the arranger-director as a producer to handle the project as a package. The packager, or producer, is given a lump sum, then he pays for music copying, studio time, tape, and musicians' wages. If any money is left, he makes something on the package for his arranging and directing. At one time, some Muzak tapes were laid down in my Los Angeles recording studio, and I observed that the arranger-director worked with great efficiency, for every one-half hour of time he could save would mean more money left for himself. To effect maximum cost savings, many of these masters were recorded *as they were read:* the "rehearsal" became the take. Quite often, the only delays in the procedure were caused, not by the inability of the musicians to sight-read the charts, but by mistakes in the copied parts.

In respect to repertoire, background music services do not hire songwriters or other kinds of composers. The material is drawn entirely from music already published, mostly standards and near-standards. Singers are not hired either; practically all background music is instrumental. As for employment of arrangers and directors, the work invariably goes to those who write fast — and cheap. No conductors are hired; all sessions are directed by the arrangers, some of whom do their own copying when they have time.

Part Five

MUSIC IN BROADCASTING AND FILM

22

MUSIC IN RADIO

PERSPECTIVE

From the beginning of commercial broadcasting in the 1920s, radio has had an enormous influence on the business and profession of music. It developed at the same time as phonograph records, and these two industries formed the first mass communications media for sound. Music could now be delivered to audiences of millions — at the speed of light. The art and business of music was never again to be the same.

The early radio broadcasts were live, of course, often featuring opera stars and other artists in the classical field. The audio quality was poor and the broadcast signals were filled with static. But audiences loved the novelty of radio and rushed out to buy the new crystal sets to receive the broadcasts in their homes. The first commercially licensed station went on the air in 1920. Entrepreneurs saw the potential of the medium, and within three years 500 stations were licensed to broadcast and the first radio network was formed.

It did not occur to broadcasters at the time that radio might become an advertising medium. But as the radio audience grew within a few years from dozens to millions, it was inevitable that business firms would step forth to sponsor programs if they could get their names mentioned on the air. By the mid-1920s, broadcast sponsorship was shared by stations, networks and advertisers.

As advertisers increased their dominance of program sponsorship, they pressured broadcasters for even larger audiences. A businessman or program director did not have to be exceptionally smart to figure out that the quickest way to draw a large audience was to broadcast popular music. And so the earlier programs that often favored classical music were now more often pointed toward middle America and the music of Broadway and Tin Pan Alley. In addition to the programs that featured stars of the Met and light opera, programming began to include vaudeville headliners. By 1926, it could be said that radio had become "show business."

Radio had developed an audience of millions, and neither broadcasters nor sponsors felt the need for audience analysis or market research. It was not yet known that within the "popular audience" were many smaller audiences comprised of persons with specialized tastes and identifiable buying habits. These significant discoveries were not made until much later in broadcasting.

Since World War II, the influence of radio over the music business has become so powerful, successful exposure via this medium can now "make" a song, a record or an artist. While publishers, record companies and performers keep searching for effective alternatives, few experience success today without radio exposure. Radio affects not only the aforementioned, but everyone else in the music business.

To understand the great dependence of the music industry on radio broadcasting, it will be helpful to summarize how the phenomenon developed historically

1864   *The basic theory of electromagnetism is set down by a British scientist, James C. Maxwell.*

1920   *The first commercially licensed radio station goes on the air (KDKA, Pittsburgh), broadcasting the presidential election returns (Harding vs Cox). At this time, only three stations are on the air.*

1922   *The first sponsor's name is mentioned on the air. The novelty of radio quickly attracts larger audiences.*

1923   *Radio broadcasting booms. Now there are 500 stations licensed to broadcast. AT&T inaugurates the first radio network.*

1926   *Radio rapidly becomes "show business." Stars of the Met and other classical artists are featured. Vaudeville headliners begin to be programmed.*

1930s   *In 1934, the FCC is set up by the Federal Communications Act. Broadcasting is turned over to "free enterprise" with minimum federal control. During the Great Depression, when people cannot afford to buy records or tickets to the movies, radio offers "free" entertainment to mass audiences. Network shows feature vaudeville headliners, movie stars and name bands. Advertising revenue soars.*

1941   *The FCC authorizes commercial FM stations, but development is delayed until after World War II.*

1945   *950 AM stations are on the air at the end of World War II.*

1946   *The post-war boom is on. 500 additional stations, AM and FM, go on the air.*

1950s   *The rapid growth of television nearly kills network radio, rapidly wiping out most live music and radio staff orchestras. As network programming fades,*

> *local stations take over, programming "electrical transcriptions" and other kinds of recorded music. The disc jockey begins to dominate.*

1960s   *The FCC authorizes multiplex broadcasting. The record business booms, largely due to the promotional medium of radio. FM stations increase in number and begin to attract special audiences.*

1970s   *FM stations turn more toward the "middle" audience in quest of a larger market share. Most AM and FM programming becomes predictable, with few programmers risking innovation. But the medium continues to earn good money.*

1980s   *FCC permits stations and networks to determine their own programming content and style: no more limits on lengths or frequency of commercials; no more requirements to cover news, public affairs or maintain program logs. FM stations proliferate, threatening survival of AM. Latter counters with stereo broadcasting. Elimination of most governmental control of broadcasting is predicted by some members of Congress.*

EXTENT OF RADIO BROADCASTING AT THE START OF THE 1980s (USA)[1]

Commercial AM stations	4,554
Commercial FM stations	3,155
Noncommercial FM stations	1,039
Total number of stations	8,748
Radio's annual revenue from time sales	$2.6 billion
TV's annual revenue from time sales	6.9 billion
Total annual time sales revenue from broadcasting	9.5 billion

TYPES OF STATIONS

AM/FM

One way to classify radio stations is by their carrier waves. AM stands for *amplitude modulation,* where the power or amplitude of the carrier wave varies but the wave frequency remains constant. FM stands for *frequency modulation,* where the carrier wave frequency varies but its amplitude remains constant. From the beginning, AM stations have dominated radio broadcasting. But in the period, 1970 to 1976, FM stations increased their share of the audience by 80 percent. A 1977 study sponsored by the NAB estimated that by the mid-1980s, FM radio would have an audience equal to that of AM. Some studies show that in the late 1970s, some age groups (for example, those 18-24) tended to listen more hours each day to FM broadcasts (1.92 hours) than they did to AM (1.62 hours). The NAB study predicted that by 1985 FM would be earning 42.6 percent of radio revenues, a remarkable increase over its share in 1975 of 17.9 percent. During the 1960s, FM was considered radio's "underground" audience. By the mid-1970s, FM had surfaced to become of great importance to broadcasting and the music industry as a whole.

1-According to *Nielsen Television Index* and *Arbitron.*

Those who favor FM over AM broadcasting point out these advantages:

1- *FM reception is almost free of electrical interference (static).*

2- *All stations within a reception range come in with equal strength.*

3- *Audio quality ("fidelity") is much higher than with AM.*

4- *More than one station can be assigned the same frequency, because FM signal coverage is much more limited than AM (FM reception is line-of-sight, as with television).*

5- *FM stations cost less to build and operate.*

FM also has certain disadvantages. Its signal cannot be received by AM sets. This has severely limited FM's use in automobiles, most of which have lacked AM/FM combination receivers. Advertisers look on FM broadcasting less favorably, as the FM audience is generally smaller than AM. Record companies have more sophisticated ways of comparing the relative promotional value of AM stations as opposed to FM. Some studies tend to show that FM audiences are more "hip," apparently more receptive to newer artists and experimental records. Promoters who believe this tend to push new product harder on FM stations. Radio programmers have gone way beyond this kind of audience analysis and have come to have abiding faith in their research, some of which may even be accurate.

For several years now, broadcasters have held to the view that radio audiences can be identified and classified with considerable precision. Much of their research is convincing, at least to those persons who need convincing, the advertisers to whom the stations sell time. Demographic research seems to show that broadcasters can predict, to a large extent, the type of audience their programs will attract. It is the type of audience a station seeks that determines its classification in the industry. The type of station that draws the most attention from record companies is generally referred to as "the youth market" station. It is this group that makes or breaks most new singles. Radio stations adopt a supremely simple programming philosophy: to attract a particular segment of the radio audience, broadcast its favorite music. It works.

YOUTH MARKET

General characteristics of youth market stations:

1- *They seek listeners in their late teens through the age, say, of 24. (Some radio stations extend this top figure to include "young marrieds;" others argue the latter are more appropriately included under "young adults" or even the "adult" market.)*

2- *75 percent to 85 percent of their programming is derived from commercially released records dominated by rock and its derivatives.*

3- *They feature "personality-type" disc jockeys who seek a personal rapport with listeners.*

4- *The commercials emphasize products and services of interest to teenagers and adults in their early twenties. Well-run stations aiming at youth capture a predominant share of the audience in many markets.*

ADULT MARKETS

In the late 1970s, radio programmers began to lose faith in their ability to identify the makeup of their audiences. Curiously, this unsettling discovery was made at a time when audience research was becoming more extensive, more carefully controlled. The principal reason for this blurred audience profile was the phenomenon of the crossover record. A station could conduct a study and be led to believe it was drawing a group of listeners predominantly in the group, say, 18 to 24 years of age. But the difficulty was that this group could not seem to decide just what kind of records it preferred.

With the approach of the 1980s, it became clear that the crossover record audience was becoming dominant and that about the only thing that could be said beyond that was, when a music lover grows out of his teens, he/she shows a tendency to prefer music that is softer than rock. This then opens up the entire range of musical styles, from pop to classical and all points in between. But stations know that their advertisers need more precise audience profiles than that. So the station going after the post-teen audience then attempts, as best it can, to carve out for itself an identifiable segment of adult listeners. This sorting out results in three rough categories of "adult" radio stations:

YOUNG ADULT STATIONS — They seek a post-teen audience that favors soft rock and the various styles that are derivative of rock. Young adult stations use less flamboyant disc jockeys. This kind of station goes after the young couples who spend the most money on cars, homes, furniture, babies, insurance and food.

Some stations say that they are "AOR," meaning their programs are dominated by album-oriented rock. The AOR classification is not consistently useful, however, because the distinction between rock on singles and rock on LPs continues to change as artists and labels experiment with the market.

MOR ("Middle Of The Road") STATIONS — They seek not only the "post-rock" listeners, but those favoring the music from Broadway shows, other "golden oldies," and pop singers accompanied by large studio orchestras featuring strings.

"GOOD MUSIC" STATIONS—Another name sometimes used interchangeably with MOR. Yet another term used for MOR music is "easy listening." These categories favor mostly instrumental music and fewer singers.

COUNTRY MUSIC

Until World War II, most stations of this type were called "country and western," and they were located almost exclusively, not in the country, not in the west, but in urban centers of the southeastern part of the United States. Since World War II, when war industries accelerated migration of southern people to the industrial north and west, broadcasters responded by locating "country" stations all over the USA. All urban centers now include one or more so-called country music stations.

This type of station initially programmed the type of popular music traditionally associated with Nashville, what oldtimers like to call *real* country. This repertoire is still widely loved and broadcast. But by the 1970s, the balance was shifting gradually to "pop country," "country rock," "L.A. country" and other stylistic mutations. Except for a few "hard-line" country stations, the broadcaster who goes after this market will program a great variety of music ranging from Nashville to pop.

Country music audiences are diverse geographically and musically. For this reason, results of demographic studies of it should be partially discounted. However, most studies of the country audience show that it is made up predominantly of persons with low income, limited education, who are Protestant, young adult, married females. In listening to the spots on country stations, one additional observation might be made, not so much about the audience as the advertisers: they seem to believe their audience is not too bright, for a high percentage of the advertising is simplistic. Country music DJ's deliver much of the ad copy themselves, live, and attempt to affect a kind of "down home" manner of talking. This approach seems to instill confidence in country music listeners, and they often respond well to the commercials. Well-managed country stations make money.

R & B — SOUL

Some stations seek a predominantly black audience. No agreement exists on the most appropriate label for such stations. Some broadcasters prefer "black music station." Others go by the old R & B label. Still other stations seeking a black audience program black gospel music and like to be known as "gospel stations." In the 1920s in the south there were a few stations that sought the black audience, but they were "underground." This was contemporaneous with (white) record companies discovering the large market for what was then called "race records." Stations outside the south began to cater to this black audience when migrations of this segment of the population accelerated during and after World War II.

Programming of black music increased during the "black revolution" period of the 1960s. Today, most urban centers have either "all soul" stations, "all gospel" stations, or stations which devote substantial portions of their air time to black music. On these stations, increasing numbers of black announcers and disc jockeys are being used. Also, management and ownership of these stations by black persons is increasing.

Recent research reveals some interesting contradictions in soul music broadcasting. Studies now show that *audiences are color blind:* most soul stations seem to have only a 10 percent to 15 percent black audience — only slightly higher than the proportion of blacks in the population as a whole. The reason for this mix of races is that more and more records are neither black nor white but cross over stylistic lines and appeal to a wide audience of diverse tastes. Whatever the size of the black audience, studies show that persons of African descent are generally more responsive to radio ads than are white persons.

SERIOUS MUSIC

Many people in the music industry think of classical music as a money loser. Sometimes it is, but certainly not always.

We have classical stations and "classical" stations. The "purist" stations eschew even the "light classics," nor will they broadcast what is known in the UK as "light music." Other so-called "classical music" stations are permissive, define the term more loosely and include even Broadway show music. Stations holding mostly to standard classical fare apportion the repertoire approximately as follows:

1- *Music to 1800 A.D. — 5 percent*

2- *Music from 1800 to 1900 A.D. — 90 percent*

3- *Twentieth century "serious music" — 5 percent*

Audiences are relatively small and advertising rates are correspondingly low. Demographic studies show that these audiences are predominantly well-educated, affluent, middle-aged, and just as snobbish in their preferences as devotees of other styles of music. Announcers are often well-informed, educated in the classical music repertoire, and able to chat with their audiences about composers, works, artists and stylistic periods. Classical music stations find it advantageous to associate themselves with the cultural life of their communities and with educational institutions. This factor contributes to building loyal audiences. The number of listeners is small, but well-run classical stations manage to find audiences who are loyal to the station's sponsors. Well-managed classical stations can profit. Radio audiences have become so satiated with the banality and redundancy of much "popular" music, one does not need a crystal ball to predict that the audience for "the real standards," as one of my students put it, will grow.

OTHERS

GOSPEL STATIONS — Stations addressing an audience attracted by music oriented toward religious faith and church activities are located predominantly in the "Bible Belt" section of the USA and its bordering states. Sometimes gospel stations are called "Christian stations." Gospel music is a style loved by blacks and whites, and some stations broadcast this kind of music exclusively. Audiences are fiercely loyal and larger in number than is generally understood. For a fuller understanding of this repertoire, read Tony Heilbut's *The Gospel Sound.* Many gospel stations are low-powered and have comparatively small audiences. Black gospel stations have no difficulty holding almost exclusively to the great supply of records available in this style. White Christian-oriented stations program songs of Christian faith, gospel music, sermons and other Christian messages. Because audiences are small, conventional advertisers do not often buy time on these stations. Sponsorship is more likely to come from a preacher or faith healer or conservative politician or publisher of religious-oriented materials.

SPANISH-SPEAKING STATIONS — A few radio stations, located predominantly in the southwestern region of the USA and in Mexico address their programming to audiences of Spanish descent. Most announcements are in Spanish, and the stations program many recordings produced in Mexico. They have low-power broadcast signals, small but loyal audiences and low-cost time rates. Another kind of station that may offer music and announcements bilingually are those located in Mexico, just across the border from the USA. They select such a location to avoid meeting the licensing requirements of the FCC. Some have extremely powerful signals which, at night, cover much of the USA.

NATIONAL PUBLIC RADIO — The FCC sets aside a segment of the FM broadcast band (88 to 92 megacycles) for schools, colleges, civic entities and others who devote all or part of their programming to education, the arts and other kinds of nonprofit enterprise.

Most public radio stations are low-powered, 10 watts or less. They address a small audience in a limited geographic area. They do not accept advertising. Stations located on college campuses are often connected with one or more campus departments, e.g., music, broadcasting, theatre. These stations are usually operated by students of the college, with or without faculty supervision.

Programming tends to lean to the personal tastes of the current group of station managers. "Undergound" music and lesser-known recording artists are sometimes featured. Promoters and agents for them are often well-received by campus stations. While pop and rock are favored, most stations are also receptive to special programming which might include chamber music, opera, electronic music, avant-garde, campus recitals and concerts featuring faculty and students. Stations also broadcast educational music programs, e.g., "Music Appreciation," "Understanding Jazz," etc.

Many public radio stations — over 200 of them — are affiliated with

National Public Radio, the equivalent of TV's Public Broadcasting System. NPR was incorporated in 1970. The network and its affiliates receive financial support from the Corporation for Public Broadcasting, the National Endowment for the Arts, cities, and states arts councils and private donations.

Some public radio stations receive support from AFM locals (Las Vegas is an example) who use this medium to foster "live" broadcasts of music and musicians. NPR has a long-standing agreement with the AFM, not only to pay union wages, but protect AFM members from unauthorized "new uses" of music originally cleared only for NPR broadcasts.

NETWORK RADIO

The Federal Communications Act defines a network or chain as "the simultaneous broadcasting of an identical program by two or more connected stations." Today, the term network or chain is used also to describe two additional types of station "networks." One is typified by the RKO radio chain, where the parent firm owns several stations, maintains some managerial control, but where each station determines its own programming. Another kind of radio network is the regional chain. The network components are owned and operated separately, but they share part of their air time in cooperative advertising. A sponsor whose product or service has a potential market larger than local but smaller than national will often contract with a regional radio network to broadcast his ads. In the United States we have about 50 regional radio networks.

The original concept of a radio network as defined by the Federal Communications Act — linked stations broadcasting the same programs simultaneously, dominated the industry to c. 1950. At that time, the networks were NBC, CBS, ABC and MBS. Star musicians and entertainers appeared regularly on radio network programs. To performers, such appearances were second only to movies in prestige and importance. In the early 1950s, network television rapidly came to dominate broadcasting, and network radio quickly faded. Live music almost disappeared; staff orchestras were either cut in size or eliminated. Networks were suddenly reduced just to feeding their affiliates news, weather reports and soap operas.

This near-demise of network programming was countervailed, in part, by the increasing dominance of local radio station programming. Almost overnight, recorded music became the dominant program material. All of the major networks active at the time television threatened their existence did manage to survive. In addition, we have today a variety of linkages, large and small. These networks share managerial responsibilities, cooperate in sales campaigns and market research. They sometimes share syndicated programs.

STATION MANAGEMENT

SALES

Sales personnel have the responsibility of selling time to local and national advertisers. Rates are determined on a "cost-per-thousand" basis. This information is shared with advertising agencies, clients and prospective clients on a "rate card." Besides just selling air time, sales departments get involved in developing advertising concepts for sponsors. They also become involved, when needed, in the actual production of advertisements and complete broadcast campaigns. No matter how large an audience the station programmers may draw, the operation cannot turn a profit without an effective sales department.

ENGINEERING

This department has these responsibilities:

1- *Mix the audio signals for transmission via leased telephone lines to the station's transmittor. Smaller stations require their disc jockeys to mix their own programs and even monitor the broadcast signal.*

2- *Maintain the equipment in the studio and at the transmitter.*

3- *Operate the transmitter station, monitor and control the broadcast signal per FCC regulations.*

4- *Assist in tape recording and rerecording program components — music, commercials, other announcements — and produce composite tapes (open reel and broadcast-type cartridges) for broadcast.*

5- *Evaluate, purchase, install and maintain equipment as needed.*

OPERATIONS

Stations are run by a general manager. He delegates responsibilities to his department heads, e.g., news, sales, engineering and programming. Yet, it is he who is ultimately responsible for all of these operations. In addition, the general manager is responsible for:

1- *The station's FCC license and its periodic renewal*

2- Office management and accounting

3- *Personnel*

4- *Finance*

5- *Audience research*

6- *Relationships with advertising agencies and their clients*

7- *Music licenses with ASCAP, BMI and SESAC*

8- *Union negotiations and contracts*

9- *Legal matters*

10- *Community relations*

The general manager is also ultimately responsible for programming, but delegates this task to his program director.

MARKET RESEARCH

In the last 10 years, advertisers have acquired great faith in the value of market research. Since broadcasting is now the dominant medium for all advertising, radio and television markets are more intensively researched than any other. All radio stations are busily engaged in trying to figure out what people like to hear. If a station can manage to accurately count and diagnose its potential audience it will make money. A station that is unable to do so will have difficulty surviving.

DEMOGRAPHY

Audience research is based on demographic studies. Demography can be defined as *the statistical science dealing with the distribution, density and vital statistics of populations.* Stations and their advertisers are interested in the location, age, sex, education, economic status and race of their potential audience. Above all, stations and their clients need to know how many people are listening to the station at various times during the day and their density per square mile. When a radio station salesperson talks to a retailer of motorcycles, he needs to be able to convince that merchant that at 5 p.m. during weekdays, his station can "deliver" 100,000 listeners who are 18 to 24 years of age, of medium income, prefer rock music and seem to be the kind of folks that like motorcycles. The salesperson asks the merchant if he would be willing to spend $10 per thousand to broadcast a sales message to those 100,000 potential customers. That may sound reasonable to the merchant. If it does, the salesperson will write $1,000 worth of radio spot announcements concerning motorcycles. If the salesperson lacked this kind of specific demographic research data, he would have much less convincing information for the prospective sponsor.

RESEARCH METHODS

Radio market research is based largely on polling samples of its audience or potential audience. In this respect, it is much like political polling, where a candidate for national office may spend $100,000 or more to try to find out how he is doing with the electorate. Nearly all polls are based on sampling. Most samples are so tiny (perhaps .01 percent of the total) that they are held suspect by many persons. It appears absurd to argue that a poll of less than 1 percent of 1 percent of a total potential radio audience could in any way provide accurate information on the makeup of the other 99.9 percent. Those that are "behind in the polls" are quick to complain that they do not believe in them. When a politician or a radio station looks good in sample polling, they are quick to assert its validity. The question of the validity of this kind of market research rests on *the quality of the sample.* When the sampling is accumulated with careful scientific controls, data yielded from the research will prove to be remarkably accurate.

Pollsters such as Gallup, Roper and the New York Times-CBS group state that their margin of error is in the range of three percent. But they admit they have been off, from time to time in the range of ± five percent. Companies sampling broadcast audiences assert their figures are also in the three to five percent accuracy range. But not all market research is this good or this useful to broadcasters and their advertisers. Research methods range from casual to scientific. The most trustworthy, systematic methods used for broadcasters attempt to determine three basic sets of statistics:

1- **Station Rating.** *This is determined by counting the percentage of the audience which is listening to a particular station at a particular time. Example: if a station has a rating of 15.2 at noon on weekdays, that means that out of every 100 listeners contacted, 15.2 were listening to that station at noon on a weekday.*

2- **Sets in use.** *This is a count of the actual number of sets turned on in the homes sampled. Example: a 62.4 sets-in-use figure indicates that of 100 homes sampled, 62.4 had their radios turned on.*

3- **Audience share.** *This statistic indicates the comparative popularity of a program being broadcast at a particular time. Example: if a show has a 34.6 share, that means that, of the homes which had their sets turned on, 34.6 percent were listening to that particular program at that particular time. The audience share is obtained by dividing the station (program) rating by the sets-in-use figure.*

If a radio station can accumulate a large enough share of the available market, it has a reasonable chance of turning a profit. If it cannot manage this, it may go under unless it receives income from sources other than its advertisers.

What is a profitable share? This may be shown by a market we'll name *Averagetown, USA.* Let's imagine that this city of opportunity comprises one million radio listeners. It is served by 15 stations, AM and FM. A glance at Figure 22.1 reveals useful information. Perhaps the most critical data show each station's share of its own special "subshare" or "submarket," e.g., each station going after the youth market can see how it compares with the other four stations also trying to reach the kids. Three stations are scrambling for the adult market. Note that two of them are doing alright, but the third one is probably losing money, just isn't making it in pulling a cumulative audience of only 30,000.

Averagetown's five most-listened-to stations, whatever their programming format, rank as follows: Rock (No's 1 and 2), Adult (No's 3 and 4), and Country (No. 5). I do not suggest that this ranking of formats typifies most American cities of this size. But Averagetown does appear to have a relatively weak country music station. We might risk the conjecture that, if an aggressive management took over one of the country stations, it might be able to increase its ratings enough to give the present top four stations a real scare.

AVERAGETOWN, USA

RADIO AUDIENCE SHARES OF 1 MILLION HOMES

15-Station Battle

Type of Station	Cumulative Audience	Share of Special Market	Share of Total Market	Station Rank	Profit/Loss
Youth Market	175,000	35%	17.5%	1	P
	150,000	30%	15%	2	P
	75,000	15%	7.5%	6	?
	50,000	10%	5%	7	L
	50,000	10%	5%	8	L
Totals	500,000	100%	50		
Adult Market	150,000	50%	15%	3	P
	120,000	40%	12%	4	P
	30,000	10%	3%	10	L
Totals	300,000	100%	30%		
Country Market	85,000	85%	8.5%	5	P
	15,000	15%	1.5%	12	L
Totals	100,000	100%	10%		
All Others	40,000	40%	4%	9	L
	30,000	30%	3%	11	L
	10,000	10%	1%	13	L
	10,000	10%	1%	14	L
	10,000	10%	1%	15	L
Totals	100,000	100%	10%		

Fig. 22.1

Besides the factor of audience share, a station will make or lose money depending on its efficiency in management. But if we assume that all 15 Averagetown stations are equally efficient and have a payroll proportional to their size of operation, we can guess that only five stations in the town are making money, with nine not breaking even, and one whose profit margin is in doubt. But it is like a horserace; the lead keeps changing. The ranking of Averagetown's stations six months later could flip-flop — those on top might be pushed under by former losers who have changed their programming or management or acquired a group of hot-shot new salespersons. This accounts in part for why 15 stations would even attempt to share so small a market. *If each of them shared equally in it, not one of them could make money.* But entrepreneurs step forth periodically because they believe they have an opportunity to show their competitors how a radio station should really be run.

Individual stations conduct their own research, but they generally call on independent research companies for studies which compare the performance of a number of stations in a given market. Several dozen firms offer this kind of service. Some function regionally, others nationally. Among the most widely used firms that operate on a national basis is the American Research Bureau, also known as ARB or Arbitron. It is based in New York City but provides data for regional and local markets. ARB uses a controlled sample of listeners who are asked to maintain weekly logs of programs they hear. These logs, or diaries, are collected periodically and analyzed.

ARB also uses a device called *Arbitron.* Sets are wired into a central receiving terminal which shows instantaneously what programs its sample homes have turned on at a particular time. Of special usefulness to radio stations is the fact that ARB can tell its clients the relative popularity of stations in a given market. For example, all the stations in Denver that contract for ARB's service receive periodic reports indicating which stations are accumulating the largest number of listeners, then the next largest, and so on. Following appearance of a station's comparative rating in a market, it revises its time rates. A station may pull only 85 percent of the audience of its top competitor. But it can still offer its advertisers about as good a time buy if its rates are 15 percent lower than the number one station in the area. If, however, an audience study shows that a station is accumulating only a five percent share of the local radio audience, its sales department will not only have difficulty selling time, even at low rates, it will have difficulty holding together its sales staff who will tend to move to other stations offering stronger competition in the market.

In addition to data bought from independent research companies, individual stations conduct their own market research. Controlled research is expensive to undertake, and a station will engage in it to the extent that its resources permit. Small stations in small towns may "research" the efficacy of their programming simply by chatting with the local hardware merchant at the weekly Rotary luncheon ("Hey, Fred, did we help you move that fertilizer last week?") The smallest stations measure their audience by informal means, for they lack the money to do it systematically.

Large stations in major markets have complete research departments, possibly headed by a Ph.D. in psychology or statistics. These expensive research operations seek the same data as Arbitron or Nielsen, but focus their full attention on what all the figures might mean for just that particular station. Station research personnel often make large numbers of telephone calls at random, inquiring if the listener has his radio turned on, to what station, how often, his or her age, sex, musical preferences, etc. Other telephone calls are made to local record distributors and retail stores, inquiring which records are selling best. Other researchers contact patrons of sponsors. For example, they might poll the shoppers of the local department store. When a shopper inquires about the sale of dresses, the station researcher may ask the clerk or the customer if the inquiry was induced through advertising heard on the station. More likely, the station's ads will be "keyed." For example, a store might advertise a new product only on the radio and only on one station in the market area. It is a simple matter to determine the efficacy of those advertisements by asking the merchant how many customers appeared to inquire about that particular product.

A radio station gets additional information on its audience size and preferences through incoming telephone calls. Disc jockeys sometimes encourage listeners to call in to express their views. Another audience information source comes from fan mail. Analysts must be cautious in interpreting incoming calls and fan mail, because they may not be reliable indicators of audience opinion.

DATA INTERPRETATION

It is one thing to accumulate the research data. It is quite another matter to interpret their meaning. The accuracy and usefulness of audience research information is widely disputed. Questions commonly raised:

1- *How good was the sample? Did it typify the market?*

2- *How weak, how strong was the program preceding/following the program being measured?*

3- *How strong, how clear was the station's signal at the time the sampled audience was listening?*

4- *How strong were the competing programs?*

5- *What was the influence of publicity?*

6- *What was it that most attracted listeners — the music, the disc jockey, a prize contest?*

It is evident to experienced audience researchers that their data must be interpreted with great care. A casual reading of the numbers can render this kind of research worse than useless. Only the larger stations can afford the staff to thoroughly analyze the meaning of research data.

Programmers and sales personnel must know what they are talking about if the station is going to accumulate a profitable share of the market.

High quality market research is essential for all business concerns. But in broadcasting, it is particularly important because its customers are invisible. How do you identify a customer you can neither see nor hear? Because of the intangible elements and the uncontrolled variables in audience analysis, stations must rely more and more on information storage and retrieval — computer technology. As they say in the computer field, "Garbage in, garbage out": stations must make sure their encoding of information is as accurate as possible. That is their only hope of deriving benefit from the decoding process. Stations which can afford to invoke the aid of computer science in market research will almost certainly come to dominate the broadcasting business, provided management knows how to use the information.

PROGRAMMING

INFLUENCES

How does a radio station determine what it will put on the air? We can identify a variety of factors that will influence a station's programming.

1- **Habit.** When a station is reasonably satisfied with its share of the market, it tends to continue its programming format. Why abandon a winning formula?

2- **Competition.** There is room in any given area for only a limited number of stations to share a particular segment of the available audience. If, for example, a station has grabbed the country music audience in a small market, another station will be ill-advised to change its moderately successful rock format and switch to country. Unless management has a lot of money for experimentation, it will tend to determine its programming format in accord with the strength of competing stations.

3- **Trade charts.** Most stations read the trade paper record charts each week to learn what records appear to be gaining or falling in national popularity. Much less known to the public, but influential with radio management are certain tip sheets, e.g., the *Gavin Report*. Stations do not agree on the usefulness of record charts in determining play lists. There is also disagreement on the objectivity of some of the trade charts.

Most charts purport to show the extent of airplay records receive, the number of records distributed and sold, the rate of rise or fall of individual records, and the geographic location where records may be breaking or fading from popularity. Stations lacking their own research resources tend to rely heavily on their favorite charts. Stations with their own research departments tend to use national charts only to corroborate their own local research.

4- **Record promoters.** Program directors receive weekly visits from record promoters. These efforts rarely influence programming policy, but record promoters do impact on how station programmers make up their play lists. If this were not so, the record industry could not function as it does today. Program directors are probably influenced most by those promoters who have *credibility* — and good records. Experienced P.D.'s have learned not to succumb to the pitch of the fast talker. But programmers can be strongly influenced by a promoter who is persistent, particularly if that promoter has the kind of records the station is seeking.

5- **Change of management.** A station will often change its programming format when new management comes in, or when a station changes ownership. New blood may bring new ideas.

New FCC Policy — Until the early 1980s, the Federal Communications Commission strongly influenced programming through its power to grant station licenses or renew them. The FCC no longer attempts to control programming or the number of commercial messages a station may put on the air. The FCC no longer requires radio stations to devote a specified amount of air time to cover news and provide public service announcements. Program logging requirements were also eliminated.

The commission came to the view that radio programming should be determined by market forces and audience preferences rather than a governmental regulatory body. Legislation is pending in the Congress which will almost totally eliminate governmental control of broadcasting.

GATEKEEPERS

Those who determine what radio stations will broadcast are perhaps the most powerful individuals in the music industry. They are the gatekeepers. Those they let pass may prosper. Those denied rights of passage will probably never rise from obscurity in the popular music field.

Who are these decision-makers? Until the late 1950s, most of the records that got on the air were selected by the disc jockeys. Following the payola scandals, station management proceeded to attempt to isolate their employees from the blandishments and bribes of record promoters.

Opinion varies on the extent of payola today. Most observers believe that whatever payola exists is offered by the smaller labels. Medium and large-sized stations rarely risk the consequences of accepting payola, now a federal crime. Large stations go to considerable effort to inform their employees about company policy. The musical director of KHJ-Los Angeles, one of the most powerful stations in the country, told me that every few weeks employees of that station receive written instructions from management specifically naming just what kinds of favors or gifts they can accept from record promoters. Employees are limited to only occasional socializing at lunch or dinner, and they can accept gifts of only modest value at Christmas. Any hint of an employee accepting dope or sexual favors brings immediate dismissal.

Most radio stations will have their programming controlled by one or more of the following types of gatekeepers:

STATION MANAGER — Very small stations have tiny staffs. The boss himself may make up the station's play list, or he may delegate all or part of this responsibility to a disc jockey. Station managers in larger stations would have only indirect influence on determination of weekly play lists.

PROGRAM DIRECTOR ("P.D.") — Larger stations generally assign their program directors the responsibility of making up the play lists. This is his principal concern, together with the selection and scheduling of his on-the-air personalities. Even in major markets, some program directors will also take their turn on the air or cover for a jock who is ill.

MUSIC LIBRARIAN — Some stations prefer the title, "Music Director" or "Music Researcher." If a station lacks a staff person bearing the title "program director," the selection of the weekly play list is assigned to the music librarian (by whatever title). Larger stations sometimes have two persons sharing this responsibility. Record promoters soon learn who the real gatekeeper is, and they focus their efforts accordingly. The musical director of KHJ sets aside one day each week to meet record promoters. Each promoter asking to see her receives about 15 minutes of her time, if needed. At the time I talked with her, she told me she will see any promoter who is professional in his approach and can show her that the record being promoted is showing action in other markets. In addition to listening to promoters, she spends at least one-half day each week calling up distributors and retailers to learn which records are moving up or down. After five days of market research, she makes up a play list of about 35 records and then discusses her recommendations with KHJ's program director. He then selects from her recommendations about 30 records for the following week's play. She volunteered, without apology, that her recommendations include records she personally likes and believes in, whether or not they are popular in KHJ's particular market. She permits herself an additional subjective judgment: she will not recommend a record even in the rock style that, in her opinion, lacks musical content. She will not accept a record just because it may have shock value.

DISC JOCKEYS — While larger stations usually deny their disc jockeys the privilege of selecting their own playlists, some air personalities are so popular and powerful that they persuade management to let them select, or at least share in the selection, of the records they broadcast. Some big name jocks insist on full control of their play lists. Small stations often lack research staffs, even music librarians. In these kinds of limited operations, the disc jockeys share in whatever needs getting done, from selling spots to sweeping out the studio. The small station's weekly play list might be improvised day to day, even hour to hour. For this reason, record promoters from The Big City frequent these local precincts, knowing that they might place a record on the local air for the price of a one-martini lunch. This kind of payola would not be likely to cause hysteria in the halls of the FCC.

PROGRAM CONSULTANTS — Larger stations that can afford it will call in, from time to time, independent programming consultants to advise them. A station that has been unable to increase its audience share, no matter what it does with its programming, turns to outsiders, when it can afford such service, hoping that a more objective viewpoint may identify what the station might be doing wrong. Programming consultants who have developed a reputation for raising stations' ratings can charge handsome fees for their advice, some of which may turn out to be correct. *Some stations may assign to an outside consultant or production company the entire responsibility for making up its weekly play lists.*

PROGRAM CONTENT

Most radio stations devote 75 to 85 percent of their broadcast time to music. The only kind of commercial station not following this programming policy is the all-news or all-talk station. Practically all music broadcast is prerecorded. Most of it derives from commercially-released records originally licensed for private use in the home.

No radio staff orchestras exist today; the last holdout was WGN-Chicago, which let go its staff orchestra years ago. Here and there a radio station might feature a local instrumentalist or small combo. A handful of stations try to keep going perhaps one low-budget live music show each week to offer air time for local artists trying to put together performing careers. But these last vestiges of live radio music, admirable as they may be, are exceptional in radio broadcasting. As a matter of fact, most of the radio stations built since about 1960 do not even have studios that can accommodate more than a three-piece band, if that.

Everyone seems to know about "Top 40 Radio." This is curious, because it can hardly be said to exist today. Several surveys show that the length of the average play list among stations seeking the rock audience is below 30 records. As pointed out, this sharp reduction in the number of records being programmed each week limits stations in the "contemporary" field to adding two to four new releases each week. This limitation has inestimable impact upon the whole music industry.

Most radio stations discovered in recent years that radio audiences tend to leave on a particular station *provided they don't hear a record they dislike.* This complacency and inertia among listeners is caused, in part, by the reluctance of a listener to bother to move to the set and punch a selector button. With car radio listening, station switching is a very different matter, because the buttons are so easy to reach. *The bulk of the radio audience seems prepared to leave a set droning on as long as it doesn't become annoying.* Many listeners will explore the radio dial, not for a particular station (most will not care which station they land on), but for a style of music they like. Studies repeatedly show that the listener will not move off a station unless a record comes on that is different in musical style, inconsistent with the other music the station typically programs. When the listener notices the station has put on a record contrary to his taste or just different from what is familiar to him, he may then punch out, searching for another station that is more consistent, less disturbing.

Radio programmers therefore do everything they can to avoid upsetting their audience. This, then is *reverse programming.* A station determines, not so much what it believes its audience will like, but what it will not dislike. This programming philosophy, when carried too far, can result in a station's sound being so predictable, so unimaginative, that listeners interested in newer artists and occasional innovation, may tend to favor a station that takes some chances. The conservative approach to programming (avoiding, at all costs, listener alienation) works only for stations that are interested mostly in maintaining their present audience share. It would be unwise to adhere to such a constricting policy for a station that is trying to find new listeners.

While some stations permit their staffs the occasional luxury of broadcasting personal favorites, most profit-making broadcasters do everything they can think of to identify what the potential audience wants to hear, then give it to them, 24 hours a day.

Few stations conceive of their establishments as art centers. Rarely does management believe it has any special obligation to educate the public to "good" music. Their FCC license states that their obligation is just "to serve the public convenience and necessity." This would exclude any feeling of obligation to push Stravinsky or Bach.

The concept of programming based on non-alienation has led to segmentation and categorization of radio stations. Nearly all broadcasters have figured out just what share of the market they want to go after — youth, young adult, MOR, etc., then hold to it as consistently as they can, so that the potential audience will eventually discover them because they offer not only what the listener likes, but *predictable* music.

This is all very neat. But the traditional classification and categorization of stations doesn't work as predictably as it once did. The difficulty is that more and more music lovers are being attracted to music that defies classification. As I stress elsewhere in this volume, the phenomenon of the crossover record has turned the music industry on its ear, so to speak. The record labels continue to produce "rock records," "country records," "R & B records," but when the music contains elements borrowed from a somewhat different style, it may attract not only its intended audience, but "outsiders" who love the record just for its sound. When this happens on a wide scale, a super-hit is born. And radio stations jump on the superhits because that is what most listeners want most to hear. Thus, a "youth market station" or "adult station" — whatever —finds itself crossing over all kinds of stylistic lines. In the process it may lose its original identity, but listeners are delighted — for the moment.

For the moment. That is the fundamental problem of all radio broadcasting. Changing public taste. Unpredictability. Not even computers can invent the future. Enterprising radio programmers have the choice of simply reacting to changing tastes — or attempting possibly to influence them.

The phenomenon of the crossover record will increase its influence on radio programming. But it appears unlikely that we will see the successful emergence of the anything-goes station, throwing together records from all styles in an effort to grab everybody who likes music. Stations will continue to try to maintain their own identities, their own personalities.

Whatever the predominant type of music programmed, stations tend to *cluster* their records, then cluster their commercials. Some studies show that this pattern of grouping tends to hold an audience more effectively than a pattern of announcement-record-commercial then announcement-record-commercial — and so on.

Programmers hold different views on how to *pace* records. Some believe that in a three-record cluster, audiences will favor a sequence of tempos, say, slow-medium-fast. Other programmers hold the view that it is best to alternate "pretty" and "aggressive" sounds. Still others are convinced the ideal sequence of music is an alternation of singers, group singers and instrumental features. Take your choice.

As I point out in the chapter on music in advertising, programmers often hold to the notion that commercial announcements are most readily accepted, meaning least-annoying, when their musical style and tempo flow into the play list "unnoticed," ostensibly as components of the musical entertainment.

Stations using cluster programming, then "back announcing," create in that format a span of air time for the disc jockey to speak continuously for awhile, thus affording him an opportunity to display his personality. He has time not only to chat about several records, he can invest his personality into the reading of commercial copy or in recommending a particular sponsor whose products he would not do without. This kind of "personality radio" seems to appeal to many listeners. With all the music being canned, about the only element of spontaneity and personality a station can provide is through its disc jockeys.

SYNDICATION

Independent production companies package complete programs, then license or sell them to stations. Such programs are said to be in *syndication,* and the packagers of them are called syndicators. The producer of syndicated programs determines a format for a show or series of shows, engages the announcers, then lays in the music tracks, interviews — whatever is to go into the programs. Most of the music used by syndicators is lifted from commercially released records. Special new music is rarely used because its cost is considered prohibitive. Syndicators draw upon music library sources when needed. These services, most of which date back to the early days of live radio drama, offer a complete catalog of music "cues," ranging from a symphonic passage to the sound of rustling leaves. Most of the music derived from library services has been recorded in Europe at rates well below those current with the AFM.

A radio station or a radio chain can order prepackaged programs delivered on open reels or on special broadcast-type cartridges. The shows provide time for insertion or addition of commercial messages of the local station. Syndicated program material can range in length from 30 seconds to several hours. It can be an individual, one-time program or series. Most syndicated programs are based on a single concept. The concept may feature one artist, or it might be based on a particular style of music, or one composer, or it might be in historical format, e.g., "The History of Rock and Roll."

Production companies are now producing more and more specials following the precedent set in the 1950s by television "spectaculars." Stations leasing or buying special syndicated programs believe their cost is offset by their quality, and they offer useful vehicles for the station to attract attention.

Radio programming has become imitative and conservative. Whether the ideas come from the station or from independent producers, broadcasters need to take more chances, engage in experimentation, reach out for audiences that have long since become bored with predictable, formula programming.

AUTOMATION

About one station in seven has turned to automated programming. Automated stations use programs that have been syndicated by an independent production company, then leased or sold to individual stations or radio networks. Automatic equipment is available that will accept, not just a 30-second spot announcement, but a whole stack of program cartridges which may run, unattended by station personnel, not just for one program, but continuously all day and all night. It is theoretically possible for a station to stay on the air for days at a time without any human being entering the studio.

Automated radio: operator can interrupt taped program with local spot announcements. *Control 16 Processor* by Broadcast Electronics Inc.

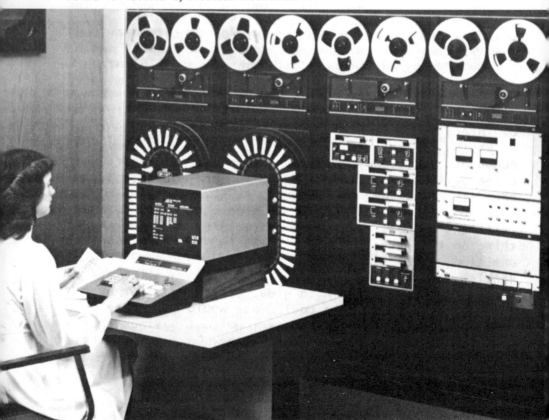

Stations turn to automation in an effort to make more money. Certainly these broadcasting robots do not demand high salaries; they have no union minimums; they don't complain about working conditions; they don't talk back to the boss, and the only thing they demand for nourishment is a fresh stack of tapes. Once a station manages to amortize the cost of the automated equipment, nearly all programming costs are limited to the fee demanded by the program packager.

Stations turn to automation for reasons other than concern over rising costs. A station may have tried various programming formats and been unable to dent a local market. An absentee owner might prefer to entrust what his station broadcasts to a recognized producer rather than local decision-makers. Whatever motivates management to switch to automation, it seems likely the trend will continue.

Automated radio broadcasting has distinct disadvantages, and most stations believe they outweigh the savings in operating costs. Automated programming denies a station flexibility in scheduling, not only in program content, but with commercials. Automation can lock you in for hours, if not days at a time; it lacks spontaneity. Audiences sometimes perceive they are being fed canned fare and may resent it.

23

MUSIC IN TELECOMMUNICATIONS

DELIVERY SYSTEMS

STATIONS AND NETWORKS

It would be impossible to adequately account for the influence of television on our lives since the late 1940s. Ninety-eight percent of American homes own at least one TV set, and most of them are in color. Nearly one-half of the homes own more than one set. The most difficult statistic to understand is that the average household has the magic box turned on more than six hours a day[1]. When a top-rated program, such as the NFL Superbowl is broadcast, nearly every set in the country (over 76 million) seems to be tuned in to it.

The three commercial networks dominate the business, and most TV stations are affiliated with one of them. A station remains independent only when it cannot arrange a network affiliation (there are about 115 independent TV stations). NBC, CBS and ABC are not very concerned about "competing" networks. A number of independent stations are linked from time to time, but these "networks" are temporary and are normally limited to special events, particularly sports

---

1-Source: A.C. Nielsen Co.

broadcasts. Program syndicators will sometimes sell several dozen stations the same program for simultaneous broadcast, but such linkages cannot be called networks. Some stations form regional groupings and share spot sales, films and transcriptions.

NBC, CBS and ABC TV networks own radio stations, too. But the FCC limits broadcasters' holdings. For example, a radio station owner may no longer acquire a TV station in the same market area, nor a TV owner a radio outlet. TV stations may no longer operate cable-TV franchises in the same city. Networks cannot own cable-TV systems at all. Newspapers, at one time in control of most local advertising, may no longer buy radio stations in the same market area.

The number of TV stations licensed by the FCC:

Commercial		Noncommercial		Total Number
VHF	UHF	VHF	UHF	
517	224	105	162	1008

Audience preferences change from year to year, and programmers invoke the aid of everything from scientific research to sheer guess-work in trying to figure out just what might win wide audience support. About 25 percent of TV viewers seem to favor suspense/mystery shows; 20 percent favor straight drama; slightly fewer go for sitcoms. Feature films attract about 20 percent to 25 percent of the audience. This leaves about 20 percent of the total audience for musical/variety shows, news, etc.

Eight-five percent of viewer time is spent watching network programs. When a new show bombs, network executives have been known to wait as long as one day to cancel the show and slam a quick fix into the ailing time slot. And the advertising revenue just keeps rolling in.

The incredible success of television can be attributed to two factors. First, it delivers a variety of entertainment and information into homes 24 hours a day, seemingly without cost to the viewer. But the more fundamental reason for TV's popularity is not just that it is an entertainment medium. Rather, it is because *TV is a magic selling machine.*

The function of the entertainment segments of the programs is not to entertain, but to separate the commercials. Ninety-two percent of all TV spots are now 30 seconds (or less) in length. The one-minute TV commercial is nearly extinct. When inflating production and time costs forced advertisers to the "half-length" commercials they learned, to their delight, that 30-second spots could move about as many goods and services as the 60-second ones.

As with radio, advertising rates for TV are determined by the size of audience a station or network can deliver. Audience measurement techniques for TV are more sophisticated, and probably much more accurate, than those available for radio. Advertisers can know before they spend their money what their "cost-per-thousand" will be to deliver a commercial message. Early in the 1950s, advertisers learned that selling via TV was much more effective and relatively less costly

MASTER CONTROL for CBS-TV network's O. & O. station KNXT, Hollywood. Engineer intercuts "network feeds" with local program material, commercials.

than print media. Clear proof of this was obvious as TV burgeoned in the early 1950s (and almost knocked out radio for a while). Meantime, mass-reader magazines (*Life, Look, Saturday Evening Post,* others) lost so many advertisers they were forced to discontinue regular publication.

TV stations and networks take in about $7 billion a year in time sales, which represents about 72 percent of all money collected for broadcasting time buys[2]. Many more dollars are spent each year by advertisers to produce the commercials and program material filling these time slots. A sizable chunk of this production money goes to musicians, entertainers, their managers and agents.

Millions of dollars are spent each year in TV for music that goes largely unnoticed except by professionals — the thousands of hours

---

2-Source: FCC.

of music that is used to underscore dramatic action. Most viewers are not aware of and do not care about background music, but if underscoring were suddenly withdrawn from dramatic programs, the shows would lose much of their impact. Good underscoring has salvaged many a weak scene — and ruined good ones. The field of TV scoring offers extensive employment for composers, copyists, cutters and instrumentalists. Wages to these artists, even at AFM scale, constitute major components of production expense.

When TV increased its use of tape and film in the 1950s, producers bought music "tracks" from Europe to avoid payment of the much higher wages demanded by union musicians in this country. But this huge loss of wages to "tracking" came to a halt with the 1978-79 season when the new AFM contract with TV and film producers came into effect. This contract is discussed in Chapter 25 where I cover music underscoring of TV and theatrical films.

STATION ORGANIZATION

Most television stations lead two lives. One is a station's local existence in its own community. Its second level of existence is as a network affiliate. This bifurcation can most clearly be observed in a station's sales department. The vice-president for sales assigns his salespersons to either local advertising or national accounts. Some personnel function at both levels. A large station will have at least a half-dozen salespersons calling on prospective local advertisers and negotiating with advertising agency account executives. Others in the sales department will handle national sales accounts, usually brought to the station by national advertising agencies who buy time and assist in scheduling broadcast campaigns. Stations affiliated with networks periodically negotiate with management to determine how much air time should be shared with the network, how much should be withheld for local advertisers, and what proportion of time should be used for national spot buyers and national advertisers whose ad agencies buy time directly from local stations.

Station sales departments sometimes get involved in conceiving, even producing, ad campaigns for sponsors. However, when produc-

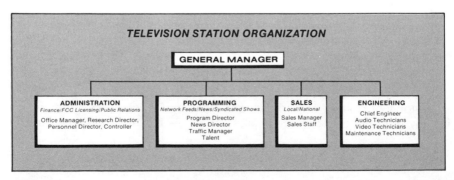

Fig. 23.1

tion begins to get elaborate, the salespeople leave such problems to the agency or to the station's programming personnel.

Television programming departments are headed by a director of programming in larger stations. But in most stations, the great bulk of station-generated program production occurs in the news department. Now that most persons favor broadcast journalism to print media as their news source, audiences have grown large enough to enable most news shows to turn a profit. Other than news, local station program production is normally limited to low-budget children's programs, audience game shows, perhaps an occasional local talent show, and public service shows turned out by news departments. The use of music in local station programming is minimal. Orchestras larger than quartets are rarely hired. If music is needed in connection with locally filmed shows, canned music tracks are used.

The engineering department of a TV station functions somewhat like its counterpart in radio, except the task in television is more than twice as complex — because the engineering department must have experts in both audio and video. In addition to maintaining increasingly sophisticated audio/visual equipment, each station needs a staff of engineers to handle film and tape transfers. The engineers must know how to operate and maintain complicated electronic image mixers, graphic equalizers, etc. Engineers also assist in racking filmed and taped material for intercutting with network feeds, etc. Anyone who has witnessed the master control room of a large network-affiliated station, with its elaborate mixing consoles, equipment racks, multiple screens and supporting hardware can well appreciate that engineers perform complicated tasks to keep the station on the air.

The office operation of a television station is comparable to that of a large radio station or other business concern which must find efficient ways to handle such departmonts and functions as personnel, accounting, research, legal affairs and community relations. Note that I did not mention music. Television stations normally do not have music "departments" or music directors. The music used on television at the local station level normally arrived by mail, imprinted on tape.

CABLE TELEVISION

While conventional stations and networks may continue to dominate television for a few more years, it is now clear that *alternative* TV delivery systems will capture large shares of the audience. Some observers believe the rapid expansion of the number and kinds of "new" delivery systems could actually eliminate most conventional TV stations and networks by the 1990s.

Television today has developed a whole new language, what the *Los Angeles Times* calls "cablespeak." Here is a list of some of the more common terms for this television era:

Basic Cable — For a moderate monthly fee this service brings into the home, via cable, traditional broadcast stations, public access channels, some cable-only networks, superstations and certain other channels.

DBS — Direct broadcast satellites are intended to beam programs directly into the home from communication satellites, bypassing both conventional TV broadcasts and cable systems. This service is expected to be available in the mid-1980s.

MDS — Multi-point distribution services send out pay-TV programming by microwave. This is for homes not connected to a cable system.

MSO — This acronym stands for "multiple system operators." These firms own more than one cable system. The 10 largest MSO's account for about 35% of the nation's cable subscribers.

Pay Cable — This service is cable-only pay-TV provided by such networks as the Time Inc. HBO system. Pay-cable programming is comprised largely of movies. Some pay TV networks also offer original shows including night club acts, sporting events and plays.

Public Access — The FCC has required cable TV firms to provide individuals and special interest groups opportunities to get on the air for minimum cost. Unknown performers, producers and directors can, for less than $50 an hour, take over a cable TV studio and present their talents to the TV audience. The hourly fee includes the studio and basic equipment, scheduled on a first-come, first-served basis.

Public access TV affords aspiring writers, performers, directors and producers a unique opportunity to test their talents and learn their craft.

STV-ON-TV — These are not cable channels, but subscription TV services. Scrambled signals are broadcast by conventional TV stations, then unscrambled by special equipment attached to the home TV set. STV-ON-TV firms broadcast movies, sports and special events.

Superstations — We have a handful of independent stations (non-network) whose signals are transmitted via satellite to cable TV systems.

Cable and subscription TV firms believe they can attract a sufficient number of paying viewers to finance programs pointed toward smaller, specialized audiences interested, for example, in opera, Shakespeare plays or chamber music. This kind of programming is referred to as *narrowcasting*. Persons impatient with the type of television produced for the mass audience eagerly await opportunities to enjoy programs addressing their individual tastes.

PRODUCTION

Networks are receiving increasingly strong competition, not only from alternative broadcast delivery systems, but from special independent program producers intent on capturing a large share of all video audiences. Some new TV programming has come from the audio record companies who have turned out video promotion tapes for their contract artists. While record promo tapes are sometimes linked together and broadcast in Europe as complete programs, the practice has not caught on in this country.

More attractive than record promo videotapes are the programs now being created for pay-TV and home videodiscs and cassettes. In the early 1980s, a TV software producer received $300,000 to $400,000 from a pay-TV firm for about two-weeks' use, during which period the broadcaster could program the material as often as he liked. Following this kind of licensing to pay-TV companies, the software producer then offered his material for manufacture and sale in the form of home videocassettes and videodiscs. Additional income was generated through licensing of this material to commercial airlines for in-flight entertainment.

THE MUSIC-VARIETY SHOW

Most employment for musicians in television comes from underscoring and from networks' music-variety programs. Concerning the latter category, the normal pattern is for a network to come up with the money to finance a particular show or series, then engage an independent producer or production company to actually package the entertainment. *Sometimes the sequence is reversed:* an independent producer or production company puts up the money, packages the entertainment, then tries to persuade a TV network or pay-TV firm to buy it.

THE PRODUCTION LINE — Whatever the financing and production plan, a network music-variety program requires the services of a large number of talented artists and business people. Here is a typical sequence of activity, which we might call the music production line:

1- The producer contracts the director, writers and performers.

2- The producer schedules a series of meetings to decide what music is to be programmed and who is to perform it. These decisions are made by the individuals invited to the production meetings: musical director, writers, choreographer, featured performers and art director. Star performers will probably bring along their own personal musical directors, perhaps their personal managers.

3- The musical director meets with the special material writers, music coordinator and featured artists to set music routines — style, key, sequence, length, etc. The music is then sketched for full scoring later.

4- The music coordinator, often doubling as the rehearsal pianist, will rehearse the featured performers, using musical sketches, confirming keys, routines, etc.

5- The musical director hires arrangers to score the charts for the orchestra, unless he has time to do some of this himself. But the musical director is usually too busy attending production meetings to write all his own charts.

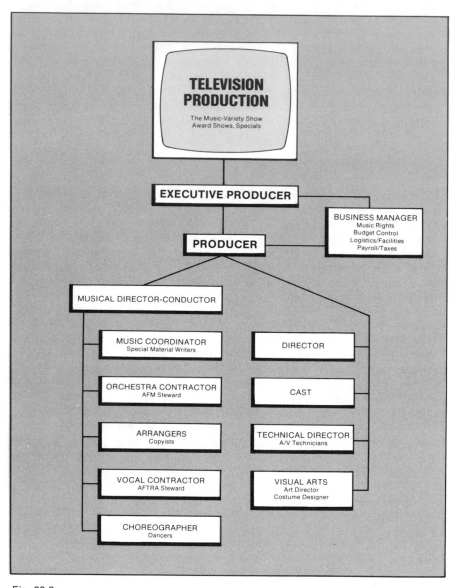

Fig. 23.2

6- If background singers are to be used, the musical director will probably hire a choral director to score the charts for the singers, hire the singers and rehearse them separately from the orchestra.

7- The arrangers hire copyists or a music preparation company to extract the parts for the instrumentalists and singers, run off multiple copies as needed, bind the scores, set up the books and deliver them to the studio for rehearsal and recording. The supervising copyist will attend the recording sessions and serve as music librarian. He will almost certainly be called upon to correct mistakes in the parts, even re-orchestrate a passage if need be.

8- Meanwhile, the musical director has hired an AFM contractor to engage the individual musicians who are to comprise the studio orchestra. The contractor and supervising copyist develop a list of "doubles" — the musicians in the orchestra who will be required to play more than one instrument. The contractor then notifies the doublers what additional instruments to bring to the sessions. This is particularly critical for woodwind players and percussionists.

9- The orchestra will prerecord most, if not all, of the show. Prerecording may be done to provide accompanying music for dancers. Featured singers may prerecord their voices too, particularly if they are called upon to dance when they sing.

10- After preliminary rehearsal, the background singers join the orchestra to record their tracks. Meanwhile, the audio engineers have been busy trying, not only to record the best possible orchestra-choral sounds, but coordinate live recording with prerecorded tracks. They are assisted in this effort by music cutters. Final master tapes are produced, which now include, not only music, but dialogue and sound effects.

The foregoing process describes how the sounds are produced for broadcast. It leaves out how the music will "appear" on the screen. Television finds it difficult to engage the eye when music is telecast. Here we have further proof that McLuhan is mistaken in arguing that TV is primarily a sound medium. It is not. It is primarily a visual medium. And to engage the eye of the viewer, TV must move its images. In this respect, good TV is like good cinema: the most engaging scenes involve the movement of the subject, the camera, or both. But most musical performance is relatively static. Good television directors know this, and they will go to absurd lengths to entertain the eye during televised musical performances. Most TV producer-directors are action-oriented and are accustomed to moving actors around. They are afraid to arrest motion to permit the viewer to focus on the musical sound. To give at least the illusion of movement, they will keep their cameras traveling, they will call for a lot of lens changes and, as often as they can, they will use a secondary image showing dancers moving behind the singer. Even these devices are considered inadequate. Directors will then take these images and split the screen electronically and/or optically, offering the viewer a kaleidoscope. When the eye becomes engaged with these events, the ear seems willing to accept almost anything. This accounts for so many actors and entertainers getting by on television as "singers." Really good singers can hold a TV audience without all these visual diversions, but even they are asked to move for the camera. TV choreographers are expected to create movements for non-dancers which are simple enough for them to pick up within an hour's rehearsal.

One of the reasons there is difficulty putting over straight musical TV performances is that television receivers have uniformly poor sound reproducing systems. TV music therefore lacks the fidelity and impact we are accustomed to through other media. Musicians pressure manufacturers to improve their TV audio systems. Manufacturers argue that their customers would probably be unwilling to pay the added cost for a good quality sound system in a TV set.

PRODUCTION PERSONNEL

In addition to the hundreds of musicians employed in television, the medium provides lucrative jobs for a variety of other personnel. Here follows a description of the individuals involved in the production of network and syndicated TV music-variety programs.

Executive Producer — This is the individual in charge of the whole undertaking and the one who then delegates responsibilities to his associates. An executive producer might well be the individual who has the financial backing for the program or the network support, or he may control a star who is to be featured.

Producer — If a program or series does not have an executive producer, the overall responsibility falls on the one simply called producer. He handles the major decisions relating to concept, budget, casting, writing and filming. The producer also has the task of licensing or selling the show he provides (if it has not been presold).

Associate Producers — Musical-variety shows have two to six individuals who execute the decisions of the producer and often make important decisions on their own in respect to such matters as minor casting, stage direction, scheduling, equipment rentals, filming remotes, rerecording, rehearsals, liaison with contractors — and anything else needed to keep the producer from going crazy. These helpers are called associate producers or production assistants. Some associate producers are merely gofors; others have more on the ball than their employers.

Director — Many TV shows, particularly news and special events, employ directors largely in a technical capacity. Such a director is responsible for calling shots he wants the video technician to punch in for actual takes. The director also instructs the floor manager in anticipating camera positions. He also supervises the lighting when needed. The director or his assistant times the segments of a show and, with the producer, supervises the final editing.

A director of a musical-variety show would delegate many of the foregoing kinds of technical supervision to an assistant director or technical director. In a production involving singers, dancers and actors he must focus his attention on their performances, block their stage movements and set camera shots. In this respect, a TV director functions like a film director.

Featured Performers — Singers, instrumentalists, actors and dancers who are cast as featured artists are engaged by the producer. The individual doing the hiring first tries to sign his stars, then he contracts for the supporting cast.

Musical Director — This person shares, with the producer and the director, the task of selecting material for the production, e.g., songs, dance music, underscoring, special material. The musical director also engages his arrangers, retains an orchestra contractor, conducts the orchestra and confers with the audio technicians If background singers are used, he will engage a vocal contractor.

Special Material Writers — Many shows engage composers and lyricists to prepare special routines for featured artists. Quite often these writers will prepare elaborate medleys, portions of which may include new music, new lyrics, bridges, patter, etc. These writers are hired by the producer or director or musical director. Most writers of this kind of special material learn their craft through experience on Broadway.

Music Coordinator — These persons assist the musical director in setting up music routines for featured artists. Sometimes they assist in locating obscure copyrights. They may assist communication among the musical director, his arrangers and the orchestra contractor. Most music coordinators have backgrounds as rehearsal pianists. If they do, they are called upon to help featured performers learn the charts. They may have participated in laying out sketches for the arrangers, setting keys, reprises, etc.

Music Editor — These individuals, sometimes referred to as "music cutters," are required whenever prerecorded music is intercut with either live music or newly-recorded tracks. They work with the other sound technicians in mixing music with dialogue and sound effects.

Songwriters — Except for the individuals hired to write special material (see above), songwriters and lyricists are not hired for TV shows. Rather, the songs used on programs are selected from material already available on the market or about to be released. A songwriter's entrée to television is through his publisher.

Composers — Those qualified to underscore drama or those who are able to compose effective music for dance routines are consistent-

Jy required for television. Musicians with these qualifications come from the ranks of established composers who perform most of their services for dramatic TV shows and feature films rather than variety shows.

Arrangers — Musical directors arrange music for their shows when they have time. But most of the scoring is done by free-lance arrangers hired by the musical director. All arrangers working on network shows are AFM members. Most of them work for AFM scale, which is high. The busiest arrangers can handle a variety of styles and they survive in this competitive field by being able to do top work, fast. Instrumentation, style, keys, overall length of charts are usually determined "by committee." This decision-making group will often include, besides the arranger, the music director, music coordinator, the star and perhaps the star's own musical director.

Copyists — Network shows use a great quantity of music, nearly all of which is in manuscript form. The musical director or the arrangers hire copyists to extract the individual parts. Because of the volume of work and pressure of time, arrangers usually engage a supervising copyist who in turn hires other copyists to assist him in meeting deadlines. All network TV shows use AFM members exclusively for copying, proofreading and library work. Much of this work is assigned to music preparation services, firms that assume the full responsibility of getting the music ready for performance.

Orchestra Contractor — This person is hired by the musical director to engage the individual musicians comprising the studio orchestra. The contractor is the union steward for the AFM and is responsible for seeing to it that the terms of the contract between the producer and the AFM members are carried out. In addition to engaging each instrumentalist (only AFM members are used) and supervising adherence to AFM work rules, the contractor is responsible for making out the payroll, calculating wages, deductions and benefits. Finally, this individual must see to it that paychecks are available when due. The contractor also assists the union in collecting AFM fees for its members for reuse and new use of music recorded for the show.

Orchestra Musicians — These artists are hired by the orchestra contractor with the advice and consent of the musical director. These musicians are drawn from a select pool of artists who can play about any style, at sight, without mistakes. First readings often sound as well as actual takes. Most delays are to correct errors in the score or parts and to make adjustments suggested by the sound engineers. Only AFM members are hired for network TV shows.

Vocal Group Director — When background singers are used, the musical director hires a vocal group director to engage the individual singers. This person is usually one of the singers in the group. The vocal director may also be the vocal arranger, cooperating with the orchestra arrangers in laying out the charts for the singers. In addition to directing the group, he doubles as the AFTRA union steward. In that capacity, he performs tasks for AFTRA quite like those performed by his AFM counterpart: he sees to it that the singers are paid, that fringe benefits are covered, work rules followed, and fees for reuse or new use are paid the AFTRA members.

Background Singers — Variety shows often use background singing groups ranging in size from gospel trios to perhaps a 16-voice mixed chorus. The vocal contractor hires his singers from a select pool of artists who are able to sing, almost at sight, any style from Renaissance polyphony to blues. All singers hired for network shows are AFTRA members. Most of them have studied voice extensively and probably started acquiring their skills in ensemble performance at an early age in school and church choirs.

Background singers for TV can be classified in two groups. "Off-camera singers" can perform as described above, but do not have the physical appearance required by the producer to sing and move on camera. These singers are heard, not seen. The second group might be called "camera-ready" singers. Besides possessing the musical talents described above, these artists have the physical appearance acceptable for on-camera exposure. They understand stage movement and can respond quickly to instructions from the director or choreographer. A select number of this group are also trained as dancers, the performers who are known affectionately on Broadway as "the kids in the show." Some of these "kids," Broadway alumni, are pushing fifty, but they maintain an appearance acceptable to the producer. These versatile artists are the first to be called and the highest paid of their kind.

Choreographer, Dancers — Variety shows with adequate budgets will engage a corps of four to 16 dancers. As pointed out earlier, even if the corps has little to do as a dance group, most producers hold the view that wiggling bodies seen behind a singer help engage the attention of the audience. Most of the top choreographers and dancers come from Broadway. The most versatile among them are qualified to perform, with very limited rehearsal, dance styles ranging from classical ballet to jazz.

Audio Technicians — After a slow start, TV networks are beginning to catch up a bit with the sophisticated kind of audio mixing associated with the recording industry. Two or more audio technicians are used on TV musical shows to supervise microphone movement, mixing, remixing, equalization, and all the other maneuvers understood by the individuals in this elite fraternity. Some of the audio technicians possess strong musical backgrounds. Others have strengths, perhaps even university degrees, in electrical engineering. Producers put together a combination of such talents to get the sounds they want.

Other Personnel — Network productions using music require the expert services of many other artists and technicians, but they relate only indirectly to music — art directors, scenic designers, lighting directors, costume designers, etc.

TV networks and production companies assign a *production manager* to handle business affairs. His duties would include budget control, logistics, securing of facilities and equipment, accounting, payroll, taxes and insurance.

ARTISTS UNIONS

Except for local stations, all instrumentalists, arrangers, copyists and musical directors employed in telecommunications are expected to be members of the AFM. Singers, dancers, actors, directors, writers and announcers are members of their respective unions or guilds.

The AFM has a number of different contracts with TV stations, networks and producers:

Local Television is under the jurisdiction of individual AFM locals, provided the musicians' services are broadcast live or "live-on-tape," not TV film.

Network and Syndicated Shows (live and live-on-tape) are controlled by contracts negotiated by the AFM's *National Contracts Division* and the employers (networks, producers, syndicators).

TV Film (not videotape) work is controlled by national contracts (covering the USA and Canada) which are negotiated by the AFM *National Contracts Division* and the film producers association. This national contract also covers musicians' work on theatrical films.

TV Commercials are covered by yet another national contract. It is discussed in my chapter on music in advertising.

Home Videocassettes, Discs — The AFM has taken the position that home video software is a "new use," and producers are not permitted, under present contracts with the musicians, to lift taped music from one medium and apply it to a new use such as home video programming. The union has also sought a share of royalties generated from home video media. The AFM and software producers have had difficulty working out a blanket contract for this sector of the industry.

AFM contracts tend to set the pace for other artists unions active in television, particularly AFTRA and SAG, in respect to wages, working conditions and benefits. As with the AFM, these other artists unions have sought some kind of royalty sharing of the income software producers receive from home videocassettes and discs.[3]

3-National contracts covering AFM members' services in television provide payments to musicians ranging from 5 percent to 45 percent of union scale when a program is syndicated *outside North America*.

HOME VIDEO

> The **marketing** of home videocassettes and discs was covered in my chapter on music merchandising. Before these products can reach the stores, the entertainment must be conceived and produced. In this chapter I shall attempt to place these events in sequence.

OVERVIEW

Any serious student of the arts and entertainment business has heard prognostications for years about home video — how it would wipe out conventional records and perhaps other modes of entertainment. Home video development has been "ready to explode" at any moment — and any musician or businessman unprepared for it was expected to find himself out in the street. Home Video did not exactly "explode," but it is true that anyone in the arts and entertainment field who remains unaware of this burgeoning medium may well be left far behind.

How fast is home video growing? How big a share of the entertainment dollar will it capture? A number of researchers and industry observers believe that by 1990, the dollars moving out of consumers' hands may reach $10 to $20 billion at the retail price level. If these crystal ball gazers are half right, home video activity by the end of the 1980s should surpass the record business in gross dollars.

Whether or not home video turns out to be bigger in the marketplace than the record industry, qualified observers are sure it will have a profound effect, not only on the record business, but *all modes of entertainment.* What will be the impact? Here is a synthesis of views of industry leaders, market analysts and investment banking institutions:

- *Home video and cable TV systems may make conventional TV stations and networks unnecessary.*

- *Movie theatres will suffer box-office erosion with the increasing use of home video.*

- *"Electronic delivery systems" for TV programs, whether via pay-TV, commercial TV, or satellite will be cheaper for viewers than buying (or renting) videocassettes and discs.*

- *By the end of the 1980s, home video products will probably contain less theatrical content and more "interactive" material.*

- *Over the long term, pay TV will have a favorable impact on the market penetration of videocassette recorders and a negative impact on the sale of videodiscs.*

- *Home TV that mimics commercial TV probably won't make it. Software producers must break new ground.*

- *In respect to counterfeiting, video products will suffer greater losses to the crooks than audio recordings.*

HOME VIDEO HARDWARE

Development of the market for home videocassettes and discs was delayed, in part, by the incompatibility of competing formats. Japanese, European and American manufacturers of video recorders and reproducers have invested tons of gold in an effort to persuade consumers their equipment was not only the best available, but destined to wipe out all competition. Neither the manufacturers nor the consumers really know which, if any, equipment now available will ultimately dominate the market.

In the early 1980s, VCRs (videocassette recorders) clearly led the hardware market. As pointed out, all research has indicated the number one attraction of VCRs has been their *time-shift capability*. VCR's early lead in the hardware market was matched by a comparable dominance in software sales.

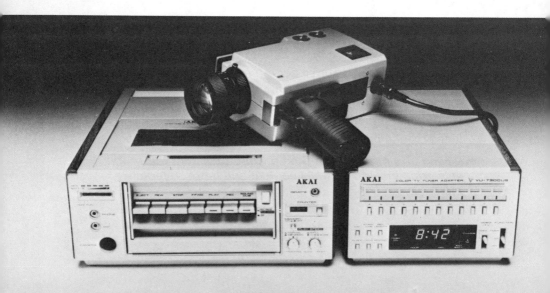

The Beta type of VCR was first on the market, and its proponents believe it offers certain technological advantages over its leading cassette competitor, VHS ("video home system"). The Philips company of the Netherlands has sought to offer Beta and VHS competition in the cassette field with its "Philips Video 2000" machine. While Philips employs one-half inch tape, as do its competitors, the Video 2000 cassette can be flipped over, as with a conventional audio-only cassette. Philips has pushed its machine strongly in Europe, claiming to be headed for at least one-half of that market.

Most videocassettes can record up to six hours of material. To achieve this, the recording tape speed must be slowed to a rate that impacts negatively on recording quality. Many consumers appear willing to sacrifice picture quality to gain the maximum recording time from a single cassette.

Those video fans particularly concerned with picture quality may opt for the *videodisc;* its proponents believe discs offer sharper pictures than cassettes. The first home videodisc was introduced in 1978 by Phlllps and MCA. It uses an optical scanner employing laser beam technology to "read" the information on the disc. Pioneer and Magnavox disc machines also use an optical (laser) scanning device and their machines are compatible. One clear advantage of optical scanners is that no stylus comes in physical contact with the disc. Consequently, videodiscs of this type, theoretically at least, do not wear out.

In 1981 RCA introduced its SelectaVision videodisc player with a very strong promotion campaign stressing the machine's availability for under $500. Engineers describe its technology as CED — "capacitance electronic disc." While the SelectaVision machine was introduced with a monophonic sound system, RCA promised it would follow with a machine with stereo capability for a slightly higher price.

Video systems in the development stage include PCM ("pulse code modulation") and VHD (which stands for "video high density").

In that a number of existing optical (laser) scanning systems are compatible, producers have found it advantageous to cooperate in promoting that medium. To facilitate these efforts, they have formed the *Laservision Association.* One of their goals is to encourage production of videodisc software which, they believe, will accelerate sales of their disc players.

PROGRAMMING

Music Rights — Every person in home video knows that the growth of the industry is dependent upon increasing the number and variety of available programs. For years, cable TV and home video software suppliers have depended heavily on feature films. But that backlog is a finite source. Many consumers have seen about as many golden oldie movies as they can stand.

In the early history of VCRs, market research showed that the number one seller among videocassettes was x-rated movies. Research indicated about one-half of videocassette player owners bought one to three porn movies, then moved on to more diverse kinds of entertainment.

All market researchers believe that the future of the home video industry lies in the production of new programs, not just replays of material borrowed from another medium. Programs created originally for home video have been slow to develop. Here are some of the reasons:

- *The market has been too small to justify budgets large enough to finance truly creative programming.*

- *Writers, directors and performing artists have held out for a share of the income generated by this medium.*

- *Producers have been uncertain how to handle music rights and copyright problems surrounding home video production.*

The video programmer in the early 1980s was often in doubt about how copyright law impacts on home video. Even the lawyers have not agreed on what the law requires; they have given conflicting advice to their producer and publisher clients. As pointed out earlier, cable TV is under a compulsory license, but videocassettes and discs are not. Rental of home video products is legal, but how are copyright owners compensated for rentals? What happens when a home video product is reproduced for a club or bar, as they frequently are? Who pays for the performance? What rights are violated when a videocassette sold for home use is televised over a commercial station, or bounced around the earth from a satellite?

The copyright act gives the purchaser of a home video product the right to do anything he wishes except duplicate it or show it publicly. But no one knows how to control the individual who permits other uses of an entertainment package intended only for home use.

As pointed out in my chapter on merchandising, manufacturers have attempted to deny merchants the right of renting home video products. But most lawyers believe such restraints are enforceable only on the first sale. So merchants find ways around the restrictions on rentals. Many observers believe manufacturers may have to abandon limitations on rentals and concede that their restrictive policy is unmanageable.

The Harry Fox Agency has offered help to music publishers when they are asked to license music rights for video. Fox emphasizes that copyright law requires videocassette and videodisc programmers to obtain, first, a right to record and synchronize the music to the production — a *synchronization license.* The publisher also must be asked to license the program manufacturer to *reproduce* and *distribute* copies of video productions containing music. Finally, Fox advises publishers that the software producer must obtain a *performance license,* either directly from the publisher or his performance licensing society, in anticipation of the video program material being performed outside the home, such as through cable TV.

Since the program producer-manufacturer can rarely anticipate all the uses his material may undergo, he is well-advised to secure the broadest possible music licensing rights from copyright proprietors.

A NEW MEDIUM

Musicians and record industry people are sound-oriented and tend to look upon videocassette and videodisc production as a matter of adding pictures to sound. It is doubtful that television audiences will be turned on by this kind of unimaginative entertainment. If recording artists are to make it on home video and cable TV, they will have to be presented to the audience by producers and directors who understand that *television is a visual medium.* Music should not be "applied" to video, it must be integrated, synthesized with the visual events.

Will musicians and record producers be able to make this switch from aural to visual thinking? Those with imagination will. The people turning out good home video entertainment have come largely from conventional television, film, and Broadway. It appears likely the demands of the market for original program material will foster the development of a new group of creative artists who approach this task unencumbered by ideas borrowed from other media.

One of the most useful tools for this new breed of producers will be digital computers used for "image processing." This computer-assisted imagery offers what can be called "visual synthesis." It can provide an unlimited number of image choices and visual combinations.

Video programs will also involve the increasing use of the art of animation. Hollywood animators are hard at work invoking the aid of digital computers to facilitate and expand their art and extend Walt Disney's techniques of combining animated figures with human actors.

Interactive TV — Another development in video entertainment is *interactive TV.* Viewers are already familiar with TV screen games that permit viewers to engage in sports or wage imaginary war with "weapons" manipulated by the participants. TV game interaction with the viewer can be extended to music and variety programs, too. For example, a viewer who had just spent $50 for a videodisc and was disappointed in his purchase could vent his anger by "attacking" the performers with "weapons" he could call up and fire across the screen. Conversely, a viewer particularly pleased with a performance might manipulate his home screen, zoom in on his favorite performer, enhance the lighting, perhaps even prolong the applause following the performance. With interactive TV, the home viewer becomes, at once, a producer-director-editor and critic, creating his own entertainment fantasies.

Arp *Quadra*

24

MUSIC IN ADVERTISING

PERSPECTIVE

We lack agreement on who first thought up the idea of using music to sell things. It may not be unreasonable to imagine that, when the Indians sold the island of Manhattan for $24, they might have brought along a few tom-toms to help put the deal over. Probably the first memorable use of "commercial music" was the radio "jingle," "Pepsi-Cola hits the spot/Twelve full ounces/That's a lot." The early jingles jangled, and the "jingle" label is still used by the AFM and first-generation advertisers who created the monotonous commercials in the early days of broadcasting. The public simply calls them commercials, of course. Advertising agencies and broadcasters call them "spots."

As pointed out in my chapters on radio and television, it would be difficult to exaggerate the importance of broadcast commercials in the field of advertising. With radio, it is sounds that sell. In TV, it is pictures and sounds that move the goods and services, and musical sounds can often be more effective sellers than verbal ones.

Advertisers continue to experiment with different kinds of spots. One season, testimonial-types, or "actuals," are in high fashion. Another season, comedy spots are in vogue. Whatever the changing fashion, one type continues to hold favor over the years — the commercial with music. Current thought holds that audiences will receive a musical commercial with little resentment, because it seems less of an interruption of the entertainment. A sounder reason, so to speak, is that ad copy that is sung is easier to remember than copy read cold. Yet another advantage of the musical spot is that audiences learn a sponsor's theme music and remember the tune and the association long after the broadcast is over. When an advertiser can find a composer to write music that sticks in the listener's head, and if the listener associates the music with the product, that sponsor is fortunate indeed. This happens often, and sponsors continue to pay for music in advertising, knowing that it is money well spent.

Writing music and lyrics for commercials is one of the most lucrative forms of music employment available. Additionally, the spot field at the local level affords good opportunities for talented, but unknown, writers to break into the commercial field. At the national level, sponsors and agencies are willing to pay fees large enough to attract hit songwriters and alumni from Broadway. Commercials were a starting point for such successful musicians as Jim Webb, Roger Nichols, Barry Manilow and Paul Williams. The huge hit for The Carpenters, *We've Only Just Begun* by Roger Nichols and Paul Williams was originally for a Crocker Bank commercial in California. Many other songs, originally scored for commercials, have been recast and have gone on to considerable success as popular songs.

MUSIC USES

The musical commercial described above can be called "thematic," the composer's goal is to form in the listener's mind a memorable association of the melody with the product. When the melody includes words identifying the product name, it is even more memorable, often inseparable in the listener's mind. Advertisers call this phenomenon "product identification."

Another use of music with commercials involves music underscoring dramatic action. Many commercials are conceived as little plays, and music is used to help create the appropriate mood or perhaps to punch up action. If the minidrama is comedic, the music may be scored in a style associated with movie cartoons, known as "Mickey Mouse."

Sometimes commercials will simply borrow music from another source. The melody may already be familiar to the listener, but the original words are discarded and new language is written to convey the advertising message. If the producer wants to borrow a copyrighted melody, he must obtain permission from the copyright owner to alter the material and use it for advertising purposes.

Another type of musical commercial might be called "starbased." A well-known person offers, by acting or singing or dancing, a "testimonial" for the sponsor. The advertiser assumes the audience will be persuaded to buy the same product the star "uses." Original music is composed for the star.

Music on commercials is sometimes sung by amateurs when an

advertiser wants to give the impression that ordinary people, "just folks," use the sponsor's product. This amateur-type of singing commercial developed in the 1960s concurrently with the popularity of folk and rock styles. The goal often seems to be to attract the ear of the listener by giving the impression that the singer just walked in off the street and is no different from his audience. To effect this nonprofessional singing style, or community-sing style, producers will instruct professionals to sing in unison, forget their voice training, and harmonize naturally, as if they were singing around a campfire. Sponsors attracted to this kind of natural singing have included Coca-Cola, Pepsi-Cola and Continental Airlines.

Music budgets for commercials range from $25 for a "needle drop" to perhaps $25,000 for an elaborate national campaign. One of the reasons the spot business is so good for musicians is that even hometown local sponsors like to massage their egos by purchasing their own theme music or product logo. Many composer-directors of limited experience break into the music spot business through low-budget jobs sponsored by the local furniture store or car dealer. That is true of local radio advertising. In local TV, custom music is rarely bought, because the small-budget sponsor must assign his dollars to production of the visuals. If the local TV advertiser wants music, he will probably use what pros still call "needle drops," a hangover phrase from the days when radio transcription libraries licensed broadcasters to a one-time, nonexclusive use of canned tracks available on 16-inch discs, before tapes were available. If an advertiser also uses local radio spots, he may lift portions of the audio tracks and transfer them to video use, thus drawing extra mileage from the money he originally invested in custom music for his radio campaign.

Nearly all local broadcast spots have limited budgets for music. But national campaigns often spend huge sums for custom music. Network campaigns are usually produced in New York, because that is where most national advertising agencies have their headquarters — and these giant firms control most advertising in this country.

STATION LOGOS

One of the most widely-used types of musical commercial is the station logo or "ID." Most radio stations and many TV stations hire an independent production company to create for them a musical "trademark" or fragment of sound which is used whenever the station announces (or shows on the screen) its call letters. Most station logos feature a small vocal ensemble. Increasing numbers of them use electronically synthesized sounds, for they are less expensive than a full orchestra. Logos are often 10-seconds long, but vary in length from a few seconds to thematic types of extended duration. The latter, sometimes called "image-type" logos, function more as theme songs and can be broadcast full-up or in the background for voice-over announcements. Wealthy stations, such as KHJ-Los Angeles, use a whole series of musical ID's, played frequently enough for the listener to learn to associate the music with the station and its call letters. For many years, the center of production of station logos has been Dallas, Texas, particularly the *T.M. Productions* company. One of the most active spot producing areas is San Diego, California. Many national advertisers prefer to have their spots produced in New York City.

THE AGENCY ROLE

Most advertising is handled through advertising agencies. These firms range in size from one-man, office-in-your-hat operations to super giants like J. Walter Thompson, whose annual billings just in broadcast media total over $300 million. Most sponsors prefer to place their radio and TV spots through ad agencies because, theoretically, the service doesn't cost them anything. Except for out-of-pocket production expense, the sponsor does not normally pay its ad agency to service the account and place its business — the ad agency receives nearly all of its fees, not from the sponsor, but from the medium in which it places its client's advertising. These fees are actually called commissions, the standard rate being 15 percent. For example, if the ad agency places $1 million worth of business with CBS TV, the network discounts the billing to the agency $150,000. When an ad agency undertakes to produce for its client a series of commercials, it will be billed, say $100,000 in production costs for such items as studio rental, actors, composers, etc. The agency, in turn, bills its client for that $100,000 and adds 15 percent for its commission. The sponsor and the agency may agree, before starting a relationship, that certain kinds of services are noncommissionable.

Sponsors retain ad agencies on the theory that companies that specialize in marketing know more about how to sell things than the manufacturer. Many small and medium-sized sponsors maintain in-house "advertising agencies" where their own employees conceive, produce and place the company's advertising. But even in-house "agencies" will often retain an external agency to assist it in spot production and media buying.

An advertising agency — a competent one, that is — offers important services to the sponsor who wants to use broadcast media. Probably the most valuable of these is creativity, that much-abused word. That term, freely translated, when used in this context, means that the sponsor leans heavily on its ad agency to conjure, invent, borrow or steal ideas to sell things. People in music and advertising often use the word "concept" to describe an advertising approach or selling angle. Some people use the word "hook" in the same way. Most ad campaigns seek some unifying ingredient or premise.

An advertiser determines what he can spend in one year for advertising, then retains an ad agency to offer advice on what part of that ad pie should be sliced for broadcast commercials. Once the radio and TV ad budget is agreed upon, the agency uses that money to implement the campaign, which is based on the advertising concept the client finds acceptable. If the ad agency is very large, it will have on its staff a radio/TV production department and its own in-house staff of writers. Large agencies also often have, in-house, their own small recording studios. While it is rare that even the largest agencies will attempt to record masters involving music in-house, they will often use their own facilities to produce demos and voice tracks.

The ad agency's next task is to farm out to others what it cannot handle in-house. This would normally include rental of filming studios, set design, acting, music and editing. Even the largest agencies will normally go outside their own shops for music. Many agencies do retain on their creative staffs individuals with some competence in music, particularly in the composition of lyrics and other kinds of copy intended for musical setting. But even here, professional composers find that a high percentage of agency-written "lyrics" or music texts are pretty awful. We hear their awkward efforts even on network spots — unnatural accents, too many words, almost unsingable phrases. These writers receive these assignments because they are cheaper — they are already on the agency's writing staff. But many of these copywriters lack qualifications to write words for music.

After the production work is completed, the agency has the responsibility of recommending to its client how and when the spots should be placed. They join with the sales departments of stations and networks to work out the best possible times, frequencies and geographic coverage. Once the client and the agency agree on these matters, the agency instructs its "media buyer" to purchase the time and the spots go on the air. Once a campaign starts, a competent agency will monitor the results of the campaign. Broadcast sales departments assist in this. If the campaign appears to be selling effectively, the sponsor will be advised to stay with whatever happens to be working. If the results of the broadcasting campaign are disappointing, the sponsor may change the commercials — or it may fire the agency. Accounts come and go. Alliances in advertising survive only as long as the sponsor is satisfied with the results he is getting.

ADVERTISING MARKETS

Advertisers attempt to focus their messages on definable groups of potential customers. As in the record business, these groups are called "markets." Identification of those advertising markets is achieved, or at least attempted, through the same kind of demographic research conducted by radio and television stations. As a matter of fact, sponsors, ad agencies and broadcasters cooperate in this research for they share the same goal, maximum profit. This shared research produces data similar to, but not identical with, the categories used in the recording industries. Sponsors of broadcast commercials try to reach one or more of the markets described on the following pages.

Children — Affluent societies provide children spending allowances, and advertisers try to influence young buyers almost from infancy. Advertisers also try to persuade children to encourage their parents to patronize the advertiser. A good example is McDonald's hamburgers. That firm addresses much of its advertising to kids, believing the youngsters can often persuade their parents where the family should go to eat.

Youth — The 12- to 19-year-old group has billions to spend in affluent societies. Advertisers go after not only this money, but show keen interest in trying to establish habits among teenagers that may well stay with them as they mature into adulthood. Among the strongest believers in this indoctrination theory are automobile manufacturers.

Adults — All research indicates the biggest spenders are the young homemakers. About half of the American households have two wage earners. This creates some "discretionary" income for the variety of goods and services needed by young homemakers. From the mid-1970s, advertisers, including publishers and record companies, observed that the number of teenagers was dropping and the size of the young adult and middle-aged populations was growing. The music industry and the advertisers continue to adjust their use of music in response to what we might risk calling "maturing musical taste."

Geritol Set — Mature adults, say, age 45 and older, have identifiable spending tendencies, e.g., blood tonics, laxatives, etc., and advertisers with such products and services hire the kind of music — usually MOR — that tends to attract their money.

Females — Girls and women spend most of the money advertisers try to get their hands on. Commercials addressed primarily to females, e.g., cosmetics, undergarments, household cleaners, infant care, etc., account for the largest share of the total advertising dollar. Individuals of masculine gender have traditionally produced most advertising campaigns. While their prevailing views of females may horrify liberated women, the male animal believes the most direct approach to attracting female spenders is through sex appeal. When ad agencies order music for "the female market," they usually ask for "something sexy." While composers have never been able to precisely identify just what degree of eroticism their creations might conjure, it is generally understood that what the sponsor wants is something that sounds soft and pretty. Which can't be all bad.

Macho — Advertisers believe in stereotypes in both males and females. Since men, whether straight or gay, buy most of the cars, trucks, stereos and beer, advertisers believe that "masculine-sounding" music will appeal to male vanity (generally believed boundless) and attract increased spending among those of the male persuasion. Here the advertiser orders up music nearly the opposite from the soft-and-pretty formula used for females. For the macho market he wants the music strong and forceful. Composers respond with big brass sections and male glee clubs barking energetically about the glories of Goodyear Tires. Sex-oriented commercials, male or female, may sound silly, but they sell.

Dumb — Research shows that the bulk of the audience appears to be, shall we say, unsophisticated. Advertisers relearn this every time they try to locate discriminating buyers. Advertisers aim most of their commercials at the lowest common denominator, the mass audience. They generally assume the mass audience is gullible, just not very bright. This accounts not only for much of the simple-minded copy we hear, but some of the lightweight music scored for the mass audience.

Ethnic — Racially or culturally identifiable market segments show up in demographic studies. About 15 percent of the broadcast audience seems to be persons of African descent. Advertisers try to buy music that is particularly appealing to this minority. Advertisers seeking an authentic "black sound" do not rely just on tokenism. The most convincing "black music" is scored and recorded by blacks.

Affluent — Fewer listeners are in the upper-income brackets. But when they spend, they spend big. Banks, insurance companies, steel merchants and computer companies try to gain the attention, not of the mass audience, but the purchasing agents, investors and managers within the mass who make the decisions regarding big spending. Advertisers believe, probably correctly, that this more affluent element in the broadcast audience is attracted by the sounds from big studio orchestras. Big ensembles just sound "richer."

Institutional — Large corporations spend millions on commercials in an attempt to inculcate in the public consciousness an image of the firm as an "institution." Advertisers seek to relate the corporate name with goodness, power, patriotism, stability. Producers engage large orchestras and choruses to help conjure up such aural images.

PRODUCTION

All advertising is concerned with persuasion. A number of theories have been propounded on the art. But all of them are related to the most widely accepted advertising formula, known in the industry as AIDA. That label should be easy for musicians, at least for those who have heard of Verdi. AIDA is an acronym for —

A *Attention*
I *Interest*
D *Desire*
A *Action*

WRITING COPY

It has been my privilege to be professionally associated with some of advertising's best writers. They not only agree with the AIDA philosophy, they make practical use of it — and go on from there. Additionally, top writers make these recommendations:

1- *Mention the sponsor's name as often as you dare.*

2- *Be economical with words. In radio, let the music say it; in TV, let the pictures "talk."*

3- *Use simple language.*

4- *Express one idea — again and again.*

One of the things done least well by advertising agencies, as pointed out, is writing copy to be set to music. It is astonishing how often even national accounts will accept music that is almost halted in its flow by the awkwardness of the words being sung. In preparing ad copy or lyrics for singers, the minimum requirement is to come up with language that permits a natural musical scan. If you don't manage this, your composer will have to set your words to unmusical rhythms.

SCORING MUSIC

If the copywriter submits lyrically-conceived texts, the melodic rhythm almost sings itself. Too often, agency copywriters lack musical sensitivity, and the composer must adjust the text to permit a rhythm that not only makes musical sense, but is naturally singable. Before starting to invent a melody, the composer must first scan the text to discover its natural speech accents. This should be accomplished by speaking the text aloud and observing on what syllables the speech accents in a phrase naturally occur. For example:

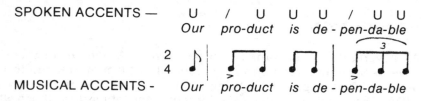

All texts for musical setting should be scanned in this manner to make sure they can be sung naturally.

A number of additional guidelines will be found useful by composers trying to get established in the commercial field. For example, words ending with consonants require tones of short duration:

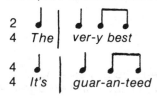

Words ending on vowels can have tones of long duration:

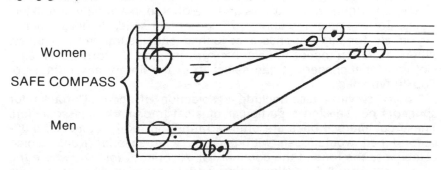

4/4 It's | all ——— for | you ———

4/4 Try ——— our | co-la ———

When composing music for commercials, the most successful musicians in the field appear to follow these guidelines:

1- *Melody should be simple, singable and memorable.*

2- *Harmony should progress, give a feeling of drawing the music forward. Stylistic consistency is essential.*

3- *Rhythm should be conceived in the musical style the producer ordered. He may be unable to describe what he wants, but he can suggest that the composer make it sound "like so-and-so."*

Instrumentation is largely determined by budget constraints. Inexperienced producers may ask for "a Stan Kenton sound." That's easy. But if he has a budget for a quartet, see if you can persuade him to settle for an imitation of the Beatles. Unlike much popular music-making, just about everything is written out for commercials. Improvisation is limited to appropriate liberties taken by the rhythm section. The arranger's main goal is to have his "front line" stay out of the way of the singers. The sponsor wants to hear the text, not the background. The cardinal rule for all arrangers scoring backgrounds for singers I learned while working for Nelson Riddle: stay out of their way. When in doubt: simplify.

Melodies appropriate for commercials have limited compass, usually one octave or less. The key for the singers must be very carefully determined. All else is sacrificed to provide the most comfortable, effortless tessitura for the lead singer. An easy working range for singing groups in the commercial field:

PRODUCTION COMPANIES

Commercial production companies specialize in radio or television, rarely both. Total production costs for national spots using music run from $25,000 to $150,000, with some going higher. These firms are typically staffed by a producer (or producer-director), a director (or director-cameraman), at least one cameraman, an art director, perhaps a graphic artist, two to perhaps six technicians (audio/video), office personnel and sales staff.

Musicians are engaged free-lance. These firms lease or own their own studios, which must provide room for at least three-camera production, sophisticated lighting, scenery/prop/graphics production, film and tape recording facilities, and A/V editing rooms. Wages to personnel and rental of facilities run to hundreds, sometimes thousands of dollars per day, depending on the extent to which the production company farms out part of the work. These are essentially video production facilities. Music is rarely recorded in them.

Companies outside of New York, Chicago and Los Angeles are typically smaller operations which serve local, regional and, occasionally, national accounts. They would probably have, in-house, a staff of two to five persons. Companies with small staffs may have modest TV filming studios or, more likely, they will rent shooting stages. Audio is recorded in recording studios, then later synchronized with tape or film.

Production companies specializing in radio commercials operate in dozens of cities, because their accounts are usually local and regional, not national. Radio spot firms range in size from one-man operations to an in-house staff of five to ten. Many have their own recording studios or ally with a recording studio by sharing offices and staff. These firms often have studios big enough to handle small choral/instrumental sessions. When a sponsor wants something on a grander scale, producers rent independent recording studios.

Firms involved in production often offer their clients complete programming services in whatever musical format the station wants — Top 40, MOR, Country, etc. In addition, full production houses also offer their clients music library services which include "commercial beds." They are 30- or 60-second music tracks that are arranged for use with whatever ad copy the station or advertiser wants broadcast These are original music tracks and are offered in a variety of musical styles. For example, the library would contain solid, dignified-sounding music for such sponsors as banks and insurance companies. When a station needs music background for a store advertising clothing for teenagers, it can select from the library any number of Top 40-type beds.

Library services also include a selection of "neutral" tracks for sponsors not seeking a particular musical trademark or association. These commercial beds are often arranged in three segments: a 60-second bed would open with perhaps a 20-second "front" which establishes the tone of the commercial. A "bridge" follows, where the music is less full in orchestration and less active in texture. This provides a musical background ("bed") that makes it easier for the listener to understand the ad copy being read. This copy can be read live by the disc jockey, or it can be prerecorded. Following this middle section, the remaining time, perhaps 10 seconds, is where the bed rises up, so to speak, offering a musical reprise of the front. This end section is often called the tag, a term borrowed from vaudeville. Tags return to the "up full" sound of the front.

Production companies can be engaged to add singers and custom copy to the front and tag sections of canned tracks of this kind. This radio commercial format was widely used in the 1950s through the early 1970s. Since the format became so predictable, more imaginative producers and advertisers now prefer a less pat format and have experimented with a variety of sequences of copy, music, reprises, cold copy, and musical trademarks.

Commercial producers, whether supplying custom spots or library services, regularly offer their clients "lifts." These are usually 10-second extrapolations from 60-second spots which were initially scored in anticipation of a short section being lifted from the full-length commercial. These lifts provide the sponsor with the option of buying 10-second time segments and having available spots of the appropriate length — with minimal additional production cost.

ARTISTS AND FEES

The creative and performing artists engaged to produce commercials range in talent from minimal to brilliant. A correlation is often found between the level of competence and the size of the market. Since job opportunities are extensive even at the local level, producers and musicians of modest gifts often get hired — because they are aggressive or because they work cheap, perhaps both. Too many small market spots are of low quality, either for the reasons just cited, or because the local production personnel lack experience or sensitivity; they tolerate weak material and unprofessional performances because they may not know better. Still, most top people making it in major markets learned their craft in the small time, then developed the competence demanded in major markets.

In fairness to the individuals producing spots in small markets, it should be emphasized that they are usually compelled to try to turn out good work on shoestring budgets. Many a sponsor is willing to hire up to three artists, provided "You can make it sound like Henry Mancini."

Sponsors and agencies are accustomed to paying "creative fees" for music and texts. While some composers charge no creative fee and charge only for their arranging, copying and conducting, it is not uncommon for a spot composer to get paid a creative fee (for one piece of material) of $500 or more for a local campaign. At the national level, creative fees vary widely, from $2,000 to perhaps $15,000 for a "buy-out."

Until recent years, composers worked for ad agencies on a buy-out basis: as employees performing "work for hire," they gave up all copyrights in their work. Since about 1975, increasing numbers of agencies have contracts with their creative people which provide that *the composer retains copyright in the music* and assigns rights for use into perpetuity to the agency or the sponsor for advertising purposes only. This kind of contract, now being widely accepted, leaves the composer free to seek exploitation of his material in other media, particularly the pop song field.

Returning for a moment to further consideration of budgets for small markets, advertisers will often seek *package deals.* A composer-arranger scratches around for an assignment and discovers a prospective client who has, say, $1,800 for a musical spot. The musician agrees to take on the complete package for that fee: he composes the music, perhaps the text too, scores the arrangement, extracts the parts, rents the studio, engages the performers — and delivers the master tape to his client. If this packager could get away with using just one singer and a three-piece band, he might end up with $300 for himself for his two-weeks' labor. Or he might have budgeted carelessly, run overtime in the studio, and end up in the hole. In national campaigns, package deals are less common. But here, instead of one individual taking on the whole project, an ad agency will engage a music production house for a flat fee. This kind of company often figures its budgets on two levels: "above the line" costs (creative fees, "talent") and "below the line" costs (out-of-pocket expense such as studio rentals, scale payments to union artists, music copying, tape, etc.).

Many music production firms are owned, or partly owned, by the composer. Such houses will offer a client, for one lump fee, composition, text, arranging, orchestration and musical direction. Such fees for national accounts range from $2,500 to $10,000 for one job.

A producer or agency may locate a naturally gifted songwriter to do the creative work for a campaign. Some of these individuals may have attracted the attention of producers through their songwriting success on pop records. Many of these individuals are musical illiterates and are helpless without the aid of competent arrangers. They will often sing their tunes into a tape recorder, then hire an arranger to pull the music off the tape and render it in correct music notation. The leadsheet thus produced is then turned over to the arranger-orchestrator-director who is hired to score the music for the recording session.

ARTISTS' CONTRACTS

Singers, instrumentalists, arrangers and copyists employed on spots scheduled for national broadcast are members of their respective unions. The total dollars earned by AFM members working in the spot field exceeds, by about 30 percent, what union musicians earn scoring TV movies and theatrical motion pictures. No other field of employment is more lucrative, hour for hour, for musicians than working on commercials. The national contract covering AFM members in this field embraces both radio and TV commercials and governs the employment of AFM instrumentalists, musical directors, arrangers, orchestrators, music librarians, proofreaders and copyists. As with certain other AFM contracts, "leaders" (musical directors, conductors) receive 200 percent of a sideman's base pay. Instrument doublers make 30 percent extra for the first double, then 15 percent for additional doubles. If the orchestra contractor is an individual other than the leader, he, too, makes 200 percent of a sideman's wages.

The employer (who may be the advertising agency or the spot producer) must also pay into the AFM/EPW (Employers Pension and Welfare Fund). Some locals add surcharges for the benefit of their members working in the spot field. For example, if the producer records his spots in Los Angeles, Local 47 tacks on a surcharge for the employer to pay into Local 47's own Health and Welfare (H & W) Fund.

Nearly all instrumentalists and copyists work for scale, as do many orchestrators and leaders. However, with major national accounts, most orchestrator-leaders either charge well over union scale or earn extra money by charging a creative fee.

The AFM contract stipulates that the employer is responsible for additional payments to the musician for uses of the music following the initial 13-week period covered by the basic fees. For such extended use (starting with the 14th week) or for each spot dubbed into a new commercial or used in a new medium, each AFM member who was employed on the original project receives a good-sized additional payment. National advertising agencies and their sponsors are accustomed to paying these extended use (or "new use") payments, and musicians lucky enough to land this kind of work make very big money over the years. But at the local and regional levels, circumvention of extended use and reuse payments is common. Many local spots are straight buy-outs by the sponsor or his ad agency for all services creative and artistic. While this is convenient for all concerned, it yields far less income in the long run for the musicians. Many AFM locals simply fail to police and enforce their contracts; many just look the other way when their members record local spots.

Concerning singers on commercials, AFTRA claims jurisdiction over radio spots, while SAG claims jurisdiction in television. The firmness of AFTRA and SAG control over spot singers relates directly to the size of the intended market: agencies and advertisers generally adhere carefully to union scales for national campaigns and most regional campaigns. AFTRA and SAG control over singers and singing actors in local markets is spotty at best, frequently nonexistent.

As with standard recordings prepared for commercial release to the public, AFTRA has set, in the spot business, special scales for group singers (two or more), group singers who "step out" from groups, soloists, and leader-contractors.

As with the AFM, one of the most critical tasks AFTRA has is *obtaining reuse payments* for its members who have recorded spots that stay on the air beyond the initial 13-week contract period. Responsibility for payment of reuse fees may devolve on different persons, depending on the terms of the initial contract for the union artsts — and sometimes upon who can be located to meet their obligations to the union. As with the AFM, AFTRA artists may well receive more income via reuse payments than they do from the initial recording sessions. When singers receive conflicting calls for jobs, they will opt for the work that appears most likely to stay on the air beyond 13 weeks. More often, however, this cannot be predicted.

The singers who get hired to record national spots are usually drawn from that select pool of vocal artists described earlier. In addition to being able to sing almost any style and sight-read like demons, spot singers must excel at clear diction. The sponsor's first concern is not *bel canto,* but clarity of language. The composer may have scored music comparable to the *Hallelujah Chorus,* but the account executive may demand it be discarded in favor of a unison jingle if he can't make out the words.

Much of the foregoing account describes spot production at the fully professional level, legitimate, unionized and above board. But the fact is that a high percentage of *local market* spots are produced without regard for AFTRA, AFM and SAG. The composer-director may be an AFM member, his sidemen may also be union musicians, the singers may be AFTRA members. But the whole project may be produced and broadcast without ever satisfying union requirements for scales, particularly, reuse payments. On the other hand, our composer-director may pay the equivalent of union wages to his musicians, but sign no AFM or AFTRA contracts, thus avoiding the responsibility of paying reuse fees.

In addition to the professionals described above, budgets for broadcast commercials must provide for a number of additional personnel. Among the highest-paid are the producer-directors of network TV commercials. Many of these individuals learned their craft turning out industrial, educational, or theatrical motion pictures, then formed their own spot production companies. Top pros earn $30,000 to $100,000 a year. In respect to announcers and actors on radio spots, most of them work for AFTRA scale. Announcers and actors who perform on camera for TV spots are under the jurisdiction of SAG. Most of these artists receive union scale. Stars get whatever fees their agents can extract from sponsors. If a TV announcer or actor is heard but not seen on film, his services usually fall under the jurisdiction of AFTRA, not SAG.

PRODUCTION SEQUENCE

Production of broadcast commercials is an involved process. Here is how the events might fall in place for the production of a network television commercial where the budget for music is large. We will assume the advertising agency retains a production company to assist.

1- The sponsor instructs its advertising agency to come up with a

TV campaign for a new soap.

2- The account executive notifies his boss that the account is ready to spring for a sizable amount of money. The agency head notifies the agency's creative director. These two call a staff meeting and invite ideas for a hook on which the campaign might be hung.

3- The concept is decided upon and a production meeting is called. Agency staff attending: creative director (chairperson), writers, TV producer, art director, and the account executive.

4- This production committee creates a storyboard for the sponsor's approval. A TV storyboard is a visual representation, measuring perhaps 24" x 36", which shows rough drawings of the sequence of events scheduled to occur on the screen. That is the visual component. The aural components are indicated (dialogue, music) below each picture on the storyboard as captions, enabling the viewer to perceive an approximation of how the eyes and ears are engaged in the 30-second spot.

5- The sponsor likes the storyboard and accepts the advertising concept for the campaign.

6- The agency develops a detailed budget to cover cost of production. The sponsor says it's too high. The agency says, "But Mr. Doe, wait till you hear the music!" Mr. Doe says, "So let me hear it."

7- The agency's creative director or house producer issues what is known in the trade as a "cattle call": recognized commercial music composers and a few "music houses" (production companies) are invited to submit for agency approval appropriate music for the campaign theme music. Composers and houses needing work at the time will compose appropriate soap-selling music — good, clean sounds — on a demo tape, on spec. This means they may even pay for out-of-pocket expenses of recording the demo. Some ad agencies will pay for costs of demo production. The agency production committee selects its favorite demo from the spec demos submitted.

8- The sponsor hears the proposed music, complaining that "The music sounds too thin," but he likes the singer and the tune. After receiving agency assurances that the final production will be fully satisfying, the sponsor approves the music and the production budget.

9- The agency producer studies the casting books in his office which have been supplied to him by the leading artists' agencies. From 8" x 10" glossies in these books he selects half a dozen actors and actresses who might look right for his cast. He calls the agents representing the artists, arranges either live or videotape auditions of them, selects his actors, perhaps his on-camera singers in this way.

10- The producer dickers with the agents for acceptable fees, then gets the sponsor's approval of casting.

11- Meanwhile, back at the agency the creative director has rejected five versions of the script, then settles on a final draft.

12- The producer notifies his composer that the sponsor and agency people liked best track three on the demo and that the creative fee for music is $2,500. The composer accepts the fee, provided he can retain all publishing rights exclusive of the advertiser's uses of the music. Agreed.

13- The producer tells the composer that he has a production budget for a 20-piece orchestra and five singers and can they record tomorrow morning? The composer-musical director offers an opinion, unsolicited, on the mental capacity of the producer, offering two alternatives. One, they can record not before the day after tomorrow. Or, two, he offers a suggestion on what the agency can do with its commercial. The producer opts for the former.

14- The producer reserves Wondersound Studios for day-after-tomorrow, and is guaranteed his favorite engineer who can handle 24 sliders on the Studio A console. The producer accepts a telephone call from his musical director, reminding him that he will not record at Wondersound unless the studio can schedule his favorite engineer for the date. The producer, having learned this in previous outings, assures his musical director that he already has it set up that way.

15- The musical director calls up his regular AFM contractor and AFTRA contractor to engage the performers. He tells the AFM contractor that the two percussionists on the date will be expected to bring every instrument they can think of short of cannon traditionally fired in the *1812 Overture.* Agreed. The AFTRA contractor is asked to hire voices that will sound "legit" on the theme, but be able to do a soul version of the commercial for an alternative track to be used in the New York, Atlanta and Detroit markets. No problem.

16- Six hours before the recording date, the composer calls his music preparation service to pick up the score and deliver it, all parts copied, to Wondersound, Studio B for the vocal rehearsal at 9 a.m., and the orchestra parts at 10 a.m. in Studio A. Any questions? Just one: does the composer understand that AFM copying scale is double after midnight? He does, and tells the music preparation service to bill the producer accordingly. But right now, more urgent is the need to call a messenger service to pick up the score and deliver it to the copyists.

17- Our musical director-composer retires for four hours sleep.

18- The morning of the date, the AFTRA contractor-vocal director rehearses the singers for 30 minutes and they take a half-hour break, waiting for the orchestra to come in at 10 a.m.

19- The orchestra starts reading through the chart. The only delay is to correct some wrong notes, which the composer-arranger insists is the fault of the careless copyists. After the engineer gets an acceptable balance of the instruments and voices, the artists record Take One. Takes continue for the two hours budgeted and the artists leave for their next session down the street.

20- The musical director, producer and account executive select the best take and instruct Wondersound to deliver three 30 i.p.s. copies to the agency by 5 p.m. that same day.

21- The producer meanwhile has filmed all his visuals, processed his opticals, created a final edit, then proceeds to lip-sync his actors with the musical track. Following adjustments in the answer print, the complete commercial is ready for the duplication lab and distribution to broadcasters.

22- The agency's media guyer has secured air time for broadcast of the campaign on all three commercial networks. Because this sponsor agreed to a major outlay for production, the agency buys most of its exposure in prime time.

23- The AFM and AFTRA contractors submit bills to the agency. The agency volunteers the view that the artists are highly overpaid, then issues the payroll checks for distribution.

24- The AFM and AFTRA unions read in the trades that the campaign was a success and that the sponsor has bought an additional 13 weeks national exposure. The unions notify the agency that their members are now entitled to reuse payments to cover the 13-week extension. The agency offers an even stronger opinion of the union demands, then issues the checks.

POSTSCRIPT — The composer's contract with the agency granted to the sponsor music rights limited to use in advertising. This leaves the composer free to find a lyricist to set new words to the ad campaign's theme music, then submit it to a publisher. He does so. A publisher accepts the song, in the hope that he can get a free ride based on the current popularity of the music generated by the broad cast campaign. Everyone is happy, even the sponsor, who now enjoys additional identity through the popularity of the pop song version of his theme music.

P-15 Moviola upright film/music editing machine.

16mm film editor. Magnasync/Moviola console Model M-77

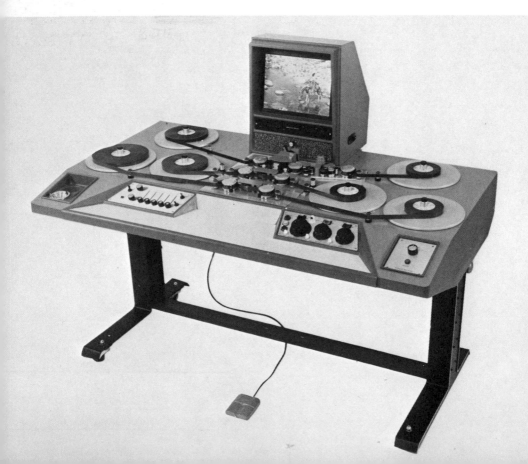

25

FILM SCORING

Many musicians consider film scoring as their ultimate professional goal. This may be because of the so-called "glamour" traditionally associated, at least in the past, with Hollywood. More likely, the stronger attraction is the money. The term "film" includes not just movies, but TV shows on film. Under the term "scoring" we include composition, arranging, orchestration, copying and recording. Professionals use the expression "film scoring" in reference to the preparation and recording of dramatic music intended to synchronize with action on the screen.

It is a cliché to say that, when an underscoring job is well done, it should go unnoticed by the audience. This is often true. But under some circumstances, that assertion makes as much sense as suggesting that the theatre audience enjoying a performance of the *Swan Lake* ballet should take no notice of Tchaikovsky's music. As a matter of fact, film composers have saved many a weak scene. The artistic contributions of our best movie composers often surpass those observed on the screen. As for public acceptance, it is not unusual for a movie sound track album to turn a bigger profit than the film itself. And some of the music scored for TV dramas will probably be remembered longer than the programs.

CANNED TRACKS

Before considering film and TV film underscoring, let's look at how music is used in educational films, documentaries, and movies produced for business and industry. Thousands of these films are turned out every year, and practically all of them use only canned music tracks. The reason is simple: low cost. A producer can underscore complete productions with "cues" (or "bridges") lifted from a canned music library (professionals use the term "cue" to describe the musical fragments scored to accompany dramatic action. They range in length from a few seconds to several minutes). Use of canned cues often creates an inartistic, even clumsy result, for the music, even when carefully selected, may not really match the picture. Most canned tracks sould like what they are — stuck on, cheap.

Library services (you can buy the whole catalog or pay for individual "needle drops") classify cues in predictable ways, e.g., "chase," "romance," "comedy," etc. Even "neutral" bridges are available. Length of these fragments is rarely critical, for the director can instruct his audio mixer to "get lost" (fade out the music) whenever the director wishes. Audio quality of canned cues is not considered critical either, by many persons. This is because the films we are talking about here are usually on 16mm or Super 8, media capable of reproducing only the middle band of the audio spectrum.

Few musicians find employment in this country preparing canned tracks, because library services have generally imported lost-cost tapes from Europe.

SCORING MOVIES, TV DRAMA

Theatrical movies and TV films rarely use canned tracks today, and the production of original, custom music to underscore these media provides high-paying jobs for hundreds of skilled musicians. The first music heard by the public on a sound movie sound track occurred in 1927 when vaudevillian Al Jolson broke into song in the middle of a film titled *The Jazz Singer.* The public loved it, and very quickly the producers began adding music and audible dialogue to their movies. At first, they simply borrowed music from other sources — Broadway, Beethoven, Liszt, Tin Pan Alley. Producers also had classical composers score original music. The list includes nearly all prestigious composers of this century with the exception of Stravinsky and Schoenberg: Erik Satie, Darius Milhaud, Arthur Honegger, Paul Hindemith, Dmitri Shostakovich, Serge Prokofiev, Mario Castelnuovo-Tedesco, Virgil Thomson, Ralph Vaughan Williams, Ernst Toch, Aaron Copland and Leonard Bernstein. This distinguished group produced a Pulitzer Prize (for Virgil Thomson's score for *Louisiana Story*) and an Academy Award Oscar (to Aaron Copland for his score to *The Heiress*). This particular group of composers has worked at film scoring only sporadically; most movies have been scored by composers who work in the field full-time.

The period of the 1930s and 1940s is known to film music buffs as "The Golden Age." All the major studios in Hollywood — MGM, 20th Century-Fox, Paramount, Columbia, Warner Brothers and RKO — had composers on salary full-time. Each major studio had a staff orchestra of almost symphonic proportions. Composers and producers in this Golden Age required these huge ensembles because the preferred musical style was neo-romantic. Producers would instruct their composers that they wanted music to sound like Tchaikovsky, Rachmaninov or Debussy. Leaders in the neo-romantic style were Alfred Newman, Franz Waxman, Bronislau Kaper and Miklos Rozsa (although the latter broke nineteenth century bonds in such period pictures as *Ben Hur*). These scores sound European because most of these composers were either from Europe or trained only in European styles. In rehearing these movie scores on the TV late show, some of them sound embarrassingly outdated.

CHANGING STYLES

Tastes began to change after World War II. In the 1950s, a number of first-rate movie music composers began to abandon the musical clichés that had helped buy their Beverly Hills swimming pools. They began to experiment with more contemporary American sounds. The leaders in this break from European romanticism included Hugo Friedhofer, David Raksin, Jerome Morros and, later, Bernard Herrmann, Alex North and Henry Mancini.

Composers of both the European and American traditions were influenced, until the 1960s, by techniques exploited by composers scoring music for movie cartoons, e.g., *Popeye the Sailor, Mortimer* (later changed to *Mickey*) *Mouse*, and Disney's *Silly Symphonies*. Producers wanted their composers to use a technique known as "catching action": if Mickey Mouse slipped on a banana peel, the composer was expected to underscore the action with a trombone glissando. When the Good Guy discovered The Bad Guy lurking in the shadows, the orchestra was expected to play what is still known in the business as a "stinger," a sforzando chord. Remnants of the old Mickey Mouse style of scoring remain here and there, but a film composer using it today can sound silly, because audiences have long since memorized these clichés.

Many of the early comedies, usually two-reelers, underscored the entire movie with a popular song droning in the background, even under dialogue. Of a higher artistic order was the practice in the 1930s of hiring Broadway and Tin Pan Alley composers to write songs for feature films. Some of these early "Hollywood musicals" spawned a fair share of the standards we know today.

The more recent discovery by film producers of the value of a good popular song occurred in 1949, when the main theme from *The Third Man* film, featuring a zither, hit the pop record charts. The message was not lost on other film producers who searched for "film composers" who could turn out hits for them to stick into their feature films.

And stuck in they were. To this day, audiences appreciative of good drama are affronted by intrusions of pop songs grafted onto sound tracks without regard for their suitability. Producers, many of whom possess the artistic sensibilities of an amoeba, hold to these rude interruptions in their films in the hope that, if the movie bombs at the box office, they just might recover their negative costs through exploitation of the score on pop records. They are sometimes right.

Composers of the old school were horrified at this pop invasion and complained that the art of film scoring was getting lost. To a large extent, they were correct. To compound this gross affront, the older film composers began to lose a lot of scoring work to the pop songwriters.

With the pop invasion, movie "composers" began to be classified in one of two categories — those fully qualified to underscore drama on film, and the pop songwriters, most of whom had not even heard of a click track. But by the 1960s, a third type of film composer emerged — comprised of a handful of artists who could not only underscore film drama appropriately, but also invent attractive melodies that could be pulled from a sound track and popularized on hit records and sheet music. This kind of versatility was new to the movies, but hardly unknown in traditional music — Mozart, Verdi, Bizet and many other theatre music composers knew how to underscore drama, then follow with a popular-type song as the occasion might demand.

Composers since c. 1960 who have enjoyed the greatest popular acceptance of their underscoring and melodic inventions include Maurice Jarre (for "Laura's Theme" from *Dr. Zhivago*), Francis Lai (theme from *Love Story*) and John Barry (for the pop hit from *Born Free*). To some ears, music that sounds this precious strikes the senses like spilt perfume.

Two other film composers, Henry Mancini ("Moon River" from *Breakfast at Tiffany's*) and particularly Michel Legrand (e.g., theme from *Summer of '42*, "Windmills of My Mind", etc.) manage to underscore their pictures with beautiful melodies when the occasion calls for them, yet hold the respect of musicians of sophistication.

One of the most significant stylistic turns in the evolution of film scoring began in the 1950s with the introduction of jazz elements. Probably the first feature film score to show clear signs of jazz influence was Alex North's music for *A Streetcar Named Desire* in 1951. One of the earliest extended uses of jazz in a feature-length theatrical film occurred in 1955 with Elmer Bernstein's *The Man With The Golden Arm*. Bernstein used ingenious combinations of symphonic and jazz-like elements. The film concerned drug addiction; many film producers of subsequent films dealing with drug abuse demanded that their pictures be underscored with jazz.

Further impetus to the use of jazz underscoring came from television. In 1959, movie producer Blake Edwards hired film composer Henry Mancini to score his new TV whodunit, *Peter Gunn*. It was agreed that Mancini would use a "big band" instrumentation playing driving jazz. It was particularly appropriate for this series, because the big city chase scenes seemed to call for the frenetic energy of jazz. It worked so well, TV and movie producers now began an earnest search for jazz composers. Another TV series about that time, *Route 66,* with a superb jazz-oriented score by Nelson Riddle, gave further impetus to the increasing popularity of the use of jazz elements for underscoring contemporary drama. Only a handful of the first generation movie composers could (or would) make the transition from European romanticism to Afro-American styles. So a new generation of film composers emerged who could do both dramatic underscoring and contemporary jazz. Some came off the road from name bands and found new homes (big ones) in Hollywood. Lalo Schifrin, European-trained but very creative in jazz styles, could not only handle dramatic underscoring, but occasionally score an entire film using improvised jazz (*The World of Insects*). For this film he brought to the scoring stage just some sketches, tone clusters and 12-tone rows, then instructed his small chamber orchestra to improvise freely on these fragments.

The best of the "second generation" of film composers (Henry Mancini, Nelson Riddle, Lalo Schifrin, Earl Hagen, Michel Legrand) continue to score movies and television. But in the late 1970s, a "third generation" of movie music writers emerged. This group includes such outstanding creative talents as Dave Grusin, John Williams, Jerry Goldsmith, Patrick Williams and Quincy Jones. Each of these composers has had extensive musical training, acquired through college studies or with private teachers.

For many years, a high percentage of successful film composers studied with the distinguished Italian-born composer, Mario Castelnuovo-Tedesco, himself a successful film composer in Hollywood. His roster of students, dating from the late 1940s, has included Henry Mancini, André Previn, George Duning, Lionel Newman, Jerry Goldsmith and Nelson Riddle. Tedesco's unique gift to his students was in the art of orchestration. Those of us who were privileged to study with him learned "transparency" in scoring ("windows for the ears"), a technique particularly suitable for film scoring where the composer must avoid covering dialogue.

The luminescence of the best film music, sometimes called "the Hollywood sound," can be largely attributed to the orchestration techniques Tedesco imparted to his students and their imitators. Probably Tedesco's most brilliant student of orchestration, Nelson Riddle, has applied these scoring techniques to his arrangements on dozens of hit albums featuring Frank Sinatra, Nat Cole and Ella Fitzgerald, among others.

Today's composers for film and television not only have strong backgrounds in traditional music and jazz, but invest their scores with the best of rock and electronic sounds. These amazingly versatile composers can score a period movie or a contemporary urban drama, creating music appropriate to the dramatic purpose. If jazz and rock seem to dominate their work, it is because the current fashion favors contemporary dramas set in urban centers, where The Bad Guys often seem to outnumber The Good Guys. In these contemporary scores we seem to have what Gershwin searched for as early as 1924 with his *Rhapsody in Blue.*

Gunther Schuller suggested in the 1950s that we might think of the classical tradition as one stream, jazz a second stream — and when the two flowed together, forming a confluence, we could call the result "Third Stream" music. We have disagreement about whether the idea should even be attempted. But whatever its aesthetic validity, the best film composers today borrow naturally, without inhibition, from the whole world of music — western, eastern, Afro-American — and it seems to come out "American." The best of it probably has more aesthetic value than the fragments coming from the post-Webern serialists and the alleged avant-garde.

The contemporary school of film composition employs the same stylistic approach for feature films as for movies produced for television. Most of the composers work in both media, but they prefer theatrical film scoring because they are allowed more time to write and it pays much better. The most successful film composers will also accept TV dramatic scoring jobs during periods when no big picture job comes along. The average fee for scoring a one-hour TV drama is about one-fifth to one-tenth the fee for a major motion picture score.

As production costs continue to rise, producers are more frequently asking their composers to score for smaller orchestras. One of the devices resulting, in part, from budget pressure, is the increasing use of sound synthesizers. Other electronically-generated music machines are being used more and more to substitute for entire orchestra sections, particularly strings.

THE CRAFT

MUSIC APPLICATIONS

Those who underscore films use many of the techniques employed for centuries by opera composers. But the unique time-lapse illusions in cinema art challenge the creative powers of film composers well beyond the more familiar techniques of scoring music for the theatre. Here are the ways film composers use music:

1- *To imply a period in history or a geographic location for a scene.*

2- *To suggest a dramatic mood or atmosphere. These techniques can intensify a mood or suggest a relaxation of tension.*

3- *To "punch up" scenes by synchronization of action and music.*

4- *To provide dramatic unity, e.g., the use of leit motif* (identifying musical fragment). *This device has been used in the movies since the 1930s.*

5- *To provide an element of comedy, ranging from satire to slapstick.*

CUE SHEETS

Before the composer starts scoring, a private screening is arranged. The first look the composer has of the movie is often in the company of the director, and often the music editor. The producer may also attend to offer his views. The director and composer watch the film roll by and discuss where underscoring might be appropriate. Just as important, they also discuss where music should *not* be used. The music editor overhears this conversation and makes notes on where the other two professionals have decided, at least tentatively, the music should be underscored. The producer has hired this particular composer to score the picture because he knows of his qualifications and track record. A climate of confidence already exists, and composers rarely encounter strong disagreement on how the movie should be scored. The composer on a major film will usually want to view the picture several times before he starts scoring. Many established composers have access to a Moviola, which is a cinema projector that can be started and stopped, reversed, frame by frame if necessary, by the composer who may want to study particular scenes in detail or in slow motion. The Moviola has a film foot counter which provides precise reference points for the composer for critical timings.

The music editor also works with a Moviola, and writes cue sheets for each reel of film. Most cue sheets contain the name of each scene calling for music, net film footage, and timings to one-third of a second. Another column on the cue sheet will provide space for indication of click tracks. The click track enables the composer to sync music to film with mathematical precision. Theatrical film moves at a rate of 24 frames per second, or 1440 frames per minute. The editor or composer divides his metronome tempo into 1440; the result is known as a "frame-click beat." For example, if the tempo is M.M. 144, 1440 ÷ 144 = 10. This results in a need for the cutter to prepare a 10-frame click which is derived from holes punched in the edge of the film. Composers can ask that the clicks be spaced equidistant on the film or at unequal spacings to provide an audible guide for music that is to be rubato, not regular, in pulse. The sound of the clicks is conveyed to the conductor and key musicians in the orchestra via head sets.

Click tracks are not used as widely as they once were, for two reasons. Scoring styles today do not often call for the composer to "catch" action, and their timings do not require such precise synchronization. The other reason is that some composers and directors believe that music scored to click tracks gives a metronomic feeling, and they prefer music that gives an impression of being less restricted.

Click tracks and Moviolas are used less today by many film composers, in that they have turned more to the use of videocassettes.

COMPOSITION

The standard contract for a full-length feature film provides that the composer shall write the music and get it on tape in 10 weeks. In actual practice, the producer is more likely to tell the composer that he has three to four weeks to complete the job. Some composers work under six-week deadlines, which may or may not include recording. In Europe, the composer has traditionally been expected to present a completed score to the copyists. In the United States, film composers normally compose orchestral sketches, perhaps three to eight lines per system, then turn over the sketch, with indications for instrumentation, to an orchestrator to render the full score. This practice developed because producers were always in a hurry, and still are. They have been willing to pay the extra costs of dividing the writing of movie scores between two persons. Bernard Herrmann, often named as one of Hollywood's finest film composers (*Citizen Kane, Fahrenheit 451*), believed the farming out of orchestration was an abomination and always insisted on doing his own.

RECORDING TO FILM

Most feature films are recorded on movie "scoring stages." These facilities are huge, upholstered barns. When I was scoring films at Paramount and 20th Century-Fox, I felt that no music-making environment could be less hospitable. These cavernous chambers are cluttered with a big projection screen, discarded equipment, dusty chairs and an old AFM contractor leering at his watch. Besides a half-acre of musicians, sound stages are attended during scoring sessions by audio technicians, a music librarian, the music cutter, assistant directors, the conductor's agent, the producer's girlfriend, and the head copyist who has the appearance of being on the threshold of a nervous collapse. But failure on the film scoring stage is rare. Occasionally, a film director will throw out a complete score, fire the composer and engage another one to redo the job. More likely, this high-tension environment proceeds with efficiency — because the stage is inhabited by pros who have paid a lot of dues for the privilege of sharing this high-paying field. The only delays, as a rule, in scoring movies are similar to the ones afflicting most other recording sessions — clams in the orchestra parts. After the composer-conductor has properly insulted the copyists, the errors are corrected. Once the recording engineers have found an acceptable balance in the control room, the film projectionist cries "Speed!" (meaning — his projector has caught up to 24 frames per second), and the recording machines roll.

Except when click tracks are used, scoring movie music is, in many respects, less critical than recording for commercial records. Where commercial recording now calls for 24- to 32-track mixing, film music recording is often done on less sophisticated equipment. Producers know that they are working primarily in a visual, not a sound medium, and have traditionally shown less concern for state-of-the-art audio tracks. Pressures of budget often cause a conductor to accept an audio "print" on the first or second take.

The final application of music underscoring occurs when the music, dialogue and sound effects are combined and synchronized with the film. These mixing sessions (sometimes referred to as rerecording) are attended by the composer, music cutter, sound effects man, and one to three recordists (mixing engineers). Some film directors attend these sessions to make sure the sounds they require are sufficiently prominent. Not infrequently, the composer approaches despair when his precious music gets lost behind shouting dialogue or screaming sirens. And when someone attempts to console him with "that's show business," his distress remains unrelieved. Until a few days later his check arrives.

Much of the labor of synchronization of music to film can be accomplished on the scoring stage through application of the cueing and timing techniques described above. But additional refinements in synchronization are necessary, and these tasks are performed in the music editing room by a music editor.

Underscoring TV drama is handled differently from films produced for theatrical exhibition. Many TV producers would use canned tracks exclusively if their contract with the AFM permitted it. Others would pay for a few hours of new recording for a series, then use and reuse the same few musical fragments throughout the run of the series. It has been the task of the music cutter over the years to take these various musical sources, then lay them in as appropriately as he could in subsequent shows in a series, doing his best to make them fit, not only new timings, but different dramatic situations. Skillful cutters camouflaged these deceits very well sometimes. But even lay listeners learned to recognize musical cues as a series progressed in its first run. These music patchwork jobs become glaringly apparent when a viewer watches reruns of his favorite shows.

HIRING PRACTICES

AFM CONTRACTS

If TV audiences tired of continuous reuse of music on a TV series, the practice was particularly obnoxious to the musicians who lost out on a lot of recording work. Some years ago, the AFM finally managed to negotiate a contract with the TV producers that imposed significant limitations on the extent to which TV music could be reused. For example, a minimum number of initial recording hours was stipulated for creation of a music library of tracks for a particular series. A minimum-sized orchestra was agreed upon for dramatic underscoring. Tracks recorded for a particular dramatic series could be used only for that series in that TV season. This contract increased, not only the employment opportunities for studio musicians, but affected artistic improvements in the application of music to TV drama.

Over the years, the AFM has continued its unrelenting battle with film and TV producers for improvement of employment opportunities for union musicians. In the summer of 1977, the AFM signed a new contract with the Association of Motion Picture Producers and the Alliance of Television Producers which caused an historic breakthrough in music underscoring practices: the TV producers agreed to discontinue use of canned tracks, starting with the 1978-79 season, for dramatic underscoring. This historic change has impacted favorably on studio musicians, and increased job opportunities for musicians trying to break into this high-paying field. It should be noted that, under this contract, TV producers are exempt from the live scoring provision for "standard cues," logos, "commercial bumpers" and "format music." But even here, no library-music recording sessions are allowed. The contract also provides certain exemptions from the live-scoring rule in the case of emergencies, such as "time or facility problems . . ."

The contract also provides for a minimum number of recording hours for a TV dramatic series. Certain "emergency tracking sessions" are permissible, but they may not be charged against the minimum number of scoring hours stipulated in the contract for a series.

The musicians' union does not set scales for composition, leaving that issue to be negotiated between the composer and the producer. But the AFM does set minimums for all other persons engaged in music preparation — arrangers, orchestrators, copyists, proofreaders and librarians. In the film field, scales are high. Union musicians earn premium rates for services performed after 8 p.m. and on holidays. Music preparation people earn the same fringe benefits as instrumentalists.

Musicians working in film receive additional income once a year from the AFM Theatrical and Television Motion Picture Special Payments Fund. This fund derives its income from producers and movie studios that sell exhibition rights to their movies to television networks.

Since the 1930s, musicians all over the world have thought of Hollywood as the land of milk and honey, not to mention sunshine and starlets. Individuals whose top priority in the profession is money have considered "making it in the studios" as the ultimate achievement. Financially, if not artistically. Those of us who have worked in and around Tinseltown for many years might agree with part of this rosy portrait. The money is great, when you can find work. But the glamour is well-tarnished. In the daily contests between artists and commercial interests, it is usually the money changers who win. Even where a musician manages to hold on to his artistic values, he often feels like a tiny component of the whole music production process. I once invited the late Hugo Friedhofer, often called the dean of film composers, to visit one of my classes at the University of Colorado. He described the production of film music as an assembly line: each musician in the chain — composer, orchestrator, copyist, player —

experiences only his particular fragment of the whole, somewhat like workers turning out Ford motorcars. TV and films rarely use "compositions," they use "cues," some of which may last as long as six seconds. And even these brief musical spasms might be buried under dialogue.

But then there's the money. Time for golf. A pleasant life for those who make it. But in 1957 all the major movie studios dropped their staff musicians. Soon, those who had "made it" found time, not only for golf, but the unemployment line. At this time, runaway film production and the rising popularity of television threatened the Hollywood film industry. But by the 1970s, the ailing industry had revived; runaway movie scoring became less threatening. Film scoring in the United States increased. Television's demand for new music increased dramatically. These developments helped create a lot of jobs for studio musicians and others related to the music industry.

Most of the musicians I have worked with in Los Angeles not only like the money, they seem to enjoy the musical experience. While some of the cues one must write or play can be musically meaningless, in almost every three-hour recording session some genuine musical satisfactions occur. They may come from an inspired phrase or stunning color. They regularly come from the thrill musicians generate for each other with their superb musicianship. In New York and Los Angeles studios are assembled, not just very good musicians, but the best musicians in the world. Writing for these artists, conducting them, playing alongside these musicians offers musical rewards unsurpassed. It makes up for the periods when no work comes along — and even the first-call musicians experience lean periods from time to time. My cheerful appraisal of the musical satisfaction and professional attitudes of studio musicians is corroborated by research conducted by Robert Faulkner, whose important book, *Hollywood Studio Musicians,* cites evidence derived from extensive interviews of several dozen musicians most active in film scoring.

PACKAGE DEALS

In the film scoring fields, producers require the services of composers, orchestrators, arrangers, copyists, librarians, instrumentalists and recordists. Until 1957, all of these services could be provided by the major film studios who retained all of these artists and technicians on staff, most of them full-time. But when the staff musicians were let go by the film studios in 1957, producers had to engage all their musicians on a free-lance basis. To make this situation manageable, producers would often negotiate "package deals" with independent contractors. This practice prevails today in the background music field and in the scoring of some theatrical film. Music packagers are not as widely used in television.

Producers like package deals because the system transfers their financial risk to the independent contractor. The background music firm or movie producer usually budgets a set figure for music. That money must cover all music production costs — composition, orchestration, arranging, copying, proofreading, library services, conducting, instrumentalists, instrument cartage, studio or sound stage rental, tape, mixing, and editing. The producer will contract with a composer-director to assume all these responsibilities and expenses for a lump sum. He has little difficulty in locating individuals to assume this risk, because he knows there is always a supply of hungry musicians.

A composer-director anxious to break into the field, or one who is already established but needs the work, is often delighted to receive an offer of, say, $10,000 to score a picture — and pay all the other music costs. The inexperienced composer-director believes this kind of money means he has really hit the big time in Hollywood. His score might be well-received, but unless the composer-packager uses a very small orchestra or pays less than AFM scale, he would have to be very efficient on the sound stage to come out well financially. Package deals for $10,000 for a picture look good until the bills come in. Some packagers learn how to budget their time and expenses and come out well on these deals. Many manage to pay full AFM scale and have enough left over for themselves to compensate for several gruelling weeks of composition and orchestration.

Well-established composers are less likely to accept package deals where they are expected to assume full responsibility for all music production costs. Big-name studio composers practically never do.

COMPOSERS-CONDUCTORS

In the field of underscoring movies and TV drama, there are many employment opportunities for the fully qualified professional. But there are no openings for anybody but the expert, seasoned pro. While some feature films are still recorded in New York, most American-made movies are scored in Los Angeles. A handful of pros with firmly established track records, e.g., Oscar winner Nelson Riddle, land their picture jobs without the help of an agent; the producer simply engages the composer directly. But the great majority of the composers are hired through film composers' agents. For many years, three or four such agents have controlled most of the best film and TV scoring. Three well-known TV/film composers — Dave Grusin, Patrick Williams and Tom Scott — have told me they get their picture assignments because of their reputations; their agents do not actually find them jobs but assist in drawing up contracts with producers and help keep their business affairs in order. Producers are accustomed to negotiating with composers' agents and place trust in their judgment.

Patrick Williams estimates that about 200 film composers are making it in Hollywood. My own view is that about half that number are "making it" full-time scoring movies and TV shows. That second one hundred, I believe, fill out their workweeks with other kinds of creative work, particularly in the recording industry.

As pointed out earlier, top film composers sometimes get so busy they find it necessary to call in helpers to meet deadlines. These assistants include, not only arrangers and orchestrators, but composers. They are paid by the musician whose name goes on the screen credits. Purists are bothered by the ghost-writing phenomenon, but this is the route this author and many others found to break into broadcasting and film scoring. Yet another way of cracking these high-paying media is to be an advanced student of a busy composer. Not infrequently, teachers farm out some of their time-pressure work to their best students who then later begin to locate their own scoring jobs in their own names.

During the period of contract studio orchestras in Hollywood (1944-1957) all the major studios employed staff conductors on a full-time basis. These individuals would occasionally score a picture themselves when production schedules became crowded, but their first responsibility was to handle the conducting of film scores and the synchronization of them to film. In the 1928-1943 period, some film composers did not pretend to also be conductors and they were expected to turn over direction of the scoring sessions to musicians specializing in that field. As the number of staff musicians lessened, increasing numbers of film composers were asked to conduct their own scoring sessions. Then and now, many of these composers lacked training as conductors. Scoring sessions under their batons were saved, and are today, by the superb skills of their orchestra players whose expertise and long experience in the studios make it possible for even the worst "conductors" to appear as if they know what they are doing.

In the Los Angeles area, the only jobs in the studios for conductors (who do not also score their own music) are found occasionally on the old movie lots, such as Universal Studios, where the tremendous volume of TV drama production sometimes requires the services of conductors hired to perform this special service.

ARRANGERS-ORCHESTRATORS

As outlined above, the busiest studio composers find it necessary to farm out some or all of their orchestration. Under pressure of time, or possibly because the producer has provided funds to pay for orchestration in addition to composition, studio composers will entrust completion of their sketches to arrangers and orchestrators who understand how the composer wants his music to sound. All arrangers and orchestrators used in these secondary capacities are selected by the composer himself, never by the producer or director.

COPYISTS

Copying of vocal and orchestral parts for network television and theatrical films scored in this country is performed exclusively by AFM members for union scale. Copyists are engaged by the composer, sometimes by the orchestrator. In the film and TV fields, it has been traditional to schedule composition and scoring sessions within a time frame calculated to produce in all concerned a maximum level of panic. Last-minute scoring sessions are the rule. Also standard in the business is the tendency for composers to begin their assignments several hours beyond the last possible minute. Thus, the copyists consistently work under intolerable time pressures. Since many scores cannot be copied by an individual in the time available, it is common practice for head copyists to turn over some or all of the work to a music preparation service.

When television shows or films are being recorded, the supervising copyist is expected to attend the sessions to serve as music librarian and, more importantly, be available to correct errors in the extracted parts during the recording.

ORCHESTRA MUSICIANS

Instrumentalists hired to score theatrical or television films produced in the United States are members of the American Federation of Musicians. Unlike the field of background music library services, only a negligible number of movies produced in the United States are scored and recorded by nonunion musicians. Except for low budget package deals where the composer himself serves as the AFM union steward, film musicians are engaged by the orchestra contractor. Just as outlined in my chapter on television, the contractor and the composer-conductor together prepare a first-call list of players, with a supplemental list of second- and third-choice players, should their favorite musicians not be available.

In New York and Los Angeles since the 1930s, the artists getting this high-paying work are selected from a small pool of musicians, perhaps 300 to 400 in each city, who have earned reputations over the years for being able to play almost anything placed before them perfectly at sight. These musicians often make the music sound better than it is.

Whenever I recorded in Hollywood, I would only authorize my contractor to hire a player I did not know personally when the contractor or some other musician whose judgment I trusted would say, "I would like to suggest you call John Doe. He can handle it without any problems at all." This kind of referral system in the studios works consistently and well.

Musicians who want to break into the studios are rarely accepted when they make a frontal attack on the inside pool of players. Those that have spent years earning their reputations resent newcomers bursting upon the scene without paying their dues. But when a new player earns his credentials by first establishing a good reputation, not just with contractors or conductors, but with the players themselves, he has a much better chance of being recommended for recording sessions.

Unknown players can become known in a number of ways. When I was a staff conductor-arranger for NBC, from time to time we would have reading sessions of chamber music by the staff string players, and unknown string players (and pupils of the staff players) would be invited to sit in. If a player could sight-read a Haydn quartet, that accomplishment would be remembered — and the next time the contractor was short a string player, that individual might receive a call.

A reputation-building medium for winds and percussion derives from the various rehearsal bands widely popular in New York and Los Angeles. The inside players are always alert to evaluate the newcomers. Another pipeline to the inside is through the teachers of unknown players. James Decker, one of the most in-demand horn players in Hollywood, is able to recommend each year several of his most advanced students for studio and symphony jobs; Decker himself is too busy to cover all the offers he receives personally and is able to "sponsor" unknown hornists.

String players, almost without exception, are alumni of major symphony orchestras. A high percentage of them are former concertmasters or first-desk players. Besides competence in standard orchestral playing, these string players understand jazz phrasing and the kind of "popular" style characteristic of what is sometimes called "the Hollywood Sound" — beautiful tone, romantically expressive, perfect intonation, entirely relaxed. As for double-bass, most studio players have, in addition to extensive traditional backgrounds, ability to play jazz, perhaps even rock, and often the electric bass. But when a really funky, Fender bass line is required, specialists in the rock or soul fields are brought in.

Brass players making it in the studios originally came from theatre orchestras and symphonies. In the 1940-1960 period, many brass players came off the road from name bands. In more recent years, some brass players have come from the nation's leading university concert bands. Some today come from top conservatories such as Juilliard, Eastman and Curtis. All brass players, whatever their backgrounds, are expected to handle not only "legit" music, but any other style from country to rock to "progressive." When brass players take their chairs in the studio or on the scoring stage, they already know among themselves who is expected to play lead, which chair, if any, is "the jazz chair," what horn player will play the lyrical solos. Even among this prestigious clique of superb artists, some players enjoy a special additional prestige. Most trumpet players are expected to play trumpets in Bb, C, or perhaps even the piccolo trumpet in D. Most double on fluegelhorn today. Hornists and trombonists are sometimes called upon in big film scores to double on Wagner tuba, euphonium or tenor tuba, even contrabass trombone.

Studio woodwind players are an elite breed, most of whom have backgrounds in professional symphony orchestras. Many of the saxophone players are aging alumni of the big band era of the 1940s who have acquired, along the way, the additional skills of "legitimate" performance styles often called for in film scoring. Since the 1960s, increasing numbers of these players have been graduates of university concert bands and orchestras.

It is generally known that woodwind and saxophone players are expected to be competent doublers on clarinet and flute, perhaps even double reeds. But this demand for doubling is less common in scoring feature films and TV movies, where the music directors prefer to engage specialists on each instrument. Another reason woodwind doubling is less common in film scoring is that the union rates for this kind of versatility are very high; it is almost as cheap to hire extra players.

Studio percussionists usually come from wide backgrounds which would include extensive study and experience in styles ranging from jazz, Latin, symphonic and rock. When a particularly authentic rock or "black" sound is wanted, sometimes specialists are brought in. If the timpani work is extensive, many contractors will engage a player with solid experience in symphony work. While nearly all studio percussionists play mallet instruments, contractors will sometimes try to hire special artists to handle elaborate solos.

Keyboard players are expected to be able to play the leading styles, sight read and improvise. Some pianists are hired for their special ability to play "comp" piano; others are known as jazz soloists or "legitimate" players. Not all studio players are yet competent on electronic keyboards. But nearly all of them are expected to be able to register and play the Rhodes electric piano and the preprogrammed performance synthesizers. Keyboard players who can handle these assignments and play an instrument like the Arp 2600 are in demand. A handful of players in the major recording centers are known for their special competence as rock keyboard players who can read well. Some specialize in rock organ and "live synthesis."

SOUND MIXERS

During the period when film scores were precisely synchronized with action, all recording was done on scoring stages on movie studio lots. These facilities are set up, not only to handle huge orchestras, but large movie screens on which the film is projected during synchronization sessions. This practice prevails today. But many films, particularly those where little or no music is precisely synchronized with action on the screen, are recorded in conventional recording studios, usually without movie screens. In this kind of situation, precise timings and other synchronizations are made by the music cutter whose work can be done at a later time in a small editing studio.

Until about the mid-1960s, music mixing on movie sound tracks failed to keep abreast of the developments concurrent in the record industry. I recall hiring a mixer (for a short time) from Walt Disney Studio when I was operating my own recording studio in Hollywood. I quickly learned that a good audio mixer from the film industry was no match for other engineers I hired whose backgrounds were in the record field. Today, some of the music mixing for films approaches the sophistication of the record industry. In the TV film field, however, low budgets and time pressures regularly force upon musical directors and mixers the acceptance of balances and timbres that would be unacceptable on records. As for personnel, mixers in films tend to work just in that particular field. This is partly because these engineers must be knowledgeable and experienced in mixing, not only music tracks, but dialogue and sound effects.

When a composer or singer known for his recorded "sound" works in films, he will sometimes attempt to bring on the lot his sound engineer.

MUSIC CUTTERS

Music cutters, or film music editors, have acquired their skills on the job. Some started out as film editors who then turned to music cutting. Others may have been composers or orchestrators in the early days of filmmaking, then switched to music cutting, out of frustration or choice. The best music cutters are amazingly versatile, possessing great musical sensitivity, a keen ear for balance, an awareness of how music can make or break a scene, all combined with a knowledge of the special technology used in synchronizing music tracks to film or tape. Since no schools exist for the training of music cutters, they are products of the film industry itself. Like so many artists and artisans in film, music cutters learned their craft, their art, as apprentices to older masters. Now that the first generation of music cutters is about gone, the second generation is accepting apprentices from the third generation of individuals who are attracted to film music-making.

COMPOSERS AND LYRICISTS GUILD OF AMERICA (CLGA)

Since the AFM claims no jurisdiction over the work of composers and lyricists, creative artists active in those fields found it advisable years ago to organize their own representation in order to bargain collectively for their services. Most established composers of dramatic underscoring for the movies and television, and most songwriters active in those media, are members of CLGA, the Composers and Lyricists Guild of America.

Until late 1971, established movie and TV producers who required the services of a composer or lyricist would only hire, with rare exceptions, CLGA members. This hiring was done under the contract in force up to that time between the CLGA and the MPTPA — the Motion Picture and Television Producers Association. The two groups had been in serious dispute for years, and no extension of the contract prevailing in 1971 could be worked out. Instead, the CLGA filed a $300 million class action suit against the producers in an effort to satisfy their grievances. The composers and lyricists charged that the producers had engaged in a conspiracy in restraint of trade, particularly in respect to the producers' alleged monopolistic control of publishing rights to music scored for their films. Of special concern to CLGA at that time was the fact that the old standard contract (not used since November 30, 1971) stipulated that the publisher selected by the producer (usually a subsidiary of the production company) was under no obligation to exploit the music.

The guild had traditionally negotiated minimum weekly fees to be paid its members working on a picture or TV program and had helped gain screen credits for guild members. The old CLGA-MPTPA contract imposed minimum requirements on the producer/publisher for distribution of printed editions. The contract specified mechanical royalties were to be paid guild members for commercial records derived from film scores. Also recognized was guild members' affiliation with ASCAP or BMI and the inherent right of guild members to receive authors' shares of royalties from performances paid through these licensing societies.

The CLGA lawsuit against the producers finally came to trial in 1978. Shortly thereafter, the parties settled their dispute out of court. The settlement left intact the producers' ownership of copyrights. But the agreement provided that, should the producer (or his publisher) fail to promote the music, the composers reserved the right to exploit the properties themselves.

Part Six

CAREER PLANNING AND DEVELOPMENT

26

CAREER OPTIONS

Hope is the thing with feathers, that perches in the soul, and sings the tune without the words, and never stops at all.
EMILY DICKINSON

The world of work is full of square pegs in round holes. This pervasive mismatch of people and jobs is particularly apparent in music and music-related employment. Students, parents, teachers and counselors hold generally distorted views of the field. Their information, what little is available, is often inaccurate and out-of-date. The bibliography appearing in the appendix lists two or three useful references. But the present volume provides the first comprehensive account of music career options and sets forth precisely how aspirants may qualify for a career in music.

The US Department of Labor lists 35,000 different occupational titles. Its Bureau of Labor Statistics publishes each year its *Occupational Outlook Handbook* which attempts to calculate what jobs might be available in future years. But the government, the MENC, NASM, AFTRA and AFM have been shamefully negligent in informing people concerning career opportunities (or lack of them) in music. While some parts of the field are tremendously overcrowded, *we have an actual shortage of qualified people in other areas*. A complete inventory of music-related occupations reveals an astonishing diversity. The individual searching for employment in music will discover that he has a very large number of career options. To provide a perspective, we shall group them as follows:

Creative Careers *Teaching Careers*
Producing/Directing Careers *Music-related Careers*
Performing Careers

Choosing the right career goal can be the most important decision in a person's life. Before proceeding to examine the options available, look at the accompanying summary (Fig. 26.1) which outlines the stages the prudent individual could go through in planning and developing a career.

CAREER PLANNING AND DEVELOPMENT

DISCOVERING YOURSELF	*Self-appraisal of temperament, talent.* *Professional assessment of your temperament, talent.*
DEFINING GOALS	*Personal needs, preferences.* *Investigation of career options.* *Short-term employment objectives.* *Long-term career goals.*
GETTING PREPARED	*Education, training.* *Apprenticeship, work experience.* *Diplomas, degrees, licenses, union affiliations.*
FINDING WORK	*Surveying the job market, current, potential.* *Predicting entry: time, place, pay, status.* *Breaking in: auditions, demos, letters, resumés, interviews.* *Self-employment options.*
CLIMBING THE LADDER	*Planning advancement: status, income, power.* *Vertical vs. horizontal job change.* *Quitting vs. hanging on.* *Attainment of career goals.* *Realization of personal goals.* *Periodic reassessment of goals.*
RETIREMENT	*When, how.* *Estimated financial requirements.* *Anticipated income; preparing for inflation.*

Fig. 26.1

CREATIVE CAREERS

Professional Songwriter
Composer of Show Music
Composer of Dramatic Music
Composer of Educational Materials
Composer of Children's Music

Composer of Serious Music
Arranger/Orchestrator
Music Editor
Music Copyist

PROFESSIONAL SONGWRITER

CAREER DESCRIPTION — The professional songwriter spends a-bout half his time composing, and his creative energies are focused on one market — *the record business*. The other half of the song-writer's workweek is usually spent promoting — trying to persuade performers and producers to record his material. Most songwriters have difficulty gaining acceptance and find it necessary to support themselves with other kinds of employment which may or may not relate to music. Genuinely talented songwriters, once they obtain initial acceptance, usually discontinue moonlighting and devote their full attention to writing and promoting their songs. When this happens, they often find themselves increasingly involved in such related activities as music publishing, record production, perhaps even artist management or show production.

Professional songwriters generally find it necessary to live and work in a major recording center where they can make direct personal contacts with publishers, record producers and recording artists. The real pros write, not just dozens of songs, but hundreds, knowing that prolific activity is required to sustain a full-time songwriter career. As for working conditions, they are ideal: the "worker" sets his own hours, vacation periods, usually writes at home, and can limit his professional contacts to the kinds of individuals he probably likes to be around — musicians and show people. Unlike most other professionals, he need not clutter his workweek with "the public," amateurs, groupies, salespersons or sponsors' wives.

QUALIFICATIONS, PREPARATION — Since the publishing/recording business requires hundreds of new songs every week, it is a common occurrence for untalented, ill-prepared songwriters to get heard — initially. But such individuals experience only brief acceptance and are soon displaced by those who are genuinely qualified. An aspiring songwriter can usually discover whether or not he possesses genuine creative talent by offering his songs to performers and producers over a period of time. If he follows the "getting started" procedures outlined in this book, he should learn, with persistent effort, whether song users judge him as really talented. If the aspirant finds no acceptance after two or three years' effort of this kind, the message becomes clear: he does not have what song users want.

Assuming for the moment that the aspirant has demonstrable creative talent, he should make certain he learns his craft. Chapter 4 treats this topic at length.

If we assume the aspirant is talented and competent, his professional success will also be dependent on whether he has the right kind of temperament.[1] Unless the aspirant is so creatively gifted that song users beat a path to his door, he will have to possess certain personal traits to survive in his chosen field. The essential personal attribute is *determination.* The writer must be strongly motivated to write songs and then more songs and then get out on the street and push his material unrelentingly, day after day. Even established pros rarely enjoy the luxury of sitting at home waiting for the telephone to ring. Songwriters learn that the world must be continuously reminded that they are still alive, still producing. Another desirable personality trait is

---

1-Throughout this chapter I shall refer repeatedly to individual temperament, for it is probably the dominant factor in a person's makeup determining success or failure in professional life. An individual must have the "right" temperament to make it in most fields of employment.

infinite patience. Some top writers waited years for recognition. A less patient temperament might have given up.

EMPLOYMENT PROSPECTS — If the aspirant is genuinely talented, professionally competent, has the temperament described and is persistent, his chances of experiencing professional success are good. But if he comes up short in even one of these areas, he should forget his first-choice career plan and turn to something else. If he makes it without these qualifications and personal attributes it would be a miracle.

Fully qualified songwriters work under contract to music publishers, either by the song, group of songs, or "on staff" exclusively for one publisher. A publisher will often set up a "draw" for a songwriter he has signed, this to be charged against royalties potentially due the writer. Writers of high promise who are broke sometimes receive almost a living wage for a year or so, pending the income of royalties from the publisher's promotional efforts in getting the material recorded. As for average incomes experienced by working songwriters, see Chapter 4.

Who "hires" songwriters? Publishers almost exclusively. A writer may hustle direct contacts on his own with recording artists and record producers, but this is really jumping the gun. The writer cannot enjoy royalties from records or printed music until a publisher has contracted for the material. Writers concerned with composing musical shows would not approach a publisher, but a show producer. Writers talented in creating "special material" would contact performing artists, artists' managers and producers.

COMPOSER OF SHOW MUSIC

CAREER DESCRIPTION — A small group of professional composers devotes most of its creative efforts to writing music for shows. Years ago, this would mean only the kind of creative work involved in mounting a Broadway production. Today, in addition to the dozens of composers working on such projects, additional show-writing opportunities occur not only off-Broadway, but "off-off-Broadway" — in regional theatres, dinner theatres, children's theatre and industrial shows.

Show music composers work differently than pop songwriters. The latter are free to invent whatever material they think might appeal to record producers. But show music composers normally start work only after a producer or writer has presented them with a script defining the nature of the show, the scenario, dialogue and, early on, the "book" for the production. The composer works sometimes on a daily basis with the show writers and producers, searching for music and lyrics that enhance the show and move it forward. Show music composers often work steadily on a project for several months, even a year or more, shaping, then reshaping the music to fit the script which is also probably undergoing constant rewriting. Completed, polished songs may have to be thrown out and new ones hastily inserted. Casting may change, and the composer may have to rethink just what type of material will best suit the new actor or actress. Show music composers may be handed a lyric and be asked to come up with the music in two or three days, even overnight. Absurd as it sounds, some great standards that were composed overnight have emerged from Broadway hits. On the other hand, Rodgers and Hammerstein (*South Pacific, Carousel, Oklahoma!* etc.) were known for working and reworking music and lyrics on just a handful of songs for a year or more until they attained their artistic goal. Composers and lyricists of stature are almost always called upon to serve as consultant to the producer in such matters as casting, dialogue, staging and orchestrations. Show music composers/lyricists are, then, men "of the theatre," and their work starts and ends with what works on-stage.

Some show music composers are occasionally called upon to write, not just show songs, but instrumental music, dance music, even dramatic music to underscore stage action. For example, the master show music composer, Richard Rodgers, was called upon to compose dramatic ballet music, *Slaughter on Tenth Avenue* for one of his Broadway shows. A composer able to handle diverse assignments of these kinds rises above the ranks of "songwriter" and becomes a "composer's composer." It is more common in most shows, however, to expect the composers-lyricists engaged for the project to be called upon only for songs, not dramatic music.

QUALIFICATIONS, PREPARATION — Show music composers must possess the same qualifications cited above for songwriters, plus one more: *a sense of theatre.* Composers lacking that sense remain just pop songwriters; they will not experience success in theatre music. Show composers are often expected to work well with collaborators, particularly lyricists. While Broadway has had a few masters who could write words and music, e.g., Cole Porter, Irving Berlin, Stephen Sondheim, most shows are created by a kind of committee involving composers, lyricists, playwrights, directors and composers. Choreographers and lighting directors also have their say. The creative artist who is comfortable only when working alone is better off staying away from the theatre.

As audiences become more demanding for meaningful musical theatre, it appears likely that composers will look more and more, not just for songwriters, but for more versatile composers such as Leonard Bernstein. For example, when Bernstein writes a theatre piece (e.g., *West Side Story*, even *Mass*), he comes up not only with great songs, but whatever music is required to further the drama.

How does an aspirant prepare himself for this level of composition? Unless he has unlimited natural talent and studies intently on his own with private teachers, such a composer would have to spend at least four to six years beyond high school studying music, probably in a university. He might major in composition and minor in theatre. He would prepare himself by getting fully involved in writing shows for campus productions, as did Stephen Sondheim, Oscar Hammerstein, Cole Porter, Richard Rodgers and many others. The "complete" show music composer would immerse himself not only in the Broadway repertoire, but also study the great "show music" composed by earlier masters such as Mozart and Wagner, not to mention Stravinsky and Copland in this century. Once the aspiring composer begins to explore theatre music at this level, he will find that study of his art and craft becomes a lifelong pursuit.

What kind of temperament must a composer have to work professionally in the theatre? I have already mentioned the need for an ability to collaborate artistically; a "loner" cannot make it in this environment. Also, the show music composer must be able to endure the sudden rejection of his material without experiencing total collapse of ego. The aspirant must have unlimited patience. He may work on one project for a year or two, then see the show fold after one performance. He must then decide whether he can endure another huge disappointment, try again and come back. The aspirant must also possess sufficient aggressiveness to search for show backers and producers. Creative musicians working in the theatre must hustle their own financial support and convince investors that the project is as good as the composers believe it is. In this aspect of a theatre composer's career, there is little room for modesty. Self-confidence and drive are as important to professional success as the musician's creative prowess.

EMPLOYMENT PROSPECTS — There is no such thing as an "employer" or a "job" for show music composers. Rather, they work on projects, perhaps for long periods without compensation, in the hope that, along the way, they can locate a financial backer. Despite the hit-flop ratio of musical shows, every season "angels" emerge, money in hand, ready to sink perhaps a million dollars into an untried, unproved musical dream. A show composer may struggle for years and never find financial backing or a receptive producer. Still, writers new and old continue to make their way in the theatre.

Elsewhere in this volume I describe potential income sources for show music. Since royalties for show music from records and print media can be huge, it is this pot-of-gold that attracts every year still more show music composers who are determined to follow the rainbow. Since the rewards are great, composers always seem willing to endure long periods of starvation waiting for that hit. Individuals engaged in this long-odds game must have outside income of some kind. Fortunately for us who love good musical theatre, we seem to have an unending supply of creative artists who are willing to keep knocking at the stage door.

COMPOSER OF DRAMATIC MUSIC

CAREER DESCRIPTION — Increasing numbers of musicians are finding careers in composing background music for television and movies. These composers are given a script, then sit with the film director and music cutter to determine where music should be underscored and just what kind of music would be appropriate for the dramatic situation. Background music composers must write at top speed. Producers may demand a score for a 30-minute TV episode, even a one-hour show, in one week. Movie producers may require the music score be written and recorded for a feature film within four to six weeks. Even well-established composers in this field experience feast and famine; they may make weekly visits to the employment office for a while, then suddenly be called upon to turn out a 13-week TV series in three months and work on a film score concurrently. Hot and cold, rich and poor, that is the pattern. TV and film composers must locate in Los Angeles, New York or a major foreign city to find work in TV and the movies.

Some composers who prefer to write for the theatre and other dramatic media do not attempt to crack the inner circle of movie composers and focus on writing ballets and operas. Professional work of this kind is almost invariably performed on commission, and the composer can live anywhere he chooses. But most dramatic music composers in the field of ballet and opera are employed as theory and composition teachers by universities.

QUALIFICATIONS, PREPARATION — Unlike other kinds of professional composing careers such as pop songwriting, where luck can play an important factor in success, the musician aspiring to a professional career scoring dramatic music must possess outstanding creative talent. He must also be highly sensitive to dramatic values, tone painting and how music can enhance theatrical experience. As for musical style, film and TV producers today prefer jazz-rock-flavored scores for contemporary drama. Historical drama and exotic settings require, of course, music appropriate for particular times and places. Composers hired to score high-tension dramas find that they can get away with a level of dissonance, including atonality, that many concert audiences even today find unpalatable. Some film composers use, from time to time, post-Webern serial techniques.

Aspiring composers in this field must know the great music of the past and present, in order to be prepared to score appropriately for any historical period. While most of our leading film music writers are amazingly versatile, they tend to be hired to score in a style in which they are particularly adept. For a contemporary romantic comedy, many producers would like to have Henry Mancini, if they could meet his price. Producers of high adventure films or space-age thrillers might try to hire John Williams, renowned composer of movies of this kind. Jerry Goldsmith seems to excel in underscoring psychological thrillers and mystery dramas.

EMPLOYMENT PROSPECTS — See Chapter 25 for a discussion of film composers' agents and suggestions on how newcomers break in to this high-paying field.

COMPOSER OF EDUCATIONAL MATERIALS

When schools and colleges accelerated their music education programs following World War II, publishers became increasingly involved in attempting to supply the print-music needs of school bands, orchestras and choruses, as well as the requirements of the individual student in search of learning materials. This print music market expanded in the 1960s to involve several hundred composers-arrangers-editors in the publication of music education materials. Nearly all professional composers in this field come from the teaching profession. Most of these pros write music only part-time and continue to hold their teaching jobs nine months a year.

This division of professional activity has developed for two reasons. First, few educational field composers can earn enough at it to support themselves; it may yield very respectable royalties but usually not enough to justify quitting a teaching post. The second reason composers in the educational field generally continue to divide their time between composing and teaching is that their jobs in schools and colleges keep them aware of this changing profession and the changing market for educational music. Further, these composers are able to maintain their professional contacts with potential customers through educational organizations, clinics and conventions.

The most successful composers of educational materials usually concentrate on the particular medium that they know best: band directors tend to compose mostly band pieces; choral directors generally limit their creative projects to choral repertoire. Our best educational field composers, e.g., Peter Mennin, Jean Berger, Vincent Persichetti, Alfred Reed, Cecil Effinger, do not limit their creative work to the educational market. All of the aforementioned composers (another two dozen could be named) are active in the general field of serious music, enjoying performances of their compositions by professional symphony orchestras, ballet and opera companies.

Very little first-class music is created exclusively for schools. Genuinely worthy compositions are more widely performed by a variety of amateur and professional artists and ensembles. But publishers will generally offer to schools and colleges special arrangements of serious compositions. This is usually necessary to assure reasonably satisfactory coverage of parts by school groups of unpredictable instrumentation. Also, school arrangements of some serious compositions must be modified to adjust their performance difficulties to a level school players can handle. Publishers engage the original composer to render these school editions when they can. More often, the publisher hires free-lance arranger-editors to prepare editions suitable for school use.

How do most educational field composers function? Simply by scoring what they believe is their best work, then making a demo tape with a school group, forwarding the score and demo to a publisher — then crossing their fingers. Publishers usually have knowledgeable chief editors who are adept at determining if a particular score shows promise. Works accepted usually receive a first printing of 1,000 copies in the instrumental field, and some composers receive advances on royalties. The standard royalty in this field differs from the pop field: usually 10 percent of sales at the *retail* price.

The largest market is in the school band field. An average five-minute concert band piece may retail for $25. Thus, if the first edition

(1,000 copies) sells out, the composer receives $2,500 in royalties. If a composer in this field can turn out several dozen reasonably good sellers, he can earn a respectable income and devote his full time to this activity if he chooses.

QUALIFICATIONS, PREPARATION — An individual who wants to become a professional composer specializing in the educational field will almost certainly major in music in college — and probably go on to graduate school for a masters degree, perhaps a D.M.A. (Doctor of Musical Arts) degree. The aspirant should have several years of experience with school ensembles as a director. He would have to become acquainted with the repertoire of the past and present which has been found suitable for educational purposes. Such experience and study may help him avoid at least the most common clichés which infect this repertoire. The aspirant would, in the course of his studies and directing experience, become thoroughly familiar with the performance capabilities of amateur musicians at various grade levels, then score his music to accommodate the needs of particular segments of the market. Besides possessing his craft, let us hope that the aspirant is also creative, capable of composing music of substance and meaning. Music scored for schools and colleges need not be as banal as much of it has been in the past.

EMPLOYMENT PROSPECTS — If a composer heading for specialization in the educational field is really talented, creative, knows his craft, and can produce acceptable demo tapes, he will find publishers receptive. That is, if he follows certain procedures. The first step is for the composer to address a specific market and medium. If the work is intended for high school concert bands of average ability, everything should be scored accordingly. Assuming the composer has written for an identifiable segment of the market, he then writes publishers active in that area, inquiring for that firm's guidelines for submission of unsolicited manuscripts. Publishers welcome this preliminary contact and are much more receptive to scores that come in which conform to their requirements. A letter accompanying submission of the full score and parts should offer a description of the piece and state for whom it is intended, together with any other information pertinent to the composition which the publisher might need to know, such as whether the piece is already covered with registration of claim to copyright. Publishers urge composers never to submit a manuscript for consideration by more than one publisher at one time. Publishers are annoyed when, after spending time examining a prospective work, they hear from the composer that he has accepted an offer from a competing firm. Submitting MSS to one publisher at a time can cause long delays in getting a piece accepted. But that may be preferable to not ever getting the work placed.

All educators complain they have difficulty locating a sufficient number of high-quality works for students to study, so the field is open to persons with real talent in this area. Few composers in the educational market will die rich, but large numbers of them will receive good royalty checks every quarter from their publishers to supplement their incomes.

Composers in the educational field cannot expect sizable incomes from performances or record royalties. Most of this repertoire does not figure in those segments of the music business. An exception would be dramatic music, such as school operettas and book shows intended for high schools and colleges. Here the composer would receive royalties from performances which generate through his publisher's granting of dramatic performance licenses.

One additional income source can be mentioned. Some composers write special material for school and college football bands — such as instrumental novelties, jazz-swing-rock "marches," etc. Since many football game shows are broadcast, performance income is thus generated. Composers' income from this kind of "educational music" can be considerable, particularly if their music is performed by college and professional bands as part of network TV broadcasts.

COMPOSER OF CHILDREN'S MUSIC

It rarely occurs to musicians that they might develop a career creating music just for children. When mass production of printed and recorded music accelerated after World War II, one of the new markets discovered was in the area of music addressed to young children and kids up to the age of about nine to twelve years. The Walt Disney people led the way in marketing special music of this kind, discovering that families who attended movies such as *Snow White and the Seven Dwarfs* became very interested in preserving some of those pleasantries by taking home, not only records of the movie score, but all kinds of printed arrangements of the songs. Since the Disney company showed the way, other publishers imitated them, for example with music for nursery rhymes and Tubby the Tuba-type of children's music. This special kind of repertoire has, in intervening years, grown to sizable proportions. Publishers and record companies now employ composers adept at serving this special audience.

A composer seeking a professional career writing children's music must understand how to score his ideas in a simple style, yet avoid the simplistic: a composer might "write down" for kids, but he shouldn't get caught at it. Competition in the field is strong, and even the simplest nursery room songs should reveal at least a hint of charm, if not originality. Song texts are essential to most music appealing to children. If the composer is not adept at composing lyrics, he will need to locate someone who knows how to handle song texts without sounding totally vacuous. Also, the aspiring composer in this field needs to know how limited in range his melodies must be for young voices.

One aspect of composing music for kids spills over into the educational field. A portion of this market includes materal that helps young children learn to count, to spell, to recognize the names of animals, etc., often correlated to music books, lavishly illustrated, with sound recordings. Some A/V material producers go the next step and correlate records with film strips. Composers interested in this kind of writing and production are involved, not just in entertainment, but in education.

QUALIFICATIONS, PREPARATION — Aspirants may find work in this field with no more qualifications than those cited above for popular songwriters — natural creative gifts. A professional arranger can always be called in to bail out the illiterate composer who is not informed in his craft. But it is more likely that publishers and record producers, given a choice, will prefer to look at the music submitted by musicians who know how to score what they invent. Competition in the field from genuinely professional composers will probably make it increasingly difficult for the ill-prepared to compete.

In order to prepare for professional work in the children's music field, the aspirant would be well-advised to write a volume of material for kids in his own community, working through nursery schools, kindergartens and elementary school teachers to discover whether the youngsters turn on to the music. If the kids and their teachers are receptive, a publisher in the field would be interested in looking at that composer's work.

EMPLOYMENT PROSPECTS — Most income in this field derives from records and printed music which follow release of a successful musical film or TV program. And some of this work is rendered by songwriters already hired by the film producers. Music publishers and record companies then follow up the film with special editions aimed at very young audiences. Composers who cannot make contact with film producers will find their next best access is through a firm such as Bowmar Inc. That firm's success has been largely based on its handsome illustrations of music in books and filmstrips and the employment of composers knowledgeable in the music education field who are adept at writing music that is particularly appealing to kids. Bowmar has prospered also because of strong marketing campaigns. The composer aspiring to work in the children's music field, once he learns he is qualified, should seek contact directly with those publishers who address most of their energies to this particular market. The quickest route to discovering just who these publishers are is to examine the children's section of a music store. Music discovered there will not compete with Beethoven's *Ninth Symphony*, but royalties it generates for composers will certainly help pay the rent. Composers successful in the children's educational field sometimes manage to earn royalties comparable to pop songwriters. Others who prefer to moonlight as teachers, arrangers, choir directors, etc., remain active in the children's music field only part-time. Some publishers and record producers like to sign composers on a work done for hire basis rather than on a royalty basis. Composers who have any pride in their work should never agree to this. Creative musicians should do all they can to perform their services strictly on a royalty basis. In the long run, royalties, even on material of only limited initial success, will accrue greater income for the composer than any job performed for just one lump sum in front.

COMPOSER OF SERIOUS MUSIC

Musicians who aspire to professional careers as composers of serious music generally view themselves as functioning outside the music "business," believing they can spare themselves direct confrontation with the commercial world. This may be possible for the composer who is fortunate enough to marry a rich widow. But most composers in the so-called classical field bump up against the rude realities of the marketplace, sometimes more often than their brothers in popular music. If we assume the serious music composer is very talented and possesses the right temperament for such a career, he should acquaint himself with the professional lives of Bach, Handel or Chopin — not to mention Schoenberg and Bartók. Each of these composers discovered that he had to devote much of his time hustling for jobs, commissions and students. In the late twentieth century, only a handful of composers devote their full workweek to composing. Either through choice or financial necessity, nearly all composers divide their time between composing, teaching, performing — and job hustling.

Practically all serious music composers find that about the only place they can find steady employment is on the teaching staff of a conservatory or university (in recent decades, Schoenberg, Bartók, Harris, Piston, Hindemith, Persichetti, Crumb, Foss, Schuller).

Once a composer starts to acquire a good reputation, he begins to receive commissions. It is not uncommon for a high school band or community symphony orchestra to commission a composer to write a piece for it, paying a commission of, say, $500 to $5,000. Sometimes a commission looks large, but if it does not include copying and reproduction of the parts, the composer may pay out more for these services than he receives to compose the music. A composer of national and international reputation, e.g., Aaron Copland, could fully support himself from commissions alone, for musicians of this stature receive more requests to compose than they can accept. But the composer aspiring to this high station may have to wait a lifetime to reach these heights.

Composers of even modest reputation enter composing contests. They come along all the time, and an energetic composer can often earn several hundred dollars a year this way. Certain contests of this kind can lead to a national reputation; through them composers develop offers of commissions, even teaching jobs. Below this prestigious group are several thousand professional composers whose names are known only regionally, but who divide their time between writing and teaching, sometimes performing as conductors or soloists. While this time-sharing is not desirable to most of these artists, they usually have summers free to write or rest and enjoy prestige in their communities.

QUALIFICATIONS, PREPARATION — To find this kind of employment, the aspirant must be highly motivated and determined to make his way in serious composition. Let us hope that he might also be talented. But how do we identify the really first-rate serious composer today? We have no consensus on this question. With the abandonment of most of the nineteenth century tradition, the adoption of atonality and serialism, not to mention sound synthesis, critics, musicologists and audiences do not agree at all on precisely which composers are outstanding and which ones just hide their limitations behind compositional systems and bleeping oscillators.

As it turns out, the composers who manage to achieve more than regional reputations are those who discover how to attract attention. Sometimes this attention is generated by using outlandish tricks (quartet for strings and cement mixer) — or "composing" pieces that are silent musically (John Cage). Or a serious (?) composer may attract attention through tricking critics (garnering rave reviews for a piece that was deliberately performed backwards).

Other serious composers get their music played because they appear as soloists or conductors. If they are really good at either, they give the impression of being first-rate at anything musical.

How does a serious composer prepare himself? Practically all of them today who get teaching jobs must have an earned terminal degree from an accredited university. Of these, the most useful is the D.M.A. - Doctor of Musical Arts, the degree now most often awarded to musicians planning professional careers as composers-teachers. Some older, more traditional universities award the Ph.D. as the terminal degree in composition. Most advanced degree candidates serve as teaching assistants to the faculty under which they are studying or teach music in a school to support themselves financially during the arduous period of graduate study. Whatever the work/study combination the degree candidate can set up, honest teachers admit that the years of advanced study in composition do not have much to do with teaching "composition" as a creative act. Rather, advanced study focuses on developing the student's craft — through extensive exercises, performances, and study of master works.

EMPLOYMENT PROSPECTS — The musician aspiring to employment as a composer of serious music cannot expect to earn his living scoring masterpieces. As outlined above, he will almost certainly find work, early in his career, primarily as a teacher of theory and composition in a college or university. As a potential pedagog, he should know that, since 1970, the supply of qualified, certified teachers has exceeded demand. The job shortage since the early 1970s has been particularly acute at the college level. And at post-secondary teaching levels, there is a large surplus of applicants in the theory and composition fields, with even an oversupply of composers holding the D.M.A., Ph.D. and Ed.D. degrees. Still, those who are sufficiently motivated will continue their quest for employment as serious composer-teachers.

Composers who land college jobs earn about the same salaries as others on post-secondary music faculties. These individuals may supplement their salaries with commissions and summer teaching jobs.

How does the aspiring composer-teacher land his first job? In these ways: 1) develop a good reputation with influential musician-teachers; 2) join the College Music Society and follow up its job-opening notices; 3) register with your alma mater's placement bureau; 4) attend professional meetings; get acquainted, set up performances of your work, seek publicity; 5) register with teacher employment services; 6) persevere for at least five years. If this combination of strategies yields no employment, consider the alternatives open to composers cited in these pages. Many composers have musically-satisfying careers writing only part-time, knowing that rent money has to come from second and third-choice professional activities.

ARRANGER-ORCHESTRATOR

Thousands of creative musicians earn most of their incomes as arrangers. They accomplish this in diverse ways, ranging from writing leadsheets to scoring motion pictures. Hundreds of arrangers make their living working for songwriters and publishers, turning out leadsheets and song copies. Earnings in this field average about $30 to $50 per hour. The AFM has scales covering this kind of work but they are often ignored because the union has few opportunities to police this kind of employment.

Publishers engage arrangers full-time or free-lance to score various editions particularly for the educational field. Astute publishers hire only specialists for this kind of work — choral arrangers for vocal editions, jazz specialists for jazz charts, and so on.

The largest number of professional arrangers work for performers. Nearly all professional performers use custom arrangements exclusively. Unlike earlier decades in the pop field when "stock" arrangements were widely used, in recent years the professional soloist or ensemble performer has understood that he must depend on himself or outside arrangers to chart his music for live or canned presentation. This has resulted in widespread employment for arrangers.

Nearly all arrangers are employed free-lance; few are retained on regular salaries. Their services are considered, under copyright law, as *work done for hire*; they receive one flat fee, in front, and do not receive royalties on copies or records sold.

Many arrangers in the pop field work on an exclusive basis for one star, e.g., George Rhodes for Sammy Davis, Jr. Arrangers such as Rhodes are actually the star's musical director, and they double as piano accompanists. Their workweek is a busy combination of helping the star select songs, scoring charts, rehearsing the house band, then conducting the star's music during performances. This kind of music director farms out the arranging when he lacks time to do it all himself.

Another type of music arranger doubles as a music director/performer with ensembles. Many of these arrangers must find ways to convey their ideas to groups that may have some members lacking music-reading ability. In the rock field, the arranger-director of the group is often the composer, too, so he has control over the choice of material and the manner of its presentation. Such individuals enjoy the highest incomes in the rock field through their royalties as composers.

Another type of arranger is employed by producers engaged in recording royalty artists. Many recording session arrangers perform double duty as music directors of the recording orchestra or vocal ensemble. Since most pop songwriters lack competence as arrangers, producers hire their favorite arranger free-lance for recording sessions. This procedure is common in the fields of pop, country and MOR.

Some of the arrangers enjoying the greatest prestige work in the film and TV fields. This type of arranger also is generally the best paid, for AFM scales are very high. Arrangers are needed to write instrumental or vocal arrangements for pop songs or they score background music to accompany drama. All such employment is performed exclusively by AFM members for at least union scale.

For many years, the AFM has attempted to educate producers and musicians as to the alleged distinctions between "arranging" and "orchestration" — without conspicuous success. While separate AFM scales prevail for these two kinds of scoring, (the scale for arranging is higher than for orchestration), composers and producers simply call in an "arranger," tell him what the job pays, and he takes it or leaves it. He takes it, then pays AFM work dues on whatever he believes he can get past the union.

Arrangers and orchestrators usually work under absurd deadlines, largely because composers and producers fail to hand over the scores with reasonable lead time. It is a very high pressure field. Panic-type time schedules are regularly relieved, however, with intermittent periods of idleness, if not starvation. But musicians attracted to the arranging field appear to love their work and manage to survive careers which are a mix of great artistic satisfaction and trips to the unemployment office.

While many musicians manage to work quite steadily just in the arranging field, a much larger number work as part-time arrangers, dividing their professional efforts among such related fields as composition, directing, producing and performing. Others are working at least part-time in such fields as publishing and management.

QUALIFICATIONS, PREPARATIONS — To qualify as a professional arranger, the individual should have thorough training in music theory. This learning can take place through private study, but college training may be preferable. The advantage of formal training is that the student can measure his progress and accomplishments against other students. He may discover he is well ahead of his peers, or he may learn he cannot really compete and should turn to some other field. Also, formalized schooling may be less costly than several years of private lessons. Formalized training will include studies in sight singing and ear training which are sometimes difficult skills to pick up outside of school.

An arranger's ear must be as finely tuned as that of a composer. Actually, nearly all professional arrangers qualify as composers, too. An arranger is expected to work fast and be able to knock out a score overnight, when necessary.

Besides schooling in music theory, the best training for aspirants is *to write* — and write and write — then hear the score in rehearsal. Then rewrite. Then rehearse the revision — and on and on over several years of experimentation, trial and error. All good writers, whether they create prose, poetry or music, recommend two basic activities: read a lot and write constantly.

EMPLOYMENT PROSPECTS — The aspiring professional arranger need not starve throughout his learning experience. All arrangers who eventually make it as pros begin to pick up small jobs early on — first for free, then maybe somebody has a few dollars for one of your charts — if you'll copy off the parts and run the rehearsal. Really talented arrangers attract attention quickly, and they begin receiving requests for their work, often from those with inability to pay much. But outstanding talents can break in. Employment prospects for them are generally good, provided they are prepared, at least early in their careers, to fill out their workweeks with other jobs. Top arrangers working in the record field for stars or busy record producers sometimes earn $50,000 a year and up. If they manage to keep abreast of ever-changing musical styles, their careers can last longer than the artists for whom they write.

A lot of arranging is done without regard for AFM scales. But in records and film, all arranging-orchestrating and copying are written (theoretically) for AFM scale. Top arrangers usually charge over scale, knowing that they must get their fees in front and not expecting any royalties, no matter how creative their work may be.

MUSIC EDITOR

Several kinds of music editors can be identified. The professional who lays music tracks to film is identified as either a music editor or music cutter, as explained earlier. Career opportunities for this kind of person are described in this chapter under Music Services. Career opportunities for writers *about* music, e.g., critics and journalists, are described under Words and Music. Here I shall discuss only the kind of music editor who prepares music manuscripts for publication.

All publishers of printed music require professional editors, because even skilled composers and arrangers are rarely knowledgeable concerning precisely how scores and parts must be edited before the music is printed. In the popular field, most publishers contract with one of the major printing houses, such as Charles Hanson Inc. to handle their music editing and paper publishing.

Music print publishers engage editors on staff and free-lance to rewrite the composers' or arrangers' scores so that they conform in content and style to the standards this country inherited centuries ago from master European engravers and printers. Regrettably, many publishers today have abandoned (or were never aware of) the art of music publishing known in earlier times. Only a handful of master engravers are left in this country, and this shortage of skilled craftsmen accounts in part for the far more prevalent music printing practices involving manuscript autography, music typewriting and photographic plate-making techniques.

Whatever technique is used to prepare music for the platemaker, the music editor must first perform his tasks of correcting, proofreading and pasteup for the platemaker's camera. This kind of work is drudgery to many music writers and they rarely stay with music editing jobs unless at least part of their work can involve actual rescoring, arranging, and even original composition. The music editors who are most in demand are almost always qualified as composers and arrangers, too. Many editors specialize in just one field, such as choral music or piano music. Publishers in educational music have several editors specializing in just marching or concert band.

When an editor acquires long experience, he is sometimes elevated by a publisher to the status of executive editor or editor-in-chief. This individual is normally employed full-time on the publisher's staff — and may even own part of the company. In larger houses, the executive editor is largely concerned with passing judgment on acquisitions. Most publishers receive large quantities of manuscripts, particularly in the classical and educational fields. It is the task of the executive editor to evaluate the scores submitted in respect to musical quality, style and market suitability. Even if the score under review appears aesthetically respectable and technically well scored, the chief editor may pass on the offering if it does not fit into his firm's needs at a particular time of year. To handle this much responsibility, the editor must be of long experience and very knowledgeable, not only in music but in music marketing.

To qualify for a job as a music editor, the individual should undertake a complete musical education in theory, history, literature and performance practices. This broad background is most readily available in universities with strong music departments. Most editors major in music theory and composition and aspire to careers as creative musicians. When this admirable goal cannot be fully attained, musicians find that they can still remain fairly close to their first career choice by seeking employment as editors of other composers' works.

No college curriculum adequately prepares a musician to become an editor. After acquiring the broadest general music education possible, the aspiring editor then finds it necessary to enter into some kind of apprenticeship arrangement with a publisher and learn on the job.

Can an aspiring music editor find employment? It will be difficult at the outset. For many musicians, particularly composers and arrangers with good educational backgrounds, music editing is a fallback position; they enter the field as a second career choice, or, more commonly, as one component of a combination career.

Nearly all free-lance editors earn part of their incomes from composing, arranging, copying, performing or teaching.

Editors-in-chief of major houses are sometimes among the high salary earners in the corporation and may also enjoy stock options and other benefits.

MUSIC COPYIST

Many musicians break into the composing and arranging fields as music copyists. Other musicians develop satisfying, good-paying careers just in the copying field itself. There is an actual shortage of fully-qualified musicians who have the knowledge and skill required of professional copyists. Since practically no school or college teaches professional music preparation (the term includes extraction of parts, duplication, collation, score preparation and other music library services), the aspirant must acquire his knowledge and skills on his own.

All professional copyists are also arrangers. They will have studied music theory just as professional arrangers, for the two professions have much in common as to craft. Good self-study books on copying are available, too. The aspiring copyist will learn also from how well musicians read his work. Working copyists not only turn out legible parts, their MSS are usually beautiful to see. Assuming legibility and appearance are in hand, the critical issue with music copying is accuracy. Professional copyists are expected to make no mistakes, and they are also expected to correct the errors in the scores they work on — scores which every copyist knows are replete with composers' carelessness, not to mention whole sections of scores left incomplete by the composer or arranger. The experienced professional copyist may not be able to reach the composer-arranger to answer his questions about illegible notes or incomplete sections. He must then have sufficient skill and knowledge to correct, then complete the score himself. Copyists who must run to their employers every 16 bars or so become an annoyance. Next week, the composer-arranger will try to call in a copyist who can simply figure the music out for himself.

A large part of copying is done outside AFM jurisdiction — for prices ranging from free to union scale. But in the film, show, and recording fields, practically all copyists are AFM members working for union scale. AFM copying scale now is very high, and fully qualified copyists can earn good money — sometimes more than arrangers.

Some copyists work rather steadily for a name composer or publishing company. Nearly all work of this kind, however, is performed free-lance, and even a copyist of fine reputation may experience irregular income.

Copying jobs exist everywhere. But the aspirant must sniff them out and make his availability known to every composer-arranger he can locate.

Most copyists supplement their income as performers. Others may also be active in music publishing, merchandising, as an agent or manager. These kinds of combination careers can often yield, in the aggregate, satisfactory incomes.

PRODUCING-DIRECTING CAREERS

Music Director-Conductor
Record Producer

Theatrical Producer-Director
Film Producer-Director

MUSIC DIRECTOR-CONDUCTOR

CAREER DESCRIPTION — All musical performers — soloists and ensemble artists — require musical direction. In the pop field, the individual serving as musical director may not be a conductor but simply a performer in the group who assumes a leadership role. Musical direction of groups of this kind is sometimes shared, but dividing this important responsibility usually leads to difficulties. As for soloists, when an artist reaches star status, he usually finds it necessary to employ a musical director, at least for appearances on tour. These individuals are almost invariably rehearsal pianists-accompanists who assist the artist by selecting material, arranging it, conducting rehearsals and live performances. Many of these pianist-conductors are not trained baton twirlers but manage to make sufficient hand gestures from their position at the piano keyboard to cue the musicians. Stars' musical directors-accompanists are usually displaced when the star records, as most record producers install their own people on those occasions.

Some jobs for musical directors in the pop field are found in major cities, particularly Las Vegas, conducting shows. Other musical directing jobs are available in the field of industrial shows. Broadway, off-Broadway and regional theatres, particularly dinner theatres, employ musical directors, most of whom are actually orchestra conductors.

Musical directors for movies and TV are almost invariably hired first as composer-arrangers; they then are expected to conduct their own music when their scores are recorded; the musician who is only a conductor rarely finds employment in these fields. This same pattern prevails in the field of syndicated music and library services: musical directors are usually serving the producers as triple-threat artists, composers-arrangers-directors.

Some musical directors are engaged by arts centers and community centers as artistic directors. They may not only conduct rehearsals and performances, they are likely also to function as organizers and supervisors of artistic and educational programs for these entities.

The conductors best known by the public, of course, are those engaged as musical directors of symphony orchestras and opera companies. Symphony orchestras in the United States are classified by the American Symphony Orchestra League according to the size of their annual operating budgets. Major orchestras normally contract for a conductor for terms of one to five years. Some are called "artistic director." It is customary for musicians holding these posts to assist management in selecting, then contracting guest conductors and guest soloists, selecting programs, working with orchestra managers in planning operating budgets, and hiring and firing musicians.

Artistic directors also become involved with the major orchestras in negotiating recording contracts for their ensembles. Because of the heavy responsibilities assumed by these kinds of musical directors, they require at least one assistant conductor. Some of the major orchestras have two or more assistant conductors who help the artistic director by conducting performances for school children and pop concerts.

Assistant conductors also are often assigned many of the summer concerts. Conductors who serve time as assistant conductors often graduate to roles of principal conductors and music directors of orchestras and opera companies.

Music directors and assistant directors have such heavy responsibilities, they rarely find time for any other professional employment. In addition to their directing, they must meet with the various committees charged with the responsibility of raising money for operations. An important part of this aspect of the work is fostering goodwill among the individuals and corporations and foundations who pledge money to support the artistic goals of the ensemble. Some conductors find these fund-raising meetings and social contacts distasteful and refuse to take part. Musical directors of this temperament don't hold jobs for long.

Thousands of musical directors are employed by churches. These professionals are usually organists, many of whom serve double duty as choir directors. Large churches sometimes call their musical directors "ministers of music." A person serving in such a capacity usually directs two to four choral groups for the institution and may also assist in directing youth activities. Where the largest churches pay their musical directors full-time salaries, smaller institutions do not, expecting them to fill out their incomes through such activities as teaching. Salaries for musical directors in the religious field compare with those for school teachers.

QUALIFICATIONS, PREPARATION — All really successful musical directors share a common attribute: as personalities, they have a commanding presence. They know how to lead, either intuitively or through training. This leadership quality is not limited to musical matters but extends to relationships with the variety of human personalities they work with in rehearsal and performance.

Musical directors achieve dominance and control over those working under them in a variety of ways. Some win over their performers through respect: the conductor is so obviously talented that the musicians follow him without question. Others may possess a particularly clear baton technique and the ensemble responds with precision. Other leaders dominate their musicians through fear, even abusive behavior. Many famous conductors have used such techniques with great success. Lesser numbers of conductors win their allegiance through charm and friendly encouragements. Leaders of this kind of temperament may achieve good results in minor posts. I do not know of any personalities of this kind that have achieved recognition and prestige at anything like the national or international level. In the musical directing field, nice guys may not finish last, but they remain relatively unknown outside their own communities. I have performed under many of the leading conductors of the world. Every one of them was a despot. They were also great leaders and superb musicians.

Besides the essential attribute of a dominating personality and leadership qualities, a successful musical director must possess musical qualities that clearly distinguish him from those he leads. The conductor must know more music, be better informed and more sensitive about styles, have better ears, know more repertoire, and have an effective baton technique. If the director lacks these distinctions, he will not be a leader but a follower. Some directors come by these leadership qualities through natural, God-given talent. Others, less endowed, must work very hard to pull themselves up above other musicians.

Nearly all successful musical directors have had very extensive schooling, often a combination of formal education and private instruction. Since musical directors must be well-informed on all aspects of music, their education, at least through the baccalaureate degree level, will be broad. Post-baccalaureate study may include emphasis in performance, composition or conducting.

In that all qualified conductors must be good score readers, they must either be pianists or at least play enough piano to dig out the inner workings of scores at the keyboard. In the classical field, conductors who are not pianists are most often string players. Through study of instrumental performance, conductors acquaint themselves with repertoire and acquire understanding of performance problems encountered by the musicians they lead.

Choral conductors are invariably voice majors or thoroughly prepared, through practical experience as singers, to understand the challenges singers face in tackling vocal music.

In the pop field, directors are almost invariably performers, too, and are usually involved in composition and arranging. A high percentage of pop music directors are occupied much of the time rehearsing and directing performances of the music they themselves have scored.

Few musical directors in the pop field function only as conductors. While pop music conductors rarely need to study extensively the serious music repertoire, they must have basic skills in conducting any musical style, for musical direction jobs often demand involvement in styles ranging from pop to the classics. This means that any individual aspiring to a career as a music director is well-advised to thoroughly prepare himself as a musician, acquire his craft. He will then be prepared to do at least a respectable job of rehearsing and conducting whatever music is placed in front of him. Accordingly, schooling for all professional conductors is basically the same.

The best environment for an aspiring musical director is a first-rate university with a strong faculty and a variety of performance groups. Additionally, most conductors start early, usually while still in college, to direct a church choir or jazz band or pop chorus or whatever group they can get their hands on. The aspiring musical director who waits until he is out of college to start doing what he wants to do is already too late; his competition has passed him.

If the aspiring musical director possesses sufficient talent and acquires a first-rate musical education, he may still lack one essential attribute: the ability to handle his responsibilities in an organized way. Above all, he must be able to organize his time because he will never have enough of it. He must understand how to draw together and manage an ensemble. Only a minority of directors enjoy the luxury of having a professional manager to handle the infinite details requiring attention. Finally, the director must possess an ability to develop financial support. A musical director won't have a group to lead unless he locates and maintains a money source.

EMPLOYMENT PROSPECTS — Job prospects for musical directors can be compared with those found in other aspects of the arts and business: there is plenty of work available for top people. In the classical field we have a worldwide shortage of first-rate symphony and opera conductors. Organizations here and abroad outbid each other for the top musical directors. The field is so understaffed, most conductors of high reputation hold down at least two conducting posts.

At the level below the top 100 conductors in the classical field, we have thousands of musicians who believe they are qualified for top jobs. Many are. A variety of reasons might account for their inability to crack the big time. They may lack a forceful personality. They may lack an enterprising manager or agent. They may have a reputation for being unable to work well with musicians or sponsoring boards. And they may lack the music directing talent required of our leading arts organizations.

Some conductors who languish in small communities conducting unknown ensembles go through their whole careers never discovering that they simply lack the special talents the big jobs require. Still others do not aspire to glamorous posts and prefer to serve smaller communities where the salaries are lower, but so are the pressures.

Musical directors in the popular field experience employment opportunities in sharp contrast to the serious music field. Nearly all musical directors in the pop and pop-related fields rise or fall, not on their abilities as conductors or leaders. Rather, it is their ability to please their employers *as writers*. A musical director who is a really competent composer and arranger can usually find work — and his ability to rehearse and conduct groups is a minor consideration. Employers tolerate incompetent leadership qualities and baton techniques when the musical director is a whiz at writing music.

In the pop field, young musical directors usually start out earning no more than the other performers in the group they direct. When the group goes union, AFM scales generally call for the leader to receive double sideman's scale. When a record producer or music library service (syndicator) production house hires a musical director, he will probably be paid AFM scale (double sideman's wages), then be paid again for any arranging he may do. In TV and film scoring, the conductor usually works for AFM scale, but makes his real money as a composer-arranger. Unlike the huge fees commanded by conductors in the classical field, such rates are unheard of in popular music.

RECORD PRODUCER

CAREER DESCRIPTION — The work of the various kinds of record producers is described in detail earlier in this book, and I will not restate that information here. Individuals employed as record producers function at a level and in a manner that reflects their particular competence. Some producers are successful largely because they are very good at locating the right musical material, then matching it to the right artists. This is why the old label for these practitioners used to be "artist and repertoire producers."

Some producers are masters of the control room. Others know how to raise money, then hire outside experts to arrange the music, mix the sound and supervise post-production. Still other producers are master musicians who make it in the field because they are creative and capture artistic performances on tape.

Most record producers don't have "careers." They just get jobs. Over half of the work is performed free-lance. The nearest thing approaching steady employment is found with major labels who hire staff producers and place them on full-time salaries. Producers float from job to job pretty much like recording artists; they get return engagements when their records sell. If they produce a string of flops, their telephones stop ringing. Greater employment continuity is found among staff producers, but even here, a label won't retain a house producer beyond a year or so unless he can produce sufficient sales to at least cover his salary.

Independent producers often own their own production companies, and they stay in the field as long as they can turn out at least occasional hits. One good hit may keep them afloat for a year or so. But without periodic successes in the marketplace, independent producers are forced to change directions or fold.

QUALIFICATIONS, PREPARATION — An individual aspiring to a career in record production should not expect to follow an orderly path. Nearly all producers who make it discover that they must first become recognized in an allied field — such as songwriting, arranging, sound mixing or musical direction. In addition to the competence in one or more of these facets of music, the record producer usually possesses some kind of leadership ability. He has a temperament that mixes well with other artists, technicians and businessmen. He may lack the personal charisma often associated with big-name conductors, but he at least handles himself in a manner that elicits cooperation from co-workers. Also, the producer must remain stable when others around him are disintegrating through frustration or fatigue. He has the additional worry of staying within budget. Budget panics are endemic with record production, and the individual in charge is totally responsible for keeping costs under control. So the record producer must be a kind of miracle man, possessing strong musical ability, technological know-how, business sense, magic ears, and the stability to remain rational under great pressures — all the while serving as referee in conflicts of ego that threaten working relationships.

EMPLOYMENT PROSPECTS — Since no one possesses all these talents, those that come close find themselves in high demand. Investors, labels and artists are always searching for a record producer who can pull all the elements together, get them on tape and on the charts. If a producer possesses the essentials of his art and craft, he will work and prosper, through in-front fees and points (royalties). But even the most successful producers have spotty careers. They work steadily, sometimes frantically, for a few years, then fade. Why? Most often because they cannot adjust their ears to changing tastes. When an established producer starts to slip, it is this very phenomenon, omnipresent in the field, that opens up work for newcomers — or for producers seeking comebacks. Labels experiment continually, ever searching for the commercial combination of producer-material-and artist. For example, when the disco craze hit in the late 1970s, a whole new group of producers came out of the woodwork, presenting themselves to labels and investors as just the right choice to produce records in this "new" style. Whenever a "new," or relatively new style comes along, this kind of shift in the business opens up jobs for new producers. Some prosper, for a while, often to be displaced later by the next new wave.

Record production, then, is not really a career, but a series of jobs. Because of the absence of employment continuity, nearly all record producers maintain other irons in the fire, just as most musicians do. They may write songs, own part of a publishing company, manage artists, function as agents, write arrangements, produce shows — whatever maintains their close contacts with music and records.

Staff producers earn weekly salaries; the best of them also have contracts providing royalties based on sales of records they produce. Some producers become wealthy through royalties. Some contracts provide for a royalty "override" — meaning that a producer's royalties don't start until royalties from his records have first covered an amount equal to his annual salary. Some producers do not start receiving royalties until the label has recovered its out-of-pocket production costs. Some independent producers are given all their production expenses by a record label and receive a flat production fee plus royalties, or possibly no fee, just royalty income.

Record producers are also required in the field of serious music. Such employment can not be said to constitute a career, for jobs are spaced few and far between. When a label such as London decides to record the Chicago Symphony performing yet another version of

Beethoven's *Eroica,* the label would normally hire, on a free-lance basis, a producer for just that job — two to six weeks' work at the most. The producer would have to confirm with London's top management that the terms of the contract between the label and the orchestra were fully understood. Then he would rent the best theatre or concert hall he could find for the sessions, engage a remote recording company for technical services, clarify the orchestra's contract with the AFM, set the recording schedule at times that do not conflict with the orchestra's other commitments, then supervise the actual recording sessions, his worried eye glancing at the clock every few minutes to allay his fears that he was going over budget. If the producer manages to actually get the complete symphony on tape, he has many more hours of work in mixing, editing, equalizing, and mastering. Other post-production tasks will probably occupy him full time for another few weeks.

The producer of serious music must possess many of the same qualifications as the pop record producer, plus a few more. He has to be as good a score reader as his conductor and know details of the score being recorded. Ideally, the producer in the booth should be the twin of the producer on the podium, so close must they understand each other and the musical interpretation the literature requires.

To qualify to produce classical music recordings, the musician must have training identical to the kind described above for serious music conductors. Additionally, he must have knowledge of technology, perhaps even acoustics, sufficient to give direction to his mixing and mastering technicians. Few record producers possess all these talents. Those who come closest are the ones the major labels call for repeatedly in this highly specialized work.

In between jobs, serious music record producers who prefer three meals a day find it necessary to be active in one or more allied musical fields, such as conducting, teaching, or composing. Record producers in the classical field are usually paid one fee and rarely receive royalties based on record sales.

THEATRICAL PRODUCER-DIRECTOR

CAREER DESCRIPTION — An individual whose interests are divided between music and theatre can develop a career that combines the two. No person, no matter how versatile, is equally talented in both fields, but those who produce and/or direct music connected with drama discover ways of functioning adequately in both arts. Producers, directors (and producer-directors) find employment in such fields as television, radio packaging, musicals, industrial shows, broadcast commercials, opera and dance theatre. Kurt Herbert Adler might be mentioned as an individual who excels in both the production and direction of musical theatre. He not only conducts performances of the San Francisco Opera Company, he is its general director.

Comparable versatility is found on Broadway in such individuals as Bob Fosse. He started in the theatre as a dancer, then became a choreographer, then a director. Since about the 1950s, the majority of successful directors of Broadway musicals have emerged from the field of choreography. Hal Prince (*A Chorus Line*) can be mentioned as a particularly successful professional who combines directing and producing. Few theatrical producer-directors come from orchestra pits as former instrumentalists or conductors. But many songwriters have successfully combined writing and producing, e.g., Richard Rodgers, Frank Loesser, others.

Less creative people get into theatrical producing and directing through their particular talent as managers. Whether they work on Broadway or in less glamorous venues, such persons are sought after because they excel at raising money, managing budgets and selling tickets. Theatrical producers of this stripe may lack skills as directors, but they surround themselves with sharp assistants to cover all bases.

Individuals involved in theatrical producing and directing find that their most important tasks (following the raising of money) are locating, then selecting, the right material and the right performers to execute the material. But this is only the beginning. Most successful individuals in the field agree that the only way to make it in the musical theatre, and certainly on Broadway, is to have all the elements right. By this, theatrical people are saying that a show hits because the book, score, cast, direction, choreography, staging and management all work together in some magic alchemy. Very often the human catalyst for this beautiful chemistry is the producer — or producer-director.

Since the hit/flop ratio is in the range of one to ten, it is clear that few individuals on Broadway or off-Broadway have possessed the talent and luck to be able to pull together all the diverse elements that go into a hit show. Few schools or colleges offer a complete curriculum in production and direction of musical theatre. Such an education would include studies in drama, music, dance, theatre management and business. A person can study these arts and professions as extensively as possible, throughout one's career — and just trust that, through demonstrated talent and lucky coincidence, producing and directing opportunities may come along.

EMPLOYMENT PROSPECTS — Beyond what has been stated above, it is not possible to generalize about job openings in this field. About all that can be said is that an individual who approximates the kind of versatility the field demands will attract the attention of employers. Only a few producer-directors are hired on yearly contracts with predictable salaries. Producers and directors don't get jobs. Rather, they take on projects; most of the time they have to invent their employment. Even established professionals in the musical theatre experience feast and famine.

As with the field of recording, the musical theatre continues to draw artists and investors because of the omnipresent possibility that they might share in a hit. Whether or not a producer or producer-director has invested in a show, he invariably shares in the royalties that accrue from a successful production. On Broadway, this sharing is guaranteed by contracts negotiated through the Dramatists Guild and can aggregate more royalties than a million-selling record album.

FILM PRODUCER-DIRECTOR

Some versatile artists who experience success in both the fields of music and theatre may turn eventually to working in film or in musical-variety shows for television. For many artists, film is their ultimate goal. Producers, directors (and producer-directors) who graduate to this level of employment will have spent many years prior in related activity, such as songwriting, musical shows, records and commercials.

Many film producers and directors become involved in movies first as screen writers. Many movie writers come to believe that film directors have, in the past, destroyed their work and henceforth demand the right to direct their own scripts. If such persons manage to succeed as writer directors, they often graduate to the status of a full-fledged "hyphenate," a writer-producer-director.

PERFORMING CAREERS

SINGER

CAREER DESCRIPTION — In the field of popular music, singers find careers, not only as soloists and recording artists, but as group singers, on commercials, and as "production" singers, singing actors or singing dancers. As most singers have already discovered, a career often starts at school or college where the individual can learn quite early whether audiences respond well. In the pop field, these amateur and semiprofessional beginnings are often combined with instrumental performance, with songwriting, sometimes both.

Steady employment in the singing field is almost unknown. Performers bounce from job to job, hoping that, over a period of time, work will come their way often enough to form reasonable continuity.

Professional singers practically never sit down very long in one city; their lives are filled with almost incessant travel. The longest engagements occur when an artist remains in one location for a month or two to complete recording an album. Stars who play Las Vegas are booked in for two to four weeks. But most other singing jobs in the pop field are strings of one-nighters or week-long engagements.

Singing careers that go anywhere invariably involve a mix of live appearances and recordings. Established recording stars also appear, occasionally, as we know, on television, sometimes in commercials and films. Few experiences are more exhausting than incessant traveling, and a professional singer's first concern, under these strains, is to stay healthy. His second concern is, or should be, finding a competent personal manager. His third priority is an ongoing search for good material.

Even singers who write most of their own songs must somehow find outside sources to feed their acts. Non-writing singers never stop searching for good songs. Writers and publishers know this and follow singers around constantly, leadsheets in hand, trying to persuade them they have just what the artist is seeking. Successful singers are also plagued with enthusiastic, even overbearing fans who want to get to them. These multiple pressures can debilitate a performer and only the hardy can survive. But those attracted to the field seem to sustain themselves on the applause and adulation of their audiences — not to mention their money.

Even singers with competent managers must give some attention every few days to business affairs, if only to define acceptable para-meters for their managers. Also, singers must work constantly with arrangers and musical directors to assure themselves that their per-formances are presented in the most effective way. Major artists must also find time for costume fittings, makeup jobs and lighting tests. All touring artists find it difficult, often impossible, to locate edible meals while traveling, and must guard their health against junk food and too many calories.

QUALIFICATIONS, PREPARATION — To qualify for a successful career as a professional singer, it is helpful for the aspirant to be able to sing. But any audit of the field will reveal that dozens of non-singers manage to make a living as "singers." Individuals with no recognizable musical talent sometimes win an audience. This usually occurs when the public becomes attracted to a performer, not for his singing ability, but because of the individual's personality. This is the only way to explain the great popularity of such "singers" as Dean Martin, Cher, even Louis Armstrong.

Some performers can sing well and also be appealing personalities, e.g., Neil Diamond, Helen Reddy. Still others have superb vocal instruments but lack charismatic personalities — Jack Jones, Ella Fitzgerald. But if an aspiring singer lacks both good singing ability and a winning personality, he would be well-advised to shift his professional goal. Even a wizard of a manager cannot sell a performer lacking strong audience appeal.

Most popular singers have achieved their following, not through special training, but through natural talent. There are some exceptions. For example, such competent singers as Florence Henderson, Vic Damone, Jack Jones, Robert Goulet have all studied singing with good teachers. But few voice coaches know how to help pop singers. Most of them inhibit naturally talented singers, and their students frequently sound worse coming out of their studios than going in. About all a singing teacher can offer naturally gifted singers in the pop field is improved breath control and help with diction.

When we turn to the kind of singing career that requires extensive vocal training, we have a very different set of circumstances. The largest number of "legitimate" singers are employed by churches and funeral directors. Opera and other kinds of musical theatre employ the next largest group of trained singers. These fields offer employment, at least part-time, not only for solo artists but for chorus singers. Broadcast commercial producers also employ many trained singers. Employment of schooled vocalists in the concert and recital field is very small and is getting even smaller.

While a handful of "natural" voices occasionally cross the line into "legitimate" singing positions, the most common route to this kind of employment is through formalized musical training in conservatories and universities. Respectable institutions of this kind accept as voice majors only those students who exhibit high promise. Following (what should be) this selective filtering process, an aspiring professional singer begins at least four years of voice training, together with studies in sight singing, music theory, literature and languages. Singers planning careers as college teachers go on to the masters and sometimes the D.M.A. degree as voice majors or as majors in choral music.

One of the reasons many singing jobs require extensive vocal training is that most of the repertoire has been long established and demands stylistically authentic interpretation. Singing "personality," universally assumed in the pop field, is often out of place in "legitimate" singing. Musical theatre is sometimes the exception.

To qualify as a legitimate singer, artists must be excellent sight readers, particularly for work in broadcast commercials. In this same field, singers are often called upon to handle a wide variety of singing styles, ranging perhaps from funky to operatic. This high-paying field also requires those singers who can produce crystal clear diction.

Aspirants to singing careers of this kind prepare themselves over many years in school recitals, church jobs, community choruses, perhaps singing at weddings and local concerts. Most colleges have performing opportunities, of course, through recitals, choral performances and opera productions. Some enlightened colleges also have curriculum in musical theatre where singers learn stage movement, dancing, acting, theatrical direction and management. Their graduates are far more employable than those emerging from most university schools of opera. Trained singers enter auditions and contests, some of which offer prize money, scholarships, even job opportunities. Whichever performing medium a singer may hope to enter, he will find Lehman Engel's book, *Getting Started In The Theatre* very useful (see bibliography). Recommended.

EMPLOYMENT PROSPECTS — The job outlook for singers ranges from grim to excellent. Unfortunately, *the fewest opportunities lie in the fields for which our universities and conservatories are turning out the most students* — opera, concerts and recitals. While the solo recital field is about dead, some 200 to 300 professional singers find at least seasonal employment. In New York City, we have about a dozen artist "managers" who provide employment to classically trained singers in opera, recitals, community concert series and with symphony orchestras. The employment prospects for the thousands of university graduates, fresh from four to eight years of study, are particularly grim. New York's artist managers are unable to keep busy the artists already in their stables and have almost no interest in auditioning new artists.

In the field of opera, artist managers place some of them; others are in such demand, they book themselves — opera companies outbid each other for their services. Unfortunately, only a few trained singers qualify for leading roles with good companies. Thousands of university graduates aspiring to careers in their fields are disappointed each year, turn to school teaching, voice coaching or church choir jobs.

Churches offer many jobs to trained singers who can also direct choirs. Jobs in this field pay from $20 to $500 a week. Some singers who are unable to develop performing careers they had planned turn to school teaching, then pick up singing jobs at weddings and funerals. Practically all of this work is nonunion.

Musical theatre sometimes offers an employment option for trained singers, particularly if the auditioners are young, of the right physical size and shape, and able to act and/or dance. While New York producers audition and hire many new singing actors each season, more extensive job opportunities are found in the dozens of regional and dinner theatres sprinkled across the land. Most of these jobs are under Actors Equity Association (AEA), which sets scales and working conditions for singers performing in musical shows and plays.

Aggregate wages paid Equity actors and singers by regional and dinner theatres exceed wages to union members working on Broadway. Aspiring singers sometimes begin their professional careers as non-Equity supporting players in regional and dinner theatres, then graduate to leading roles and Equity wages. The best of these go on to Broadway. Job prospects for really talented singers who can also act or dance or both, are reasonably good. Versatile artists of this kind who are relatively young, physically attractive and highly motivated are probably going to develop professional careers in the musical theatre.

When it comes to job prospects for straight pop singers, we have yet another set of conditions. The difficulty here, as pointed out, is that large segments of the public fail to distinguish between the truly gifted singer and the non-singer who gets by just on personality — or sex appeal or publicity. The aspiring pop singer does not know whether he has a really fine instrument — he rarely bothers to get objective appraisal from a qualified teacher. He thinks he's really good and insists on trying to crack the entertainment business.

The only way he can test his personal appeal is to expose himself repeatedly before all kinds of audiences, even for free, for at least two or three years. If audiences have not demonstrated a strong favorable reaction, and if no artist's manager has stepped forth enthusiastically to take his career in hand, the performer should probably change his professional goal.

A pop singer is probably wasting his time if he attempts to bypass a test of his talent in his local community. It is risky to ignore local receptivity, make a fancy demo, then present his talents to big city record producers. Producers don't need the aspiring singer who has not yet proved himself with the hometown audience. If the home folks don't love him, who will?

Yet another difficulty for the straight pop singer is that several million other young people believe that they, too, are qualified to make it professionally. So these countless hordes compete for the same recognition, the same jobs. The career prospects for the untrained singer who lacks some of the versatility cited above, are grim.

Among the most sought-after singers are those who double as instrumentalists with rock bands. If the performer sings well enough, many rock acts will welcome him even if his abilities in instrumental performance are limited. But double he must, for few rock groups can afford to carry a performer who only sings.

Finding work as a straight singer in the pop field is difficult, but those who survive in the business below the star level get busy qualifying themselves in such related fields as acting, dancing, musical direction and arranging. Through extensive training and preparation of this kind, the pop singer doubles, perhaps quadruples, his chances of developing a professional career in music.

In addition to these recommendations, a pop singer today has one other way to break in that beats them all: composing songs. Since the Beatles in the mid-1960s, the preponderant number of new singing artists breaking big in the business have been performing composers. These artists may not be either great singers or top composers, but the combination enchants audiences and these versatile artists sell most of the records today.

Singing composers have two ways to gain recognition. Some break through initially as writers of songs for others. Some gain initial recognition as performers. These versatile individuals can divide their time between hustling publishers and hustling agents. Also, as songwriters they come in contact with other performers who can occasionally open career doors for them.

INSTRUMENTALIST

CAREER DESCRIPTION — Among the recognized professions, music is unique. Unlike such fields as medicine, law and engineering where one can easily define a "professional," in music we classify as professional musicians individuals whose talents and employment are worlds apart. At one end of the scale we might find the saloon musician who plays for tips and drinks. At the other end might be the studio musician who earns $100,000 a year. In between these two extremes lie about 400,000 other instrumentalists whom we might classify as professionals or semiprofessionals.

The semiprofessional musician tries to keep employed full-time at a non-music job and picks up occasional playing gigs when he can. The semiprofessional usually works for very low wages and accepts long hours and low pay because he views music as an avocation, even recreation. Most semiprofessionals lack the talent, training, opportunity or ambition to become full professionals. But then we have some amateurs and semipros whose talents equal those of top performers, but they prefer non-music careers.

When we leave the ranks of the semipro and examine the careers of individuals who consider themselves professional musicians, we find that the majority of them are occupied only part-time as instrumentalists. Even musicians who say they are employed as instrumentalists "full-time" average only three to four hours per 24 and fill out the balance of their workweek with other professional activities.

Practically all professional musicians do at least some teaching. Accomplished musicians often have more students waiting for openings than they can accept. Student fees not only offer income to supplement playing jobs, but can often provide at least minimum sustenance during periods when the musicians cannot find playing jobs.

The working hours of a full-time professional may average only three hours a day, but most musicians are busy at least 40 hours a week. Besides setting hours aside for teaching, professionals usually engage in regular daily practice, continuing throughout their careers to polish their skills, expand their repertoire. In addition to these musical activities, a large percentage of professional musicians are actively employed partly or entirely outside of music. From choice or necessity, many pros moonlight (more often, daylight) at jobs whose hours can be flexible, thus providing release time for them to accept whatever music jobs come along. For this reason, many musicians combine music careers with sideline work in sales, e.g., real estate and insurance.

Many professional musicians manage a different kind of moonlighting: they accept every attractive playing job that comes along, then fill in the balance of their workweek in music-related employment such as composition, arranging, copying, perhaps artist management or record production. Many professional musicians work fairly regularly as instrumentalists, while filling their daytime hours as music merchants — selling instruments, equipment, etc. Thousands of musicians combine playing and non-playing careers and enjoy double incomes.

Playing jobs vary widely in prestige and pay. Employers seem to find an endless supply of musicians who will perform long hours for low wages — apparently because many performers think of their pay as secondary to the pleasure of performing, whatever the circumstances. It is this avocational, unprofessional attitude of musicians that makes it impossible for the AFM to control a lot of musical employment. Also, many musicians do not understand the advantages of what unionists call collectivism. So musicians outside the AFM usually accept work for shamefully low rates, rarely graduating to professional fees and professional working conditions.

Another aspect of union vs. nonunion employment is found among AFM members who will accept jobs below union scale whenever they believe they can get away with it. These individuals try to have it both ways — and often do. The extent of union control of professional musicians varies greatly among AFM locals. Critics of the AFM argue that the union could do a better job of controlling professional employment if it would make lesser demands upon the employers. AFM officials counter with the argument that musicians, despite periods of training comparable to medical doctors, are still asking hourly wages (except in recording) that are generally lower than those for union plumbers and truck drivers.

AFM headquarters lacks summary data relative to the total number of dollars its members earn each year. But we can gain a perspective on this from figures reported to the AFM-Employers Pension and Welfare Fund. Union musicians working under AFM-EPW contracts (local and national) have earned about $220 million per year at union scale. Of this total, single and "casual" engagements have yielded about $90 million a year, TV and radio commercials $22 million, theatre work some $14 million. AFM wages earned in motion picture scoring (writing and playing) have totalled around $12 million a year. *These figures exclude employment under the many AFM locals whose members perform services which are not covered by the aforementioned AFM-EPW contracts.* The AFM informs me it lacks such figures.

It should be noted that data from the EPW Fund *exclude* some 9 to 15 percent earned additionally by AFM members in fringe benefits, income from the Special Payments Fund, overscale payments and royalties.

It should also be noted that union musicians are required to pay "work dues," what AFM members call "tax." This tax averages 3.5 percent of scale, varying according to local rates and whether or not the work is covered by an AFM national contract.

Except for solo recitalists and those artists who prefer symphonic work, the ultimate professional goal of many musicians is in the recording field. Practically all of this work is regulated by national contracts negotiated by the AFM and the record manufacturers or film producers.

An important consideration for those planning careers as performers is the matter of travel. Most musicians must move around a lot. It can be fun when you are young, but become intolerable after several years of the gypsy life. Another important concern is the seasonal aspect of most performing careers. Many symphony, opera and dance company musicians are laid off in the summer months. Broadway pit musicians know only seasonal employment, which generally means the life of a particular show. Instrumentalists working clubs on so-called "steady engagements" are delighted when a job extends beyond a few weeks.

Another unattractive aspect of the performing instrumentalist's career is that he is often called upon to perform music he doesn't like. Many symphony musicians suffer greatly when recording commercial jingles or country music. The jazz musician often feels excruciating pain when working a rock or country music date. Even in the symphonic field, most orchestras today cheapen their repertoire with a pop series each year. They will program anything that will sell tickets, and the symphony musicians who spent 15 years learning how to play

Mozart suffer deeply.

QUALIFICATIONS, PREPARATION — Aspiring musicians rarely have a clear understanding of what is required of them to succeed as professionals. Many music teachers also lack adequate information. The difficulty here is the distinction among the variety of playing careers available. The semiprofessional or part-time professional may have little or no trainng but sufficient natural talent to get occasional jobs. But if the young instrumentalist has ambitions for a full-time, fully professional playing career, he must qualify at an entirely different level. First, he will have to be endowed with outstanding musical talent. His instrumental study should begin in early childhood and continue throughout his professional life.

Until recent decades, many performers in the serious field aspired to careers as solo recitalists and concert artists. Those who did not attain those goals usually ended up as section players in symphony orchestras. To qualify for concert or symphonic work, the aspirant today will normally enroll in a conservatory for two to four years, undertaking concentrated studies in music performance and repertoire. Tuition costs at good conservatories are out of reach for most students, however, and the great majority of them enroll in a college or university.

To qualify for the concert and symphonic field, students today will usually complete at least the masters degree, often the doctorate, in performance (conservatory graduates normally complete a "diploma" program). Whatever amount of formal training the musician might undergo, it is expected that he is familiar with performance practices of both serious and popular music. Even symphony string players today, the last group to enter the twentieth century, are now called upon to perform in pop, if not jazz, styles. Practically all symphony orchestras have a pops series where travelling artists bring in charts ranging in style from blues to country. And musicians in the theatre and recording fields are expected to be able to perform any musical idiom in the correct style. The old days of the "classical" and "jazz" musician are about gone. All pros now must cross the line.

Young musicians, particularly from the folk, country, soul and jazz fields, often ask if they really have to be good readers. We still have non-readers in these fields, some of whom are financially, occasionally artistically, very successful. But their success is often based more upon their personality, composing, or strong natural talent. The great majority of full-time professional instrumentalists are expected to be musically literate and read at sight what is placed before them.

Whatever professional goal the musician aspires to, whatever his talent and training, to build a career with continuity the instrumentalist will discover the field demands a particular kind of temperament. Besides having a personality that helps him work well with others, the real pro must be willing to work very hard for long years and persevere during periods of disappointment. Just "liking music" is not enough. Most truly accomplished professional artists reach their goal through a love, even a passion, for music-making.

Yet another personal attribute is essential for the instrumentalist who shoots for the highest-paying fields, particularly symphony and studio work: *strong nerves.* Young musicians shooting for the big time are generally unaware of the working atmosphere particularly in the recording field, which is one, not so much of high tension as sheer terror. Those jobs demand perfection in performance. There is minimum tolerance for error and none whatever for carelessness. A top studio player is allowed an occasional flub, but he is quickly displaced, sometimes forever, by a competitor who can demonstrate even greater reliability. Nerves of steel come in handy, but before the faint-of-heart abandon their dreams of the big time, it should be reassuring to remember that artists of international stature — musicians, dancers, actors, have told us that controlled tension aids artistic performance.

EMPLOYMENT PROSPECTS — While we have thousands of unemployed and underemployed musicians, the truth is that we are actually undersupplied in some areas. Employment prospects depend, not only on a musician's talent and training, but his particular instrument:

Keyboard Players — We are greatly oversupplied by first-rate concert pianists and recitalists. Our conservatories and colleges continue to turn out thousands of these artists, but their employment prospects are not just poor, they are almost zero. Even the old strategy of "buying" a New York Town Hall debut rarely works anymore. We also have an oversupply of piano teachers in most communities, except those who have acquired the innovative pedagogical techniques of group instruction. Most communities are oversupplied with restaurant, club and saloon pianists. But where are the pianists who play really artistically, *even in one style?* Traveling extensively in this country and Europe, I am continually astonished to rediscover just how incompetent most working pianists are — they may know the popular standards, but they play the wrong chords, wrong tempos, wrong style, wrong melody, can't improvise creatively, and would be hard-pressed to get through an easy piece of Chopin. Our conservatories and universities have graduated tens of thousands of "pianists," but very few of them even approach the level of versatility and competence required of the working professional keyboard artist. We have M.A.'s and even D.M.A.'s who, if asked to improvise "Happy Birthday" in two different keys, would risk cardiac arrest.

Our schools do graduate good pipe organists, but many of them would stand dumbfounded in front of a modern electronic organ or keyboard synthesizer — standard hardware today for keyboard players. In the theatre music field, we have a shortage in most communities of keyboard artists who can sight-read a traveling Broadway show book, handle the written-out parts and also play comp style. In the recording field, we have brilliant keyboard artists, but an actual shortage in most cities of musicians who can handle such diverse styles as jazz, pop and rock. Even more scarce are those pianists who can handle these styles and Mozart or Chopin or Gershwin's concert pieces. If a keyboard artist seeks work in the recording field (and even in pit orchestras), his employability will be increased by facility in at least some of the less sophisticated performance synthesizers. Some keyboard players work regularly now just specializing in performing real-time synthesis.

Guitarists — We have a huge oversupply of amateur and semiprofessional guitarists who want to become full-time *professionals*. Many of these individuals do not understand the difference between an amateur and truly *professional* performing artist. Most of them have been misled by the rock guitarists whose entire repertoire consists of three chords. We have an actual *shortage* of guitarists who can perform artistically, even in one style. We have even fewer guitarists who can negotiate, at a fully professional level, three or four of the basic musical styles. Probably less than 10 percent of our guitarists can read music at a level expected of other professional musicians. Any guitarist who is a good reader and who can perform artistically in the basic idioms of jazz, blues, rock and country will probably have to engage a telephone answering service to handle his job offers. This kind of competence and versatility is in demand everywhere, from the neighborhood saloon to the big-time recording studios.

Percussionists — Even before rock and roll, the world was oversupplied with drummers. But still today, we have in most communities an *undersupply* of fully competent, versatile percussionists. Directors and contractors can rarely find a drummer/percussionist who can really read well and who can handle, not only conventional percussion, but mallet instruments and timpani. Many drummers play great jazz or rock or Latin rhythms, but don't really know how to play concert or show music.

Few percussionists take the time to seriously study the art of timpani tuning and playing or know much about non-western musics. The percussionists who can do most, or all of the basic musical styles well, and are good readers, are rare in most areas and in high demand. Percussionists who are the next most active group are those who come closest to the prowess and versatility of the "complete professional percussionist." Drummers who are unwilling to undertake this level of training will continue to compete with thousands of other drummers of like mind. Competition among "average" musicians will always be great.

Wind Instrument Players — The bloated school band programs of the last three decades have produced a large surplus of good wind instrument performers. We even have an oversupply of fully-qualified wind players with masters, even doctors degrees. When an opening is advertised by a professional symphony orchestra on, say, clarinet or trumpet, it is not unusual to see 100 applicants seeking to audition. A respectable percentage of that group would have professional experience that would qualify them for serious consideration. In the recording studios, we also find a large oversupply of wind players scrapping for those high-paying jobs. One area of wind playing is not overcrowded, as a rule: saxophone players who can *really* play the clarinet, flute and, perhaps, a double-reed instrument. Extensive woodwind doubling is expected in the show music field and in recording. Woodwind doubling by saxophone players is much less common in film scoring. Since it takes a lifetime to master even one instrument, it is understandable why top doublers are so scarce. Those that come closest to really playing several winds get a lot of work — and when they do, they earn, through their doubling ability, 25 percent to 100 percent above basic scale.

String Players — In this country we have a serious shortage of top professional string players (violin, viola, 'cello, double bass). Proof of this is readily observed with a glance at the "Help Wanted" ads in the *International Musician,* official journal of the AFM. When the school band movement swelled following World War II, kids took up the flute and trumpet, not the violin and 'cello. This national shift away from strings cut off much of the supply, and practically all our major orchestras now outbid each other for the services of string players who can meet the stringent demands of symphonic playing.

Our conservatories continue to accept and graduate performers who believe they are headed for a career as a solo concert artist or recitalist. Teachers warn their students that the field is difficult to crack. But they should not say that employment prospects are poor, they should say that they are about zero. Booking agents already have overcrowded stables of fine concert artists, and they rarely take a chance on a newcomer. So the thousands of disappointed solo artists, some of them outstanding talents, look around for a line of retreat.

Instrumentalists often search for a symphony orchestra job. While we have a surplus of qualified wind and percussion players, the employment picture in the symphonic field is not entirely bleak. We have over 200 professional symphony orchestras in this country and Canada now offering employment for 15,000 musicians. The American Symphony Orchestra League classifies 34 of these orchestras as "major." Each of them offers annual employment contracts to some 80 to 105 players, providing 30 to 52 weeks of work. Fringe benefits are generally excellent now, and most major orchestras are developing increasingly attractive retirement funds, sometimes in cooperation with the AFM. We also have what the American Symphony Orchestra League classifies as "regional orchestras" and "metropolitan orchestras" that offer employment to some 7,000 musicians. Occasional employment is also offered, at least to first chair players, by some of the 550 "community orchestras" active in this country and Canada.

Performers heading for careers as soloists in the classical field will find it difficult to break in without the aid of an agent or manager. Concert agents and management companies most active are listed in the annual directory of *Musical America.* That useful publication also includes the names and addresses of symphony orchestras and opera companies here and in Europe.

It is not unusual for classical musicians to first achieve prominent recognition abroad. Instrumentalists seeking work with a symphony orchestra in Europe should locate the German publication, *Das Orchester* (B. Schott's Soehne Musikverlag, 65 Mainze Weihergarten,

P.O. Box 36-4-, Mainz, Germany). It provides information on openings in European symphony orchestras.

The most direct route for an instrumentalist in any field to find work is by establishing a reputation for being able to handle whatever opportunities come along — and a reputation for being better quali-fied than the competition. An instrumentalist of genuine ability be-comes known throughout the musical community very quickly. He is almost immediately conspicuous — and other players, directors and contractors mark him as the one to call. Jobs can be scarce, but when they come along the really good players are in demand.

A musical reputation can work even more quickly the other way around: less talented performers, weak readers, undependable music-ians, earn overnight reputations, too. They may never learn why their telephone does not ring, for who wants to notify an individual that he can't cut it, that he is unprofessional?

Musicians who want to earn a full-time income just from playing their instruments will have to struggle in an overcrowded field. More playing jobs may come along as a result of the growth fields of pay TV and home video. Also, as workers gain shorter workweeks, they will have more time for music and entertainment. And audiences one day may become satiated with canned music and return more to live entertainment. All of these factors could increase the number of jobs for musicians.

TEACHING CAREERS

Studio Teacher
School Music Educator
Music Education Supervisor

College Music Instructor
Music Therapist

Every musician is a teacher. Composers, performers, directors — all those who make music are involved, directly or indirectly, in teaching others to do what they do. No other sector of the music profession includes within its ranks so diverse a group of individuals, ranging from the inspiring master teacher to the outright charlatan. This disparity in quality of music teaching will probably continue because practitioners are not examined, except in grades K through 12, for their qualifications, nor are they licensed.

STUDIO TEACHER

The land is populated with neighborhood music teachers who offer "Lessons in Your Home or Mine on Accordion, Violin, Piano and Voice." Perhaps five percent of these practitioners are really qualified at the professional level. The others should be avoided by the serious student. Quite another kind of private teacher is the real pro who is an active performer or writer engaged in teaching as a sideline. Practical-ly all active professionals teach at least part-time. The best of them fill every vacant hour in 40- to 60-hour workweeks and experience excellent income. Others, unable to stand an unending stream of kids passing through their studios, will accept only a limited number of pupils.

Fully professional teachers are able to demonstrate artistic performance to their students, teacher and student often performing side by side during the lesson. Some teachers have developed new pedagogical techniques in group teaching. Those who have mastered this kind of pedagogy claim that they can teach a group of three to five students more effectively than one-to-one.

Genuinely qualified music teachers have completed four to eight years of college-level music study, are competent writers or performers themselves, possess sound pedagogical techniques, and know how to motivate students. Persons so qualified have no difficulty finding students.

Unfortunately, students and parents often are unable to distinguish between the dilettante and the fully professional teacher. This often accounts for the hordes of talented kids whose families dump thousands of dollars into music lessons only to come out the tube several years later with minimum competence. Professional musicians should support the movement to require accreditation and licensing of private music teachers. Fraud is presently widespread. "Consumers" need protection in this field.

How does a qualified musician build up student clientele? By building a strong reputation in the community, first as a musician, second, as a teacher. Students will find such a person over a period of time. That musician will also become known to school music educators and they will recommend his services to their pupils.

SCHOOL MUSIC EDUCATOR

CAREER DESCRIPTION — Music teachers employed in grades K (kindergarten) through six have responsibilities different from those working in junior and senior high schools. Most school districts try to finance a sufficient number of general music teachers for the lower grades to provide at least some music listening and participation for every child: singing, movement to music and improvised performance on simple rhythm instruments and toys. In the early 1970s, innovative music educators discovered that many students could be taught academic subjects, including reading and arithmetic, through music. Teachers skilled in these new techniques are in demand.

Teachers in the junior and senior high schools divide into two groups. One teaches mostly "general music" — music appreciation, music reading, perhaps some singing. The second type of music educator at this level is generally either a choral director or instrumental music director. Choral directors in many schools will be in charge of developing mixed choruses, boys' glee club and girls' glee club.

Since the late 1960s, students have pressured their teachers to direct "show choirs." Some of the most popular show choirs, particularly in high schools, rehearse and perform pop standards, sometimes current pop tunes, then choreograph their movements and stage their performances (shows) with costumes, special lighting, sometimes even scenery or rear projections. Few show choirs are content with just piano accompaniment; most of them also use percussion, bass and guitar. Joint programs with the high school's "stage band" are common. Students and parents in many communities get as turned on by these activities as they do by the school's athletic teams.

Some choral directors feel that the show choir is commercial and unrelated to "music education." Some of these same critics, however, have organized "jazz choirs" or "jazz choruses." They generally disdain straight pop music and search for charts that are more jazz- or blues-oriented. Some groups of this kind even get into singing jazz improvisations. Jazz-type singing groups also use rhythm section accompaniments. These kinds of contemporary choral activities have attracted large numbers of aspiring music educators who favor twentieth century repertoire.

Students who get turned on to band music in high school and junior college often decide that their best opportunity to become professional musicians is to major in music education with a concentration in instrumental music pedagogy. They have observed at firsthand the kind of work their high school band director performs and that is what they want most to do: direct a concert band, marching band, pep band, and, probably, what educators unfortunately call a "stage band." From August through November, high school band directors' lives are generally consumed by charting, arranging and rehearsing their football bands. During these frantic weeks, music educators often feel they are not so much musical directors as drill sergeants, arrangers, copyists and entertainment directors for the school's athletic department. Following football season, these teachers must hastily prepare a Christmas program, then springtime music festivals involving their concert bands and stage bands. When summer vacation finally arrives, they may spend a week or two with their families, then use the balance of the "summer off" trying to get equipment repaired and shows planned for the fall football season.

While bands dominate music education, some teachers have the added responsibility of organizing and directing string ensembles and orchestras. If the community lacks a strong "feeder" program, high school instrumental directors find it necessary to start string players from scratch. High school music educators are accustomed to 60-hour workweeks, but they appear to thrive on their heavy loads.

Most school districts employ at least one "music supervisor" to administer K-12 educational programs in their districts. The general practice is to hire one supervisor for choral, and one supervisor for instrumental music programs. The role of the supervisor is to guide formulation of educational policy, assist school principals in hiring new teachers, fight for and control music budgets, and offer pedagogical guidance to the music educators employed in their districts. Music supervisors also administer acquisition and circulation of central music lending libraries for their districts. These individuals are also involved in organizing music festivals, reading clinics and contests. Some supervisors are employed, not for the school year, but on 12-month contracts.

QUALIFICATIONS, PREPARATION — Except for the field of music therapy, school music teaching is the only kind of employment where applicants are required to have a college degree in music. School music teachers (grades K through 12) in practically all states are also required to have a teaching "certificate" or teaching "credential." Some states will automatically certify a teacher in a particular music teaching field if he holds a baccalaureate degree in music from a state-accredited college or university. Other states require that college graduates in music also successfully pass a state-administered certifying examination. Types of teaching certificates vary from state to state, but usually include "general music certificate," "elementary school certificate," "general secondary credential," "choral music certificate," "instrumental music certificate," and "junior college music teaching certificate."

In addition to a college degree and teaching license, those who do most of the music teacher hiring (school principals usually) look for one or more of these qualifications or attributes: a good reputation as a teacher; high grades in college and on the certifying examination; outgoing personality — and an applicant who works cheap. Many principals will hire a low-cost teacher over a teacher of long experience because they want to (or must) keep down their payroll expenses. For this reason, fine teachers of long experience sometimes find it more difficult to change jobs than teachers fresh out of college who will accept minimum salaries. This shameful practice saves money, but deprives students of the best instructors.

EMPLOYMENT PROSPECTS — Until about 1970, a reasonably talented college student majoring in "music education" could expect to find a full-time teaching position upon graduation. Until the early 1970s, we had more job openings in many fields, including music, than qualified applicants. But since that time, the employment prospects for school music teachers have changed radically, and no improvement is anticipated in the near future. A handful of top universities with distinguished track records of turning out fine teachers continue to place most of their graduates. But even they, and nearly all the other post-secondary institutions offering music teaching degrees, are having increasing difficulties placing their students. Jobs that are open now usually occur in rural communities with poor school financing histories — or inner-city ghettos where most teachers find teaching very difficult.

Pressure on school budgets from inflating costs will probably continue the trend in most states of decreasing employment opportunities for individuals seeking teaching jobs in music and the other arts.

COLLEGE MUSIC INSTRUCTOR

CAREER DESCRIPTION — Before describing careers in college and university music teaching, I shall discuss the junior colleges, or community colleges, most of which offer a two-year degree called "associate in arts." Most junior colleges offer such courses as music appreciation, music theory, class piano, perhaps class guitar, band and "stage band." Junior colleges that offer an associate in arts degree in music may also offer such courses as music arranging, music history — and music business courses (rare). Individuals aspiring to employment in one of these junior colleges are usually required to teach about 20 contact hours a week, almost double the teaching load of music instructors in four-year colleges and universities. Because of this extremely burdensome schedule, few junior college music teachers have adequate time to prepare for their classes and rehearsals, and they are among the most overworked teachers in the music education field.

Quite a different kind of employment is found at four-year colleges and universities, where full-time music faculty members average about 12 contact hours a week. Practically all music instructors at this level specialize in one particular aspect of music, and most, if not all their teaching and directing responsibilities relate to that specialty, e.g., theory, choral music, instrumental music, applied music instruction, music history, perhaps jazz education. They may only teach three or four different classes or ensembles a week, but their "off time" is filled with preparation for their hours in the classroom or rehearsal hall. Most university-level music teachers claim to have a workweek that averages well above 48 hours. Teachers who have attained higher academic rank, e.g., associate or full professor, are normally assigned somewhat lighter teaching loads. But the senior professors are often even busier than their colleagues of lower academic rank — engaged in research and other creative activities such as writing music, articles and books.

QUALIFICATIONS, PREPARATION — Practically all states require that their junior college teachers have not only a masters degree in music from an accredited institution but, in addition, a junior college teaching certificate. Musicians applying for "the choral job" or "the band job" at a particular junior college are expected to have established reputations in their field of specialization. Such reputations are usually acquired first at the high school level before the aspirant is considered for a faculty position in a junior college. Prospective faculty members are normally hired by the junior college president, upon recommendation of his resident music faculty.

Four-year colleges and universities normally hire only those individuals who have earned a terminal degree in music, e.g., D.M.A., Ed.D. or Ph.D. Some prestigious schools occasionally hire faculty members who lack a terminal degree, but whose reputations as performers, composers or scholars are equal in prestige to a doctor's degree. Many colleges and universities will not consider prospective faculty who lack publications; either music compositions/arrangements or writings about music or music-related topics are considered "publications." These same institutions tend to waive this requirement when they are evaluating prospective members for their "applied music" faculty.

EMPLOYMENT PROSPECTS — During the 1960s, when college enrollments more than doubled, quite a number of additional instructors were hired. When college enrollments tapered off, then leveled or dropped in the mid-1970s, teaching job openings fell sharply. In some colleges and universities, funding for new faculty positions was halted. Some institutions were even forced to fire tenured instructors. The number of music majors in American colleges in the 1970s was also influenced by increasing awareness that many college-level music studies appeared to lead to no job. But the individual aspiring to college-level music teaching would be mistaken to conclude that no career opportunities exist. While we are over-supplied with aspirants holding even doctoral degrees in theory, history, musicology, piano, and choral directing, some colleges and universities have difficulty finding fully-qualified instructors (with doctorates) in certain specialties. Though the job picture is far from promising, the areas of specialization that are least crowded include ethnomusicology, music therapy, jazz education, electronic music, pop choral music, improvisation, sound synthesis, recording, and the music business. If more of our colleges and universities decide to change their curriculums in response to the radical changes in the music profession since the development of mass media, musicians aspiring to college teaching in the areas just listed will be in great demand. But even they will probably be expected to earn doctoral degrees — and "be published" or have respectable track records as professionals in contemporary music and the music business. This development is incredibly slow in coming. It may continue to limp along until sufficient pressure comes from students who seek an education that relates to what is really going on in the outside world of music-making.

MUSIC THERAPIST

Another kind of music educator is a music therapist. The National Association for Music Therapy Inc. defines the profession as involving "the use of music in a prescribed manner to help individuals with emotional and/or physical disabilities function more successfully in the world in which they live." Music has been used from the beginning of time to change human behavior or heal. But following World War II, the trained music therapist became a recognized professional.

Since about 1950, qualified music therapists have been using musical techniques therapeutically in a prescribed scientific manner. A variety of techniques are employed. The National Association for Music Therapy (NAMT) listed these examples: "Group ensembles using folk or traditional instruments, orchestras and bands, choruses, individual instruction, rhythmic activities, music theory and composition instruction, general music. Participation can be either passive or active, but active involvement usually develops as the therapy sessions progress."

To qualify as a professional music therapist, the aspirant must graduate with 128 semester-hours credit in a university accredited to offer this specialized curriculum. NASM has accredited about 32 universities which offer four-year degrees in the field (some universities offer masters and doctors degrees related to therapy). Candidates should possess strong motivation for a life of teaching, even healing. Because of the nature of the therapists' clientele, therapists must possess a lot of self-confidence, emotional stamina, patience and perseverance. Love of people would certainly be helpful.

NAMT believes that employment opportunities are presently good for fully qualified therapists and that the field will continue to grow. Among the employers of music therapists: psychiatric hospitals, mental retardation centers, physical disability hospitals, physical disability schools (for the blind, deaf, etc.), community mental health centers, day care centers, special education schools, nursing homes and special service agencies.

Part of the therapist's training occurs in the senior (or fifth) year of university study when the candidate interns in an institution such as listed above and gains clinical experience under the supervision of a registered music therapist. Upon completion of an accredited course of study and the internship, the therapist can become a "registered" music therapist (most employers hire only registered music therapists). Professionals in the field generally earn salaries comparable to public school teachers but rarely enjoy privileges of tenure. The total enrollment of students in music therapy programs is around 2,500.

Detailed information on the profession may be obtained from NAMT (see appendix) and the Urban Federation of Music Therapists, c/o School of Education, NYU, 777 Education Building, Washington Square, New York, N.Y. 10003. NAMT publishes *Journal of Music Therapy,* which can be obtained from that association and in large libraries.

MUSIC-RELATED CAREERS

Some of the careers listed here relate directly to music, others only indirectly. Some are open to trained musicians; others offer employment opportunities to non-musicians. The more prevalent music-*related* careers are discussed in the pages following.

WORDS AND MUSIC

LYRICIST — Individuals who are talented in expressing themselves lyrically can develop careers writing words to songs. It is not possible

MUSIC-RELATED CAREERS

WORDS AND MUSIC
Librettist
Lyricist
Playwright
Music Critic/Journalist
Writer/Editor

MUSIC SERVICES
Music Coordinator
Music Copyist
Music Cutter/Editor
Music Librarian
Talent Coordinator

MANAGERIAL/EXECUTIVE
Artists Personal Manager
Artists Agent (Talent Agent)
Arts Administrator
Artists Union Officer
Audience Research Director
Broadcasting Executive
Company Manager (TV, Theatre)
Concert Promoter
Development Director (Arts)
Educational Director
Entertainment Director
Film Producer
Home Video Producer
Market Research Director
Orchestra Manager
Personnel Director
Product Manager (Records)
Production Manager
Professional Manager
Program Director
Programming Consultant
Project Director
Publisher
Record Company Executive
Record Producer
Recording Studio Manager
Road Manager
Stage Manager
Talent Agency Manager
Talent Coordinator
Television Producer
Traffic Manager

BROADCASTING/ADVERTISING
Account Executive
Composer/Lyricist
Creative Director
Disc Jockey
Graphic Artist
Music Librarian
Musical Director
Producer/Director
Program Director
Program Supervisor
Publicist
Research Director
Salesperson

Spot Producer/Director
Ticket Sales Manager/Agent
Visual Synthesist
Writer

BUSINESS/MERCHANDISING
Broadcasting Station Broker
Concert Promoter
Music Merchant/Salesperson
Music Rights Manager
Music Wholesaler/Distributor
Publicist
Talent Agent
Ticket Sales Manager

MUSIC PRODUCTION
(Theatre, Film, Telecommunication)
Audio Technician/Engineer
Choreographer/Dancer
Costume Designer
Director
Floor Manager
Lighting Designer
Music Coordinator
Orchestra Contractor
Producer/Executive Producer
Property Master
Scenic Designer
Singer/Actor
Special Material Writer
Stage Director
Stage Manager
Talent Coordinator
Technical Director
Theatrical Producer
Variety Artist
Visual Synthesist
Writer/Composer/Lyricist

SCIENCE AND TECHNOLOGY
Audiologist
Equipment Designer
Equipment Maintenance Technician
Instrument Designer/Manufacturer
Piano Tuner/Technician
Record Mastering Technician
Sound Engineer/Technician
Studio Designer/Acoustician

LEGAL SERVICES
Copyright Researcher
Copyright Lawyer
Entertainment Business Lawyer
Paralegal

ARTS/GRAPHICS
Commercial Artist
Graphic Artist
Theatrical Scenic Designer
Music Engraver
Music Calligrapher

to describe a typical career for a lyricist because no two are alike. The first difficulty in attempting to make it as a lyricist is the same one confronting the pop singer: just about everyone thinks he can do it. This conceit among songwriters, particularly lyricists, is reinforced every day by the quick popularity gained by songs lacking even basic craftsmanship, let alone any artistic quality. Public acceptance of the banal in songs is probably most readily explained by the fact that the popularity of most musical entertainment is based, not so much on the material an artist may use, but his personality and presentation.

Even though the popular song business continues to accept far too many poor songs with dumb words, increasing numbers of publishers and artists are seeking material containing more value. Those persons believing the world waits for their lyrics should know that there is a decreasing market for the ancient Tin Pan Alley clichés of "moon-spoon-and-June" and "charms-in-my-arms."

As stressed in Chapter 4, the songwriters who enjoy careers with continuity are the ones who really work at it. They study the great standards and learn the difference between what goes into a flash hit as opposed to songs of lasting quality. Employment prospects of lyricists aspiring to full-time careers are not promising for anyone lacking distinctive creative talent with words. Unless a writer is richly endowed, his career may sustain continuity of income only if he becomes professionally active also as a composer or in some other music-related work such as publishing, producing, artist management, etc.

Some lyricists are discontented with just churning out words for pop songs and aspire to writing for the musical theatre. If these writers have a genuine sense of theatre and a love for what takes place there, they will probably associate themselves with other creative talents of similar tastes and professional goals. This often occurs, as it did with Cole Porter, Richard Rodgers and others, when the writer is still in college, where student-written shows provide vehicles for novices to learn their craft.

When a writer has a feeling for how a song can contribute to the progress of the drama on stage, he will probably take the next step and become involved in collaborating with others in writing the "book" for shows, a term used on Broadway for the text of a musical play. Among the most distinguished (and wealthy) lyricists who have also written (or helped write) books for successful Broadway shows are Ira Gershwin, Oscar Hammerstein II and Alan Jay Lerner. The field of writing for the professional musical theatre is very difficult to break into, but the rewards, artistic and financial, can be incomparable.

CRITIC/JOURNALIST/EDITOR — Some of history's most distinguished musicians have used their creative energies, not just for composing, but in writing about music. While few musicians have managed to perform these two tasks as well as Richard Wagner, in the twentieth century hundreds of creative persons have fashioned rewarding careers as music critics, journalists and editors. Those who follow one of these paths find that their work schedules are filled with attending concerts about eight nights a week, their workdays occupied in reviewing endless stacks of new recordings and books on music. The most conscientious critics make an effort to study new scores before attending premiere performances; some try to attend rehearsals and recording sessions to inform themselves on how creative and interpretive artists prepare new works or rework old pieces.

To qualify as a music critic in the classical field, the individual should have a thorough musical education, acquiring this through formalized university-level study or through individual effort. Our most distinguished critics have grown into their work after long years of observation and study. They not only develop penetrating insights on compositions and performances but manage to write in a style that communicates effectively with a broad general readership. But many professional critics lack these qualifications and inflict their incompetence on ignorant editors and a gullible public. It is not unusual for a newspaper to assign a news reporter, even a sports writer, to cover concerts and review recordings. The smartest among this group of fakers are those that avoid writing about the music itself and focus on the composers' or performers' personalities or personal habits. Other music critics, not qualified to write about music, tend to focus on the words to songs, for if they have any right at all to comment about a performance, it might be that they may know something about language. Critics of this stripe are more accurately described as journalists or reporters, and they are particularly active in the pop-rock and jazz fields. Some of these reporters are very clever writers and they accommodate the interests of music lovers who enjoy reading about the performers' personalities and the show-biz aspects of music.

What about careers in writing about music? All major newspapers and most popular magazines employ one or more critics or music journalists. We have a shortage of fully qualified, versatile music critics who can write well. Those aspiring to the field will probably have to begin their efforts to break in to full-time professional writing by volunteering occasional reviews for neighborhood newspapers, perhaps college newspapers or small magazines. Really good writers-about-music will probably attract a responsive readership and perhaps graduate to more prestigious, better-paying newspapers and magazines.

Only about 100 critics are employed full-time in the United States, and only the major papers offer really top salaries. But the great majority of critics and music reporters are rather poorly paid and earn salaries comparable to most other journalists, which are not high. Some "stringers" work for shamefully low free-lance fees. Critics and music reporters, even if employed full-time, often find it necessary to moonlight in other fields, such as teaching. Some are college students who get started in the field by reviewing concerts and records for their campus newspaper.

If an individual is more interested in journalism than music criticism, he may be able to land a job on a newspaper in an editorial capacity.

Some of these jobs carry the title, "music editor" and, as such, usually provide full-time employment for the person hired. Most newspapers receive dozens of canned publicity releases every week from publicity chairpersons of performing groups, and most newspapers assign their "entertainment editor" or music editor to select the pieces most deserving of publication. This gatekeeper is also expected to edit, even rewrite these canned articles coming in from outside writers, most of whom are amateurs. This kind of editorial work can be drudgery for the person who aspires to being a music critic. But until that more prestigious position can be attained, writers on music will usually find it necessary to serve some time in more humble tasks such as rewriting other writers' work. Sometimes a modest salary is partially compensated when the music writer is granted a by-line — his name at the head of his pieces. If the newspaper is unionized, the contract may stipulate that, when a piece bears a by-line, the paper is not permitted to rewrite the copy. Nonunion papers rarely show this much respect for their journalist's timeless prose.

Individuals wishing to pursue the various kinds of employment available in writing about music can obtain further information from the Music Critics Association (see appendix).

MUSIC SERVICES

MUSIC CUTTER — Full-time careers can be developed in the field of music cutting, sometimes called music editing. As explained in my chapter on film scoring, music cutters are the individuals who are responsible for selection, timing and synchronization of music tapes to TV or movie film. They assist film directors and movie composers in scheduling and timing music sound tracks, then work with audio engineers in rerecording music, dialogue and sound effects to film (or videotape).

Those qualified to work as music cutters have usually acquired their craft and art as apprentices, working alongside other more experienced cutters who, themselves, learned in a master-apprentice relationship over many years. Some good cutters are expert musicians. Others are simply very sensitive to how music can enhance dramatic events and do expert work without having acquired formal musical training. The individual seeking a career as a music cutter should expect to follow the time-honored apprenticeship-kind training, perhaps getting started on amateur movies, educational or sales films.

Supply and demand for music cutters is presently in about equal balance. But as the media of CATV and home video grow, it is likely that employment opportunities will increase for persons possessing the ability to sync music to pictures. Additional jobs should also develop in the growing field of producing A/V teaching materials. For further information on getting into the field, contact the Motion Picture Editors Guild, Local 776, I.A.T.S.E. (see appendix).

MUSIC LIBRARIAN — Librarians are employed in a variety of settings in contemporary music. The most familiar is the individual working in college and public libraries as a music specialist. Some of these jobs involve little more than clerking. At the other end of the scale are the trained music cataloguers and researchers who apply knowledgeable judgments and perform sophisticated, occasionally even scholarly tasks. All but the smallest libraries employ paraprofessionals and professionals. For the former, college degrees are sometimes required. For individuals aspiring to careers as fully professional music librarians, they should plan to acquire a baccalaureate degree in music, preferably with a concentration in music history and literature. Then they should plan on acquiring a masters degree in library science, preferably from a university with a well-respected curriculum. Few libraries will consider applicants lacking these credentials.

Quite a different kind of music librarian is found at radio stations, where the responsibilities include cataloging the station's discs, cartridges, cassettes and tapes. Some station librarians also perform sound transfers, e.g., disc to reel or disc to broadcast-type cartridges. Stations involved in automated programming keep their librarians and engineers busy in these ways.

At many radio stations, the music librarian is heavily involved in audience research concerning listener preferences in music. The most prestigious career for a music librarian is at those stations where that individual is an important decision-maker relative to weekly play lists for broadcast. These individuals, sometimes called "music directors," meet with hordes of record promotion personnel and either succumb to their blandishments or resist. Some music librarians (or directors) perform their jobs so well they work up to program director positions. On small stations, one person may perform all of these tasks.

To qualify for a job as a radio station music librarian, the aspirant should be knowledgeable about recorded music, recording artists, demographic research methods and the vagaries of public taste. If the aspirant possesses some of these qualities, he may perform in the job quite well without any special music training. The individuals who accept these jobs should have one additional personal attribute: the ability to handle continuous pressure from record promoters — and still make objective judgments about what to broadcast.

Another kind of music service that offers some career opportunities is in the field of music preparation. This is the appellation commonly used in reference to the companies that offer mass-produced music copying, music duplication, music writing supplies and music library services, including delivery of scores and parts to customers. Music preparation companies are located in all major recording centers and employ copyists, proofreaders, arrangers, orchestrators and clerical help. All but clerical helpers and delivery people are AFM members who work for union scale. Proprietors of these service companies are the supervising copyists, and invoices to their clients (arrangers, composers, producers) include a surcharge for supervision, this surcharge amounting to at least the AFM minimum (usually 25 percent).

Persons seeking a career in the music service field will normally start out as free-lance copyists, develop a reputation for dependability and good work, then get hired by an established company. Most are employed, however, on a piece-work basis — being called in when outside help is needed to meet deadlines. Many individuals in this field also work free-lance elsewhere in music or music-related fields.

SCIENCE AND TECHNOLOGY

SOUND ENGINEER/TECHNICIAN — Individuals employed in the technical aspects of sound reinforcement, recording and broadcasting are generally referred to as "engineers." Some are, but many in the field are only *technicians.* The appellation audio "engineer" should be reserved for university graduates who hold degrees in electrical engineering or, perhaps, physics, audiology, acoustics or computer science. These engineers or scientists engage in such work as research and development of audio equipment, studio and equipment design, record mastering, equipment maintenance and sound mixing. Most of these scientists and engineers are employed full-time by equipment manufacturers, sound reinforcement companies, recording studios, radio and TV stations and film studios. Some engineers are assigned only one type of work, e.g., design or maintenance or audio mixing. In smaller firms, audio engineers perform a variety of tasks.

Employers also hire audio technicians who may or may not have done university-level study of electrical engineering. Many audio technicians and mixers are simply talented, self-taught handymen who, through years of apprenticeship, earn job assignments that involve sophisticated technology. Many of these largely self-taught technicians do more effective equipment maintenance work than graduate engineers. Most engineers and technicians are attracted to these music-related jobs by their love for music and some of them hold college degrees in music or have studied music informally. The art of sound mixing demands considerable musical knowledge and the ability to make sensitive aural judgments.

To qualify for employment as a sound engineer, university degrees in electrical engineering and music would be ideal, but few professionals are so prepared. With the increasing sophistication of audio equipment, employers more and more require, not just audio technicians, but sound engineers and computer scientists.

Individuals who want to go to the top in recording technology and sound engineering should not only study as much music as they can, but go on to at least some studies in acoustics. Such persons would be called upon to design and build state-of-the-art recording studios and then perhaps displace those who, in the past, have faked their way in such enterprises and wasted much money on poorly-designed facilities. The professionals who come closest to this kind of preparation will be in high demand and experience career continuity with good earnings.

INSTRUMENT DESIGN/MAINTENANCE — From earlier times, the inventors and designers of musical instruments have held a distinguished place in the history of the art. While the basic design of most musical instruments was set centuries ago, scientists and technicians continue, not only to improve instruments, but invent new ones. Persons interested in the physics of sound, acoustics and electronics manage to develop music-related careers. While it cannot be said that there is a big demand for instrument designers, positions can be found for qualified persons with manufacturing companies, particularly those involved in developing ever-new electronic instruments.

When we consider careers in the field of instrument maintenance, we have a shortage in most communities of competent instrument repair technicians. It is simply impossible to find sufficient numbers of real craftsmen. Qualified repairmen can just about choose where they want to live, then knock on the door of the nearest instrument repair shop and go to work the same day.

Other jobs await qualified maintenance personnel in school systems, colleges and universities, not to mention the armed services. Persons aspiring to such careers can acquire their training in some junior colleges and some universities. It is more common, however, for repairmen to learn their craft as apprentices to masters.

Repairmen often specialize in keyboard instruments. Many communities lack fully qualified piano technicians/tuners. The best of them have been factory-trained or learned their craft as apprentices. Piano tuners today do not even have to have a true sense of pitch. Tuning can be accurately handled with the use of electronic pitch-measuring machines which are readily available with piano repair kits. Piano technicians are almost always independent contractors working out of their homes; they set their own hours and vacation periods. The competent ones are in demand and make good livings.

We also have a shortage of electronic keyboard maintenance personnel. Persons knowledgeable in the technology of electronics are usually so busy repairing amps, speakers and tape recorders they cannot find time to fix electronic organs, electric pianos and keyboard synthesizers. Persons who acquire competence in repairing electronic keyboard instruments will be able to find steady employment at good pay. And those with musical backgrounds will, on most jobs, be able to do a better job than just straight technicians.

With the proliferation of lower-cost electronic musical equipment of all kinds, it is safe to predict that steady employment at good pay will be available to those persons who take the time to educate themselves in electronics and music. This is clearly a growth area of employment.

MANAGERIAL/EXECUTIVE

Individuals not involved directly in music-making can develop successful careers in the business and managerial sectors of the arts and entertainment industry. Dozens of options await them. The simple truth is, *the music business has never had an adequate supply of people who are qualified to run things.*

It is not possible to predict career patterns in music and arts management. The person who aspires to becoming an artists' manager may start out in music publishing and end up in record production. The individual who believes he wants to run a talent agency may experience his greatest success as a TV executive. Rapid change is so pervasive in the music business, it is rarely possible, even desirable, for a manager or executive-type person to hold with one job throughout his working life. Fast learners who are quick on their feet will seize career opportunities as they develop. The most creative executives won't wait for job offers; *they will create their own opportunities.*

QUALIFICATIONS, PREPARATION — Until recent years, most music business jobs have been held by individuals who walked in off the street and learned on the job. Practically no musicians were available who had sufficient backgrounds in management, so the big firms turned to ex-salesmen, lawyers and accountants for their leadership.

In recent years, some of the people with these kinds of backgrounds have been joined at the middle management level by a new kind of professional: the college or university graduate who has gone through an educational program that *integrates* music and business and the recording arts. These graduates are the ones I described earlier as "the new professionals." Several dozen colleges and universities in the United States and Canada now offer these kinds of curriculums, and their graduates are finding their places in the arts and entertainment industry.[2]

A profession directly related to music business management is arts administration. Our educational institutions have only recently begun to develop degree programs leading to professional employment in that area. The early leaders in the field have been UCLA, the University of Wisconsin-Madison, Yale and NYU. Persons considering arts administration should inquire directly of these institutions and others that may interest them, because curriculums in arts administration are now proliferating. Most of these degree programs are at the masters degree level. Candidates are normally expected to present a baccalaureate degree to start these graduate programs.

How does one qualify as an arts administrator? A masters degree will probably help. For a fuller answer to this question, review Chapter 14. Of all the music-related career options available, arts administration may present one of the greatest challenges to an individual's versatility and imagination — and the field offers a unique opportunity to achieve something that might turn out to be important.

2-These educational institutions, practically all of which use this book as their music business text, are listed in the appendix.

EMPLOYMENT PROSPECTS — The persons who take the time to prepare themselves in business and music will be among the most sought-after executives throughout the 1980s. One indication of this is that the graduates of the University of Miami's Music Merchandising curriculums (bachelors' and masters' degrees) all find jobs in the music business before they graduate).

Fast talkers and off-the-street types will continue at least for a while to find work. But the music business is now so large and diverse, increasing numbers of corporations will refuse to turn over their affairs to dilettantes. Too much money is now on the line. Seat-of-the-pants operations, uninformed decision-making can no longer be tolerated in this huge industry. Those hoping to land managerial-executive positions in the field will have to have first-class credentials in the decade ahead.

BROADCASTING/ADVERTISING

The fields of broadcasting and advertising in the United States are so closely allied that they will be considered here as inseparable. A person aspiring to a career in either of these fields will very likely become professionally involved with the other. Even so-called "public broadcasting," although nonprofit, is dependent upon large corporations which grant money to PBS and local nonprofit stations in the form of "institutional" ads — prominent corporate name identification at the beginning and end of programs.

Of the five kinds of employment listed just above, the role of the disc jockey is most obvious.

DISC JOCKEY — The individual who masters the ceremony of getting records identified and on the air is the key figure in radio broadcasting. With over 8,000 stations on the air, we have about 25,000 DJs working full-time and another 5,000 or more performing part-time. As explained in Chapter 22 disc jockeys in major markets are often confined to introducing records and making commercial announcements, these proceedings interrupted by ad-lib comments by the jock about the entertainment, the performers, or most anything else he believes might engage his listeners.

In addition to time the DJ logs on the air, he is usually occupied in a variety of tasks relating to the operation of his station. Most station managers try to increase their community visibility by encouraging their air personalities to become involved in such activities as being an MC for shopping center openings and judging beauty contests. Many jocks are involved in promoting, even acting as MC for rock concerts. Some DJs assist their station's PR activities by involving themselves in charities and other public services.

Disc jockeys in smaller markets are often called upon to perform every conceivable task at their stations, from making up play lists to sweeping out the studio. In many markets, jocks assist in writing and producing commercials and may even sell spots. A station with a limited budget will also require its DJs to run the audio engineering board concurrently with physically handling the discs and tapes.

One way to get started as a disc jockey is to enroll in a technical school that offers training leading to acquisition of what the FCC calls a third-class license, required of all individuals handling audio monitoring of radio broadcasts. But some disc jockeys get started with little or no professional training. Some self-taught air personalities (or on-the-job apprentices) rise to the top of their profession. But the life expectancy of a disc jockey is short, comparable to that of a professional athlete or ballet dancer. Few DJs remain on the air after their mid-thirties, for two reasons. First, they tend to lose touch with their predominantly young audiences. Second, the best air personalities tend to move up to become program directors, even station managers.

While it is not difficult to get some kind of modest start as a disc jockey, individuals planning a career in broadcasting should take time out to earn a college degree or two in broadcasting, communication, or an allied field such as music, theatre, perhaps even journalism. The quality and usefulness of curriculums in these disciplines varies widely across the country. But a graduate of even a second-rate institution will have placed himself in a position competitive with the tens of thousands of other aspiring broadcasters pouring out of our colleges who hold at least a baccalaureate degree. Those who qualify themselves with a good education will almost certainly rise faster in their broadcasting careers than others whose backgrounds may limit their potential for leadership roles.

The essential qualification for a disc jockey is, as everyone knows, to possess the type of personality on the air that causes radio fans to want to hear him. If the station management believes the individual under consideration has the particular kind of air personality suitable for the station, the individual will probably be offered a job. Then, if it turns out that the DJ is effective also in selling what the station advertises, the job at that station may turn into a career.

What are employment prospects? Quite good, because stations in this country continue to hire and fire people in their unending quest for larger audiences. A station knows that if a new DJ can increase the rating of a show by just a fraction of one percent, he can earn his salary many times over.

Jocks change jobs as often as musicians. The disc jockey just starting will find opportunities on very small stations for some kind of tryout, partly because such stations (even some larger ones) pay their inexperienced jobs only the minimum wage. Youngsters working for free on a campus station will leap at the chance to get started as a professional on a commercial station.

Young performers often feel it is quite glamorous to be an air personality and will work for very low wages — for a while. Those that stick with it are motivated by the awareness that, once a disc jockey begins to attract a strong following, his station or, more likely, a competing station, will soon recognize this and start paying him commensurate with his commercial value. Stations live by ratings and will attempt to hire away any individual whom they believe might help them meet and beat their competition.

Most DJ jobs are landed through the submission of airchecks accompanied by the individual's resumé. A home tape recording won't do: a station manager wants to hear how the individual sounds on the air during an actual broadcast. Airchecks submitted for audition should have most of the music edited out, retaining only a few seconds to enable the auditor to hear how the performer gets in and out of the music.

Those seeking their first job and those changing jobs can learn of available openings by word-of-mouth and through the trades.

Top DJs in major markets can earn $100,000 a year and more.

BROADCAST PRODUCERS/DIRECTORS — No disc jockey gets on the air without the services of the producers, directors and account executives who make commercial broadcasting work. The individual most closely connected with music in broadcasting is the program director, who spends most of his time selecting recordings for his play lists and scheduling the jocks to handle the shows. Some P.D.'s perform their tasks effectively with minimum musical backgrounds, perhaps none at all. Such P.D.'s depend on their musical intuition as to what their audience might prefer, or they may rely wholly on demographic research to guide, even dictate, their play lists. In large stations, some P.D.'s refuse to meet with record promoters and assign that duty to their "musical director" or "music librarian," as some are called. In smaller stations, sometimes all of these three "hats" are worn by the same individual. Whoever is assigned the task of dealing with record promoters and play lists works with the sales department of the station to form a liaison with sponsors.

An individual heading for a sales position in radio and TV often becomes involved with music programming. He functions sometimes as a go between for the station and its sponsors to ascertain whether the advertisers are satisfied with the music broadcast for them. But this linkage is more regularly found between the station's sales department and commercial producers. Music is an integral component of both local and national spots, and everyone in broadcasting becomes involved eventually with the production, use, and broadcast of musical commercials. Most really good local commercials, and practically all network spots, are put together and produced for broadcasting by the "creative directors" of advertising agencies. These individuals spend their workweeks creating concepts and "hooks" on which to hang music and advertising messages. They are, first of all, advertising copywriters. Most creative directors lack musical expertise but may be adept at selecting qualified composers and performers for their broadcast spots.

Advertising agencies employ "account executives" to function as liaison between the agency and its clients. The account executives are primarily salespersons, not producers or musicians. Yet they have been found essential in seeking out their clients' preferences, then keeping them informed on how their spots are progressing in production and how they are to be scheduled for broadcast.

All the aforementioned persons in broadcasting and advertising fields change rapidly and competition is intense. Stations and ad agencies keep hiring and firing personnel in the hope that new blood may do a better job for them in their eternal quest for larger audiences and bigger profits.

QUALIFICATIONS, PREPARATION — The individual aspiring to a career in broadcasting and/or advertising must, first of all, possess a temperament that can adjust to the wild ups and downs which are endemic in these fields. Anyone unable to handle at least temporary professional failure should consider trying to go to work for the post office. Secure it isn't. Risky it is, but with the dangers of failure come exciting opportunity and the possibility for high income. Experts do well and work steadily.

Persons aspiring to leadership roles in broadcasting and advertising usually are college graduates. Some have degrees in broadcasting and marketing. Now that broadcasting is a multibillion-dollar enterprise, there is just too much money at stake to be handled by individuals lacking sophisticated knowledge and expertise in such areas as communication theory, accounting, economics, market research, mass psychology, perhaps even computer science.

EMPLOYMENT PROSPECTS — The numbers of jobs available in broadcasting and advertising will continue to grow in our post-industrial economy. But our universities are graduating far more students in broadcasting and marketing than these fields can handle. Yet, newcomers often find opportunities to at least get started, particularly as disc jockeys and salespersons, at low pay. But once the foot is in the door, the newcomers must outperform their competitors or step aside. To rise above this level of employment, most aspirants will be required to have a good university education — if only because employers can readily find applicants with strong academic backgrounds and even stronger ambitions.

I have repeatedly asserted that there is a need in music and broadcasting for fully qualified people. My views are reinforced by Bill Drake, whose firm, Drake-Chenault Enterprises, is one of the most successful radio program packagers in the world, serving over 250 stations. Drake attributes the success of his company to the fact that his clients say they cannot locate enough fully qualified talent in their local communities to meet their needs, and they find it necessary to retain outside programming experts.

BUSINESS/MERCHANDISING

Thousands of careers in the music business are available for individuals who prefer to involve themselves in the marketing of goods and services relating to the industry. Even live music is a "product" which must be advertised, packaged and sold. Music merchandising is a multibillion-dollar enterprise and talented persons will probably be able to develop full-time careers in it — if they apply their energies in the right places.

Career patterns cannot be described here, because products and markets change overnight. Jobs come and go; merchants sink or swim. Even in periods of economic depression, employers will always take on an employee who can sell — if not on salary, at least on commission. The music industry requires peddlers as well as top executives.

Most music merchants, whether working as employer or employee, enjoy satisfactory careers because they know how to hustle; they do not wait for the telephone to ring or for the unemployment check. They are out on the street, on the telephone, ever searching for something to buy or sell. But work in this field can be frustrating, exhausting, sometimes frightening. The strongest operatives survive, because ever-new opportunities come along.

QUALIFICATIONS, PREPARATION — Until recent years, a music merchant or talent salesman did not require a university diploma to succeed in the music business. Such a person could often make it, at least for a while, just being "street smart," quick on his feet. But as the music business tends more and more toward large corporations, even international conglomerates, the person who wants to rise to the top may find an acute need for a strong academic background. Corporate boards no longer want to entrust the buying and selling of merchandise and musicians to mom and pop. The small community will still need the small businessman. But the big money prizes are now going to the merchants and agents and promoters who are informed in such fields as market research, advertising, accounting, even computer technology.

EMPLOYMENT PROSPECTS — Individuals who are fully prepared and motivated for work in contemporary business will find good career opportunities. Particularly employable today are persons with strong university training in music and business. Those who go on to earn the M.B.A. degree start at high salaries, particularly if they graduate from a prestigious school of business such as those at Stanford and Harvard.

Whatever the educational background a musician-merchant may acquire, his ultimate achievements will probably be governed more by his imagination and drive. If he possesses these two attributes, he will create his own "luck." As more than one person of achievement has expressed it, "The harder I work, the luckier I get."

LEGAL SERVICES

Each year the music business requires the services of more and more legal experts, because every aspect of the industry involves copyright law and the negotiation of contracts. While all law schools train their students in contracts, it is often impossible for an attorney in general practice to be sufficiently well informed to handle certain kinds of music business contracts. In the field of copyright, the attorney lacking expertise often gets in over his head and is unable to counsel clients adequately. For these reasons, increasing numbers of lawyers now specialize in entertainment law and copyright.

Even music business specialists are often hard-pressed to keep abreast of the complexities of the industry. In the copyright field, even with the clarifications provided in the 1976 copyright statute, lawyers, clients and adversaries continue to do battle over the meaning of the fine print.

Despite the increased demand for music business attorneys, most law schools still do not offer specialized training in the field. However, law students wanting to study copyright will find an outstanding curriculum at NYU. Also, USC and UCLA give special attention to entertainment law.

What are the employment prospects? The brightest, best-informed entertainment law attorneys have plenty of clients and high incomes. Those of considerable experience often get full-time positions as legal counsel for such firms as publishers, record companies and film studios. Others go into artist management. But our law schools turn out about twice as many lawyers as we can accommodate. Attorneys of lesser talents (or ambition or luck) may find it necessary to go into some field other than law. But this kind of second-choice career may not be bad, for in our complex society, it is to everyone's advantage to possess an understanding of law.

The individual who is attracted to the law may not be able to gain admission to a good law school or lack sufficient funds to complete his education. Such a person can often find employment as a copyright researcher, music rights agent or as a paralegal. Still others may already be working in some aspect of the music business and attend law school concurrently. Upon admission to the bar, persons of this kind of background would probably find themselves more readily employable than their competitors.

For an extensive treatment of the role of lawyers in the music business, review Chapter 9.

ARTS/GRAPHICS

Creative persons in the aural and visual arts have often worked in close alliance. Some have been talented in both fields, e.g., Schoenberg and Gershwin were good painters; Stravinsky worked closely with Picasso in stage design and costuming. Today, musical performers must be attractively staged and costumed. Music merchandise must be packaged to sell. These circumstances create many career opportunities for talented individuals interested in graphics and other visual arts. Record companies alone require the services of hundreds of graphic artists they employ on staff or free-lance. Printers and commercial art companies employ artists who have a feeling for music and how visual impressions — packaging and displays — can move people to buy music.

STARTING YOUR OWN BUSINESS

Many persons of independent mind do not choose to work as an employee and prefer to "go it alone." They become entrepreneurs of one kind or another. As I have suggested repeatedly in this book, if you can't find a job, create your own! Now you may not be able to set up your own TV network or movie studio, but it is possible, with a limited amount of capital, to start your own music-oriented company, e.g., a production firm, concert promotion organization, management company or publishing business.

The type of music business easiest to get started and least expensive to finance is publishing. This fact is reconfirmed all the time by hundreds of new firms being set up, usually by songwriters frustrated after repeated turn-downs of their material by others. They decide to strike out on their own.

Here is a step-by-step approach to setting up a publishing company in the popular music field.

1- RESEARCH — Study this book and the publications concerning business management listed in the bibliography.

2- ACQUISITIONS — You have to acquire "properties" before you can start publishing. In addition to your own copyrights, search out other qualified writers and gain their confidence and assistance in your publishing plans. Retain a lawyer to assist in drawing up contracts. Use the guidelines listed in Chapter 5.

3- STRUCTURE YOUR FINANCING You have three basic options in structuring your company and its capitalization, as explained in Chapter 13. Once you have determined whether you will be organized as a sole proprietorship, partnership or corporation, you know what working capital you will have and you can now tentatively select a firm name.

4- CONTACT ASCAP, BMI OR SESAC — Request an application for affiliation as a publisher. The organization may ask you to supply your first choice and alternate choices for your firm name. The licensing organization will not accept into membership a firm with a name identical to or similar to an established publishing company.

5- REGISTER YOUR FIRM NAME — Call on your county clerk and recordor's office and search the records to learn if your choice of firm name has been previously registered in the county. Duplications will not be accepted. Unless you identify the company with your own full legal name, you will be required to register a "fictitious firm name" (some counties use the term, "trade name"). For example, if your name is John Doe, the county will record your firm as "John Doe DBA Hit Publishing Company" (DBA is an acronym for "doing business as"). The county clerk will also require this filing to be published in a "legal newspaper" in the county. Procedures and applicable fees vary county to county.

6- AFFILIATE WITH ASCAP, BMI OR SESAC — Requirements are explained in Chapter 7.

7- ESTABLISH YOUR COMPANY BANK ACCOUNT — Your bank will not open your account until your firm name has been published as described above. Do not commingle personal funds with your company account, even if you are the sole proprietor. Commingled accounts make difficult problems in accounting and tax matters.

8- BUSINESS LICENSE — If you limit your firm's activities just to publishing, you will not require a business license, for the U.S. Constitution guarantees citizens the right of a free press. But if your company should branch out into artists agency work, most states would consider that as a kind of employment agency, and all states license and regulate employment agencies.

9- ARRANGE OUTSIDE SERVICES — Since most new publishing companies start on a shoestring, proprietors generally do not attempt, at the outset, to handle everything themselves. Outside companies are available to handle just about any service a business needs — mail handling, telephone answering, secretarial, bookkeeping, accounting, etc. Most small publishers in New York, Nashville and Hollywood share a small office (perhaps three to six firms) along with the costs of rent, a secretary, etc. Even a publisher as large as Chappell houses within its offices a large number of subsidiary publishing companies.

10- PREPARE YOUR MATERIALS — A songwriter sometimes manages with leadsheets and demos prepared by amateurs. But now that you are a publisher, everything you present to a producer or artist must be prepared by qualified professionals.

11- YOUR FIRST SUCCESS — The essence of the publishing business in the pop field is getting material recorded and released. When you accomplish this feat with your first song, it can be said that you have really become a publisher. While you may grant a recording license under the compulsory licensing provisions of the 1976 Copyright Act, it is much more common for publishers and record companies to negotiate directly, settling on mutually agreeable terms. Most publishers use their own mechanical license form.

12- FORMS, CONTRACTS — Copyright forms are readily available, without cost, from the U.S. Copyright Office. When you negotiate writers' publishing contracts, retain a qualified music business attorney — or use the draft contract discussed in Chapter 5 as a basis for your discussions with an attorney less experienced in the music field.

13- SUBPUBLISHING — If your first recorded song hits, you may want to publish it in printed form. For this, you will probably license a music printing company to handle this for you. See Chapter 5. Also, reread there how to set up subpublishing deals abroad through licensing agreements with firms active internationally.

14- YOUR SECOND COMPANY — Just as soon as your first company gets under way, establish a second one so that you can accommodate properties from writers affiliated either with ASCAP or BMI. Except for the preliminaries outlined here, the procedures for setting up a second firm are the same as your first venture.

15- CONTINUITY — Once your new firms start to get their copyrights licensed and recorded here and abroad, don't sit waiting for royalty checks. Real profitability comes along when a firm can achieve continuity year to year, building catalogs of hundreds, eventually thousands of songs. So the search for new writers and new properties goes on and on. That is the publishing business.

©NARAS

From upper right, clockwise: National Academy of Recording Arts and Sciences (NARAS) *Grammy*; Academy of Motion Picture Arts and Sciences (AMPAS) *Oscar*; the Country Music Association Award; the Antoinette Perry *Tony* Award of The League of New York Theatres and Producers. Center: Academy of Television Arts and Sciences (ATAS) *Emmy* award. Used with the permission of the copyright owners.

27

CAREER DEVELOPMENT

DEFINING GOALS

Recent studies reveal that music is one of the most frequently named career goals. This pervasive enchantment with the world of music came with the rapid growth of the recording and broadcasting industries since 1950. Millions of young people are drawn to music and want somehow to become part of the profession. But many of these dreams are ill-defined. Aspirants appear attracted by the alleged "glamour" and big money of the music and entertainment fields, but have no clear idea of how they might break in. Most teachers and counselors also lack current information.

The world of music and entertainment has always had a certain mystique. Most of those who are visible in these fields seem to be rich and famous. Producing and selling music can be enjoyable and profitable, but here we are more concerned with what goes on back-stage, off-camera. Here we uncover thousands of individuals no one has ever heard of, most of them employed quite regularly, earning respectable incomes — and probably enjoying what they are doing.

It is important to distinguish between a *job* and a *career*. To borrow from Gertrude Stein, a job is a job (is a job). But a career, properly defined, is more likely an ongoing series of jobs, which, if related, add up to an employment sequence that has continuity and development. Unfortunately, large numbers of musicians simply bounce from job to job, giving little thought to how their pattern of employment might develop into a career offering a potential for planned growth and advancement.

Some fortunate people have been able to determine at an early age just what kind of work they want to do. James Levine, musical director of the Metropolitan Opera Company, had decided at the age of six that he was going to become a professional musician. Many young people are not so clearly directed or motivated.

Concurrently with defining career goals, the individual should try to define *himself* — analyze not only his interests, but individual temperament and personality. Along with this personal discovery should come measurement of aptitudes and talents. In addition to doing all he can to discover who and what he is, the individual should obtain outside appraisals from qualified professionals. *Probably more than one-half the work force is miscast.* Whole lifetimes can be spent in frustration and failure. While many different causes may be identified for these unsuccessful lives, very often the individual got started off on the wrong foot, before he knew who he was or measured his talents or considered whether he could meet the competition. Well-planned careers do not always work out either. But if the individual proceeds sensibly, with all available information, at the very least that person has reduced the probability of failing in his chosen field.

Early on, I recommend the individual search out the best available counseling. Despite the reports of unsatisfactory experiences many individuals have had with professional counselors, they are probably the most competent persons in the community to offer professional help, what we can call structured intervention. Most counselors have information concerning career options and statistical projections of employment prospects. One of the useful services a qualified counselor can offer is assisting the individual in finding out who he is. Counselors can offer a battery of aptitude tests, interest measurements and temperament tests. The objectivity and value of these tests and measurements remain in dispute, but they are almost always partially helpful, and the individual should avail himself of every possible opportunity to find out where he may excel and just what makes him tick.

For individuals out of high school and college, counselors are available through state employment services. In larger communities, professional career counselors, independent of government, are available, with payment of a fee.

Many of my students have used a form, Discovering Yourself, which I devised particularly for individuals interested in careers in the arts and the music business. If the reader uses the form (Figure 27.1) it should be remembered that there is no "passing" or "failing" score. Rather, the individual's answers should be interpreted and evaluated in light of the information set forth in these pages concerning music-related careers and the kinds of talents and personalities that have been found appropriate in pursuing certain careers. For example, if the individual's answers show that he dislikes travel, is frightened by the thought of not always having a steady job, he would be unhappy and unsuccessful attempting to build a career as a performing musician. On the other hand, if the individual discovers that his highest priority is being free to create, that he is not worried too much about job security, he might be a strong candidate for building a career as a composer or record producer.

Besides seeking to understand one's own interests and value system, it is equally important at this early stage to conduct an inventory of personal strengths, weaknesses and talents. The accompanying form (Figure 27.2) can assist the individual in these assessments; they must be rendered as objectively as possible to be useful.

DISCOVERING YOURSELF

Effective career planning should begin with careful self-appraisal. What is important to you? What makes you most effective? What kinds of talents do you have? Place a number from 1 to 10 in the appropriate spaces below. Think of number 1 as "low," "little" or "poor," depending on the nature of the category. Use a number 5 for "average." Number 10 means "high," "a lot" or "very important." After you have indicated your own appraisals, seek *outside professional opinion* to learn if others view you as you see yourself.

MY VALUE SYSTEM

	MY ESTIMATE	OUTSIDE ESTIMATE
Need for respect from others		
Need for prestige, status		
Need for audience approval		
Desire for peace of mind		
Need to be liked		
Desire to be loved		
Need for artistic freedom		
Concern for health		
Desire for leisure time		
Desire to have children		
Importance of artistic achievement		
Importance of job security		
Importance of money		
Tolerance for jobs demanding travel		
Desire for personal development		
Desire for artistic development		

Fig. 27.1

MY STRENGTHS, WEAKNESSES, TALENTS

This form can be revealing for both musicians and people in business. Use the one-to-ten numbering system described for Figure 27.1.

	Today		When Fully Developed	
	My Estimate	Outside Estimate	My Estimate	Outside Estimate
Motivation, ambition				
Self-confidence				
Creative talent				
Performing ability				
Musical knowledge				
Business sense				
Effectiveness as an oral communicator .				
Effectiveness in written communication .				
Ability as an organizer				
General leadership ability				
Musical leadership ability				
Capacity to accept direction				
Ability to work with others				
Understanding of the music profession .				
Understanding of the music business ...				
Emotional stability, health				
Intelligence				
Capacity for musical growth				
Capacity for personal growth				
Personal habits				
Ability to adjust to change				

My strongest personal attribute _____

My strongest talent _____

Fig. 27.2

Inaccurate talent appraisals are readily available. For example, a musician who works every Saturday night at the local American Legion Hall can offer a "professional" opinion, but he may have no idea what level of talent is required in the recording studios. The local singing teacher may hold an advanced degree in music, but not know what would be expected of her voice students seeking work in broadcast commercials. Many of our university professors of music composition do not know the level of talent (and craft) demanded of film composers.

If the aspiring musician discovers, through systematic appraisal of his temperament and talent that he may lack what it takes to make it in music, he still has scores of career options in music-related fields.

CLIMBING THE LADDER

No two persons hold the same views on just what constitutes "success." To most persons, the professional who earns a good living has achieved "success." But in the arts, many individuals place a higher value on personal fulfillment, artistic idealism. They refuse to be seduced by the dollar; they won't go "commercial," preferring to hold to their conception of artistic integrity, whatever the consequences. Psychologists would describe this kind of idealist as one who is more concerned with "psychic rewards" than financial security.

How many persons in the world of work are happy with what they do for a living? Many surveys have been made; most of them indicate that *more than half* of those interviewed stated they were unhappy with their jobs. Unhappiness over low pay was rarely the number one concern. Those interviewed have most often complained they felt trapped in their jobs, and that they had little confidence they had a chance to "get ahead." A majority of those asked stated that, if they had the opportunity, they would change their line of work. Anyone planning a career related to the arts knows at the outset that he is engaging in a high risk enterprise. But while careers in the arts, particularly music, often provide only minimum security, few would give up the personal rewards the field offers to trade for more stable employment. One of the great things about a music-related career is that the individual, through careful preparation and planning, can often have it both ways — personal satisfaction and employment continuity.

As the individual contemplates climbing the music career ladder, it will be helpful to be aware of the following:

1- Most music-related careers are *combination careers*; most people work at more than one job at the same time.

2- Most persons experience *serial careers*; they move from job to job, not necessarily because they quit or get fired, but because of the nature of the profession. Typical example: a person starts out as a gofor, then begins to get a few music copying jobs; he may then progress to arranging, composing, perhaps get into the publishing business and eventually become involved in artist management and record production. Each job helps the individual prepare for his next step up the ladder.

3- The music business offers decreasing opportunities for the ill-prepared. The jobs offering the best potential for advancement go more and more to the well-educated, genuinely competent individuals.

4- Males dominate the business. Women are often under-recognized, under-utilized and underpaid.

5- Young people tend to dominate the creative and performing aspects of popular music. Persons of more mature years tend to dominate the field of serious music, music teaching, the business and managerial facets of both popular and serious music.

6- All professions, all fields are characterized by rapid change. But in music, career opportunities change every day. New jobs, new opportunities keep coming along.

7- Music-related careers often lack employment continuity. But musicians, at least union musicians, can usually earn more per hour than can those in any of the other arts and more than those in most other lines of work.

The Bureau of Labor Statistics estimates that in the 1975-1985 decade, 5.2 million new jobs will have come along each year and that by 1985 about 29 percent of the jobs available will require applicants to have four or more years of college education. By 1985, one out of five persons will be a college graduate (compared with one out of seven in the mid-1970s).

Many jobs available by the mid-1980s had not even been conceived in the mid-1970s. The U.S. Bureau of Labor Statistics believes we have just over one million writers, artists and entertainers in the work force — with seven percent to eight percent unemployed. Within this one million are 151,000 "musicians and composers" (104,000 male, 47,000 female). These U.S. Bureau of Labor statistics may be the best available, but they form an inaccurate picture. As the National Endowment for the Arts has pointed out, the data fail to take into account the rapid shifts in music-related employment and, particularly, its seasonal aspects. More significant, it appears that the Department of Labor has not yet conducted any real research on the extent of employment and career opportunities available (and projected) in fields related to music. Astonishingly, neither have the artists' unions and music trade organizations.

The Bureau of Labor Statistics offers the prediction that, by 1985, American colleges will graduate 13 million persons for 12 million available jobs. Such prognoses have encouraged many observers to complain that too many people are becoming "over-educated." While this may be true in some fields, in the music business it is precisely the opposite. Because of the unique demands of the music business, where practitioners must be well-informed in both the art and business of music (not even mentioning the technology), no career ladder-climber can ever learn quite enough. The more education the better, provided the schooling and training are intermixed with practical work experience.

One additional observation can be made: no research I know of shows any strong correlation between education acquired and employment pursued. As a matter of fact, one study conducted by the

Higher Education Institute of Los Angeles showed that, of 4,000 men and women who entered college, one-half of them changed their career goals following completion of their college education. Other studies show only minimal correlation between what a person studies and what he does for a living. This further strengthens my argument for all persons considering careers in music-related fields: enroll in a good university, study music and business, perhaps even law. But before you escape the ivy-covered halls, also take time to acquire a strong background in the liberal arts. With this kind of educational breadth, you will be best prepared for career opportunities that lie ahead.

In the music field, the shift from schooling to employment is rarely sudden. Unlike such professions as law, engineering and medicine, people heading for careers in the music business break in gradually, land part-time jobs or become involved in various projects while still in school. As a matter of fact, it has been my observation that the student who waits until he has "completed" his education to get going professionally probably won't make it anyway. A person becomes a pro in the music business gradually, as a rule. As he acquires skills and know-how, he starts out part-time, perhaps semiprofessionally, then moves on to full-time work. Composers and performers begin to find work by *building their reputations.* Talented people find work. Persons more interested in the business end of music often get started as pros by inventing their own projects.

It makes little difference in the music business at just what "level of entry" the newcomer breaks into the field. His associates will quickly assess his competence and the individual's career will rise or fall accordingly. The business changes so rapidly, anyone with real talent will climb the ladder. But to continue to climb and not fall back, the individual will certainly have to possess more than raw talent. As we have stressed time and again here, artistic and financial success in the music business are possible, even likely, when the aspirant can present this package to the world:

- *He has genuine talent.*
- *He has the right temperament.*
- *He gets the important information.*
- *He works with qualified associates.*
- *He has the will to win.*

Hang in there.

Part Seven

APPENDIX

COPYRIGHT FORM PA

APPLICATION FOR COPYRIGHT REGISTRATION
for a
Work of the Performing Arts

FORM PA

UNITED STATES COPYRIGHT OFFICE
LIBRARY OF CONGRESS
WASHINGTON, D.C. 20559

HOW TO APPLY FOR COPYRIGHT REGISTRATION:

- **First:** Read the information on this page to make sure Form PA is the correct application for your work.

- **Second:** Open out the form by pulling this page to the left. Read through the detailed instructions before starting to complete the form.

- **Third:** Complete spaces 1-4 of the application, then turn the entire form over and, after reading the instructions for spaces 5-9, complete the rest of your application. Use typewriter or print in dark ink. Be sure to sign the form at space 8.

- **Fourth:** Detach your completed application from these instructions and send it with the necessary deposit of the work (see below) to: Register of Copyrights, Library of Congress, Washington, D.C. 20559. Unless you have a Deposit Account in the Copyright Office, your application and deposit must be accompanied by a check or money order for $10, payable to: *Register of Copyrights.*

WHEN TO USE FORM PA: Form PA is the appropriate application to use for copyright registration covering works of the performing arts. Both published and unpublished works can be registered on Form PA.

WHAT IS A "WORK OF THE PERFORMING ARTS"? This category includes works prepared for the purpose of being "performed" directly before an audience or indirectly "by means of any device or process." Examples of works of the performing arts are: (1) musical works, including any accompanying words; (2) dramatic works, including any accompanying music; (3) pantomimes and choreographic works; and (4) motion pictures and other audiovisual works. Note: This category does not include sound recordings, which should be registered on Form SR. For more information about copyright in sound recordings, see the reverse side of this sheet.

DEPOSIT TO ACCOMPANY APPLICATION: An application for copyright registration must be accompanied by a deposit representing the entire work for which registration is to be made. The following are the general deposit requirements as set forth in the statute:

    Unpublished work: Deposit one complete copy or phonorecord.

    Published work: Deposit two complete copies or phonorecords of the best edition.

    Work first published outside the United States: Deposit one complete copy or phonorecord of the first foreign edition.

    Contribution to a collective work: Deposit one complete copy or phonorecord of the best edition of the collective work.

These general deposit requirements may vary in particular situations. For further information about the specific deposit requirements for particular types of works of the performing arts, see the reverse side of this sheet. For general information about copyright deposit, write to the Copyright Office.

THE COPYRIGHT NOTICE: For published works, the law provides that a copyright notice in a specified form "shall be placed on all publicly distributed copies from which the work can be visually perceived." Use of the copyright notice is the responsibility of the copyright owner and does not require advance permission from the Copyright Office. The required form of the notice for copies generally consists of three elements: (1) the symbol "©", or the word "Copyright", or the abbreviation "Copr."; (2) the year of first publication; and (3) the name of the owner of copyright. For example: "© 1978 Alexander Hollenius". The notice is to be affixed to the copies "in such manner and location as to give reasonable notice of the claim of copyright." Unlike the law in effect before 1978, the new copyright statute provides procedures for correcting errors in the copyright notice, and even for curing the omission of the notice. However, a failure to comply with the notice requirements may still result in the loss of some copyright protection and, unless corrected within five years, in the complete loss of copyright. For further information about the copyright notice, see the reverse side of this sheet. For additional information concerning the copyright notice and the procedures for correcting errors or omissions, write to the Copyright Office.

DURATION OF COPYRIGHT: For works that were created after the effective date of the new statute (January 1, 1978), the basic copyright term will be the life of the author and fifty years after the author's death. For works made for hire, and for certain anonymous and pseudonymous works, the duration of copyright will be 75 years from publication or 100 years from creation, whichever is shorter. These same terms of copyright will generally apply to works that had been created before 1978 but had not been published or copyrighted before that date. For further information about the duration of copyright, including the terms of copyrights already in existence before 1978, write for Circular R15a.

FORM PA
UNITED STATES COPYRIGHT OFFICE

REGISTRATION NUMBER
PA   PAU

EFFECTIVE DATE OF REGISTRATION

....
Month   Day   Year

DO NOT WRITE ABOVE THIS LINE. IF YOU NEED MORE SPACE, USE CONTINUATION SHEET (FORM PA/CON)

1
Title

TITLE OF THIS WORK:

NATURE OF THIS WORK:
(See instructions)

PREVIOUS OR ALTERNATIVE TITLES:

2
Author(s)

IMPORTANT: Under the law, the "author" of a "work made for hire" is generally the employer, not the employee (see instructions). If any part of this work was "made for hire" check "Yes" in the space provided, give the employer (or other person for whom the work was prepared) as "Author" of that part, and leave the space for dates blank

1

NAME OF AUTHOR:

Was this author's contribution to the work a "work made for hire"?   Yes   No

DATES OF BIRTH AND DEATH:
Born _____ Died _____
(Year)   (Year)

AUTHOR'S NATIONALITY OR DOMICILE:
Citizen of _____ } or { Domiciled in _____
(Name of Country)   (Name of Country)

AUTHOR OF: (Briefly describe nature of this author's contribution)

WAS THIS AUTHOR'S CONTRIBUTION TO THE WORK:
Anonymous?   Yes   No
Pseudonymous?   Yes   No
If the answer to either of these questions is "Yes," see detailed instructions attached

2

NAME OF AUTHOR:

Was this author's contribution to the work a "work made for hire"?   Yes   No

DATES OF BIRTH AND DEATH:
Born _____ Died _____
(Year)   (Year)

AUTHOR'S NATIONALITY OR DOMICILE:
Citizen of _____ } or { Domiciled in _____
(Name of Country)   (Name of Country)

AUTHOR OF: (Briefly describe nature of this author's contribution)

WAS THIS AUTHOR'S CONTRIBUTION TO THE WORK:
Anonymous?   Yes   No
Pseudonymous?   Yes   No
If the answer to either of these questions is "Yes," see detailed instructions attached

3

NAME OF AUTHOR:

Was this author's contribution to the work a "work made for hire"?   Yes   No

DATES OF BIRTH AND DEATH:
Born _____ Died _____
(Year)   (Year)

AUTHOR'S NATIONALITY OR DOMICILE:
Citizen of _____ } or { Domiciled in _____
(Name of Country)   (Name of Country)

AUTHOR OF: (Briefly describe nature of this author's contribution)

WAS THIS AUTHOR'S CONTRIBUTION TO THE WORK:
Anonymous?   Yes   No
Pseudonymous?   Yes   No
If the answer to either of these questions is "Yes," see detailed instructions attached

3
Creation and Publication

YEAR IN WHICH CREATION OF THIS WORK WAS COMPLETED:
Year _____
(This information must be given in all cases.)

DATE AND NATION OF FIRST PUBLICATION:
Date _____
(Month)   (Day)   (Year)
Nation _____
(Name of Country)
(Complete this block ONLY if this work has been published.)

4
Claimant(s)

NAME(S) AND ADDRESS(ES) OF COPYRIGHT CLAIMANT(S):

TRANSFER: (If the copyright claimant(s) named here in space 4 are different from the author(s) named in space 2, give a brief statement of how the claimant(s) obtained ownership of the copyright.)

• Complete all applicable spaces (numbers 5-9) on the reverse side of this page
• Follow detailed instructions attached
• Sign the form at line 8

DO NOT WRITE HERE
Page 1 of .... pages

CONTINUATION SHEET FOR FORM PA

FORM PA/CON
UNITED STATES COPYRIGHT OFFICE

- If at all possible, try to fit the information called for into the spaces provided on Form PA.
- If you do not have space enough for all of the information you need to give on Form PA, use this continuation sheet and submit it with Form PA.
- If you submit this continuation sheet, leave it attached to Form PA. Or, if it becomes detached, clip (do not tape or staple) and fold the two together before submitting them.
- **PART A** of this sheet is intended to identify the basic application. **PART B** is a continuation of Space 2. **PART C** is for the continuation of Spaces 1, 4, or 6. The other spaces on Form PA call for specific items of information, and should not need continuation.

REGISTRATION NUMBER
PA   PAU
EFFECTIVE DATE OF REGISTRATION
(Month)   (Day)   (Year)
CONTINUATION SHEET RECEIVED
Page _____ of _____ pages

DO NOT WRITE ABOVE THIS LINE. FOR COPYRIGHT OFFICE USE ONLY

(A) Identification of Application

IDENTIFICATION OF CONTINUATION SHEET: This sheet is a continuation of the application for copyright registration on Form PA, submitted for the following work:
- TITLE: (Give the title as given under the heading "Title of this Work" in Space 1 of Form PA.)
- NAME(S) AND ADDRESS(ES) OF COPYRIGHT CLAIMANT(S): (Give the name and address of at least one copyright claimant as given in Space 4 of Form PA.)

(B) Continuation of Space 2

NAME OF AUTHOR:
Was this author's contribution to the work a "work made for hire"?   Yes   No

DATES OF BIRTH AND DEATH:
Born _____ (Year)   Died _____ (Year)

AUTHOR'S NATIONALITY OR DOMICILE:
Citizen of _____ (Name of Country)   } or { Domiciled in _____ (Name of Country)

WAS THIS AUTHOR'S CONTRIBUTION TO THE WORK:
Anonymous?   Yes   No
Pseudonymous?   Yes   No
If the answer to either of these questions is "Yes," see detailed instructions attached.

AUTHOR OF: (Briefly describe nature of this author's contribution)

NAME OF AUTHOR:
Was this author's contribution to the work a "work made for hire"?   Yes   No

DATES OF BIRTH AND DEATH:
Born _____ (Year)   Died _____ (Year)

AUTHOR'S NATIONALITY OR DOMICILE:
Citizen of _____ (Name of Country)   } or { Domiciled in _____ (Name of Country)

WAS THIS AUTHOR'S CONTRIBUTION TO THE WORK:
Anonymous?   Yes   No
Pseudonymous?   Yes   No
If the answer to either of these questions is "Yes," see detailed instructions attached.

AUTHOR OF: (Briefly describe nature of this author's contribution)

NAME OF AUTHOR:
Was this author's contribution to the work a "work made for hire"?   Yes   No

DATES OF BIRTH AND DEATH:
Born _____ (Year)   Died _____ (Year)

AUTHOR'S NATIONALITY OR DOMICILE:
Citizen of _____ (Name of Country)   } or { Domiciled in _____ (Name of Country)

WAS THIS AUTHOR'S CONTRIBUTION TO THE WORK:
Anonymous?   Yes   No
Pseudonymous?   Yes   No
If the answer to either of these questions is "Yes," see detailed instructions attached.

AUTHOR OF: (Briefly describe nature of this author's contribution)

(C) Continuation of other Spaces

CONTINUATION OF (Check which):   ☐ Space 1   ☐ Space 4   ☐ Space 6

EXAMINED BY:	APPLICATION RECEIVED:	
CHECKED BY:		
CORRESPONDENCE: ☐ Yes	DEPOSIT RECEIVED:	FOR COPYRIGHT OFFICE USE ONLY
DEPOSIT ACCOUNT FUNDS USED: ☐	REMITTANCE NUMBER AND DATE:	

DO NOT WRITE ABOVE THIS LINE. IF YOU NEED ADDITIONAL SPACE, USE CONTINUATION SHEET (FORM PA/CON)

PREVIOUS REGISTRATION:

⑤ **Previous Registration**

- Has registration for this work, or for an earlier version of this work, already been made in the Copyright Office? Yes .... No ....

- If your answer is "Yes," why is another registration being sought? (Check appropriate box)

  ☐ This is the first published edition of a work previously registered in unpublished form.
  ☐ This is the first application submitted by this author as copyright claimant.
  ☐ This is a changed version of the work, as shown by line 6 of the application.

- If your answer is "Yes," give: Previous Registration Number .... Year of Registration ....

COMPILATION OR DERIVATIVE WORK: (See instructions)

⑥ **Compilation or Derivative Work**

PREEXISTING MATERIAL: (Identify any preexisting work or works that the work is based on or incorporates.)
....
....
....
....

MATERIAL ADDED TO THIS WORK: (Give a brief, general statement of the material that has been added to this work and in which copyright is claimed.)
....
....
....
....

DEPOSIT ACCOUNT: (If the registration fee is to be charged to a Deposit Account established in the Copyright Office, give name and number of Account.)

Name: ....

Account Number: ....

CORRESPONDENCE: (Give name and address to which correspondence about this application should be sent.)

Name: ....

Address: .... (Apt.)

.... (City) .... (State) .... (ZIP)

⑦ **Fee and Correspondence**

CERTIFICATION: * I, the undersigned, hereby certify that I am the: (Check one)

☐ author ☐ other copyright claimant ☐ owner of exclusive right(s) ☐ authorized agent of ....
(Name of author or other copyright claimant, or owner of exclusive right(s))

of the work identified in this application and that the statements made by me in this application are correct to the best of my knowledge.

Handwritten signature: (X) ....

Typed or printed name .... Date ....

⑧ **Certification (Application must be signed)**

☞

| MAIL CERTIFICATE TO | ⑨ **Address For Return of Certificate** |

.... (Name)

.... (Number, Street and Apartment Number)

.... (City) (State) (ZIP code)

(Certificate will be mailed in window envelope)

* 17 U.S.C. §506(e) FALSE REPRESENTATION - Any person who knowingly makes a false representation of a material fact in the application for copyright registration provided for by section 409 or in any written statement filed in connection with the application, shall be fined not more than $2,500.

☆ U. S. GOVERNMENT PRINTING OFFICE: 1977 O – 248-636

Nov. 1977 – 1,000,000

COPYRIGHT FORM SR

APPLICATION FOR COPYRIGHT REGISTRATION
for a
Sound Recording

FORM SR

UNITED STATES COPYRIGHT OFFICE
LIBRARY OF CONGRESS
WASHINGTON, D.C. 20559

HOW TO APPLY FOR COPYRIGHT REGISTRATION:

- **First:** Read the information on this page to make sure Form SR is the correct application for your work.

- **Second:** Open out the form by pulling this page to the left. Read through the detailed instructions before starting to complete the form.

- **Third:** Complete spaces 1-4 of the application, then turn the entire form over and, after reading the instructions for spaces 5-9, complete the rest of your application. Use typewriter or print in dark ink. Be sure to sign the form at space 8.

- **Fourth:** Detach your completed application from these instructions and send it with the necessary deposit of the work (see below) to: Register of Copyrights, Library of Congress, Washington, D.C. 20559. Unless you have a Deposit Account in the Copyright Office, your application and deposit must be accompanied by a check or money order for $10, payable to: *Register of Copyrights.*

WHEN TO USE FORM SR: Form SR is the appropriate application to use for copyright registration covering a sound recording. It should be used where the copyright claim is limited to the sound recording itself, and it should also be used where the same copyright claimant is seeking to register not only the sound recording but also the musical, dramatic, or literary work embodied in the sound recording. Both published and unpublished works can be registered on Form SR.

WHAT IS A "SOUND RECORDING"? With one exception, "sound recordings" are works that result from the fixation of a series of musical, spoken, or other sounds. The exception is for the audio portions of audiovisual works, such as a motion picture soundtrack or an audio cassette accompanying a filmstrip; these are considered an integral part of the audiovisual work as a whole. For further information about "sound recordings" and the distinction between "sound recordings" and "phonorecords," see the reverse side of this sheet. For additional information about copyright in sound recordings, write for Circular R56.

DEPOSIT TO ACCOMPANY APPLICATION: An application for copyright registration must be accompanied by a deposit representing the entire work for which registration is to be made. For registration on Form SR, the following are the general deposit requirements:

Unpublished work: Deposit one complete phonorecord.

Published work: Deposit two complete phonorecords of the best edition, together with "any printed or other visually perceptible material" published with the phonorecords.

Work first published outside the United States: Deposit one complete phonorecord of the work as first published.

Contribution to a collective work: Deposit one complete phonorecord of the best edition of the collective work.

These general deposit requirements may vary in particular situations. For further information about the deposit requirements for sound recordings, see the reverse side of this sheet. For general information about copyright deposit, write for Circular R7.

THE COPYRIGHT NOTICE: For published sound recordings, the law provides that a copyright notice in a specified form "shall be placed on all publicly distributed phonorecords of the sound recording." Use of the copyright notice is the responsibility of the copyright owner and does not require advance permission from the Copyright Office. The required form of the notice for phonorecords generally consists of three elements: (1) the symbol "℗" (the letter P in a circle); (2) the year of first publication of the sound recording; and (3) the name of the owner of copyright. For example: "℗ 1978 Rittenhouse Record Co." The notice is to be "placed on the surface of the phonorecord, or on the label or container, in such manner and location as to give reasonable notice of the claim of copyright." Unlike the law in effect before 1978, the new copyright statute provides procedures for correcting errors in the copyright notice, and even for curing the omission of the notice. However, a failure to comply with the notice requirements may still result in the loss of some copyright protection and, unless corrected within five years, in the complete loss of copyright. For further information about the copyright notice, see the reverse side of this sheet. For additional information concerning the copyright notice and the procedures for correcting errors or omissions, write for Circular R3.

DURATION OF COPYRIGHT: For works that were created after the effective date of the new statute (January 1, 1978), the basic copyright term will be the life of the author and fifty years after the author's death. For works made for hire, and for certain anonymous and pseudonymous works, the duration of copyright will be 75 years from publication or 100 years from creation, whichever is shorter. These same terms of copyright will generally apply to works that had been created before 1978 but had not been published or copyrighted before that date. Sound recordings fixed before February 15, 1972 are not eligible for registration, but may be protected by state law. For further information about the duration of copyright, including the terms of copyrights already in existence before 1978, write for Circular R15a.

FORM SR

UNITED STATES COPYRIGHT OFFICE

REGISTRATION NUMBER	
SR	SRU

EFFECTIVE DATE OF REGISTRATION

....
Month   Day   Year

DO NOT WRITE ABOVE THIS LINE. IF YOU NEED MORE SPACE, USE CONTINUATION SHEET (FORM SR/CON)

① **Title**

TITLE OF THIS WORK:

Catalog number of sound recording, if any

PREVIOUS OR ALTERNATIVE TITLES:

NATURE OF MATERIAL RECORDED:
(Check Which)

☐ Musical   ☐ Musical Dramatic
☐ Dramatic   ☐ Literary
☐ Other

② **Author(s)**

IMPORTANT: Under the law, the "author" of a "work made for hire" is generally the employer, not the employee (see instructions). If any part of this work was "made for hire" check "Yes" in the space provided, give the employer (or other person for whom the work was prepared) as "Author" of that part, and leave the space for dates blank.

1

NAME OF AUTHOR:

Was this author's contribution to the work a "work made for hire"? Yes...... No......

AUTHOR'S NATIONALITY OR DOMICILE:
Citizen of .... } or { Domiciled in ....
(Name of Country) (Name of Country)

AUTHOR OF: (Briefly describe nature of this author's contribution)

DATES OF BIRTH AND DEATH:
Born .... Died ....
(Year) (Year)

WAS THIS AUTHOR'S CONTRIBUTION TO THE WORK:
Anonymous? Yes...... No......
Pseudonymous? Yes...... No......
If the answer to either of these questions is "Yes," see detailed instructions attached.

2

NAME OF AUTHOR:

Was this author's contribution to the work a "work made for hire"? Yes...... No......

AUTHOR'S NATIONALITY OR DOMICILE:
Citizen of .... } or { Domiciled in ....
(Name of Country) (Name of Country)

AUTHOR OF: (Briefly describe nature of this author's contribution)

DATES OF BIRTH AND DEATH:
Born .... Died ....
(Year) (Year)

WAS THIS AUTHOR'S CONTRIBUTION TO THE WORK:
Anonymous? Yes...... No......
Pseudonymous? Yes...... No......
If the answer to either of these questions is "Yes," see detailed instructions attached.

3

NAME OF AUTHOR:

Was this author's contribution to the work a "work made for hire"? Yes...... No......

AUTHOR'S NATIONALITY OR DOMICILE:
Citizen of .... } or { Domiciled in ....
(Name of Country) (Name of Country)

AUTHOR OF: (Briefly describe nature of this author's contribution)

DATES OF BIRTH AND DEATH:
Born .... Died ....
(Year) (Year)

WAS THIS AUTHOR'S CONTRIBUTION TO THE WORK:
Anonymous? Yes...... No......
Pseudonymous? Yes...... No......
If the answer to either of these questions is "Yes," see detailed instructions attached.

③ **Creation and Publication**

YEAR IN WHICH CREATION OF THIS WORK WAS COMPLETED:

Year ....
(This information must be given in all cases.)

DATE AND NATION OF FIRST PUBLICATION:

Date ....
(Month) (Day) (Year)
Nation ....
(Name of Country)
(Complete this block ONLY if this work has been published.)

④ **Claimant(s)**

NAME(S) AND ADDRESS(ES) OF COPYRIGHT CLAIMANT(S):

TRANSFER: (If the copyright claimant(s) named here in space 4 are different from the author(s) named in space 2, give a brief statement of how the claimant(s) obtained ownership of the copyright.)

- Complete all applicable spaces (numbers 5-9) on the reverse side of this page
- Follow detailed instructions attached
- Sign the form at line 8

DO NOT WRITE HERE	
Page 1 of .... pages	

EXAMINED BY:	APPLICATION RECEIVED:	FOR COPYRIGHT OFFICE USE ONLY
CHECKED BY:		
CORRESPONDENCE: ☐ Yes	DEPOSIT RECEIVED:	
DEPOSIT ACCOUNT FUNDS USED: ☐	REMITTANCE NUMBER AND DATE:	

DO NOT WRITE ABOVE THIS LINE. IF YOU NEED ADDITIONAL SPACE, USE CONTINUATION SHEET (FORM SR/CON)

PREVIOUS REGISTRATION:

- Has registration for this work, or for an earlier version of this work, already been made in the Copyright Office? Yes . . . . No . . . .

- If your answer is "Yes," why is another registration being sought? (Check appropriate box)
  - ☐ This is the first published edition of a work previously registered in unpublished form.
  - ☐ This is the first application submitted by this author as copyright claimant.
  - ☐ This is a changed version of the work, as shown by line 6 of the application.

- If your answer is "Yes," give: Previous Registration Number . . . . Year of Registration . . . .

⑤ Previous Registration

COMPILATION OR DERIVATIVE WORK: (See instructions)

PREEXISTING MATERIAL: (Identify any preexisting work or works that the work is based on or incorporates.)

. . . .
. . . .
. . . .

MATERIAL ADDED TO THIS WORK: (Give a brief, general statement of the material that has been added to this work and in which copyright is claimed.)

. . . .
. . . .
. . . .

⑥ Compilation or Derivative Work

DEPOSIT ACCOUNT: (If the registration fee is to be charged to a Deposit Account established in the Copyright Office, give name and number of Account.)

Name: . . . .

Account Number: . . . .

CORRESPONDENCE: (Give name and address to which correspondence about this application should be sent.)

Name: . . . .

Address: . . . .
(Apt.)

(City)   (State)   (ZIP)

⑦ Fee and Correspondence

CERTIFICATION: ✱ I, the undersigned, hereby certify that I am the: (Check one)

☐ author ☐ other copyright claimant ☐ owner of exclusive right(s) ☐ authorized agent of . . . .
(Name of author or other copyright claimant, or owner of exclusive right(s))

of the work identified in this application and that the statements made by me in this application are correct to the best of my knowledge.

Handwritten signature: (X) . . . .

Typed or printed name: . . . . Date: . . . .

⑧ Certification (Application must be signed)

MAIL CERTIFICATE TO

. . . .
(Name)

. . . .
(Number, Street and Apartment Number)

. . . .
(City)   (State)   (ZIP code)

(Certificate will be mailed in window envelope)

⑨ Address For Return of Certificate

✱ 17 U.S.C. § 506(e): FALSE REPRESENTATION—Any person who knowingly makes a false representation of a material fact in the application for copyright registration provided for by section 409, or in any written statement filed in connection with the application, shall be fined not more than $2,500.

☆ U.S. GOVERNMENT PRINTING OFFICE : 1977 O—248-637

Nov. 1977—200,000

ASCAP WRITER APPLICATION

W

APPLICATION FOR WRITER-MEMBERSHIP
IN THE
AMERICAN SOCIETY of COMPOSERS, AUTHORS and PUBLISHERS
One Lincoln Plaza, New York, N.Y. 10023

FULL ☐   STANDARD ☐   AUTHOR ☐
I hereby apply for membership as a ASSOCIATE ☐ POPULAR PRODUCTION ☐ COMPOSER ☐
in the American Society of Composers, Authors and Publishers. If elected, I agree to be bound by the
Society's Articles of Association, as now in effect and as they may be amended, and I agree to execute
agreements in such form and for such periods as the Board of Directors shall have approved or shall
hereafter approve for all members.

The following information is submitted in support of this application:

1. Full Name: Mr. Miss

    Mrs. Ms. _____
                    (First Name)   *(Middle Name or initial)*   *(Last Name)*

2. Pseudonyms, if any (no more than four)

    _____

    _____

3. Home Address:
☐ _____
    (Street)   *(City)*   *(State)*   *(Zip Code)*   *(Area Code & Tel. #)*

    Business Address (if same as above, write "same"):

☐ _____
    (Street)   *(City)*   *(State)*   *(Zip Code)*   *(Area Code & Tel. #)*

Please check to which address your mail is to be sent.

4. Date of Birth: _____
                        (month)   *(day)*   *(year)*

    Place of Birth: _____

5. Citizen of: _____

6. Social Security #: _____

7. I am ☐, or have been ☐, a member or affiliate of ASCAP, BMI or SESAC, or of a foreign performing
    rights licensing organization. (Check one if applicable)
    If you have checked one of the boxes above, please state the name of the organization with which
    you were affiliated and the period of your affiliation, and attach a copy of your release: _____

    _____

8. I have ☐, do not have ☐, a relative (including brother, sister, husband, wife, child or any other relation)
    who is affiliated with an organization referred to in item 7. (Check the applicable box)

    If you answered affirmatively, please give the name of any such person, relationship to you and

    organization with which affiliated: _____

9. I have ☐, have not ☐, paid to have the works submitted by me on behalf of this application published
    or recorded. (Check the applicable box)
    If you have answered affirmatively, please indicate which works submitted by you were the subject of
    such payment and to whom payment was made:

    _____

    _____

10. The musical works of which I am the composer or author are listed on the reverse side.   I represent
    that there are no existing assignments or licenses, direct or indirect, of non-dramatic performing
    rights in or to any of the works so listed, except with publishers of such works. If there are assignments
    or licenses other than with publishers, I have attached true copies. I have read the Society's Articles
    of Association and make this application with full knowledge of their contents.

    I warrant and represent that all of the information furnished in this application is true. I acknowl-
    edge that any contract between ASCAP and me will be entered into in reliance upon the representa-
    tions contained in this application, and that the contract will be subject to cancellation if the infor-
    mation contained in this application is not complete and accurate.

Signature _____   *Date* _____

ASCAP PUBLISHER APPLICATION

P

APPLICATION FOR PUBLISHER-MEMBERSHIP
IN THE

AMERICAN SOCIETY of COMPOSERS, AUTHORS and PUBLISHERS
One Lincoln Plaza, New York, N.Y. 10023

I(we) hereby apply for membership, as a ☐ Standard/ ☐ Popular Production Music Publisher, in the American Society of Composers, Authors and Publishers. If elected I (we) agree to be bound by the Society's Articles of Association as now in effect, and as they may be amended, and I (we) agree to execute agreements in such form and for such periods as the Board of Directors shall have approved or shall hereafter approve for all members.

The following information is submitted in support of this application:

1. Firm Name _____

2. Business Address _____

             City   State   Zip Code

   Telephone(   )_____

3. Check and complete *one* of the following to indicate organization of company:

   A. CORPORATION ☐   Corporate I.D. No. _____

      State of Incorporation _____ Date of Charter _____

      Stockholders (list all stockholders)

Name	Soc. Sec. No.	Home Address & Zip Code	Percentage of Ownership

      Officers (list all officers)

Name	Soc. Sec. No.	Home Address & Zip Code	Office Held

   B. PARTNERSHIP ☐ (list all partners)   Year Business Established _____

Name	Soc. Sec. No.	Home Address & Zip Code	Percentage of Ownership

   C. INDIVIDUAL OWNERSHIP ☐ Year Business Established _____

     Name _____ Soc. Sec. No. _____

     Home Address _____
             City   State   Zip Code

     Telephone Number: (   ) _____

4. Cities In Which Branch Offices Are Maintained

_____

_____

City	State	Address	Area Code & Telephone #

5. If any owner, stockholder, officer, or employee with executive responsibilities, has been or is now connected with any publishing company, songwriter's agency, recording company, performance rights licensing organization (as an employee), or any other organization engaged in the solicitation, publication or exploitation of music, please fill in the information requested below:

Name of Individual	Name of Company	If Publishing Company Indicate performance rights affiliation	Position Held	Years of Association

6. If you have made, or intend to make, any charge to an author (lyricist), or composer in connection with the examination, publication, recording or exploitation of any composition published or to be published by you, please state the nature of the charge and the service to be performed.

7. I (we) have read ASCAP's Articles of Association and make this application with full knowledge of their contents. I (we) understand that any agreement entered into between ASCAP and me (us) will be in reliance upon the information contained in this application and attached schedules. I (we) understand that the agreement will be subject to cancellation if any information contained in this application is not fully and correctly provided or if the true name of each owner, stockholder, and officer is not provided as requested.

Firm Name

_By_

Title

Date _____
     month   _day_   _year_

DO NOT FILL IN BELOW

Received:	Presented:	Recommended by Membership Committee
		For _____ Date _____

ASCAP AGREEMENT WITH WRITER OR PUBLISHER

1976-1985

Agreement Between

Composite sample page only. DO NOT USE.

AND

American Society
OF
Composers, Authors & Publishers

1 LINCOLN PLAZA
NEW YORK, N. Y. 10023

AGREEMENT made between the Undersigned (for brevity called "*Owner*") and the AMERICAN SOCIETY OF COMPOSERS, AUTHORS AND PUBLISHERS (for brevity called "*Society*"), in consideration of the premises and of the mutual covenants hereinafter contained, as follows:

1. The *Owner* grants to the *Society* for the term hereof, the right to license non-dramatic public performances (as hereinafter defined), of each musical work:

Of which the *Owner* is a copyright proprietor; or

Which the *Owner*, alone, or jointly, or in collaboration with others, wrote, composed, published, acquired or owned; or

In which the *Owner* now has any right, title, interest or control whatsoever, in whole or in part; or

Which hereafter, during the term hereof, may be written, composed, acquired, owned, published or copyrighted by the *Owner*, alone, jointly or in collaboration with others; or

In which the *Owner* may hereafter, during the term hereof, have any right, title, interest or control, whatsoever, in whole or in part.

The right to license the public performance of every such musical work shall be deemed granted to the *Society* by this instrument for the term hereof, immediately upon the work being written, composed, acquired, owned, published or copyrighted.

The rights hereby granted shall include:

(a) All the rights and remedies for enforcing the copyright or copyrights of such musical works, whether such copyrights are in the name of the *Owner* and/or others, as well as the right to sue under such copyrights in the name of the *Society* and/or in the name of the *Owner* and/or others, to the end that the *Society* may effectively protect and be assured of all the rights hereby granted.

(b) The non-exclusive right of public performance of the separate numbers, songs, fragments or arrangements, melodies or selections forming part or parts of musical plays and dramatico-musical compositions, the *Owner* reserving and excepting from this grant the right of performance of musical plays and dramatico-musical compositions in their entirety, or any part of such plays or dramatico-musical compositions on the legitimate stage.

(c) The non-exclusive right of public performance by means of radio broadcasting, telephony, "wired wireless," all forms of synchronism with motion pictures, and/or any method of transmitting sound other than television broadcasting.

(d) The non-exclusive right of public performance by television broadcasting; provided, however, that:

(i) This grant does not extend to or include the right to license the public performance by television broadcasting or otherwise of any rendition or performance of (a) any opera, operetta, musical comedy, play or like production, as such, in whole or in part, or (b) any composition from any opera, operetta, musical comedy, play or like production (whether or not such opera, operetta, musical comedy, play or like production was presented on the stage or in motion picture form) in a manner which recreates the performance of such composition with substantially such distinctive scenery or costume as was used in the presentation of such opera, operetta, musical comedy, play or like production (whether or not such opera, operetta, musical comedy, play or like production was presented on the stage or in motion picture form): provided, however, that the rights hereby granted shall be deemed to include a grant of the right to license non-dramatic performances of compositions by television broadcasting of a motion picture containing such composition if the rights in such motion picture other than those granted hereby have been obtained from the parties in interest.

(ii) Nothing herein contained shall be deemed to grant the right to license the public performance by television broadcasting of dramatic performances. Any performance of a separate musical composition which is not a dramatic performance, as defined herein, shall be deemed to be a non-dramatic performance. For the purposes of this agreement, a dramatic performance shall mean a performance of a musical composition on a television program in which there is a definite plot depicted by action and where the performance of the musical composition is woven into and carries forward the plot and its accompanying action. The use of dialogue to establish a mere program format or the use of any non-dramatic device merely to introduce a performance of a composition shall not be deemed to make such performance dramatic.

(iii) The definition of the terms "dramatic" and "non-dramatic" performances contained herein are purely for the purposes of this agreement and for the term thereof and shall not be binding upon or prejudicial to any position taken by either of us subsequent to the term hereof or for any purpose other than this agreement.

(e) The *Owner* may at any time and from time to time, in good faith, restrict the radio or television broadcasting of compositions from musical comedies, operas, operettas and motion pictures, or any other composition being excessively broadcast, only for the purpose of preventing harmful effect upon such musical comedies, operas, operettas, motion pictures or compositions, in respect of other interests under the copyrights thereof; provided, however, that the right to grant limited licenses will be given, upon application, as to restricted compositions, if and when the *Owner* is unable to show reasonable hazards to his or its major interests likely to result from such radio or television broadcasting; and provided further that such right to restrict any such composition shall not be exercised for the purpose of permitting the fixing or regulating of fees for the recording or trans-"ibing of such composition, and provided further that in no case shall any charges, "free plugs", or other consideration be required in respect of any permission granted to perform a restricted composition; and provided further that in no event shall any composition, after the initial radio or television broadcast thereof, be restricted for the purpose of confining further radio or television broadcasts thereof to a particular artist, station, network or program. The *Owner* may also at any time and from time to time, in good faith, restrict the radio or television broadcasting of any composition, as to which any suit has been brought or threatened on a claim that such composition infringes a composition not contained in the repertory of *Society* or on a claim by a non-member of *Society* that *Society* does not have the right to license the public performance of such composition by radio or television broadcasting.

2.   The term of this agreement shall be for a period commencing on the date hereof and expiring on the 31st day of December, 1985.

3.   The *Society* agrees, during the term hereof, in good faith to use its best endeavors to promote and carry out the objects for which it was organized, and to hold and apply all royalties, profits, benefits and advantages arising from the exploitation of the rights assigned to it by its several members, including the *Owner*, to the uses and purposes as provided in its Articles of Association (which are hereby incorporated by reference), as now in force or as hereafter amended.

4.   The *Owner* hereby irrevocably, during the term hereof, authorizes, empowers and vests in the *Society* the right to enforce and protect such rights of public performance under any and all copyrights, whether standing in the name of the *Owner* and/or others, in any and all works copyrighted by the *Owner*, and/or by others; to prevent the infringement thereof, to litigate, collect and receipt for damages arising from infringement, and in its sole judgment to join the *Owner* and/or others in whose names the copyright may stand, as parties plaintiff or defendants in suits or proceedings; to bring suit in the name of the *Owner* and/or in the name of the *Society*, or others in whose name the copyright may stand, or otherwise, and to release, compromise, or refer to arbitration any actions, in the same manner and to the same extent and to all intents and purposes as the *Owner* might or could do, had this instrument not been made.

5.   The *Owner* hereby makes, constitutes and appoints the *Society*, or its successor, the *Owner's* true and lawful attorney, irrevocably during the term hereof, and in the name of the *Society* or its successor, or in the name of the *Owner*, or otherwise, to do all acts, take all proceedings, execute, acknowledge and deliver any and all instruments, papers, documents, process and pleadings that may be necessary, proper or expedient to restrain infringements and recover damages in respect to or for the infringement or other violation of the rights of public performance in such works, and to discontinue, compromise or refer to arbitration any such proceedings or actions, or to make any other disposition of the differences in relation to the premises.

6.   The *Owner* agrees from time to time, to execute, acknowledge and deliver to the *Society*, such assurances, powers of attorney or other authorizations or instruments as the *Society* may deem necessary or expedient to enable it to exercise, enjoy and enforce, in its own name or otherwise, all rights and remedies aforesaid.

7.   It is mutually agreed that during the term hereof the Board of Directors of the *Society* shall be composed of an equal number of writers and publishers respectively, and that the royalties distributed by the Board of Directors shall be divided into two (2) equal sums, and one (1) each of such sums credited respectively to and for division amongst (a) the writer members, and (b) the publisher members, in accordance with the system of distribution and classification as determined by the Classification Committee of each group, in accordance with the Articles of Association as they may be amended from time to time, except that the classification of the *Owner* within his class may be changed.

8.   The *Owner* agrees that his classification in the *Society* as determined from time to time by the Classification Committee of his group and/or The Board of Directors of the *Society*, in case of appeal by him, shall be final, conclusive and binding upon him.

The *Society* shall have the right to transfer the right of review of any classification from the Board of Directors to any other agency or instrumentality that in its discretion and good judgment it deems best adapted to assuring to the *Society's* membership a just, fair, equitable and accurate classification.

The *Society* shall have the right to adopt from time to time such systems, means, methods and formulae for the establishment of a member's status in respect of classification as will assure a fair, just and equitable distribution of royalties among the membership.

9.   **"Public Performance" Defined.**   The term *"public performance"* shall be construed to mean vocal, instrumental and/or mechanical renditions and representations in any manner or by any method whatsoever, including transmissions by radio and television broadcasting stations, transmission by telephony and/or "wired wireless"; and/or reproductions of performances and renditions by means of devices for reproducing sound recorded in synchronism or timed relation with the taking of motion pictures.

10.   **"Musical Works" Defined.**   The phrase *"musical works"* shall be construed to mean musical compositions and dramatico-musical compositions, the words and music thereof, and the respective arrangements thereof, and the selections therefrom.

11.   The powers, rights, authorities and privileges by this instrument vested in the *Society*, are deemed to include the World, provided, however, that such grant of rights for foreign countries shall be subject to any agreements now in effect, a list of which are noted on the reverse side hereof.

12.   The grant made herein by the owner is modified by and subject to the provisions of (a) the Amended Final Judgment (Civil Action No. 13-95) dated March 14, 1950 in U. S. A. v. ASCAP as further amended by Order dated January 7, 1960, (b) the Final Judgment (Civil Action No. 42-245) in U. S. A. v. ASCAP, dated March 14, 1950, and (c) the provisions of the Articles of Association and resolutions of the Board of Directors adopted pursuant to such judgments and order.

SIGNED, SEALED AND DELIVERED, on this.........................day of.., 19........

Society {

AMERICAN SOCIETY OF COMPOSERS, AUTHORS AND PUBLISHERS.

Owner {

By ....
                    President

BMI WRITER APPLICATION

APPLICATION FOR WRITER AFFILIATION
BROADCAST MUSIC, INC.
PERFORMING RIGHTS ADMINISTRATION

320 WEST 57th STREET
NEW YORK, N. Y. 10019

PLEASE PRINT

1. NAME: MS.
   MR.
   MRS...
   MISS   (First Name)   (Middle Name or Initial)   (Last Name)

2. ☐ HOME ADDRESS.

   ....
   (Street)   (City)   (State)   (Zip Code) (Phone Number)

   ☐ BUSINESS ADDRESS (If same as above, write "same")
   (Include Company Room No. if necessary)

   ....
   (Street)   (City)   (State)   (Zip Code) (Phone Number)
   (Check one address above to which all mail is to be sent)

3. DATE OF BIRTH: .... CITIZENSHIP: ....
                 Month   Day   Year   Country

4. EDUCATIONAL BACKGROUND, ACADEMIC & MUSICAL: ....
   ....

5. DO YOU WRITE WORDS, MUSIC OR BOTH?..

6. LIST ALL PEN NAMES AND PSEUDONYMS WHICH YOU HAVE USED OR WILL USE:
   ....

7. Are you now or have you ever been a writer member or writer-affiliate of BMI, ASCAP, SESAC, or of any foreign performing rights licensing organization? If so, state name of organization and the period during which you were a member or affiliate. ....
   ....

8. Is your spouse, parent, brother, sister, child or any other relative or writer-member or writer-affilate of any organization specified in Paragraph 7? If so, give name, realtionship to you, and organization. ....
   ....

9. Have you ever written music or lyrics for a fee or in consideration of any payment from a composer or writer of the music or lyrics? Please state the circumstances under which you performed such services ....
   ....
   ....

10. Please list on the reverse side of this form at least one but not more than three compositions heretofore written by you, either alone or in collaboration with others, which are placed with a publisher, commercially recorded, being performed or likely to be performed.

STATE OF .... ⎫
                        ⎬ ss. :
COUNTY OF .... ⎭

On the .... day of .... 19......

before me came

to me known and known to me to be the individual described in and who executed the foregoing
instrument, and (s)he duly acknowledged to me
that (s)he executed the same.

I warrant and represent that all of the information furnished on this application is true. I acknowledge that any contract consummated between me and BMI will be entered into in reliance upon the representations contained in this application, and that the contract will be subject to cancellation if any question herein contained is not answered fully or accurately.

....
         Notary Public

Date ....

Social Security No. ....

Signature ....

APPLICATION WILL NOT BE ACCEPTED UNLESS IT IS NOTARIZED

AND ALL QUESTIONS ARE FULLY ANSWERED

Return Completed Application to BMI, Attention of PERFORMING RIGHTS ADMINISTRATION
WR201-78

BMI WRITER AGREEMENT

BROADCAST MUSIC, INC.

320 West 57th Street   New York, N.Y. 10019

Date

Dear

The following shall constitute the agreement between us:

1. As used in this agreement:

(a) The word "period" shall mean the term from   to
                                          , and continuing thereafter for additional terms of two years each unless terminated by either party at the end of said initial term or any additional term, upon notice by registered or certified mail not more than six months or less than sixty (60) days prior to the end of any such term.

(b) The word "works" shall mean:

(i) All musical compositions (including the musical segments and individual compositions written for a dramatic or dramatico-musical work) composed by you alone or with one or more collaborators during the period; and

(ii) All musical compositions (including the musical segments and individual compositions written for a dramatic or dramatico-musical work) composed by you alone or with one or more collaborators prior to the period, except those in which there is an outstanding grant of the right of public performance to a person other than a publisher affiliated with BMI.

2. You agree that:

(a) Within ten (10) days after the execution of this agreement you will furnish to us two copies of a completed clearance sheet in the form supplied by us with respect to each work heretofore composed by you which has been published in printed copies or recorded commercially or which is being currently performed or which you consider as likely to be performed.

(b) In each instance that a work for which clearance sheets have not been submitted to us pursuant to sub-paragraph (a) hereof is published in printed copies or recorded commercially or in synchronization with film or tape or is considered by you as likely to be performed, whether such work is composed prior to the execution of this agreement or hereafter during the period, you will promptly furnish to us two copies of a completed clearance sheet in the form supplied by us with respect to each such work.

(c) If requested by us in writing, you will promptly furnish to us a legible lead sheet or other written or printed copy of a work.

3. The submission of clearance sheets pursuant to paragraph 2 hereof shall constitute a warranty by you that all of the information contained thereon is true and correct and that no performing rights in such work have been granted to or reserved by others except as specifically set forth therein in connection with works heretofore written or co-written by you.

4. Except as otherwise provided herein, you hereby grant to us for the period:

(a) All the rights that you own or acquire publicly to perform, and to license others to perform, anywhere in the world, any part or all of the works.

(b) The non-exclusive right to record, and to license others to record, any part or all of any of the works on electrical transcriptions, wire, tape, film or otherwise, but only for the purpose of performing such work publicly by means of radio and television or for archive or audition purposes and not for sale to the public or for synchronization (i) with motion pictures intended primarily for theatrical exhibition or (ii) with programs distributed by means of syndication to broadcasting stations.

(c) The non-exclusive right to adapt or arrange any part or all of any of the works for performance purposes, and to license others to do so.

5. (a) The rights granted to us by sub-paragraph (a) of paragraph 4 hereof shall not include the right to perform or license the performance of more than one song or aria from a dramatic or dramatico-musical work which is an opera, operetta, or musical show or more than five minutes from a dramatic or dramatico-musical work which is a ballet if such performance is accompanied by the dramatic action, costumes or scenery of that dramatic or dramatico-musical work.

(b) You, together with the publisher and your collaborators, if any, shall have the right jointly, by written notice to us, to exclude from the grant made by sub-paragraph (a) of paragraph 4 hereof performances of works comprising more than thirty minutes of a dramatic or dramatico-musical work, but this right shall not apply to such performances from (i) a score originally written for and performed as part of a theatrical or television film, (ii) a score originally written for and performed as part of a radio or television program, or (iii) the original cast, sound track or similar album of a dramatic or dramatico-musical work.

(c) You retain the right to issue non-exclusive licenses for performances of a work or works (other than to another performing rights licensing organization), provided that within ten (10) days of the issuance of such license we are given written notice of the titles of the works and the nature of the performances so licensed by you.

6. (a) As full consideration for all rights granted to us hereunder and as security therefor, we agree to pay to you, with respect to each of the works in which we obtain and retain performing rights during the period:

(i) For performances of a work on broadcasting stations in the United States, its territories and possessions, amounts calculated pursuant to our then current standard practices upon the basis of the then current performance rates generally paid by us to our affiliated writers for similar performances of similar compositions. The number of performances for which you shall be entitled to payment shall be estimated by us in accordance with our then current system of computing the number of such performances.

It is acknowledged that we license the works of our affiliates for performance by non-broadcasting means, but that unless and until such time as feasible methods can be devised for tabulation of and payment for such performances, payment will be based solely on broadcast performances. In the event that during the period we shall establish a system of separate payment for non-broadcasting performances, we shall pay you upon the basis of the then current performance rates generally paid by us to our other affiliated writers for similar performances of similar compositions.

(ii) In the case of a work composed by you with one or more collaborators, the sum payable to you hereunder shall be a pro rata share, determined on the basis of the number of collaborators, unless you shall have transmitted to us a copy of an agreement between you and your collaborators providing for a different division of payment.

(iii) All monies received by us from any performing rights licensing organization outside of the United States, its territories and possessions, which are designated by such performing rights licensing organization as the author's share of foreign performance royalties earned by your works after the deduction of our then current handling charge applicable to our affiliated writers.

(b) We shall have no obligation to make payment hereunder with respect to (i) any performance of a work which occurs prior to the date on which we have received from you all of the information and material with respect to such work which is referred to in paragraphs 2 and 3 hereof, or (ii) any performance as to which a direct license as described in sub-paragraph (c) of paragraph 5 hereof has been granted by you, your collaborator or publisher.

7. We will furnish statements to you at least twice during each year of the period showing the number of performances as computed pursuant to sub-paragraph (a) (i) of paragraph 6 hereof and at least once during each year of the period showing the monies due pursuant to sub-paragraph (a) (iii) of paragraph 6 hereof. Each statement shall be accompanied by payment to you, subject to all proper deductions for advances, if any, of the sum thereby shown to be due for such performances.

8. (a) Nothing in this agreement requires us to continue to license the works subsequent to the termination of this agreement. In the event that we continue to license any or all of the works, however, we shall continue to make payments to you for so long as you do not make or purport to make directly or indirectly any grant of performing rights in such works to any other licensing organization. The amounts of such payments shall be calculated pursuant to our then current standard practices upon the basis of the then current performance rates generally paid by us to our affiliated writers for similar performances of similar compositions. You agree to notify us by registered or certified mail of any grant or purported grant by you directly or indirectly of performing rights to any other performing rights organization within ten (10) days from the making of such grant or purported grant and if you fail so to inform us thereof and we make payments to you for any period after the making of any such grant or purported grant, you agree to repay to us all amounts so paid by us promptly on demand. In addition, if we inquire of you by registered or certified mail, addressed to your last known address, whether you have made any such grant or purported grant and you fail to confirm to us by registered or certified mail within thirty (30) days of the mailing of such inquiry that you have not made any such grant or purported grant, we may, from and after such date, discontinue making any payments to you.

(b) Our obligation to continue payment to you after the termination of this agreement for performances outside of the United States, its territories and possessions shall be dependent upon our receipt in the United

States of payments designated by foreign performing rights organizations as the author's share of foreign performance royalties earned by your works. Payment of such foreign royalties shall be subject to deduction of our then current handling charge applicable to our affiliated writers.

(c) In the event that we have reason to believe that you will receive or are receiving payment from a performing rights licensing organization other than BMI for or based on United States performances of one or more of your works during a period when such works were licensed by us pursuant to this agreement, we shall have the right to withhold payment for such performances from you until receipt of evidence satisfactory to us of the amount so paid to you by such other organization or that you have not been so paid. In the event that you have been so paid, the monies payable by us to you for such performances during such period shall be reduced by the amount of the payment from such other organization. In the event that you do not supply such evidence within eighteen (18) months from the date of our request therefor, we shall be under no obligation to make any payment to you for performances of such works during such period.

9. In the event that this agreement shall terminate at a time when, after crediting all earnings reflected by the statements rendered to you prior to the effective date of such termination, there remains an unearned balance of advances made to you by us, such termination shall not be effective with respect to the works then embraced by this agreement unless and until sixty (60) days after the unpaid balance of advances shall be repaid by you or until sixty (60) days after a statement is rendered by us at our normal accounting period showing that such unearned balance of advances has been fully recouped by us.

10. You warrant and represent that you have the right to enter into this agreement; that you are not bound by any prior commitments which conflict with your commitments hereunder; that each of the works, composed by you alone or with one or more collaborators, is original; and that exercise of the rights granted by you herein will not constitute an infringement of copyright or violation of any other right of, or unfair competition with, any person, firm or corporation. You agree to indemnify and hold harmless us and our licensees from and against any and all loss or damage resulting from any claim of whatever nature arising from or in connection with the exercise of any of the rights granted by you in this agreement. Upon notification to us or any of our licensees of a claim with respect to any of the works, we shall have the right to exclude such work from this agreement and/or to withhold payment of all sums which become due pursuant to this agreement or any modification thereof until receipt of satisfactory written evidence that such claim has been withdrawn, settled or adjudicated.

11. (a) We shall have the right, upon written notice to you, to exclude from this agreement, at any time, any work which in our opinion (i) is similar to a previously existing composition and might constitute a copyright infringement, or (ii) has a title or music or lyric similar to that of a previously existing composition and might lead to a claim of unfair competition, or (iii) is offensive, in bad taste or against public morals, or (iv) is not reasonably suitable for performance.

(b) In the case of works which in our opinion are based on compositions in the public domain, we shall have the right, upon written notice to you, either (i) to exclude any such work from this agreement, or (ii) to classify any such work as entitled to receive only a fraction of the full credit that would otherwise be given for performances thereof.

(c) In the event that any work is excluded from this agreement pursuant to paragraph 10 or subparagraph (a) or (b) of this paragraph 11, all rights in such work shall automatically revert to you ten (10) days after the date of our notice to you of such exclusion. In the event that a work is classified for less than full credit under sub-paragraph (b) (ii) of this paragraph 11, you shall have the right, by giving notice to us, within ten (10) days after the date of our letter advising you of the credit allocated to the work, to terminate our rights therein, and all rights in such work shall thereupon revert to you.

12. In each instance that you write, or are employed or commissioned by a motion picture producer to write, during the period, all or part of the score of a motion picture intended primarily for exhibition in theaters, or by the producer of a musical show or revue for the legitimate stage to write, during the period, all or part of the musical compositions contained therein, we agree to advise the producer of the film that such part of the score as is written by you may be performed as part of the exhibition of said film in theaters in the United States, its territories and possessions, without compensation to us, or to the producer of the musical show or revue that your compositions embodied therein may be performed on the stage with living artists as part of such musical show or revue, without compensation to us. In the event that we notify you that we have established a system for the collection of royalties for performance of the scores of motion picture films in theaters in the United States, its territories and possessions, we shall no longer be obligated to take such action with respect to motion picture scores.

13. You make, constitute and appoint us, or our nominee, your true and lawful attorney, irrevocably during the term hereof, in our name or that of our nominee, or in your name, or otherwise, to do all acts, take all proceedings, execute, acknowledge and deliver any and all instruments, papers, documents, process or pleadings that may be necessary, proper or expedient to restrain infringement of and/or to enforce and protect the rights granted by you hereunder, and to recover damages in respect to or for the infringement or other violation of the said rights, and in our sole judgment to join you and/or others in whose names the copyrights to any of the works may stand; to discontinue, compromise or refer to arbitration, any such actions or proceedings or to make any other disposition of the disputes in relation to the works, provided that any action or proceeding commenced by us pursuant to the provisions of this paragraph shall be at our sole expense and for our sole benefit.

14. You agree that you, your agents, employees or representatives will not, directly or indirectly, solicit or accept payment from writers for composing music for lyrics or writing lyrics to music or for reviewing, publishing, promoting, recording or rendering other services connected with the exploitation of any composition, or permit use of your name or your affiliation with us in connection with any of the foregoing. In the event of a violation of any of the provisions of this paragraph 14, we shall have the right, in our sole discretion, by giving you at least thirty (30) days' notice by registered or certified mail, to terminate this agreement. In the event of such termination no payments shall be due to you pursuant to paragraph 8 hereof.

15. No monies due or to become due to you shall be assignable, whether by way of assignment, sale or power granted to an attorney-in-fact, without our prior written consent. If any assignment of such monies is made by you without such prior written consent, no rights of any kind against us will be acquired by the assignee, purchaser or attorney-in-fact.

16. In the event that during the period (a) mail addressed to you at the last address furnished by you pursuant to paragraph 19 hereof shall be returned by the post office, or (b) monies shall not have been earned by you pursuant to paragraph 6 hereof for a period of two consecutive years or more, or (c) you shall die, BMI shall have the right to terminate this agreement on at least thirty (30) days' notice by registered or certified mail addressed to the last address furnished by you pursuant to paragraph 19 hereof and, in the case of your death, to the representative of your estate, if known to BMI. In the event of such termination no payments shall be due you pursuant to paragraph 8 hereof.

17. You acknowledge that the rights obtained by you pursuant to this agreement constitute rights to payment of money and that during the period we shall hold absolute title to the performing rights granted to us hereunder. In the event that during the period you shall file a petition in bankruptcy, such a petition shall be filed against you, you shall make an assignment for the benefit of creditors, you shall consent to the appointment of a receiver or trustee for all or part of your property, or you shall institute or shall have instituted against you any other insolvency proceeding under the United States bankruptcy laws or any other applicable law, we shall retain title to the performing rights in all works for which clearance sheets shall have theretofore been submitted to us and shall subrogate your trustee in bankruptcy or receiver and any subsequent purchasers from them to your right to payment of money for said works in accordance with the terms and conditions of this agreement.

18. Any controversy or claim arising out of, or relating to, this agreement or the breach thereof, shall be settled by arbitration in the City of New York, in accordance with the Rules of the American Arbitration Association, and judgment upon the award of the arbitrator may be entered in any Court having jurisdiction thereof. Such award shall include the fixing of the expenses of the arbitration, including reasonable attorney's fees, which shall be borne by the unsuccessful party.

19. You agree to notify our Department of Performing Rights Administration promptly in writing of any change in your address. Any notice sent to you pursuant to the terms of this agreement shall be valid if addressed to you at the last address so furnished by you.

20. This agreement cannot be changed orally and shall be governed and construed pursuant to the laws of the State of New York.

21. In the event that any part or parts of this agreement are found to be void by a court of competent jurisdiction, the remaining part or parts shall nevertheless be binding with the same force and effect as if the void part or parts were deleted from this agreement.

Very truly yours,

BROADCAST MUSIC, INC.

ACCEPTED AND AGREED TO:

By ....

....

9/80

BMI PUBLISHER APPLICATION

APPLICATION FOR PUBLISHER AFFILIATION

BROADCAST MUSIC INC.

Performing Rights Administration
320 West 57th Street
New York, N.Y. 10019

FEE (For BMI Use)

☐ CHECK

☐ MONEY ORDER

☐ CASH

REC'D ....

NOTE:

ALL QUESTIONS MUST BE ANSWERED

APPLICATION MUST BE SIGNED ON LAST PAGE

1. NAME OF YOUR PROPOSED PUBLISHING COMPANY:

(In order to eliminate confusion it is necessary to reject any name identical with, or similar to, that of an established publishing company. Also, any name using INITIALS as part of your company name cannot be accepted.)

1st Choice: ....

2nd Choice: ....

3rd Choice: ....

2. BUSINESS ADDRESS:

.... Zip Code ....

⬜⬜⬜ ⬜⬜⬜ – ⬜⬜⬜⬜
AREA CODE   TELEPHONE NO.

3. LIST 1 OR 2 TITLES of music owned by your publishing company which have been commercially recorded or are likely to be broadcast or performed in concerts or otherwise publicly performed.

TITLE	FULL NAME(S) OF WRITER(S)	WRITER(S) PER. RIGHTS AFFILIATION BMI, ASCAP, SESAC OR OTHER	COMMERCIAL RECORDING	
			NAME OF LABEL	RELEASE DATE
....	....	....	....	....
....	....	....	....	....
....	....	....	....	....
....	....	....	....	....

IF CUE SHEETS ARE NECESSARY, PLEASE SUBMIT.

4. COMPLETE A, B OR C TO INDICATE HOW YOUR COMPANY IS ORGANIZED:

    A. INDIVIDUALLY OWNED:

        Name of Individual .... Soc. Sec. No. ....

        Home Address ....

        .... Zip Code ....

Are you now or have you ever been a writer member or writer-affiliate of BMI, ASCAP, SESAC, or of any foreign performing rights licensing organization? If so, state name of organization and the period during which you were a member or affiliate.

....

    B. PARTNERSHIP:

        List all Partners

NAME	HOME ADDRESS & ZIP CODE	SOC. SEC. NO.	PERCENTAGE OF OWNERSHIP

    C. FORMALLY ORGANIZED CORPORATION:
        (Complete only if corporation is now in existence)

        State in which Incorporated..

        List all Stockholders

NAME	HOME ADDRESS & ZIP CODE	PERCENTAGE OF OWNERSHIP

        List all Officers

NAME	HOME ADDRESS & ZIP CODE	OFFICE HELD

5. LIST ALL OTHER EXECUTIVE EMPLOYEES, if any
    (such as professional manager, contact man, etc.)

NAME	HOME ADDRESS & ZIP CODE	POSITION HELD

6. If any owner, stockholder, officer or executive employee has been or is connected with any record company, publishing company, songwriters' agency, or any other organization engaged in the solicitation, publication or exploitation of music, please give the following information:

Name of Individual	Name of Company	If Publishing Co., is it BMI?	Position Held	Years of Association	
				From	To

7. Have you charged or do you intend to charge a fee to a songwriter for examining, publishing, recording or exploiting his songs? Please answer by checking the appropriate box below. If you answer yes, you *must* state the amount of the fee and what it is for.

NO ☐   YES ☐

N O T I C E

IT IS ACKNOWLEDGED THAT ANY CONTRACT CONSUMMATED BETWEEN APPLICANT AND BMI WILL BE ENTERED INTO IN RELIANCE UPON THE REPRESENTATIONS CONTAINED IN THIS APPLICATION. THE CONTRACT WILL BE SUBJECT TO CANCELLATION IF ANY QUESTION HEREIN CONTAINED IS NOT ANSWERED FULLY AND ACCURATELY OR IF THE TRUE NAME OF EACH OWNER, STOCKHOLDER, OFFICER AND/OR EXECUTIVE EMPLOYEE IS NOT REPORTED IN QUESTIONS 4 AND 5 HEREOF.

IMPORTANT

In the case of a partnership or corporation, please insert in the space provided below, the Tax Account number assigned to your company by the Internal Revenue Service. If you do not as yet have such a number, secure it by filing Internal Revenue Form No. SS4.

Account No.: ....

Signature ....

Date ....

BMI PUBLISHER AGREEMENT

BMI

AGREEMENT made on .... between BROADCAST MUSIC, INC. ("BMI"), a New York corporation, whose address is 320 West 57th Street, New York, N.Y. 10019 and

....,

a .... doing business as ....

....("Publisher"), whose address is..

....

W I T N E S S E T H :

FIRST: The term of this agreement shall be the period of five (5) years from..

to ...., and continuing thereafter for additional periods of five (5) years each unless terminated by either party at the end of such initial period, or any such additional five (5) year period, upon notice by registered or certified mail not more than six (6) months or less than three (3) months prior to the end of any such term.

SECOND: As used in this agreement, the word "works" shall mean:

A. All musical compositions (including the musical segments and individual compositions written for a dramatic or dramatico-musical work) whether published or unpublished, now owned or copyrighted by Publisher or in which Publisher owns or controls performing rights, and

B. All musical compositions (including the musical segments and individual compositions written for a dramatic or dramatico-musical work) whether published or unpublished, in which hereafter during the term Publisher acquires ownership or copyright or ownership or control of the performing rights, from and after the date of the acquisition by Publisher of such ownership or control.

THIRD: Except as otherwise provided herein, Publisher hereby sells, assigns and transfers to BMI, its successors or assigns, for the term of this agreement:

A. All the rights which Publisher owns or acquires publicly to perform, and to license others to perform, anywhere in the world, any part or all of the works.

B. The non-exclusive right to record, and to license others to record, any part or all of any of the works on electrical transcriptions, wire, tape, film or otherwise, but only for the purpose of performing such work publicly by means of radio and television or for archive or audition purposes and not for sale to the public or for synchronization (1) with motion pictures intended primarily for theatrical exhibition or (2) with programs distributed by means of syndication to broadcasting stations.

C. The non-exclusive right to adapt or arrange any part or all of any of the works for performance purposes, and to license others to do so.

FOURTH:

A. The rights granted to BMI by subparagraph A of paragraph THIRD hereof shall not include the right to perform or license the performance of more than one song or aria from a dramatic or dramatico-musical work which is an opera, operetta, or musical show or more than five (5) minutes from a dramatic or dramatico-musical work which is a ballet if such performance is accompanied by the dramatic action, costumes or scenery of that dramatic or dramatico-musical work.

B. Publisher, together with all the writers and co-publishers, if any, shall have the right jointly, by written notice to BMI, to exclude from the grant made by subparagraph A of paragraph THIRD hereof performances of works comprising more than thirty (30) minutes of a dramatic or dramatico-musical work, but this right shall not apply to such performances from (1) a score originally written for and performed as part of a theatrical or television film, (2) a score originally written for and performed as part of a radio or television program, or (3) the original cast, sound track or similar album of a dramatic or dramatico-musical work.

C. Publisher retains the right to issue non-exclusive licenses for performances of a work or works (other than to another performing rights licensing organization), provided that within ten (10) days of the issuance of such license BMI is given written notice of the titles of the works and the nature of the performances so licensed by Publisher.

FIFTH:

A. As full consideration for all rights granted to BMI hereunder and as security therefor, BMI agrees to make the following payments to Publisher with respect to each of the works in which BMI has performing rights:

(1) For performances of works on broadcasting stations in the United States, its territories and possessions BMI will pay amounts calculated pursuant to BMI's then standard practices upon the basis of the then current performance rates generally paid by BMI to its affiliated publishers for similar performances of similar compositions. The number of performances for which Publisher shall be entitled to payment shall be estimated by BMI in accordance with its then current system of computing the number of such performances.

It is acknowledged that BMI licenses the works of its affiliates for performance by non-broadcasting means, but that unless and until such time as feasible methods can be devised for tabulation of and payment for such performances, payment will be based solely on broadcast performances. In the event that during the term of this agreement BMI shall establish a system of separate payment for non-broadcasting performances, BMI shall pay Publisher upon the basis of the then current performance rates generally paid by BMI to its other affiliated publishers for similar performances of similar compositions.

scribed in subparagraph C of paragraph FOURTH hereof has been granted by Publisher, its co-publisher or the writer.

SIXTH:. BMI will furnish statements to Publisher at least twice during each year of the term showing the number of performances of the works as computed pursuant to subparagraph A(1) of paragraph FIFTH hereof, and at least once during each year of the term showing the monies received by BMI referred to in subparagraph A(2) of paragraph FIFTH hereof. Each such statement shall be accompanied by payment of the sum thereby shown to be due to Publisher, subject to all proper deductions, if any, for advances or amounts due to BMI from Publisher.

SEVENTH:

A. Nothing in this agreement requires BMI to continue to license the works subsequent to the termination of this agreement. In the event that BMI continues to license any or all of the works, however, BMI shall continue to make payments to Publisher for so long as Publisher does not make or purport to make directly or indirectly any grant of performing rights in such works to any other licensing organization. The amounts of such payments shall be calculated pursuant to BMI's then current standard practices upon the basis of the then current performance rates generally paid by BMI to its affiliated publishers for similar performances of similar compositions. Publisher agrees to notify BMI by registered or certified mail of any grant or purported grant by Publisher directly or indirectly of performing rights to any other performing rights organization within ten (10) days from the making of such grant or purported grant and if Publisher fails so to inform BMI thereof and BMI makes payments to Publisher for any period after the making of any such grant or purported grant, Publisher agrees to repay to BMI all amounts so paid by BMI promptly on demand. In addition, if BMI inquires of Publisher by registered or certified mail, addressed to Publisher's last known address, whether Publisher has made any such grant or purported grant and Publisher fails to confirm to BMI by registered or certified mail within thirty (30) days of the mailing of such inquiry that Publisher has not made any such grant or purported grant, BMI may, from and after such date, discontinue making any payments to Publisher.

B. BMI's obligation to continue payment to Publisher after the termination of this agreement for performances outside of the United States, its territories and possessions shall be dependent upon BMI's receipt in the United States of payments designated by foreign performing rights licensing organizations as the publisher's share of foreign performance royalties earned by any of the works. Payment of such foreign royalties shall be subject to deduction of BMI's then current handling charge applicable to its affiliated publishers.

C. In the event that BMI has reason to believe that Publisher will receive or is receiving payment from a performing rights licensing organization other than BMI for or based on United States performances of one or more of the works during a period when such works were licensed by BMI pursuant to this agreement, BMI shall have the right to withhold payment for such performances from Publisher until receipt of evidence satisfactory to BMI of the amount so paid to Publisher by such other organization or that Publisher has not been so paid. In the event that Publisher has been so paid, the monies payable by BMI to Publisher for such performances during such period shall be reduced by the amount of the payment from such other organization. In the event that Publisher does not supply such evidence within eighteen (18) months from the date of BMI's request therefor, BMI shall be under no obligation to make any payment to Publisher for performances of such works during such period.

EIGHTH: In the event that this agreement shall terminate at a time when, after crediting all earnings reflected by the statements rendered to Publisher prior to the effective date of such termination, there is an indebtedness from Publisher to BMI, for advances or otherwise, such termination shall not be effective with respect to the works then embraced by this agreement unless and until sixty (60) days after such indebtedness shall be paid by Publisher or until sixty (60) days after a statement is rendered by BMI at its normal accounting period showing that the amount of such indebtedness has been fully recouped by BMI.

NINTH:

A. BMI shall have the right, upon written notice to Publisher, to exclude from this agreement, at any time, any work which in BMI's opinion (1) is similar to a previously existing composition and might constitute a copyright infringement, or (2) has a title or music or lyric similar to that of a previously existing composition and might lead to a claim of unfair competition, or (3) is offensive, in bad taste or against public morals, or (4) is not reasonably suitable for performance.

B. In the case of works which in the opinion of BMI are based on compositions in the public domain, BMI shall have the right, at any time, upon written notice to Publisher, either (1) to exclude any such work from this agreement, or (2) to classify any such work as entitled to receive only a stated fraction of the full credit that would otherwise be given for performances thereof.

(2) For performances of works outside of the United States, its territories and possessions BMI will pay to Publisher all monies received by BMI in the United States from any performing rights licensing organization which are designated by such organization as the publisher's share of foreign performance royalties earned by any of the works after the deduction of BMI's then current handling charge applicable to its affiliated publishers.

(3) In the case of works which, or rights in which, are owned by Publisher jointly with one or more other publishers who have granted performing rights therein to BMI, the sum payable to Publisher under this subparagraph A shall be a pro rata share determined on the basis of the number of publishers, unless BMI shall have received from Publisher a copy of an agreement or other document signed by all of the publishers providing for a different division of payment.

B. Notwithstanding the foregoing provisions of this paragraph FIFTH, BMI shall have no obligation to make payment hereunder with respect to (1) any performance of a work which occurs prior to the date on which BMI shall have received from Publisher all of the material with respect to such work referred to in subparagraph A of paragraph TENTH hereof, and in the case of foreign performances, the information referred to in subparagraph B of paragraph FOURTEENTH hereof, or (2) any performance as to which a direct license as de-

C. In the event that any work is excluded from this agreement pursuant to subparagraph A or B of this paragraph NINTH, or pursuant to subparagraph C of paragraph TWELFTH hereof, all rights of BMI in such work shall automatically revert to Publisher ten (10) days after the date of the notice of such exclusion given by BMI to Publisher. In the event that a work is classified for less than full credit under subparagraph B(2) of this paragraph NINTH, Publisher shall have the right, by giving notice to BMI within ten (10) days after the date of BMI's notice to Publisher of the credit allocated to such work, to terminate all rights in such work granted to BMI herein and all such rights of BMI in such work shall revert to Publisher thirty (30) days after the date of such notice from Publisher to BMI.

TENTH:

A. With respect to each of the works which has been or shall be published or recorded commercially or synchronized with motion picture or television film or tape or which Publisher considers likely to be performed, Publisher agrees to furnish to BMI:

(1) Two copies of a completed clearance sheet in the form supplied by BMI, unless a cue sheet with respect to such work is furnished pursuant to subparagraph A(3) of this paragraph TENTH.

(2) If such work is based on a composition in the public domain, a legible lead sheet or other written or printed copy of such work setting forth the lyrics, if any, and music correctly metered; provided that with respect to all other works, such copy need be furnished only if requested by BMI pursuant to subsection (c) of subparagraph D(2) of this paragraph TENTH.

(3) If such work has been or shall be synchronized with or otherwise used in connection with motion picture or television film or tape, a cue sheet showing the title, composers, publisher and nature and duration of the use of the work in such film or tape.

B. Publisher shall submit the material described in subparagraph A of this paragraph TENTH with respect to works heretofore published, recorded or synchronized within ten (10) days after the execution of this agreement and with respect to any of the works hereafter so published, recorded, synchronized or likely to be performed prior to the date of publication or release of the recording, film or tape or anticipated performance.

C. The submission of each clearance sheet or cue sheet shall constitute a warranty by Publisher that all of the information contained thereon is true and correct and that no performing rights in any of the works listed thereon has been granted to or reserved by others except as specifically set forth therein.

D. Publisher agrees:

(1) To secure and maintain copyright protection of the works pursuant to the Copyright Law of the United States and pursuant to the laws of such other nations of the world where such protection is afforded; and to give BMI prompt written notice of the date and number of copyright registration and/or renewal of each work registered in the United States Copyright Office.

(2) At BMI's request:

(a) To register each unpublished and published work in the United States Copyright Office pursuant to the Copyright Law of the United States.

(b) To record in the United States Copyright Office in accordance with the Copyright Law of the United States any agreements, assignments, instruments or documents of any kind by which Publisher obtained the right to publicly perform and/or the right to publish, co-publish or sub-publish any of the works.

(c) To obtain and deliver to BMI copies of: unpublished and published works; copyright registration and/or renewal certificates issued by the United States Copyright Office; any of the documents referred to in sub-section (b) above.

E. Publisher agrees to give BMI prompt notice by registered or certified mail in each instance when, pursuant to the Copyright Law of the United States, (1) the rights granted to BMI by Publisher in any work shall revert to the writer or the writer's representative, or (2) copyright protection of any work shall terminate.

ELEVENTH: Publisher warrants and represents that:

A. Publisher has the right to enter into this agreement; Publisher is not bound by any prior commitments which conflict with its undertakings herein; the rights granted by Publisher to BMI herein are the sole and exclusive property of Publisher and are free from all encumbrances and claims; and exercise of such rights will not constitute infringement of copyright or violation of any right of, or unfair competition with, any person, firm, corporation or association.

B. Except with respect to works in which the possession of performing rights by another person, firm, corporation or association is specifically set forth on a clearance sheet or cue sheet submitted to BMI pursuant to subparagraph A of paragraph TENTH hereof, Publisher has exclusive performing rights in each of the works by virtue of written grants thereof to Publisher signed by all the authors and composers or other owners of such work.

TWELFTH:

A. Publisher agrees to defend, indemnify, save and hold BMI, its licensees, the advertisers of its licensees and their respective agents, servants and employees, free and harmless from and against any and all demands, loss, damage, suits, judgments, recoveries and costs, including counsel fees, resulting from any claim of whatever nature arising from or in connection with the exercise of any of the rights granted by Publisher in this agreement; provided, however, that the obligations of Publisher under this paragraph TWELFTH shall not apply to any matter added to, or changes made in, any work by BMI or its licensees.

B. Upon the receipt by any of the parties herein indemnified of any notice, demand, process, papers, writ or pleading, by which any such claim, demand, suit or proceeding is made or commenced against them, or any of them, which Publisher shall be obliged to defend hereunder, BMI shall, as soon as may be practicable, give Publisher notice thereof and deliver to Publisher such papers or true copies thereof, and BMI shall have the right to participate by counsel of its own choice, at its own expense. Publisher agrees to cooperate with BMI in all such matters.

C. In the event of such notification of claim or service of process on any of the parties herein indemnified, BMI shall have the right, from the date thereof, to exclude the work with respect to which a claim is made from this agreement and/or to withhold payment of all sums which may become due pursuant to this agreement or any modification thereof until receipt of satisfactory written evidence that such claim has been withdrawn, settled or adjudicated.

THIRTEENTH: Publisher makes, constitutes and appoints BMI, or its nominee, Publisher's true and lawful attorney, irrevocably during the term hereof, in the name of BMI or that of its nominee, or in Publisher's name, or otherwise, to do all acts, take all proceedings, and execute, acknowledge and deliver any and all instruments, papers, documents, process or pleadings that may be necessary, proper or expedient to restrain infringement of and/or to enforce and protect the rights granted by Publisher hereunder, and to recover damages in respect of or for the infringement or other violation of the said rights, and in BMI's sole judgment to join Publisher and/or others in whose names the copyrights to any of the works may stand, and to discontinue, compromise or refer to arbitration, any such actions or proceedings or to make any other disposition of the disputes in relation to the works; provided that any action or proceeding commenced by BMI pursuant to the provisions of this paragraph THIRTEENTH shall be at its sole expense and for its sole benefit.

FOURTEENTH:

A. It is acknowledged that BMI has heretofore entered into, and may during the term of this agreement enter into, contracts with performing rights licensing organizations for the licensing of public performing rights controlled by BMI in territories outside of the United States, its territories and possessions (hereinafter called "foreign territories"). Upon Publisher's written request, BMI agrees to permit Publisher to grant performing rights in any or all of the works for any foreign territory for which, at the time such request is received, BMI has not entered into any such contract with a performing rights licensing organization; provided, however, that any such grant of performing rights by Publisher shall terminate at such time when BMI shall have entered into such a contract with a performing rights licensing organization covering such foreign territory and shall have notified Publisher thereof. Nothing herein contained, however, shall be deemed to restrict Publisher from assigning to its foreign publisher or representative the right to collect a part or all of the publishers' performance royalties earned by any or all of the works in any foreign territory as part of an agreement for the publication, exploitation or representation of such works in such territory, whether or not BMI has entered into such a contract with a performing rights licensing organization covering such territory.

B. Publisher agrees to notify BMI promptly in writing in each instance when publication, exploitation or other rights in any or all of the works are granted for any foreign territory. Such notice shall set forth the title of the work, the country or countries involved, the period of such grant, the name of the person, firm, corporation or association entitled to collect performance royalties earned in the foreign territory and the amount of such share. Within ten (10) days after the execution of this agreement Publisher agrees to submit to BMI, in writing, a list of all works as to which Publisher has, prior to the effective date of this agreement, granted to any person, firm, corporation or association performing rights and/or the right to collect publisher performance royalties earned in any foreign territory.

C. In the event that BMI transmits to Publisher performance royalties designated as the writer's share of performance royalties earned by any of the works in any foreign territory, Publisher shall promptly pay such royalties to the writer or writers of the works involved. If Publisher is unable for any reason to locate and make payment to any of the writers involved within six (6) months from the date of receipt, the amounts due such writers shall be returned to BMI.

FIFTEENTH:

A. Publisher agrees that Publisher, its agents, employees, representatives or affiliated companies, will not directly or indirectly during the term of this agreement:

(1) Solicit or accept payment from or on behalf of authors for composing music for lyrics, or from or on behalf of composers for writing lyrics to music.

(2) Solicit or accept manuscripts from composers or authors in consideration of any payments to be made by or on behalf of such composers or authors for reviewing, arranging, promotion, publication, recording or any other services connected with the exploitation of any composition.

(3) Permit Publisher's name, or the fact of its affiliation with BMI, to be used by any other person, firm, corporation or association engaged in any of the practices described in subparagraphs A(1) and A(2) of this paragraph FIFTEENTH.

(4) Submit to BMI, as one of the works to come within this agreement, any musical composition with respect to which any payments described in subparagraphs A(1) and A(2) of this paragraph FIFTEENTH have been made by or on behalf of a composer or author to any person, firm, corporation or association.

B. Publisher agrees that Publisher, its agents, employees or representatives will not directly or indirectly during the term of this agreement make any effort to ascertain from, or offer any inducement or consideration to, anyone, including but not limited to any broadcasting licensee of BMI or to the agents, employees or representatives of BMI or of any such licensee, for information regarding the time or times when any such BMI licensee is to report its performances to BMI, or to attempt in any way to manipulate performances or affect the representative character or accuracy of BMI's system of sampling or logging performances.

C. Publisher agrees to notify BMI promptly in writing (1) of any change of firm name of Publisher, and (2) of any change of twenty percent (20%) or more in the ownership thereof.

D. In the event of the violation of any of the provisions of subparagraphs A, B or C of this paragraph FIFTEENTH, BMI shall have the right, in its sole discretion, to terminate this agreement by giving Publisher at least thirty (30) days' notice by registered or certified mail. In the event of such termination, no payments shall be due to Publisher pursuant to paragraph SEVENTH hereof.

SIXTEENTH: In the event that during the term of this agreement (1) mail addressed to Publisher at the last address furnished by it pursuant to paragraph TWENTIETH hereof shall be returned by the post office, or (2) monies shall not have been earned by Publisher pursuant to paragraph FIFTH hereof for a period of two consecutive years or more, or (3) the proprietor, if Publisher is a sole proprietorship, shall die, BMI shall have the right to terminate this agreement on at least thirty (30) days' notice by registered or certified mail addressed to the last address furnished by Publisher pursuant to paragraph TWENTIETH hereof and, in the case of the death of a sole proprietor, to the representative of said proprietor's estate, if known to BMI. In the event of such termination, no payments shall be due Publisher pursuant to paragraph SEVENTH hereof.

SEVENTEENTH: Publisher acknowledges that the rights obtained by it pursuant to this agreement constitute rights to payment of money and that during the term BMI shall hold absolute title to the performing rights granted to BMI hereunder. In the event that during the term Publisher shall file a petition in bankruptcy, such a petition shall be filed against Publisher, Publisher shall make an assignment for the benefit of creditors, Publisher shall consent to the appointment of a receiver or trustee for all or part of its property, Publisher shall file a petition for corporate reorganization or arrangement under the United States bankruptcy laws, Publisher shall institute or shall have instituted against it any other insolvency proceeding under the United States bankruptcy laws or any other applicable law, or, in the event Publisher is a partnership, all of the general partners of said partnership shall be adjudged bankrupts, BMI shall retain title to the performing rights in all works for which clearance sheets shall have theretofore been submitted to BMI and shall subrogate Publisher's trustee in bankruptcy or receiver and any subsequent purchasers from them to Publisher's right to payment of money for said works in accordance with the terms and conditions of this agreement.

EIGHTEENTH: Any controversy or claim arising out of, or relating to, this agreement or the breach thereof, shall be settled by arbitration in the City of New York, in accordance with the Rules of the American Arbitration Association, and judgment upon the award of the arbitrator may be entered in any court having jurisdiction thereof. Such award shall include the fixing of the expenses of the arbitration, including reasonable attorney's fees, which shall be borne by the unsuccessful party.

NINETEENTH: Publisher agrees that it shall not, without the written consent of BMI, assign any of its rights hereunder. No rights of any kind against BMI will be acquired by the assignee if any such purported assignment is made by Publisher without such written consent.

TWENTIETH: Publisher agrees to notify BMI's Department of Performing Rights Administration promptly in writing of any change in its address. Any notice sent to Publisher pursuant to the terms of this agreement shall be valid if addressed to Publisher at the last address so furnished by Publisher.

TWENTY-FIRST: This agreement cannot be changed orally and shall be governed and construed pursuant to the laws of the State of New York.

TWENTY-SECOND: In the event that any part or parts of this agreement are found to be void by a court of competent jurisdiction, the remaining part or parts shall nevertheless be binding with the same force and effect as if the void part or parts were deleted from this agreement.

IN WITNESS WHEREOF, the parties hereto have caused this agreement to be duly executed as of the day and year first above written.

BROADCAST MUSIC, INC.

By _____

....

By_____
(Title of Signer) ....

10/80

AGAC POPULAR SONGWRITERS CONTRACT

AMERICAN GUILD OF
AUTHORS & COMPOSERS

NOTE TO SONGWRITERS: (A) DO NOT SIGN THIS CONTRACT IF IT HAS ANY CHANGES UNLESS YOU HAVE FIRST DISCUSSED SUCH CHANGES WITH AGAC; (B) FOR YOUR PROTECTION PLEASE SEND A FULLY EXE-CUTED COPY OF THIS CONTRACT TO AGAC.

POPULAR SONGWRITERS CONTRACT
© Copyright 1978 AGAC

AGREEMENT made this   day of   , 19   , between

....

(hereinafter called "Publisher") and ....

....

(Jointly and/or severally hereinafter collectively called "Writer");

WITNESSETH:

Composition
(Insert title
of composition
here)

(Insert number
of years here)

1. The Writer hereby assigns, transfers and delivers to the Publisher a certain heretofore unpublished original musical composi-tion, written and/or composed by the above-named Writer now entitled ....

(hereinafter referred to as "the composition"), including the title, words and music thereof, and the right to secure copyright therein throughout the entire world, and to have and to hold the said copyright and all rights of whatsoever nature thereunder existing, for .... years from the date of this contract or 35 years from the date of the first release of a

not more than 40

commercial sound recording of the composition, whichever term ends earlier, unless this contract is sooner terminated in accordance with the provisions hereof.

Performing
Rights Affiliation

(Delete Two)

2. In all respects this contract shall be subject to any existing agreements between the parties hereto and the following small performing rights licensing organization with which Writer and Publisher are affiliated:
(ASCAP, BMI, SESAC). Nothing contained herein shall, or shall be deemed to, alter, vary or modify the rights of Writer and Publisher to share in, receive and retain the proceeds distributed to them by such small performing rights licensing organization pursuant to their respective agreement with it.

Warranty

3. The Writer hereby warrants that the composition is his sole, exclusive and original work, that he has full right and power to make this contract, and that there exists no adverse claim to or in the composition, except as aforesaid in Paragraph 2 hereof and except such rights as are specifically set forth in Paragraph 23 hereof.

Royalties
(Insert amount
of advance here)

4. In consideration of this contract, the Publisher agrees to pay the Writer as follows:

(a) $...........................as an advance against royalties, receipt of which is hereby acknowledged, which sum shall remain the property of the Writer and shall be deductible only from payments hereafter becoming due the Writer under this contract.

Piano Copies

(b) In respect of regular piano copies sold and paid for in the United States and Canada, the following royalties per copy:

Sliding Scale
(Insert percentage here)

..........% (in no case, however, less than 10%) of the wholesale selling price of the first 200,000 copies or less; plus

..........% (in no case, however, less than 12%) of the wholesale selling price of copies in excess of 200,000 and not exceeding 500,000; plus

..........% (in no case, however, less than 15%) of the wholesale selling price of copies in excess of 500,000.

Foreign Royalties
(Insert percentage here)

(c) ....% (in no case, however, less than 50%) of all net sums received by the Publisher in respect of regular piano copies, orchestrations, band arrangements, octavos, quartets, arrangements for combinations of voices and/or instru-ments, and/or other copies of the composition sold in any country other than the United States and Canada, provided, however, that if the Publisher should sell such copies through, or cause them to be sold by, a subsidiary or affiliate which is actually doing business in a foreign country, then in respect of such sales, the Publisher shall pay to the Writer not less than 5% of the marked retail selling price in respect of each such copy sold and paid for.

Orchestrations and
Other Arrangements,
etc.

(Insert percentage here)

(d) In respect of each copy sold and paid for in the United States and Canada, or for export from the United States, of orchestrations, band arrangements, octavos, quartets, arrangements for combinations of voices and/or instruments, and/or other copies of the composition (other than regular piano copies) the following royalties on the wholesale selling price (after trade discounts, if any):

..........% (in no case, however, less than 10%) on the first 200,000 copies or less; plus

..........% (in no case, however, less than 12%) on all copies in excess of 200,000 and not exceeding 500,000; plus

..........% (in no case, however, less than 15%) on all copies in excess of 500,000.

Publisher's
Song Book,
Folio, etc.

(e) (i) If the composition, or any part thereof, is included in any song book, folio or similar publication issued by the Publisher containing at least four, but not more than twenty-five musical compositions, the royalty to be paid by the Publisher to the Writer shall be an amount determined by dividing 10% of the wholesale selling price (after trade discounts, if any) of the copies sold, among the total number of the Publisher's copyrighted musical compositions included in such publication. If such publication contains more than twenty-five musical compositions, the said 10% shall be increased by an additional ½% for each additional musical composition.

Licensee's
Song Book,
Folio, etc.

(ii) If, pursuant to a license granted by the Publisher to a licensee not controlled by or affiliated with it, the composi-tion, or any part thereof, is included in any song book, folio or similar publication, containing at least four musical compositions, the royalty to be paid by the Publisher to the Writer shall be that proportion of 50% of the gross amount received by it from the licensee, as the number of uses of the composition under the license and during the license period, bears to the total number of uses of the Publisher's copyrighted musical compositions under the license and during the license period.

(iii) In computing the number of the Publisher's copyrighted musical compositions under subdivisions (i) and (ii) hereof, there shall be excluded musical compositions in the public domain and arrangements thereof and those with respect to which the Publisher does not currently publish and offer for sale regular piano copies.

(iv) Royalties on publications containing less than four musical compositions shall be payable at regular piano copy rates.

Professional Material and Free Copies

(f) As to "professional material" not sold or resold, no royalty shall be payable. Free copies of the lyrics of the composition shall not be distributed except under the following conditions: (i) with the Writer's written consent; or (ii) when printed without music in limited numbers for charitable, religious or governmental purposes, or for similar public purposes, if no profit is derived, directly or indirectly; or (iii) when authorized for printing in a book, magazine or periodical, where such use is incidental to a novel or story (as distinguished from use in a book of lyrics or a lyric magazine or folio), provided that any such use shall bear the Writer's name and the proper copyright notice; or (iv) when distributed solely for the purpose of exploiting the composition, provided, that such exploitation is restricted to the distribution of limited numbers of such copies for the purpose of influencing the sale of the composition, that the distribution is independent of the sale of any other musical compositions, services, goods, wares or merchandise, and that no profit is made, directly or indirectly, in connection therewith.

Mechanicals, Electrical Transcription, Synchronization, All Other Rights

(Insert percentage here)

(g) ....% (in no case, however, less than 50%) of:

All gross receipts of the Publisher in respect of any licenses (including statutory royalties) authorizing the manufacture of parts of instruments serving to mechanically reproduce the composition, or to use the composition in synchronization with sound motion pictures, or to reproduce it upon electrical transcription for broadcasting purposes; and of any and all gross receipts of the Publisher from any other source or right now known or which may hereafter come into existence, except as provided in paragraph 2.

Licensing Agent's Charges

(h) If the Publisher administers licenses authorizing the manufacture of parts of instruments serving to mechanically reproduce said composition, or the use of said composition in synchronization or in timed relation with sound motion pictures or its reproduction upon electrical transcriptions, or any of them, through an agent, trustee or other administrator acting for a substantial part of the industry and not under the exclusive control of the Publisher (hereinafter sometimes referred to as licensing agent), the Publisher, in determining his receipts, shall be entitled to deduct from gross license fees paid by the Licensees, a sum equal to the charges paid by the Publisher to said licensing agent, provided, however, that in respect to synchronization or timed relation with sound motion pictures, said deduction shall in no event exceed $150.00 or 10% of said gross license fee, whichever is less; in connection with the manufacture of parts of instruments serving to mechanically reproduce said composition, said deductions shall not exceed 5% of said gross license fee; and in connection with electrical transcriptions, said deduction shall not exceed 10% of said gross license fee.

Block Licenses

(i) The Publisher agrees that the use of the composition will not be included in any bulk or block license heretofore or hereafter granted, and that it will not grant any bulk or block license to include the same, without the written consent of the Writer in each instance, except (i) that the Publisher may grant such licenses with respect to electrical transcription for broadcasting purposes, but in such event, the Publisher shall pay to the Writer that proportion of 50% of the gross amount received by it under each such license as the number of uses of the composition under each such license period during each such license period bears to the total number of uses of the Publisher's copyrighted musical compositions under each such license during each such license period; in computing the number of the Publisher's copyrighted musical compositions for this purpose, there shall be excluded musical compositions in the public domain and arrangements thereof and those with respect to which the Publisher does not currently publish and offer for sale regular piano copies; (ii) that the Publisher may appoint agents or representatives in countries outside of the United States and Canada to use and to grant licenses for the use of the composition on the customary royalty fee basis under which the Publisher shall receive not less than 10% of the marked retail selling price in respect of regular piano copies, and 50% of all other revenue; if, in connection with any such bulk or block license, the Publisher shall have received any advance, the Writer shall not be entitled to share therein, but in part of said advance shall be deducted in computing the composition's earnings under said bulk or block license. A bulk or block license shall be deemed to mean any license or agreement, domestic or foreign, whereby rights are granted in respect of two or more musical compositions.

Television and New Uses

(j) Except to the extent that the Publisher and Writer have heretofore or may hereafter assign to or vest in the small performing rights licensing organization with which Writer and Publisher are affiliated, the said rights or the right to grant licenses therefor, it is agreed that no licenses shall be granted without the written consent, in each instance, of the Writer for the use of the composition by means of television, or by any means, or for any purposes not commercially established, or for which licenses were not granted by the Publisher on musical compositions prior to June 1, 1937.

Writer's Consent to Licenses

(k) The Publisher shall not, without the written consent of the Writer in each case, give or grant any right or license (i) to use the title of the composition, or (ii) for the exclusive use of the composition in any form or for any purpose, or for any period of time, or for any territory, other than its customary arrangements with foreign publishers, or (iii) to give a dramatic representation of the composition or to dramatize the plot or story thereof, or (iv) for a vocal rendition of the composition in synchronization with sound motion pictures, or (v) for any synchronization use thereof, or (vi) for the use of the composition or a quotation or excerpt therefrom in any article, book, periodical, advertisement or other similar publication. If, however, the Publisher shall give to the Writer written notice by certified mail, return receipt requested, or telegram, specifying the right or license to be given or granted, the name of the licensee and the terms and conditions thereof, including the price or other compensation to be received therefor, then, unless the Writer (or any one or more of them) shall, within five business days after the delivery of such notice to the address of the Writer hereinafter designated, object thereto, the Publisher may grant such right or license in accordance with the said notice without first obtaining the consent of the Writer. Such notice shall be deemed sufficient if sent to the Writer at the address or addresses hereinafter designated or at the address or addresses last furnished to the Publisher in writing by the Writer.

Trust for Writer

(l) Any portion of the receipts which may become due to the Writer from license fees (in excess of offsets), whether received directly from the licensee or from any licensing agent of the Publisher, shall, if not paid immediately on the receipt thereof by the Publisher, belong to the Writer and shall be held in trust for the Writer until payment is made; the ownership of said trust fund by the Writer shall not be questioned whether the monies are physically segregated or not.

Writer Participation — (m) The Publisher agrees that it will not issue any license as a result of which it will receive any financial benefit in which the Writer does not participate.

Writer Credit — (n) On all regular piano copies, orchestrations, band or other arrangements, octavos, quartets, commercial sound recordings and other reproductions of the composition or parts thereof, in whatever form and however produced, Publisher shall include or cause to be included, in addition to the copyright notice, the name of the Writer, and Publisher shall include a similar requirement in every license or authorization issued by it with respect to the composition.

Writers' Respective Shares — 5. Whenever the term "Writer" is used herein, it shall be deemed to mean all of the persons herein defined as "Writer" and any and all royalties herein provided to be paid to the Writer shall be paid equally to such persons if there be more than one, unless otherwise provided in Paragraph 23.

Release of Commercial Sound Recording (Insert period not exceeding 12 months) — 6. (a) (i) The Publisher shall, within...................months from the date of this contract (the "initial period"), cause a commercial sound recording of the composition to be made and released in the customary form and through the customary commercial channels. If at the end of such initial period a sound recording has not been made and released, as above provided, then, subject to provisions of the next succeeding subdivision, this contract shall terminate.

(Insert amount to be not less than $250) — (ii) If, prior to the expiration of the initial period, Publisher pays the Writer the sum of $........(which shall not be charged against or recoupable out of any advances, royalties or other monies theretofor paid, then due, or which thereafter may become due the **(Insert period not exceeding six months)** Writer from the Publisher pursuant to this contract or otherwise), Publisher shall have an additional............months (the "additional period") commencing with the end of the initial period, within which to cause such commercial sound recording to be made and released as provided in subdivision (i) above. If at the end of the additional period a commercial sound recording has not been made and released, as above provided, then this contract shall terminate.

(iii) Upon termination pursuant to this Paragraph 6(a), all rights of any and every nature in and to the composition and in and to any and all copyrights secured thereon in the United States and throughout the world shall automatically re-vest in and become the property of the Writer and shall be reassigned to him by the Publisher. The Writer shall not be obligated to return or pay to the Publisher any advance or indebtedness as a condition of such re-assignment; the said re-assignment shall be in accordance with and subject to the provisions of Paragraph 8 hereof, and, in addition, the Publisher shall pay to the Writer all gross sums which it has theretofore or may thereafter receive in respect of the composition.

Writer's Copies — (b) The Publisher shall furnish, or cause to be furnished, to the Writer six copies of the commercial sound recording referred to in Paragraph 6(a).

Piano Copies, Piano Arrangement or Lead Sheet (Select (i) or (ii) — (c) The Publisher shall
□ (i) within 30 days after the initial release of a commercial sound recording of the composition, make, publish and offer for sale regular piano copies of the composition in the form and through the channels customarily employed by it for that purpose;
□ (ii) within 30 days after execution of this contract make a piano arrangement or lead sheet of the composition and furnish six copies thereof to the Writer.
In the event neither subdivision (i) nor (ii) of this subparagraph (e) is selected, the provisions of subdivision (ii) shall be automatically deemed to have been selected by the parties.

Foreign Copyright — 7. (a) Each copyright on the composition in countries other than the United States shall be secured only in the name of the Publisher, and the Publisher shall not at any time divest itself of said foreign copyright directly or indirectly.

Foreign Publication — (b) No rights shall be granted by the Publisher in the composition to any foreign publisher or licensee inconsistent with the terms hereof, nor shall any foreign publication rights in the composition be given to a foreign publisher or licensee unless and until the Publisher shall have complied with the provisions of Paragraph 6 hereof.

Foreign Advance — (c) If foreign rights in the composition are separately conveyed, otherwise than as a part of the Publisher's current and/or future catalog, not less than 50% of any advance received in respect thereof shall be credited to the account of and paid to the Writer.

Foreign Percentage — (d) The percentage of the Writer on monies received from foreign sources shall be computed on the Publisher's net receipts; provided, however, that no deductions shall be made for offsets of monies due from the Publisher to said foreign sources; or for advances made by such foreign sources to the Publisher, unless the Writer shall have received at least 50% of said advances.

No Foreign Allocations — (e) In computing the receipts of the Publisher from licenses granted in respect of synchronization with sound motion pictures, or in respect of any world-wide licenses, or in respect of licenses granted by the Publisher for use of the composition in countries other than the United States, no amount shall be deducted for payments or allocations to publishers or licensees in such countries.

Termination or Expiration of Contract — 8. Upon the termination or expiration of this contract, all rights of any and every nature in and to the composition and in and to any and all copyrights secured thereon in the United States and throughout the world, shall re-vest in and become the property of the Writer, and shall be re-assigned to the Writer by the Publisher free of any and all encumbrances of any nature whatsoever, provided that:

(a) If the Publisher, prior to such termination or expiration, shall have granted a domestic license for the use of the composition, not inconsistent with the terms and provisions of this contract, the re-assignment may be subject to the terms of such license.

(b) Publisher shall assign to the Writer all rights which it may have under any such agreement or license referred to in subdivision (a) in respect of the composition, including, but not limited to, the right to receive all royalties or other monies earned by the composition thereunder after the date of termination or expiration of this contract. Should the Publisher thereafter receive or be credited with any royalties or other monies so earned, it shall pay the same to the Writer.

(c) The Writer shall not be obligated to return or pay to the Publisher any advance or indebtedness as a condition of the re-assignment provided for in this Paragraph 8, and shall be entitled to receive the plates and copies of the composition in the possession of the Publisher.

(d) Publisher shall pay any and all royalties which may have accrued to the Writer prior to such termination or expiration.

(e) The Publisher shall execute any and all documents and do any and all acts or things necessary to effect any and all re-assignments to the Writer herein provided for.

Negotiations for New or Unspecified Uses

9. If the Publisher desires to exercise a right in and to the composition now known or which may hereafter become known, but for which no specific provision has been made herein, the Publisher shall give written notice to the Writer thereof. Negotiations respecting all the terms and conditions of any such disposition shall thereupon be entered into between the Publisher and the Writer and no such right shall be exercised until specific agreement has been made.

Royalty Statements and Payments

10. The Publisher shall render to the Writer, hereafter, royalty statements accompanied by remittance of the amount due at the times such statements and remittances are customarily rendered by the Publisher, provided, however, that such statements and remittances shall be rendered either semi-annually or quarterly and not more than forty-five days after the end of each such semi-annual or quarterly period, as the case may be. The Writer may at any time, or from time to time, make written request for a detailed royalty statement, and the Publisher shall, within sixty days, comply therewith. Such royalty statements shall set forth in detail the various items, foreign and domestic, for which royalties are payable thereunder and the amounts thereof, including, but not limited to, the number of copies sold and the number of uses made in each royalty category. If a use is made in a publication of the character provided in Paragraph 4, subdivision (e) hereof, there shall be included in said royalty statement the title of said publication, the publisher or issuer thereof, the date of and number of uses, the gross license fee received in connection with each publication, the share thereto of all the writers under contract with the Publisher, and the Writer's share thereof. There shall likewise be included in said statement a description of every other use of the composition, and if by a licensee or licensees their name or names, and if said use is upon a part of an instrument serving to reproduce the composition mechanically, the type of mechanical reproduction, the title of the label thereon, the name or names of the artists performing the same, together with the gross license fees received, and the Writer's share thereof.

Examination of Books

11. (a) The Publisher shall from time to time, upon written demand of the Writer or his representative, permit the Writer or his representative to inspect at the place of business of the Publisher, all books, records and documents relating to the composition and all licenses granted, uses had and payments made therefor, such right of inspection to include, but not by way of limitation, the right to examine all original accountings and records relating to uses and payments by manufacturers of commercial sound recordings and music rolls; and the Writer or his representative may appoint an accountant who shall at any time during usual business hours have access to all records of the Publisher relating to the composition for the purpose of verifying royalty statements rendered or which are delinquent under the terms hereof.

(b) The Publisher shall, upon written demand of the Writer or his representative, cause any licensing agent in the United States and Canada to furnish to the Writer or his representative, statements showing in detail all licenses granted, uses had and payments made in connection with the composition, which licenses or permits were granted, or payments were received, by or through said licensing agent, and to permit the Writer or his representative to inspect at the place of business of such licensing agent, all books, records and documents of such licensing agent, relating thereto. Any and all agreements made by the Publisher with any such licensing agent shall provide that any such licensing agent will comply with the terms and provisions hereof. In the event that the Publisher shall instruct such licensing agent to furnish to the Writer or his representative statements as provided for herein, and to permit the inspection of the books, records and documents as herein provided, then if such licensing agent should refuse to comply with the said instructions, or any of them, the Publisher agrees to institute and prosecute diligently and in good faith such action or proceedings as may be necessary to compel compliance with the said instructions.

(c) With respect to foreign licensing agents, the Publisher shall make available the books or records of said licensing agents in countries outside of the United States and Canada to the extent such books or records are available to the Publisher, except that the Publisher may in lieu thereof make available any accountants' reports and audits which the Publisher is able to obtain.

(d) If as a result of any examination of books, records or documents pursuant to Paragraphs 11(a), 11(b) or 11(c) hereof, it is determined that, with respect to any royalty statement rendered by or on behalf of the Publisher to the Writer, the Writer is owed a sum equal to or greater than five percent of the sum shown on that royalty statement as being due to the Writer, then the Publisher shall pay to the Writer the entire cost of such examination, not to exceed 50% of the amount shown to be due the Writer.

(e) (i) In the event the Publisher administers its own licenses for the manufacture of parts of instruments serving to mechanically reproduce the composition rather than employing a licensing agent for that purpose, the Publisher shall include in each license agreement a provision permitting the Publisher, the Writer or their respective representatives to inspect, at the place of business of such licensee, all books, records and documents of such licensee relating to such license. Within 30 days after written demand by the Writer, the Publisher shall commence to inspect such licensee's books, records and documents and shall furnish a written report of such inspection to the Writer within 90 days following such demand. If the Publisher fails, after written demand by the Writer, to so inspect the licensee's books, records and documents, or fails to furnish such report, the Writer or his representative may inspect such licensee's books, records and documents at his own expense.

(ii) In the further event that the Publisher and the licensee referred to in subdivision (i) above are subsidiaries or affiliates of the same entity or one is a subsidiary or affiliate of the other, then, unless the Publisher employs a licensing agent to administer the licenses referred to in subdivision (i) above, the Writer shall have the right to make the inspection referred to in subdivision (i) above without the necessity of making written demand on the Publisher as provided in subdivision (i) above.

(iii) If as a result of any inspection by the Writer pursuant to subdivisions (i) and (ii) of this subparagraph (e) the Writer recovers additional monies from the licensee, the Publisher and the Writer shall share equally in the cost of such inspection.

Default in
Payment or
Prevention of
Examination

12. If the Publisher shall fail or refuse, within sixty days after written demand, to furnish or cause to be furnished, such statements, books, records or documents, or to permit inspection thereof, as provided for in Paragraphs 10 and 11 hereof, or within thirty days after written demand, to make the payment of any royalties due under this contract, then the Writer shall be entitled, upon ten days' written notice, to terminate this contract. However if the Publisher shall:

(a) Within the said ten-day period serve upon the Writer a written notice demanding arbitration; and

(b) Submit to arbitration its claim that it has complied with its obligation to furnish statements, books, records or documents, or permitted inspection thereof or to pay royalties, as the case may be, or both, and thereafter comply with any award of the arbitrator within ten days after such award or within such time as the arbitrator may specify;

then this contract shall continue in full force and effect as if the Writer had not sent such notice of termination. If the Publisher shall fail to comply with the foregoing provisions, then this contract shall be deemed to have been terminated as of the date of the Writer's written notice of termination.

Derivative Works

13. No derivative work prepared under authority of Publisher during the term of this contract may be utilized by Publisher or any other party after termination or expiration of this contract.

Notices

14. All written demands and notices provided for herein shall be sent by certified mail, return receipt requested.

Suits for
Infringement

15. Any legal action brought by the Publisher against any alleged infringer of the composition shall be initiated and prosecuted at its sole cost and expense, but if the Publisher should fail, within thirty days after written demand, to institute such action, the Writer shall be entitled to institute such suit at his cost and expense. All sums recovered as a result of any such action shall, after the deduction of the reasonable expense thereof, be divided equally between the Publisher and the Writer. No settlement of any such action may be made by either party without first notifying the other; in the event that either party should object to such settlement, then such settlement shall not be made if the party objecting assumes the prosecution of the action and all expenses thereof, except that any sums thereafter recovered shall be divided equally between the Publisher and the Writer after the deduction of the reasonable expenses thereof.

Infringement
Claims

16. (a) If a claim is presented against the Publisher alleging that the composition is an infringement upon some other work or a violation of any other right of another, and because therof the Publisher is jeopardized, it shall forthwith serve a written notice upon the Writer setting forth the full details of such claim. The pendency of said claim shall not relieve the Publisher of the obligation to make payment of the royalties to the Writer hereunder, unless the Publisher shall deposit said royalties as and when they would otherwise be payable, in an account in the joint names of the Publisher and the Writer in a bank or trust company in New York, New York, if the Writer on the date of execution of this contract resides East of the Mississippi River, or in Los Angeles, California, if the Writer on the date of execution of this contract resides West of the Mississippi River. If no suit be filed within nine months after said written notice from the Publisher to the Writer, all monies deposited in said joint account shall be paid over to the Writer plus any interest which may have been earned thereon.

(b) Should an action be instituted against the Publisher claiming that the composition is an infringement upon some other work or a violation of any other right of another, the Publisher shall forthwith serve written notice upon the Writer containing the full details of such claim. Notwithstanding the commencement of such action, the Publisher shall continue to pay the royalties hereunder to the Writer unless it shall, from and after the date of the service of the summons, deposit said royalties as and when they would otherwise be payable, in an account in the joint names of the Publisher and the Writer in a bank or trust company in New York, New York, if the Writer on the date of execution of this contract resides East of the Mississippi River, or in Los Angeles, California, if the Writer on the date of execution of this contract resides West of the Mississippi River. If the said suit shall be finally adjudicated in favor of the Publisher or shall be settled, there shall be released and paid to the Writer all of such sums held in escrow less any amount paid out of the Writer's share with the Writer's written consent in settlement of such action. Should the said suit finally result adversely to the Publisher, the said amount on deposit shall be released to the Publisher to the extent of any expense or damage it incurs and the balance shall be paid over to the Writer.

(c) In any of the foregoing events, however, the Writer shall be entitled to payment of said royalties or the money so deposited at and after such time as he files with the Publisher a surety company bond, or a bond in other form acceptable to the Publisher, in the sum of such payments to secure the return thereof to the extent that the Publisher may be entitled to such return. The foregoing payments or deposits or the filing of a bond shall be without prejudice to the rights of the Publisher or Writer in the premises.

Arbitration

17. Any and all differences, disputes or controversies arising out of or in connection with this contract shall be submitted to arbitration before a sole arbitrator under the then prevailing rules of the American Arbitration Association. The location of the arbitration shall be New York, New York, if the Writer on the date of execution of this contract resides East of the Mississippi River, or Los Angeles, California, if the Writer on the date of execution of this contract resides West of the Mississippi River. The parties hereby individually and jointly agree to abide by and perform any award rendered in such arbitration. Judgment upon any such award rendered may be entered in any court having jurisdiction thereof.

Assignment

18. Except to the extent herein otherwise expressly provided, the Publisher shall not sell, transfer, assign, convey, encumber or otherwise dispose of the composition or the copyright or copyrights secured thereon without the prior written consent of the Writer. The Writer has been induced to enter into this contract in reliance upon the value to him of the personal service and ability of the Publisher in the exploitation of the composition, and by reason thereof it is the intention of the parties and the essence of the relationship between them that the rights herein granted to the Publisher shall remain with the Publisher and that the same shall not pass to any other person, including, without limitations, successors to or receivers or trustees of the property of the Publisher, either by act or deed of the Publisher or by operation of law, and in the event of the voluntary or involuntary bankruptcy of the Publisher, this contract shall terminate, provided, however, that the composition may be included by the Publisher in a bona fide voluntary sale of its music business or its entire catalog of musical compositions, or in a merger or consolidation of the Publisher with another corporation, in which event the Publisher shall immediately give written notice thereof to the Writer; and provided further that the composition and the copyright therein may be assigned by the Publisher to a subsidiary or affiliated company generally engaged in the music publishing business. If the Publisher is an individual, the composition may pass to a legatee or distributee as part of the inheritance of the Publisher's music business and entire catalog of musical compositions. Any such transfer or assignment shall, however, be conditioned upon the execution and delivery by the transferee or assignee to the Writer of an agreement to be bound by and to perform all of the terms and conditions of this contract to be performed on the part of the Publisher.

Subsidiary
Defined

19. A subsidiary, affiliate, or any person, firm or corporation controlled by the Publisher or by such subsidiary or affiliate, as used in this contract, shall be deemed to include any person, firm or corporation, under common control with, or the majority of whose stock or capital contribution is owned or controlled by the Publisher or by any of its officers, directors, partners or associates, or whose policies and actions are subject to domination or control by the Publisher or any of its officers, directors, partners or associates.

Amounts

20. The amounts and percentages specified in this contract shall be deemed to be the amounts and percentages agreed upon by the parties hereto, unless other amounts or percentages are inserted in the blank spaces provided therefor.

Modifications

21. This contract is binding upon and shall enure to the benefit of the parties hereto and their respective successors in interest (as hereinbefore limited). If the Writer (or one or more of them) shall not be living, any notices may be given to, or consents given by, his or their successors in interest. No change or modification of this contract shall be effective unless reduced to writing and signed by the parties hereto.

The words in this contract shall be so construed that the singular shall include the plural and the plural shall include the singular where the context so requires and the masculine shall include the feminine and the feminine shall include the masculine where the context so requires.

Paragraph
Headings

22. The paragraph headings are inserted only as a matter of convenience and for reference, and in no way define, limit or describe the scope or intent of this contract nor in any way affect this contract.

Special
Provisions

23.

Witness: ....

....

Witness: ....

....

Witness: ....

....

Witness: ....

....

Publisher ....

By ....

Address ....

Writer ....(L.S.)

Address ....

Soc. Sec. # ....

Writer ....(L.S.)

Address ....

Soc. Sec. # ....

Writer ....(L.S.)

Address ....

Soc. Sec. # ....

FOR YOUR PROTECTION,
SEND A COPY OF THE FULLY SIGNED CONTRACT TO AGAC.

* * * * *

Special Exceptions to apply only if filled in and initialed by the parties.
☐ The composition is part of an original score (not an interpolation) of
☐ Living Stage Production   ☐ Motion Picture   ☐ Night Club Revue
☐ Televised Musical Production
which is the subject of an agreement between the parties dated   , a copy of which is hereto annexed. Unless said agreement requires compliance with Paragraph 6 in respect of a greater number of musical compositions, the Publisher shall be deemed to have complied with said Paragraph 6 with respect to the composition if it fully performs the terms of said Paragraph 6 in respect of any one musical composition included in said score.

REQUEST FOR PERMISSION TO ARRANGE

STANDARD FORM RECOMMENDED BY:

Music Educators National Conference, Music Teachers National Association, National Association of Jazz Educators, National Association of Schools of Music, Music Publishers' Association of the USA and National Music Publishers' Association.

REQUEST FOR PERMISSION TO ARRANGE

PART I

INSTRUCTIONS

This form is to be prepared in duplicate. After completing Part I and signing both copies where indicated, forward both to the publisher who will complete Part II of the form and return it to you. If the publisher indicates a payment for the right you request, and if the conditions are agreeable to you, remit the amount to the publisher together with the original copy, which he will have signed, whereupon the agreement will be completed.

To: _____ Date: _____

_____
(Name of Publisher)

_____
(Address of Publisher)

Gentlemen:

We hereby request your permission and non-exclusive license to arrange the following musical composition:

By: _____

_____ (words)

_____ (music)

(hereinafter referred to as "The Arrangement")

1. The Arrangement will be for _____ in

_____
(number of instruments and/or vocal parts)

_____
(type of Arrangement)

_____ . We will produce _____

copies of The Arrangement for use and performance only by our

_____
(teachers, students, members, congregation, etc.)

for which no admission fees shall be charged,

or for performance otherwise exempt under the provision of the U.S. Copyright Law.

2. No right to record or to reproduce additional copies is granted to us. We understand that if we wish to record The Arrangement a separate license will be required. We agree not to distribute (except for use of copies as provided in Paragraph 1), sell, loan or lease copies of The Arrangement to anyone.

PART II

3. All copies of The Arrangement shall bear the following copyright notice and the words "Arranged by Permission":

at the bottom of the first page of music of each part of The Arrangement. We will furnish you with a copy of The Arrangement upon completion.

(over)

---

4. We will have The Arrangement made by a person connected with us as our employee for hire, without any payment, obligation on your part, and our signature below, together with yours, in The Arrangement; and the copyright in The Arrangement together with the sole right of registering the copyright as a work made for hire in your name or the name of your designee.

5. Additional provisions (if applicable):

_____

6. In consideration of your permission to arrange, we will pay you $ _____ upon the granting by you of the permission herein requested.

7. This license agreement sets forth our entire understanding and may not be modified or amended except by written agreement signed by both of us.

Very truly yours,

_____
Name of Institution

_____
Address

By: _____

Permission Granted:

By: _____
Publisher

Permission denied because:

☐ 1. Arrangement available for sale.

☐ 2. Arrangement in process of publication for sale.

☐ 3. May not be arranged because of contractual commitments.

☐ 4. Other: _____

PROFESSIONAL ORGANIZATIONS

Afro-American Music Opportunities Ass'n
2801 Wayzata Blvd., Minneapolis MN 55405
American Ass'n for Music Therapy
777 Education Bldg., NYU
Washington Square, 35 W. Fourth St.
New York, NY 10003
American Composers Alliance
170 W. 74th St., New York, NY 10023
American Council for the Arts
570 Seventh Ave., New York, NY 10018
American Federation of Musicians
1500 Broadway, New York, NY 10036
American Federation of Television and Radio Artists
1350 Ave. of The Americas, New York, NY 10019
American Guild of Authors and Composers
40 W. 57 St., New York, NY 10019
American Guild of Musical Artists
1841 Broadway, New York, NY 10023
American Music Conference
1000 Skokie Blvd., Wilmette, IL 60091
American Musicological Society
Dept. of Music, University of Chicago
Chicago, IL 60637
American Record Producers Association
952 E. 13 St., Brooklyn, NY 11230
American Society of Composers, Authors and Publishers
1 Lincoln Plaza, New York, NY 10023
American Society of University Composers
250 W. 57 St., New York NY 10019
American Symphony Orchestra League
P.O. Box 669, Vienna, VA 22180
Amusement and Music Operators Ass'n
35 E. Wacker Dr., Chicago, IL 60601
Association of College, University and Community Arts Administrators Inc.
P.O. Box 2137, Madison, WI 53701
Association of Professional Vocal Ensembles
1830 Spruce St., Philadelphia, PA 19103
Audio Engineering Society Inc.
Lincoln Bldg., 60 E. 42 St., New York, NY 10017

Black Music Association
1500 Locust St., Philadelphia, PA 19102
Broadcast Music Inc.
320 W. 57 St., New York, NY 10019

California Copyright Conference
6381 Hollywood Blvd., Los Angeles, CA 90028
Central Opera Service
Metropolitan Opera
Lincoln Center, New York, NY 10023
College Music Society
Regent Hall, Box 44
University of Colorado
Boulder, CO 80309
Composers and Lyricists Guild of America
10999 Riverside Dr., North Hollywood, CA 91602
Country Music Association Inc.
7 Music Circle N., Nashville, TN 37203
Country Music Foundation Inc.
4 Music Square E., Nashville, TN 37203

Harry Fox Agency
110 E. 59 St., New York, NY 10022

Independent Label Association
2125 Eighth Ave. S., Nashville, TN 37204
Institute of Audio Research Inc.
64 University Pl., New York, NY 10003
International Association of Auditorium Mgrs.
1 Illinois Center, 111 E. Wacker Dr., Chicago, IL 60601
International Confederation of Societies of Authors and Composers
11 Rue Keppler, 75116 Paris, France
International Music Industries, Ltd.
1414 Ave. of the Americas, New York, NY 10019
International Society of Performing Arts Administrators
c/o Columbia Music Festival Ass'n, 1527 Senate St., Columbia, SC 29201

League of Composers
c/o American Music Center, 250 W. 57 St., New York, NY 10019

Metropolitan Opera Nat'l Council
Lincoln Center, New York, NY 10023
Motion Picture Editors Guild, Local 776
I.A.T.S.E., 7715 Sunset Blvd., Los Angeles, CA 90046
Mu Phi Epsilon
7440 W. 89 St., Los Angeles, CA 90045

Music Critics Association
6201 Tuckerman Lane, Rockville, MD 20852
Music Educators National Conference
1902 Association Dr., Reston, VA 22091
Music Industry Educators Ass'n
c/o Prof. Paul Kelly, Music, Elmhurst College, Elmhurst, IL 60126
Music Library Ass'n Inc.
343 S. Main St. Ann Arbor, MI 48108
Music Performance Trust Funds of the Recording Industry
810 Paramount Bldg., 1501 Broadway, New York, NY 10036
Music Publishers Ass'n of the U.S.
130 W. 57 St., New York, NY 10019
Music Teachers National Ass'n Inc.
408 Carew Tower, Cincinnati, OH 45202

NARAS Institute
c/o Prof. James Progris, P.O. Box 248165, Coral Gables, FL 33124
Nashville Songwriters Ass'n Int'l
25 Music Square W., Nashville, TN 37203
National Academy of Popular Music & Songwriters Hall of Fame
1 Times Square, New York, NY 10036
National Academy of Recording Arts & Sciences
4444 Riverside Dr., Burbank, CA 91505
National Ass'n for Music Therapy Inc.
P.O. Box 610, Lawrence, KS 66044
National Ass'n of Broadcasters
1771 N. St. N.W., Washington, DC 20036
National Ass'n of Jazz Educators
P.O. Box 724, Manhattan, KS 66502
National Ass'n of Music Merchants Inc.
35 E. Wacker Dr., Chicago, IL 60601 or 500 N. Michigan Ave., Chicago, IL 60601
National Ass'n of Negro Musicians
4330 Fullerton, Detroit, MI 48238
National Ass'n of Recording Merchandisers
1080 Kings Hwy. N., Cherry Hill, NJ 08034
National Ass'n of Schools of Music
11250 Roger Bacon Dr., Reston, VA 22090
National Ass'n of Teachers of Singing
250 W. 57 St., New York, NY 10019
National Entertainment & Campus Activities Ass'n
P.O. Box 11489, Columbia, SC 29211
National Federation of Music Clubs
310 S. Michigan Ave., Chicago, IL 60604
National Music Council
250 W. 57 St., New York, NY 10019
National Music Publishers Ass'n Inc.
110 E. 59 St., New York, NY 10022

National Opera Ass'n
Hotel Wellington, Seventh Ave. & 55 St., New York, NY 10019
National Opera Institute
John F. Kennedy Center, Washington, DC 20566

Opera America Inc.
1010 Vermont Ave. N.W., Washington, DC 20005

People-To-People Music Committee Inc.
John F. Kennedy Center, Washington, DC 20566
Phi Mu Alpha Sinfonia
10600 Old State Rd., Evansville, IN 47711
Piano Technicians Guild Inc.
P.O. Box 1813, Seattle, WA 98111
Practicing Law Institute
810 Seventh Ave., New York, NY 10019

Radio & TV Registry
850 Seventh Ave., New York, NY 10019
Recording Industry Ass'n of America
1633 Broadway, New York, NY 10036

SESAC
10 Columbus Circle, New York, NY 10019
Society of Professional Audio Recording Studios
215 S. Broad St., Philadelphia, PA 19107

United States Copyright Office
Library of Congress, Washington, DC 20559

Young Audiences Inc.
115 E. 92 St., New York, NY 10028

MUSIC BUSINESS STUDIES IN HIGHER EDUCATION

Over 80 institutions in the USA and Canada now offer studies in the music business and related fields. Practically all of these schools have adopted *Music Business Handbook and Career Guide* as a required text.

Anderson College, Anderson, IN
Appalachian St. Univ., Boone, NC
Ashland College, Ashland, OH
Augustana Col., Sioux Falls, SD
Barrington Col., Barrington, RI
Bellevue Com. Col., Bellevue, WA
Belmont College, Nashville, TN
Benedictine Col., Atchison, KS
Bethane-Cookman Col., Daytona Beach, FL
Birmingham S. Col., Birmingham, AL
Bradley University, Peoria, IL
Brevard College, Brevard, NC
Bunker Hill Com. Col., Charlestown, MA
Cal. St. Univ., Dominguez Hills, CA
Carroll College, Waukesha, WI
Centr. Mich. Univ., Mt. Pleasant, MI
Col. for Rec. Arts, San Francisco, CA
College of Santa Fe, CA
Columbia College, Chicago, IL
Com. Col. of Finger Lakes, Canandaigua, NY
Cumberland College, Williamsburg, KY
East. Kentucky Univ., Richmond, KY
Eastman School of Music, Rochester, NY
Edinboro State Col., Edinboro, PA
Elizabeth City St. Univ., Eliz. City, NC
Elmhurst College, Elmhurst, IL
Emporia State Univ., Emporia, KS
Fairmont St. College, Fairmont, WV
Fanshawe College, London, Ontario
Five Towns College, Merrick, NY
Fontbonne College, St. Louis, MO
Gavilan College, Gilroy, CA
Georgia State University, Atlanta, GA
Golden W. Col., Huntington Beach, CA
Hartt Col. of Music, W. Hartford, CT
Heidelberg College, Tiffin, OH
Hinds Junior College, Raymond, MS
Hofstra Univ., Hempstead, NY
Indiana State University, Terre Haute, IN
Iowa Lakes Com. Col., Estherville, IA
James Madison Univ., Harrisonburg, VA
Kearney State College, Kearney, NE
Lewis University, Romeoville, IL
Long Beach City Col., Long Beach, CA
Loyola-Mary Univ., Los Angeles, CA
Loyola University, New Orleans, LA
Madonna College, Livonia, MI
Mansfield State College, Mansfield, PA
Memphis State Univ., Memphis, TN
Messiah College, Grantham, PA
Miami-Dade Com. Col., Miami, FL
Mid. Tenn. St. Univ., Murfreesboro, TN
Millikin University, Decatur, IL
Milwaukee Tech. Col., Milwaukee, WI
Miss. Univ. for Women, Columbus, MS
Mohawk College, Hamilton, Ontario

New Col. of Calif., San Francisco, CA
New England College, Henniker, NH
New Sch. for Soc. Research, New York, NY
New York University, New York, NY
N. E. Missouri St. Univ., Kirksville, MO
Northland College, Ashland, WI
North Park College, Chicago, IL
Ohio State University, Columbus, OH
Olivet College, Olivet, MI
Plymouth State College, Plymouth, NH
Ramapo Col. of N. Jers., Mahwah, NJ
Red Deer College, Red Deer, Alberta
St. Catherine College, St. Paul, MN
St. Louis Com. Col., Kirkwood, MO
Sch. of the Ozarks, Point Lookout, MO
Seattle University, Seattle, WA
Shenandoah Col./Cons./Music, Winchester, VA
South. Illinois Univ., Carbondale, IL
South Plains College, Levelland, TX
Southwestern Col., Chula Vista, CA
State University College, Fredonia, NY
State University College, Oswego, NY
State University College, Potsdam, NY
Syracuse University, Syracuse, NY
Temple University, Philadelphia, PA
Tex. South. Univ., Houston, TX
Trebas Inst. of Record. Arts, Montreal,
   Quebec and Ottawa, Ontario
Union College, Barbourville, KY
University of California at Los Angeles
University of Colorado at Denver
University of Hartford, Hartford, CT
University of Miami, Coral Gables, FL
University of Nebraska, Omaha, NE
Univ. of New Orleans, New Orleans, LA
Univ. of N. Alabama, Florence, AL
Univ. of Portland, Portland, OR
University of Puget Sound, Tacoma, WA
University of Rochester, Rochester, NY
Univ. of S. Calif., Los Angeles, CA
Univ. of S. Miss., Hattiesburg, MS
University of Texas at San Antonio, TX
Univ. of the Pacific, Stockton, CA
University of Wisconsin-Oshkosh
Utica College, Utica, NY
Valparaiso Col., Valparaiso, IN
Vanderbilt University, Nashville, TN
Walla Walla College, College Place, WA
Washington University, St. Louis, MO
Wayne State University, Detroit, MI
Webster College, St. Louis, MO
Wesleyan College, Macon, GA
William Paterson College, Wayne, NJ
Wingate College, Wingate, NC
Winston-Salem St. Univ., NC
Yankton College, Yankton, SD

GLOSSARY

— A —

AAAA. Association of Actors and Artists of America.

AFM. American Federation of Musicians of the United States and Canada.

AFTRA. American Federation of Television and Radio Artists.

AGAC. American Guild of Authors and Composers.

AGMA. American Guild of Musical Artists.

AGVA. American Guild of Variety Artists.

AM station. Radio station using an amplitude modulation signal.

AMC. American Music Conference.

AOR. Album-oriented rock.

ARB (Arbitron). 1. American Research Bureau, an audience research organization. 2. Electronic device attached to a home TV set to inform researcher what stations are turned on at a particular time.

ASCAP. American Society of Composers, Authors and Publishers.

Above-the-line. Special production expenses, e.g., salaries for featured artists, creative fees, above-scale wages. Contrasts with below-the-line expense.

Account executive. Liaison person between an advertising agency and one of its clients.

Acoustic instrument. A natural-sounding instrument, as contrasted to one using an amplifier.

Airplay. Radio broadcast of a commercially-released music recording.

Annual billing. Amount invoiced time buyers for the calendar year by broadcasters.

Arbitration clause. Provision in a contract requiring the parties to submit disputes to an impartial arbiter, usually the American Arbitration Association.

Arms length. 1. A relationship between two parties not on close terms. A relationship other than one between, e.g., a lawyer and client, or between a person and a trustee; other than a fiduciary relationship.

Art music. Repertoire associated with opera, ballet, symphony and chamber music. Often used interchangeably with "classical" music and "serious" music.

Assignment. Turning over of a contract or copyright to another person's control or ownership.

Audience share. Comparative popularity of a broadcast program, determined by dividing the program rating by the number of sets in use at a particular time.

Automated radio. Station whose programming is almost entirely on prerecorded tapes, the tapes being controlled for broadcast by a sophisticated transport system that requires minimum attention from an operator.

— B —

BMI. Broadcast Music Incorporated.

Back-announce. In radio broadcasting, the accumulation of a group of announcements following several uninterrupted playings of recorded music.

Bed. (Advertising) Musical background for a commercial announcement.

Bel canto. Fine singing; the Italian tradition of classical vocal production.

Below-the-line (expense). Predictable costs in production budgeting, e.g., union scale wages, equipment and facilities rentals, etc.

Belt. To sing a pop song or show tune with gusto, utilizing, in women, chest-tone resonance.

Berne Union. Ch. 6.

Beta (Betamax). A type of videocassette recorder-reproducer.

Bio. Slang for "biography" — a written summary of an individual's professional background.

Board. Synonym for recording console.

Boilerplate. (Slang) Redundant language in a contract used by lawyers seeking extra protection in an effort to avoid legal disputes.

Book. In a musical play, the scenario and dialogue for a production.

Breach. "The breaking or violating of a law, right, or duty, either by commission or omission." (Black, p. 235)

Breach of contract. "Failure, without legal excuse, to perform any promise which forms the whole or part of a contract." (Black, p. 235)

Bridge. Musical phrase in a song following the "hook," sometimes called "release" or "B phrase."

Buy-out. Purchase of rights in a property, as opposed to taking a percentage.

— C —

CATV. Community Antenna Television.

CPB. Corporation for Public Broadcasting.

CPM. Conference of Personal Managers.

Camera-ready. All elements in graphic art assembled in final form, ready for the platemaker's camera.

Canned. Prerecorded or filmed, in contrast to "live."

Canned release. Copy written for the press.

Canned spot. A prerecorded broadcast commercial.

Canned track. Prerecorded segment.

Casting couch. (Slang) Office furniture used ostensibly by a producer or casting director to "audition" a performer's "talents."

Catch action. Compose a musical cue to synchronize with specific action on the screen.

Cattle call. Producer's announcement of open auditions.

Charge-back. An expense assessed by a record company against an artist's royalties.

Chart. 1. Musical arrangement. 2. Trade paper list of records currently most popular on radio or in record stores.

Clam. Wrong note in the copied parts or a note performed incorrectly.

Classical music. The repertoire associated with symphony, opera, ballet, and chamber music.

Click track. Audible guide used by musicians scoring music to aid synchronization with film.

Close-miking. Recording with a microphone close to the sound source.

Cluster programming. Radio broadcast of several records uninterrupted by announcements.

Cold. In advertising, copy read without musical introduction or background.

Collective work. Ch. 6.

Commercial bed. See "bed."

Comp style. An improvised piano accompaniment often characterized by syncopated, block chords.

Competent party. Of sound mind and body; not demented or otherwise unable to act responsibly.

Compressor. Electronic sound device that limits the dynamic response to create a more constant, even dynamic level.

Compulsory license. Chs. 6, 7.

Consideration. "The inducement to a contract, the cause, motive, price, or impelling influence which induces a contracting party to enter into a contract. The reason or material cause of a contract." (Black, p. 379)

Contingent scale payment. Royalties on record sales paid to certain AFTRA members.

Contractor. In unions, the steward who hires performers, supervises their working conditions, and confirms they are properly paid.

Copyright formalities. Ch. 6.

Copyright notice. Ch. 6.

Copyright proprietor. Same as copyright owner.

Copyright transfer. Ch. 6.

Cost-per-thousand. The expense of delivering a commercial message to 1000 readers, listeners or viewers.

Coterminous. Two or more contracts that end on the same date.

Creative director. 1. In an advertising agency, the individual in charge of creative advertising concepts, supervising writers, graphic artists and audio-video producers. 2. Person in charge of creative services for a production company or record label.

Creative fee. Money paid a composer or copywriter by an advertising agency, producer or production company.

Creative services. Division of a record company that provides marketing concepts, graphic art, sales aids, editorial services and advertising materials.

Cross-collateralize. Shift of royalties earned by one property to the credit or debit of another property, resulting in a net total of royalties earned by all of them.

Crossover record. A record focused on one market segment that achieves sales in one or more additional markets.

Cue. Short musical passage composed to accompany dramatic action or underscore dialogue.

Cure. Satisfy a complaint or resolve a dispute concerning a contract.

Cut-in. Owner of a property shares ownership.

Cutter. Film (or tape) editor of music recorded for synchronization with film or videotape.

— D —

DBS. Direct broadcast satellite.

Date. Appointed time and place for a recording session. Or simply a recording (or performing) job.

Decay. Diminution of sound pressure (audible volume).

Default. Failure to perform under a legal contract.

Demo. Demonstration record.

Demography. The statistical method used in researching the characteristics of populations.

Digital recording. Audio or video recording made with the aid of digital computer technology.

Discharge. To void a contract, cause it to be non-binding.

Double. The second (sometimes third) instrument a union musician is called upon to play. For example, a flute is a common double required of saxophonists.

Down time. A period when recording or filming equipment is not functioning properly, thus unusable.

Dramatic music (dramatico-musical). Music closely related to drama or a scenario, particularly opera, a musical play, ballet, narration.

— E —

EPW. Employers Pension and Welfare Fund of the AFM.

EQ. Abbreviation for equalization.

Echo-send. Electronic control on a recording console to direct sound to a reverberation chamber.

Engineer. University graduate holding a baccalaureate degree in a field such as electrical, architectural or civil engineering. Often used (incorrectly) in reference to an audio mixer or sound technician.

Equity. Actors Equity Association.

Executive producer. Top administrator and/or financier of a production.

Executory, executory provision. A requirement of performance to be rendered following disengagement from (termination of), a contract.

Exploit. In the entertainment field, to promote, advertise, publicize and advance an artist or a property.

Extended use. A prerecorded tape or film used for a period longer than the one initially paid for.

— F —

FCC. Federal Communications Commission.

FM radio. Radio broadcasting using a frequency modulation signal.

Fader. A recording console control used to effect changes in sound level.

Fair use. Ch. 6.

Fiduciary. 1. A person who manages money or other things of value for another person and in whom the second party has a right to place trust. 2. A situation or relationship between persons where one acts for another in a position of trust.

Ex.: a lawyer or agent acting on behalf of an artist.

Find. To decide and declare.

Finding. "The result of the deliberations of a jury or a court." (Black, p. 758)

First call musician. Performer a contractor prefers to hire above all others available.

Flack. A publicist.

Flat. A natural sound, without coloration or alteration of highs and lows.

Four-fund system. See ASCAP, Ch. 7.

Four-walling. Producer rents a performance facility where the landlord offers only the venue — no stagehands, ushers, box-office help.

Franchised agent. A talent agent or booker licensed by an artists' union or guild.

Front line. Melodic instruments in a band or orchestra, as opposed to the rhythm section.

— G —

Get lost. Slang expression to indicate the conductor or recording engineer should fade music out.

Ghost writer. A writer or composer who does work for hire under the name of another writer or composer.

Gold record. A single record certified by RIAA as having sold one million copies, or an album that has sold 500,000 units. Tapes are counted as album "units."

Golden Age. In movie music, the 1930s and 1940s period when film producers hired high-priced composers to score music in the grand style for large orchestras.

Grand right. Performance right in dramatic music.

Graphic equalizer. A sound control that provides adjustment of a signal over a broad range of frequencies.

— H —

H & W Fund. AFM's Health and Welfare Fund.

Harmonizer. A signal processing device that creates delay effects and changes the pitch of a sound without affecting its tempo.

Head. Start of a tape or film reel.

Head set. Ear phones.

Hook. 1. (Song) Memorable melodic (or lyrical) phrase. 2. (Advertising) Campaign slogan or concept.

House agency. Advertising department within a company.

House producer. One of the company's salaried staff employees.

Hyphenate. Artist providing more than one service, e.g., producer-director, singer-songwriter.

— I —

ID. (Station) See "station logo."

In-house. Done within a company, itself; not hired out.

Immaterial. "Not material, essential, or necessary; not important or pertinent." (Black, p. 884)

Institutional ad (or spot). A commercial announcement intended to impress the public with a firm's or organization's merit.

— J —

Jingle. Original term for a broadcast commercial containing music. More common today is the use of the term "commercial" or "spot."

Joint venture. A business partnership of limited duration set up for a limited purpose.

— L —

Leadsheet. Music manuscript containing the melody for a song, its text and chord symbols.

Legal consideration. "One recognized or permitted by the law as valid and lawful; as distinguished from such as are illegal or immoral." (Black, p. 379). The term is sometimes used as equivalent to "good" or "sufficient" consideration.

Legit. Slang for "legitimate." Style of music or performance in the classical, formal tradition.

Library service. A collection of a large quantity and variety of recorded passages which are available for use in productions not using original or "custom" music.

Lift. In broadcast commercials, a short taped segment drawn from a longer one.

Light music. Used in the U.K. in reference to popular music.

Limiter. Signal processing device that reduces peaks but affects overall dynamics less than a compressor.

Live-on-tape. A television production performed live, with TV recording occurring at the same time for later editing prior to broadcast.

Local. 1. Branch office of a national union or guild. 2. A market or audience contained within the area of one city.

Logo. A musical or visual symbol used repeatedly in an effort to reinforce public recognition of a product or organization.

— M —

MENC. Music Educators National Conference.

MDS. Multipoint distribution service, a pay-TV system.

MOR. Middle of the road type of music.

MPA. Music Publishers Association.

MSO. Multiple system operator, a type of cable TV company.

Market. A particular group of buyers (or a type of audience) that can be identified by demographic research and/or analyses of preferences.

Master purchase agreement. A contract used by a record company to obtain exclusive rights in a master tape recording which has been produced by another person, such as an independent producer.

Mastering. The process of transferring sounds on tape to a lacquer disc for the purpose of manufacturing records.

Material. "Important; more or less necessarily; having influence or effect; going to the merits; having to do with matter, as distinguished from form." (Black, p. 1128)

Mechanical license. Legal permission given by a publisher to a producer to make a commercial recording of the publisher's copyrighted music.

Mechanicals. 1. Royalties paid by a record manufacturer to the owner of a music copyright. 2. Overlay of elements comprising graphic art assembled for the printer's camera.

Media buyer. Salaried employee who contracts for print ad space or broadcast time buys.

Mickey Mouse music. A type of music associated with filmed cartoons; sometimes silly, exaggerated.

Mix. To combine and equalize, into one or two channels, a larger number of separate tracks of recorded sounds.

Mixer. Recording technician who operates a console. Often referred to (incorrectly) as an engineer.

Music coordinator. Production assistant keeping track of musical elements.

Music cue. Short musical fragment used to bridge dramatic scenes or provide musical background.

Music cutter. Same as film music editor.

Music house (or music supply house). A company of composers and arrangers offering creative services (and recording) for buyers of "custom" music.

Music preparation. Music manuscript proofreading, extraction of parts from the score, collation, reproduction, score binding and delivery.

Music supplier. See "music house."

Mutuality of agreement. Parties to an agreement understand their commitments, obligations.

— N —

NAB. National Association of Broadcasters.

NMPA. National Music Publishers Association.

Narrowcasting. Contrasts with *broad*casting: program material produced and delivered to audiences of special tastes.

National account. Customer of an advertising agency or production company that advertises nationwide.

National Contracts Division. Group of AFM officials charged with negotiating agreements for musicians' services with producers of movies, network television, broadcast commercials, and syndicated programs.

Needle drop. Brief recorded passage (orchestral or a sound effect) drawn from a transcription library which a producer uses for a dramatic program or broadcast commercial.

Negative cost. Expense of producing a movie or TV show and delivering it to a customer; excludes costs of promotion.

Negotiated license. In the record industry, a right to record worked out between a music publisher and a record publisher. Contrasts with a statutory compulsory license.

New use. Application of recorded music tape or film to a medium different from the one originally intended, e.g., a record album to be used in a film.

Nielsen rating. Share of the broadcast audience drawn by a particular program or network, according to A.C. Nielsen, a research company.

— O —

O. & O. station. A radio or TV station owned and operated by a commercial broadcasting network.

Off-Broadway. Low-budget, often experimental, professional theatre, produced in New York City venues, but outside its Times Square theatre district.

One-stop. Record distributor/wholesaler offering a large number of record companies' merchandise to retailers and juke-box operators.

Opticals. Visual effects created for film or videotape.

Outboard equipment. Recording hardware external to the recording console which is patched into it to enhance the mixer's options of controlling sounds.

— P —

P.D. 1. Program director. 2. Public domain.

Package deal. Combined goods and/or services delivered under one price tag.

Pan pot. Recording console control (fader) used to place a signal to the left, right, or center of the stereo image.

Paper business. Printed editions sector of a music publishing company.

Paper the house. (Concert promotion) Issue free tickets to ensure a full audience for a performance.

Pass on. Make a negative judgment; to turn down, reject.

Pay TV. Cable television delivery system.

Performance right. Chs. 6, 7.

Phonorecord. Same as phonograph record or prerecorded tape.

Platinum record. An album certified by RIAA as having sold at least one million units (units include albums and all tape configurations), or a single record that has sold at least two million copies.

Play list. Radio station's recorded music schedule for broadcast.

Power of Attorney. "An instrument authorizing another to act as one's agent or attorney; a letter of attorney." (Black, p. 1334)

Production manager. Business affairs head for a production.

Promo kit. See promo pack.

Promo pack. Package of promotional materials.

Punch in. To record a passage by replacing the original performance while the tape continues to roll.

Punch up. Add emphasis to music or script.

— R —

Rack up. TV film and tape presets which may then be called up by a technician for broadcast.

Release phrase. See "bridge."

Remedy. Solve a problem or cure a default under a contract.

Rhythm section. The "motor element" of a band or orchestra, normally comprised of piano, bass, drums and guitar.

— S —

SESAC. Society of European Stage Authors and Composers.

Sampling. (Music performances) Technique used by music rights societies to estimate total performances by examining a limited number of performances.

Scale. Specified minimum union wage.

Scaling the house. Determining what quantity of available seats in a performance facility are to be priced the least expensive, the next most expensive, and so on.

Score (a film). Compose, perform and record music to synchronize with a motion picture.

Second engineer. Assistant to the head audio engineer.

Secondary transmission. Cable TV broadcast of an originating program source, such as from a commercial television station.

Sel sync. The ability of a tape recorder to record on one track at a time in synchrony with previously recorded tracks.

Self-contained group. Small ensemble that writes its own material, or an organized ensemble that performs together regularly without outside members.

Selling agent. Person or firm offering printed music or merchandise for sale at the retail level, under a royalty contract or for commission.

Session musician. Instrumentalist employed in recording studios.

Sideman. An instrumentalist other than the leader or contractor.

Slate. Chalk board ID of a filmed or videotaped segment.

Small right. Performance right in nondramatic music.

Spec., Speculation. Employed without assurance of getting paid.

Special material. Music, lyrics, dialog, patter specially written for a particular artist's performance.

Split copyright. Copyright proprietor shares his ownership with one or more persons.

Split publishing. One party shares his publishing rights with one or more persons.

Spot. 1. A broadcast commercial announcement. 2. Theatrical spotlight. 3. To place in a particular position.

Station logo. Broadcast station's musical signature, identification.

Steward. Hires performers and supervises enforcement of their union contract with the producer.

Stinger. Accented chord played by an orchestra to underscore a dramatic moment on the screen.

Stock arrangement. Published edition; not a custom chart.

Storyboard. Series of informal drawings depicting sequence of visual events planned for a TV commercial.

Strip show. A series of weekly broadcasts scheduled several times a week at the same hour each day.

Studio musician. Same as session musician.

Subpublisher. Firm affiliated with a prime publisher in providing publishing services here, perhaps abroad.

Supervising copyist. Copyist who directs the services of additional copyists working on the same job.

Sweep week. Seven-day period during which research firms collect data concerning broadcast audience size.

Sweeten. Record additional sounds by overdubbing.

Synchronization license. Ch. 6.

Syndication. Non-network broadcasts of programs which individual stations schedule to use at times convenient to them.

— T —

Tail. End of a tape or film reel.

Take. One version of a recorded performance, as in "The second take was best."

Teaser announcement. Brief press release providing preliminary information about a forthcoming event.

Technical rider. Addendum to a performance contract stipulating requirements for staging, sound reinforcement, equipment, etc.

Telecommunications. Production and delivery of all modes of televised entertainment and information.

Term. The time interval embraced by a legal agreement.

Tessitura. Prevailing pitch and range of a melodic line.

Tight. Slang for a well-rehearsed, cohesive performance.

Time-buyer. Advertising agency employee who purchases time on a broadcast station or network for a sponsor.

Time shift. Capacity of a VCR to record a TV program off the air and move its playback to a time more convenient for the viewer.

Track. One recorded portion of combined tracks, as in "24-track" recording; the sound on one track, as in "the bass track."

Tracker. Record label employee following the progress of a record release — airplay, chart action, sales, etc.

Tracking session. Taping session following the recording of basic tracks; overdubbing.

Trading fours. Jazz musicians taking turns improvising alternate four-bar phrases.

Transcription. Ch. 7.

— U —

Underscore. To place recorded music behind a movie or TV film.

Union steward. An agent who supervises the employment of union artists and provides liaison for them with their employer.

Up-front payment. Money advanced prior to completion of a job or production.

Up full. Background music crescendo to foreground.

— V —

VCR. Videocassette recorder.

Venue. Place of performance.

Voice-over. Language spoken by an actor or announcer who is not seen on the screen.

— W —

WCI. Warner Communications Incorporated.

Weighting formula. Evaluations of a performing rights society used in determining the relative value of various kinds of music performances, in order to judge what royalties are due a writer or publisher.

Work made for hire. Ch. 6.

BIBLIOGRAPHY

1- American Symphony Orchestra League. THE GOLD BOOK (Vienna, VA: ASOL).
2- H. Wesley Balk. THE COMPLETE SINGER-ACTOR (Minneapolis 1977: Univ. Minnesota Press).
3- David Baskerville. "Career Programs in Higher Education," MUSIC EDUCATORS JOURNAL Mar., 1977 (Reston, VA 1977: MENC).
4- ---JAZZ INFLUENCE ON ART MUSIC, Ph.D. dissertation (Ann Arbor 1966: Univ. Microfilms).
5- Lee Eliot Berk. LEGAL PROTECTION FOR THE CREATIVE MUSICIAN (Boston 1973: Berklee Press). Also see supplement.
6- Billboard Publications. INTERNATIONAL BUYERS GUIDE (annual) (NY: Billboard).
7- Henry Campbell Black. BLACK'S LAW DICTIONARY (Chicago 1968: West Co.).
8- BMI. THE SCORE, a film (NY: BMI).
9- Richard Bolles. WHAT COLOR IS YOUR PARACHUTE? (Berkeley: Ten Speed Press).
10- Center For Arts Administration. ARTS ADMINISTRATION TRAINING IN THE U.S. (Madison 1977: Univ. of Wisc. Grad. School of Business).
11- John Davidson and Cort Casady. THE SINGING ENTERTAINER (Sherman Oaks, CA 1979: Alfred Publishing Co.).
12- Clive Davis. INSIDE THE RECORD BUSINESS (NY 1975: Ballantine).
13- R. Denisoff. SOLID GOLD (New Brunswick 1975: Transaction Books).
14- John Eargle. SOUND RECORDING (New York 1980: Van Nostrand Reinhold Co.).
15- Lehman Engel. GETTING STARTED IN THE THEATRE (NY 1973: Macmillan).
16- Entertainment Law Institute, USC. RECORD AND MUSIC PUBLISHING FORMS OF AGREEMENT (NY 1971: Law-Arts Publishers).
17- --- LEGAL AND BUSINESS PROBLEMS OF THE RECORD INDUSTRY (NY 1975: Law-Arts Publishers).
18- ---REPRESENTING MUSICAL ARTISTS: LEGAL, BUSINESS AND PRACTICAL ASPECTS (Los Angeles 1975: Entertainment Law Institute, USC).
19- Mark Evans. SOUND TRACK: THE MUSIC OF THE MOVIES (NY 1975: Hopkinson and Blake).
20- Robert Faulkner. HOLLYWOOD STUDIO MUSICIANS (NY 1971: Aldine-Atherton).
21- Leonard Feist. POPULAR MUSIC PUBLISHING IN AMERICA (New York 1980: National Music Publishers Assoc.).
22- Ford Foundation. THE FINANCES OF THE PERFORMING ARTS, 2 vls. (NY 1974: Ford Foundation).
23- Foundation Center. ABOUT FOUNDATIONS: HOW TO GET THE FACTS YOU NEED (NY: Foundation Center).
24- Xavier M. Frascogna, Jr. and H. Lee Hetherington. SUCCESSFUL ARTIST MANAGEMENT (New York 1978: Billboard).
25- Charlotte Georgi. THE ARTS AND THE WORLD OF BUSINESS, A SELECT BIBLIOGRAPHY (Metuchen 1973: Scarecrow Press). Supplement available through UCLA's Graduate School of Management.
26- Charles Gillett. THE SOUND OF THE CITY (NY: Dutton).
27- Earl Hagen. SCORING FOR FILMS (NY 1971: Criterion Music Corp.).
28- Claude and Barbara Hall. THIS BUSINESS OF RADIO PROGRAMMING (NY 1977: Billboard).
29- Carroll Knudson. CLICKTRACK BOOK (North Hollywood: Vallé Music).
30- Dennis Lambert with Ronald Zalkind. PRODUCING HIT RECORDS (New York 1980: Schirmer Books).
31- Music Educators Journal. CAREERS IN MUSIC, reprint of March, 1977 issue (Reston 1978: MENC).
32- Charles A. Nelson and F. J. Turk. FINANCIAL MANAGEMENT FOR THE ARTS (NY 1975: ACC Publications).
33- Danny Newman. SUBSCRIBE NOW! (NY: Theatre Communications Group).
34- Dick Netzer. THE SUBSIDIZED MUSE: PUBLIC SUPPORT FOR THE ARTS IN THE UNITED STATES (New York: Cambridge Univ. Press).

35- New York University Law School. THE COMPLETE GUIDE TO THE NEW COPY-RIGHT LAW (Dayton 1978: Lorenz Press).

36- Henry Pleasants. SERIOUS MUSIC — AND ALL THAT JAZZ (NY 1969: Simon and Schuster).

37- Arthur Prieve. ADMINISTRATION IN THE ARTS: AN ANNOTATED BIBLIOGRAPHY OF SELECTED REFERENCES (Madison 1973: Center for Arts Administration, University of Wisconsin).

38- Harvey Rachlin. THE SONGWRITER'S HANDBOOK (NY 1977: Funk and Wagnalls).

39- Diane Sward Rapaport. HOW TO MAKE AND SELL YOUR OWN RECORD (New York 1979: Quick Fox).

40- Alvin H. Reiss. THE ARTS MANAGEMENT HANDBOOK (NY 1974: Law-Arts Publishers).

41- Larry J. Rosenberg. MARKETING (Englewood Cliffs 1977: Prentice-Hall).

42- C. A. Schicke. REVOLUTION IN SOUND: A BIOGRAPHY OF THE RECORDING INDUSTRY (Boston 1974: Little, Brown).

43- Neal A. Roberts, David I. Matheson and Harry A. Goldgut, editors. MUSIC INDUSTRY: CONTRACT NEGOTIATIONS AND THE LAW (Toronto 1980: York University).

44- R. Runstein. MODERN RECORDING TECHNIQUE (Indianapolis 1974: Howard W. Sams).

45- George Seltzer. THE PROFESSIONAL SYMPHONY ORCHESTRA IN THE U.S. (Metuchen 1975: Scarecrow Press).

46- Sidney Shemel and M. Wm. Krasilovsky. THIS BUSINESS OF MUSIC, 4th ed. (NY 1979: Billboard).

47- --- MORE ABOUT THIS BUSINESS OF MUSIC, rev. ed. (NY 1974: Billboard).

48- Marlin Skiles. MUSIC SCORING FOR TV AND MOTION PICTURES (Blue Ridge: Tab Books).

49- Geoffrey Stokes. STARMAKING MACHINERY: THE ODYSSEY OF AN ALBUM (Indianapolis 1976: Bobbs-Merrill).

50- Joseph Taubman. IN TUNE WITH THE MUSIC BUSINESS (New York 1980: Law-Arts Publishers).

51- --- PERFORMING ARTS MANAGEMENT AND LAW, 4 vls. (NY 1972: Law-Arts Publishers).

52- UCLA Extension. THE RECORDING CONTRACT — 1980 (Los Angeles 1980: UCLA Extension).

53- United States Government. OCCUPATIONAL OUTLOOK HANDBOOK (Washington: Bureau of Labor).

54- --- STARTING A SMALL MUSIC STORE (Washington 1969: U.S. Government Printing Office).

55- --- STARTING AND MANAGING A SMALL RETAIL MUSIC STORE (Washington 1970: U.S. Government Printing Office).

56- Alec Wilder. AMERICAN POPULAR SONG (NY 1972: Oxford).

57- John Woram. THE RECORDING STUDIO HANDBOOK (Plainview 1976: Sagamore).

JOURNALS, MAGAZINES, NEWSPAPERS

Advertising Age	International Musician	Record World
Billboard	Journal of Music Therapy	Recording Engineer/Producer
Broadcasting	Music Retailer	Rolling Stone
Cash Box	NAJE Educator	Songwriter
Country Music	Overture	Symphony News
Down Beat	Performance	Up Beat
Entertainment Law Reporter	Programming	Variety
The Gavin Report	Radio and Records	

Sources for special books on music and film: *Cinemabilia,* 10 W. 13th St. NY 10011; *Cinema and Theatre Bookshop,* 6658 Hollywood Blvd., Los Angeles, CA 90028.

INDEX

THE AUTHOR —

The author is professor of music at the University of Colorado at Denver, where he heads the music management program.

Background: Ph.D. from UCLA; staff composer-conductor for NBC-Hollywood; arranger-orchestrator for Nelson Riddle, 20th Century-Fox Studios and Paramount Pictures; television producer-director for the BBC-London; president of Sherwood Recording Studios, Los Angeles (subsequently operated by Warner Bros. Records); trombonist with the Seattle Symphony, Los Angeles Philharmonic and the NBC-Hollywood staff orchestra.

Dr. Baskerville has been a visiting lecturer or consultant to Chicago Musical College, USC, UCLA, Hartt College of Music and The Ohio State University. Presently, the author is consultant to the Entertainment Division of Walt Disney Productions.

ASCAP AWARD PRESENTATION   The author (right) receives *ASCAP's Deems Taylor Award*, given each year for outstanding books on music. The presentation is by Hal David (left), President of ASCAP and Academy Award-winning songwriter.